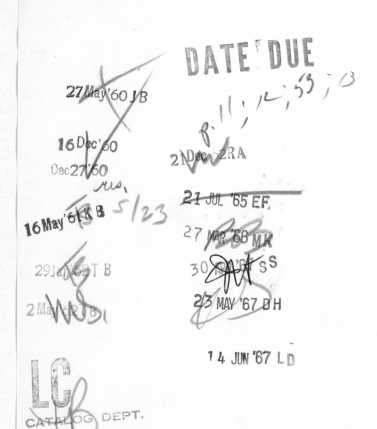

Stalin and the Soviet Communist Party

Stalin
and the
Soviet Communist Party

A Study in the Technology of Power

by

ABDURAKHMAN AVTORKHANOV

Published for the INSTITUTE FOR THE STUDY OF THE USSR

Frederick A. Praeger · *Publishers* · New York

BOOKS THAT MATTER

Published in the United States of America in 1959
by Frederick A. Praeger, Inc., Publishers,
15 West 47th Street, New York 36, N. Y.

© 1959 by the
Institute for the Study of the USSR, Munich, Germany

All Rights Reserved · Printed in Germany

Library of Congress catalog card number 59-8145

This book is Number 85 in the series
of *Praeger Publications in Russian History and World Communism*

Table of Contents

Foreword

In the introduction to his book, *Stalin*, Trotsky asserted that Stalin had taken possession of power not by virtue of his personal ability, but by virtue of an impersonal machine. It was not Stalin, said Trotsky, who created the machine, but the machine that created Stalin.

The facts as set forth in my book prove exactly the opposite: first, that in the mastery of power (and this is the main element in politics) Stalin surpassed not only Trotsky but Lenin himself; and second, that it was Stalin who created the machine which in turn made him what he was. Before this could take place, Stalin completely destroyed the existing Party machine and the Party cadres established by Lenin. Only through such a course of action lay the road to one-man rule.

Stalin will go down in history not only as a tyrant and Grand Inquisitor but also as a phenomenal tactician, strategist, and master of the science of power. The essence of Stalinism, as practiced by himself and his pupil Khrushchev, is the technology of power. A large part of the book is devoted to this theme.

I have examined the problem historically, that is, in connection with and on the basis of an analysis of the most significant intra-Party events of the thirty years from 1928 to 1958.

The book as a whole discusses the process of the formation of a Party of a new type. This is the Party of Stalin – the Communist Party of the Soviet Union.

The reader will observe that I have chosen a somewhat unusual method of presentation, consisting of a synthesis of personal recollections and historical research. As an historian, I was tempted to remain within the framework of impersonal academic analysis, but as a direct observer of Soviet events, I felt compelled to record my personal experiences to the extent that these bore on the problem.

What official Stalinist critics will say about this book is of complete indifference to me. To learned skeptics who may reproach me with bias toward events and personalities, I reply in the words of Goethe: "I can promise to be honest, but I cannot promise to be impartial."

Munich, March, 1959   *A. Avtorkhanov*

Chapter I

A Special Lecture at the Institute of Red Professors

At lunch hour in the Institute of Red Professors, where I was a graduate student, we were told that a special and very important lecture would be given at six o'clock that evening. The date was May 28, 1928. Neither the subject of the lecture nor the name of the lecturer were announced, but we were warned that all students were required to be present. Only holders of Party tickets and student registration cards would be admitted.

The strict check on attendance and the unusual fact that the lecturer's name was not announced aroused general interest. Guesses were made, opinions voiced; some students even went personally to Professor Pokrovsky, the President of the Institute, but in vain.

The Institute building, which before the Revolution had housed the Tsarevich Nicholas School at 53 Ostozhenka Street in Moscow, underwent all the preparations for an important occasion. Slogans were quickly thought up and carefully painted in white letters on red muslin, oil paintings of the founders of Marxism, borrowed from other institutions, were hung in prominent places. Cleaning women gave an extra wash and polish to the floors, workmen cleaned up the yard, the librarians displayed their best books, chimneysweeps climbed on the roofs, professors lined up at the barber's.

We students tried to guess what all the excitement was about. The older cleaning women told us that preparations of the same kind had been common on the occasion of royal visits, but that such present persons of prominence as Zinoviev, Bukharin, and Uglanov had come to the Institute without any fanfare. Therefore, said the cleaning women, our visitor must be Soviet President Mikhail Kalinin, "Kalinych" himself. However, even though in the eyes of the man on the street Kalinin was the "Red Tsar," we at the Institute of Red Professors had our own scale of values, political and theoretical, regarding the revolutionary leaders. From our point of view, "Kalinych" was a kindly old man perhaps, but overshadowed as a politician and a nonentity as a theorist. Nevertheless, even a visit by the President would be an event of importance for the Institute. We were ready to listen rather condescendingly to what Kalinin might have to say.

I left my room in the Institute dormitory in Pirogovka Street early in order not to be late for the important lecture. When I arrived half an hour before the time set, to my surprise I found the Institute wrapped in an atmosphere of deep mourning. The students jammed the corridors, whispering mysteriously. The professors, freshly shaved, were glumly discussing the history of the ancient

Babylonians, a non-Party subject clearly chosen as a means of escape into the depth of ages from the disagreeable present. The cleaning women, by now wearing white overalls and red kerchiefs, were throwing quick glances first at the students, and then at the professors, apparently trying to fathom the meaning of the sad faces on the eve of a great occasion.

Only our general favorite, the doorman Dedodub, stood in imperturable calm at his "revolutionary post." He liked to repeat, not without a trace of pomposity: "I have faithfully served four tsars, and have outlived all four of them."

"The last tsar was Nicholas the Bloody. How old are you then, Dedodub?" I had asked him one day.

He had dodged a direct answer. "The last was Lenin," he had said.

I had tried repeatedly to educate Dedodub by saying that Lenin had not been a tsar, but merely a quite ordinary man chosen by the Revolution to be its leader. The old man always smiled sardonically and said:

"You are right, of course. Nicholas was a man, Lenin was a man, I am also a man. But you people are bookworms, pedants. You were born in books and in books you'll die and you won't have given yourself the chance to serve tsars or men or even yourselves . . . Wretched people, these bookworms!"

But this day was Dedodub's name-day and he was getting ready to display full dignity in opening the door for the fifth tsar, Kalinin, unaffected by the Institute's atmosphere of gloom.

After rummaging about in some emigre newspapers in the Party office, I went off to the lecture room, passing on my way people whispering in corners. But the lecture hall was locked and barred. The door was guarded by a stranger in civilian clothes. I went back and asked: "What's the matter? Will there be a lecture?"

At first no one paid any attention. Then my friend Sorokin, an older fellow-student, came up to me and whispered in a barely audible tone:

"Things are bad, very bad . . ."

"Meaning what?"

"I don't know."

"Why do you think things are bad, then?"

"I don't think — I know."

"Well then, tell us, what is it about!"

"I don't know."

I gave up hope of getting a sensible answer from Sorokin and made my way to the Institute office. Our secretary, Yelena Petrovna, always cheerful and obliging, was for once in a bad mood.

"Toothache?" I queried.

"Worse," she replied.

"Will there be a lecture?"

"I don't know."

"I'm sorry, Yelena Petrovna, but I can't understand anything any more. What is this—a conspiracy of the deaf and dumb, or what? Or are we on the eve of a general catastrophe?"

"You've hit it."

"What do you mean?"

"I mean there's both a conspiracy and a catastrophe." Her voice betrayed not a hint of irony.

At that moment Orlov, the Secretary of the Institute Party cell, came in and asked that Professor Pokrovsky be informed that a Party meeting would be held in the study and that everyone was waiting for him.

"And what about the lecture?" I asked.

"It will be at seven o'clock."

"Can I be present at the Party meeting, Comrade Orlov?"

Orlov mumbled something into his moustache which sounded like, "why are you pestering me like a noon-day fly?" and went out.

Yelena Petrovna went to give the message to Pokrovsky, while I, tormented by curiosity, decided to try my luck again and went off to the Party office.

I caught up with Orlov almost at the door. Orlov was a last year student, "five minutes to professor" as we used to say of the students who were about to take their final examinations. He looked me up and down as if he had never seen me before, but said nothing. We had taken an instant dislike to each other when we had first met—I disliked him for his arrogance and he disliked me for my lack of respect. I entered the Party office.

The office was filled with people, all sitting in silence. I again started rummaging around in the same newspapers as before, waiting for something to happen, no longer out of curiosity, but simply from stubbornness. If Orlov says, "Get out," I'll stay; if he doesn't, I'll go.

But Orlov had no time for me. When Pokrovsky came in, accompanied by Nikitin, the Secretary of the Krasnaya Presna District Committee, there was a general stir. Orlov asked all to take their seats and declared the meeting open. His speech was short but to the point.

"The monstrous crime we have just heard about can be traced back to a gang of White Guard oppositionists . . . ."

It seemed to me that at the words, "White Guard gang," he glanced at me in the same threatening way as when I had spoken to him at the office door. The thought flashed through my mind that it had just so happened that I had been rummaging through some "White Guard" papers that very day.

"We must catch that gang and destroy it . . . . It has its agents even in the Institute."

As Orlov said "agents" our eyes met—it seemed to me hardly by accident. But the more he allowed himself to be carried away by his eloquence, the more I became convinced that it had really been accidental. He seemed to be asking each one in turn: "Are *you* an agent?" To the general relief, Pokrovsky interrupted the speaker to say that before throwing the subject open for discussion, he considered it essential to look at the lecture hall, as not all those present knew what it was all about.

When we entered the lecture hall on the second floor, I understood what was the matter. Hanging on the wall, behind the lecturer's chair, was a portrait of Stalin, painted, I think, by the famous Brodsky. It was a full-length portrait, but, alas, headless. The head, crudely cut out with a blunt instrument, was lying nearby on the floor. Affixed to his breast, above the hand held in a Napoleon-like gesture inside his overcoat, was the following inscription, made of letters cut from a newspaper:

"The Proletariat has nothing to lose but Stalin's head. Proletarians of all lands, rejoice!"

Several of those present at the meeting argued that "Stalin's execution" was a provocative demonstration by anti-Party groups within the Institute. It was decided to limit administrative action for the time being to the appointment of a Party investigating commission. The Secretary of the District Committee went so far as to recommend not taking too seriously something which was perhaps nothing but an "act of hooliganism." Now it was my turn to stare pointedly at Orlov. If he had been good at reading faces he could easily have read in mine: "There you are, you always like to exaggerate; it is not a question of White Guards—but of ordinary hooliganism."

A new portrait was brought from somewhere to take the place of the headless Stalin. It was a copy of the well-known photograph in which Stalin is pictured with Lenin in the city of Gorky in 1922. Another portrait of Lenin, hanging by itself, now had to be removed. Marx and Engels were also given new places. The portrait of A. I. Rykov, Chairman of the Council of People's Commissars, had also appeared from somewhere, though it had not been hanging on the wall before. The Institute brightened up.

In the meantime guests began to arrive: students of the Sverdlov Communist University and students and staff members of the Communist Academy and the Russian Association of Social Science Research Institutes who had also been instructed to attend the lecture. Not having been told beforehand that all four universities would be represented, our interest in the lecture became livelier. The Sverdlovians and the members of the Communist Academy were as much in the dark on its subject as we. Several of them asked us who was going to give it and what it was going to be about.

The lecture hall was full. Many had to stand in the aisles and along the sides; those who were late were not admitted at all. My friend Sorokin and I sat down in the front row, but Pokrovsky came along and told us politely that the front row was reserved for guests.

"Discrimination against the rights of men and citizens," declared Sorokin, and with a spiteful look at the supposed guests, the Sverdlovians and the Communist Academicians, he vacated his seat. But when these guests moved forward in a mass to occupy the front row, Pokrovsky explained that the Sverdlovians and Communist Academicians were not guests but were in the same class as the rest of us. The guests would soon arrive. In the meantime, we were able to occupy seats in the third row, vacated by the Sverdlovians who had rushed to the first.

Suddenly Sorokin said: "They're coming."

I turned toward the door. People began clapping loudly and there were cries of "Long live the Leninist Central Committee! Long live Lenin's pupils and companions-in-arms! Long live the Politburo!" Cries of "Hip, hip, hurrah!" and the clapping of hands grew louder and louder. When one of the guests shouted out: "Long live the Institute of Red Professors, Headquarters for Theorists of the Central Committee of the Communist Party!," the genuine enthusiasm became ecstatic. The guests applauded us and we applauded them. Orlov shouted from the rostrum: "Long live the collegiate leader, teacher and organizer of the All-Union Communist Party, the Leninist Central Executive Committee! Hip, hip, hurrah, comrades!"

"Hip, hip, hurrah!" we all screamed.

Pokrovsky appeared at the rostrum and took his seat as chairman. His gray beard was quivering. A bell rang, and the guests sat down. We sat down too. There was dead silence.

The chairman said quietly, but very distinctly: "Comrade Stalin will now speak." The subject of the lecture was, "The Grain Front."[1] For the first time I saw the man of whom I had previously heard merely that he held the position of Secretary-General of the Central Committee and that he was a Georgian by nationality. Often enough I had carefully studied his lectures on "Foundations of Leninism," delivered in 1924 in Sverdlov University. Although Stalin had then spoken simply as a commentator on Lenin, it had seemed to me that the commentator showed iron logic in his interpretation of Leninism and sober realism in his own conclusions.

At the time of Stalin's lecture it occurred to no one that Stalin was "the Lenin of today," as Henri Barbusse said later. If Stalin had died then, he would by now have long since been forgotten, even within his own party. Not only was Stalin not yet Lenin, he was not yet even himself. Historically he had only one thing to his credit, or discredit, his participation in the October Conspiracy, but in a role far below that of Trotsky and very little above that of people like Shkiryatov. In 1928 Stalin was what Mussolini had been before the March on Rome, and Hitler before January 30, 1933. True enough, in knowledgeable circles he was invariably known as "the shashlyk maker"—less in allusion to Georgian cooking than to his profession as butcher. But for the majority Stalin did not exist—there was only Djugashvili.

We were disappointed by the fact that the talk was going to be about the "grain front"—not a very academic subject. We were expecting something like

---

[1] "From a Talk to the Students of the Institute of Red Professors, the Sverdlov University and the Communist Academy," in J. V. Stalin, *Voprosy leninizma* (Problems of Leninism), 11th ed., Leningrad, 1940—47, (hereafter cited as Stalin, *Voprosy leninizma*).

"The Chinese Revolution," a very popular subject at the time, or "The Tactics and Strategy of the Comintern," but instead we were being asked to chew our daily bread, and to listen to statistical data besides! Alas, two years later the real significance of the lecture had been fully grasped by every peasant in the land. As it turned out, we were witnessing a historic event; Stalin expounded for the first time and to us his plan for the "kolkhoz revolution," the compulsory creation of collective farms, and thus inaugurated the beginning of the end of the NEP (New Economic Policy).

Stalin evidently realized our attitude to the subject, and before beginning his lecture made a number of reservations.

"You probably expect," he said, "that I shall deliver a theoretical lecture on some fancy subjects. But I must disappoint you . . . . To begin with, I am a man of action, not of theory. Secondly, I keep to the Marxist rule: 'One really revolutionary step forward is worth more than a dozen theoretical programs.' And so the subject I have chosen to talk on here, on the recommendation of the Central Committee, is the practical but revolutionary one: grain. On the way in which we shall solve the grain problem hangs not only the fate of the Soviet regime, but also that of the World Revolution. *For, after all, the World Revolution can only be sustained by Soviet grain.*"

These last words have remained firmly fixed in my memory.

Stalin spoke quietly, monotonously, and with long pauses as if trying not so much to choose the right words and phrases as to avoid saying anything he should not. He gave the impression of reading aloud an unwritten text. He had a Georgian accent which was particularly noticeable when he grew excited but which became less conspicuous when he was speaking calmly, on unemotional subjects.

After his introductory remarks, Stalin read the prepared text of his lecture. He used his favorite method of questions and answers. Most of the "questions" had been prepared beforehand and represented the kind of queries that might be expected to come from the audience, while many of the questions actually raised following the lecture were omitted from the report published in the press.

The basic question raised by Stalin was this: "What should the Soviet government do to obtain as much grain from the peasants as possible and to obtain it, as far as practicable, for nothing? In other words: is it possible to turn the peasant, a free worker on his own private plot, into a producer working on state-owned land?"

In answer to this question Stalin outlined for the first time his program of collective farms (kolkhozes) and state farms (sovkhozes). As usual in such cases, he repeatedly referred to Lenin. He attempted to prove that the only way for the Soviet government to increase the production of marketable grain was to introduce collective management, that is, to collectivize the peasantry. Regarding the complete liquidation of the kulaks, he said nothing at the time; he merely made use of the Leninist formula: "Support for the poor peasants, alliance with the

6

moderately rich peasants and war on the kulaks." In a word: the NEP was over. "Socialist industrialization in the city, a kolkhoz revolution in the country," was the essence of his talk.

Stalin himself could hardly have had any clear idea at the time what concrete forms this complicated process would take and at what cost. We students of theory had even less.

Stalin spoke for about two hours without stopping. He frequently drank water from a glass. Once, when he lifted the pitcher, it was empty. Someone laughed. One of the presiding officers handed Stalin a new pitcher. Stalin gulped down almost a full glass, then turned to the audience and said, with a mischievous laugh:

"There, you see, he who laughs last, laughs best. Anyway, I have welcome news for you: I have finished."

Everyone clapped.

The chairman announced a ten-minute recess, during which questions were to be submitted in writing. We left the hall.

"All we did was to put Stalin's portrait to death. What Stalin did was to bury the spirit of Leninism," volunteered Sorokin as a summary of his general impression of the lecture. His remark infuriated me. I knew Sorokin to be an incorrigible nihilist, for whom all earthly authorities counted as nothing if they ran counter to his own theories. About Lenin he repeated in season and out of season the same stock phrase: "Lenin, too, made mistakes." How could Stalin possibly compete with Sorokin!

"Comrade Sorokin, wisest of men! Tell me where you find the spirit of Leninism being buried by Comrade Stalin," I asked officiously.

"You never even noticed?"

"I did not."

"There you are, brother, never noticed the main thing, sticking out a mile. Tell me now, what is the essence of Lenin's 'cooperative plan'?"

"Stalin just explained it to us," I replied.

"He didn't explain it, he distorted it. In other words, he simply falsified it."

"Don't try to be clever," I insisted. "But tell me exactly how Stalin falsified it."

"Lenin's cooperative plan does not mean kolkhozes or sovkhozes or communes, it means a cooperative system of labor in the country, with the key positions held in the hands of the proletarian state. Lenin's cooperative plan deals with the exchange of goods, and Stalin wants it to deal with production; that is why he had to invent three forms of cooperation, to deal with supply, consumption, and kolkhoz production. He said that this last form of cooperation was regarded by Lenin as the highest form, which we must now adopt. But this is making fun of Lenin, it is juggling with concepts. Lenin never heard of the word *kolkhoz*, but Stalin says the whole plan was Lenin's. He is a real eagle, your compatriot, isn't he?" added Sorokin bitterly.

7

"You are right," I said not without pride, "the Caucasus is the home of eagles."

"But I believe there are a few donkeys in the Causasus, too," he retorted.

A bell rang and we went back to the hall. A pile of slips of paper lay on the table in front of Stalin. He grouped the questions into three categories: "basic," "technical," and "irrelevant." (The Bolsheviks always included in this last category everything that they considered for any reason embarassing or dangerous.) Stalin said that he would answer the questions belonging to the first two categories and ignore those belonging to the third as having nothing to do with the case. But the audience was particularly interested in the "irrelevant" questions and made Stalin read all the questions aloud.

I have a very vague recollection of the questions. I remember well only the fact that the questioners concentrated on the central theme of the report and asked Stalin: "What are kolkhozes and how do you think they should be organized?" One of the notes phrased the question about as follows: "If the peasants refuse to accept your collectivization plan voluntarily, do you consider they should be collectivized by force?"

Stalin answered by quoting Lenin's formula: "The dictatorship of the proletariat is absolute power based upon force."

"In other words, down with the NEP and back to War Communism," shouted someone in the hall.

Stalin made no answer.

Another note, an anonymous one, read: "Lenin said that we had introduced the NEP as a real change, on a long-term basis, and demanded that the peasantry be organized on a cooperative basis, super-slowly and super-carefully, while you call for collectivization at forced speed. Who is right, Lenin or you?"

To this Stalin answered sharply: "Leninism is dialectics, it is not a Bible. The only constant in our policy is our strategy—the fight for Communism. We have changed our tactics in the past and shall always change them, even radically, when the interests of strategy dictate. If the author of the note does not understand this, I advise him to leave the Institute and begin his professorial career by studying the ABC of Leninism in a Soviet Party School."

The author of the note was Sorokin.

I can recall only two of the "irrelevant" questions. The author of one asked Stalin to tell them the contents of the last letter written by the Trotskyite Joffe immediately before he committed suicide; another, also anonymous, asked for an explanation of why the OGPU was allowed, contrary to specific orders, to organize its own network of agents within the ranks of the Party itself.

Both these questions remained unanswered.

The lecture was over. Those sitting in the front row stood up. Pokrovsky, obviously greatly pleased by the success of the meeting, smiled like a benign bearded patriarch as he shook Stalin warmly by the hand. Then he turned to the audience and said: "My friends, let us thank Josif Vissarionovich for his interesting speech, and our dear friends, the members of the Central Committee, for their visit to us."

Those sitting on the platform—Molotov, Uglanov, the Party Thucydides Yemelian Yaroslavsky, somewhat dry and with an invariable air of concentration, and Skvortsov-Stepanov, editor of the government newspaper organ *Izvestia*—began to clap. The applause was taken up by the front row of Stalin's supporters—Pospelov, Adoratsky, Savelyev, Stetsky, Krinitsky—and continued by all of us who made up the audience. The audience clapped to be polite, the front rows from conviction, and the honored guests to uphold the principle of solidarity. Orlov was sublime: when the general clapping ceased he continued alone, his face crimson with effort.

Stalin's retinue rushed up to its leader. Some waxed eloquent over the profound thought behind the lecture, others expressed indignation regarding the "irrelevant" subjects. Stalin smiled politely, without commenting. Slightly to one side was Molotov, standing next to Pokrovsky and trying to prove a point; I discovered for the first time that Molotov had a slight stammer. In answer to a request by Pokrovsky, Molotov turned to Stalin and asked him a question. What it was I did not hear, but I saw Stalin turn to Pokrovsky and nod his head in approval, whereupon the chairman, addressing the audience still standing in the hall, said: "I should like to see all members of the Board of the Institute Party cell, all."

Sorokin was called up by Stalin himself. He had known Sorokin at the time of the Civil War and as a member of the Central Committee Secretariat. They exchanged greetings, and Stalin gave a fatherly clap on the shoulder to the man to whom, without knowing it, he had delivered a deadly blow only a few minutes before in his answer. When the top figures in the Institute began to gather around the Central Committee members, Sorokin said good-bye to Stalin and walked away.

As the various persons were introduced, Pokrovsky, gasping from asthma, gave brief details:

"Orlov, economist, Secretary of the Institute Party cell."

Tall and gaunt, with the mannerisms of an actor, our local leader rushed up to Stalin, stretched out his hand without waiting for Stalin to do so, and held on long after Stalin wanted to greet the next in line.

"Yudin, philosopher, member of the Board of the Institute Party cell."

Yudin's greeting was stiff and formal. This was Stalin's first meeting with his future theoretist.

"Konstantinov, philosopher, member of the cell Board."

"Shcherbakov. writer and historian, member of the cell Board."

This man's literary activities consisted in writing lengthy secret reports about the Institute to the Central Committee, as a result of which he had risen to the rank of member of the Politburo. He himself never spoke at Institute Party meetings.

"Pankratova, historian, former student of the Institute and lecturer in Russian History."

Stalin obviously wanted to begin a discussion with her, but the "bourgeois liberal" as we used to call her at that time, a thin, spare little woman, melted away. (Later on this "bourgeois liberal," after a number of victories and defeats, disclosures and self-flagellations—an art in which she was unexcelled—reached the Stalinist Olympus.)

"Mitin, philosopher."

Lean and unattractive, with the face of one who suffers from tuberculosis, Mitin bowed low before Stalin, like a court servitor before his liege lord. (Later on he, too, became a member of the Central Committee.)

Sten, Karev, Mekhlis all greeted Stalin like old friends.

The introductions were over.

While we were getting our coats and hats from the checkroom, Stalin left with his retinue. A long caravan of automobiles wound its way along Sadovaya Street.

Dedodub was still standing solemnly at his post!

"Well, Grandpa, did you see the Tsar?" asked Sorokin.

"Kalinin wasn't there. I know him personally," said the old man discontentedly.

"But Stalin is also a tsar," insisted Sorokin.

"Perhaps he is," replied the old man drily, "but he is not Kalinin."

Chapter II

Stalin's Siberian Plan

The decision to collectivize agriculture actually had its origin not in the Politburo, or even in Moscow, but in Siberia. It is true that the decision to organize kolkhozes dates back to the Fifteenth Party Congress in December 1927,[1] but it remained on paper until Stalin himself took up the matter. I learned the complete story from Sorokin, who was present at its inception.

In the fall of 1927, against the opposition of Bukharin, Rykov, Tomsky, Uglanov and, I believe, Kalinin, the Politburo decided to adopt "extraordinary measures" to assure grain deliveries. The leading members of the Party Central Committee and of the Council of People's Commissars were sent as "extraordinary delegates" to the country's main grain areas—the Ukraine, the Central Black Earth Region, the North Caucasus, and Siberia. As a rule these delegates had the right to issue decrees locally and on any subject in the name of the Party Central Committee and the Council of People's Commissars. They had at their disposal a large staff of assistants running the gamut from Chekists, technical experts, and propagandists to typists, all individually employed in Moscow by the various extraordinary delegates.

One of those sent as a delegate to Siberia in 1928 was Stalin, and his staff of specialists included the Siberian-born Malenkov and Sorokin. Stalin's plenary powers were limited to the Ural area, but he had no intention of going there and merely summoned the heads of the Ural Party organization to Novosibirsk, his future Siberian headquarters. The Siberian and Ural Party organizations received telegrams informing them of Stalin's impending arrival armed with plenary powers.

When Sorokin reached Novosibirsk and joined the Central Committee's "patrol brigade," Syrtsov, the Secretary of the Siberian Oblast Committee, was still trying to put his house in order. Schools were beginning to give regular lessons, hospitals were being disinfected, responsible officials were taking off their neckties ("Stalin, they say, is absolutely allergic to neckties"), and the local garrison's volunteer orchestra was rehearsing revolutionary anthems (there were as yet none about Stalin).

---

[1] The relevant part of the Fifteenth Party Congress resolution reads as follows: "In the present period the task of combining small individual peasant holdings and transforming them into large collectives must become the main task of the Party in the villages." See Molotov's report, "Work in the Countryside," at Fifteenth Party Congress, in *VKP(b) v rezolyutsiyakh i resheniyakh sezdov, konferentsii i plenumov TsK* (The All-Union Communist Party of Bolsheviks in Resolutions and Decisions of the Congresses, Conferences, and Plenums of the Central Committee), 2 vols., 2nd ed., Moscow, 1933, Vol. II, p. 251 (hereafter cited as *VKP(b) v rezolyutsiyakh*).

Stalin finally arrived with his retinue, and, avoiding the villages prepared for display, went straight to the real villages in search of Siberia's one and only object of interest—grain. According to Sorokin, Stalin had immediately asked Syrtsov to give him a local map showing the richest grain areas and a brief report on the fulfillment of the grain delivery plan.

He was given both. Stalin toured only the areas which were shown on the map as being poor in grain. He would stop at a village, have friendly chats with the peasants, and visit barns, stables, and threshing floors, all on the pretence of seeing how they were getting along. He asked the peasants what complaints they had, and whether those at the top were treating them well. Every such conversation ended with the question: "Well, I see your grain is just rotting away, all for nothing; why don't you want to sell it to the state?" In one village he received the reply: "Well, I've heard you have manufactured goods in Moscow, just rotting away, all for nothing; why don't you want to sell them to the peasants?" Stalin "failed to hear" this reply.

Another reply, however, he not only heard but kept firmly in mind. He mentioned it at a Central Committee plenary session in April 1929 but tactfully transferred the incident from Siberia to Kazakhstan, and used an impersonal "agitator" as the speaker instead of himself. However, even in Stalin's corrected version, the event described was recognized as important.[2]

> Once, after one of our agitators in Kazakhstan spent two hours attempting to persuade grain-owners to deliver their grain, a kulak came up with a pipe in his mouth and said: "Let me see you dance, young fellow, and then I will give you a bushel or two."

None of his hearers at the plenary session doubted that the "young fellow" was Stalin himself.

Later Stalin toured the areas where the grain delivery goal had been met. Then, by adding the data provided by his experts to his own observations, he was able to make a general estimate of the situation, and to draw some specific conclusions. The conclusions concerning Siberia were, in effect, that the "grain deficient areas" were in fact the richest in grain. The peasants in those areas were not delivering grain because it was being requested instead of being taken. As to the areas where the plan had been fulfilled, the situation was, according to Stalin, even worse; the plan had been fulfilled because the targets were too low. Those areas could and must deliver again as much grain as they had already provided. How was this to be done? Meetings of poor and medium-rich peasants should be organized to discuss the self-imposition of delivery quotas. Kulaks would be excluded from the meetings. The meetings must pass resolutions authorizing the "voluntary delivery" by peasants of all grain surpluses to the state. At the same time, the kulaks must be given hard and fast commitments with nonfulfillment punishable under Article 107 of the Criminal Code of the RSFSR.

---

[2] Stalin, *Voprosy leninizma*, p. 260.

Stalin's next step was to inform the bureaus of the Ural District and Siberian Oblast Party Committees of his plans and intentions. In one of his speeches, kept secret from the rest of the country, he said:

> I have been sent here to Siberia for a short visit. My mission is to help you fulfill the grain delivery plan. I have also been asked to discuss with you the possibilities for agricultural development and the plans for the development of kolkhozes and sovkhozes in your area.... You tell me that your grain delivery plan is too high, that it cannot be fulfilled, [but] look at the kulak households: there the granaries and barns are filled with grain and grain is lying out in the open for lack of storage space. I saw dozens of your people. Nearly all live in the households of kulaks, are supported by kulaks, and naturally try to live in peace with them. When I asked them about it they said that the kulaks had cleaner houses and provided better food. Obviously while that state of affairs lasts we cannot expect those legally responsible to do anything sensible or useful for the Soviet regime. It is less obvious why these people have not yet been removed and replaced by others. I propose: (1) that immediate delivery of all grain surpluses from kulaks at state prices be required and (2) in case the kulaks refuse to comply with the law, that they be prosecuted under Article 107 of the Criminal Code of the RSFSR and their grain surpluses be confiscated with the proviso that 25% of the confiscated grain be distributed among the poor and the less well-to-do peasants.[3]

To ensure the success of the operation, Stalin proposed that all Communists found consorting with kulaks and profiteers be dismissed from responsible posts and expelled from the Party. This would include all Communists living in kulak households, married to the daughters of kulaks, or otherwise connected with "alien elements" or those of "socially alien" origin.

The alarmists were proved right; Stalin had hardly left when a campaign was launched both in Siberia and in the Urals against "chameleons" and "aliens," who were dismissed from their positions by the hundreds and expelled from the Party. No allowance was made for anyone or anything. Among those purged were former partisans with good service records, Red Guards, "revolutionary sailors," and "Lenin recruits" (labor members admitted to the Party at the time of Lenin's death). The reasons for expulsion were always the same—"consorting with alien elements," "relaxation of revolutionary vigilance," and sabotage of grain deliveries. Former "revolutionary services" were of no avail. The well-known formula: "We thank you for the past, you answer for the present," dates from that time.

Those expelled were replaced by persons without a past or with a very dark past, even from the point of view of the Bolsheviks themselves, but who were ready to do whatever was required of them by the Party, that is, by Stalin. And all that he required at first was grain.

These organizational measures represented only one side of the story. To make them effective, the peasantry had to be given some incentive. For this purpose Stalin decided to divide the peasants into groups or classes. There were

[3] I. V. Stalin, *Sochineniya* (Works), 13 vols., Moscow, 1946–54, Vol. XI, pp. 1–4. (Hereafter cited as Stalin, *Sochineniya*.)

six such groups: (1) landless agricultural laborers, (2) poor peasants, (3) the less well-to-do peasants, (4) medium peasants, (5) well-to-do peasants, and (6) kulaks. The first two groups were completely freed from obligations to deliver grain for the purposes of the plan, the third group was to make a "symbolic contribution," the fourth would deliver grain at a standard rate amounting to about a quarter of the grain owned, the fifth and sixth would surrender all their grain. The methods proposed by Stalin for confiscating the grain were no less original. They were called "self-taxation" and "specific obligation."

The new system was introduced by calling "meetings of poor peasants" of a given village to approve the division of the inhabitants into the various classes. Lists were drawn up and after these were approved "assistance commissions" were elected, whose function it was to ratify in the name of the peasants the grain delivery plan proposed from above and to collect the grain from the peasants, a task which involved visits to farms, searches, and confiscation. To encourage the poor to fight the main body of the peasants, now called kulaks (a term in practice extended to include the "well-to-do"), Stalin proposed that the poor be given "a number of privileges."[4] A part of the peasantry, chiefly the poor and irresponsible, whom the Bolsheviks themselves called loafers, became government contractors on a percentage commission. Aided by the OGPU, they took the grain from the well-to-do peasants and retained 25% for their own use. If the well-to-do peasants resisted, they were tried in criminal court. Later on Stalin wrote, quite correctly: "The extraordinary measures were effective; the poor and the medium peasants joined in the fight against the kulaks, the kulaks were isolated, and the resistance of both kulaks and speculators was broken."[5]

Important as the revision of the grain delivery system was, the chief aim of Stalin's mission was quite different. Ever since disagreements had arisen within the Politburo on the subject of agricultural policy, particularly with reference to the development of agriculture, the Soviet government had been faced with a problem of much more than theoretical importance: should there be evolution or revolution, peace with the peasants, or repression of the peasants? In short, "Who whom?"—as Stalin phrased the Leninist formulation of the problem. In his view, the Soviet regime had by now become sufficiently strong to repeat the method used in the October Revolution against capitalists and landowners, but using it this time against the well-to-do and medium peasants. He explained his view as follows, in the speech referred to above: "For the consolidation of the Soviet regime and the victory of the socialist regime in our country, it is not sufficient merely to socialize industry. What we need is to pass on from the socialization of industry to the socialization of agriculture."[6]

What form should this socialization of the peasants take? Stalin supplied the following answer: "All the administrative districts of our country without ex-

<hr/>

[4] *Istoriya VKP(b). Kratky kurs* (Short Course in the History of the Communist Party of Bolsheviks), Moscow, 1945, p. 279. (Hereafter cited as *Istoriya VKP(b). Kratky kurs*.)

[5] *Ibid.*

[6] Stalin, *Sochineniya*, Vol. XI, 1949, p. 6.

ception must be covered with a network of kolkhozes and sovkhozes, able to take the place not only of the kulaks, but of all individual peasants as purveyors of grain to the state."[7]

At the Fifteenth Party Congress a month before Stalin's speech in Siberia there had been no mention of kolkhozes, and there was, therefore, no directive to authorize Stalin's proposal "to cover all the administrative districts of our country, without exception, with a network of kolkhozes." All that had been said on the subject was that "new measures must be taken to limit the development of capitalism in the villages and to direct the peasant economy toward socialism."[8] But now Stalin was proposing "total collectivization" and "the liquidation of kulaks as a class on this basis." In the course of the discussion in the Siberian Oblast Party Committee, Stalin was supported by Syrtsov (secretary of the Ural District Committee), Kabakov (chairman of the Ural District Executive Committee), and Sulimov (member of the Ural District Executive Committee).

On leaving Siberia, Stalin took with him a resolution of the Siberian and Ural Party Committees demanding that the tempo of collectivization be forced in accordance with the proposed plan. A short time later the following Party committees supported the resolution: the Central Black Earth Oblast Committee (Secretary, Vareikis), the Nizhny Novgorod District Committee (Secretary, Zhdanov), the Central Committee of the Ukrainian Communist Party (Secretary, Kaganovich), and still later, the North Caucasus District Committee (Secretary, Andreyev).

After Stalin's departure from Siberia, Moscow was flooded with innumerable letters and telegrams from both peasants and workers in Siberia and the Urals, complaining of the "revolution" initiated by Stalin. As what Stalin called his experiment began to be imitated in other areas on direct instructions from Stalin, issued in the name of the Party Central Committee, there arose the possibility of a large-scale peasant revolt. This development forced Bukharin's group to raise the peasant question again in the Central Committee, with the aim of calling Stalin to order. As a result, the Politburo adopted the following unequivocal resolution signed by Stalin himself: "All talk of our having abolished the NEP and introduced compulsory food distribution, liquidation of the kulaks, etc., is nothing but counterrevolutionary gossip which must be resolutely opposed. The NEP represents the basis of our economic policy and will continue to do so for a long period of history."[9] A year after this definite promise to his own Party, Stalin abolished the NEP.

Later on Sorokin gave me additional details regarding Stalin's visit to Siberia and of Sorokin's own share in the task of putting the "Siberian experiment" into effect. Of particular interest were details about the Party leaders in Siberia and the Urals which throw light on their subsequent careers. It was from him that I first heard of Malenkov. At the time in question Malenkov was working in the Party

---

[7] *Ibid.*

[8] *VKP(b) v resolyutsiyakh*, Vol. II, p. 260.

[9] Stalin, *Sochineniya*, Vol. XII, 1949, p. 15.

15

Central Committee as a member of Stalin's personal secretariat, without interrupting his studies in the Moscow Higher Technical School. While still a student, Malenkov had acquired a reputation as an "activist" in the fight against the Trotskyite opposition, and as far back as 1924 had become head of the Party organization in the school.

Malenkov's career reached a turning point early in 1925. When his Party unit in the school was providing almost unanimous support of Trotsky's program, Malenkov was one of the few Communists fanatically to support the "Leninist leadership" of Stalin and Bukharin. The unit held a meeting at which he was accused of being an opportunist and bootlicker, and a resolution was passed dismissing him from his post as secretary of the Party unit. Malenkov complained to the district committee, but was told that the committee would neither set aside the resolution nor reinstate him as secretary, as such action was contrary to Party regulations. After appealing in vain to the Moscow City Committee, Malenkov lodged a complaint with the Central Committee, in which he accused the district and Moscow City committees of failure to help him expose the Trotskyite conspiracy in the Moscow Higher Technical School. Soon after he was summoned by Kaganovich, then Chief of the Organization and Training Section of the Central Committee. What Malenkov told Kaganovich turned out to be of historic importance. The Party cells in the University and the Moscow Higher Technical School, said Malenkov, were supporting the Trotskyites mainly because Trotskyite students enjoyed special privileges at the hands of the district and the Moscow City committees, the latter of which did not allow "malicious Trotskyites" to be expelled from the Party, but demanded that they be "re-educated," while Khodorovsky, the Chief of the Education Committee in the People's Commissariat of Education, was appointing inveterate Trotskyites as university presidents. Helpless "factory proletarians" were being sent to lecture to forums of the district and Moscow City Committee cells, while those sent by the Communist Academy and the Institute of Red Professors were Trotskyites. To Kaganovich's question as to how the universities and the university-level institutes could be purged of Trotskyites, Malenkov replied with a concrete plan.

"We must use an iron broom," said Malenkov, "to sweep out not only the university auditoriums but also the studies of the university presidents. And here is a plan for doing it." With these words Malenkov took from his briefcase a detailed memorandum addressed to the Party Central Committee. Kaganovich did not read the memorandum immediately. He promised to look it through and invited Malenkov to return a week later (allowing time to make inquiries about Malenkov in the Special Sections of the Party Central Committee and the OGPU). There is no doubt that the young Malenkov, who was then only 23 years old, had made a most favorable impression on Kaganovich. When Kaganovich received him again, he surprised him by saying: "Comrade Stalin wants to meet you."

Stalin received Malenkov without ceremony ("I felt as if he were a father as soon as I met him," said Malenkov to Sorokin), asked him how he was getting on in his studies, how he liked his food and his dormitory, whether his parents were still alive, and so on. Not a single business or political question was raised. The talk ended with a complete surprise for Malenkov. "Comrade Kaganovich and I," said Stalin, "have decided to take you on to work in the office of the Central Committee. Have you any objections, Comrade Malenkov?"

"I live for the Party," replied Malenkov.

Malenkov's recommendations formed the basis for the directives on purging university and institute cells issued in 1925, and Malenkov himself became one of the executors of the purge. In that one year, 92,000 students and Soviet functionaries were expelled from the Party.[10] From that time on until his removal by Khrushchev, Malenkov held important positions in the Party Central Committee.

On Stalin's staff Malenkov's duties were those of a personal aide. He kept a detailed diary in which he entered Stalin's impressions of his journeys, and took down his questions and answers, directions and instructions; he was present at all of Stalin's closed meetings with provincial executive officers, wrote down parallel minutes of such meetings for Stalin's personal use, and acted as observer at certain departmental meetings which Stalin was unable to attend. But he never became involved in discussions, even though in the absence of Stalin he often asked pertinent questions on subjects under discussion.

In many respects Malenkov was like his master. He had the same reticence, the same ability to concentrate, the same lack of sympathy for academic or theoretical views, the same unconcealed rough-and-ready realism bordering on cynicism, the same pragmatic approach to the solution of the most abstract problems, and the same amazing capacity for adaptation and maneuver when required by the interests of himself or his work. Two other qualities inherited from his master— a deeply concealed cunning and a readiness to commit any act of disloyalty, however extreme, including treachery to Stalin himself—fill out the picture of Malenkov's character.

Before leaving Malenkov, a few words should be said on the question of theory. As I have already said, theory was not his strong point. One of the responsible functionaries of the Party Central Committee told me some time later that Malenkov once said to him in the course of an informal conversation: "You theorists pride yourselves on your knowledge of Marxism, but all I have read is the whole of Stalin, not all of Lenin, and only the *Communist Manifesto* of Marx and Engels, but I know Marxism as well as any of you theoretical scribblers." It is quite possible that Malenkov did not confess his ignorance of Marxism quite so openly, but I have no doubt at all that the story is essentially true to fact. I have known many members of the Party Central Committee—practical workers and even Party functionaries—who used to justify their ignorance of Marx's theories by the difficulty they experienced in understanding Marx's *Capital* or Engels' *Dialectics of Nature*. No one who has studied Stalin's "theoretical works"

---

[10] *Istoriya VKP(b). Kratky kurs*, pp. 257, 263.

can help being astonished at his quite unconscious schoolboy errors in the fields of philosophy and economics. Later, however, these errors were presented as "a further development of Marxism."

Weakness in theory or at least the absence of a propensity for theorizing without any natural gift for it was probably an advantage for such Communist figures as Malenkov. The Russian Revolution, in fact, swallowed up all its theorists and particularly during its Bolshevik period, when it did away with such theorists as Plekhanov, Bogdanov, Trotsky, Bukharin, Preobrazhensky, and others. Before the victory of the Revolution, it was they who established the tone, the program, and the ideology of the movement, but after the victory, when practice had to take the place of theory, they proved to be incapable of anything except further theorizing. It was for this reason that the helm of the new ship of state was taken over by sober-minded captains who recognized neither infallibility nor old dogmas, nor the validity of their prophets. Stalin was an outstanding pragmatist and enemy of dead dogma. "There is," he said a few months before the Bolsheviks came to power, "a dogmatic Marxism and a creative Marxism. I support the latter." It was just such "creative Marxists" that Stalin began to collect round himself as soon as he took over the bridge of the Bolshevik ship. Malenkov happened to be a "Marxist" of this type without having read Marx. Another important quality of Malenkov's was his ability to read the minds of others. All who knew his close collaborators said that Malenkov needed only a brief conversation to complete a faultless diagnosis, including an analysis of the person's ideals and capabilities. In this regard Malenkov made fewer mistakes than Stalin.

There is a classic example of Malenkov's superiority to Stalin in his analysis of people. It occured in connection with Syrtsov's candidature for the post of Chairman of the Council of People's Commissars of the RSFSR in 1930, in place of Rykov. Stalin's first intimate acquaintance with Syrtsov took place during his visit to Siberia. As the struggle with the Bukharin group had already begun by then and Stalin was trying to work out a plan for appointing replacements for his future victims, he decided to study the leading Siberian functionaries as possible candidates for promotion. On the eve of his departure from Novosibirsk, Stalin agreed, of course very secretly, that Syrtsov might possibly be called to Moscow to fill a responsible position. Stalin informed Syrtsov that such an appointment would depend upon his loyalty to the Party Central Committee, that is, to Stalin, and on effective support in the struggle against the Right-Wing Deviationists then in progress within the leadership of the Party Central Committee and the Council of People's Commissars. Syrtsov agreed without knowing exactly what was involved. However, Malenkov warned Stalin politely but insistently that Syrtsov was not to be trusted. Stalin paid little attention to Malenkov's warning and had Syrtsov appointed Chairman of the Council of People's Commissars of the RSFSR and supported his candidacy as a member of the Politburo. Some six months later, when Syrtsov broke with Stalin, he was expelled from the Central Committee, while Malenkov's star rose accordingly.

Chapter III

The Institute of Red Professors:
The "Theory Headquarters" of the Party Central Committee

The scientific research curriculum of the Institute of Red Professors provided the main postgraduate course for future red professors in universities and institutes in the fields of sociology and economics. The Institute had been created at the initiative of Pokrovsky, the leading Marxist historian and in Stalin's day a member of the Academy of Sciences of the USSR.

Pokrovsky had become well known as a Marxist historian long before the Revolution. Immediately after graduating from Moscow University he had made a name for himself as the representative of Marxism in Russian historiography. His main work, *Russian History from the Earliest Times*, in four volumes, had appeared as far back as 1907–1912. In it he had taken radical issue with all the existing schools of history in his interpretation of this historical process. He had invented a methodology of historical materialism of a type peculiar to himself, which his left-wing opponents called "economic materialism." He analyzed historical events from the point of view of class interests.

Pokrovsky had been a member of the Bolshevik Party since 1905. After the Revolution he had been appointed Vice-Commissar of Education, in charge of all educational institutions and presiding officer of the State Council for Research and Education under the Commissariat of Education. He was ipso facto official head of Soviet historiography. But there were no proponents of this school of historiography in Soviet Russia, apart from Pokrovsky himself and one or two historians who were members of the Party. Representatives of the traditional Russian historical schools refused to recognize either Pokrovsky's historical concept or Pokrovsky as an authority. In fact, it was for this reason that history as a science had had for a time to be abolished altogether in Russia. History departments in the universities had been closed and history as a subject no longer taught in the schools, its place being taken by what was called the science of society, and similar subjects.

The Soviet government had thus been faced with a pressing task—creation of a new staff of scholars, not only in history but in all other branches of the social sciences. This task had had to be solved by new organizations created at the initiative of Pokrovsky, including the Communist Academy, the Institute of Red Professors, and various Communist universities.

Pokrovsky provided a short but vivid summary of his new concept of history in a one-volume work entitled *A Brief Sketch of Russian History*, which appeared in ten editions between 1921 and 1931 alone. Lenin had immediately grasped the significance of Pokrovsky's "revolution" in Russian historiography, and had congratulated him on his success in the following letter:

To Comrade Pokrovsky: My sincere congratulations on your success. I greatly appreciate your new book, *A Brief Sketch of Russian History*. The original construction and exposition make for most interesting reading. It will have, I think, to be translated into European languages. I shall, if I may, make one small remark. If it is to become *a textbook (and it must)*, it should have a chronological index added. The student must know both your book and the index . . . . Yours, Lenin.[1]

(In 1934 Stalin declared this book by Pokrovsky to be anti-Leninist.)

The decree authorizing the creation of the Institute of Red Professors was signed by Lenin on February 11, 1921. It is described as follows in the *Large Soviet Encyclopedia*:

The Institute of Red Professors was founded by a decree of the Council of People's Commissars of the RSFSR of February 11, 1921, signed by Lenin. The decree of the Council of People's Commissars assigned the Institute the task of training red professors to teach theoretical economics, historical materialism, the development of social forces, modern history, and socialist construction in the universities of the Republic ("Collection of Laws and Ordinances of the Workers' and Peasants' Government," 1921, No. 12, p. 79). The following departments were organized: as of 1922, Economics, History, and Philosophy; as of 1924, Law; and as of 1926, Party History. Annual admissions to the Institute in 1921-29 were 75 to 140 persons, chiefly postgraduates . . . . Work in the Institute consists in attendance at lectures and seminars. The total course lasts three years. At the end of the course students have to take state examinations.[2]

One of the many reasons why it was necessary to create the Institute which I attended and others like it was simply that the older scholars and scientists were boycotting the Soviet regime. Many of the older professors refused to serve the Soviet regime and joined the ranks of the "internal emigration." Others openly declared war on the Soviet regime, fought in the anti-Bolshevik Volunteer Army, and when the war ended with a Bolshevik victory, emigrated entirely. Still others were expelled from Russia by the Bolsheviks, in order to rid themselves of future "conspirators."

However, those who stayed in Russia also failed to gain the confidence of the Soviet regime. "Once a wolf, always a wolf," was a proverb which I frequently heard applied by Soviet ideologists to the older professors. Even those of the surviving old professors who were the most conscientious from the point of view of the Soviet regime never went beyond the favorite formula: "We are a-political and therefore loyal." The simple loyalty which was quite sufficient during the Civil War was considered entirely inadequate after the Bolshevik victory. Besides, a "loyal professor" could only teach the young to be merely loyal. This the Soviet regime could not allow. "Communist Education of Youth" was the slogan proclaimed by Lenin at the Third Congress of the Komsomol (League of Communist Youth) in 1920. The conclusion drawn by the Bolsheviks was that it was necessary to create their own staff of red professors, who would learn Marxist theory from

---

[1] M. N. Pokrovsky, *Russkaya istoriya v samom szhatom ocherke* (A Brief Sketch of Russian History), Moscow, 1933, p. XI.

[2] *Bolshaya Sovetskaya Entsiklopediya* (Large Soviet Encyclopedia), 1st ed., 1937, Vol. XXXIV, p. 600–601. (Hereafter cited as *BSE*).

the leaders of the All-Union Communist Party and factual knowledge from "loyal professors." When they were well enough trained, they would take the places of the "bourgeois professors." "Communist education" would then be in safe hands.

By the beginning of 1928 the Institute of Red Professors had departments of History, Philosophy and Natural Science, Economics, History of Literature and Literary Criticism, World Politics and World Economics, and a General Department. Later, these departments were reorganized into independent Institutes of Red Professors, according to the fields of specialization. The professors included the most prominent scholars in the country, both Party and non-Party, and leading members of the All-Union Communist Party and Comintern organizations. The faculty included the following professors, many of whom were famous at the time, or later on:

Non-Party Scholars: Rozhkov, Platonov, Sergeyev, Gratsiansky, Bakhrushin, Tarlé, Grekov, Struve, Krachkovsky, Marr, Meshchaninov, Rubin, Groman, Bazarov, L. Axelrod, Deborin, Preobrazhensky, Mishulin, Kosminsky, and the younger Timiryazev.

Communist Party Professors: Bukharin, Pokrovsky, Lunacharsky, Yaroslavsky, Radek, Krumin, Kviring, Ye. Preobrazhensky, Vyshinsky, Krylenko, Pashukanis, Berman, Varga, Mif, Bela Kun (for Eastern Europe), Ercoli-Togliatti (for Southwestern Europe), V. Kolarov (for the Balkans), W. Pieck (for Central Europe), Kuusinen (for Scandinavia), Strakhov (a Chinese Communist writer with a Russian pseudonym, for China), and several other Chinese and Japanese. From time to time lectures were given by Stalin, Kaganovich, Kalinin, Manuilsky, Bubnov, Eideman, and others.

Lecturers were carefully selected. Candidates for competitive examinations were named in decrees of the Mandate Commission of the Party Central Committee. As a rule, candidates were required to have had a university education or the equivalent. Before taking an oral examination, each candidate had to submit a study in writing. On the basis of these preliminaries, the examining board of the Institute reported to the Mandate Commission of the Party Central Committee on the degree to which the candidate met the academic requirements of the Institute. The Mandate Commission in turn reported to the Organization Bureau of the Central Committee, which made the final decision. A new faculty appointee was immediately included in the card index of "active Party members." Thereafter no changes in his career, such as transfers, assignments, appointments, dismissals, or arrest, could take place without the knowledge and by approval of the Central Committee.

The Institute, as the "theoretical staff" of the Central Committee, supplied many workers both for Stalin and for his opponents. How and why some became Stalin's pupils and supporters while others turned into "enemies of the people" will appear later. At this point it will be sufficient to list a few names.

The following Institute graduates became Stalin's enemies and died in the cells of the NKVD or in solitary confinement in concentration camps: Slepkov, Astrov (editors of the periodical *Bolshevik* and Bukharin's colleagues on the board of *Pravda*), Eikhenwald, Maretsky, Kraval (Bukharin's secretary), Stetsky (member of the Party Central Committee and responsible head of the Department of Agitation and Propaganda of the Party Central Committee), Sten (member of the Central Control Commission), Karev, Bessonov, A. Kon (faculty member of the Communist Academy), K. Butayev, K. Tabolov, Samursky, Mikhailov (secretaries of oblast committees), Madyar, Lominadze, Shatskin (Comintern). The list could be extended to include a hundred names.

The following graduates became Stalin's intimate collaboraters: A. Shcherbakov (died as member of the Politburo in 1945), Mekhlis (member of the Party Central Committee of the All-Union Communist Party and at one time Minister of State Control), Abalin (Editor-in-Chief of *Kommunist*), Fedoseyev (at one time Editor-in-Chief of *Bolshevik*), Alexandrov (member of the Central Committee and at one time propaganda chief), Suslov (Secretary of the Central Committee), Pospelov (at one time Editor-in-Chief of *Pravda*, later Director of the Marx-Engels-Lenin Institute, then Secretary of the Central Committee), Ilyichev (at various times Editor-in-Chief of *Izvestia* and *Pravda*, alternate member of the Central Committee), Mitin (member of the Central Committee), Yudin (member of the Central Committee and Editor-in-Chief of the Cominform press organ, later Ambassador to China), Konstantinov (head of the Central Committee Department of Agitation and Propaganda), Surkov (a head of the Writers' Union). This list could also be extended.

The above list of persons who after graduation played important parts in the pro- and anti-Stalin struggle is a good illustration of the extent to which the Institute of Red Professors bore out its nickname of "theory headquarters," in which both sides, the Stalinists and the anti-Stalinists, worked out with equal zeal the "ideological strategy" of future wars within the Party. In my period in the Institute the war was to center about Bukharin.

There is as yet no good biography of Bukharin although his influence in shaping the ideology and program of the October Revolution was certainly greater than Stalin's and at least equal to that of Trotsky, who became a real Bolshevik only after the revolt of July 1917. In the realm of theory as well as in the work of drawing up the Party program, the main burden of the struggle against Trotsky and Zinoviev was borne not by Stalin, but by Bukharin. A biographical sketch by D. Maretsky in the 1927 edition of the *Large Soviet Encyclopedia* is the only available source of uncensored information about Bukharin and his life before the Revolution, and if that volume of the encyclopedia had appeared a year later we would have been deprived of even this valuable source. In the following sketch the basic facts are taken from this biography. However, the real drama of Bukharin's life, and the real history of his career as a politician and founder of a distinct ideology, date only from 1927.

Nikolai Ivanovich Bukharin was born on October 10, 1888, in Moscow, where his father was a primary school teacher. At the age of 17 Bukharin joined a circle of revolutionary students and in 1906 was admitted to the Bolshevik Party in the Zamoskvorechye sector of Moscow. He became a professional Party propagandist and in 1907 entered Moscow University, where he studied economics and law while continuing his underground work. By 1908 his reputation was such that he was elected member of the Moscow Committee of the Party. In 1909 he was twice arrested for illegal revolutionary activity. After his third arrest in 1910, he was exiled to Onega, from which he escaped. Shortly after, he emigrated to Germany and for a time lived in Hanover.

He first met Lenin in Cracow in 1912. From then on the close association between the two men remained unbroken in spite of frequent differences of opinion on political and theoretical matters. Soon after their meeting, Lenin invited Bukharin to become an active contributor to the Bolshevik papers, *Pravda* and *Prosveshcheniye*. Bukharin accepted, but on condition that he be given freedom to express his theoretical views. Later in the year he went to Vienna where, while taking a lively interest in the life of Bolshevik emigres, he attended lectures by Böhm-Bawerk and Wieser, began work on his first theoretical study, *The Political Economy of the Rentier*, and published a number of critical works on Struve, Tugan-Baranovsky, Oppenheimer, and his former teacher, Böhm-Bawerk. It was in Vienna that Bukharin first met his future executioner, Stalin, who had just escaped from exile. He helped Stalin to compile his *Marxism and the National Question* which first appeared under the title of *Social Democracy and the Problem of Nationalities*, a work which earned the author great fame as a Marxist expert on nationalities. Bukharin found and translated for Stalin suitable quotations from R. Renner and Otto Bauer, and edited the entire book before it was accepted by Lenin for publication in 1913 in the magazine *Prosveshcheniye*. Shortly before the outbreak of war in 1914 he was arrested as a Russian spy by the Austrian police, but was released thanks to intervention on his behalf by the Austrian Social Democrats, whom he and Stalin were castigating in *Prosveshcheniye*. From Austria he was expelled to Switzerland.

In 1915, using a forged passport, Bukharin emigrated to Sweden by way of France and England. In Sweden he joined forces with the Swedish left-wing Social Democratic group headed by Höglund, and led a campaign of international Leninist propaganda against the war. He was again arrested, this time by the Swedish police, as an agent of Lenin and dispatched to Norway. In 1916 he entered the United States illegally and became editor of *Novy Mir*, a political emigre organ. After the February Revolution in 1917, he returned to Russia via Japan. He at once plunged into the activity that led to the October coup d'etat, joined the Central Committee, organized the October uprising in Moscow, became editor-in-chief of *Pravda*, and delivered his famous speech to the Constituent Assembly on behalf of the Central Committee of the Bolshevik Party.

At the time of the separate peace negotiations with Germany at Brest-Litovsk he sharply criticized Lenin's policy, founded in Moscow a "group of Left Communists" with its own newspaper organ, *Kommunist*, and resigned his post as editor-in-chief of *Pravda*. He rejoined Lenin after the unsuccessful uprising of the Left Social Revolutionaries. With Lenin, Zinoviev, and Trotsky he was a co-founder of the Comintern and was until 1929 a regular member of its presidium.

Bukharin began writing early in life, and, as he himself used to say, learned German in order to read in the original the classics of the German philosophers and, of course, Marx and Engels. His first scientific work, *The Political Economy of the Rentier*, was written when he was only 24. As an economist and sociologist he had no peer in the Bolshevik Party. Frequently he was more orthodox in his views than Lenin, with whom he often disagreed on the theoretical interpretation of such varied subjects as imperialism, the theory of the blowing-up of the state, the nature of the proletarian state, the economics of the period of transition, the problem of nationality, and so on. In these arguments Lenin was often compelled to admit the orthodoxy of Bukharin's views and did so, either personally or through his wife, as, for instance, on the eve of the Sixth Party Congress in August 1917, when he was in hiding.

Bukharin's capacity for work was astounding. From December 1917 to April 1929 (with a short break in 1918 during the Brest-Litovsk crisis) he edited *Pravda*, usually writing the leading article, took an active part in the work of the Politburo and the presidium of the Comintern, in both of which he was a member, lectured at innumerable conferences and to University students, edited the magazines *Bolshevik* and *Prozhektor*, was (from 1928) a member of the Academy of Sciences of the USSR, carefully followed trends in both Russian and foreign literatures, and, with it all, found time to write highly scholarly and at the same time extremely popular books. It was hardly surprising that the young "October" generation should regard Bukharin as a "theoretical Hercules." Active and alert, he was physically very strong. From childhood on he engaged enthusiastically in gymnastics, and even during his wanderings as a political emigre never omitted physical exercise.

Although he was a fanatical admirer of Marx and Engels (of the two, he rated Engels higher than Marx as a philosopher), Bukharin did not quote them chapter and verse. He was as well informed on post-Marxian sociological literature as any university professor. While having a penchant for abstract theorizing on political economy and sociology, he was a "seeking" Marxist, like Kautsky and Plekhanov, and a popularizer of Marx in the Bolshevik spirit, through such books as *The ABC of Communism*, and *The Theory of Historical Materialism*. He was very ambitious and believed that it was his mission to provide a modern version of Marxism applicable to political economy and philosophy at the beginning of the twentieth century. He began writing on the economic aspects of this subject during Lenin's lifetime, but set his work aside during the fight with Trotsky. I was told by a person who had occupied a neighboring cell in the Lubyanka Prison that Bukharin, while in solitary confinement, completed a philosophical monograph on this subject. None of his writings on economics were published after Lenin's death, except for the introduction to this study, which appeared separately under the title of "Marx and the Contemporary World," published, as I recall, by the Academy of Sciences of the USSR in 1933 in a collection of articles dedicated to Marx on the fiftieth anniversary of his death. And even this introduction, after being screened by Stalin, bore little resemblance to the original, all Bukharin's "anti-Marxist heresies" having been thrown out wholesale and the remaining text mutilated by the addition of new material from the pens of the watchful censors of the Politburo—Mekhlis, Mitin, and Yudin.

Chapter IV

The Right-Wing Group in the Institute of Red Professors

My fellow-student Sorokin introduced me to the local group of the political Right. We frequently met in an apartment belonging to Zinaida Nikolayevna Koroleva, a fairly well-known member of the group.

Zinaida Nikolayevna was not one of the famous "cooks" of whom Lenin was speaking when he said that they must "learn to govern the state." She belonged, by social origin, to the gentry, and her education was that of a real lady, but in her political views, even in her high school years, she had become a radical revolutionary. In 1916 she had left medical school to go to the front as a nurse. The February Revolution had caught up with her at a hospital near Kiev. She joined one of the soldiers' revolutionary committees which were springing up everywhere. Though officially only a secretary, in fact she carried out very important assignments as author and editor of the local committee appeals, orders, and demands addressed to the soldiers, the people, and the government.

The soldiers had taken a liking to her simplicity of manner, even though they could not keep from mistrusting her a little. "A bourgeois herself," they used to say, "and yet she hasn't a kind word to say for them; there is something queer about it." On one occasion, when she had heard about remarks of this kind, she asked the chairman of the soldiers' committee to call a special meeting at which she could pass on some useful information. The atmosphere of the time has been well described by Artem Veseley. "There is a revolution in Russia. . . . All Russia is one political meeting." At the front, soldiers lived for the sake of political meetings, at which they were assailed by two slogans: "War to a victorious end," from the Right, and "Peace to the cottages, war to the palaces," from the Left. Both slogans seemed too extreme, and the average soldier felt instinctively that there must be another more moderate and rational solution to the problem of war and peace. They were therefore open to new resolutions and suggestions.

This readiness to listen may have been the reason why the meeting called by Zinaida Nikolayevna was so well attended that at first she had hesitated, and had thought it might be best to abandon her intention of speaking to such a vast audience. But her friends in the soldiers' committee urged her on, and the closing words of the chairman's introductory speech were well chosen. "You will now be addressed by Revolyutsiya (Revolution) Nikolayevna, formerly Koroleva." The ice was broken, Zinaida Nikolayevna spoke.

Afterward, when telling about it, she used to say:

> I cannot remember a word of what I said. It was my revolutionary debut, and you cannot imagine how nervous I was. When I had suggested calling a meeting,

I had intended to tell the soldiers something about Russian revolutionary "bourgeois women"—Vera Figner, Sophia Perovskaya, Vera Zasulich, Ekaterina Kuskova, and the "grandmother of the Russian revolution," Breshko-Breshkovskaya—in order to destroy this kind of prejudice. But of what I said I simply cannot remember a word. All I can remember is from that memorable day onward, my friends called me Revolyutsiya Nikolayevna.

In my time, in 1928, she was working in the Commissariat of Foreign Affairs and had considerable influence among its top figures. She knew Sorokin and was quite friendly with him, while he spoke with her with equal lack of hesitation on political matters or on "freedom of the sexes." It might be mentioned at this point that even in later years, when reaction had set in and every Old Bolshevik or Civil War hero was being hounded by half a dozen Stalinist agents, relations among the Old Bolsheviks remained friendly, thus causing both a great deal of harm.

I often accompanied Sorokin when he went to see her, and I treated her with all the veneration of a young enthusiast for a revolutionary hero. My close acquaintance with her dated from an evening spent in her apartment, to which only a few guests were invited: a soldier with badges of rank, whom the other guests addressed simply as "General," his female companion with a pale face and impudent eyes, Reznikov, a member of the Moscow Committee who, many thought, would end up as a member of the Politburo, People's Commissar N., really only Vice-Commissar but called "Commissar" out of courtesy, his wife, Sorokin, and I. The table was set in a typically Russian way, with plenty of food but no pretense at refinement.

After the usual drinking, and several toasts, Zinaida Nikolayevna moved the party into the neighboring room and sat down at the piano.

"Well," she said, fingering the music, "what shall I play for you, my friends?"

"A funeral march," replied Sorokin imperturbably. His words were drowned in laughter.

"Willingly, Vanya, only tell us what we are to bewail," said the hostess, half in annoyance and half in approval.

"The miserable end of the great Revolution," replied the not quite sober Sorokin.

Everyone looked thoughtful. Sorokin's words had a sobering effect. Even the General shook his head slowly and despondently as if to say, "this is the bitter truth."

After dinner and music we got down to business. I now found out that I was present at what was anything but an ordinary birthday celebration. After a few introductory remarks, the hostess introduced Reznikov, a member of the Moscow Party Committee, as the speaker of the evening.

It was only the second time that I had seen Reznikov, but I had heard from Sorokin that he was an eminent Party functionary with an opinion of his own. During the October Revolution he had been the representative of the Petrograd Military and Revolutionary Committee to the Navy, with direct responsibility to Trotsky for military matters and to Lenin for Party affairs. "Lenin was the brain, Trotsky the soul, and Reznikov the body of our Revolution," said the General in discussing the driving forces behind the Bolshevik Revolution. During the Civil War Reznikov had fought against Kolchak, been twice wounded, both times seriously, and been taken prisoner. He was to have been shot, but was saved in the nick of time by the personal intervention of Lenin and exchanged for ten Kolchak officers seized by the Bolsheviks. There was only one blot on his Party record: during the Kronstadt uprising in 1921, Reznikov had opposed Trotsky's proposed ultimatum to the rebels with its threat to destroy Kronstadt if they refused to accept it. "Every shot at Kronstadt," Reznikov had said, "is a shot at the Revolution." When the Party Central Committee was discussing the question of sending a delegation to urge the Kronstadt rebels to agree to a peaceful solution of the conflict, Lenin again thought of Reznikov. He was told that Reznikov was sitting in a Cheka prison as a "moral collaborator" of the rebels.

"Come now, comrades," said Lenin, "if people like Reznikov are considered anti-revolutionaries, we are all anti-revolutionaries." And for the second time Reznikov was saved by Lenin as he was about to be shot.

From that time on, Reznikov was a loyal follower of Lenin, but a secret and implacable enemy of Trotsky and the Cheka. During Stalin's struggle against Trotsky and his opposition group, Reznikov was in the forefront. The Stalinist Central Committee showed its gratitude by making Reznikov one of the Moscow Party leaders.

"Zinaida Nikolayevna," began Reznikov, "has asked me to tell her friends what I know of the situation within the Party and particularly the situation within our Moscow organization. I have willingly agreed, especially as the Party press is not in a position to give any information to its own Party."

After this introduction, Reznikov took a notebook from his briefcase and thumbing through the pages gave us a report lasting almost an hour on behind-the-scenes events in the Moscow Party Committee and the Party Central Committee. Everything that he told us was completely new to me.

As he told it, from the very beginning of 1928, that is, immediately after the liquidation of the Left, a concealed but stubborn fight on almost all fundamental questions concerning the domestic and foreign policy of the Party had been in progress both in the Politburo and among the leaders of the Moscow Party Committee. The debate had really begun over Trotsky, who by then had been banished to Alma-Ata,[1] from where he continued to make trouble for the Party Central Committee by articles and statements.[2]

---

[1] On his way from Alma-Ata to Constantinople, Trotsky learned from Soviet newspapers that Stalin had not found it easy to banish him. "The newspapers we get on our way comment on the big new campaign against the Trotskyites. The struggle at the top on the subject of my banishment can be guessed at between the lines. Stalin's group is in a hurry. It has good enough reason. It must surmount physical, not to speak of political, difficulties." L, Trotsky, *Moya zhizn* (My Life), 2 vols., Riga, 1930, Vol. II, p. 316. (Hereafter cited as Trotsky, *Moya zhinzn.*

[2] "During the period April—October 1928, we dispatched from Alma-Ata 800 political letters, including a number of large studies. We sent out 550 telegrams. We received about a thousand political letters and about 700 telegrams, most of them collectively signed." *Ibid.*, p. 305.

Trotsky's information sheets, mimeographed in Moscow, were distributed not only among Party members, but also among the non-Party intelligentsia. (I myself obtained one of these articles in the Communist Academy, where there was an illegal Trotskyite cell. I may add that I kept it for nearly ten years, until 1937, when in the course of weeding out all anti-Stalinist literature from among my papers in case of a possible house-search and arrest, I found it, reread it carefully, made a mental note of Trotsky's prophetic wisdom, and burned it.) In view of Trotsky's continuous "anti-revolutionary" activities, Reznikov continued, Stalin proposed to the Politburo that he be tried. Everyone understood that this time Stalin wanted to bring about the physical destruction of his opponent. Of all the Politburo members, only Molotov and Voroshilov supported Stalin. Rykov, Bukharin, and Kalinin opposed bringing Trotsky to trial. Finally a compromise solution was reached under which Trotsky was to be exiled.

For a long time Stalin had refused to accept this compromise, until he was assured by Menzhinsky, head of the OGPU, that his department did not care where Trotsky was, whether in Alma-Ata, in Lubyanka Prison, or in Madagascar: "He will be in our hands wherever he is." He was, of course, to be proved right.

Another argument concerned the so-called Shakhty Case. Late in 1927, Yefim Georgievich Yevdokimov, the OGPU representative in the North Caucasus, had presented Menzhinsky, chairman of the OGPU board, with a detailed secret report making it plain that there was an illegal counterrevolutionary sabotage group in the city of Shakhty in the North Caucasus. Its members were said to be oldtime engineers. The report presented evidence tending to prove that the persons concerned were in touch with the former owners of the Shakhty mines, now living abroad, and that they planned to wreck the mines by systematic sabotage. The Lubyanka headquarters was very skeptical. As the case was an important one, and as he well knew his colleagues' propensity to build their careers on the basis of mythical cases, Menzhinsky had asked Yevdokimov to let him have material evidence. Yevdokimov had thereupon gone to Menzhinsky himself, taking with him the "evidence," which included private letters addressed by residents abroad to some of the accused engineers. Menzhinsky was unconvinced. Yevdokimov insisted that the letters were written in code.

"All right, did you decode them then?" asked Menzhinsky.

"No," replied Yevdokimov.

"Why not?"

"The key to the code is in the possession of the addressees."

"Well then?"

"Well then, we want the board's permission to arrest some of the mine managers," said Yevdokimov.

"I will give you a fortnight," said Menzhinsky. "Either you will decode these letters without preliminary arrests, or I shall put you and your agents on trial for sabotage." And with these words he threw Yevdokimov out of his office in true Cheka style. It was now clear to Yevdokimov that unless he could provide proof of the counterrevolutionary activities of the Shakhty group, his own Cheka career would come to an end. In desperation he went to Stalin, to whom he reported the entire matter, including his conversation with Menzhinsky. But as Stalin did not then occupy an official post in the government, Yevdokimov asked him to apply pressure on Menzhinsky through Rykov, who was then Chairman of the Council of People's Commissars.

"Nonsense," said Stalin, "go back to the North Caucasus and immediately adopt whatever measures you consider necessary. From now on send all your information to me only, and we will take care of Comrade Menzhinsky ourselves." (Stalin represented the Party Central Committee on the OGPU board.) Having thus been given carte blanche, Yevdokimov dashed off to Rostov, the capital of the district in which Shakhty was located. Two days later, the leading engineers in Shakhty were arrested as a group. Although the arrests spread to the Donbas, prosecution of the case was left in the hands of the North Caucasus OGPU.

In Moscow the affair created a tremendous commotion. The All-Union Council of National Economy, the OGPU, and even the Council of People's Commissars demanded of the North Caucasus OGPU an immediate explanation. Yevdokimov kept silent. But when Rykov, Menzhinsky, and Kuibyshev, the chairman of the All-Union Council of National Economy, suggested sending to the North Caucasus a special commission of the Party Central Committee and the Council of People's Commissars, Stalin vetoed the proposal. Matters now came to a head. The question was referred to a special session of the Politburo, at which Menzhinsky and Kuibyshev joined hands with Rykov to accuse Stalin of exceeding his authority. Stalin countered by showing the Politburo a telegram from Yevdokimov in which the latter not only reported the existence of counterrevolutionary activities in Shakhty, but also hinted that the strings led to Moscow. Kuibyshev beat a hasty retreat, Menzhinsky fell silent, and Rykov merely looked questioningly at Bukharin and Tomsky. No decision was taken, but Stalin's victory was beyond doubt.

Stalin, having become morally responsible for the prosecution of the Shakhty case, took direct supervision over it. Stalin and Yevdokimov had become partners. Yevdokimov entrusted investigation of the case to his assistant, Kursky, who was instructed to obtain a "sincere confession" from the accused and to make the case one of importance at state level. Such was the genesis of the famous OGPU "methods."

Before beginning the actual investigation, Kursky's staff, including his assistant, Fedotov, also a person considered gifted in the world of the Cheka, worked out the necessary mechanics for carrying out the investigation. These took the form made famous by Yezhov, and consisting in torture.

Kursky's methods proved effective. The accused told of monstrous crimes which were widely taken at face value. What the "sincere confession" of the accused was really worth was known only to one person in Moscow—Stalin, and by only one organization outside the provinces—the staff of Yevdokimov, Kursky, and Fedotov in Rostov-on-Don. Stalin's triumph was complete. Neither the Council of People's Commissars nor its head, Rykov, nor the "rotten" theorist Bukharin, nor even Menzhinsky, supreme head of the OGPU, had revealed the counterrevolutionary activities of the Shakhty engineers, but Stalin, with his "brilliant flair" as a professional revolutionary, had exposed the conspiracy by the bourgeois engineers. Stalin "took care" of Menzhinsky, but made it as plain to the members of the Politburo as if they had been schoolboys that he had been saving their skins while they were sabotaging his efforts. "If you continue to be obstinate," he was saying in effect, "I shall do without you." The Party Central Committee in a confidential letter to the Party organization praised Stalin's "vigilance," and tactfully avoided all mention of the government's efforts to "sabotage" exposure of the Shakhty Case. When Stalin prepared a new case—the "Case of the Industrial Party" headed by Professor Ramzin—there was nothing left to the saboteurs but to agree to everything.

However, Stalin's victory was of very little help to him as such, even if it contributed toward discrediting his future opponents in the "right-wing opposition." The liquidation of the Shakhty engineers, who had been entirely unknown until then, or of the Ramzin group, who were very little known, had even less significance. Stalin's real victory consisted in finding the magic key to the public annihilation of all enemies of the regime, including the purely imaginary. The trial was Yevdokimov's laboratory for testing Kursky's methods. And Stalin was generous in his gratitude: Yevdokimov received two Orders of the Red Banner, one after the other—for the Shakhty engineers and for the Ramzin group—to add to the three he already had, was appointed First Secretary of the North Caucasus District Committee of the All-Union Communist Party (a rare occurrence in the Party at the time), and was made a member of the Party Central Committee, although entirely unknown within the Party. All the Chekists on Kursky's staff were rewarded with the Order of the Red Banner and badges marking them as "Honorary Chekists." (To anticipate, it may be said that when Stalin began preparing the ground for Yezhov's reign of terror, he recalled Kursky.) Kursky, who was still a provincial, middle-ranking Chekist, was in 1936 appointed Vice-Commissar of the NKVD. Some time later the newspapers published a short obituary: "The sudden death is announced of Comrade Kursky, faithful son of the Party." The oral version, stemming from official circles, was that he had committed suicide because he had lost his nerve. The task he had been assigned had been enough to cause the hardiest person to lose his nerve; it was not simply the framing and destruction of a dozen Shakhty engineers, but of applying the same treatment to five million enemies of the people, over a million of whom had at one time been members of the Communist Party.

These and similar differences of opinion between members of the Politburo, on organizational grounds, as Reznikov said, had gradually developed into differences of policy. Rykov, Bukharin, and Tomsky had perceived behind Stalin's tactics a desire to rule the country and the state with the help of the OGPU and the Party, by-passing the Soviet government and the trade unions. The result was the formation of two groups within the Politburo: one headed by Bukharin and one by Stalin. Bukharin's group had originally included Rykov and Tomsky. Kosior, Chubar, and Mikoyan had occupied what Reznikov called a "buffer" position; they either attempted to reconcile the two groups or abstained from voting at decisive moments. Stalin had temporarily refrained from openly attacking Bukharin's group, and was concentrating all his efforts on breaking it up internally, by pitting its members against each other.

Two examples of Stalin's divide-and-rule policy within the Politburo, cited by Reznikov, became deeply embedded in my mind. The first example concerns its application to Tomsky and Kuibyshev. In addition to "organizational" differences of opinion within the Politburo, there was constant friction among various government departments, sometimes for quite trivial reasons. Whenever important persons were concerned, such as People's Commissars, Central Committee members, and so on, it had been customary in Lenin's time to refer such disagreements to a higher authority for arbitration, with the final decision in the hands of the Politburo. After the Politburo reached a decision, agreement was imposed on both sides. After Lenin's death, Stalin expanded the practice in order to play the convenient and profitable role of permanent umpire in his capacity as Secretary-General of the Party, although he was not chairman of the Politburo. (Lenin was permanent Politburo chairman, after his death the members of the Politburo presided in turn, and after the liquidation of the right wing, Stalin became permanent chairman of the Politburo, and Molotov of the Orgburo or Organization Bureau).

Disagreements constantly occurred between the All-Union Council of National Economy, whose chairman was Kuibyshev, and the All-Union Central Trade Union Council, whose chairman was Tomsky. Essentially it was a quarrel between employer and employees. The trade unions still cherished the illusion that it was their duty to defend the interests of the workers, even against the Soviet government, but the interests of the Stalinist state demanded precisely that for which Trotsky had been condemned, namely the complete subjection of the trade unions to the state, i.e., their transformation into organs of state. However, things were not called by their right names. In the next five-year plan, drawn up by Kuibyshev, the role of the trade unions was reduced in practice to that of technical sections of the state administration, although on paper they remained independent. All current measures — "economy," "rationalization," "encouragement of innovators and innovation," and "collective agreements" — were studied and adopted from the point of view of the interests of the state. In this connection Tomsky, at Stalin's suggestion, accused Kuibyshev of being a "Soviet Zubatov," while to Kuibyshev, Stalin suggested that Tomsky be labelled a "rotten trade unionist."

An obvious blunder committed by Stalin and his assistants in editing Stalin's *Works* provides documentary proof of this double-crossing. In a letter to Politburo member Kuibyshev, dated 1928, and recently published for the first time, Stalin writes about Politburo member Tomsky:

... I have heard that Tomsky wants to injure you. What a wicked, spiteful man he is, and not quite clean! It seems to me he is wrong. I have read your report on rationalization. Very appropriate. What else does Tomsky want of you?[3]

With Stalin's letter in his pocket Kuibyshev boldly attacked Tomsky. Stalin said nothing, and Kuibyshev found himself thrown out of Bukharin's group.

The second example concerns Rykov and Bukharin. Bukharin's famous conversation in the summer of 1928 with the disgraced Kamenev was interpreted by Stalin as a conspiracy against the Soviet government (Rykov) and the Party Central Committee (Stalin). Suitable data obtained by agents provided substantiation. The entire affair was purposely made to appear to be a revolt by Bukharin against Rykov, and Stalin and his group attacked Bukharin on this basis. "Rykov," argued Stalin, "is not simply a member of the Politburo, he is also head of the Soviet government. We, therefore, cannot allow even Rykov's friends to conspire against him." Rykov refused to swallow this particular bait, and something else had to be tried.

The press organs not directly responsible to Bukharin and Rykov were charged with the task of initiating a criticism of Bukharin's theoretical writings. Attempts were made to carry this attack through the periodical *Bolshevik*, the theoretical and political organ of the Party Central Committee, but its editorial board included Astrov and Slepkov, both disciples of Bukharin. They informed Bukharin that they were under pressure from Stalin's personal secretary, Poskrebyshev, to publish articles criticizing Bukharin's *Economics of the Transition Period* and *Theory of Historical Materialism*. The critical articles were already in the hands of the editorial board. Bukharin was indignant. He copied the articles and rushed off to Stalin. The latter answered quite coolly that he knew nothing about the order given by Poskrebyshev, and rang for his secretary. Poskrebyshev came in and also said calmly that this was the first he had heard of the articles.

"Even if one of our colleagues has telephoned to the editors and spoken to them in my name, I fail to regard this as a crime," said Poskrebyshev.

"Don't forget," burst out Bukharin, "that I am not your colleague, but a member of the Politburo."

Poskrebyshev made no answer, and Stalin asked Bukharin to leave the articles with him, so that he could look into the matter. Stalin, of course, had not only read them but had himself ordered them to be written. Some time later Astrov and Slepkov received a "severe reprimand" from the Organization Bureau of the Central Committee warning them not to attempt to discredit the Committee's authority. The articles against Bukharin were not published immediately but on the other hand the Bukharinites had received a severe blow.

Stalin's trial of strength with the *Komsomolskaya pravda* was more successful. Here Stalin's action was simple. He called in Chaplin, the secretary of the Central Committee of the Komsomol, and said: "Have this article published by your editor without mentioning either me or the Central Committee. If there is

---

[3] Stalin, *Sochineniya*, Vol. XI, 1949, p. 200.

trouble the editor will be personally responsible, but he must not mention your name either." Chaplin fully grasped the meaning of his assignment. On the following day the *Komsomolskaya pravda* carried an article thundering against the theoretical sins of "right-wing opportunism," which were connected in veiled form with the opinions expressed by the Politburo member, Bukharin. For the Party as well as for Bukharin, the attack was entirely unexpected. Bukharin again went to see Stalin. The latter looked surprised and immediately demanded a copy of the issue of the *Komsomolskaya pravda* in question. (Though there was usually a stack of newspapers on Stalin's desk, there were none that day).

"Oh yes, that really is scandalous," said Stalin, and then asked almost amicably: "And what would you advise doing now, Nikolai Ivanovich?"

Bukharin demanded that the question be discussed in the Politburo.

"I think it should be," replied Stalin.

At the next meeting of the Politburo the responsible editor of the *Komsomolskaya pravda* received a severe reprimand for having published a Trotskyite article "without the permission of the Central Committee." But the Central Committee decided that it was "tactically disadvantageous" to publish a denial.

Stalin found much stiffer and quite unexpected opposition in the Moscow City organization of the Party. Information received by the OGPU from its agents, and intelligence gathered by the Central Committee itself, agreed in indicating that the influence of Bukharin, Rykov, and Tomsky was strongest in the Moscow organization. Efforts by Stalin's agents to recruit the secretaries of the Moscow district organizations or even the members of the Moscow City Committee against Bukharin's group were a complete failure. At the end of 1938, when the Bukharinites had been physically liquidated, Stalin wrote:

> At the same time when it was carrying on its political activities, the Bukharin-Rykov group was also occupied in organizing its supporters. Through Bukharin, it was bringing together bourgeois youth, such as Slepkov, Maretsky, Eikhenwald, Goldberg, and others [members of the editorial board of the Party theoretical and political organ *Bolshevik*]; through Tomsky the top-level trade union personnel in process of being bureaucratized (Melnichansky, Dogadov, etc.); and through Rykov the top Soviet personnel in process of being corrupted (A. Smirnov, Eismont, V. Shmidt, and others). By this time the Bukharin-Rykov group had gained support of the top personnel of the Moscow Party organization (Uglanov, Kotov, Ukhanov, Ryutin, Yagoda, Polonsky, etc.). At the same time a part of the right-wing opposition remained masked and did not openly attack the Party line.[4]

Because they knew nothing of this, or possibly because they did, the leading persons in the Moscow district committees and the Moscow City Committee began to attack the left-wing group which was attempting to discredit the Leninist Central Committee under the guise of criticising "Bukharin's errors." The Central Committee's decision, mentioned above, served as the "general line." This was, I believe, the only case in which Stalin committed a serious mistake, but he quickly recognized the fact and announced the famous slogan:

---

[4] *Istoriya VKP(b). Kratky kurs*, p. 281.

"For criticism and self-criticisim without respect for persons." At the same time he began quietly to prepare for special elections to the Moscow district committees. A part of this preparation centered about the famous Frumkin letter. Moses Frumkin had belonged to the Leninist Bolshevik Guard, had taken an active part in illegal work in tsarist Russia, had been repeatedly arrested and banished and had played a prominent part in the Bolshevik Revolution of 1917. After the Bolshevik victory, he had held a number of responsible posts, and during the period of which Reznikov was speaking was Vice-Commissar of Finances of the USSR, where he was in a position to become well acquainted with conditions in agriculture and industry.

After making a careful analysis of the status of agriculture, on the basis of official data supplied by his Commissariat, Frumkin wrote a letter in July 1928, addressed first to the Politburo and then to all the members of the Party Central Committee. His main points were that (1) the country's agriculture was on the decline; (2) the entire countryside, with the exception of a few of the poor peasants, were in opposition; and (3) the "policy of extraordinary measures," i.e., the policy of compulsory grain confiscation being carried out by the Central Committee, might result in the destruction of the Soviet regime.[5] He accordingly demanded that the Central Committee reverse its agrarian policy in the direction of liberalization. The absence of a liberal agrarian policy, said Frumkin, and the return to the methods employed during the period of War Communism, that is, to open looting of the middle peasants disguised as a struggle against kulaks, to attempts to set one group of peasants against the other under the guise of developing the class struggle, and, finally to adopting Stalin's system of compelling the peasants, with the help of the police, to give up their grain to the state without compensation (the so-called Siberia-Urals system introduced by Stalin during his visit to Siberia)—these were the reasons for the grain crisis. "We demand an increase of the sown area," said Frumkin, "and when the peasants increase it, we call them kulaks. We demand an expansion of trade, and when people open small booths, we call them speculators. We demand an expansion of industry, and when people open up shoe-making shops we call them NEP-men. We demand Soviet democracy, and when people point out to us how undemocratic we are, we throw them into OGPU prisons."

When Frumkin distributed his letter to the members of the plenary session of the Party Central Committee, Stalin attempted to influence action on it by inducing the Politburo to adopt a special resolution. In its original draft the effect of the resolution was to "condemn sharply Frumkin's right-wing opportunist attack on the Party" and to draw the necessary organizational conclusions, that is, to remove Frumkin from his position as Vice-Commissar of Finance of the USSR. Bukharin's group refused to oppose the resolution. When they saw that Stalin had the support of a majority of the Politburo, Bukharin, Rykov, and Tomsky walked out of the meeting. Stalin pointed to this action as evidence of their "conciliatory attitude" towards the right-wing deviation. Frumkin was admonished, but for the time being left in his position.

[5] Stalin, *Voprosy leninizma*, p. 271.

After receiving Frumkin's letter, the Party Central Committee approved the "unanimous Politburo resolution on the subject of the letter." The fact that three members of the Politburo had attacked the resolution and had left the meeting was concealed not only from the Party but also from the members of the Central Committee. As the three dissidents were bound by Party and group discipline within the Politburo, they could not relay their views to the Party in general or even to the members of the Central Committee.

Having thus prepared the ground, Stalin took occasion of the plenary session of the Moscow City Committee, in October, to strike out against the right-wing group there, which meant that he was also striking out against the right-wing element in the Central Committee. But this proved to be no easy task. A number of those present at the plenary session, led by Zapolsky, accused Stalin of "adopting as an excuse a struggle against a mythical right-wing deviation" and of instigating together with his friends a number of artificial "intrigues and quarrels." The Party Central Committee, said Berzin, was poking its nose into the work of the local Party organizations and thus infringing Party regulations. Ryutin openly told Stalin that the right-wing deviation was something that he had invented in order to get rid of the Politburo members whom he did not like. They then asked Stalin: "Can you tell us if there are any Rightists in the Politburo?"

"There are neither Rightists nor Leftists," Stalin replied.

When the members of the session, dissatisfied with Stalin's reply, demanded that the minutes of the meeting of the Politburo be read at which Frumkin's July letter attacking the Central Committee had been discussed, Stalin cited the resolution of the Politburo calling for unity in the Politburo, which, he said, had been signed by all members present. To the question: "What members were present," he replied cryptically: "All those who were there!"[6]

The effect of this entire maneuver, built around Frumkin's letter and making use of the principle of "unity within the Politburo," was that the supporters of Bukharin, Rykov, and Tomsky were disillusioned regarding the effects of maintaining "unanimity" with Stalin.

[6] *Ibid.*, pp. 203—13.

Chapter V

First Arrests in the Institute of Red Professors

When the first arrests took place in the Institute, the students quipped: "Better late than never." There was not a single professor among those who were arrested; all were students from the History Department or the Department of Philosophy and Natural Science. Most of them were last-year students with whom I was little acquainted. The cell secretary, Orlov, and a representative of the Party, B. Tal as I recall, explained to us the reasons for the arrests at a meeting specially called for the purpose. Orlov's speech boiled down to something like this: A small group of Trotskyite traitors which had taken root in the Institute had tried, with the support of the right-wing element from the Moscow City Party organization, to use the Institute as a weapon against the Leninist Central Committee. Alert Chekists had unearthed the plot and purged the conspirators from the Institute just in time. We should help the OGPU to uproot all Trotskyite tendencies. Tal, if it was he, did not say a word about Trotskyites, but emphasized the extent to which the right-wing elements constituted a danger. "Revolutionary Trotskyism has been destroyed physically and ideologically, we must now finish off its right-wing rivals."

After these contradictory statements, we were completely in the dark as to who had been arrested and even if they were members of the Right or of the Left. The Central Committee representative was, of course, in a better position to know than Orlov, who was secretary of the Party organization in the Institute, was directly subordinate to the Central Committee, and received his orders from it. The meeting immediately became unruly. Orlov and the Central Committee representative were flooded with questions.

"Who actually has been arrested—anti-revolutionaries or simply deviationists, Leftists or Rightists?"

"What connection is there between the arrests and what happened to Stalin's portrait?"

"When and where have Bolsheviks with years of service behind them ever been herded into the dungeons of the Bolshevik OGPU without as much as preliminary discussion of their Party allegiance?"

"Was it known in the Central Committee that almost all those arrested had been active participants in the Revolution and the Civil War?"

"All those arrested are Communists with years of service behind them who have fallen victim to a plot by Orlov's group: if these arrests are sanctioned, what guarantee will any of us here in this hall have that we will not be arrested tomorrow upon denunciation by Orlov, or, on the other hand, if we fail to approve the arrests, what guarantee will we have that we will not be arrested today, upon denunciation by Orlov?"

This last question was asked by Sorokin. Orlov lost his temper, frowned, fixed his large gray eyes directly upon Sorokin, and cried out hoarsly:

"Comrade Sorokin, your clever wisecracking does not say much for your courage. If you really want to show your solidarity with these bandits who have been arrested, then say so openly like a real Bolshevik; there is no room for demagoguery and provocation at a Party meeting!"

Sorokin calmly rose, came to the rostrum, and addressed the meeting without asking the chairman's permission.

"If there is a bandit, agent provocateur, and coward within these walls, it must be Orlov himself. The meeting is perhaps unaware of certain facts, but having been provoked by Orlov, I must give a frank explanation. During the difficult years of the Revolution when, in obedience to the orders of the Central Committee I went underground and worked in the areas occupied by Denikin, Orlov was General Erdeli's aide-de-camp and used to sell his chief's secrets to me for cash. Here are the documents."

Sorokin threw into the face of the Central Committee's representative a bundle of documents discolored by time and made up of receipts, reports, and newspaper clippings.

There was a great commotion in the hall, and loud shouts for and against Orlov. The Central Committee representative called the meeting to order. Sorokin continued his speech on Orlov's career with the White Army.

"My short stay with the White Army is known to the Central Committee," replied Orlov.

"Unfortunately, however," Sorokin went on, his voice shaking, "the Central Committee is still unaware that you have remained faithful to your old profession of informer, provocateur, adventurer. . . . Not the Party, not the Central Committee, not even the OGPU, but you, Orlov, have thrown your enemies into dungeons. . . . It is too bad that you are not the only one, there is a whole army of you professional time-servers. . . ."

The audience listened to Sorokin with bated breath. For most his speech was a revelation.

Without giving Sorokin time to finish, the Central Committee representative asked for permission to make a special statement. Sorokin left the rostrum. The audience came to attention. The Central Committee representative launched forth.

"The Party destroyed the power of Trotsky, Zinoviev, and Kamenev not because they had deserved less of the Party than Comrade Sorokin, but because they had taken advantage of their past services to harm the Party's present general line. We have a good proverb which says: 'We thank you for the past, you answer for the present.' The Soviet regime is not a commercial 'Trotsky & Co.' It is the state system of the dictatorship of the proletariat. The Leninist Central Committee is the brains of the dictatorship. Whoever is against the Central Committee is against the Party and against the proletariat, because our Party is the advance guard of the proletariat. And therefore let Comrade Sorokin, whose past services we all recognize, not forget that the Party now applies different standards by which to measure people."

"Long live the White Guard Bolsheviks!" shouted someone in the hall.

"Wait," continued the Central Committee representative, "I shall say something about this too. We know that our Party contains Mensheviks, Social Revolutionaries, and even people whom chance for a time tossed among the Whites. Many of them have proved and are still proving in practice that their past was both mistaken and governed by chance. But past mistakes and errors can be forgiven only when people show in the present an infinite devotion to the Leninist Central Committee. Therefore to speak of White Guard or Menshevik Bolsheviks means attacking the Party. The Party will not tolerate such attacks, just as it will not tolerate the attempts of right-wing elements to make it stray from the Leninist path, and it will not take into account any services in the past. You cannot argue with a bandit whose finger is on the trigger of his gun, and who is aiming straight at your heart; you must anticipate his shot. The Party anticipated the shot from the Right. That is why the Party—not Orlov—removed the counterrevolutionaries within the Institute. It is true that at first glance it looks as if Party regulations have been infringed because before arresting these people we did not let you discuss their expulsion from the Party. But here I must say that, first, Party regulations are not the statutes of an order of knighthood but are an instrument of the Party's will; second, why should enemies within the Party have the advantage over the enemy outside the Party and be forewarned of coming repression? The Central Committee members are not knights with a false conception of honor, but active revolutionaries. . . . The Central Committee, as the executive organ of the Party, has the right to expel any Party member. It expelled those who were being arrested, without a hearing and before they were arrested."

The Central Committee representative proposed that the meeting ratify "the only correct decision, as made by the Central Committee."

The question was put to vote without further debate. It was phrased as follows: "Who is for the Central Committee's resolution on the expulsion from the Party of enemies of the Party and of the people. . .?"

A small majority voted for the resolution. No one, I think, voted against it. About thirty persons were recorded as abstaining. Some simply did not take part in the voting. Those who abstained were required to give their reasons.

"Personally," said Sorokin, "I abstained not because I was against the Central Committee, but because the Central Committee does not observe the right sequence of action; it should first have put people like Orlov, and then crypto-Trotskyites, into OGPU prisons, and then we could talk about pseudo and real Rightists."

38

"Who," asked one of the presiding officers, "do you have in mind when you talk of crypto-Trotskyites?"

"You know better than I," replied Sorokin, and sat down.

There was enough truth in the reference to crypto-Trotskyites to sting Stalin's faithful supporters in the hall to the quick. Among the rank and file of the Party there was evident alarm at the way in which the most radical of Trotsky's demands on the home fronts, regarding the peasantry, the NEP, and industrialization, were becoming the program of action of the anti-Trotskyite Central Committee. Some were even seriously discussing the question of Trotsky's "voluntary retirement" from the Politburo and Stalin's adoption of Trotsky's plan for the liquidation of the NEP. Trotsky had been too well aware of the fact that Stalin was ambitious to attempt to make use of that weakness. He had decided to win a victory for his idea at the cost of his own ambition. As he saw it, unless he gave way, Stalin's lust for power would be stronger than any ideal, and then everyone and everything would go down—Stalin and Trotsky and the entire Revolution. As Stalin had had no other program and no other course of action for his path to power, Trotsky had felt obliged to help Stalin to reach his goal for the sake of the Revolution. However, Trotsky's program had included not only "superindustrialization" and the "permanent revolution," which were well known to Stalin and with which he was in sympathy; Trotsky had also worked out down to the most minute details the application of his program to real life. The general program was lying on a table in the Politburo, while the methods were locked in Trotsky's mind. Trotsky, it was thought, would unlock his mind only on the day after Stalin's collapse as a result of failure in his attempt to apply Trotsky's program. The Party would then remove Stalin and Trotsky would be triumphantly invited to occupy the throne.

As Trotsky saw it, the "extraordinary measures" adopted in the grain collection campaigns of 1927 and 1928 were proof that Stalin had by then created a conflict between the Party and the peasants, and would create a conflict between the Party and the working class when he came to implement the first Five-Year Plan. Stalin was rushing headlong toward catastrophe, while Trotsky was on the eve of a return from abroad.

Only one thing was true in this set of illusions: Stalin did adopt Trotsky's program with certain minor adjustments, although he did so in order to bury Trotsky ideologically. But how great is the power of illusion! Even the most careful thinkers were apparently captivated by it. Trotsky himself said later: "The *Times* stated afterward that I had gone to Constantinople by agreement with Stalin in order to prepare, while there, the seizure of the Near East by force. The six years' struggle between me and the leaders of the Revolution was presented as a mere comedy, with the parts all distributed beforehand. Who will believe this, an optimist may ask, and yet people did."[1]

In fact, the entire difference between Stalin and Trotsky lay not in their programs, but in their tactics. Had Lenin remained alive, even this difference

---

[1] Trotsky, *Moya zhizn*, Vol. II, p. 319.

between them would have disappeared. When it was necessary to make a sharp and often unexpected change in tactics, Lenin, after becoming head of the Party and later of the state, sometimes attacked the very policy he had supported the day before. "Either we shall change our policy and our tactics," he would say at critical moments in the Russian Revolution and the life of the Soviet regime, "or we shall disappear as a Party." This was true in 1906–07, it was true in April 1917, after the February Revolution, and it was true in 1921, with the NEP.

Stalin had learned well this lesson of unlimited tactical flexibility, which was the real essence of "Leninist dialectics." Trotsky on the other hand was never able to grasp it, to the very end of his life; and when Stalin began waging his war against the Right and was accordingly forced by the logic of events to borrow his ideas from the Trotskyite arsenal, he did not let himself be frightened by the outcries of the Rightists to the effect that he had adopted the Trotskyite program.

Stalin understood perfectly well that he would never succeed in ruling by democratic methods a country of 170,000,000 people, most of them peasants. Only after economically stifling peasant democracy could he easily rule the country politically. Therefore Stalin was as resolute in liquidating the NEP as Lenin had been in introducing it five years before. The NEP represented a considerable element of freedom which Lenin had been forced to give the peasants because he was weak, but Lenin had been able to rule the country even with the NEP, because he had been backed by the majority in the Party. Stalin, who from the very start had been eyed with suspicion as a leader, both by Lenin in his "Political Testament" and by the Party, including both the Trotskyites and the right-wing National Deviationists, could not have entrenched himself in power if he had allowed Lenin's "inner-Party democracy" to exist within the Party and peasant freedom to exist within the country.

Now, after the Trotskyites had been swept aside with the evident approval of the peasants and the support of the peasant members of the Party, it was necessary to kill off the Rightists ideologically in order to finish off the NEP and "inner Party democracy" at the same time. There was no other road to personal dictatorship. Here Stalin added a new chapter to the history of political tactics as written by Lenin. The problem was difficult, the danger was great, enemies were numerous, but even Stalin ran no risk; he knew his enemies too well to fear them. If his Rightist enemies should win, Stalin would repent and there the matter would rest. At the very worst, he would be removed from Moscow and placed at the head of a cooperative union in Georgia. If he should win, he would bury both the Right and the Left in order to rule the country alone.

In his progress along this thorny and blood-stained path to power Stalin proved to be a master tactician of the Leninist school, and a great expounder of Party strategy, while Stalin's pupils themselves proved to be worthy of their teacher.

Such was precisely the course of events in the Institute of Red Professors. Sorokin thought he was safe in saying: "You know the crypto-Trotskyites better than I do," but one of the presiding officers, a tall red-haired man with grey eyes like Orlov's, said boldly in a deep voice:

"Comrade Sorokin, either you will prove that I know the crypto-Trotskyites in the Party or else you will bear the responsibility for your slander. Sorokin must remember," he went on, "that whoever doubts the correctness of the general line of the Leninist Central Committee follows only one path—a path that leads into the camp of the counterrevolutionaries. And with such persons the Party speaks in the language of the Cheka. That is how the Party has dealt with those who have just been arrested and that is how it will deal with all those who attack it. Let Sorokin not console himself with the thought that he has supporters. These are vain hopes. Either you go with the Party or against it! There is no middle way! The fate of the Left lies in store for the Right unless they see the truth. The Right banked on the Institute of Red Professors to act as its headquarters in the ideological battle, but they have been defeated; we must now tear off the mask from their henchmen in our midst. I move that we now discuss the anti-Party behavior of Comrade Sorokin."

His speech was greeted with loud protests from the majority and applause from a few. The speaker was P. F. Yudin, later member of the Central Committee but at that time secretary of the Party cell in the Department of Philosophy and Natural Science.

The chairman had difficulty in restoring order. Everyone tried to speak at once. The audience stood up and formed a number of groups which shouted rather than argued; some made themselves heard if not listened to.

"This is suppression of criticism!"

"A state of siege in the Institute!"

"Yudin's demagogy!"

"Throw him out of the Presidium!"

"Sorokin is a conspirator!"

At last the chairman shouted, "I adjourn the meeting until tomorrow."

The adjournment in fact lasted for three days. In the meantime all the members of the bureau of the Institute cell and the cell secretaries of all the departments were summoned to the Central Committee.

Among those summoned there were, in addition to Orlov, Yudin, Shcherbakov, and Sorokin, also several former students who had become professors—Sten, Mitin, Vanag, Karev, Luppol, Troitsky, and Pokrovsky himself. They were received by Kaganovich, in the presence of Krinitsky, Stetsky, and B. Tal. Sorokin told us later that the minutes of the meeting of the Institute cell were lying on Kaganovich's desk, where he had apparently been studying them. Many passages were marked with a red pencil and the margins had numerous notes. Kaganovich, who was generally in a good mood, this time pretended to be displeased and irritated and assumed the pompous air of a man who knew his own value. He turned over the pages of the minutes, sometimes pretending to be surprised as if he were reading them for the first time, sometimes frowning, and sometimes wrinkling his brow as if trying to understand the innermost meaning of what he was reading.

The session lasted in this manner for about a quarter of an hour, in dead silence. No one sat down except Pokrovsky. When Kaganovich had finished reading, he glowered at the entire group and asked them to take their seats around a long table placed at right angles to his desk. The discussion lasted for about an hour, and was summarized by Stetsky, the Assistant Chief of Agitation and Propaganda. The Central Committee had decided to recall Orlov from the Institute before the termination of his assignment and to place him at the disposition of the Central Committee (he was later appointed instructor in the Organizational Department of the Central Committee). It had been "recommended" that the Party cell of the Institute be given a new bureau to be composed of Yudin, Mitin, Shcherbakov, Petrov, Konstantinov, Sorokin, Pokrovsky, and others, with Yudin as cell secretary. At the time it was not clear who had won the skirmish. But we did not have to wait long for new events to provide an answer to the riddle.

Chapter VI

The Special Assignments of the Theory Brigade

The removal of Orlov was interpreted as a definite victory for Sorokin, but the reason for the appointment of Yudin as cell secretary was not understood at the time. Neither was it clear why Sorokin had been made a member of the bureau. Everyone knew that the two were not only hostile to each other, but were complete opposites in character. Yudin repeated everything by rote like a parrot, he was a careerist who knew on which side his bread was buttered. His pronouncements on theory were naive and his ability as a researcher was only fair. But these weaknesses only became evident in academic seminars; in the Party life of the Institute he had few rivals. Persons like Yudin had one quality which enabled them, if they used it correctly, to make dazzling careers. It consisted in a gift for correctly interpreting resolutions of the Central Committee already adopted and for predicting resolutions to come. In Lenin's time, it had not been particularly difficult to predict Party weather, but later, with all the oscillations of the Stalin barometer, to keep track of it and to make invariably correct forecasts became very difficult. One had to be both in spirit and body an unseen part of Stalin himself in order to be sensitive to the workings of his mind. "I am not Lenin, but I am contained in Lenin," wrote the poet Bezymensky in *Party Ticket*. People like Yudin could say of themselves: "We are not Stalin, but we are contained in Stalin." It was for this reason that persons like Yudin set the tone at Party meetings and received from the more opportunistic Party professors the highest academic marks on the supposition that they were the future Party stars.

People like Sorokin dealt with theory in the same manner in which they had dealt with problems in the civil war: they attacked it openly and directly, paying little heed to local conditions and "meteorological communiqués" on Party weather, and inevitably they stumbled.

I remember two striking examples.

The first was as follows: The outline of *A History of the All-Russian Communist Party of Bolsheviks*, by Yaroslavsky, Mints, and Kin, was being discussed in a seminar on the history of the revolutionary movement in Russia in the nineteenth and twentieth centuries. In order to stress the significance of Lenin's "April Theses" and illustrate the wavering of the Party in its attitude to the Provisional Government of Lvov and Kerensky, the authors had argued that before Lenin's arrival from abroad the Russian Bolsheviks, represented by the former Duma deputies, the Russian Bureau of the Central Committee, the Petrograd Committee of the Bolshevik Party, and the newspaper *Pravda*, had taken a rather opportunistic point of view and had been in favor of appeasement.

All these high Party organs had supported a slogan which ran: "We will support the Provisional Government to the extent that it conforms with the will of the people." The outline pointed out that "even Stalin did not see clearly on this problem," and that the Leninists themselves had been the first to say clearly: "No support for the Provisional Government." Some of the students and professors, including Yudin, protested categorically against the words "even Stalin," on the basis that we were writing past history for the present, and that at present Stalin was Lenin's successor in the Party leadership. Since the words "even Stalin" were somewhat critical of Stalin, this part of the outline should be deleted. Yaroslavsky and Mints countered by arguing that history was a science and science must be objective. Moreover, there was nothing extraordinary in the fact that Lenin's genius made it possible for him to see farther and clearer than the ordinary Party leaders. This argument was accepted and the outline was approved in general. Yudin's followers did not object, and the Central Committee remained "neutral." But what Yudin and his followers had foreseen occurred a few years later. In 1931 in a letter to the editor of the magazine *Proletarian Revolution*, Stalin criticized Yaroslavsky's *History of the All-Union Communist Party of Bolsheviks*, which was the name under which the book finally appeared, for its "historical errors and errors in principle." Yaroslavsky and Mints and their fellow-thinkers had to recant, while Yudin and his followers were acclaimed.

As to the second example, in 1928 M.B.Mitin, a former student at the Institute of Red Professors and a lecturer in philosophy at the Krupskaya Academy of Communist Education submitted to the Department of Modern Philosophy of the Institute a study with what was still at the time an unusual title, *Lenin and Stalin as Continuators of the Philosophy of Marx and Engels*. Professors Deborin, Luppol, and Karev severely criticized the book and even ridiculed Mitin for having referred to Lenin and Stalin as philosophers, since Lenin's only philosophical work, *Materialism and Empirio-Criticism*, was not, they said, a philosophical study at all but merely a collection of critical notes written in popular style, while Stalin had written nothing at all on any philosophical theme. Yudin, who was secretary of the Party cell in the Department of Philosophy, had a different opinion. He strongly opposed his professors and took the matter up with the Central Committee. The Central Committee merely replied: "Tell Yudin and Mitin that the subject is very interesting, although it is not of immediate interest." But three years later, it was of immediate interest. Chapters of the work began to appear in *Pravda*, in *Under the Banner of Red Marxism* and in *Bolshevik* over the signatures of Mitin, Yudin, and Raltsevich.

To return to developments in the Institute, Sorokin was made a member of the Bureau of the Institute cell where he had to work, as I have said, with Yudin. I do not know whether the Central Committee suspected that Sorokin was becoming too critical of the Party's official policy and was forming connections with many of the Rightists in the Moscow Committee and the Central Committee. I have no doubt that Yudin had repeated his accusations of Sorokin to the Central Committee. Nevertheless Sorokin had been recommended for appointment as a member of the Institute Party leadership and it was rumored that Yudin and

Orlov had been reprimanded by the Central Committee for "deviationism" while Sorokin had not been. In any case Yudin's relationship with Sorokin changed and although Sorokin maintained his former attitude, Yudin became courteous and correct. He followed Sorokin around, flattered him, and took his advice while the students watching Yudin's incredible metamorphosis said: "Yudin has fallen a victim to Hegel's second law of dialectics: quantity has turned into quality and he has fallen in love with Sorokin." As Sorokin did not respond, we who knew both Sorokin and Yudin could foresee more changes.

After a month of quiet, we were faced with another riddle: the members of the cell bureau disappeared without trace. We soon discovered that some of the lecturers had also disappeared. The Institute buzzed with rumors. Pokrovsky volunteered no information and the wives of those who had disappeared came to us to ask if we knew on what "missions" their husbands had been sent. Various theories were advanced:

"They have been sent to China to help Borodin in his work in Chou-Teh's headquarters . . ."

"The Comintern has been sent to Western Europe . . ."

"The OGPU has arrested . . ."

The scaremongers became panicky. "If things go any farther," they said, "Dedodub will be the only one to remain at liberty."

At last Pokrovsky decided to set our minds at rest. "The bureau members and some of the lecturers," he said, "have gone on leave." With the term in full swing this was impossible to believe. I was not particularly worried about Sorokin's absence, as I knew that while he was in such company he could at least not have been picked up by the OGPU. I could guess that Sorokin's departure had been very sudden, as otherwise he would have told me what was happening. It was strange that he had not at least written me.

I went to see Zinaida Nikolayevna. When I told her about Sorokin's absence, she turned pale and asked: "Do you think he has been arrested?" I replied that this was being rumored in the Institute, but that I myself did not believe it, as all the new members of the bureau had disappeared with Sorokin. Zinaida Niko-layevna was visibly relieved, but she telephoned Reznikov to tell him the news. Reznikov seemed to know all the facts about Sorokin's diappearance and proceeded to explain them to her. Zinaida Nikolayevna kept repeating: "Wonderful!" When their talk was over I saw that she was no longer worried. "Reznikov," she said, "tells me that our friend is away from Moscow and is doing an important job. He will tell us all about it himself when he gets back." I left without questioning her farther.

Six weeks later, at the end of October 1928, almost all of the bureau members, including Sorokin, returned. I immediately noticed how greatly he had changed. He looked wan and thin. His natural high color, typical of a Siberian, had disappeared. I told him at once what I thought of his changed appearance. "Just the strain before a jump," he said significantly, and quickly changed the subject to speak about matters concerning the Institute.

When I told him that some people thought they had all been arrested, Sorokin laughed. "Yudin and Mitin arrested? Come, come now. You might as well dismiss the OGPU from your mind."

Sorokin said not a word about his work and I did not inquire as I was sure that when he was ready he would tell me of his own accord. And so he did.

One evening he invited me to his home and from there we went together to Zinaida Nikolayevna's. She was apparently expecting guests. We were the first to arrive. Reznikov and the General came separately, soon after. In the course of the conversation, I learned the extraordinary reason for the unexplained absence of Sorokin and his fellow students, although at the time none of us realized its full significance.

What had happened was this: Soon after the new bureau was appointed, the Central Committee summoned a group of senior students, including almost the entire membership of the new bureau, and also several lecturers. Each had a personal interview with I. Vareikis, the head of the Central Committee Press Department. He informed them, in confidence, that the Central Committee had decided (actually there had been no such decision, but there had been an order by Molotov, issued no doubt at Stalin's instigation) to set up a "theory brigade" to review and criticize all the articles, speeches, and books written by Bukharin before and after the Revolution. The Central Committee Secretariat had prepared a detailed outline of the project. Each member of the brigade was assigned a specific subject. (Some of the reviews were later published in the form of pamphlets, under such titles as: "The Philosophical Basis of Right-Wing Opportunism," "The Kulaks and the Right-Wing Deviation," "The Right-Wing Restorers of Capitalism," "The Class Struggle and the Theory of Equilibrium," "Social Democracy and Right-Wing Opportunism," and "The Comintern and Right-Wing Deviation.")

Although Bukharin was a member of the Politburo, the Party as a whole, it appeared, knew nothing of the struggle in progress within the Politburo between the Bukharin and Stalin groups. As I have said, Stalin in October 1928 categorically denied the existence of right-wing elements or "appeasers" within the Politburo. In fact, however, there were such elements, but Stalin was not yet ready to deal with them immediately either in the field of theory, by exposing them, or of organization, by repression. He, therefore, had kept silent while making preparations for the coming struggle.

As Bukharin was considered the Party's official and principal theorist, Stalin had decided to launch his first attack on this front. Although the Institute of Red Professors was itself much under the influence of the "Bukharin school," it had been decided that a few professors and senior students could be made to serve the purposes of the Central Committee in its struggle with Bukharin. These half-educated "red professors" were conspicuous neither for intellectual gifts nor for their academic qualifications, but such defects could easily be made up for by their pretentious omniscience and more particularly by the force of orders from the Central Committee. "Vareikis," said Sorokin, "told me that we must prove one simple axiom, to wit, that as a theorist Bukharin's value is nil and politically he is a nonentity." The same axiom had evidently been repeated to the other members of the brigade as well.

A week later, all those who had been sent for, including Sorokin, had disappeared from the Institute to carry out what they had been told was a special assignment by the Central Committee. Under threat of expulsion from the Party, they were warned not to divulge either the character of their work or where it was being done. The brigade was sent to Leningrad where it worked under the direct supervision of Pozern. In addition to Stalin and Kirov, Molotov and Kaganovich were the only Politburo members who knew of the brigade's work. The bulk was finished in six weeks and its results reported to Stalin. The brigade had produced ten long articles and a complete bibliography of Bukharin's writings, with a detailed index showing what Bukharin had written on any particular subject and where it was to be found. A separate index of subjects dealt with in the writings of Marx and Engels and of Lenin had also been prepared, to facilitate comparison. For the time being the entire material was withheld from publication and reserved for the personal use of Stalin. The members of the brigade promised to continue their work individually, and to produce additional pamphlets for possible future publication, while maintaining the necessary precautions.

Even before his departure to take part in the project, Sorokin had let Bukharin know through Reznikov of the bombshell being prepared for use against him by Stalin at the next plenary meeting of the Central Committee. Bukharin paid no particular attention to the information and perhaps even doubted its truth, as he considered it impossible that Stalin would try to settle accounts with him on grounds of theory at a time when opinions within the Central Committee were split along political and not theoretical lines. He completely failed to give due weight to the reasoned warnings by both Reznikov and Uglanov, a candidate member of the Politburo, to the effect that the attack would be directed against Bukharin's theories in order to pull him down from his pedestal as one of the leaders of the Party, and that it was therefore in the domain of theory that Bukharin should deliver his counterblows.

After receiving a detailed account from Sorokin, Reznikov arranged a meeting between Sorokin and Uglanov, who not only shared Bukharin's views but was a personal friend. The meeting took place in the flat of D. Maretsky, a member of the editorial board of the magazine *Bolshevik* and a student of Bukharin's. Uglanov failed to appear, but Bukharin did. Sorokin gave Bukharin a detailed account of the work of the "theory brigade" in Leningrad. Bukharin expressed real interest only in the role played by Kaganovich and Kirov, and Sorokin described this to him.

"Can you give me a written account of what you have told me?" asked Bukharin.

Sorokin handed him a letter which he had written in advance and at the same time told him that in accordance with the advice of Reznikov he had signed it with a pseudonym in order to avoid unpleasant repercussions. Bukharin was obviously displeased, but did not ask Sorokin to sign his real name.

Sorokin was right: within a few months the letter was in Kaganovich's files.

Chapter VII

Stalin's Party Within the Party

It may be well at this point to review briefly the stages through which the Revolution passed before reaching the period of which we are speaking, when the mass proletariat was marching on the scene and a man of mediocre talents was in process of becoming the feared ruler of a great state and the striking symbol of an entire epoch.

The key to the understanding of this period is not to be found in the ancestry of Bolshevism, the psychology of the Bolsheviks, the Messianism of the Russian soul, the temper of the Georgian character, or the social conditions of the time. While there is no single key, there is one fact which may be taken as a point of departure, the fact that Stalin had great insight into the nature of the mass proletariat and a genius for ruthless politics.

To look back briefly, the February Revolution gave power to the people, the October Revolution nationalized the wealthy but did not enrich the poor, War Communism completed the proletarianization of the cities and began the proletarianization of the countryside. With the NEP there began the process which culminated in Stalin's seizure of sole power.

The NEP favored the strong but did nothing for the many. Its slogans were: "Help for the Villages," "Learn How to Trade," "Get Rich!" The masses dropped down a step to become a mass proletariat which lined up at the employment offices, not to find work, but to give voice to threats: "What have we been fighting and spilling our blood for?" "Hang Lenin and put Trotsky against the wall!"[1]

A ferment of ideas, unknown to the world outside, splintered the top of the Party. Some tended to go Left, others Right, yet others drifted rudderless between the two.

Lenin's vacant seat continued to be unoccupied, but, like nature, abhorred a vacuum. Trotsky's slogan, "Let the collective will and collective brain of Lenin's Central Committee take the place of Lenin," turned out to be devoid of meaning. The interregnum continued until Stalin could master the mass proletariat and the political techniques of Machiavelli. In destroying the Left by making use of the Right and the "repenters," and destroying the "repenters" by making use of a *Lumpenproletariat* leading from Yezhov to Malenkov, Stalin out-Lenined Lenin.

---

[1] In the mid-twenties, the State Circus in Moscow presented a satire well known to all Muscovites. Portraits of Lenin and Trotsky were lying on the stage. One clown told another to take them away. "Where shall I put them?" "Hang Lenin and put Trotsky against the wall!"

48

The final weapon in Stalin's hands was a party within the Party. This "inner-Party party" was recruited from professional political activists who had to possess every human virtue except that of a moral brake. The idea may have originated with Lenin, who proposed in *What Shall We Do?* the creation of "a core of professional revolutionaries," but the technique of creating and using such a core was worked out by Stalin, long before he actually came to power.

I cannot but recall a story told me by an old Georgian Social Democrat who had been a fellow-student of Stalin's in the seminary while Stalin was still Djugashvili. He had been sent to the same tsarist prison in Kutaisi, and 35 years later was living out his last days in a Stalinist prison.

"Once," he said, "our ancient history teacher gave us the assignment of writing an essay on the cause of Caesar's downfall. The most original essay was that written by Djugashvili. After faithfully repeating the explanation of Caesar's downfall given us in school he added his own interpretation that the real reason was that Caesar lacked an apparatus of personal power to control the apparatus of state power, that is, the power of the Senate. Djugashvili appended to his essay a diagram with blank spaces enclosed in red brackets. The blank spaces were the vulnerable points where Caesarism was open to attack while the red brackets were defensive measures to avert the blows. In his notes on the diagram Djugashvili stated that the provincial governors had so much independent power that they had less fear of the Senate than of the sword of Damocles in the hands of Caesar. Caesar's struggle with the Senate noblesse, said Djugashvili, ended in full pardon for his enemies and in preservation of the Senate as the collective symbol of power, thus rendering illusory Caesar's rights as permanent dictator. Besides, Caesar had sought friends to share his power with him instead of executors of his will obliged to obey. So he perished at the hands of his friends, Cassius and Brutus, undefended by iron brackets of faithful executors. When the teacher asked, 'Doesn't your diagram resemble that of an absolute monarchy,' Djugashvili replied, 'No, a monarch's personal power is based on the apparatus of state power; in my diagram the apparatus of state power is itself dependent on the apparatus of personal power!'"

Later on, Stalin used to refer to his early statements of this kind on the "dictatorship of the proletariat" as those of "a yet unformed Marxist." (See, for instance, the Preface to Volume I of his *Works*.) But I have always thought, and still do, that these school-day essays by Djugashvili contain the whole philosophy of Stalin.

If we had no other proofs, Trotsky's memoirs would remove all shadow of a doubt that from April 1922 on, that is, from the day when he was appointed Secretary-General of the Party Central Committee, Stalin worked methodically and persistently to realize the diagram which he had drawn in his seminary days. As a first step, Stalin rebuilt the entire Party apparatus from top to bottom and placed it above the Party. The first to guess the secret of Stalin's "new course," while Lenin was still alive, was Trotsky. In a letter to the Central Committee in October 1923, Trotsky openly accused the heads of the Central

Committee apparatus of adopting a "group policy," an accusation also made in the "Declaration of the 46." According to Trotsky, the essence of Stalin's group policy was that "in spite of the Party's ideological development, the Party apparatus stubbornly continues to think and decide for all," whereas, in Trotsky's view, "the Party should make the apparatus subordinate to itself."[2] However, neither Trotsky's warnings, nor the "Declaration of the 46," nor the warning of the sick Lenin to "be careful at turning points," could hold Stalin back from the course which he had adopted.

Trotsky writes as follows:

> Lenin summoned me to his office in the Kremlin, and spoke of the horrifying growth of bureaucracy in our Soviet apparatus and of the necessity of finding a lever for dealing with the problem correctly. He proposed the creation of a special commission of the Central Committee and invited me to take an active part in the work. I replied: "Vladimir Ilyich, in my opinion, in the present struggle with bureaucracy in the Soviet apparatus it must not be forgotten that both locally and at the center a new set of civil servants and specialists, both Party and non-Party, is now being created around certain leading Party groups and personalities, in the provinces, in the districts, and in the center, that is, in the Central Committee. When you bring pressure to bear upon a civil servant, you meet a Party man who has a specialist at his heels, and under such circumstances I cannot undertake work of this kind.[3]

Lenin agreed with Trotsky's view of the matter and suggested that they create a Lenin-Trotsky bloc against Stalin.[4]

This incident shows how far Stalin had advanced, and how powerful his apparatus had become, even before Lenin's death.

The magnificently organized coordinated work of Dzerzhinsky as head of the Cheka and of Stalin as head of the Secretariat of the Central Committee was of great assistance to Stalin. When it became impossible to ignore Trotsky's accusation that a dictatorship of the Party apparatus was being created, Stalin proposed to the Politburo that a "neutral Party commission" headed by Dzerzhinsky be organized to examine the complaints of Trotsky and "The 46." The commission did all in its power to whitewash "Stalin's apparatus" and to discredit Trotsky, but a plenary session of the Central Committee in October 1923 passed a resolution recommending to the Politburo that all possible measures be taken to ensure harmonious cooperation.

As to the manner in which this order was carried out, Stalin reported to the Thirteenth Party Conference, in 1924, as follows:

> I must state, Comrades, that in the years after the October Session we took every possible step to ensure harmonious cooperation with Comrade Trotsky, although I must say that this was far from easy. We had two private conversations

---

[2] L. Trotsky, quoted in Stalin, *Sochineniya*, Vol. V, pp. 384—385 and Vol. VI, pp. 13—15.

[3] L. Trotsky, *Stalinskaya shkola falshifikatsii* (Stalin's School of Falsification), Berlin, 1932, pp. 85—86.

[4] *Ibid.*

with Comrade Trotsky during which we discussed all economic and Party problems, and came to certain conclusions which left no room for doubt. One result of these private conversations and attempts to organize harmonious cooperation within the Politburo was, as I reported yesterday, the creation of a three man subcommission. This subcommission prepared a draft resolution which later became the resolution of the Central Committee and the Central Control Commission on democratization. That is how the matter stood. We thought that after the unanimous adoption of the resolution there would be no more reason for arguments or for inner-Party strife. That in fact was how matters stood until Comrade Trotsky's new statement on the day following the publication of the Central Committee's resolution. This statement was made independently of the Central Committee and over its head, thus ruining the entire matter and radically changing the situation.[5]

Thus did Stalin complain about Trotsky, although at the same time he admitted the significant fact that the October plenary session had recommended in essence that he, not Trotsky, put an end to the practice of creating a party of his own within the Party, and this even though Dzerzhinsky's commission had attended the plenary session armed with Stalin's statements regarding "Trotsky's slander" against "the Party apparatus and the Leninist Party personnel." Trotsky based his statement, made "over the head of the Central Committee," on the fact that after putting the plenary session's resolution under lock and key in the Central Committee, Stalin had continued to organize and strengthen "the dictatorship of the Party apparatus" as if no resolution had been adopted.

After Trotsky's statement, the rank and file of the Party reacted very sharply to Stalin's behavior, in spite of terror and pressure by the Stalin-Dzerzhinsky apparatus whose creation had by then been almost entirely completed. At conferences of "Moscow proletarian cells"—the strongholds of Stalinism—Stalin and Dzerzhinsky, even by making use of Lenin's name, obtained only 9,843 votes against Trotsky. Trotsky's accusations against Stalin were supported by 2,223 persons who voted for condemnation of Stalin. An even greater number of Party members, fearing to find themselves the following day either in Dzerzhinsky's dungeons or at least in the line of unemployed at the labor exchange, refrained from taking part in the discussion.

Stalin suffered a catastrophic defeat in the Party organization of the Moscow institutions of higher education. Of 72 university cells, 32, with 2,790 members, voted for the Central Committee and 40, with 6,594 members, voted for the opposition.[6]

In the provinces Stalin fared even worse. Many provincial organizations definitely demanded that an end be put to Stalin's "new course." If there was as yet no unanimous revolt within the Party against its own apparatus the reason was the immense personal authority of Lenin, who was deprived by his illness of the possibility of giving the Party any explanation. The Party waited for his health to be restored. Stalin waited for his death. But as early as the Twelfth Party

[5] Stalin, *Sochineniya*, Vol VI, pp. 32—33.

[6] A. Bubnov, "VKP(b)" (The All-Union Communist Party of Bolsheviks), in *BSE*, 1st ed., Vol. XI, col. 499.

Conference, Stalin adopted prophylactic measures for shuffling the personnel of the disobedient Party: at his suggestion the conference decided to invite 100,000 new members, taken from the factories, to join the Party, while refusing entry into the Party by petty bourgeois elements. The "petty bourgeois elements" included the provinces (peasants) and the higher educational institutions (students). Stalin was inviting the factory proletarians to join the mass proletariat in order to destroy more completely the "saboteurs" of his attempt to create a party within the Party.

Three days after the Twelfth Party Conference Lenin died, on January 21, 1924. The appeal to the Party written by Stalin on this occasion included the following passage:

> Let our enemies gloat over our loss. Poor miserable wretches! They do not know what our Party is. They hope that the Party will fall to pieces. But the Party will go firmly forward! Because it is a Leninist Party. Because it has been brought up and tempered in battles! Because we have in our hands the testament bequeathed to it by Comrade Lenin.[7]

The reader will recall the contents of the testament to which Stalin was referring. It leaves no doubt that if Lenin had remained alive, if only for a few months, Stalin's political life would have come to an end. Lenin's decision on this matter would have been final, and, as always, without room for appeal. Stalin knew this better than the rest and for this reason was organizing the apparatus to serve as an opposition group to block the carrying out of Lenin's will. Would Stalin have been successful? It is doubtful. And here there arises the question raised by Trotsky in his biographical sketch of Stalin, namely, did Stalin himself kill Lenin, a question which Stalin prevented Trotsky from answering by dispatching Trotsky's murderer to Mexico.

Trotsky relates how Stalin, after one of his regular visits to the sick Lenin, told the Politburo that Lenin had asked for poison in order to commit suicide. Stalin's statement met with indignation on the part of the members of the Politburo. Stalin did not reveal his own reaction to Lenin's request. Trotsky comments that Lenin was well aware who was capable of giving him poison and indeed stood to benefit from such an act. Did Stalin actually accede to Lenin's request? Trotsky tacitly admits the possibility, though he does not dwell on it. Persons who know Stalin's character and the nature of his system of government would agree that it is possible. As far back as 1927, Lenin's widow, Mme. Krupskaya, dropped a comment which had wide circulation in the Party: "If Ilyich [Lenin] were alive today, Stalin would imprison him." It is well known that not a single follower of Lenin ever emerged alive from a Stalinist prison. Why then should he not have killed Lenin himself? Of all the members of Lenin's Central Committee elected at the Sixth Party Congress in August 1917, how many are now alive?

---

[7] *Kommunisticheskaya partiya Sovetskoga Soyuza v rezolyutsiyakh i resheniyakh sezdov, konferentsii i plenumov TsK, 1898–1954* (The Communist Party of the Soviet Union in Resolutions and Decisions of Congresses, Conferences, and Plenums of the Central Committee, 1898–1954), 3 vols., Moscow, 7th ed., 1954, Vol. I., p. 806. (Hereafter cited as *KPSS v rezolyutsiyakh.*)

1.	Lenin	Died
2.	Kamenev	Shot
3.	Trotsky	Assassinated by Stalin's order
4.	Stalin	Died
5.	Zinoviev	Shot
6.	Sverdlov	Died
7.	Nogin	Died
8.	Rykov	Shot
9.	Bukharin	Shot
10.	Bubnov	Shot
11.	Uritsky	Assassinated by a terrorist
12.	Milyutin	Shot
13.	Kollontay	Died
14.	Artem (Sergeyev)	Died
15.	Krestinsky	Shot
16.	Dzerzhinsky	Died
17.	Joffe	Committed suicide
18.	Muralov	Shot
19.	Sokolnikov	Imprisoned
20.	Smilga	Shot
21.	Shaumyan	Shot (by the British)
22.	Berzin	Shot
23.	Stasova	Imprisoned (later freed)
24.	Lomov	Shot

Accordingly, of the twenty-four members of the Central Committee which had organized the Bolshevik Revolution in October 1917, Stalin survived until his death in 1953, six died a natural death, eleven were shot by order of Stalin, one was killed by order of Stalin, two were imprisoned, one was killed by enemies, and one committed suicide. Would Stalin have shown mercy to Lenin himself, if he had no compunctions against destroying the entire Leninist elite?

To return to the events following Lenin's death, I have recounted earlier Trotsky's description of the manner in which Stalin had created his own party within the Party with Lenin looking on. Lenin's death merely accelerated the process. To begin with, immediately after Lenin's death the Central Committee decided to call more factory workers into the Party. This was the so-called "Lenin call-up," under which the Party ceremoniously accepted as many as 250,000 workers who sympathized with the new Stalin Party line. By May 1924, the Party had grown until it contained 730,000 members. At the same time the Stalinists undertook to purge the Party of members who during the 1923 discussions had voted against Stalin and for Trotsky.

The purge was naturally applied first of all to university cells, the majority of which had sided with Trotsky. (Stalin and the Central Committee accused Trotsky, among other things, of having announced the slogan, "Youth is the Party's Barometer," merely in order to flatter young people and set them against the "old members.") By the end of 1925, after the purge, the Party had only 640,000 members left. Stalin had expelled from the Party about 100,000 students, professors and university officials by application of the "Malenkov Plan" of which I have already spoken, on the basis of their lack of confidence in him.[8] Those expelled from the Party were immediately expelled from the universities.

This cruel lesson which Stalin had taught the "proletarian students" was in the mind of everyone when matters concerning the Rightists began to be discussed within the walls of the Institute of Red Professors. Most Institute students were openly sympathetic to the right-wing group, but the Stalinist minority worked in a Stalinist manner to create within the Institute its own Party organization based on the same principles as those on which Stalin was creating his own party within the Party.

"Give us organized professional revolutionaries and we shall turn Russia upside down," Lenin had said in 1902, in *What Shall We Do?* This thesis continued to be Stalin's central guideline in his pursuit of personal power and his struggle with the opposition, although in place of "professional revolutionaries" he used the term "Party activists." This was not only a magic expression, but a magic idea as well. Some twenty years later *Pravda* reminded the Party apparatus of the identity of the originator of the idea and how significant it had been in the history of the Stalinist revolution: "Comrade Stalin," said *Pravda*, "points out that activists, if rightly used, can represent an enormous force, capable of working miracles."[9] In fact, during the struggle with Trotsky the activists did represent an "enormous force" and did "work miracles," when they succeeded so easily in disparaging Trotsky's authority within the Party and within the country, although this authority had until then appeared unshakable. It is true that many of the old activists turned out to be Trotskyites, but as a whole the activists proved to be equal to their task.

The only conclusion which Stalin drew from this experience was that activists must be selected and organized in the manner in which Lenin had selected and organized his group of professional revolutionaries. No potential enemies of the "general line" could be admitted to activist membership. Activists must be selected not for their former services to the Revolution but for their present qualities, depending on what the given Communist was capable of doing at the present time. "The Central Committee was guided by Lenin's brilliant idea that the main factor in any organizational work is the choice of men and the control of performance," said Stalin.[10] When purging the post-Trotskyite activists in the 1920's Stalin let the Party understand that he would limit membership in this group to persons who were obedient and would mercilessly persecute the old Party heads. Local Party committees received directives telling them who was to be purged from activist membership and how this should be done.

On the surface, the purge of activist membership was so carried out as to make it appear that the Party was discharging only "bureaucrats" and "harmless

---

[8] *BSE*, 1953, Vol. II, p. 653.
[9] *Pravda*, July 25, 1952.
[10] Stalin, *Voprosy leninizma*, p. 479.

babblers." In fact, however, those purged were possible allies of Bukharin and the right wing, although the rank and file of the Party did not as yet know that such a group existed. Those dismissed from their posts were automatically removed from activist membership even if they had been well-known Party members before the Revolution, during the Revolution, and during the Civil War. Thus they ceased to exert any influence on inner-Party affairs.

The secret purge of activists had been carried out and the persons able to support Stalin's leadership in the Central Committee against the followers of Bukharin had been selected when Stalin decided to take his quarrel with the right-wing group out of the Politburo and place it before the Party activists. At the end of 1928, a first attempt of this kind was made in the Party cells of Moscow. But who should in fact be considered a member of the activist group either locally or centrally, in districts and in oblasts? Would the name apply to the so-called "nomenclature officials" of district committees, oblast committees, and the Central Party Committee, in other words to bureaucrats within the Party, the administration, or the industrial and agricultural, trade union, or military organizations? Not all members of this bureaucracy were included in the category of activists. Who would choose the few who did belong? The Party apparatus. Only those who received personal invitations from the Party apparatus (district, oblast, or Central committees) could take part in meetings of Party activists. To whom did the Party apparatus send such invitations? Only to leading Communists who did not have black marks against their names in lists kept by the Special Sections of the Party committees. There were many cases in which deserving and well known Communists, who still occupied important posts in administrative or industrial organizations, were not invited to attend activist meetings if their loyalty to Stalin's Party line was in question.

Their omission was understandable, for the activists formed the elite of the Party and the correctness of the political line taken by Stalin and the Central Committee was confirmed at their conferences, at which they spoke in the name of the Party as a whole. Activists served to create public opinion within the Party in the same manner as *Pravda* did for the press. Any decision by Party activists was automatically considered to be the will of the whole Party. Therefore, the name "activist" symbolized both loyalty to the Stalinist line and membership in the Party elite. In order to be able to make a career for himself within the Party and the state, a Communist had to be an activist. Thus was created the party within the Party which gave Stalin his easy victory over the right-wing elements.

Immediately after the return of the Central Committee's "theory brigade" from Leningrad, there took place in the Communist Academy the first meeting of activists of the so-called "theory front" of the USSR. Invitations to the meeting were issued directly by the Agitation and Propaganda Department of the Central Committee. I do not recall how many tickets were sent to the Institute of Red Professors, but I do remember that many students as well as professors of the "Bukharin school" were not invited. The Bukharinites who had formerly been included in the group of activists and who had in fact done much for Stalin and

Bukharin during the struggle with Trotsky now created a great uproar. They accused Yudin and Orlov, who had deleted their names from the invitation list handed to the Central Committee, of forming a clique. Pokrovsky undertook to clear up the matter in the Central Committee, but was told that although the Central Committee was not to blame for the "annoying mistakes" they could not now be corrected: there were no more tickets. The activists who felt insulted were ready to lynch Yudin, but in spite of everything they did not succeed in attending the meeting legally. I myself, being a newcomer, was not included among the activists, but I sympathized with those who felt themselves slighted.

If it had not been for the uproar in the Institute, I would probaly not have been much interested in hearing the speeches which were to be made. But when Sorokin suggested that he might be able to get me a ticket I willingly agreed to attend the meeting with him. The meeting took place in the large auditorium of the Communist Academy on the Volkhonka. The meeting was attended not only by members of the Communist Academy and professors and students of the Institute of Red Professors and of the Russian Association of Scientific and Research Institutes but also by leading functionaries of the Central Committee, headed by Kaganovich, who had just been transferred from the Ukraine to Moscow to accept appointment as Secretary of the Party Central Committee. Pozern, Kirov's propaganda chief, had come specially from Leningrad. The Central Committee functionaries, although not members of the Communist Academy (only Kaganovich and Stetsky were, as I remember) sat at the head table. On the floor of the hall and in the gallery I saw many of the dissidents who had been able to attend the meeting in spite of all difficulties. (I subsequently discovered that they had pulled strings to get admitted.) None of those present except Central Committee members and members of the "theory brigade" knew why and in what connection the meeting had been arranged. The chairman of the meeting was Professor Pokrovsky, who was, and remained to the end, a personal friend of Bukharin. (It might be added here that at Pokrovsky's funeral in 1932 Bukharin was appointed by the Central Committee to deliver the official eulogy, on which occasion he made a long speech on the Red Square praising Pokrovsky as a scholar and referring to Stalin as "field-marshal of the proletarian forces.")

Pokrovsky declared the activist meeting open and announced as the subject for discussion, "The Theoretical Errors of Bukharin and His School." The unusual nature of the subject was probably the reason why Pokrovsky omitted the usual introductory speech and immediately introduced Kaganovich. The audience became attentive. Kaganovich approached his subject indirectly. "Lenin," he said, "did not fight for any kind of science but only for a Party science, a Bolshevik science. Lenin recognized no authorities when the interests of Marxism were at stake. Lenin had no equal in fulminating against enemies and striking against friends in the struggle for a Marxist science. Think of *Materialism and Empirio-Criticism* . . . . If we want to be pupils worthy of Lenin we too must be merciless toward those in our midst who think they can teach not only us but Lenin himself. . . . After Lenin's death no one can lay claim to filling the role of our teacher in questions of Marxism: we have one teacher, Leninism, and only one laboratory of Lenin's political and theoretical thought, the Central Committee. However, there are among us self-appointed would-be theorists who think that they have in their pockets the key to Marxism-Leninism. This category of would-be theorists includes Bukharin and his school . . . ."

At this moment a group of persons quietly made their way through the long hall to the head table, acknowledging greetings right and left as they went. The audience became slightly restive. Whispering swelled into general conversation. Someone in the gallery shouted in a deep voice: "Long live the one beloved in the Party as man and theorist, Comrade Bukharin!"

"I am sorry, Lazar Moiseyevich [Kaganovich]," said one of the newcomers, with exaggerated irony, "I am afraid I have interrupted your learned dissertation at a most interesting point."

It was Bukharin.

As a member of the Politburo, and also a member of the Presidium of the Communist Academy, Bukharin outranked Kaganovich and took the seat which Kaganovich had been occupying. Pokrovsky was obviously embarrassed, but Adoratsky, the vice-chairman of the meeting, ordered silence in the gallery and the hall, while Kaganovich, addressing himself to the audience and not to Bukharin, exclaimed rudely but pompously: "You are wrong again, Comrade Bukharin, if you think anyone has been interested in grubbing in a manure heap without a chance of finding a pearl hidden in it."

"It shows you are poor sanitary engineers," said Bukharin.

The audience laughed appreciatively. The unexpected appearance of Bukharin and his friends had clearly spoiled Kaganovich's introduction to this speech on the errors of Bukharin's school.

While Kaganovich was still speaking, one of the presiding officers, Shkiryatov, I believe, left the hall and went to the office of the chairman of the Academy Party Presidium. As soon as Kaganovich finished, Shkiryatov, who had by then returned, came up to him and whispered in his ear. Kaganovich picked up his heavy commissar's briefcase from the table in front of Bukharin and accompanied Shkiryatov quickly to the office from which Shkiryatov had just returned. The chairman and vice-chairman hesitated, at a loss what to do next, whether to call upon someone to speak or to await the return of Kaganovich and Shkiryatov.

Voices called from the gallery:

"Let Nikolai Ivanovich [Bukharin] speak!"

"We want Comrade Bukharin!"

Bukharin beamed good-naturedly and shook his head in the direction of the chairman's office as if to say, "Let's wait till the chief comes back."

But the chief did not come back, the audience wanted the meeting to continue, and the gallery was becoming frantic.

"Let Nikolai Ivanovich speak!"

Shkiryatov came back and restored calm by saying, "Nikolai Ivanovich, you are wanted on the telephone."

Bukharin left the hall.

In the chairman's office, Bukharin had a fairly long telephone conversation with Stalin. Later on, the text of the conversation was made a part of the record of the case of the Right Opposition when it was first brought up in the plenary session of the Central Committee in February 1929. The conversation was approximately as follows:

Stalin : The Central Committee does not consider it desirable for you to be present at the discussion on theory, because it does not want the discussion to assume a political character.

Bukharin : Kaganovich has already given it a political character and, besides, the fact that almost the entire Central Committee is present hardly testifies to the "theoretical" character of the meeting.

Stalin : Kaganovich is there not as a representative of the Central Committee, but on the personal invitation of the Communist Academy; the others also came because they were invited by the Academy, of which you, too, are a member.

Bukharin : But I am also a member of the Politburo, and the Politburo has passed no resolution about even a "theoretical discussion." How could Kaganovich have initiated a discussion of any kind on his own initiative and without the knowledge of the Central Committee?

Stalin : The initiative apparently does not come from Kaganovich, but from the Academy itself. The Central Committee cannot, after all, forbid a scholarly body to engage in scholarly debates even if these deal with persons like you and me who are members of the Politburo. But your presence as a member of the Politburo may hamper the freedom of discussion once it has begun. I have, therefore, consulted with other members of the Politburo and we have decided that it would be better if you left the meeting, so that it will not assume a political character.

Bukharin : First, are all the members of the Politburo of your opinion, and second, does this request apply to the other members of the Central Committee as well—to Kaganovich, Pozern, Krinitsky, Stetsky, Yaroslavsky, Shkiryatov?

Stalin : As you know, Rykov and Tomsky are not in Moscow, Kalinin is ill, and the others have all been asked to give their opinions. They insist that you think of the political consequences of your failure to obey the general will of the Politburo. We did not discuss the question of Kaganovich and the others, but will talk about this later.

Bukharin : I demand a definite answer: have you, as Secretary of the Central Committee, given orders for holding a discussion, even of a theoretical nature, directed against me?

Stalin : Of course not, but neither can I forbid anyone to hold one, even if it were directed against me.

Bukharin : I am staying on at the meeting.

Stalin : In that case, you must blame yourself for the consequences.

Bukharin, pale and obviously upset, returned to the hall and resumed his seat. Kaganovich and Shkiryatov were still absent. Soon Pozern and Yaroslavsky went out to join them. A few minutes later, Pokrovsky was also sent for.

During the interval, discussions broke out here and there among various groups. All guessed that telephone conversations were in progress with the Central Committee. Some came up to the head table and attempted to find out what it was all about. Bukharin was plunged deep in the reading of a newspaper and made no answer to inquiries. After half an hour, the members of the Central Committee returned.

"I declare the meeting closed," said Pokrovsky, without giving any reason for his action.

Chapter VIII

The Defeat of the Moscow Party Committee

On the morning of the second day after the ill-fated meeting described in the preceding chapter, as I was strolling through the corridor of the Academy building I stopped as usual to take a look at the notice board of the Institute Party cell. Posted on the board was a printed list of students and professors who were "urgently" requested to report to the cell office. My name was on the list. However, I was scheduled to attend a lecture, so I went there with the intention of reporting to the cell office during the intermission. The class session, a lecture on philosophy by Mme. Axelrod-Ortodoks, had hardly begun when the secretary of the cell bureau interrupted the lecture to read the same list as that posted on the board, and to say that those whose names were called were to go to the office at once. About ten persons, including myself, stood up and left the lecture hall, asking each other the meaning of the summons. A number of persons from other departments were waiting when we got there.

In the cell office was Yudin, the new cell secretary, frowning and trying to look important as he ran his fingers through his thick red hair. His dull gray eyes, usually far from flashing with "Bolshevik fire," were now gleaming with both fire and malice. When one of his fellow-students tried deliberately to deflate the secretary's self-importance, Yudin said sharply: "We are not in a bar; we are in the cell office."

"Can't you take a joke, Pavlusha?" asked the student, trying to repair his mistake.

"My name is Yudin," he replied curtly, obviously displeased at being addressed familiarly as Pavlusha.

His fellow-student fell silent.

We were silent too.

Yudin checked the list. All the students had turned up, but there were no professors. The office secretary returned to report that the professors were busy with their seminars.

"Call them in," Yudin ordered.

A few minutes later the professors appeared, no less puzzled than we.

"All the comrades whom I have summoned must go to the Central Committee offices at 6 p. m.," Yudin announced.

When the students and professors asked him what was going on and whom they should ask for, Yudin replied sharply: "You will find out when you get there."

Various possibilities rushed through my mind:

"Denunciation by Orlov?"

"Return to the Caucasus?"

"Taking part in Stalin's decapitation?"

"Or something better?"

But what could be better than being allowed to continue my courses? I decided to take the following rule as a guide: Hope for the best but be prepared for the worst. Still, I had not decapitated Stalin, I had not been one of the Trotskyites. What else might I have done, perhaps even worse? As always in such circumstances, I dashed off to see Sorokin. As bad luck would have it, he was absent. I tried to find out from one of the office secretaries but she merely replied that she had first heard the news from me. I went back to my classroom. There the aged Mme. Axelrod was talking about Nietzsche: "There are the chosen few and the crowd, masters and slaves. The chosen few are called upon to make history. The urge for power is the driving force for human development. Only the chosen few possess it." How original and timely!

Fresh thoughts and the soft voice of the lecturer, "the last of the Mohicans of the philosophy of independent Marxism," as we called her, distracted my thoughts. I sat through my other lectures without hearing them. Often I caught myself thinking about Orlov, Yudin, and the Central Committee. I ate my dinner without appetite. Immediately after dinner, I skipped a German lesson and went to Sorokin's apartment, but he was not in. I found him at Zinaida Nikolayevna's.

Reznikov came in, looking even more pale and upset than myself. "I have terrible news for you," he said. "Both Uglanov and Kotov have been dismissed today, as well as the secretaries of the Rogozhsko-Simonov, Krasnaya Presna, and Khamovniky district committees. A Central Committee commission has been appointed with Molotov as chairman to investigate the entire top staff of the Moscow organization." (This had been done at the end of October 1928.)

"This is awful! It should not be allowed," said Zinaida Nikolayevna in a hushed, sad voice. Tears were in her eyes. Reznikov nodded assent and sank wearily on the sofa.

"This is awful! It should not be allowed," Zinaida Nikolayevna repeated sobbing. I was sorry for her, and gave her a chair and a glass of water. She sat down, but refused the water.

"But you do not understand, comrades, this is the beginning of a real counter-revolution," she said, gradually recovering.

"For some it is the beginning, for others the end," Sorokin declared laconically.

I felt that Sorokin saw more clearly than she the significance of the events which were taking place, that he could look farther ahead and that he probably experienced them more keenly and deeply, but was trying not to give himself away. He was obviously unsuccessful.

"How did it happen and what is the reaction in the Moscow Committee," Sorokin asked Reznikov, with difficulty suppressing his emotion.

Reznikov then related that about three days earlier, to the complete surprise of the members of the Moscow Party Committee bureau, certain members of the Committee, including Voroshilov, Menzhinsky, Bulganin, Karavayev, and Bauman, a member of the committee bureau, had proposed calling an extraordinary meeting of the bureau and the top activists to make an important announcement. Uglanov, who was also a Secretary of the Central Committee, tried to find out what was going on, but was only told that this would be announced at the meeting itself. When Uglanov had followed the matter up in the Central Committee, Molotov, ostensibly acting in the absence of Stalin, after first saying that the Central Committee was in the dark, pointed out that every member of the Moscow Committee as well as of the Central Committee had the right to request that a meeting be called. The Central Committee, for its part, would willingly send representatives to the meeting if the members of the Moscow Committee concerned had anything important to say.

Uglanov had opened the meeting at 10 o'clock at night. Stalin, Molotov, Kaganovich, and a large group of Moscow Committee members and activists who were not members of the bureau had come to the meeting. At the very beginning, the Central Committee members had questioned the right of the activists to be present. Kotov and Reznikov had opposed their admission. Bauman, who was also head of the Rural Section of the Moscow Committee, had supported their inclusion. Molotov had interrupted to say that it would be an infringement of the spirit of "inner-Party democracy" if the Moscow Committee activists were forbidden to be present merely on the basis of the letter of Party law.

Although it was obvious that the Moscow Committee members and the activists had come for a definite purpose, and Reznikov continued to protest, Uglanov had ruled that the meeting was open to "the Moscow Committee bureau, together with the leading activists." Bulganin who was then the director of the Moscow Electic Power Plant, but had always been a member of the group of "Cheka activists," had requested permission to make a "brief statement on behalf of the Moscow Committee and Central Committee members on the work being done by right-wing elements in the Moscow organization." His statement had declared that "right-wing opportunists" and their immediate followers and tools, who were attempting to divert the Party into paths leading to the restoration of capitalism, were active in the Moscow organization among the top personnel of the more important establishments and institutions, in research institutes and universities, in a number of district committees and even within the Moscow Committee itself. The statement had asserted that not only Uglanov but also Kotov, Ukhanov, Penkov, Reznikov, and Ryutin, all members of the Moscow Committee bureau, who talked so much about the "general line," were in fact right-wing elements. The authors of the statement had demanded in the name of the district activists and the members of the Moscow Committee that (1) the top Moscow personnel be forced to resign, and (2) a special commission be appointed to check the Party background of the top personnel of all Moscow institutions and enterprises and of the Soviet and Party apparatuses.

Bulganin's statement had been, said Reznikov, entirely unexpected, not only to the members of the Moscow Committee bureau but even to Uglanov. Uglanov adjourned the meeting and demanded the right to hold a private conference with the members of the Central Committee Secretariat (Stalin, Molotov, and Kaganovich were present, not as members of the Politburo, but as secretaries of the Central Committee). Kaganovich categorically opposed Uglanov's proposal. Uglanov appealed to Stalin, but Stalin merely looked puzzled. Then Molotov spoke up.

"As early as February of this year the Central Committee warned the Moscow Committee as well as Uglanov personally about the possibility that matters would come to the pass to which they have come. The Central Committee received many hints and even direct requests from Moscow district organizations calling for improvement in the Moscow Committee leadership, but we wished to refrain from interfering in your affairs in the hope that the members of the Moscow Committee bureau would change their minds, but all in vain. Now there is no longer any other way out—the question which has been openly raised must be openly discussed." Molotov suggested that the statement be discussed further.

Uglanov now proposed to Stalin that the question be discussed at a closed meeting of the Moscow Committee bureau and the Central Committee Secretariat and, if necessary, at a meeting of the Politburo. Stalin replied evasively: "I do not find that the situation is so tragic as to call for another special conference, although I have no objections in principle."

Stalin's statement instilled new hope in Uglanov and he officially declared the conference reopened. A discussion began. All the members of the Moscow Committee and the Central Committee, as well as the activists, unanimously supported Bulganin's statement. A member of the Moscow Committee bureau, Polonsky, I think, suggested as a compromise that since the conference had no right to discuss the question of the Moscow Committee leadership, an extraordinary plenary session of the Moscow Committee and the Moscow Control Commission be held to consider the statement submitted by the members of the Moscow Committee. Uglanov suggested that this proposal be put to a vote. All members of the Moscow Committee bureau, except Bauman, voted for the proposal, all the activists against it. The secretaries of the Central Committee did not vote. Kaganovich, resourceful as ever, reversed the results of the voting.

"According to the rules of order governing today's joint meeting of the Moscow Committee bureau and the activists," he said, "I consider that the proposal to call a plenary session has been rejected, as an absolute majority of those present have voted against it."

Uglanov jumped up from his seat and asked loudly and indignantly: "Who is secretary of the Moscow Committee here, I or you, Comrade Kaganovich?"

"You are, Comrade Uglanov, for the time being," replied Kaganovich with perfect composure.

"Let me tell you then, that I am such no longer. You can now continue with your farce. . . ."

Uglanov picked up his briefcase and stalked out of the room. Stalin followed immediately, but soon returned without him.

"Where is Comrade Uglanov," asked Molotov.

"He has rushed off to see Bukharin," replied Bulganin, in anticipation of Stalin's answer.

Kaganovich proposed that the meeting continue in order to approve the resolution of the Moscow Committee. Members of the Moscow Committee bureau, including Reznikov, argued that it was impossible and illegal to discuss the statement with Uglanov absent. Stalin then addressed the meeting. He expressed regret that such bitter argument and passion should have been aroused, for, he said, the question was not one of individuals, but of a certain ideological and political current within the Party which was highly dangerous for the cause; the question concerned a deviation from Marxism, a right-wing, kulak, reactionary deviation. It was quite unimportant, said Stalin, who was at the head of this deviation or reflected its tenets, but it was absolutely essential for all Communists to understand that the main danger to the Party was no longer represented by the left-wing Trotskyite deviation, now exposed for what it was, but by the right-wing opportunist deviation. That danger must be exposed and liquidated. Stalin did not agree with Bulganin that the members of the Moscow Committee bureau, headed by Uglanov, formed a right wing. This was an exaggeration which overshot the mark. But Stalin did not consider it possible for the Moscow Committee bureau, under the present circumstances, to combat the right-wing danger sucessfully, particularly as the Moscow activists, as had been made clear by Bulganin's statement and the speeches made at the present meeting, were opposed to the present membership of the Moscow Committee bureau.

Stalin dwelt on Uglanov personally, mentioned his great services in the revolutionary underground before the Revolution, his active participation in the Revolution and the Civil War, his bitter struggle against Trotskyism, and his well-deserved high authority in the Party. He ended his speech by saying: "After all, we Bolsheviks are used to listening to the voice of the masses and especially to the voice of the Party masses: if the Party activists want to change their leaders, the Central Committee is ready to recall Uglanov and other members of the Moscow Committee bureau ... " Kaganovich, who had continued to act as chairman after Uglanov had left, struck the iron while it was hot. He proposed the following resolution:

"Those present at the joint meeting of the Moscow Committee bureau and activists: (1) regret that Uglanov left the meeting in open violation of Party discipline; (2) request the Central Committee to recall the members of the present Moscow Committee leadership; (3) propose the calling of an extraordinary plenary session of the Moscow Committee to elect a new leadership; (4) recommend that V. Molotov, Secretary of the Central Committee of the Communist Party, be made Secretary of the Moscow Committee."

"Not until now," said Reznikov, after this description of the meeting, "have we understood why the extraordinary session was called and why Bulganin had invited the secretaries of the Central Committee to attend it."

"I think," replied Sorokin, "that even now you do not understand what it is all about and what actually took place at the meeting. You think that the initiative came from the activist Bulganin, but it is much more subtle than this; the initiative came in fact from the Central Committee. Actually it was the apparatus of the Central Committee, the Secretariat, which prepared both the joint meeting of the Moscow Committee and the activists and the 'statement by the group.' In fact, as is clear from what you have just said, the parts to be played by the secretaries of the Central Committee behind the back of the Politburo had been assigned beforehand. Molotov was to be 'the moderate,' Kaganovich 'the aggressor,' and Stalin 'the benevolent arbitrator.' But in order to act all this comedy as successfully as possible to the very end, it was essential to exasperate Uglanov sufficiently to induce him to leave the meeting. Stalin's hypocritical words about Uglanov's merits were the smoke screen for a successful attack."

"Oh no," broke in Reznikov, "this time Stalin was sincere."

"Indeed! Just as sincere as when, for the first anniversary of the October Revolution, he wrote in *Pravda* that 'the successful preparation and the accomplishment of the October coup d'etat were due first and foremost to Comrade Trotsky.' Where has he now driven the 'Father of October' to? Trotsky now refers to us all in his writings as the heroes of October because Stalin quite seriously assured him that without him there would have been no October. But Stalin did not write this to make it sound good and or even to lick his boots, but with his own aims in view, namely, to lull the suspicions of his enemy (for Trotsky was his enemy even then), to gain his trust, to penetrate his fortress, and then to blow up the fortress together with its commandant. This was the way in which he dealt with Lenin when he became Secretary of the Central Committee, this is how he dealt with Trotsky after Lenin's death, this is how he is now dealing with Bukharin. . . . He was insincere in his dealings with Bukharin. 'We shall defend our little Bukharin,' shouted Stalin at the time. He defended Bukharin vehemently and praised him to the skies. During the struggle against Trotsky, Stalin even created artificially a cult of Bukharin and Bukharin's fame."

"Stalin never said a word about Bukharin at the meeting," said Reznikov again.

"Oh, yes, he did. All the good things he said about Uglanov were in fact a bomb hurled at Bukharin as well as Uglanov and all of us. 'Step by step' is Stalin's favorite expression; he does everything carefully, cunningly, but well. He always used to call Trotsky Judas, but now it should be clear to us that he was actually reflecting his own nature. If he should ever praise you and you should fail to fall on your knees like a faithful subject, you can be sure that you will remain on your feet only until he is strong enough to throw you into the abyss. Shall we fall on our knees? This is a question which we will soon have to answer."

Sorokin spoke for a long time, with occasional bitter reproaches directed at Reznikov. Reznikov answered rarely and without conviction, and obviously only for the sake of an answer. Deep within himself, he felt guilty for having given up so easily at the meeting.

"What should we have done," he asked Sorokin suddenly.

"Go, as Uglanov did, leaving Stalin with his hirelings. There would have been a row, and Stalin was not ready for a row."

Reznikov made no reply.

Zinaida Nikolayevna remained silent throughout the conversation. As I was leaving, Sorokin asked me to go to the General's house in the Moscow suburbs to tell him that he was expected in Zinaida Nikolayevna's apartment. As it was late, I had to tell Sorokin why I could not carry out his errand. This meant that I had to divulge the reason for my visit.

"I have been called," I said, "to the Central Committee, together with other students, for six o'clock tonight and I shall hardly have time to do what you have asked me to."

"Why have you been called," he asked.

As Sorokin himself did not know the meaning of the summons, there was no use of my talking with him further. I went off to the Central Committee.

Chapter IX

My Interrogation at the Central Committee and Krinetsky's Speech on Bukharin

The Central Committee headquarters was only a short distance away. I arrived in plenty of time. There were several people in the corridor but none belonging to our group. The information desk was to the right of the elevator and near it was a bulletin board on which were listed the various departments of the Central Committee and the offices of the secretaries. The procedure for seeing someone was still wonderfully democratic. The days and hours for interviews with the secretaries were indicated: "J. Stalin (or Molotov, or Kaganovich, or Kubyak) receives on . . . (days) from . . . to . . . (hours)." No special permits were required, nothing at all, you just produced your Party card, went straight to Stalin's Secretariat, and asked for an interview! (The procedure had altered when I last visited the Central Committee in 1940. Cheka men in uniform and plain clothes sat in the waiting room; a special pass to the Central Committee valid only for admittance to a stated department had to be attached to the Party card, but even that was insufficient. Before filling in the pass the Cheka officer rang up the Party bureaucrat whom you wished to see, and if the latter, on his own responsibility, allowed you to enter the building, a special questionnaire was filled in and only then were you allowed to enter the Holy of Holies. The bulletin boards giving the office hours of Stalin and the other secretaries were taken down in the early thirties.)

The elevator took me to the third floor and I went down the hall in the direction of the Agitprop, the Department of Agitation and Propaganda, to which our Institute was directly subordinated. In the hallway I met some of our students, who were just coming out of the Agitprop office, and tried to find out whom we were to see and what the whole affair was about. All they could tell me was that I was going to the right office and would be told there what to do.

When I entered the waiting room of the chief of Agitprop I found a few more of our students there. I was at once approached by a thin bespectacled man with red hair:

"Are you from the Institute of Red Professors, Comrade?"

"Yes."

"What is your name?"

I told him. The red-haired skeleton went through a list, on which opposite my name I saw a letter and number in red ink.

"Fourth floor, such and such an office." This in a hollow, consumptive voice.

When I reached the fourth floor and found the required office, I was immediately struck by the dead silence all around. The doors of the outer office and the private offices were covered with leather tacked over padded felt. Inlaid mosaic paths stretched down the passage before me like a ribbon. No names on the doors, only numbers. When I knocked on the soft leather door of the outer office I well knew that no one could hear me inside, nor would I hear anything in the passage. So I made up my mind and stepped inside. To my great surprise I found Orlov seated at the desk in a soft but well worn chair. Stupidly and bluntly I exclaimed, "How did you get here?" "In a different way from you," replied the clever and astute Orlov.

He went straight to the point.

"In the name of the Central Committee and under pain of expulsion from the Party, and that includes expulsion from the Institute of Red Professors, I must warn you to answer my questions truthfully. We know the whole truth but if you should attempt to conceal it from the Central Committee, you will leave here minus your Party ticket."

He paused and began to leaf through the papers in his file box.

His impressive tone, the serious inner-Party atmosphere, but especially this mysterious Central Committee office all produced the desired effect. It suddenly dawned on me that my fate was in the hands of this jaundiced and short-sighted man. Scenes from "Stalin's execution," Zinaida Nikolayevna's party, my friendship with Sorokin, today's meeting with Reznikov, flashed through my mind. Obviously Orlov knew about all these things but on the other hand the dilemma in which he had placed me was equally obvious: if I revealed all I knew, I would stay in the Institute of Red Professors; "if not, I would be expelled both from the Institute and from the Party." I could see that Orlov was watching me closely. I was nervous and knew that I was spoiling my chances. Finally I made up my mind to answer all his questions with a resolute "No," in the name of Zinaida Nikolayevna, Sorokin, and Caucasian honor. Let them expel me! Let them banish me to Siberia! Let them do what they like!

My thoughts were interrupted by a sudden question flashed at me by Orlov.

"Did you attend the meeting at the Communist Academy yesterday?"

"I did."

"Who gave you a ticket?"

"I got it at the Institute."

"Who actually gave it to you?"

"Sorokin."

"Why did he pick you out?"

"Ask him!"

"I am asking you."

"You have my answer."

"Did you applaud Bukharin?"

"Yes."

"Why?"

68

"Because he's a member of the Politburo."

"Did you cheer Bukharin?"

"It would be better for you to tell me why I have been called here, as I consider it superfluous to answer these silly questions."

"Please remember that you are in the Central Committee and must answer my questions," replied Orlov threateningly.

By now I was feeling more sure of myself. After all, Orlov's interrogation was nothing more than a kind of routine police investigation with no serious charges behind it. I plucked up courage and counterattacked.

"I set eyes on Bukharin for the first time in my life yesterday and only applauded when everyone else applauded, including the presiding officers. If in the meantime something has gone wrong with Bukharin, do not blame me, blame the Central Committee of which he is a member."

"And did you applaud Kaganovich," suddenly asked Orlov.

"I did, and for the same reason."

"Do you share the theoretical outlook and political opinions of Bukharin?"

I leaped from my chair indignantly and threatened to complain directly to Stalin about Orlov's questions. But my threats were of no avail.

"Stop behaving like an hysterical old woman and stop trying to act like a demagogue. You can't fool me about your anti-Party views. And another thing: don't threaten to complain to Stalin while you are working against him. What utter nonsense! Teach me my job, will you, you greenhorn! Now then, are you prepared to give real answers to my questions?"

Orlov was now shouting at me. He uttered the last sentence syllable by syllable. His jaundiced face turned into a question mark. His last words had struck at my pride with the impact of a bullet. I saw red; I had reached the stage where I was ready to commit murder—to die. (To be called an old woman is the greatest insult one can offer a Causasian.)

"Citizen Orlov, you always were and still are a low-down detective and careerist, and for men like you there should be no room in the apparatus of the Leninist Central Committee. Either I lose my Party ticket or you get thrown out."

With this I rushed out of his office, and forgetting about the elevator, began to run down the stairs. I had barely reached the third floor when I heard quick footsteps behind me. Someone shouted my name, "Comrade Avtorkhanov, Comrade Avtorkhanov!" I halted. A middle-aged man whom I had never seen before, in uniform, with no badges of rank, a Caucasian from his looks, was coming toward me. Smiling broadly, as if we were old friends, he asked me to come to his office. In vain I tried to find out what he wanted of me; the only answer he would give was a repetition of his request to accompany him to his office. Back we went to the fourth floor, past Orlov's office. Two or three doors farther on, he politely ushered me in. The room was similar to Orlov's. To an elderly woman typing at a desk, my guide casually said: "If anyone calls, I'm busy." We crossed the room and entered another office; still smiling he offered me a seat and sat down beside me in an armchair, less dilapidated than Orlov's. Two telephones, one for inside calls and the other a direct outside line, indicated that he was higher in rank. "Of course, you do not know me—my name is Tovmassian, Central Committee responsible instructor," said the stranger, "but I have heard of you from my colleague, Central Committee responsible instructor Karib. You know him; not long ago he was giving a course on the North Caucasus and Dagestan. He thinks very highly of you and predicts that you will go far. I had heard that you had been called to the Central Committee to see Orlov about some business connected with the Institute and I asked Orlov to introduce me to you after his interview, but now it appears that you have quarrelled. What about? What happened?" I had no wish to discuss Orlov with Tovmassian, but he was so curious and insistent that I ended by telling him the whole story.

"You know, Comrade Avtorkhanov," he commented, "on the face of it you may be right, he did insult you, and if he had known how quick we Caucasians are in using our daggers, it would not have happened; but you are wrong in principle. You lost your temper too quickly and only made matters worse for yourself. If the story gets to the Central Control Commission, you will be the one to suffer, and not Orlov. We are a hot-tempered people and they make allowances for us in Moscow, but we are supposed to use our tempers against the enemies of the Party, not our friends."

"If the Party has an enemy, it is Orlov," I snapped back.

"You are mistaken, he may not be a diplomat or a theorist, but he is devoted to the Party heart and soul."

"He was just as devoted heart and soul to the intelligence service of the Whites," I said.

"What do you know about that?"

"I've read the files."

"Yes, but that is an old story. It was investigated many times by the Central Control Commission without anything incriminating being brought to light. After all, what was in the past is not so important; what matters is what one is now. We have in the Party a good many members from before the Revolution, but what good are they if they keep on looking back, not forward. It might even be correct to say that Party members like that do more harm than good."

Tovmassian was looking me straight in the eye and could not help noticing my surprise.

It was the first time that I had heard a blunt and cynical statement to the effect that old Party members might be harmful today! I was completely bewildered, nor was it clear to me why Tovmassian was telling me. Surely he had not brought me back to his office merely to make this extraordinary statement.

He was waiting in silence for me to speak but I had nothing to say and felt it was useless to argue. When he realized that I was not prepared to talk he broached what was apparently the main subject of our conversation.

"Are you familiar with the views of the Rightist leaders on the national question," he asked. (The "national" question referred to peoples of non–Russian nationality.)

"It is the first time that I have heard of the existence of Rightist leaders," I replied innocently.

"I am talking about Bukharin's school of theorists in your Institute," explained Tovmassian.

"I can only say that I heard this school mentioned for the first time yesterday by Kaganovich."

I do not know whether he believed me, but I had been in fact quite unaware of any separate Right approach to the problem of the nationalities. I had heard that Lenin had criticized Bukharin's views on a number of legal and tactical matters, such as the theory of the state, the Brest-Litovsk Peace Treaty, the question of nationalities, historical materialism and dialectical materialism, but I had no idea whether Bukharin still held any separate views on the national policy of the Party. At one time Pyatakov and Bukharin had been known to have independent views on the right of the nationalities to self-determination, but this was now a thing of the past.

It turned out that the national theory of the Right, as explained by Tovmassian, who kept on using the term "Right," was very much what I had imagined it to be when I had first met Sorokin at the Institute of Red Professors.

The Right, went on Tovmassian, held that the Central Committee had become de-Russianized. It had previously been dominated by Jews and was now being managed by Caucasians, the Jews (Trotsky, Zinoviev, and Kamenev) having been replaced by Caucasians (Stalin, Mikoyan, and Ordzhonikidze). The Right had declared war on the Caucasus. A victory of the Right within the Party would mean not merely the triumph of Russian supra-state chauvinism, but also of Russian super-imperialism. Those who were taking action against Stalin—the originator of Lenin's policy on nationalities—were plotting against their own peoples. "You," continued Tovmassian, "are still young and inexperienced in politics, but let me tell you that all this concerns us Caucasians very closely. And because the Russian Orlov is fighting this chauvinist ideology together with us it is wrong to treat him as an enemy and to inquire too closely into his past life."

The interview was coming to an end. Tovmassian brought it to a close by a concrete proposal: I was to report any information I might have about Rightist plots in the Institute of Red Professors.

"Do you suggest that I am aware of a plot by unspecified Rightists and that I am concealing from the Central Committee my knowledge of this plot?" I asked indignantly.

"No, no! Your standing is above suspicion, but is the same true of your friends?" replied Tovmassian reassuringly.

His telephone buzzed; he picked up the receiver in leisurely fashion and answered in monosyllables, "Yes," "No." I had a feeling that the discussion was about me, but could not make out whether the "Yes" and "No" referred to me. Tovmassian put down the receiver and, dropping the previous subject, told me that we were about to hear something of interest.

"Whom are we going to see," I inquired involuntarily.

"Kaganovich," he answered indifferently, as if he were referring to a chat with our Dedodub. As an afterthought he added, "Kaganovich is a clever fellow who will never let one of us down."

My head was by now so full of the day's impressions, my nerves so taut, that I longed for a welcome "you are free to go," but I was aware how useless it was to decline this great honor. Meekly I followed Tovmassian and a few minutes later we both entered Kaganovich's waiting room. (The offices of the Party secretaries were in the southern wing of the fourth story; their doors were adorned with nameplates: "J. Stalin," "L. Kaganovich," "V. Molotov," "N. Kubyak.")

All of us who had been summoned to the Central Committee had gathered in the visiting room, both students and professors, including Yudin and Orlov. Everyone was silent except these two, who were conversing in whispers at the far end of the room. We rose as Kaganovich and Krinitsky entered and then resumed our seats at a sign from Kaganovich. Still standing, he made a short speech to the effect that the Institute of Red Professors had always been and still was the principal theory mainstay of the Central Committee in its struggle against the enemies of Leninism, and he called on those present to be worthy of the Red Professors and the high calling conferred by membership in that group. Owing to pressure of work he would have to leave, but Krinitsky would acquaint us with the object of the meeting. Nodding abruptly, he turned the meeting over to Krinitsky and left the hall.

"Yesterday's demonstration in the Communist Academy against the Central Committee," began Krinitsky, "is a definite indication of unrest in the Institute of Red Professors. Most of you, in one way or another, shared in this demonstration. You must understand clearly that we cannot tolerate the presence within the Institute of any person who sides with deviationists attempting to destroy the purity of Marxism-Leninism. What may be overlooked on the part of a workman at his lathe is unforgivable when it comes from the future theorists of the Party. It is quite likely that some of you are mistaken about the character of Comrade Bukharin, but let me tell you that the Central Committee has nothing against Bukharin as an individual. What we shall do, however, is to fight, as we have done in the past and will do in the future, against the anti-Leninist ideology and theory of Bukharin, even though he is a member of the Politburo. The times are too grave to allow us to view with equanimity a revision of Leninism by representatives of Right opportunism in the Party. The leader of this opportunism is Comrade Bukharin. It would, of course, be far easier to expel Comrade Bukharin from the Politburo or even from the Central Committee, but Right opportunism is an ideology which does not lend itself to mere mechanical expulsion. It is an ideology of the old restorationist classes. It must be destroyed by the tempered steel of Leninism. We call on Comrade Bukharin to do this himself and trust that sooner or later he will choose this way. However, the Central Committee cannot afford to wait until Comrade Bukharin makes up his mind. The Central Committee is responsible both to the Party and to the Comintern for any deviation from

72

Leninism by its members. Because of this fact the Central Committee considers the danger from the Right as the main danger to the Party and herewith brands any tendency at compromise as a Party crime."

The end of Krinitsky's speech sounded like a mixture of threat and command: either we students and teachers in the Institute of Red Professors would actively join the fight against the danger from the Right within the Institute being conducted in the press and at Party and workers' meetings in Moscow, or the Central Committee would take steps to re-examine the personnel of the Institute.

It was well after eleven o'clock when we left the building.

Chapter X

The Meeting at the Institute of Red Professors

It was thus that the attention of the Central Committee had quite unexpectedly been focused on the Institute of Red Professors. Looking back, the reasons were obvious. First, the Institute contained the best propaganda brains of the Party; second, until recently Bukharin had been considered at the Institute as the undisputed authority on matters concerning Marxist theory. The Party members of the faculty were all, after the removal of the Trotskyites, regarded as followers of Bukharin, while Bukharin himself had been a leading professor of political economy and the theory of Soviet economics from the very inception of the Institute. It was therefore of crucial importance to the Central Committee that the campaign to discredit Bukharin as a theorist should begin spontaneously and at the bottom, and that it should begin in the Institute of Red Professors.

It was only much later that I was able to grasp the real reasons which had prompted the Central Committee to adopt this roundabout way of dealing with Bukharin instead of simply branding him as a heretic and consigning his school to anathema. When all was said and done, Krinitsky was right: it was not a question of Bukharin as a person but of the extent to which his influence had spread in the theoretical and academic circles of the Party, and the need to ascertain promptly what were the supporting factors on which he relied and which would have to be liquidated together with him. The agitation against Bukharin was not so much a trial balloon as a well-planned reconnaissance of his existing and potential army. The Central Committee, or rather the Secretariat of the Central Committee, was engaged in bringing about a clearcut division in the Party of those for and those against Bukharin. The lower strata of the Party were by now firmly controlled by Stalin's Party apparatus, but higher up the relative strength of the opposing forces was as yet unclear. The preliminary screening of Bukharin, so far limited to theory, was being made use of as a means of provoking a split among the Party activists. The meeting of the Communist Academy had been called for this purpose, while other meetings of Party activists were being planned for Moscow, Leningrad, Kiev, Minsk, Sverdlovsk, Baku, Tiflis, and other large Party centers. It was, however, evident that our trial balloon meeting at the Academy, which the Central Committee had regarded as very important, had proved a failure, and there was no overlooking the unfavorable impression which it had produced on the Stalinists. It was clear that Bukharin could count on a larger following and consequently on a greater measure of potential support among the activists than had at first been anticipated by the more optimistic members of Stalin's entourage. As a result Party directives and political pressure began to be exerted upon the rank and file Party members.

The first blow was dealt to the Moscow leadership on November 27, 1928, when the leaders of the Moscow Party Committee, including its chairman Uglanov, were removed from office without official explanation. As I have already said, the fate of both the committee and its chairman had been decided at the end of October, some time before the actual purge. At the same time that Uglanov and his fellow committeemen were removed, it was announced that Molotov had been elected Secretary of the Moscow Committee while retaining his post as Second Secretary of the Central Committee of the Communist Party of the Soviet Union. Accordingly, it can be accepted as true that, as an "Appeal by the Moscow Committee to the Members of the Party" stated a year and a half later, in April 1930, "it was in the Moscow Committee itself that Right opportunists who had attempted to attack the general Party line were first decisively defeated."

The fact that the leaders of the Moscow Committee had been removed for Right opportunism was never actually mentioned in the Party press either in 1928 or before the close of 1929; it was only hinted that the Moscow leadership contained a certain number of unnamed Right sympathizers. After his dismissal, Uglanov was appointed a People's Commissar of the USSR (if I am not mistaken, for Labor) while Ukhanov, chairman of the Moscow Soviet, retained his position until the end of 1930, when he was replaced by Bulganin—the "hero" in the unmasking of Uglanov. In inner circles of the Party, however, and certainly in the Party leadership, the fact that the members of the Moscow Committee had been removed for supporting Bukharin was a matter of common knowledge, as was the appointment, for the sake of appearances, of its members to positions that were important, but less dangerous from the point of view of the Central Committee.

The events described were the first real blow to the opposition headed by Bukharin and constituted a serious warning. While it was clear to all that the defeat of the Moscow organization was a definite triumph for the Central Committee Party apparatus, it was recognized that it might eventually prove to be a Pyrrhic victory if put to the test of a free vote of the Party rank and file.

Futhermore, the relative strengths of the contending ideologies were quite unpredictable and would be the subject of heated debate at the next plenary meeting of the Central Committee, when the existence of a Right danger, personified by Bukharin and Uglanov, would be openly discussed. Nothing was known about the position of Rykov and Tomsky. Quite recently Bukharin and Uglanov, supported by the entire leadership of the Central Committee, had resolutely opposed the Trotskyites and the Left deviation. Viewed from this angle the struggle against Trotsky had been a two-edged sword, as the broad masses of the Party ascribed the relatively easy victory over Trotsky to the theoretical soundness and Leninist logic of Bukharin, not Stalin. Bukharin's prestige as an exponent of orthodox Party theory had gained enormously during this struggle. It might prove a difficult task to convince the Party that Bukharin was really a worthless theorist and anti-Party deviationist. How could this be done? Even Stalin's logic, let alone ordinary human logic, could hardly explain the retroactive damning of all of Bukharin's anti-Menshevik and anti-Trotskyite writings as anti-Leninist doctrine, especially as these writings had been published during Lenin's lifetime and many of them had even been edited and approved by Lenin himself. And, finally, what explanation could be found for Stalin's repeated assertions during debates against Trotsky that he would defend Bukharin from attacks from any quarter whatever?

The Party apparatus would now want to know what had happened to compel the Central Committee to brand Bukharin unexpectedly as the most dangerous enemy of the Party. His former activities, said the Party activists, were not at stake; what mattered was his present attitude as expressed in the Politburo. What then, the apparatus would ask, was his attitude? At the meeting of the Party activists in the Communist Academy, Bukharin had been denied the right to speak, and everything that Kaganovich had said had been quite irrelevant, while the proceedings at the joint meeting of the Secretariat of the Moscow Committee and the Party apparatus had been veiled in secrecy. The fact that the disgraced members of the Moscow Committee had been given government posts entailing greater legal responsibility (an intentional though a temporary measure) had misled both the Party and the victims. The one unquestionable fact was the presence of another crisis in the Party, involving a choice between Stalin and Bukharin. The list of Stalin's supporters was known, but that of Bukharin's adherents was not. And even more obscure was the real cause of the crisis. The Central Committee Agitation and Propaganda Department attempted to pour oil on the troubled waters by applying the formula: "You can't go wrong by voting for Stalin." The more zealous among us countered with the quotation from Trotsky: "It is not the Party, but Stalin's voting herd."

The Party apparatus was brought to bear in an intensive and highly organized campaign, canvassing public opinion, frightening the "appeasers" and terrorizing the "deviationists."

The academic life of the Institute, to all intents and purposes, came to a standstill. Non-Party professors and academicians withdrew to their studies and libraries, while the students and Party members crowded into Party meetings and discussions. The decision was made and carried out to convene meetings, similar to the one just held by the activists of the Communist Academy, at other educational institutions at various levels—the Institute of Red Professors, the Russian Association of Social Science Research Institutes, Sverdlov University, and the Stalin Communist University for Workers of the East. At these meetings only one standard subject was discussed: "The Lenin Plan for Cooperatives, the Class Struggle, and the Errors of Bukharin's School." The principal speakers were invariably members of the "theory brigade."

At the meeting of the Institute of Red Professors the speaker was Mekhlis, who was steadily ascending the Party ladder. The meeting was purposely spread over two or three days in order to allow a larger number of professors and students to air their views. By basing every statement on an interminable series of quotations, long and short, from Marx and Engels, and particularly from Lenin, Mekhlis brilliantly performed his task. At the end of his speech he dwelt on agriculture and discussed the so-called "two paths" of agricultural development—the capitalist and the socialist. He then asserted, less successfully, and with less assurance, that Bukharin's school was leading the Party toward capitalist development. As proof, he quoted long passages from Bukharin's books, *Economics of the Transitional Period* and *The Problem of Trotskyism*. He wound up by reminding his audience that at the beginning of 1928, at the joint plenary meeting of the Moscow Committee and the Central Control Commission of the Party, Stalin had stressed the fact that in the Politburo no member belonged either to the Right or to the Left and that the point at issue was the past theoretical and political errors of Bukharin. However, this reference to Stalin and his statements spoiled the effect of Mekhlis' speech, and, what was more important, disrupted the long-term plans of Stalin, Molotov, and Kaganovich. Both the overt and the secret followers of Bukharin at once seized upon this tactical error. The remarks of Comrades Sten, then a member of the Central Control Commission, and Sorokin, are still fresh in my mind. Sten openly shared the latest views of Bukharin, but Sorokin was at the time still regarded as belonging to the ranks of the orthodox. Now was the time for everyone to lay his cards on the table. I wondered what Sorokin would do. Very few of us knew that he was incensed and resentful at what now appeared to be the "pro-Trotsky" policy of the Central Committee. Many believed that this man with his honesty, lofty idealism, and personal courage, would do anything rather than shun the discussion of dangerous topics or engage in conspiratorial double-dealing.

Several days had elapsed since I had last seen him at Zinaida Nikolayevna's apartment. Just before the meeting we met face to face in one of the passages of the Institute, but he passed me without as much as a greeting. I was both perplexed and hurt, and wondered if he suspected me of having spoken of him unfavorably in the Institute or if someone had whispered that I had informed on him. In either case I felt abused and ran after him to demand an explanation, but lost him in the crowd. At the meeting which began a little later, I took a seat in one of the back rows, not knowing what stand he would take and anxiously awaiting his speech.

He was one of the first to reply to Mekhlis. He began by questioning the honesty and validity of the whole report. His opening words still ring in my ears, "I never thought that anyone, not even Mekhlis, was capable of making so colorless and politically feeble a statement." These words immediately aroused the attention of the entire audience, and were followed by breathless silence. He then proceeded to analyze Mekhlis's speech point by point and to accuse him of either having willfully falsified Marxist-Leninist theory or of being patently incapable of correctly interpreting it. In answer to Mekhlis's insistent protests about playing to the gallery, Sorokin expressed his readiness to apologize provided Mekhlis would help him to clarify one point; he then read a fairly long quotation crammed with Marxist deductions on the growth of modern capitalism. Then in a challenging tone he asked Mekhlis, "Comrade Mekhlis, would you tell us whether you agree with these ideas?"

"I certainly do," answered Mekhlis.

"In that case may I congratulate you. I have just quoted from Mussolini."

The entire assembly rocked with laughter. Taking full advantage of the impression he had made on his listeners (later we always referred to this episode as the "quotation incident") he exclaimed: "A person who cannot tell red from black, who cannot distinguish between Lenin and Mussolini, is now trying to initiate us into the intricacies of Marxist theory. How low must our theory have fallen if we are reduced to listening to an ignoramus like Mekhlis! In my opinion," continued Sorokin, "Mekhlis is pushing us in the wrong direction, wittingly or unwittingly, when he tells us that we are assembled here merely to discuss Bukharin's former errors, and that these errors have no connection with the present state of affairs in the Politburo. They have, I repeat a thousand times, they have! Bukharin was wrong in his theory of the state in 1916; Bukharin was wrong in his reactions to the Peace of Brest-Litovsk in 1918; he was wrong again when the trade union question was being examined in 1921; and he could be wrong again today, in 1928. If that is the case we are justified in criticizing Bukharin, not for his alleged or past errors, but for his present political errors. The past merely serves to illustrate the present but of itself does not define the political personality of Bukharin as we see him today. Besides, can anyone in the assembly name a single member of the Politburo who has not committed some error in the past? Revolutionaries may err, but not the Revolution. Men like Mekhlis, whose sole delight lies in rummaging through old archives, never make revolutionaries. Instead of giving us a straightforward analysis of Bukharin's position today, he is furtively looking for an answer in his files. These grandmothers' tales are unworthy of Bolsheviks. Either, or! Either Comrade Bukharin is truly guilty of pushing the Party in the direction of the eventual restoration of the capitalist order of society, in which case he should be a member of a stock exchange, not of the Politburo, or Comrade Bukharin disagrees with the present policy of the Central Committee, in which case he should be required to state his views openly to the entire Party, as has been past practice in similar cases. But a delicate task of this nature should not be entrusted to such a loud-mouthed demagogue as Comrade Mekhlis. In politics a game of hide and seek can only lead to catastrophe, especially if it is played by people of similar views." Sorokin brought his speech to an unexpected conclusion by suggesting that the Central Committee invite Comrade Bukharin to state in the press his views on the current policy of the Party, or that in the event of a refusal by Comrade Bukharin, the Central Committee be invited to examine the question of his expulsion from the Politburo.

Sorokin had hardly finished speaking when loud protests were heard throughout the hall. "Exaggerator!," "Butcher!," "Trotskyite!" Even Mekhlis, accustomed as he was to internal intrigues in the Party, was completely taken by surprise at the totally unexpected conclusion of Sorokin's speech.

Instead of taking full advantage of Sorokin's radical offer, the chairman, Comrade Yudin, made a few noncommittal remarks about Bukharin's services to the Party, carefully omitting to talk about Bukharin himself. The most unprincipled and craftiest of the "appeasers," Mitin, while fully endorsing Sorokin's recognition of Bukharin's errors, nevertheless considered the suggestion of expelling

Bukharin from the ranks of the Politburo as a Trotskyite move "at this stage of the debate." Luppol, the vice-rector of the Institute, unversed in political intrigue, called Sorokin's statement "catastrophic." Others, such as Konstantinov, Leontiev, Fedoseyev, and Gladkov, argued that Sorokin's outburst showed a painful lack of responsibility.

Sorokin, however, had gained his objective of sowing dissention among the Stalinists. Among the speeches made by members of the Institute teaching staff, I recall those by Varga and Sten. (Mitin, as an instructor in the Krupskaya Academy of Communist Education, at a lower level than the Institute, was debarred from lecturing at the Institute.) Varga, in a monotonous and grammatically faultless speech, delivered with a strong foreign accent, treated us to a lengthy dissertation on Marx's theory of crises, which as far as I could see, had no bearing on the subject at all. The tall, elegant Sten, as red-haired as Yudin, a powerful orator and dialectician and brilliant in theoretical debate, steered the meeting back to Mekhlis' speech.

"When persons," said he, "who were only yesterday the first disciples of Bukharin and his devoted weapon bearers, tell us of the sinful errors of their master and confess to their reasons for betraying him, they leave only a sense of disgust. In persons of this kind a flair for temporary political advantage may compensate for their lack of theoretical soundness, but this by no means enhances their moral rectitude. You know as well as I do that up to the past few days both Mekhlis and Stetsky were literally more ready to swear by Bukharin than by Lenin. Personally, for Mekhlis, the authority of Lenin as a theorist never carried any weight, because Bukharin was his one and only god. Today we see Mekhlis executing a right face, but in that case it is perhaps permissible to ask him: What is the secret of your amazing transcendental intuition? Let us be frank with each other; Bukharin is admittedly a sinner, but this was discussed and debated long ago, at the time when you were licking his boots (if you will allow me this philosophical expression); would you tell me whose boots you find more palatable today? Nature protects the weak; it has endowed the chameleon with all the colors of the rainbow, the hedgehog with needles, the tortoise with armor, but, as our proverb says, it 'has deprived the butting cow of horns.' If you want us to believe your childish twaddle about Bukharin's errors, I suggest you begin by telling us how you changed your colors in the Party and became a renegade among Bukharin's followers."

During Sten's speech, Mekhlis sat nervously fidgeting or ruffling his hair. When Yudin asked if there were any more speakers, Sorokin stood up and called for an end to the debate and a vote on his recommendation. Renewed protests were heard in the hall. Someone suggested that Mekhlis be given the opportunity to answer Sorokin and Sten.

Mekhlis requested an adjournment until the following day, but his request was rejected. He then refused to make any statement at all, at which there was another uproar in the hall.

"Feeble, feeble," shouted the audience. "He wants to ask the new boots for advice," cried a voice. Yudin lost his head and did nothing. The situation was getting out of hand. Amid the general hubbub, someone at last suggested: "In view of the refusal of Comrade Mekhlis to make a closing statement, this meeting will now put Comrade Sorokin's proposal to a vote." Yudin glanced questioningly at Mekhlis. The latter was in a quandary. He was aware that the mere fact of a vote of this nature would spell his political death in the Central Committee. It was not that he was unduly perturbed by Sten's jibes; he could cleverly, though perhaps unconvincingly, parry them. But in order to deal with Sorokin's proposal, he would be forced to exceed the instructions which he had received regarding the meeting, namely, to have it request the Central Committee to expel Bukharin from the Politburo. He was perfectly aware that for a long time Bukharin had been attempting, against the categorical refusal of the Central Committee, to defend in the press his basic theoretical and political views. "The Central Committee," said Kaganovich later on regarding this matter, "cannot take the direction of committing political hara-kiri."

Mekhlis, however, lacked courage to combat the resolution and finally made up his mind to be guided by the political formula popular at the time: "Better go too far than not far enough!" So taking a chance for the first time in his life, he made up his mind to speak. Yudin heaved a sigh of relief, while the assembly settled down in tense silence to await events. Mekhlis, as was only to be expected, vented the whole of his wrath on Sten. "I was indeed," he said, "a disciple of Bukharin's, and his sword bearer as long as he used it to cut down the Trotskyites, but when his sword lost its edge I threw it away. You, Sten, picked it up when it was pointed at the heart of the Party. You cannot break the Party, but you may well get your own head broken." Referring to the first part of Sorokin's speech, he dubbed it an essay in popularity; then quite unexpectedly to the assembly, and as I later concluded, to himself as well, he seconded Sorokin's recommendation that a vote be taken on Bukharin's continued membership in the Politburo. At this an indescribable uproar broke out in the hall.

"We are not here to judge the members of the Politburo!"

"This is not a meeting of the Central Committee!"

"Bukharin is not a Sorokin or a Mekhlis, but a leader of the Party!"

What the result of this uproar would have been it is difficult to imagine, if Pokrovsky had not resorted to his well-worn device: "Comrades," he said, "I declare the meeting adjourned until tomorrow, as my lecture on 'Trotskyism and the Russian Historical Process' [an uncontroversial subject] is scheduled to begin in a few minutes." Of course none of us cared at all about the lecture, but it was obvious that Pokrovsky, as Rector, was doing his best to save the face of the Academy. We trooped out of the stuffy hall, mentally thanking our savior. Old Dedodub, as usual, stood majestically at his post by the door; Yelena Petrovna, one of the office secretaries, flitted down the corridor like a swallow. Outside, late autumn was visibly turning into belated winter and in the sky, equally pale and unhappy, the moon, with an effort to break away from the enfolding grasp of threatening thunderclouds, was slowly gliding off into an infinite future.

Into what future were we gliding?

Chapter XI

Stalin's Invention of a Right Opposition

The Central Committee relentlessly continued to pursue the task of unmasking, or rather provoking, what it called "Right opportunism" within the Party. Every effort was made to give the impression that this was not an attack on individual members of the Central Committee, the Moscow Committee, or local committees in the provinces, but a campaign directed against an ideological trend which had made its appearance both within the Party and in the country at large. The entire machinery of propaganda, both verbal and press, was used to drive home this point. The hidden motives behind the vague and seemingly senseless campaign were beyond the comprehension of the average Party member or the man in the street. With no individual opportunists in the Central Committee or elsewhere in the Party on whom to throw the blame, people looked for other explanations for the existence of this evil. The problem was much discussed in the Institute. It was even suggested that a small group within the Central Committee might be suffering from a persecution mania or some form of political hallucination and had conjured up imaginary "Rightists" and Right opportunism. But the Central Committee apparatus was implacable. All secret letters sent by the Central Committee Secretariat to Party organizations in the course of the year 1928 repeated: "The danger from the Left has been overcome; the Party is now faced with a new and graver danger—this time from the Right. The entire fire and the entire wrath of the Party and the people are centered on Right opportunism."

Had these letters not been signed by Stalin, the lower strata of the Party would undoubtedly have supposed that the chief Right opportunist was, in all probability, Stalin himself. It was Stalin who had criticized Trotsky for Left deviation and attacked the idea of the "permanent revolution"; it was Stalin who had defended the NEP and the economic freedom of the peasants against Trotsky's desire to "rob the peasantry"; it was Stalin who had upheld against Trotsky's demand for "statifying" of the trade unions their sacred right to defend the professional and material interests of labor against the bureaucratic apparatus of the Soviet state; it was Stalin who had called for joining the League of Nations and entering the world trade union movement and allying with Chiang Kai-shek. Who of the Bolsheviks then but Stalin could possibly be a Rightist?

But if Stalin was not leading the attack against Right opportunism it must be someone else. But who? The names of the members of the Politburo, the Secretariat, the Central Committee, the Central Control Commission, and lastly the Comintern, Profintern, Peasant International, and International Organization for Aid to Revolutionary Fighters (MOPR) were canvassed one by one. All were to the Left of Stalin. This chaotic state of affairs had been further aggravated by Stalin's declaration at the joint plenary meeting of the Moscow Committee and the Moscow Control Commission in October 1928, that "we have neither Leftists nor Rightists in the Politburo." Possible Rightists were sought in the central committees of the Union republics and in the oblast committees, but with no better success. In brief, there were no Rightists and yet there was this deadly menace of a threat from the Right. Where did it come from? All the Communists and all the leaders needed to be looked into. According to Stalin any of them might be a potential Rightist, hence the necessity for a ruthless war against these possible enemies. As no one aspired to go to Siberia, every individual did everything within his power to insure himself against such an eventuality. The whole Party, a million strong, was shouting "Stop Thief!" at the top of its voice. It had become an obsession. Toward the end of 1928 every speech by a member at a Party meeting, every article in the press, a routine broadcast, a limerick sung on the stage or a slapstick joke by a clown, was sure to contain some reference to the theme "The Right Danger is the Greatest Danger." Within one year the publicity given to this undefined danger acquired such proportions that the more orthodox members of the Party began to rage: "Enough of this talk about danger from the Right; give us the Rightists so we can massacre them!"

At the October joint plenary meeting of the Moscow Committee and the Moscow Control Commission, Stalin drew attention to the mass psychosis which he himself had created in the Party. He said:

> Nor are those comrades correct who, in discussing the Right deviation, center their attention on the individuals who represent the Right deviation. They want the names of these individuals in order to deal with them. This is the wrong approach. While admitting the relative importance of the individual, we should remember that the conditions which give rise to a Right deviation within the Party are far more dangerous. Individuals can be removed but by so doing we would not destroy the roots of this danger within the Party. Unquestionably the influence of the individual is important, but it is not decisive. In this connection it is impossible to avoid mention of an episode which occured in Odessa at the beginning of 1920. Our troops had just driven the Whites out of the Ukraine and were mopping up the remnants of Denikin's armies in Odessa. Some units of the Red Army were zealously trying to find the "Entente," under the impression that the capture of this "Entente" would mean the end of the war.[1]

Nevertheless, the campaign of psychosis attained its goal—Stalin named his first victim, Bukharin. Even the Party activists were staggered: this brilliant theorist of Bolshevism, the darling of the Party, the terror of Trotsky, the "savior" of Stalin, the extreme Leftist of Left Communism in 1918, had become a Right champion of capitalism, a supporter of the kulaks, and an enemy of the Party! In spite of elaborate preparations and lavish propaganda the Party refused to be convinced. But retreat was no longer possible—it was either Stalin or Bukharin. There was no other alternative.

---

[1] Stalin, *Voprosy leninizma*, p. 204.

Bukharin enjoyed the confidence of the Party, was popular with the government (Rykov), had the support of the trade unions (Tomsky) and was a man of intelligence and education. Stalin had none of these advantages. He possessed, however, something worth more than the Party, the trade unions, government support, or scholarship—an overwhelming desire for power and a splendidly organized team of professional conspirators within both the Party and the government. He developed two lines of attack: mobilization of the Party activists against Bukharin, and the tricking of Bukharin into making anti-Party outbursts. As it was not possible to destroy Bukharin for his past mistakes, which Lenin himself had known and had forgiven, it was necessary to prove new errors or to unearth old errors hitherto unrevealed. (This was done later, when it was charged that, in alliance with the Social Revolutionaries, Bukharin had sought to kill Lenin, Stalin, and Sverdlov in 1918!)

The general reaction to the first line of attack was typified by our Institute. Like the Communist Academy, we were not greatly impressed by the propaganda spewed out by the Central Committee, a fact to be explained by the nature of the faculty and student body of the Institute and the personal influence and connections of Bukharin in both these institutions. In other organizations, especially those in the provinces, which were subservient to the Center, the attack was, however, more effective. By the end of 1928 the Central Committee had successfully introduced into all the large centers of the country groups of Party activists, small at first for reconnaissance purposes, but later increased in size. One standard subject, "The Rightist Danger and the Errors of Bukharin," was discussed at every meeting. Speakers at these meetings were armed with officially prepared statements and supplied with prepared texts of resolutions approved by the Central Committee for submission to the voters. A spate of suitable resolutions soon flooded the Central Committee: "We decisively condemn the errors of Comrade Bukharin," "We unreservedly support Lenin's Central Committee," "We decisively demand the disarming of Bukharin," "We decisively demand that Comrade Bukharin be brought to justice by the Central Committee," and so on.

However, it was not always as easy to obtain similar resolutions in the political bodies where Bukharin had followers, such as the Ural, Kharkov, and Ivanovo-Voznesensk, Party Committees. Here the statements prepared by the Central Committee were thrown into the wastepaper baskets or unceremoniously rejected, and openly anti-Stalinist resolutions were passed. For instance, at meetings of activists in Sverdlovsk, where the oblast committee secretary was Kabakov, and in Ivanovo-Voznesensk, where the oblast committee secretary was, as I recall, Komarov, resolutions were voted demanding "maintenance of unity and cessation of intrigues by the apparatus against tested leaders of the Party."

In the Politburo itself and in the Presidium of the Central Control Commission, Bukharin was at first supported by Tomsky and Rykov, and later by Ordzhonikidze, Kalinin, Shvernik, Yenukidze, and Yaroslavsky. At joint meetings of the Politburo and the Presidium of the Central Control Commission Lenin's widow,

N.K. Krupskaya, who had once burned her fingers over Trotsky (at one time Stalin had almost expelled her from the Party for her support of Trotsky) sat stubbornly silent. It was rumored that after these meetings she used to go to the homes of either Rykov or Bukharin and weep for hours. "I am silent for the sake of Volodya [Lenin]," she would wail. "This Asiatic monster will end by throwing me into the Lubyanka and bringing shame upon the Party in the eyes of the world." After calming down she would repeat the famous complaint made when Trotsky was under attack: "But what can I do? If Volodya were alive today he would jail that horrible scoundrel. He is taking revenge on Lenin's friends because of what Ilyich said about him in his will."

The second line of attack was designed to provoke the future Rightists into making statements regarding the main lines of current Party and government policy. This policy had been laid down at the last two Party congresses, in the field of industrialization at the Fourteenth Party Congress in 1925, and in the field of collectivization at the Fifteenth Party Congress in 1927. Stalin's later allegation that the Rightists were opposed to official policy regarding industry and agriculture was entirely unfounded. Those whom he attacked as Rightists did not differ from Stalin regarding the need of moving toward socialism, or the need of promoting industrialization, or the need of socializing agriculture, but on the manner and means of doing these things. Although Stalin was not to furnish any definite answer to the crucial question of manner and means until December 1929, he demanded an answer from the purported Rightists as early as June 1928, immediately after his speech in the Institute of Red Professors.

Two commissions of the Politburo were now created, an industrial commission presided over by the head of the Soviet government, Rykov, with Kuibyshev as deputy, and an agricultural commission under the chairmanship of the Second Secretary of the Central Committee, Molotov, with Yakovlev as vice-chairman. Stalin and Bukharin were made members of both commissions. The industrial commission was charged with the task of drawing up an outline for the first Five-Year Plan, while the agricultural commission was to examine problems connected with collectivization. Both commissions had at their disposal imposing staffs of experts from Gosplan (the State Planning Commission) whose chairman was Krzhizhanovsky, and from the Central Statistical Administration, headed by Osinsky. On the question of what should be done, both commissions reached unanimous agreement, namely, that the Five-Year Plan and collectivization should be carried out. The task of reporting on the vital and crucial question of how and by what means these policies were to be put into effect were delegated by the commissions to Rykov and Bukharin respectively. The two reporters submitted written outlines based on the findings of the experts. These outlines were intended to become, after approval by the commission, decisions of the Politburo and decrees of the Central Committee. It was thus that the long-sought-for Rightists in the Politburo were pushed onto the political scene.

The basic points of Rykov's memorandum concerned industrialization and the maintenance of a proper balance between heavy and light industry. While recognizing that the goal was the development of heavy industry, Rykov regarded the development of light industry as a stimulus for and a main means of increasing the development of heavy industry, with the development of both types proceeding at an equal pace. Forced labor, being economically unsound, should be discontinued. Bureaucratic interference from above was to be avoided as far as possible and local initiative fostered, especially in the development of local industries and the manufacture of consumer goods. Two variants of the Five-Year Plan goals should be adopted—an optimum and a minimum—the former desirable but unrealistic, the latter possible and realistic. The optimum should be aimed at in order to meet the minimum. Since the Five-Year Plan was a first attempt and a grandiose enterprise for the entire national economy, the first two years should be treated separately and a separate Two-Year Plan for the development of agriculture prepared as a first step toward the fulfillment of the Five-Year Plan as a whole.

Bukharin's memorandum called for the development of socialized agriculture, that is, for organization of cooperatives of three main types: production, trade, and distribution. A uniform rate of development for the three types should be aimed at, completely free from all administrative coercion. Collectivization should be genuinely voluntary, not state directed. He suggested liberal credits and subsidies for those willing to enter production cooperatives, and heavier taxation of the kulaks to force them to abandon private farming and accept collectivization —that is, "peaceful conversion of the kulak to socialism." Various incentives, such as reduction of taxation, lowering of wholesale prices, and provision of credit for commercial cooperatives, would be adopted to enable the collectives to undercut private traders represented by the NEP-men. Prices would be raised for agricultural produce and lowered for industrial goods, within a system of state controlled commerce, in order to develop distributors' cooperatives and stimulate agriculture in general. In short, he proposed to give peasant Russia the motto: "Get rich!"[2]

When the memorandums prepared by Rykov and Bukharin were submitted for approval to a regular meeting of the Politburo (a few members of the presidium of the Central Committee usually attended such meetings with the right to cast advisory votes) Kuibyshev and Molotov rudely and arrogantly declared that the recommendations were pure expressions of Right opportunism. The actors in ensuing heated debates, all well coached by Stalin, Kaganovich, Voroshilov, Mikoyan, and Kirov, then spoke their parts as pre-arranged: they not only approved the criticism leveled at the memorandums but demanded that the Central Committee and then the whole Party be informed that the Politburo now contained Rightist elements, namely, Rykov and Bukharin.

The discussion was now carefully led away from consideration of acceptance or rejection of Bukharin's and Rykov's recommendations to the problem of revealing and accusing the hitherto unknown Right opportunists. Stalin, as was usual in such cases, maintained an attitude of neutrality until the reactions of Bukharin and Rykov should become clear and the alignment of forces should

---

[2] *KPSS v resolyutsiyakh*, Vol. II, p. 445.

become definitely established. Tomsky openly sided with Bukharin and Rykov, while Ordzhonikidze, Shvernik, Kalinin, and Yaroslavsky argued that the accusations of Kuibyshev and Molotov were without basis and demanded that the recommendations be accepted or rejected after serious study. Stalin continued to remain noncommittal and as the votes were fairly equally divided the session ended inconclusively. A committee was now appointed to examine the proposals in detail. The "neutral" Stalin was elected chairman, Bukharin and Rykov were included, Tomsky was passed over, and all the other members of the committee were chosen from among those who had attacked the proposals at the meeting. Bukharin and Rykov were now faced with a solid hostile majority under a chairman of undefined opinion but questionable impartiality.

Although the Politburo meeting was supposedly a closed session and officially the entire matter was studiously veiled in secrecy, the details were being discussed in the Institute of Red Professors two days later. A rumor began to circulate that Stalin himself was among the Rightists and had been forced into authorizing a formal cross-examination of Bukharin by pressure from the majority in the Politburo. I have no way of knowing whether this rumor was deliberately circulated or was mere hearsay. In any case, it was emphatically denied by the followers of Bukharin, but not, for reasons best known to themselves, by the Stalinists. Stalin repeated his earlier statement that there were no Rightists in the Politburo:

> We have had occasion to come upon supporters of Right deviation in our basic institutions . . . If you should go higher, to county and province Party organizations, you could easily find bearers of danger from the Right . . . . If you should go still higher and raise the question about the Central Committee, it must be recognized that in the membership of the Central Committee there are undetected, very insignificant to be sure, elements with a compromising attitude toward the Right danger . . . . And what about the Politburo? Is it free from all deviation? In the Politburo we have neither Rightists nor Leftists nor compromisers with either. This must be categorically said here. It is time to put an end to gossip . . . .[3]

In December 1928 the political situation was further clarified. At a meeting of the committee appointed to study the recommendations, Stalin submitted counter-proposals to Rykov's and Bukharin's plans for collectivization and industrialization. These proposals were adopted by the committee against the dissenting votes of Rykov and Bukharin. The new proposals differed radically from Rykov's and Bukharin's central theses and, which was even more important, ran counter to the directives of the Fourteenth and Fifteenth Party Congresses, precisely on points concerning the ways, means, and pace of implementing the Five-Year Plan in relation to industry and agriculture. The committee, after accepting Stalin's counter-proposals, did however authorize Bukharin and Rykov to state their objections in a written memorandum, for submission to the next session of the Politburo. While Rykov was against making use of this offer, Bukharin, strongly supported by Tomsky, wished at all costs to prove the unprovable and succeeded in forcing Rykov to give in.

---

[3] Stalin, *Voprosy leninizma*, pp. 211–12.

Such was the origin of the counter-counter-proposals by "the three," dealing with all main aspects of Party economic policy. The Central Committee apparatus at once multigraphed these counter-counter-proposals and distributed them to local Party organizations as "the platform of the Rightists" even before they were debated in the Politburo. Stalin's proposals, described as resolutions adopted by the Central Committee but being resisted by the three were appended. Stalin had thus succeeded in making the Rightists into a "legal entity," against which the Party activists could proceed.

Before Stalin found it possible to convene a meeting of the Politburo the Central Committee was inundated by a flood of resolutions stemming from provincial organizations: "We condemn the Right deviationists – Bukharin, Rykov, and Tomsky"; "We demand their expulsion from the Politburo," "We decisively demand... demand... demand...." At the height of this flood of resolutions and of "Party indignation" directed against the Rightists, a meeting of secretaries of oblast, district, and national republic central committees was called with the object of bringing to a head the campaign of condemnation of the "platform of the Rightists." The meeting, in spite of many abstentions and a few dissenting votes, passed a resolution demanding that the entire matter be placed before the Politburo and the Presidium of the Central Control Commission. Stalin now convened the Politburo and reported on the resolutions passed by local Party organizations and by the general meeting held under the auspices of the Central Committee.

After the wavering members of the Politburo and the Presidium had submitted to the "will of the Party," Rykov, Bukharin, and Tomsky found themselves completely isolated. It was then that Rykov made the remark which I have cited earlier: "How often did I tell Nikolai Ivanovich [Bukharin] that it was a mistake to set down his views in writing!"

Much later, in February 1937, Rykov was to repeat this remark. He still did not realize that Bukharin's restless hand had been guided by the invisible will of Stalin. Stalin had needed documentary evidence (he could, of course, have achieved his aims without it, but with more difficulty) and knowing of Bukharin's passion for writing, had shrewdly exploited this weakness. From then on, whenever the Rightists showed signs of resistance, Stalin could always obtain the desired effect by saying to them: "There, Comrades, are the documents bearing your signatures."

Chapter XII

Bukharin's Search for Allies

The struggle which had broken out between the Right and the Stalinists placed the followers of Trotsky and Zinoviev before a difficult decision. In the quarrel between Stalin and Bukharin, they were ideologically closer to Stalin and his view that "the Right danger is the main danger, both within the Party and in the country at large." On the other hand they could not, if only for psychological reasons, support Stalin, as the wounds he had inflicted on them, in alliance with Bukharin, were much too severe. A political orientation toward Stalin and his followers would spell disaster, as this time it would entail voluntary capitulation and complete ideological surrender. If such a course were adopted they would lose prestige and would no longer be able to uphold their previous claims to being the representatives of orthodox Leninism in the Party. But Bukharin's group was even less acceptable to them. It was Bukharin, not Stalin, who had been the leading ideological theorist in discrediting the platforms of the Trotskyites and the Zinovievites, and later, in 1926, that of the "combined Trotskyite-Zinovievite bloc." Without the support of Bukharin's propaganda machine and theory laboratory, Stalin would have been destroyed in his first trial at arms with the Trotskyites, not to mention his battle with the joint Trotskyite-Zinovievite bloc. It must be borne in mind that in the first quarrel over "Lenin's heritage," that is, in the struggle for power, the conflict centered in the realm of theory and future Party policy. It was only after the winning of the ideological victory over the followers of Trotsky and Zinoviev at the Fifteenth Party Congress in December 1927 that the apparatus of the OGPU was put into motion to apply physical reprisals. Such reprisals were dealt out to the Trotskyites and Zinovievites in 1928, after which they were deported by the hundreds. It was as discredited anti-Leninist elements, especially after the anti-Stalinist demonstrations organized on November 7, 1927, by Trotsky in Moscow and by Zinoviev in Leningrad in connection with the anniversary of the October Revolution, that they had fallen easy prey to the OGPU, leaving Bukharin to face Stalin alone and unsupported.

Stalin had launched his attack by besieging the Bukharin school with theoretical criticism. He had followed it up by assaulting the entire Bukharin group with political criticism. It was under these circumstances that the Trotskyites and Zinovievites had to find an answer to the thorny question of their attitude to the attack on Bukharin.

At the beginning of the campaign against Bukharin, many of the principal leaders of Trotskyism, including Trotsky himself, had been deported, although Trotsky still had at his disposal a number of underground cells in Moscow which carried on clandestine work against Stalin. Several of his followers who had been restored to Party membership after signing statements of surrender and thus avoiding exile were active members of these cells. The status of Zinoviev's followers was quite different. Here the rank and file had been effectively suppressed, although Zinoviev and Kamenev had been allowed to remain unmolested in Moscow after both had capitulated unconditionally, had acknowledged Stalin as "the great leader," and had branded Trotsky as an "historical enemy of the people." Stalin, of course, never placed any faith in these protestations of loyalty, but at the time found useful such self-castigation by Old Bolsheviks and flattering adulation by trusted companions-in-arms of Lenin.

Faced with the split in the Politburo, which came to both as a complete surprise, Zinoviev and Kamenev were confronted with the problem of allegiance and the choice of a policy. As to the followers of Bukharin, they, in their search for supporters, realized only too well that by appealing to the old opposition groups in their struggle with Stalin they themselves ran the risk of becoming known as unprincipled political bankrupts. If they veered toward Trotskyism, they would place in the hands of Stalin invaluable tactical trumps, while gaining little support for Bukharin, since Trotsky's followers and Trotsky himself were isolated physically as well as politically. Moreover, coalition with Zinoviev and Trotsky was possible only on the basis of a joint political platform dealing with all the main questions of internal and external policy and with Trotsky no such common platform could be found.

The Bukharinites also realized that Zinoviev was quite unfitted for clandestine negotiations. He had twice formed coalitions with Trotsky and at the critical stage had twice betrayed him. When victory was assured he was an ardent revolutionary leader, but when the time came for risking his neck he fell easy prey to panic. For instance, on the decisive eve of the October coup d'état, he and Kamenev had both voted, in secret meetings of the Central Committee on October 10 and 16, 1917, against the proposed armed uprising. Having provided himself with a convincing alibi, he was nowhere to be found, although his friend Kamenev, together with Trotsky, had personally directed events from the Smolny Institute. It is therefore hardly surprising that the Rightists turned to his friend Kamenev rather than to him when they began to discuss the formation of a coalition against Stalin and his followers. The Rightists would have preferred to exclude him from the new political grouping if Kamenev and his followers could have been brought to agree on a joint policy without him.

Talks on the possibilities of a coalition were initiated by Bukharin and Kamenev in the summer of 1928. All the usual trappings of conspiracy were observed and the meetings took place in Kamenev's apartment, with only one other person, Sokolnikov, the go-between and friend of Kamenev, present. Bukharin began by giving Kamenev a detailed account of the divergence of views in the Politburo and the attitudes of its various members, and then proceeded to make a concrete offer of collaboration. Feeling it his moral duty to give Zinoviev an exact account of this interview, Kamenev noted down Bukharin's revelations and handed them the same day to Zinoviev. Pleasantly surprised by these disclosures, Zinoviev sensed that they offered possible advantages which he could exploit for a return to power. But somehow or other Kamenev's original notes fell soon after into the hands of Stalin. His elation at having this damning evidence in his possession may well be imagined. "The Rightists are safely boxed up in their coffin! All we lack is the grave," he is said to have exclaimed.

After this fiasco, Bukharin's followers viewed all offers by leaders of former opposition groups with extreme suspicion. Nevertheless, both as an ideological force and as fanatical anti-Stalinists the Trotskyites enjoyed a better reputation than the Zinovievites, in the eyes of Bukharin. Despite their political defeat and the exile of their leaders, they were still persevering in their implacable war against "the heroes of October" and the "Stalin reaction." Unlike the Zinovievites, the Trotskyites were known for their courage and their readiness for personal sacrifice. From this point of view, the Trotskyites might have been of real value as allies, but the ideological chasm which separated the Leftists and the Rightists was to some extent a no-man's-land into which neither the dogmatic sympathizers of Bukharin nor the idealistic Trotskyites ventured to tread. Only a few members of the two groups rose above the implications of their respective doctrines and were able to view the situation in historical perspective. The issue of the struggle was power, not Leninism, a fact which neither the Left nor the Right seemed to grasp. To Stalin, on the other hand, the situation was perfectly clear. Because they persisted so stubbornly in clinging to the letter of Leninism, the Leftists and the Rightists were rushing headlong into the abyss, while Stalin was rapidly ascending to the summit of power. He was to reach his goal a year later, in December 1929, when *Pravda* for the first time told the nation that "Stalin is the leader of the Party and the most brilliant of Lenin's disciples," and thus fixed in print a turning point in history.

Meanwhile the Trotskyites had radically altered their tactics as soon as the government had begun a mass deportation of their comrades and particularly of their leaders. As open opposition to the Stalinist Central Committee was no longer politically practicable, they had ceased to resist the Party openly, and had resorted to underground methods. Whether this policy was adopted with or without the connivance of their leaders remains obscure. The Fifteenth Party Congress in December 1927 had decreed that Trotskyism was incompatible with membership in the Party; consequently, former followers of Trotsky who still wished to remain in, or to return to, the Party had no alternative but to declare their open agreement with the general line, and to recognize Stalin as the leader and Trotsky as an enemy of the Party. False protestations of loyalty were made by the Trotskyite leaders in the press and by the rank and file at Party meetings. These forced statements were repugnant to their political thinking, but there was no other course open for membership in the Party. Although Stalin regarded the repentant return of the Trotskyites with suspicion, he accepted it at face value as a convenience in his struggle with Bukharin. Large numbers of Trotskyites were brought back from exile and some were placed in positions of reponsibility. Only Trotsky and a few of his personal friends continued their stubborn resistance. It need hardly be added that the recognition accorded Stalin by the majority of the Trotskyites was only formal and was made with a view to furthering Trotsky's cause.

"Repentant" Trotskyites could now be found in many government departments with the exception, however, of the Party apparatus and the organs of the Political Police. They continued to exercise great influence upon Moscow student circles in spite of the defeat suffered in connection with Malenkov's Plan. Nearly half the lecturers in the social sciences in the Moscow institutions of higher education were present or former Trotskyites, while the other half openly sided with Bukharin. The workers and peasants were the classes least affected by Trotskyism and among them support for Bukharin could only be found in isolated cases.

After their return to the Party, their repentance for their former sins, and their adoption of the new tactics in their fight against Stalin, the Trotskyites were organized in small groups and circles, entirely recruited from among Communists. Their immediate aim was underground propaganda both in the Party and among the workers. New methods were developed, such as anti-Stalin propaganda directed at individual members in the Party and systematic mass distribution of proclamations, pamphlets, and slogans among the workers. The first pamphlets, signed by Trotsky, were sent out from Alma-Ata. These were followed by appeals addressed to Moscow "Leninist Bolsheviks" by Muralov, the former commander of the Moscow Military District, and to former "companions-in-arms and sympathizers" by Mrakhovsky and others. In Moscow, this underground material was hectographed and distributed by devious means throughout the country through the Central Administration for the Distribution of Printed Matter, either by insertion in official publications, or by registered mail to local Party organizations and their chairmen, or even as wrapping paper for parcels dispatched by commercial and cooperative organizations. The pamphlets published in Moscow were anonymous or bore such fictitious names as the "Group of Leninist Bolsheviks," "Lenin Group," "Group of Bolsheviks," or "Group of Bolshevik Workers."

Organized groups of Trotskyites could also be found in many of the research institutions of the Communist Academy, where they called themselves "Leninist Bolsheviks" as opposed to "Stalinist Bolsheviks."

Chapter XIII

The Installation of Political Commissars
and Resistance in the Trade Unions

While Bukharin was searching for allies among the Trotskyites and Zinoviev-ites, Stalin was engaged in strengthening his forces. After succeeding in having the political platform of the Right opposition condemned by the Politburo, he effected the necessary changes in organization made possible by the victory. The immediate effect of the change was to place the three leaders — Rykov, Tomsky, and Bukharin — under strict control by "political commissars" in order to make sure that the "general line" of the Party was strictly followed in the Council of People's Commissars of the USSR, whose chairman was Rykov, in the All-Union Central Council of Trade Unions, whose chairman was Tomsky, in *Pravda*, whose editor-in-chief was Bukharin, and in the Comintern, where Bukharin held the chief office, that of Secretary of the Political Secretariat, the office of Chairman of the Executive Committee of the Comintern having been abolished after the removal of Zinoviev.

The political commissars were selected from Stalin's immediate entourage, and their futures as members of the Politburo were assured on condition that they carried out their alloted tasks of supervising the Rightists and compromising them as leaders. Sergo Ordzhonikidze was assigned as first vice-chairman to Rykov, Savelyev (later replaced by Mekhlis) to watch over Bukharin and Kaganovich, a member of the presidium of the Trade Union Council, and also Third Secretary of the Party Central Committee, to supervise Tomsky. Supervision over Buk-harin's activity in the Comintern was entrusted to Manuilsky and at the same time a tighter control, in the hands of Molotov, was instituted over the USSR delega-tion in the Comintern, consisting of Stalin, Manuilsky, Molotov, Kaganovich, Pyatnitsky, Kuusinen, Skrypnik, Shatskin, and Lominadze. Bukharin, although not officially removed from the delegation, was forbidden all contact with other delegations and sections of the Comintern.

The government departments headed by Right leaders were now actually controlled by these political commissars, officially known as representatives of the Central Committee. For instance, no order issued by Rykov, the Chairman of the Council of People's Commissars, had legal force unless it also bore the signature of Ordzhonikidze. No copy of *Pravda*, even though already set up, and signed by Bukharin as editor-in-chief, was sent to the printing presses unless it had first been censored by Savelyev. No resolution of the presidium of the Trade Union Council, although passed by a majority vote of its members, reached the trade unions if it had been vetoed by Kaganovich. Molotov, as Second Secretary of the Central Committee, was instructed to organize a system of control by the Party apparatus over the state apparatus, wherever officials were working who might be connected with the Right in any way. This measure adequately limited any effective activity by the Rightists. The leaders of the Right, although members of the Politburo and nominal heads of government departments, were compelled to appeal to "deputies" who were not even members of the Politburo, and to coordinate with them every act, from daily editorials in *Pravda* to verbal orders to the commissars.

By their constant use of the right of veto the deputies paralyzed all effective government, trade union, or editorial work. The entire range of disputed decisions had to be submitted to the Politburo for arbitration, and the arbitration invariably resulted in a decision in favor of the deputies. It was obvious that such a system was unworkable and could not long endure. As a countermove, the Rightists first retaliated by adopting a form of unofficial self-effacement, in which they approved only instructions issued by their deputies, or accepted decisions sponsored by the deputies at conferences. These tactics led to complaints to the Politburo by the deputies against their chiefs who, they claimed, were staging a sit-down strike. The Politburo reacted by threatening the recalcitrant leaders with stronger measures of administrative coercion.

The Bukharinites now decided to act. They offered to resign from all positions of authority: Rykov from his chairmanship of the Council of People's Commissars, Tomsky from his chairmanship of the Trade Union Council, and Bukharin from his post as editor-in-chief of *Pravda*. It looked as if Stalin had at last achieved his aim: the voluntary withdrawal from the political scene of the Right opposition.

However, on Stalin's recommendation, the Politburo refused to accept the offers of resignation, instructed those concerned to remain at their posts, and drew up a new indictment accusing them of capitulation. The Rightists were accused of capitulation to the class enemy, fear of "our growing pains," desertion of "the front of socialist construction," and activity as "strikebreakers of socialism." To activists in Party circles sympathetic to the Rightists, it now appeared that the leaders of the Right were victims of a skilful plot intended to goad them into submitting their resignations and thus laying themselves open to these fresh indictments.

Bukharin's followers and others who sympathized with the Right opposition believed that their leaders would now cling to their responsible posts until the next regular Party congress. There was a widespread belief among the anti-Stalin activists in the Party that Bukharin, Rykov, and Tomsky were preparing a bombshell for Stalin's conspiratorial group at the Sixteenth Party Congress. But the leaders were indulging in a game of parliamentary chicanery and by their rash offers to resign had irrevocably lost their moral prestige. The situation was somewhat retrieved by Stalin's refusal to accept their resignations, as this allowed them time to plan for the future. It was absolutely essential for them that the congress be convened at the earliest possible moment, since the Central Committee would be forced to obtain from it a ruling on the questions at issue, in view of the reasons submitted by the Rightist leaders for tendering their resignations.

Although it was true that the Rightists had offered to resign, they had by no means capitulated. They contended that the Central Committee, by usurping their authority and wilfully creating untenable conditions of work, had forced them to relinquish their posts. They persisted in maintaining that the disastrous policy pursued by the majority in the Central Committee was contrary to all previous Party directives and, in particular, to those of the Fourteenth and Fifteenth Party Congresses. They reserved the right to put their views before the next congress and to defend them there. The gist of a long statement made by "the three" on the subject of their resignations was as follows: "The present line of policy adopted by the majority in the Central Committee will inevitably lead to dictatorship by a Party oligarchy and result in the enslavement and exploitation of the workers by the state, and also to feudal armed robbery of the peasants. We have previously warned the Central Committee and we now wish to warn the entire Party against this policy, fatal to both the Party and to the Soviet state. All this talk about a Right opposition is merely a smoke screen laid with a view to blinding the Party to the danger of this greatest of all menaces. What is the way out? One only: Back to Lenin, in order to go forward with Lenin. There is no other way, and we are confident that we can convince the Party of this truth. We therefore demand that a Party congress be immediately convened."

Although the statement was not made public at the time, the Party was acquainted with its contents. (It was first revealed at the April 1929 plenary session of the Central Committee, when it was submitted as an incriminating document damaging to the Rightists.) As a means of bringing the Trotskyites and Bukharinites closer together, it was of considerable value. The Trotskyites believed that even though Bukharin might have capitulated to Stalin, his conduct was also a capitulation to Trotsky, whose "new course" had laid the foundations for the current policy of the Central Committee, albeit Bukharin had taken four years to arrive at the same conclusions. In effecting their rapprochement, the Trotskyites were headed by the well-known Soviet philosopher, N. Karev, and the Rightists by Sten, the leader of the group in our Institute of Red Professors. Both were rated as stars of the first magnitude in matters of theory. As the Trotskyites were debarred from coming out into the open, Karev had perforce to capitulate to Sten. Karev advised his group to desist from quarrelling with the Rightists and suggested that, for the future, theoretical pronouncements against Stalinism should be made to comply with the principles of Bukharin's school of thought. The same policy was adopted in other educational and scientific institutions, by Madyar in the Communist Academy, Mif in the Association for the Study of National and Colonial Problems, attached to the Stalin Communist University for Workers of the East, Plotnikov in the All-Russian Association of Scientific Research Institutes in Social Sciences, and so on.

Thus the contact between the two opposition groups which Kamenev and Bukharin had not succeeded in imposing from above was established without difficulty by leaders of local groups. The same type of contact was established with the supporters of Zinoviev in his former base in Leningrad, where O. Tarkhanov, G. Safarov, Raltsevich, and others gave support to Bukharin. Skrypnik's national Communists in Kharkov were also won over. In addition the Rightists had groups in the national republics of Central Asia, where they had the support of Secretary of the Uzbekistan Central Committee Ikramov, chairman of the Council of People's Commissars Faizulla Khodzhayev and chairman of the Turkmenistan Council of People's Commissars Kurbanov, in Azerbaidzhan with Akhundov, Musabekov and Bunait-Zade and in Georgia with Budu-Mdivani, a Trotskyite, and Orekhalashvili, a Bukharinite. Among members of non-Russian nationality groups in Moscow opposed to Stalin were Ryskulov, Korkmasov, vice-chairman of the Committee for a New Alphabet, Nurmakov, deputy secretary of the Central Executive Committee of the USSR, and others.

As I have pointed out earlier, large numbers of oblast Party committee secretaries at first openly supported Bukharin and his group. But after the meeting in the Central Committee they ceased to air their views. Their future conduct, and that of many others at the coming Party congress was a matter of speculation. Only the holding of an early Party congress could prevent them from being swallowed up by the Central Committee apparatus. The dismissal of several secretaries in the Moscow and other districts was an ominous warning. There was no time to lose. But the greater the insistence of the Rightists on the need for a new congress, the more they aroused Stalin's suspicions, and time was on his side.

Party regulations, however, provided for another way of hastening the calling of a congress. In the event of refusal by the Central Committee to call a special congress, the Rightists could, on demand by several Party organizations, create an organizing committee empowered to summon such a congress. The question facing the Rightists was whether they could find the necessary support in the oblast organizations. In the light of subsequent events it is probable that this would have been possible. However, no attempt was made to take advantage of the right to call a special session under this procedure. Bukharin, Rykov, and Tomsky feared that in the event of defeat they would be accused of having attempted to splinter the Party. They wished to preserve at all costs the semblance of "legality" and to bury Stalin with his own "legal" consent. Little did they know Stalin, whereas he knew them only too well! In threatening to charge them with splintering the Party and making use of the authority of Party legality, Stalin was acting strictly according to Party law. Meanwhile, using Molotov as a tool, he was mercilessly purging the Party and Soviet apparatuses of declared and suspected Bukharinites.

It was under these circumstances that the Eighth Congress of the All-Union Central Trade Union Council met, in December 1928, at which the first serious trial of strength between the Rightists and Stalinists in the trade union movement took place.

For the country at large and the working class in particular there was nothing extraordinary about this routine trade union congress. But for Stalin's majority and Bukharin's minority in the Central Committee, it was an all-important test of their respective strengths.

It must be borne in mind that the Bolshevik Central Committee claimed to rule for the proletariat, by the proletariat, and in the name of the proletariat. The state itself was called a workers' state and its social character was expressed in the awe-inspiring title of "dictatorship of the proletariat"—not of the Bolshevik Party but of the proletariat. Zinoviev once wrote, before he fell into disgrace, that when all was said and done it was a Party dictatorship, as it was the Party that ruled the country. Stalin subsequently used this statement for an attack on Zinoviev and the "new opposition." "What does he mean by dictatorship of the Party?" he asked. "We have no dictatorship of the Party, we have a dictatorship of the proletariat."

This very proletariat, as represented by delegates elected at local congresses was now meeting in Moscow to discuss its needs and desires. In view of the split in the Politburo it is easy to realize the importance that Stalin attached to this congress. His influence in the Central Trade Union Council and its presidium was very small, being limited to a group consisting of Shvernik, Andreyev, Lozovsky, Leps, and the recently appointed Kaganovich. The other members of the Council, its presidium, and the chairmen of branch committees were supporters of Tomsky. That the situation was the same in the provinces had been shown by the strong Rightist majority delegated in local elections. The result was a paradoxical situation, in which the Politburo, which had not yet revealed to the workers the fact that their leader Tomsky was a Right opportunist and "Western trade-unionist," was attempting to have the proletariat condemn Tomsky and his friends Rykov, Bukharin, and Uglanov as Right deviationists but could not do this openly at so clearly a Rightist congress. But the resourceful and inventive experts of Stalin's school were never at a loss for expedients. Under the guise of "criticism and self-criticism" an endless succession of Stalin's supporters sought to reveal "a trend toward bureaucracy" on the part of the Trade Union Council, harped on the betrayal of the interests and needs of the workers by the leaders of the Council, deplored the growth of a foreign bourgeois ideology among the rank and file of the workers and a deviation toward western trade-unionism by their leaders, and warned against the danger from the Right in trade union life. The real target of this spate of trumped-up criticism was of course Tomsky and his colleagues in the council—Dogadov, Melnichansky, Artyukhina, Polonsky, Shmidt, and others.

At separate meetings of the Party members present at the Congress, criticism was bolder and more outspoken. Kaganovich demanded adoption of a resolution condemning the policy of the Trade Union Council presidium, in the hope of wrecking Tomsky's chances of re-election as Council chairman. However, on the first count, only a bare dozen of the 300 Party delegates voted in favor of his resolution. Here was an open rebellion of the "proletariat" against its own dictatorship. For the first time during his entire period of service under Stalin, Kaganovich, who had been selected to replace Tomsky, had failed to carry out a mission. Molotov, Second Secretary of the Central Committee, sent in to save the situation, promptly disavowed him.

Molotov reminded the congress that Tomsky was a member of the Politburo and had been appointed by the Party. While admitting that Tomsky, like others, might have been guilty of mistakes, Molotov said that in his opinion Kaganovich had committed a mistake in condemning the conduct of the presidium of the Trade Union Council, incidentally showing that Kaganovich too was subject to error. Although Kaganovich had received a public reprimand, Molotov had redeemed the prestige of the Central Committee. On the other hand the enforced retreat of the Central Committee showed clearly that Tomsky was not the only Rightist in the trade unions; that, in fact, the entire proletariat membership of the unions, including its Communist vanguard at the congress, was tainted with bourgeois ideology, and that the proletariat, if left to its own course, was unable to appreciate its blessings and must be taught to do so by coercion. Stalin now realized that the application of parliamentary rules for settling matters in dispute and the removal of unwanted rivals by parliamentary means were essentially bourgeois methods. Having saved its face and avoided a civil war with the proletariat, the Central Committee hastened to wind up the congress.

(When the next congress, the Ninth, met, only the dozen delegates who had voted in favor of Kaganovich's resolution were reelected. Kaganovich himself was not made head of the Trade Union Council. Shvernik, who was appointed to this post by the Central Committee, was endowed with a valuable asset—the ability to remain silent when matters appeared to be getting out of hand.)

I first met Tomsky at a New Year's party at his summer house in the suburbs of Moscow at the end of 1928, immediately after the Eighth Congress of the Trade Union Council. It was there too that I had my second encounter with Bukharin. When Sorokin and I arrived, Bukharin was engaged in a lively conversation in one of the rooms next to the large drawing room. I have forgotten the subject, but I have a vivid memory of how he was interrupted by the entrance of a massive individual, dressed in a gaudily embroidered shirt, bright red sash and elegant high boots. Dark and tanned, rather Mongolian in type, our host looked like a stoker, or a Tatar merchant. With a lordly wave of his hand in the direction of the dining room, he asked his guests to be seated. People trooped in from the adjoining rooms and sat down where they pleased.

The lights were switched off and candles lit. The hands of a massive oak grandfather clock pointed to five minutes to twelve. Our host took his place at the head of the table, looked at his watch and called for attention: "Comrades!"

All conversation ceased. The silence was broken only by the hurried ticking of the clock, witnessing the headlong rush of time.

"To the happiness of all nations! To the happiness of the working class! To the happiness of the Party! To the New Year! To new happiness!"

He uttered these hopeful words without enthusiasm, in a dull, lifeless tone.

The clock struck twelve. We clinked glasses.

Our host was Tomsky.

A printer by trade, Tomsky was a typical representative of the Russian prerevolutionary trade union movement. Strongwilled and determined, of an eminently practical turn of mind, he might well have become a Russian Bebel had he not been handicapped by a lack of education. Straightforward by nature, and devoid of the tactfulness he might have acquired at a school or university, he spoke his mind frankly in political discussions and debates. Although ready to admit the intellectual superiority of the more educated leaders of the Bolshevik movement, he attempted to get at the truth through his own "worker's mind" and was not prone to bow to authority. Even Lenin he thought was too much of an "intellectual" to appreciate properly the workers' mentality, and on several occasions criticized him in public, as, for instance, at a trade union debate, after which Lenin in a fit of temper banished Tomsky, the "workers' leader," to the desert wastes of Turkestan.

The arid sands apparently had a soothing effect, for later, in the struggle with Trotsky, Tomsky feebly raised his voice from distant exile in support of Stalin. This support earned him an immediate return to Moscow and reinstatement in his previous post as leader of the trade unions. Stalin's calculated move was soon justified. Under Tomsky's leadership the trade unions became, to use Stalin's words, a conveyor belt for carrying the Party to the working masses. Tomsky's reward was not long delayed and he was promoted to membership in the Politburo. If, however, he entertained a hope that he had been brought in to become a trade union leader of the English type, playing in the leadership of the "workers' party" the role of independent representative of the Soviet trade unions, he was greatly mistaken. What Stalin wanted was to use him both as a "labor screen" and a "labor tool," for purposes of his own which, at the time, were unsuspected by Tomsky as well as by many others. When he finally realized what Stalin had in mind, he threw the weight of his influence as leader of the trade unions against Stalin, and thus created for a time a dual regime—a labor regime in the Palace of Labor (the seat of the All-Union Central Council of Trade Unions) on the one hand, and a Party regime in the Kremlin, on the other.

The existence of this "dual regime" had been a dominant feature of 1928, and it had appeared that Stalin's days were numbered when the official Soviet regime, represented by the Chairman of the Council of People's Commissars, Rykov, and the Party theorist-in-chief and editor of *Pravda*, Bukharin, had joined forces with the leader of the Trade Union Council, Tomsky, against Stalin's wing of the Central Committee. Accordingly, at the end of the old year, Tomsky was in an optimistic mood, although he had already conditionally tendered to the Politburo his resignation as head of the Trade Union Council if the newly appointed "commissar" to the trade unions, Kaganovich (modestly described as "member of the presidium"), were retained in office, or if Stalin refused to abandon the Trotskyite program for making the trade unions a part of the state apparatus.

Our New Year's party at Tomsky's summer house passed off quietly, with the usual entertainment and telling of anecdotes. At some time between three and four in the morning the man whom I have called the General arrived, looking unusually serious. Very soon after his arrival the General withdrew with Bukharin and Tomsky to a neighboring room. The guests dispersed, filled, in spite of

Tomsky's optimism, with heavy forebodings regarding what the New Year held in store. Not ease or happiness, thought those who had a feeling for politics and had seen the General arrive cold sober on New Year's Eve.

Why should the General's views carry so much weight? Not so much on account of his personality as on account of his position.

At the time of the October Revolution the man who was now the General had been a sailor on one of the ships of the Baltic Fleet, and had taken an active part in the Bolshevik coup d'état in Petrograd. With this his naval career came to an end, but during the Civil War he was promoted from junior naval officer (midshipman, I believe) to general, there being no particular demand for admirals in those days. His brilliant career in the Civil War set him apart as one of the ablest generals of Frunze's school in the Red Army. In 1925, Frunze superseded Trotsky as commander-in-chief and had the General transferred to Moscow. In 1919, when Stalin was laying his plans for the removal of Trotsky, he had resolved to entrust the military leadership of the country to one of his own men, i. e., to a member of the so-called Military Opposition made up of Yegorov, Voroshilov, Budenny, Shchadenko, and Minkin, which, while pretending to oppose Trotsky alone, was in fact being used by Stalin in his campaign against both Lenin and Trotsky.[1]

When at the Eighth Party Congress in March 1919 the Military Opposition, after obtaining a guarantee of support from Stalin, made a concerted attack on Trotsky, who was then chairman of the Revolutionary Military Council and People's Commissar of Land and Naval Forces, Lenin curtly showed his displeasure and demanded that the congress condemn the attack. The shrewd and calculating Stalin swiftly altered his tactics and defended Trotsky at the congress. Later on, after the Trotskyites were purged from the Red Army, he repaid his debt to his military friends by appointing them to the vacant military posts. Many of them, even so, ended their days in the cells of the NKVD.

It is of interest that Stalin, who devoted so much space in his writings to "oppositions" of various kinds, was studiously silent on this episode of the Military Opposition. Even in his *Short Course in the History of the Bolshevik Party* he refers to it only in passing and in a highly characteristic fashion: "At the congress the so-called 'military opposition' made its appearance—but together with representatives of the defeated 'left Communism,' the 'military opposition' included workers who had never participated in any opposition whatever but

---

[1] Trotsky writes on this subject: "Tsaritsin, where the military were grouped around Voroshilov, was of particular importance to the Red Army and the Military Opposition. In the circle of Voroshilov's friends, the military experts, staff officers, and higher headquarters in Moscow were always alluded to with unconcealed hatred. Stalin spent several months in Tsaritsin. He successfully dovetailed his secret plotting against me with the amateurish opposition of Voroshilov and his closest associates, but was careful to keep a path open for retreat in case of need . . . . As soon as Lenin fell ill, Stalin, by means of his allies, succeeded in having Tsaritsin renamed Stalingrad. The significance of this change, of course, escaped the broad masses, as they had no idea what the name actually implied. If Voroshilov is today a member of the Politburo, it is only thanks to the fact that in 1918 I forced him into submission by threatening to dispatch him to Moscow under guard." In Trotsky, *Moya zhizn*, Vol. II., pp. 171—75.

were dissatisfied with Trotsky's leadership in the army."[2] Stalin's aim here was, of course, to rehabilitate his supporters in the Military Opposition, primarily Voroshilov.

In 1925 Frunze died under the scalpel of Stalin's political surgery, and Voroshilov was appointed People's Commissar for Land and Naval Forces. When the commissariat was filled with Voroshilov's followers, the General was transferred to the headquarters staff of the State Security Section in the Kremlin.

By decision of the Central Committee, the members of the Kremlin Commandant's staff and the State Security Section consisted exclusively of Party members completely unconnected with politics. They were Communists, of course, but persons who had never been members of any faction in the Central Committee.

The duties of the Security Section consisted in protecting the lives and safety of members of the government and in safeguarding its legal status quo. The Central Committee was well acquainted with instances in Russian history when the palace guards had been used to bring about a palace revolution. The instinct for self-preservation dictated caution. Officially the Security Section was under the jurisdiction of the government through the OGPU–NKVD but in practice it took its orders from the Kremlin Commandant. Appointments to the staff of the Kremlin Commandant were made individually by the Special Section of the Organization Bureau of the Central Committee and formally ratified by the government in accordance with the rules governing appointments to the top posts in the OGPU. In other words, there were two OGPUs, quite independent of each other—an external OGPU for control over the population at large and an internal OGPU for supervising the government.

The internal OGPU had at its disposal an independent network of secret agents under its direct control, who reported on outside affairs, including the external OGPU. The latter, however, was kept entirely in the dark regarding this intelligence activity and knew nothing about the secret work of the internal OGPU, that is, of the Kremlin Commandant and the State Security Section. A system of this kind presented many advantages, but, in particular, it shielded Stalin from plots hatched outside the Kremlin, including those which might originate in the external OGPU. This unusual division of labor was employed in the Central Committee itself, particularly after the death of Lenin. It need hardly be added that the General belonged to the staff of the internal OGPU, and was accordingly in an extraordinarily favorable position to keep informed on the course of events.

---

[2] *Istoriya VKP(b). Kratky kurs*, p. 224.

Chapter XIV

"Stalin's Cabinet" and its Powers

After the expulsion of the Trotskyites and Zinovievites and before the appearance on the political scene of the Right Opposition, Stalin did not control majorities in all of the principal organs of the Central Committee.

As of December 1927 the members of the important Politburo were Bukharin, Voroshilov, Kalinin, Kuibyshev, Molotov, Rykov, Rudzutak, Stalin, and Tomsky and the alternate members were Petrovsky, Uglanov, Andreyev, Kirov, Mikoyan, Kaganovich, Chubar and Kosior. The members of the Organization Bureau or Orgburo were Stalin, Molotov, Uglanov, Kosior, Kubyak, Moskvin, Bubnov, Artyukhina, Andreyev, Dogadov, A. P. Smirnov, Rukhimovich, and Sulimov and the alternate members were Lobov, V. M. Mikhailov, Lepse, Chaplin, and Shmidt. The members of the Secretariat were Stalin (Secretary-General), Molotov, Uglanov, Kosior, and Kubyak and the alternate members were Moskvin, Bubnov and Artyukhina.[1]

Of the nine full members of the Politburo Stalin could rely only on three—himself, Voroshilov, and Molotov. Bukharin could also count on three votes—those of himself, Rykov, and Tomsky. The remaining three members—Kalinin, Rudzutak, and Kuibyshev—shifted back and forth and at decisive moments might support either Stalin or Bukharin. In the Orgburo, Stalin commanded five votes—those of himself, Molotov, Kosior, Andreyev, and Rukhimovich; Bukharin could count on an equal number—those of Uglanov, Dogadov, Smirnov, Sulimov, and Kubyak. Bubnov, Artyukhina, and Moskvin were neutral. Only in the Secretariat did Stalin have a small but secure majority of three—Stalin, Molotov, and Kosior—against two—Uglanov and Kubyak.

Accordingly, although he was not full master of all the Central Committee chief organs, Stalin was master of the Secretariat, the supreme organ of the Party, which framed the policy of the Party and the government. The Politburo and Orgburo were merely asked to give post factum approval to decisions previously reached by the Secretariat. What was most important was that Stalin had usurped the authority of the Orgburo in matters concerning the organizational policy of the government. All matters dealing with appointments to and recall from the higher posts in the Party apparatus, the national economy, the army, the trade unions, and the Commissariat of Foreign Affairs, i.e., all branches of government under the supervision of the Orgburo, were now decided

---

[1] *VKP(b) v rezolyutsiyakh*, Vol. II, p. 455.

by the Secretariat of the Central Committee. This usurpation of the proper functions of the Orgburo in fact amounted to usurpation of the authority of the Politburo, which had become a screen for the all-powerful Secretariat. The members of the Politburo frequently received from outsiders news of what was going on in the Secretariat.

Appointments to the state apparatus—that is, to the Party apparatus and the state administration—were made without the knowledge of the Politburo and entirely on the basis of the new Party statute which stated that "current executive and organizational work are directed by the Secretariat." In fact, what other body could have assumed this duty? The Politburo and the Orgburo met only periodically and were made up of persons outside the Central Committee, while the Secretariat was a permanent living and functioning organ of the Central Committee.

If the Secretariat was Stalin's legal organ of authority, the Central Committee apparatus, hand-picked by him as Secretary-General of the Party, was the powerful weapon with which he was able to strengthen and maintain this authority. Having step by step rid the Central Committee apparatus of Old Bolshevik members, Stalin proceeded to reconstruct it. Under Lenin's leadership the Central Committee Secretariat and its working apparatus had only technical and executive functions. The business of the officials at the head of the Secretariat and the apparatus was limited to seeing to it that resolutions passed by the Politburo, the Orgburo, and plenary sessions of the Central Committee were carried out.

The Secretariat and even more so the Central Committee apparatus made no independent decisions not based on directives from the above-mentioned organs. For this reason, those appointed or elected to the Central Committee Secretariat and apparatus were persons known as good executors. Stalin himself had been put there as an "executor," not, to be sure, upon recommendation by Lenin, as the Stalinists later asserted, but as a result of a conspiracy by Zinoviev, Kamenev, and Stalin against Lenin and Trotsky. Now, having first rid himself of Trotsky and then of Kamenev and Zinoviev, Stalin was preparing for his final skirmish with Bukharin by imperceptibly but radically clearing the Central Committee apparatus of Bukharin's supporters.

In order to avoid arousing the suspicions of the officials thus purged, and to escape protests by Bukharin, the persons relieved were, as has been noted, given responsible posts in administrative or economic fields, as a step toward their utter destruction. When questioned by his followers as to the wisdom of this method, Stalin used to comment that it was the results that counted. By the beginning of 1929 reorganization of the Central Committee apparatus had resulted in the creation within the Central Committee itself of what was called at the time "Stalin's unofficial cabinet." Stalin's cabinet was later given official status in Party documents under the name of "Comrade Stalin's Secretariat." A resolution of the Central Committee stated that "reorganization of the Central Committee and the apparatuses of local Party organizations is made necessary mainly by the greatly increasing complexity of problems facing Party leaders in the conditions prevailing in the period of reconstruction, especially in the fields of selection, allocation, and training of cadres."[2]

The reconstructed Central Committee apparatus now comprised sections for organization and instruction, allocation (personnel), culture and propaganda, and agitation and mass campaigns. The heads of sections were chosen from among Central Committee members faithful to Stalin, including Kaganovich, Bauman, Stetsky, Vareikis, and D. Bulatov. "Stalin's cabinet" on the other hand was composed of young fanatics who were not Central Committee members. At first no one paid particular attention to these men, who were generally regarded as technical collaborators of Stalin and as devoted workers with no aspirations to engage in "higher politics." They were occupied in writing up minutes of the meetings of the Central Committee, or supplying information on a variety of subjects, or passing tea and sandwiches at meetings, or sharpening the pencils of their chiefs. As was fitting for well-trained flunkeys (even in the Party) they were exaggeratedly humble, obedient, and sickeningly attentive to members of the Central Committee:

"Would you permit me to call your car, Nikolai Ivanovich [Bukharin]?"

"At your service, Alexei Ivanovich [Rykov]!"

"May I suggest another sandwich, Mikhail Pavlovich [Tomsky]?"

"Yes, yes, Comrade Stalin!"

It was persons of this type that Stalin picked for his secret cabinet. They included Tovstukha, Poskrebyshev, Smitten, Yezhov, Bauman, Pospelov, Mekhlis, Shub, Malenkov, Tovmassian, Peters, Uritsky, Varga, and later Umansky. Each was given some kind of official title. In the lists of Central Committee employees Tovstukha was carried as "Assistant Secretary of the Central Committee," a kind of office manager with no policy functions, of a type found in local Party organizations. Poskrebyshev was an assistant to an assistant, appointed to assist the man in charge of control and information. After the death of Tovstukha, Poskrebyshev was made assistant to the Central Committee Secretary and head of the Special Section, while Smitten, his assistant, previously in charge of keeping Party statistics, was given Poskrebyshev's former post.

Yezhov was placed in charge of the Personnel Section, Pospelov in charge of the Propaganda Section, with Mekhlis as his assistant, Tovmassian in charge of the Nationalities Section (at one time this post was occupied by Dimanshtein and then by Rakhimbayev, who later became Chairman of the Tadzhikistan Council of People's Commissars and a vice-chairman of the Central Executive Committee of the USSR). Malenkov, at first Poskrebyshev's deputy in the Special Section and Recording Secretary of the Politburo, was later appointed head of the Personnel Section, when Yezhov was placed in charge of the Personnel Department of the People's Commissariat for Agriculture, in 1929. Shub, as I remember, was head of the Political and Administrative Section and after 1935, when Andreyev

---

[2] *BSE*, 1953, Vol. LX, p. 552.

was elected as one of the secretaries of the Central Committee, became his personal secretary, with the title of Assistant Secretary of the Central Committee. Peters was head of the Military Section and Varga of the Foreign Section.

I have pointed out earlier that Stalin's secret cabinet was later legalized and given the official name of "Comrade Stalin's Secretariat," not to be confused with the Secretariat of the Central Committee. Every single question concerning internal or external policy was examined and in practice predecided by Stalin's cabinet before being submitted to the principal organs of the Central Committee and then passed to the appropriate sections. The resolutions of these sections, which merely put the stamp of official approval on the recommendations of the technical experts in Stalin's cabinet, were then passed on for ratification by the Central Committee Secretariat, the Orgburo, and the Politburo. In case of a serious difference of opinion on any subject in these departments—as frequently occurred—the question at issue was passed to permanent or ad hoc Politburo committees. These committees, which consisted mainly of members of the Central Committee not included in the permanent apparatus, were nevertheless wholly dependent on the permanent apparatus, i.e., on Stalin's cabinet, in matters relating to draft proposals and, particularly, to their passage through the relevant higher Party organ. A vicious circle was thus formed, which only Stalin, as Secretary-General of the Central Committee, could break by sabotaging any resolution that did not suit him.

The organizational policy of Stalin's cabinet was based on a tried principle, which, two years later, Stalin proclaimed as the slogan of the Party: "Everything depends on personnel."

Stalin's future historians, if they have access to the files of his cabinet, will be able to establish the simple but amazing fact that the internal and world policy of the USSR was directed, not by the Politburo, composed of Old Bolsheviks, but by Stalin's technical cabinet of unimpressive young men, little known to the Party and to the country at large, but who were the docile executors of their master's will. And this was achieved by "selection, allocation, and training of cadres." The cabinet selected the personnel of the Party, the army, and the state. The cabinet was primarily a "laboratory for filtering personnel." The career and future fate of every member of the Party, from the secretary of a local Party committee to a People's Commissar of the USSR, depended on the relevant section of the cabinet.

In order to appoint new men, the former occupants of posts had first to be removed with the least possible publicity. This was the task of the Special Section directed by Poskrebyshev. There had earlier been in the apparatus of the Central Committee a Secret Section in charge of the secret files of the Party and the government. Its role was that of Party strong box, or safe. When Stalin's cabinet finally took shape the Secret Section had died a natural death, only to be resurrected and integrated into the cabinet again under the mysterious name of Special Section. From now on its activities were really secret. It was not officially brought to the notice of the Party until the Seventeenth Party Congress, in 1934, after Stalin's conclusive victory.

What were the functions of the Special Section? The answer cannot be found in official Party documents. Unofficially the following is known: The Special Section was created as a special organ of control over members at the summit of the Party, the army, and the government and, of course, the NKVD itself. It had at its disposal an independent network of secret agents and a separate subsection for personnel matters covering all Party officials regardless of rank. This allowed Stalin, whether in his office or on vacation in the country, to be constantly informed on the private lives and clandestine activities of the Party and government heads in Moscow. Even the personal correspondence of the more responsible officials, including that of Stalin's closest associates, was also subject to vigilant censorship by the Special Section, exactly as in the days of Metternich or of the Black Cabinet of the tsarist Okhrana. Stalin was aware of every secret thought and move of friend and enemy alike in his immediate entourage. The fate of any high official was predecided by the Special Section as soon as the black marks against his record had begun to accumulate in his personal file. The final and official decision was made by the appropriate official organ of the Central Committee depending on the rank of the victim: if he was a member of the Central Committee, action was taken by the Secretariat or in rare cases by the Orgburo; if he was a high-ranking civil servant but not a member of the Central Committee, he was simply removed by the competent department of the Central Committee. In cases which Stalin feared might make trouble or attract unwanted publicity, material incriminating a high Party member or even a member of the Central Committee was placed before the official Party tribunal—the Central Control Commission (later the Commission of Party Control)—consisting of the "irremovable judges"—Shkiryatov, Yaroslavsky, Solts, Yanson, and Ordzhonidze.

By such means the Special Section created vacancies in responsible posts which were immediately filled by the Personnel Section, first under Yezhov and then under Malenkov. It is therefore hardly surprising that People's Commissars quailed before Tovstyukha and Poskrebyshev while members of the Central Committee licked the boots of Yezhov and Malenkov, in spite of the fact that the persons who wielded such authority and their colleagues were listed merely as "technical employees" of the Central Committee. "In a period of reconstruction technology decides everything," said Stalin on one occasion. His own use of technology in operating the Central Committee through the Poskrybyshevs and Malenkovs in Moscow definitely decided the fate of the Party. Such then was the situation in the Party when Stalin moved into final battle for Lenin's heritage. What counted was not the elected Party members but the secretaries of oblast and district committees and of Party central committees of the local national republics, all of whom had been appointed by the Personnel Section, and the iron will and desire for sole power of the chief "constructor" of the conspiracy.

Stalin's seizure of working control of the Central Committee was parallelled by an even more meticulous process of quietly building up a strong body of permanent officials, completely devoted to him, in the oblasts, districts, and national republics. From 1928 on it was literally impossible to find a secretary of any local Party organization who had been elected according to the procedure laid down by the Party statutes and required by the much vaunted "inner-Party democracy." Under one pretext or another the secretaries elected under the old rules were removed from Party work, sometimes, as in Moscow, to be given responsible administrative, diplomatic, or more usually industrial or agricultural posts; anything, in fact, that would rid the Party apparatus of their presence. The posts thus vacated were filled by bought Stalinists, appointed by the Personnel Section through the legal organ of the Central Committee, the Organization and Instructor Section.

When the local Party organizations, accustomed as they were to talk about "inner-Party democracy" and in accordance with the Party rules still nominally in force, began to refuse to accept the secretaries "recommended by Moscow," the Central Committee, again breaking these rules, adopted the practice of appointing local secretaries from above. In order to ensure peaceful acceptance of the nominees by the local Party committee plenums, each new secretary was accompanied to his post by an "instructor" from the Central Committee. The instructor explained to the local committee that this particular appointment expressed "the will of the Leninist Central Committee."

Such a "will" was not easy to oppose. If any local Party organization openly criticized this newly invented procedure, or expressed displeasure at the appointment of an utter stranger as its chairman, the machinery of the Special Section immediately built up a case against an "anti-Party group" in the particular organization, which usually ended in expulsion of the trouble makers from the Party by action of another organ directly under Stalin—the Party Collegium of the Central Committee.

In selecting and appointing local Party secretaries Stalin was acting in accordance with Machiavelli's wise precept to avoid placing supreme authority in the hands of local inhabitants, who being prone to separatism, might easily betray the Prince, and also to avoid allowing them to stay long in one place, but to move them around frequently. Stalin adhered strictly to these rules when building up his body of supporters in the local Party central committees.

By the end of 1928 the process of remodeling the lower Party apparatus had been completed. Henceforward the basic cadre of secretaries of oblast, district, and national republic central committees was composed of men screened by the Special Section and appointed to their posts by the Personnel Section of Stalin's cabinet. In local apparatuses from oblast committees up, "special sections" were created, invariably headed by persons sent from Moscow by the Special Section and the Personnel Section of the Central Committee. Officially these emissaries were subordinate to the secretaries of the local committees but in practice they were answerable only to Stalin's cabinet. Each local special section was provided with a network of Party informers, independent of the Party committee, and a staff of three to ten highly skilled workers in the apparatus of the Party committee, including a chief, one or two instructors, a code clerk, a recording secretary, a special typist, etc. At the time, the local special sections were granted no administrative rights, and this is still true. Their one duty was to supply authentic and exhaustive information for use by the Special Section of the Central Committee in Moscow.

The chief of a local special section was always present at sessions of the bureau and secretariat of the local Party committee in the capacity of recording secretary and was attended by the special typist, who was also a stenographer. Official liaison between the Central Committee and the local committees was maintained through the local special sections. Telegrams in code and secret directives from the Central Committee were channelled through the local special section, which decoded them and passed them on to the secretaries. The local committee secretary channelled his secret reports, replies, and decisions to Moscow through the same section. In addition to the usual postal services and state telephone and telegraph lines, the Special Section had at its disposal special field messengers, a kind of internal diplomatic courier service, attached to the NKVD–MVD, which carried important Party and government papers to and from Moscow and enjoyed greater immunity from unwelcome interference than any minister in the Soviet government. They were provided with mandates signed by the cabinet officer in charge of State Security which not only guaranteed their personal immunity from arrest, but authorized them to require, in the execution of their duties, assistance of every kind from both Party and government authorities at every level.

Chapter XV

Stalin's Cabinet in Action: The Campaign of Provocation

By the beginning of 1929 events had reached a stage at which the powers of Stalin and his cabinet, described in the foregoing chapter, were to be put to the test.

Throughout the fall of 1928 Bukharin, Rykov, and Tomsky had argued over the advisability of placing their conflict with Stalin before a plenary session of the Central Committee. Rykov, supported by Bukharin, wished to avoid the appearance of bringing into the open a Party split of which the Party at large was as yet unaware. Tomsky, on the other hand, wished to reach a clearcut solution and considered that a joint resignation would be the best method of demonstrating their disapproval of the course taken by Stalin. Tomsky hoped that Stalin would not dare to accept their resignations, while the Central Committee would wish to know the reasons for the step. In November 1928 Rykov and Bukharin at last accepted his view and handed in their resignations. Stalin, as was to have been expected, refused to accept them, without even informing the Central Committee itself. For some time, Bukharin and Tomsky sabotaged their own work in *Pravda* and in the Trade Union Council, but they were ultimately starved into submission: Rykov, followed by Tomsky and Bukharin, returned to work. Had Stalin genuinely wished for peace in the Politburo the whole matter might have come to an end at this stage of his struggle within the Party. But he had other intentions. What he really desired was to provide the Party apparatus and the Party activists with the means of destroying his enemies—the new Right Opposition—in open battle. Throughout the history of the All-Union Communist Party of Bolsheviks the cry of "Opposition!" had been a much sought-for target against which it had been possible to mobilize both the undiscriminating Party masses and the completely informed Party careerists. The entire course of Stalin's policy was aimed at setting up such a target, but he wished to set it up in his own way and by using his own methods of skillful conspiracy and expert provocation. The conspiracy has been described. The following incident, as later reported by the General, not only provides an illustration of Stalin's use of provocation but carries a step farther the story of Stalin's march to sole power.

On the same night when Bukharin and Tomsky were attending the New Year's party at Vera Nikolayevna's, the members of Stalin's secret cabinet, including the General, were meeting at Kaganovich's summer house on the other side of Moscow. The host presided and the opening talk was given by Stalin, the "chief" of a group of attentive and loyal followers. Following Stalin's opening statement, the listeners threw in questions brief and to the point, to which Stalin gave answers equally brief and to the point.

To begin with, Stalin drew a horrifying picture of the threatened annihilation of the Party apparatus by the plotters against the Party—Bukharin, Rykov, Tomsky, Uglanov and their supporters. He attempted to prove to his listeners that the plotters intended to disrupt the entire Party from top to bottom, and that the first victims of this annihilation would be the Party apparatus. Moreover, he went on, the conspirators intended to destroy the military cadres of the Party and to replace them with Trotskyites and professional soldiers from the former tsarist army. Both for their own advantage and on the basis of their beliefs the conspirators had as their political program the restoration of capitalism in the country, and because this aim could not be attained without first destroying the Party apparatus, the first blow was being directed at Stalin and his listeners. The conspirators were clever enough to understand that the Leninist apparatus of the Party could not be shattered by the normal methods of free discussion, either in plenary sessions of the Central Committee or in a Party congress. They were, therefore, forced to resort to methods of trickery and provocation, and had gone as far as to attempt to blackmail individual members of the Central Committee and officers of the Red Army. Taking advantage of past failures or mistakes on the part of some of the leading comrades, the Bukharinites were preparing to attack them. This attempt was made easier by the fact, Stalin added significantly, that in some strange manner copies of all the files on Party personnel from the Special Section had fallen into the hands of Bukharin.

When Smitten, who was in charge of personnel matters, attempted to clear himself by arguing that Bukharin could not possibly have such copies in his possession, Stalin cast an inquiring glance at Poskrebyshev.

"I am sorry to say that Josif Vissarionovich is quite right," answered Poskrebyshev smugly.

"Then what can we do? How can we remedy this mistake on the part of our apparatus and at the same time render the Bukharinites harmless?" asked Stalin and at once supplied the answer. "Lazar Moiseyevich [Kaganovich], Vyacheslav Mikhailovich [Molotov] and I have decided that before the Bukharinites have time to make use of the stolen files, we must warn our supporters—our members in the Central Committee and the leaders of the Red Army—of the acts of provocation which the Bukharinites are preparing to use against them. There is only one way to do this effectively: members of the Central Committee's apparatus who are cleared for work in the Special Section must immediately go to the local centers to acquaint the comrades there with the excerpts from their personnal files which the Bukharinites intend to use against them." Stalin closed with a stern warning that the excerpts were to be brought to the attention of the comrades concerned, not as excerpts from their personnal files, but as materials intercepted from the Bukharinites by the Central Committee. After acquainting the comrades with the excerpts, the persons dispatched on these missions must obtain from each person interviewed a written reply to the following two questions: (1) What has the comrade to say to justify himself regarding the substance of the charges brought against him, and (2) If he rejects the compromising evidence, what explanation can he give for the conduct of Bukharin's group? Assignments were then made and the New Year's gathering came to an end.

The General had then gone immediately to the party at Tomsky's house where he had passed on to Tomsky and Bukharin a full report of the meeting he had just attended. I later heard it from Sorokin, who had been in the room when the General had made his report.

Sorokin never told us how Bukharin and Tomsky reacted to these revelations, but I have a vivid recollection of the effect they produced on Zinaida Nikolayevna and her friends when we were discussing them a few days later in her apartment. We had all arrived rather late in the evening, but as the General, who had called the meeting, had not yet made his appearance, we killed time by talking about Tomsky's party. The discussion lagged, especially as Sorokin took no part in the conversation in spite of all efforts by Zinaida Nikolayevna. The only cheerful person in the room was a People's Commissar, who kept bragging about his exploits on a recent hunting expedition, most likely fictitious because at each report of a successful shot Sorokin incredulously shook his head or made a face. When the People's Commissar, having killed off countless ducks, partridges, and hares and a couple of foxes, began to take aim at a wolf, Sorokin rudely spoiled his shot:

"Let's forget these imaginary shots. Just tell us why you ran out of powder at the meeting of the Moscow activists, when you should have taken a shot at Kaganovich!"

"I never tried to shoot two rabbits with one shot, as you did at the meeting of activists at the Institute of Red Professors," replied the Commissar angrily.

"And I have never known one rabbit to hunt another," answered Sorokin.

"Don't talk such rubbish," said Zinaida Nikolayevna in an effort to pacify them. To the relief of everyone, the front door bell rang and the General came in.

"I am sure Zinaida Nikolayevna and the rest of you will forgive me for being late if I tell you my story; but I shall have to begin at the end," said the General. He then proceeded to tell us that he had just been at a briefing in the Central Committee and was flying to the Caucasus early the next morning to brief Party leaders there. He went on to fill in the details of Stalin's plan and went so far as to tell us the names and destinations of the members of the Central Committee apparatus who were being dispatched to put it into effect.

"The whole thing is an invention intended to destroy the Leninist Guard," he concluded.

"In that case, why are you going?" asked Zinaida Nikolayevna in surprise.

"But hasn't Sorokin told you?"

"No, he only mentioned that Bukharin refuses to believe that the plan will succeed, that Rykov agrees with him, and that Tomsky, as usual, has rushed to the other extreme. He never said anything about your trip."

"It was only yesterday that I was told that I was being sent and where I was going to."

"Do our people know?"

"Of course they do."

"Well . . .?"

"Oh! What is the use of going over the whole thing, Zinaida? 'The flowers have bloomed and the leaves have fallen,' and, anyway, what kind of revolutionaries are we," said the General with a sigh, and added: "Tomsky is the only one among us who has kept faith with the Revolution and himself; all the others, if you will forgive me for saying so, are only a pack of old women."

"I believe Nicolai Ivanovich [Bukharin] is quite right in thinking that the members of the Party Central Committee are wise enough to see through this cheap attempt to compromise them," cut in Reznikov.

"Yes," put in the People's Commissar, "they are old birds that have been shot over before, and are not likely to fall for Stalin's poisoned bait."

"But this is not just poisoned bait, but a set of very serious charges discrediting members of the Party and making us responsible for bringing the charges."

"I refuse to believe it," persisted the People's Commissar.

With a visible effort at self-control the General slowly removed from his briefcase a few sheets of official Central Committee stationery inscribed: "Excerpts from Evidence Prepared by the Right Opposition," and began to read:

"Belov: Commanding Officer of the North Caucasus Military District; formerly a Left Social Revolutionary; corresponds with exiled Trotskyites; has frequent love affairs with the wives of his staff officers . . ."

"Andrei Andreyev: Secretary of a Party District Committee; before the Revolution was an activist in a Menshevik trade union; during the war was a defeatist; after the Revolution misappropriated large sums belonging to the Central Committee of the Railway Union, but was not brought to trial; chronic drunkard . . ."

"Philip Makharadze: President of the government of Georgia; in association with national deviationists and exiled Georgian Mensheviks; is secretly working for the secession of Georgia from the USSR . . ."

"Mirzoyan: Secretary of the Central Committee of the Azerbaidzhan Communist Party; was employed by the British Secret Service in the Caucasus; had his children christened in the Armenian Church . . ."

"Fabricius: Commanding Officer of the Special Caucasian Red Army; Bonapartist; morphine addict."

The list was long and filled with spicy details, and was received with increasing dismay by the listeners. Political charges against each individual alternated with accusations of moral vice—drunkenness, addiction to drugs, embezzling, debauchery, adultery. In those days moral and political offenses were regarded as on a par and the moral charges were no less serious than the political. After reading through his list of charges, the General looked inquiringly at the Commissar. But the latter could only remark sadly: "From what I personally know about some of the comrades mentioned, I must agree that the facts, as stated, are correct."

"But don't you understand that although the evidence has been compiled, not by us, but by the Central Committee apparatus, it is to be put before the comrades as originating with us. What can you call this but a vile trick and rank blackmail," hotly retorted the General in an effort to make the People's Commissar see the point. But the latter stuck to his guns. "Facts are facts, however they are presented," he replied. Reznikov nodded in approval, while Sorokin and Zinaida Nikolayevna exchanged bewildered glances.

After an all-night discussion, the General took his leave and drove off to the airport.

Chapter XVI

The Removal of Bukharin as Editor of *Pravda* and Tomsky as Chairman of the Trade Union Council

The campaign of provocation initiated by the dispatch to local committees of envoys from Stalin's cabinet was eminently successful. Bukharin, who had viewed with some scepticism the information imparted by the General regarding the campaign against the Rightists, was soon forced to realize that the threat was both serious and real. Correspondence received from his own supporters, as well as from "neutrals"—questioning, surprised, and frankly indignant—convinced him that this time Stalin was in earnest. If on other occasions the lower layers of the Party had been content, under pressure from the Secretariat of the Central Committee, to submit stenciled resolutions against the Rightists, now the entire Party in the provinces was seething with anger. Silence, under the circumstances, could lead only to political suicide.

Before proceeding to a description of Bukharin's counterattack and its outcome, a few words must be said regarding further preparations which Stalin had made long before to meet just such a situation.

According to the Party statutes, neither the Presidium of the Central Control Commission nor the Presidium of the Comintern was legally empowered to sit in judgment on the conduct of the Central Committee Politburo and Orgburo; on the contrary, and dating back to the days of Lenin, the Politburo—again not by statute, but by Bolshevik unwritten law—was both the supreme court and the supreme legislature for all other Party organs. On paper, the All-Union Communist Party of Bolsheviks modestly described itself as "a section of the Comintern," and the Central Control Commission as "the supervisor of Party unity," but this was only on paper.

The statutes adopted by the Fourteenth Party Congress in 1925 stated:

The Central Control Commission has as its chief task the maintenance of Party unity and the strengthening of the ranks of the Party, for which purpose the Central Control Commission is entrusted with:

(1) Assisting the Central Committee of the All-Union Communist Party of Bolsheviks in strengthening the proletarian composition of the Party . . .;

(2) Preventing infringement of the Party program, the statute of the All-Union Communist Party of Bolsheviks and decisions of Party congresses by members;

(3) Vigorously combating all possible anti-Party groups and all signs of factionalism within the Party, and also forestalling and assisting in the elimination of conflicts;

(4) Combating uncommunist offenses: accumulation of property, moral laxity, etc.;

(5) Guarding against the spread of bureaucratic practices in the Party apparatus and bringing to justice those guilty of obstructing the putting into effect of the principle of inner-Party democracy in the functioning of Party organs.[1]

The most important of these points—items 1, 3, and 5—directly applied to the methods used by Stalin and his secret cabinet in the Central Committee and it was in order to deal with these items that Stalin moved his first line reserve—the Central Control Commission—into the Party battle. He did not, however, make use either of the entire Central Control Commission, since of the 195 members elected at the Fifteenth Party Congress at least half were supporters of Bukharin, Rykov, and Tomsky, or of the 21 members of the Presidium of the Central Committee, among whom Bukharin also had followers. He utilized only a small number of picked leaders of the Central Control Commission. By following this course Stalin was, moreover, complying with a provision of the Party statutes which authorized the Presidium of the Central Control Commission to delegate three members and three alternates to the Politburo and five alternates to the Orgburo. These delegates attended sittings of these top Party organs with advisory votes. At the Fifteenth Party Congress the farsighted Stalin had introduced a few apparently minor but actually radical changes. An amended clause reading "The Presidium of the Central Control Commission delegates to the Politburo not three but four of its members and four candidate members" failed to include a previous provision giving the delegates the right to an advisory vote. A second amendment was apparently equally innocuous, but in fact of equal potential importance. The old statutes had provided that in intervals between plenary sessions the Presidium of the Central Control Commission was to be the sole supreme directing organ of the Commission, in charge both of its Secretariat and its Party collegium. The Party collegium of five members and two candidate members was in practice the supreme Party tribunal. Formally dependent on, and subordinate to, the Presidium of the Central Control Commission, which, as has been noted, was mainly composed of Bukharinites, the Party collegium was under the amended statutes made independent of the Presidium of the Central Control Commission. Its verdicts were now final. A third amendment of great importance was the addition of a provision that "members of the Party refusing to reply truthfully to questions by a control commission are subject to immediate dismissal from the Party."[2]

At the end of 1928 the Presidium of the Central Control Commission was headed by Ordzhonikidze, who had by now thrown in his lot with Stalin. This supreme and now independent Party tribunal was headed by Yaroslavsky, Shkiryatov, Solts, Zemlyachka, and Yanson. The members of the permanent delegation of the Central Control Commission to the Politburo—Ordzhonikidze, Yaroslavsky, Shkiryatov, and Solts—were selected from among these Party

[1] *VKP(b) v rezolyutsiyakh*, Vol. II, p. 223.
[2] *Ibid.*, p. 451.

stalwarts. Following plenary sessions of the Central Committee in July and November 1928, with their evidence of a critical struggle within the Politburo, Stalin felt obliged to throw into the fray this reserve.

Arguing that the absence in the Politburo of a clear majority on the main problems of policy was hindering Party work Stalin proposed that the Central Committee adopt the practice of holding joint meetings of the Politburo and the Presidium of the Central Control Commission. A resolution to this effect was adopted in November or December 1928 with little or no opposition from the Bukharinites, since, as I have already said, in the Presidium of the Central Control Commission the forces of Bukharin and Stalin were equally balanced. But Stalin managed to get the better of the deal. When, as before, out of the 21 members of the Presidium only four—Ordzhonikidze, Yaroslavsky, Shkiryatov, and Solts—turned up at the first joint meeting of the Politburo and the Central Control Commission Presidium, Bukharin, in genuine surprise, inquired: "Where are the others?" Stalin replied quite reasonably: "According to the Party statutes a delegation of four members and four alternates represents the Presidium of the Central Control Commission at meetings of the Politburo."

The outwitted Rightists, of course, protested loudly. Their protests, however, were in vain; and merely succeeded in gaining them the hostility of the delegates who were present. As a special concession, the "peace-loving Stalin" did agree to the addition of one more member to the delegation of the Central Control Commission, a Bukharinite—Yenukidze. This concession was a real infraction of the Party statutes, which plainly stated that the delegation from the Central Control Commission should consist of four members only. But, after all, why not, if such an infraction would help matters? Tal had been right in telling us in the course of a lecture at the Institute: "Our Party statutes are not the statutes of an order of knighthood!"

What concrete measures were taken by Bukharin and his followers to avert what Bukharin called "this organizational encirclement" by Stalin? Except for Bukharin's ill-fated interview with Kamenev, practically none. And this in spite of the balance of forces in the Politburo, the sympathy and support, in some cases open, in some potential, of strong groups in the Central Committee and Central Control Commission, the sympathy and support of the entire apparatus of the Central Trade Union Council, Bukharin's good standing with the Red Army, the activity and support of prominent Party theorists and propagandists, and, finally, the sympathy and potential support of the peasantry, i.e., of the bulk of the population. These objective factors were all in Bukharin's favor. But one factor, called by Lenin the "subjective factor," he unfortunately lacked—an organized following of inspired revolutionaries. Bukharin was too much of a theorist, Rykov a pedant, and Tomsky a lone wolf. The leaders of the Right Opposition were deathly afraid of acting outside the legal framework of the Party, which Stalin was unabashedly smashing to bits under their very eyes. They feared to be accused of splintering the Party, while Stalin, in their presence, was building up a faction of his own—"a party within the Party." They feared to appeal to the broad masses of the Party over the heads of Stalin and his apparatus, while he, in a stream of correspondence and instructions, was not only appealing to the Party masses over the heads of both the Politburo and the Orgburo, but with no compunctions whatever was dispersing the locally elected officals in order to replace them with persons appointed from Moscow. Stalin lacked the "objective factors" possessed by Bukharin, but he had on his side Lenin's "subjective factor," a dynamic organization of trained workers, ready for any venture, prepared to use any methods, and avid for power. Their strength lay in the fact that in the pursuit of this power they were prepared to go to greater lengths than Bukharin and Trotsky together; even to the point of desecrating Lenin's tomb and anathematizing Marx and Engels if by so doing they could ensure victory.

Such was the status of affairs within the Party when Bukharin, goaded by Stalin's dispatch throughout the country of envoys selected by his secret cabinet and intent on provocation, at last decided to strike back. He began by proposing to a group of his supporters in the Central Committee that they issue a joint statement demanding the convening of an extraordinary plenary session of the Central Committee. Rykov flatly refused to adopt "a splintering method of struggle." The Right was now split in two, a "left" group of Rightists—Bukharin, Tomsky, Uglanov, Kulikov, and Reznikov—and a "right" group of Rightists—Rykov, Mikhailov, Ukhanov, and Kotov. To avoid giving Stalin the satisfaction of witnessing a "schism among the schismatics," Bukharin resolved to submit the statement alone. This he did on January 30, 1929.

It is a great pity that this extremely important document, stating the political program of the Right Opposition, was never published in the USSR. Neither did it find its way abroad, as far as I know, although isolated sentences from it have been cited in foreign writings on Bukharin, such as the assertion that "Stalin's agricultural policy is a policy of armed feudal robbery of the peasants." Stalin even forbade the members of the Party to read it. Only the top Party activists who in the opinion of the Stalinists were sufficiently immune to the influence of "anti-Party heresies," having reached a satisfactory stage of "pro-Stalinism," were allowed to peruse it in an appendix to the stenographic report of the joint plenary session of the Central Committee and Central Control Commission held April 16–23, 1929. Moreover, even the resolution of this plenum regarding Bukharin's group was kept secret until the publication in 1933 of the decision on the Rightists made by the joint session of the Politburo and of the Presidium of the Central Control Commission and the decision of the plenum. And these decisions, as published, omitted Bukharin's declaration of January 30, 1929, and a "platform of the three" of February 9, 1929. The extent to which these documents were post facto abridged and amended may be judged by the fact that with few exceptions most of the most colorful and biting parts of Bukharin's statement were omitted. Even in this mutilated form they are, however, of value in helping to reproduce the original text.

The main subjects of Bukharin's statement of January 30 were Stalin and the Secretariat of the Central Committee, with other leading Central Committee organs omitted. By carefully avoiding criticism of the Politburo, the Orgburo, and the Central Committee as a whole, Bukharin, both openly and by reference to the current methods employed by the Central Committee apparatus, accused Stalin of carrying on what was essentially a conspiracy against the Party line. His accusations may be summed up as follows:

(1) Stalin's peasant policy was based on the slogan which he had announced at the July plenum of the Central Committee, namely, "tribute, that is, armed and feudal exploitation of the peasantry." Stalin's aim, based on methodical and legalized robbery of the peasantry, the basic class of the population, was directed toward industrialization. He was striving toward this aim by two types of means—enforced collectivization and "reassessment of taxation."

(2) In disregard of repeated decisions of the Party concerning stimulation of the development of peasant agriculture and raising the agricultural yield by methods of encouragement, Stalin was resorting to methods of a directly contrary type—the practice of reintroducing "War Communism" in the countryside by using measures of severe administrative repression in connection with grain deliveries, such as the wholesale confiscation of peasant grain, while simultaneously refusing to manufacture consumer goods for the rural population, as required by previous decisions of the Party.

(3) In connection with the entire policy for the country as a whole and for the peasantry in particular, "congresses, conferences, and plenary meetings of the Party Politburo decide matters in one way while Stalin's apparatus carries them out in another."

(4) In matters of inner-Party policy in general and organizational Party policy in particular, "congresses, conferences, and plenary meetings of the Central Committee and the Party statutes provide one set of rules, while Stalin's apparatus sets rules of its own." As a result "inner-Party democracy has become a fiction while the appointment of Party secretaries from above has become the law." Accordingly, "in the Party there are no longer elected secretaries, but there are Party bureaucrats appointed by and removeable by Stalin's apparatus." The aim of this method of selecting secretaries was to create a Stalinist faction of picked bureaucrats in order to disrupt the Leninist Party from within. The aim was to create "a party within the Party," or, as Bukharin put it, "a picked set of secretaries."

(5) The same process of Party bureaucratization had been introduced by the Stalinists into the state apparatus. The role of the local soviets or councils had been reduced to that of a supplementary mechanism in the Party apparatus. The bureaucratization of the state apparatus was being put into effect along the same lines as the bureaucratization of the Party. This "bureaucratic regeneration" of the proletarian state and the Leninist Party was not spontaneous but was being methodically organized by "Stalin's cabinet."

(6) In cases in which Stalin and the Stalinists had not succeeded in seizing and paralyzing the state, Party, or trade union apparatus by the vice-like grip

of their faction, Stalin and his henchmen had resorted to the planned and calculated method of "organizational encirclement," that is, to the appointment of "political commissars" such as Kaganovich in the Central Trade Union Council, Ordzhonikidze in the Council of People's Commissars, Savelyev and Manuilsky in *Pravda*; Molotov and Manuilsky in the Comintern, etc. and this was being done not by decision of the Party acting through a plenum of the Central Committee, the Politburo, or the Orgburo, but by decision of "Stalin's cabinet," ratified pro forma at meetings of the Secretariat of the Central Committee.

(7) A similar policy of bureaucratization and selection of bureaucrats was being pursued by the Stalinists in relation to the Comintern. Selection of rank and file workers and leaders was no longer based on the Leninist principle of promoting professional revolutionaries, but on the Stalinist system of picking hired functionaries. Devoted Comintern personnel were being expelled from fraternal parties if they showed signs of independence in judgment or in work. Stalin's activity in the Comintern was not carried on by seeking to convince people or to educate them, but by a policy of dictatorship. If foreign Communists dared to criticize personal orders from Stalin's apparatus, they were at once branded as "oppositionists" or "compromisers," "Social Democrats" or "turncoats," and were expelled from the Party, not by their own national parties, but by Thalheimer or Brandler in the Comintern in Moscow, or if their expulsion was likely to cause personal embarassment for Stalin, they were simply summoned from their native countries to Moscow, as "compromisers," as in the case of Ewert and Eisler.

(8) While these things were being done by methods "normal to Stalin's apparatus," another course, now being taken by Stalin, was one which could not be tolerated by any party made up of politically like-minded persons—the course of monstrous provocation, falsification, extortion, instigation of one group of leaders and Central Committee members against another, and of all against the organizational principles and the theoretical bases of Leninism. Behind the backs of the Party and its supreme organs, Stalin was pursuing a policy aimed at liquidation of the Leninist Party. This "Stalinist regime is no longer tolerable in our Party."

In short, Bukharin's statement declared that the immediate removal of Stalin and of his entire "cabinet," in full conformity with the terms of Lenin's testament, offered the only possibility of restoring health to the Party and reestablishing the policy of Lenin.[3]

Bukharin's statement struck Stalin like a bombshell. If it were allowed to explode at a plenary session of the Central Committee, it might easily destroy not only him, but several others as well. It was imperative to avert the explosion at all costs or at least to delay it sufficiently to allow time to complete the consolidation of a line of defense. This he did by unexpectedly cancelling the Central Committee plenary meeting scheduled for the end of January, the last meeting having been held in the preceding November. Meanwhile he searched diligently

---

[3] *KPSS v resolyutsiyakh*, Vol. II, pp. 437, 445.

for a compromise. The psychological advantage of such a search was obvious. To those who persisted in calling him the chief aggressor, Stalin could now reply: "Here is Bukharin, who has declared war at a time when I am offering peace, for after all a bad peace is better than a good war."

However, behind the veil of Party peacemaker there lurked the ceaseless aggressor, crafty and cunning. No sooner had Bukharin presented his statement than Stalin created a Politburo commission (I do not know who its members were—most probably the mediators: Kalinin, Kuibyshev, and Rudzutak) which, evidently with his assistance, drew up terms for "compromise and peace" in the Politburo. On February 7 the commission notified the two contesting groups— Stalin, Molotov, and Voroshilov on the one hand and Bukharin, Rykov, and Tomsky on the other—of its terms for reaching a compromise. The paper throws light both on the drama of the events in progress and on Stalin's skill as a Party tactician. Regardless of whether the Bukharinites accepted the offer or rejected it, the victor would clearly be Stalin, as the terms set forth by the commission were bound decisively to influence in his favor the weight of opinion in the Politburo and in the plenum of the Central Committee. Having allowed the draft compromise to produce the desired effect, Stalin locked it up in the steel safe of the Politburo. It was first published twenty years later, in 1949. It reads as follows:

From an exchange of views in the commission it was ascertained that:

(1) Bukharin admits that his negotiations with Kamenev were a political error;

(2) Bukharin admits that the statement made in his declaration of January 30, 1929, in which he claims that the Central Committee is following a policy of "armed and feudal exploitation of the peasants," and that the Central Committee is disrupting the Comintern and encouraging the spread of bureaucracy in the Party, was unconsidered, made in the heat of argument, that he no longer stands by these claims and confirms that he has no further differences with the Central Committee in regard to these matters;

(3) On the basis of the above, Bukharin recognizes the possibility and necessity of friendly work within the Politburo;

(4) Bukharin withdraws his resignation from *Pravda* and the Comintern;

(5) In consideration of this, Bukharin withdraws his declaration of January 30.

In consideration of the above the commission finds it possible not to submit to a joint session of the Politburo and the Presidium of the Central Committee the draft resolution with its political evaluation of Bukharin's errors, and proposes that all documents on hand (stenographic reports of speeches, etc.) be withdrawn from use.

The commission proposes that the Politburo and the Presidium of the Central Control Commission furnish Bukharin all the conditions necessary for him to carry on normal work as editor-in-chief of *Pravda* and Secretary of the Executive Committee of the Comintern.[4]

Acceptance of such a compromise by the Bukharinite group would have meant unconditional capitulation to Stalin and admission that the group had

---

[4] Stalin, *Sochineniya*, Vol. VII, 1950, pp. 6–7.

been in error in criticizing Stalin's policy and that of the Stalinist apparatus. On the other hand, rejection would serve to emphasize the aggressive intent of the group toward the "peace-loving" Stalin, particularly in view of his proposal for "friendly work within the Politburo" and the provision of normal working conditions for Bukharin on *Pravda* and in the Comintern.

Recognizing the danger from a frontal attack, Bukharin declined to accept the so-called compromise. But he failed to appreciate the possibility of a flank attack, a failure of which Stalin was later to take advantage.

The Politburo commission's compromise proposal having been rejected, Bukharin's declaration had to be dealt with in some other way. Stalin's next move was to present Bukharin's statement to a joint meeting of the Politburo and the delegation from the Presidium of the Central Control Commission for their examination. His reasons for doing so were quite simple. After the grant of a casting vote to each of the four members of the delegation of the Presidium of the Central Control Commission, the balance of forces in the Politburo had altered sharply in Stalin's favor, being now seven to three, even if Kuibyshev, Kalinin, and Rudzutak continued to act as "mediators." His calculations proved to be right: at the session of February 9, the seven members unitedly opposed Bukharin and, of the three mediators, the indoctrinated Kuibyshev hastened to join the seven.

The session declared that Bukharin's letter constituted the political platform of the three opposition leaders—Bukharin, Rykov, and Tomsky—and a libel upon Stalin and the Party. (This was, incidentally, the first time that Stalin was identified with the Party.) The session resolved that Bukharin's statement should be withheld from the full membership, the so-called plenum, and that he be forbidden to make another statement to the plenum along the same lines. Bukharin and Tomsky replied by repeating their intention to resign their posts immediately in order to safeguard their right to defend their indictment of Stalin's leadership before the plenum. Rykov, however, refused to join them in this step. His refusal had a restraining effect on Bukharin but incited Tomsky to attack Stalin with greater vehemence and to accuse his friend Rykov of inconsistency. Uglanov, a Secretary of the Central Committee and an alternate member of the Politburo, ranged himself on Tomsky's side.

Stalin's triumvirate of Stalin, Molotov, and Voroshilov now decided to profit by the discord among the leaders of the Right Opposition and to strike while the iron was hot. They introduced before the session the following resolution:

> (1) To declare Bukharin's criticism of the Central Committee absolutely without basis. (By discrediting the line of the Central Committee and for this purpose of all kinds of gossip concerning the Central Committee, Comrade Bukharin was inclining toward the introduction of a new line.)
>
> (2) To propose to Comrade Bukharin that he disavow the line of Comrade Frumkin in the field of internal policy and that of Comrade Ember-Dro in the field of foreign policy.
>
> (3) To decline to accept the resignations of Comrades Bukharin and Tomsky.

(4) To propose to Comrade Tomsky that he loyally obey all decisions of the Party and its Central Committee.[5]

Stalin diplomatically avoided mention of Rykov and thereby reduced Bukharin's opposition from three to two. He did not refer at all to Uglanov. Matters were obviously moving toward a breakdown in the internal structure of the Right Opposition, as Rykov enjoyed the support of many of its members, both in the Central Committee and in the middle echelons of the Party and the Soviet organs. Aware of the danger, Bukharin, Tomsky, and Uglanov presented Rykov with an ultimatum that he sign the draft declaration of the three members of the Politburo which they had once withdrawn. The ultimatum called upon Rykov to make a clear choice between Stalin and the Bukharin group. Rykov acceded, and signed the joint indictment of Stalin, but with a heavy heart. Such was the origin of the "Statement of February 9," later described by Stalin as expressing the political platform of the Rightists.

In content the new statement differed little from Bukharin's statement of January 30. It was attached to the minutes of the joint session of the Politburo and the Presidium of the Central Control Commission. Stalin intended to consign it in this manner to the archives. As it was submitted toward the close of the session, he attempted to ignore it completely, while the Rightists continued to press for the immediate convention of a plenary session of the Central Committee to examine their statement. Stalin made promises, but did nothing. He had just won a battle within the Politburo, and was facing another; but for this he needed time to prepare.

From Stalin's viewpoint it was essential to prove that the criticism by Bukharin's group was in fact directed at the Central Committee and not merely at himself and his apparatus. The members of the Central Committee plenum must somehow be convinced that Bukharin's disclosures and his criticism of Stalin's organizational practices were slander based on nothing but rumor. For this purpose Stalin proceeded to have a lengthy resolution drawn up by the joint session. Being by now convinced that in spite of all his efforts to postpone the convening of a plenum Bukharin and his followers were this time determined to state their case to the members of the Central Committee, he prepared a special statement addressed to the plenum and appended to the resolution, explaining why he had concealed from the Party and its Central Committee the existence of two hostile groups in the Politburo although only three months earlier at the October plenum of the Moscow Committee he had solemnly stated that there were in the Politburo neither Leftists nor Rightists nor persons who were trying to mediate between such groups. His statement attempted to justify his failure to report on the split by arguing that, while differences had of course existed, they were of a temporary nature, and that, therefore, "the Politburo of the Central Committee and the Presidium of the Central Control Commission did not find it necessary to report to the plenum of the Central Committee on differences which had already been cleared up," and "this

---

[5] *VKP(b) v rezolyutsiyakh*, Vol. II, p. 529.

circumstance made it possible to oblige all the members of the Politburo to affirm in their speeches in the plenum and outside it that there was no divergence of views within the Politburo."[6]

Another six weeks were to elapse before Stalin, having completed his preparations, at last consented to convene the Central Committee plenum, which met April 16, ended on April 23 and became famous in Party history as the April Plenum. Five months had passed between the two plenums although, as noted earlier, the Party statutes called for a plenary meeting at least once every two months. His preparations included not only the public and collective "working over" of the Rightists at meetings of Party activists and through the press, but also the secret and individual recruiting of members of the Central Committee and the Central Control Commission, and army leaders, for his campaign against Bukharin through such means as those involved in the General's mission.

It should be noted that in the Central Committee, and even more so in the Central Control Commission, there were fairly large groups of members who had not as yet taken a stand either for Stalin or for Bukharin. The political philosophy of these groups was "live and let live." The luxury and comfort afforded their members by the new régime were taken for granted and they were only too happy to live on the proceeds of the political capital invested many years ago by the Bolshevik Old Guard. Old enthusiasms and idealisms were forgotten in the lush surroundings of Soviet state apartments, and the members of these groups were grateful to the Revolution for having realized the hopes of the most rabid among them—the right to lord it over an immense empire as members of its supreme legislative body. All else automatically followed. These men clung to power, externally so imposing, internally so valuable, by every means within their grasp, at the cost of any sacrifice, even that of their former ideals. Politically, they were a quagmire, and Stalin was past master of the art of wading through it.

The beat of the heart of this quagmire was, obviously, quickened by Bukharin, but the sobering instinct characteristic of a Party herd directed its members into Stalin's camp. When all was said and done the Red Square and the Lubyanka Prison were only one block apart, and the terrifying memory of the fate that had befallen the Trotskyites was still all too vivid.

At the April Plenum of the Central Committee it was the quagmire that came to Stalin's rescue. The Bukharinites began by openly censuring Stalin's group and its manner of dealing with the basic problems of foreign and domestic policy. This criticism, in the main, followed the line of Bukharin's statement of January 30 and the joint statement by Bukharin, Rykov, and Tomsky of February 9. Personal attacks against Stalin were toned down, particularly by Rykov, but the cutting edge of the weapon was not in the least blunted. In the course of the debate Bukharin accused Stalin of Trotskyism and apparently touched him to the quick, for his indignation was quite genuine when he exclaimed: "And this is said by Bukharin, who only a short time ago was a pupil

---

[6] *Ibid.*

of Trotsky's, who only yesterday was attempting to form a common bloc with the Trotskyites against the Leninites, and who crept in at the back door to visit them. This, Comrades, is really ridiculous!"[7]

Stalin then reported Bukharin's refusal in early February to accept the "compromise" prepared by the Politburo commission. He asked: "Why did the comrades of Bukharin's opposition—Bukharin, Rykov, and Tomsky—refuse to accept the compromise offered them by the Politburo commission on February 7 of this year? Is it not a fact that this compromise gave Bukharin's group a perfectly acceptable way out of the impasse into which it had driven itself . . . in order thus to dispel the tension within the Party and create conditions favorable to unanimous and friendly collaboration in the Politburo?"[8]

After thus sharpening the issue and citing a general observation by Lenin on opportunism, Stalin paused significantly. Apparently satisfied with this lyrical overture to his triumphal march, he proceeded to answer the question: "Yes, Comrades, we must face up to realities, no matter how painful they may be. May God shield us from being infected by fear of the truth. And, in this case, the truth resides in the fact that we have no common line of policy. On the one hand we have a revolutionary line; on the other we see a second line, the line of Bukharin's group, which fights the Party line by making statements aimed against the Party, by resignations, by slander, and by secretly undermining the Party. This second line is the line of opportunism."[9]

Throughout the meeting Stalin maintained an unexpected but shrewdly planned stoical calm in the face of attacks on the Central Committee apparatus, on his close supporters, on his real (and not merely alleged) underhand activities, even on his own person, as Secretary of the Central Committee. At the very beginning of his speech he declared: "I shall not dwell on the personal factor, although this personal factor has been heavily stressed in speeches by several comrades in Bukharin's group. I consider the personal factor trivial."[10] When Bukharin called him the Genghis Khan of the Party, Stalin replied: "This is trivial." When Bukharin asserted that Stalin had conspired against his own Party, he again replied: "This is trivial." When Bukharin declared that Stalin was a fabricator of lies, Stalin replied: "This is trivial." Stalin's aim was to show that his only wish was to defend Lenin and the Leninist Party, while Bukharin was trying to draw him off by stressing "personal factors." "They would like to substitute political chicanery for real policy but this trick will not work," he countered. This deliberate self-effacement, this absence of any attempt at self-justification, this magnanimous and even condescending treatment of "trivialities," combined with a fervent, convincing, and logically consistent defense of Lenin and Leninism against the ideological assault by Bukharin—this in itself provided Stalin with a political alibi in the eyes of the Central Committee. He needed nothing more.

---

[7] Stalin, *Voprosy leninizma*, p. 253.
[8] Stalin, *Sochineniya*, Vol. XII, 1949, pp. 6—7.
[9] *Ibid.*, p. 9.
[10] *Ibid.*, p. 1.

Stalin did not, however, limit himself to accusing Bukharin of opportunism and of being anti-Leninist in his theories. He reminded him of his "betrayal" in 1918 in connection with the Brest-Litovsk negotiations for a separate peace with Germany, when Bukharin had headed a group of so-called Left Communists opposed to the treaty. *"Bukharin has mentioned here the absence of collective leadership in the Central Committee*. I must point out that this is not the first time that Bukharin has ignored the elementary demands imposed by loyalty and collective leadership. An example is recorded in the history of the Party when, at the time of the Brest peace negotiations, Bukharin, caught in the minority, ran over to the Left Social-Revolutionaries and tried to form a joint anti-Lenin bloc with their support. What he discussed with the Left SR's at the time is, unfortunately, still unknown."[11] (The use of the words "still unknown," if correctly reported, was not accidental or merely a polemical trick; it was no doubt intended to be an ominous reminder of the fate of the Left SR's, who had all been sentenced to death and shot.)

Having disposed of Bukharin as a politician, Stalin thought the time ripe to disavow him as the theorist of the Party. He proceeded to quote from Lenin's Testament the following excerpt dealing with Bukharin: "I should like to say a few words about the younger members of the Central Committee, Bukharin and Pyatakov. In my opinion they stand out among the younger men and I should like to point out the following in connection with them: *Bukharin is not only the Party's most valuable and greatest theorist, but he is also rightly regarded as the favorite of the entire Party*. The orthodoxy of his Marxism must, however, be treated with grave suspicion, for there is something scholastic in him (he never studied and, I think, never understood dialectics)." Stalin stressed the last words and triumphantly exclaimed: "And so, Bukharin is a scholastic theorist, a theorist with no dialectics; but dialectics are the very soul of Marxism!"[12]

Stalin thus succeeded in turning the original "trial of Stalin" into a "trial of Bukharin's group." Only a few members of the Central Committee and the Central Control Commission—Uglanov, Mikhailov, Kotov, Ugarov, Rozit, Kulikov, and of the younger members, Sten from our Institute—actively supported Rykov, Bukharin, and Tomsky, while the quagmire reluctantly followed the lead of Stalin. Outside Moscow, the Party oblast and district secretaries, and the secretaries of the national republics, whose jobs were at the mercy of Stalin and his cabinet, all began clamoring, as they had done before, for the immediate expulsion of Bukharin and Tomsky from the Politburo. In answer to their demands Stalin was able to assume the pious role of peacemaker. "Some comrades," said Stalin, "are insisting on the immediate expulsion of Bukharin and Tomsky. *I disagree with these comrades*. In my opinion, *at the present time* we can dispense with so extreme a measure."[13]

---

[11] *Ibid.*, pp. 100–01. The words "still unknown" were probably inserted later to demonstrate Stalin's amazing foresight concerning Bukharin's betrayal in 1918.

[12] *Ibid.*, p. 69.

[13] *Ibid.*, p. 107.

The plenum resolved:

(1) To relieve Tomsky and Bukharin of their posts and warn them that, in the event of the slightest attempt to disobey the decisions of the Central Committee, the latter would be compelled to exclude them from membership in the Politburo.

(2) Not to make public the resolution concerning Bukharin and his group, and to disclose its contents to Party organizations only.[14]

Stalin angrily reprimanded Rykov for his infringement of the "collegiate principle" in the government leadership, and for following Bukharin's line against the accepted line of the Party, but did not demand that he be punished. He even went farther and appointed Rykov chief reporter on the Five-Year Plan at the Sixteenth Party Conference, which opened the same day.

Rykov thereupon reverted to his former lukewarm attitude, enabling Stalin to go ahead with still greater assurance. His first need was to draw the organizational consequences from his victory over Bukharin. This required the removal of potential Bukharinites from the Party and from responsible posts in the army. He ordered a "general purge of the Party," with definite instructions that it be completed by the time of the forthcoming Sixteenth Party Congress. (There were at the time 1,500,000 Party members.)

A resolution endorsing this order was correspondingly passed by the Sixteenth Party Conference after a report by Yaroslavsky. The purge was to be carried out by the apparatus of the Central Control Commission, under the direction of the Secretariat of the Central Committee. The resolution plainly stated: "The check and purge of the Party ranks to be undertaken will thus make the Party more homogeneous. . . . The purge must ruthlessly eliminate from the ranks of the Party all elements foreign to it . . . and supporters of anti-Party groups . . . without regard to rank or persons. . . ."[15]

The conference closed on April 29 and the first plenary session meeting of the Central Committee met on the same day to ratify its decisions. All were ratified unaltered save for one amendment: Uglanov was removed from the Secretariat of the Central Committee and replaced by Bauman, chief of the Rural Section of the Moscow Committee. Kubyak waded through the quagmire to Stalin's side. The entire Secretariat of the Central Committee was now firmly in Stalin's grasp.

---

[14] *VKP(b) v rezolyutsiyakh*, Vol. II, pp. 520–21.
[15] *Ibid.*, pp. 566–67.

Chapter XVII

Stalin's Attack on Bukharin as a Theorist

We in the Institute of Red Professors followed reports of proceedings at the joint plenary session of the Central Committee and the Central Control Commission with the keen interest usually reserved for communiqués about the fate of a beleaguered fortress. At first the communiqués were very reticent and often contradictory, in spite of the fact that the plenum was attended by leaders of the Moscow group–Reznikov, the General, and Sten–in addition to representatives of the Right Opposition.

Every day, according to established practice, Yudin informed us of progress. However, his information was indirect and obtained at second hand. He and other leaders of central Party institutions were daily summoned to the Agitation and Propaganda Section of the Central Committee, where they were supplied with official communiqués and commentaries intended to help them suitably to indoctrinate the Party masses. During the course of previous plenums we had obtained such communiqués at first hand from Sten, one of our own professors and a member of the Central Control Commission. But now Sten had been relieved of this "honorable burden." We eventually learned from Yudin why Sten, although a member of the Central Control Commission, was no longer allowed to share with his colleagues and students at the Institute his impressions of the work of the plenum. It transpired that Sten had subjected Stalin to detailed criticism at the plenum, and, as Yudin put it, "had endeavored to explain the philosophical basis of Right opportunism." As to what this "philosophical basis" really meant Yudin knew as little as we. We were therefore more eager than ever to hear Sten's reports on the plenum at first hand. We informed Yudin of this wish at one of our routine sessions, but, although he may have known little about Sten's philosophy he was only too well versed in the philosophy of Stalin. "If anyone," he said, "doubts the Central Committee communiqués he had better apply to the Central Committee's enemies direct. It is not my duty to act as go-between in this business."

Yudin was a fanatic and no diplomat (although later he became a diplomat!), and this fact invariably weakened his popularity among the rank and file, although on the other hand it enhanced his prestige in top circles. His unguarded answer quoted above gave rise to an argument which, I am sure, was not entered on the agenda. It began when Belov, the chairman of my group, an old Party member and commander in the Red Army (even in the Institute he appeared in uniform, with a regimental commander's badge of rank on his collar) asked Yudin quite seriously: "Then in your opinion Comrade Sten is an enemy of the Party?"

"I said enemy of the Central Committee."

"But I understood you to say that he was an enemy of Stalin, not the Central Committee."

"That is one and the same thing!"

"It therefore follows that the Central Committee is Stalin?"

"That is quite correct."

"But, in that case, the Party is also Stalin?"

"That, too, is quite correct."

"In which case I must remark that Sten is not the only enemy of the Party," concluded Belov.

Yudin did not argue the point any farther, but there were loud calls of approval from the hall. Gathering up his papers and making for the door, he said: "I declare the information session closed." His exit was followed by shouts and questions and he was surrounded on all sides, but somehow evaded envelopment and safely made his escape.

"He is playing at Stalin," somebody remarked.

"Yudin is the Party," said Belov, making his point even clearer.

Yudin's information sessions took place every evening, but we gleaned from them very little real information on the work of the plenum. The last-year students hardly ever took the trouble to be present, as they probably had better sources of information than Yudin. Sorokin, too, was never to be seen, although he had been granted a couple of visitors tickets for admission to the plenum. The scantier the information the greater became our curiosity. That Stalin's apparatus in the Central Committee would mislead the Communists through such underlings as Yudin was clearly understood by all of us whether friends or foes of the apparatus. But why the Rightist members of the Central Committee should conceal from their friends the facts of the beating to which they were being subjected at the plenum was quite incomprehensible.

A month after the closing of the plenum, the stenographic report solved the riddle. (Shorthand reports of Central Committee plenums were supplied in one copy to the Party organizations of the Institute and were consequently read to, or by, groups of professors and students of the various departments of the Institute.) At the very beginning of the meeting Stalin had succeeded in pushing through an extraordinary resolution, to the effect that "special measures will be adopted providing for secrecy of the resolutions passed by the Central Committee and Politburo and the prevention of leakage of information to the Trotskyites on matters concerning the Politburo and Central Committee, under penalty of exclusion from the Central Committee and the Party."[1] The purpose of this resolution was obvious: to prevent any member of the plenum, even a member of the Politburo, from divulging to the Party matters concerning internal Party politics, unless specially authorized by the Agitation and Propaganda Section of the Central Committee. It was for this reason that Yudin, the secretary of the

---

[1] *VKP(b) v rezolutsiyakh*, Vol. II, p. 521.

Institute Party cell, was allowed to report to the Communists while Sten, a member of the Central Control Commission and Bukharin, a member of the Politburo, were reduced to silence.

The stenographic report also provided us with the meaning of Sten's "philosophy of Right opportunism." Sten had chosen an original way of "philosophizing." By making use of everything that Stalin had written and said about the Trotskyites during his struggle with Trotsky, and taking that as his premise, Sten argued that Stalin's actual policy, aimed at super-industrialization by robbing the peasants like any feudal war-lord, contained nothing original and peculiar to Stalin; that it was, in fact, "a second amended and amplified edition of Trotskyism," by Stalin. All the amendments and amplifications could be reduced to one thing: the declaration of open civil war in the countryside, while slandering Trotsky and distorting Lenin. He further contended that, if the Central Committee followed the path traced by Stalin, a Soviet Pugachev would succeed in wringing all our necks and drowning the Russian Revolution in the blood of a peasant Vendée. Stalin's primitive knowledge of theory, said Sten, prevented him from seeing the wood for the trees, the wood which was the great, peasant Russia. The Russian Revolution had been saved by the peasants; the peasants were in the last analysis equally capable of wrecking it. If the Party had no desire to prepare its own funeral, Stalin and his supporters should be told: "Back to the NEP!" As regards the peasants this would entail abrogation of the extraordinary measures then in force to ensure grain deliveries, revision of the policy of excessive taxation, freedom for cooperation, raising of grain prices and guaranteed supplying of the rural market with industrial goods at normal prices. Such a policy, he declared, would lead along the pathway to winning the support of the peasants through the Soviet ruble. Admittedly it was a long and arduous pathway, but it was the pathway of Lenin. There was, of course, another pathway, short and tempting: the pathway of the police, subjection of the peasants by the bayonets of the OGPU forces. The first pathway had been bequeathed to us by Lenin. Stalin was marching down the second. In that case we could not journey together.

At this point, according to the stenographic report, someone shouted: "You are fellow travellers of Kamenev!" "Stalin and Molotov have been fellow travellers of Kamenev all their lives," answered Sten, hinting at their activities in the Duma bloc of the Bolshevik Social Democrats and in *Pravda*, where Molotov had been secretary of the editorial office and Stalin assistent editor while Kamenev was editor.

Throughout Sten's speech he was subjected to similar interruptions by supporters of Stalin who had rehearsed their parts in advance. From the report it was difficult to judge of the effect which Sten's speech had produced on the plenum, but we in the Institute were tremendously impressed. For sheer biting power it was undoubtedly the most telling speech delivered, next to those of Bukharin and Uglanov.

The statement by Tomsky was cruder and more forthright, but followed the same line of argument. Rykov, on the other hand, dwelt mainly on practical questions of economic policy and barely touched on the subject of "pure politics." We were therefore not in the least surprised when we heard that Rykov had been appointed to report on the Five-Year Plan at the Sixteenth Party Conference at the suggestion of Stalin and over the objections of his own friends.

Sten also argued vigorously with Stalin at the plenum when Stalin was losing his way in the jungle of theory. A couple of these exchanges, much mutilated and consequently rather unintelligible, have found their way into Stalin's work. The question at issue concerned an article by Bukharin published in 1916 in the Comintern journal *Youth International* in which he stated that Social Democracy must stress its basic hostility to the state. Lenin's reply in another article criticized this view by arguing that the theory of hostility to the state, the theory of the blowing-up of the State, was not a Marxist theory, but an Anarchist theory. The Marxists, he said, while believing in the existence of two kinds of state, a "bourgeois" and a "proletarian," maintained that the Social Democrats should treat the latter as their own; that a state of this kind under a "dictatorship of the proletariat" did not, of necessity, have to be blown up but would gradually die away of itself, as Engels had said in his *Anti-Düring*. Referring to these polemics between Lenin and Bukharin, Stalin concluded: "The essence of the matter is fairly clear, as is also the semi-anarchical mess in which Comrade Bukharin has landed."

Sten: "At that time Lenin had not yet definitely formulated the inevitable necessity of blowing up the state, and Bukharin, although guilty of making a few Anarchist errors, was really trying to define the problem."

Stalin: "No, that is not the point; the point at issue is the broad approach to the problem of the state, and the fact that, in Bukharin's opinion, the working class must, as a matter of principle, regard itself as the enemy of any state, including a state of the working class."

Sten: "Lenin at that time only mentioned in general terms the manner in which a state could be exploited, and said nothing at all about Bukharin's criticism of the theory of a 'blowing up.'"

Stalin: "You are wrong; this theory is an anarchist formula, not Marxist. Allow me to assure you that it was precisely Bukharin's intention to make it clear that in his opinion (and in the opinion of the Anarchists), the workers should at all times emphasize their hostility to any form of state and consequently to the state of the transitional period, i.e., to the working class."[2]

In brief, what Stalin was saying was that Bukharin was opposed to the dictatorship of the proletariat. The facts in the case were, of course, quite the opposite. There is incontrovertible documentary evidence that the 1919 Party program on the subject of the dictatorship of the proletariat had been jointly drawn up by Bukharin and Lenin and that it was Bukharin who, with the assistance of Lenin, formulated the theory of the "blowing-up" of the bourgeois state.

Infuriated by Sten's exposure of his distortion of Lenin, Stalin resorted to his old trick of putting up a smoke screen so dense that both he and his opponent

---

[2] Stalin, *Sochineniya*, Vol. XII, 1949, p. 72.

were hidden from view. He began to quote Lenin at length, but his ill-chosen quotations merely strengthened Bukharin's position.[3] He then resorted to quoting Bukharin, with the obvious intention of proving to the plenum that Bukharin considered himself a better theorist than Lenin. Pursuing his argument with Sten, but turning to the plenum, Stalin said: "You probably think I am not speaking the truth, Comrades. In which case please listen to this." He then proceeded to quote a footnote by Bukharin to his article in *Youth International* which had been reprinted after the Revolution in a collection entitled *Revolyutsiya prava* (The Revolution of the Law). In this note Bukharin had said: "Lenin has adversely criticized my article in *Youth International*. It is easy to see that I am not to blame for the errors of which I am accused, as I plainly foresaw the necessity for the dictatorship of the proletariat; on the other hand, from what Ilyich says, it is obvious that at that time his views on the blowing-up of the state (bourgeois of course), were incorrect, for he did not distinguish between this problem and that of the gradual decay of the dictatorship of the proletariat. . . ."

"When I returned from America to Russia I met Nadezhda Konstantinovna [Lenin's wife] at our secret Sixth Congress when Lenin was in hiding, and her very first words were 'Vladimir Ilyich has asked me to tell you that he no longer disagrees with you on the question of the state.' Apparently, after studying the problem, Ilyich had reached the same conclusions as I on the subject of the 'blowing-up,' but had broadened it and further elaborated the doctrine of dictatorship to the point where his thinking marked an era in the development of theoretical thought in this direction."[4]

Here Stalin sarcastically remarked: "Up to the present we have always thought of ourselves as Leninists; it would, however, appear that both Lenin and we pupils of his are disciples of Bukharin. . . ."[5]

The discussion closed with these groundless accusations that Bukharin regarded himself as superior to Lenin.

[3] *Ibid.*, Vol. XII, pp. 74–76.
[4] *Ibid.*, p. 77.
[5] *Ibid.*, p. 78.

Chapter XVIII

The Aftermath of the April Plenum

The Sixteenth Party Conference and the April Plenum of the Central Committee had ended in complete victory for Stalin and his supporters in the Politburo and in the Stalinist apparatus in the Central Committee. Nine tenths of this victory was a personal victory for Stalin. Until this time it had been the generally accepted opinion that Stalin was far from being one of the outstanding leaders of the Bolshevik Party, and was a mediocre politician. At best he was credited with being a good executor of the will of others. Trotsky spoke of him in these terms, and even the circumstances surrounding Lenin's death did little to unravel the mystery surrounding the sphynx-like Stalin. His personal victory at the April Plenum made him a recognized figure of major importance.

Much of Stalin's success resulted from his "specifically new" attitude to politics. Politics, tactics, and strategy were interpreted by the Stalinists in a manner peculiarly their own. They considered their party as a party of an original and novel kind. Complete abandonment of the old accepted forms of policy-making was an indispensible attribute for anyone who wished to make his way boldly through the sombre labyrinths of the new system. The fact that Stalin was familiar only at second hand with the basic principles of former Party policy was one of his major assets, as he was freed of "the childish disease" of naiveté in politics, and of all the accepted moral and ethical conventions of the political game.

In connection with the "new policy" as well as the "new Party," Stalin refused to recognize either the romantic influence of historic memories, or the laws of historical succession. Though he accused Trotsky of harboring what were in reality his own plans for the future (a maneuver to which he often had recourse on other occasions and for different reasons) and charged that Trotsky wished to dethrone Old Bolshevism by striking Lenin from history for his own self-aggrandizement, he was himself devoid of all respect or reverence for Lenin. In applying the "new policy," Stalin always steered toward all that was "newest." The following remark in this connection is typical: "It is quite likely that the upholders of respect due to rank will not approve of this manner of acting. What business is that of mine? I am not a great lover of bowing to rank."[1] This, too, explains why Stalin recognized the Old Bolsheviks only to the extent that they were capable of becoming "new." "If we are called Old Bolsheviks just because we are old," he said at the April Plenum, "the outlook is bad, Comrades. Respect is rendered to the Old Bolsheviks not because they are old in years, but because of their ability to remain forever new.[2]

---

[1] Stalin, *Sochineniya*, Vol. XII, 1949, p. 114.

[2] *Ibid.*, pp. 1–2.

It was also to Stalin's advantage that, as Trotsky pointed out, he was no great theorist and was quite ignorant of Marxism, for he was thus unburdened by the dogmatic fetters of Marxist orthodoxy. "There is dogmatic Marxism and creative Marxism: I stand by the latter," Stalin had said at the Sixth Party Congress on the eve of the October Revolution. Stalin became acclaimed as a "master of theory" only after he had risen to power. In his early years he was fully aware of his limitations and had no ambitions in this respect. On occasions when his innumerable admirers turned to him for pronouncements on questions of Marxist theory, philosophy, political economy, language, literature, and art, he unabashedly confessed to his incompetence in matters of theory and Marxist criticism. A few early confessions are contained in his published works; in a letter to the author Bezymensky he wrote: "I am no literary expert and, of course, no critic."[3] In another letter, to Maxim Gorky, he was even more outspoken: "I cannot grant Kamegulov's request. No time! Besides, devil take it, what kind of a critic am I?"[4] Paradoxical as it may appear, this particular weakness enhanced Stalin's strength as a "politician of the new type." He did not rack his brain trying to solve the obtuse intricacies of the "scientific socialism" of the future but stood with both feet firmly planted on the ground. Brought down to this level, socialism was not an end in itself, but a means to an end—to power at the price of any methods, at all costs.

There was also another basic difference between Stalin and Lenin. Lenin rose to power as a result of a struggle with classes hostile to the Party; Stalin first endeavored, and eventually succeeded, in seizing power in a fight with his own Party. But Lenin had taught, and Stalin agreed, that the seizure of power was only half the battle; the important and most difficult task was to hold it after it was won. For Lenin there existed but a single way of successfully solving the problem—the political isolation and subsequent physical destruction of the hostile classes. Stalin applied Lenin's teaching to his own Party. He knew that the actual seizure of power could be attained with comparative ease, but he also realized that in order to maintain himself in power he would have to follow Lenin's principle by politically isolating and bodily destroying political foes and hostile groups in the Bolshevik Party.

The April Plenum marked the dividing line between two campaigns. Prior to the plenum Stalin had been mainly engaged in the seizure of power. At the April Plenum he was beginning his campaign to hold power by the "political isolation" of his enemies with an eye to their subsequent removal when his new regime of personal dictatorship was definitely consolidated. It may be contended that Lenin would have acted in the same way if he had been forced to deal with numerous enemies inside the Party. Addressing himself to Tomsky in the discussion in the plenum, Stalin admitted as much and added that he, Stalin, and his followers in the Central Committee were more liberal than Lenin. "You all remember," he said, "how Lenin drove Tomsky into the wastes of Turkestan over some paltry

---

[3] *Ibid.*, Vol. XII, p. 200.
[4] *Ibid.*, p. 177.

trifle!" And to Tomsky's retort: "Yes! Thanks to Zinoviev's intrigues, and not without your kind help," Stalin replied: "You are wrong if you think it was so easy to convince Lenin of something of which he was not already convinced."[5]

Finally, in Stalin's dialectics, at least during the first years of his struggle with the opposition, terror was not the decisive factor. In all his actions he was guided by a profound understanding of the mentality of a radically new Party elite, straining every nerve to dash onto the political stage.

The practical consequences of the April Plenum began to appear immediately.

Signs of unrest among the Rightists became manifest at the Institute as soon as it became known that Bukharin had been removed from *Pravda*, and Tomsky relieved of his post as chairman of the Central Trade Union Council. Many who but recently had been upholding the justice of the Rightist cause or had been diplomatically waiting to see how events would develop were now vociferously proclaiming the legal soundness of the general line of the Party and its Secretary-General. The job hunters with their extraordinary flair for interpreting the fluctuations of the Party barometer, the camp followers with their amazing gift of adaptability, and the gamblers, those talented jobbers of the Party exchange, all moved into the fray, forsaking conscience, honor, and common decency in order to stake their claims under the rising sun of Stalin. The passions of these gentry were further kindled by the announcement of a forthcoming general reexamination of loyalties, not only in the Party but also in the multiple branches of the state apparatus, including the government, the trade unions, and the army. In the April Plenum, Stalin had heated the iron to melting point and made it fit for forging. His henchmen in the Party now set busily to work.

When, a few days after the Sixteenth Party Conference and the April Plenum, Kaganovich, the Secretary of the Central Committee, delivered a report to the Party theorists and propagandists in the Communist Academy, the atmosphere in the hall was totally different from that of the previous December, while Kaganovich himself was at less pains to contradict the theories of the Rightists. The Rightists, he said, had been politically buried at the Party plenum. If mentioned at all they should be referred to as dead. But not in the sense of the old-fashioned, opportunist saying, that one should say nothing but good of the dead, because such an attitude was quite out of place. On the contrary, if the dead were evil, they should be spoken of evilly. If he was going to speak of them, it was in order to use them as a warning to the hidden enemies of the Party whose spokesman was Bukharin. To them, said Kaganovich, we say: "Your tricks have failed, are failing, and will always fail. The Party will always sweep you out with an iron broom. And those of you who want to hide behind the scenes in the hope of better times, while the Party is waging a fierce battle for the building of socialism in our country, are making a great mistake. We will seize you by the scruff of the neck, drag you up to the fire and give you the choice between going into battle for the cause of the Party, or being thrown out of the Leninist Party."

---

[5] *Ibid.*, Vol. XI, p. 324.

"The Party," he continued, "has learned to read its members' minds by their deeds. Those who cherish the hope of deceiving the Party will be bitterly disappointed; when in the bitterness of their frustration they look for solid ground on which to stand, they will not find it; they will be at the bottom of the Trotskyite–White Guard pit, where there is plenty of room for officials of all kinds."

The challenging, threatening, and victorious note struck by the speech was less an exhibition of strength based on past victory than a finger pointing to the dawn of a new era in the history of Bolshevism. Of this new era Kaganovich said to his deathly silent and servilely tense audience: "Our Party is now stronger than ever before. It is strong because after the death of Lenin, and the test of tremendous upheavals and cruel tribulations, it has at last found a true, strong-minded, and courageous leader. This leader is Comrade Stalin!"

These last words were uttered with such enthusiam that the strain of the meeting was broken. A storm of applause broke out in the hall, where only a few months before the same listeners had tempestously applauded the mere appearance of Bukharin and had insolently wrecked Kaganovich's meeting. He was now taking sweet revenge.

Kaganovich's speech was long and convincing. He spoke in terms of political clichés when he sought for applause; he was formal when he asserted the greatness of Stalin; he was imperative when he identified the Party with Stalin.

In a sense Kaganovich was delivering an Order No. 1 for the Theoretical Front: "For the Cult of Stalin!" For the cult of Stalin in the Party, for the cult of Stalin in politics, for the cult of Stalin in history, for the cult of Stalin throughout the country. He did not, of course, use these words, but such was his meaning. Up to the present, he asserted, it had been customary to speak of the "collective leadership" of the Party, of the "Leninist Central Committee," of the "Party leaders," of the "disciples and companions-in-arms of Lenin." Now a new formula was in process of birth: "The leader of our Party, Comrade Stalin." This was final, there were no other "leaders of our Party!" (Other formulas, it might be noted, would be born, though much later, when the Party would no longer be called the "Leninist Party" but "The Party of Lenin-Stalin," when the "disciples and companions-in-arms of Lenin" would be the "disciples and companions-in-arms of Stalin," and the "disciples of Marx-Engels-Lenin" the "disciples of Marx-Engels-Lenin-Stalin," until finally the stage would be reached when Lenin was merely "great," while Stalin was "the greatest.")

The "greatness" of Stalin was first "discovered" by three members of the Central Committee—Kaganovich, Molotov, and Voroshilov—and three men of the ideological front—Mekhlis, Yudin, and Mitin. It was these last three who picked up the order to Science to exalt Stalin which Kaganovich had just issued.

"Up to the present," said Mekhlis, the first speaker in the discussion, "it has been usual in broad circles of the Party to consider Bukharin responsible for unmasking the theory and philosophy of Trotskyism; we must state quite frankly that this is only a myth invented by the Bukharinites. After Lenin, the chief and only theorist of our Party has always been and still is Comrade Stalin. The Party is indebted to Stalin, and to Stalin alone, for destroying the theoretical strongholds of Trotskyism. The eclectic and pedantic Bukharin could never have shouldered this task; he never even attempted to do so. The theoretical vigor and Marxist depth of Stalin's analysis can only be compared with the genius of Lenin. In order to unmask the spurious legend of Bukharin as a theorist, we must inform the entire Party that it now possesses a brilliant theorist in Comrade Stalin. We are all aware of Comrade Stalin's exceptional modesty in anything touching himself personally or his service to the Party. We also know of Comrade Stalin's aversion to all forms of self-advertisement and his dislike of being advertised by others. Therefore we Bolsheviks have no intention of doing so in order to herald the birth of a new false legend. What we wish to do is to call the attention of the Party to the immensely important historical fact, so carefully concealed by the Bukharinites, that in the field of theory Lenin's one and only successor is Stalin! The Party must at last be made alive to this truth, even if, in order to do this, we are forced to disregard Stalin's simplicity and modesty, for he belongs as much to the Party as the Party belongs to him."

Such, then, was Mekhlis' description of Stalin as a theorist—the same Stalin who only two years before had been unanimously blackballed as a candidate member of the Communist Academy "because of lack of specialized research in the realm of Marxism." (It can be readily understood that the new deputy editor-in-chief of *Pravda* did not long remain in this secondary capacity, but was soon to be promoted by the "modest Stalin" to the post of editor-in-chief!)

Yudin and Mitin suggested in their speeches an elaborate "publishing plan" for workers on the "theoretical front." Under this plan, new philosophical works on the subject of "The Importance of Lenin and Stalin in Raising Marxism to Its Present High Level" were to be prepared and published.

The dam was breached. Economists—Leontiev, Ostrovityanov, Varga, Laptev, and others—addressed the meeting to prove that it was Stalin who had evolved the principles of "the political economy of socialism." Historians—Mints, Pankratova, Kin, Knorin, and others—found in Stalin's works the key to the proper understanding of the evolutionary process of mankind. Philosophers—Mitin, Yudin, Raltsevich, Rozental, Konstantinov, and others—were amazed at the "depth and universality of Stalin's dialectical method." Where Kaganovich, by explaining the real meaning of the upheaval in the Central Committee, had promoted Stalin to virtual leadership of the Party, the members of the Communist Academy had in retrospect now turned him into a sinless and omnipresent academic god!

The meeting lasted well into the night. Of some two dozen speakers, not one uttered so much as a word of criticism or asked an insidious question. All expressed the opinion that the "theoretical front" was not facing up to the demands of the Party in this "reconstruction period" and that, because of the deliberate distortion of Marxism-Leninism by Bukharin and his school, the attention of the "theoretical front" had been diverted from the concrete problems involved in laying "the foundations of socialism in our country." The meeting approved a resolution providing for reorganization of the work of the Communist Academy and revision of the curriculum of the research institutes and higher schools of social studies along the lines of Kaganovich's speech and the decisions of the April Plenum. The plan presented by Mekhlis, Yudin, and Mitin for taking preliminary steps toward the publication of theoretical works on the manner in which Lenin and Stalin had raised to the highest level the teaching of Marx and Engels on Communism and the proletarian revolution was also approved.

This seeming unanimity by no means meant that no ideological Bukharinites were present at the meeting, but it did indicate that they had been reduced to hopeless silence. When at the close of the meeting it was moved that a message of greetings be sent to the Secretary-General of the Central Committee of the Soviet Union, Comrade Stalin, someone shouted: "I move that greetings also be sent to the Chairman of the Council of People's Commissars, Comrade Rykov." The presiding officer, Yaroslavsky, replied cooly: "You are too late, I declare the meeting closed."

And for Rykov, it was really too late; we had just witnessed his burial, although nominally he continued to hold his post as head of the government.

Chapter XIX

The Podolsk Conference

I spent the May Day holiday with Sorokin. Later on, at the end of May, we decided to visit a friend of his who lived somewhere outside Moscow. Sorokin, to arouse my curiosity, did not tell me where we were going and whom we would see, and I retaliated by not asking him.

I had thought that the victory of the Stalinists in the Central Committee, the ignominious capitulation of the Communist Academy to Kaganovich, the dispersion and disheartenment of the Bukharin school in the Institute of Red Professors, the complete triumph of people like Mekhlis and Yudin on the "theoretical front," would finish off Sorokin as well.

But never had I seen him so assured as in those days of the victorious advance of the members of the Party apparatus, the so-called apparatchiks, of the rapid reorientation of those best able to adapt themselves to the changed circumstances, of the greedy rush of the Party careerists.

My first question after the stirring events of the past months was: "How are things now, Ivan Ivanovich?"

"They could hardly be better."

"Come now, Ivan Ivanovich," I said, genuinely puzzled, "we are in a terrible mess." Sorokin looked surprised and gazed at me with his shrewd eyes as if I were about to tell him news of a catastrophe of which he was quite unaware.

"Our people are being defeated everywhere," I explained. Sorokin laughed his familiar laugh, so that for a moment I thought that it was possible that our people were not being defeated and that our people were not our people. But when Sorokin asked: "Whom do you call our people?" I immediately answered, "Kaganovich and Yudin, of course." Sorokin looked sour, as if I had pronounced the names not of persons whom he knew but of something unclean. Then, walking up and down the room, his hands behind his back, he began to talk as if to himself. "Politics, like nature, does not permit a vacuum. There is a gaping void at the top level of the Party. Stalin is compelled to fill it with pseudo-entities, persons like Kaganovich and Yudin, while subjecting everything that is idealistic to the control of his apparatus. I have heard of the speeches made by Kaganovich and the others at the Communist Academy. I have heard how Stalin became a great leader and a wise theorist but the tragedy is that neither Kaganovich nor Mekhlis believe in the slightest in what they themselves say about Stalin when they praise him to the skies. People like Yudin are simply fools with pretensions to scholarship, as politicians they are merely parrots, and as scholars past masters at comparing quotations from Marx with quotations from Lenin. Do not expect from them a single original idea or a single live expression, even when they talk about Stalin. These people have been created to think in quotations and to speak in clichés."

"Is that how you look at the results of the plenum?" I asked impatiently.

"Wait a moment, that is what I was going to talk about. Kaganovich's threat to destroy the old revolutionaries, and the wholesale purge of the Party that has just been announced, bring us nearer to the ultimate end."

"The end has already come."

"That is not true."

"How do you mean not true, if Bukharin and Tomsky have been kicked out of their jobs, and Rykov has been disarmed?"

"Rykov will also be kicked out, but do not forget that the Central Committee is under the hard control of someone who is stronger than all the Kaganovichs taken together, and that someone is the Russian peasant. He cannot be kicked out, either by Kaganovich's purge or Yudin's quotations or Stalin's wisdom. The April Plenum passed a resolution which would put him back into serfdom. This is the historical significance of the plenum. But will they succeed? Perhaps not, if we get to the Sixteenth Congress."

"And what if we do not get there?" I asked.

"Then the return to serfdom will cause the destruction of the Soviet régime and the ideas of socialism will be discredited in Russia forever and ever."

Sorokin believed that the Right had not been finally defeated. He admired the bold and consistent line taken by Bukharin and Tomsky in the plenum. He was pleased, too, with Uglanov and Kotov, while his comment on Sten was short—"an intelligent man"—an expression which for him was the highest praise. The condition on which the Rightists were to be left at their posts was that they should accept the "general line." Only Rykov had partially done so. The Stalinists had, therefore, left him in office but only conditionally. On the other hand, in spite of all preliminary preparations and the many "local demands," the Stalinists and Stalin did not dare to expel the Rightists from the Politburo and the Central Committee.

"Besides," said Sorokin, "immediately after the plenum Stalin went to see Rykov and spent the night drinking vodka with him and talking of his friendship for him and his love for Bukharin. Victors do not act like this. But if Stalin imagines himself to be a knight in shining armor, there is every reason to fear some fresh villainy from him. His ability to disguise such villainy as friendly devotion and human decency amounts to genius. If our friends do not see through this duplicity of Stalin and the Stalinists, the end will come."

"To spend twenty years with Stalin in an illegal Party, to be with him during the decisive days of the Revolution, to sit at the same table in the Politburo for ten years after the Revolution and still fail to know Stalin is really the end," I said.

Sorokin obviously brightened up. I saw that he was pleased by the way in which I had deliberately sharpened and exaggerated the problem of the end. He only wanted me to be consistent and was forcing me to be consistent. Questions followed in rapid succession. Whenever I sounded a false note, he caught me up immediately. "You are being a parrot, you are repeating other people's words, you say this but you do not believe it."

Under his taunts I was losing my temper. Suddenly he stopped, turned toward me, and asked sharply: "Do you believe that Stalin is a villain?"

"After what the General told us, I have never doubted it."

"Well then, remember: all else being equal, only villains succeed in politics."

"In that case, the end has already come," I concluded.

"This is where you are wrong, the end has not come. Stalin is approaching it by stealth, but he can be forestalled in true Stalinist fashion, that is, his villainy can be met with villainy and, besides, he can be forestalled prophylactically too, by using the surgeon's knife."

As he uttered these words, Sorokin looked at me questioningly. I did not answer, but the words "surgeon's knife" remained engraved on my memory. Sorokin paused, as if giving me time to digest what he had said.

"A coup d'état is not a counterrevolution," explained Sorokin. "It is merely an attempt to rid the Party of its own villainy at one stroke. There is no need even to have the garrison troops of a Bonaparte in the capital. All that is needed is the dagger of a Soviet Brutus and a few words about the deceased before a crowd of indignant fanatics."

Sorokin paused again, longer this time. I still kept silent, but my silence was so eloquent that it betrayed me completely.

"Why did you turn pale, as if you had just murdered Stalin?" he asked, jerking my shoulder.

I made no answer. Sorokin continued: "Every friend is a potential Brutus, but to become a Brutus in Roman style you must forget your past, hate your present, and renounce your future in the name of your personal Rome. No country is as rich in Brutuses of this kind as ours. But they must be aroused. The Roman Brutus ruined Rome; ours will save it. And this will constitute the immortal greatness of the potential Soviet Brutus."

Sorokin developed this theme further and deeper, thinking up counter-arguments and relentlessly rejecting them. I felt that as usual he was trying to convince himself rather than me.

The thought of a palace revolution directed against Stalin was not in itself new, particularly among young people. But the leaders of the Right were reso-lutely against it. I remember on another occasion being present at a meeting of a number of the persons to whom Stalin referred as "undisarmed opportunists," that is, potential opponents not yet rendered harmless. The meeting, held in Sorokin's apartment, took place on the eve of the Sixteenth Party Congress. Buk-harin was among those present. He was in a gay mood and cracked jokes with everyone, as if it were Stalin and not he who was to be buried at the congress. The idyll was broken by an unpleasant question.

"Nikolai Ivanovich, life has confirmed your gloomiest predictions in every sphere of domestic politics, and the peasants, driven to despair, have voted for you with their blood. Do you really, in spite of all this, intend to vote for Stalin at the Sixteenth Congress?"

Bukharin's forced gaiety, his feigned composure, and his mask of political indifference suddenly deserted him. He had probably been asked this question many times in the course of the last few months. It was equally probable that he had found no satisfactory answer. He was like a general who after brilliantly winning a battle in the field, has offered to capitulate because he was unaware of his own victory.

"Attacks against Stalinists directed from above have not been successful. The Party line can only be straightened out from below," was all Bukharin could say.

"But the whole point is that there is no Party, but only the apparatus, before which the Party cards of the rank and file and the peasants' pitchforks in the villages are equally powerless," put in Sorokin.

"What is your conclusion?" asked Bukharin.

"Surgery!" replied Sorokin.

A tense silence followed—one of those moments of silence which can decently be broken only by a powerful argument. But even Bukharin failed to find such an argument. We continued to look at each other in silence. Bukharin felt that he had to answer.

"A knife in the hands of a careless surgeon can destroy the life of a young organism together with the ulcer it is trying to remove," he said at last.

Sorokin immediately rejected this argument. "If the ulcer is mortal," he said, "such an operation can only be an act of mercy for the organism itself."

Again there was silence. And again it was Bukharin himself who had to break it. This time he tried an indirect approach.

"In our Revolution," said Bukharin, "a distinction must be drawn between two of its facets: its transient form represented by the government at the summit and its permanent content represented by its social structure. The ideals of socialism and social justice, in whose name we made the Revolution, cannot be sacrificed to a struggle between groups at the Party summit. A first-class automobile may be badly driven by an inefficient driver, but this is no indication that the automobile is defective. It is absurd to smash the automobile merely to remove the driver." Bukharin lectured to us in this vein for nearly an hour. It was clear that although he had no intention of capitulating to Stalin at the Sixteenth Party Congress, he had no thought of resuming his attacks upon the driver.

The struggle within the Party had now reached such a pitch that the opposition had no resource left but an appeal to the people, while the people were against the entire social system. I gained the impression that Bukharin feared the people no less than did Stalin. The ideological teacher of the Soviet peasants with his cautious motto "Get rich!" appeared to fear that the peasants might force him to become the leader of a peasant rebellion, a second Pugachev. Neither Bukharin nor his friends were capable of leading such a rebellion.

To return to my May Day trip with Sorokin, we left Moscow fairly late, reached our place of destination—Podolsk—within an hour, and went to the apartment which had been prepared for us. We were received by an elderly man, tall, thin, and dark, an intellectual, with an Ukrainian accent and a German name. Later I discovered that he was an old railway man, a member of the board of the People's Commissariat of Ways of Communication. There we also met the General. That night Sorokin went off somewhere with the General and the railway man, and I retired to bed. When I was called for breakfast in the morning I found a number of persons already assembled, including some of our Moscow friends. One of them had a birthday and they had come together to celebrate it as well as the 20th or 25th anniversary of membership in the Bolshevik Party by a man whose name was Viktor. Viktor was a fairly well-known member of the Party and of the Central Committee. He had been invited to Podolsk for the celebration because it was there that he had begun his revolutionary career. But the celebration was merely an official excuse for a conference of several Moscow groups supporting or connected with the Rightist leaders. The meeting dealt with the results of the Central Committee plenum and of the Sixteenth Party Conference, as well as with the tasks facing the opposition in connection with the forthcoming Sixteenth Party Congress. The main speaker was Viktor himself, who had taken part in the plenum and in the Sixteenth Party Conference. I had never seen him before, but I had often heard his name and knew that he occupied an important position in the government hierarchy. He spoke very little of what had occurred at the plenum, but described in some detail the whole backstage struggle of the Soviet apparatus and the Central Control Commission against the Rightist elements.

"After what has taken place," said Viktor, "we are faced with a dilemma: either we surrender and throw ourselves on the mercy of Stalin and his group and in that case we bear the same responsibility as he for the foundering of the Revolution; or we go over from empty catchwords to more active forms of struggle in which case there is a good possibility of saving the Revolution and the country. If we are able to inform the Party and the people of our program, over the heads of the apparatus, our efforts will be crowned with complete success. To the possible objection," he continued, "that by choosing the second alternative we run the risk of being politically and probably physically isolated as was the case with the Trotskyites, I repeat: we would be isolated even if we chose the first alternative, that of capitulation. It is merely a matter of time. Whoever says the opposite knows nothing of the experience of history or of the logic of political struggle or, of course, of Stalin's character. But it is better to perish consciously fighting for a just cause than to commit suicide after a miserable capitulation. Each of you here must decide for himself how he will solve this dilemma, in full knowledge of the risk he is running. Oh, yes, we stand a good chance, but there is also a great risk of losing. But at least anyone who is capable of staking his own life on the chance of victory avoids one risk—that of losing his honor as a revolutionary."

Victor's words were convincing and stirring, perhaps as they had been at the time when he was risking his life at the hands of another kind of police, that of the tsar. His reputation as a fearless revolutionary of the past gave weight to his every word. The discussion was earnest and to the point. Two questions had to be solved: should the struggle against the Stalinist wing in the Party be continued and if so, then how and with what means. To the first question there was only one answer: the struggle must be continued. Opinions regarding the second question differed widely, reflecting the contradictions existing among the leaders of the opposition on this question. These included the activists, the supporters of decisive action—Bukharin, Tomsky, Uglanov, Rozit, Mikhailovsky, and others— and the pacifists, supporters of "waiting inaction," as Trotsky would have expressed it—Rykov, Kotov, Kulikov, Ukhanov, Yenukidze, and their friends. Viktor belonged to the activists, as did Sorokin, the General, and, to a certain extent, Reznikov. Zinaida Nikolayevna wavered, while the Commissar was both a pacifist and an opportunist.

The first to voice his opinion was the General. He supported Viktor's views on the necessity of going over to active forms of opposition and asked him to make practical suggestions. Two or three others spoke in the same vein. The pacifists waited to hear the practical suggestions. Sorokin proposed the following plan of action:

(1) Preparation of a detailed program of Opposition demands for submission to the Party Congress.

(2) Appointment of an organizational committee to call an extraordinary congress to which the delegates would be elected by direct and secret ballot.

(3) Establishing as the aim of the Congress not the adoption of resolutions but the election of an inner-Party Center to conduct the Party referendum on the program of the Opposition and the policy of the Stalinists.

Sorokin pointed out that his plan did not infringe the Party statutes but was in direct accordance with them in providing for the appointment of an organizational committee alongside the Central Committee, for the purpose of summoning an extraordinary congress in case the Central Committee should refuse to summon one or if there was no clear majority within the Central Committee itself, or if the Central Committee considered it necessary to consult the Party on the correctness of its policy.

"If Stalin rejects your plan, and he certainly will, what should be done then?" asked somebody.

"Then we must summon it over Stalin's head," answered Sorokin.

Viktor nodded approvingly. "Right," interjected the General, and the stranger who had asked the question—obviously a pacifist—made a sour face.

Reznikov supported the plan in general on condition that it be accepted by all the leaders of the Opposition.

The last to speak was the one who had questioned Sorokin. He considered that the time for action was not suitable. He argued that Stalin would break his own neck without any effort on our part, and that he would do it when he made his second attempt to put into practice his plan of enforced collectivization. Therefore, while criticizing Stalin's policy within the framework of "legality," it was essential to wait for events to ripen. As was to be expected, the Commissar supported him.

Viktor summed up the results of the conference as recognizing the necessity for action and gave his unreserved support to Sorokin's plan, of which he had in all probability been co-author. It was resolved by a majority, without formal vote, to accept Sorokin's plan and to communicate it to the Opposition leaders. A list of five persons was drawn up, to make up a subcommittee on program to be appointed by the inner-Party center.

Although Sorokin's plan for presenting demands to the Central Committee was accepted with little objection, as amended by Reznikov, a proposal by Viktor that a subcommittee on organization be appointed caused an open split. Viktor, supported by the General and Sorokin, believed it necessary to create such a committee analogous to the subcommittee on program to coordinate the efforts of opposition groups acting independently in Moscow and outside. Reznikov, supported by a number of those present, including the railway man, sharply rejected this proposal. His arguments boiled down to the view that by creating a standing committee on organization we would be handing over to the Stalinists a powerful trump. We would be accused of organizing a bloc within the Party, which would be enough to destroy us immediately even without study or discussion of our political platform.

"You know," pleaded Reznikov, "that the fate of all such blocs within our Party irrespective of whether they were right or wrong has always been one and the same: political isolation. We must not consciously court such isolation."

"If you are afraid of wolves, keep out of the forest," remarked the General.

"Perhaps, but there is only one conclusion to be drawn," replied Reznikov, "before you go into a forest with its wolf packs, you must arm yourself."

"With scraps of paper?" asked the General contemptuously.

"If," continued Reznikov irritably, "you think that our political requirements in the shape in which we have given them and which we want to communicate to the entire Party are only a scrap of paper, I cannot understand why we have come here at all. These demands could be presented even without creation of a separate bloc within the Party. No one is as interested in making us into a separate bloc as Stalin. He has a legal mandate to do away with blocs, given him by the last Party congresses, and signed by ourselves. But political demands by a certain section of the Party and its Central Committee and presented within the framework of legality and the Party statutes would make it impossible for the Stalinists to deal with us as if we constituted an anti-Party bloc. I hold that such a procedure would not only be expedient, but would give us far greater peace of mind."

Sorokin, who was waiting with great impatience for the end of Reznikov's speech, now asked for permission to speak himself. A feeling of alarm spread through the room. Viktor, who was acting as chairman, tried to prevent Sorokin from voicing his opinions too harshly, by asking him to speak briefly and to keep to the essentials of the point under discussion.

Sorokin took the chairman's advice. His speech was not couched in harsh terms. But he took issue with Reznikov about the bloc. "However angelic our behavior within the 'framework of legality,'" he said, "Stalin and his apparatus will declare, in fact are already declaring, that we are an anti-Party bloc. Reznikov must have a very low opinion of Stalin if he thinks that he is dealing with a Party Secretary-General who is in love with his Party's statutes. Stalin is an apparatus above the Party. We can fight this particular apparatus and defeat it in one way only: by creating an anti-Stalinist apparatus within the Party." After defending this thesis by reference to the manner in which Stalin's own bloc had been created within the Party, Sorokin addressed a few words to Reznikov personally.

"As a person I can follow Reznikov's arguments about peace of mind, but as a revolutionary I cannot accept them. Reznikov is, of course, wrong. Only Prutkov was right: 'Many people would have more peace of mind if all unpleasantness could be charged to the public exchequer.'"

The chairman smiled in spite of himself, but the others present were not greatly amused.

Reznikov did not react in any way; in fact, I sensed that he was much pleased to be so easily rid of Sorokin.

Sorokin was punished: the conference rejected Viktor's proposal for creation of a committee on organization. Viktor reserved the right to bring it up again under "more suitable circumstances."

Late that night we returned to Moscow.

Chapter XX

Bukharin's Expulsion from the Comintern

Until the dissolution of the Comintern during World War II, the title sheet of the membership ticket of a member of the Soviet Communist Party bore at the top the inscription, "Proletarians of All Lands Unite!" In the middle was, "Party Ticket," and at the bottom, "VKP(b) [All-Union Communist Party of Bolsheviks] Section of the Communist International." Ever since the Second Congress of the Comintern, when Lenin's famous "21 Conditions" for the acceptance and continued membership of foreign parties in the Comintern were agreed upon, the wording at the bottom of the Soviet Party ticket had been an anachronism. The Soviet Communist Party was not a section of the Comintern, but the Comintern was a section of the Soviet Communist Party, or more specifically, of the International Department of the Soviet Party Central Committee.

During World War I Lenin had taken steps toward creating the Comintern out of groups of "Left Zimmerwaldians," which included all the extreme Left elements of the then existing western Social Democratic parties. There were those like the Russian Bolsheviks and the German Independents (later Spartacists), who stressed their international affiliations and supported Lenin's slogan about "turning the imperialist war into a civil war." Lenin's persistent attempts during the war to create a Third Communist International were quite unsuccessful. The victory of the Bolsheviks in Russia in October 1917 sharply changed the situation. Not only the political and moral conditions created by the victory of Lenin's tactics and strategy but—which was the main factor—all the material conditions were now present to ensure success. Lenin again raised the subject of the creation of the Comintern with Soviet Russian funds. It was one of history's ironies that what then occurred was the exact opposite of what Trotsky had in 1906 predicted when he had written: "Without the direct state support of the European proletariat, the Russian proletariat will not be able to hold its power and turn its temporary grip on the situation into a lasting socialist dictatorship."[1] Lenin proved the opposite: that it was possible to create a world Communist movement with the support of Communist Russia.

It is highly significant that the decision to create the Comintern was first made not by the Central Committee of the Russian Communist Party (the predecessor of the Communist Party of the Soviet Union) but by the Soviet parliament itself—the Central Executive Committee. On December 24, 1917, the Party Central Committee passed a resolution to send abroad a delegation including the

---

[1] Trotsky, quoted in Stalin, *Voprosy leninizma*, p. 87.

Bolsheviks Bukharin, Radek, Berzin, and Kollontay and the Left Social Revolutionaries Ustinov and Natanson, "to undertake preliminary steps for the convocation of an international conference consisting of representatives of the left wing of the International, who share the Soviet régime's attitude on the necessity of fighting imperialist governments within each of the belligerent nations."[2]

This delegation did not, of course, succeed in going abroad, but an international conference in Petrograd in January and February 1918 passed the following resolution:

> An international socialist conference must be convoked on the following conditions:
>
> 1. Organizations and parties must agree to fight against their own governments and for immediate peace.
>
> 2. The October Revolution and the Soviet régime must be supported.[3]

To such foreign parties and groups the Soviet régime gave generous aid. They formed one of the reserves from which the Bolsheviks obtained personnel for the Third International. No less important was another reserve of the Comintern which consisted of former prisoners of war in Russia, including Germans, Austrians, Rumanians, Czechs, Slovaks, Bulgarians, and others. Immediately after the February Revolution of 1917, the Bolsheviks began an energetic propaganda campaign of "Communist education" among the prisoners of war, and after the October Revolution a "Federation of Foreign Groups" of Communists under the Central Committee, organized by languages, was formed. The Federation was composed of nine groups, including "free foreigners," such as the "Anglo-American group." It was headed by the famous Bela Kun.

Lenin considered this reserve to be exceptionally important. At the Seventh Party Congress in 1919 he said:

> I must draw your attention to the activities of the Federation of Foreign Groups ... I must say that here we can see the real basis of all that we have done for the Third International. The Third International was founded in Moscow at the Second Congress, on which a detailed report will be given by Comrade Zinoviev. If we were able to do so much in such a short space of time at the congress of Communists in Moscow, that was due to the fact that a gigantic preparatory work had been performed and carried out by the Central Committee of our Party and by the organizer of the congress, Comrade Sverdlov. Propaganda and agitation has been developed among many of the foreigners in Russia and a number of foreign groups have been organized. Dozens of members of these groups have been informed of the basic plans and general tasks of our policy in its main outline. Hundreds of thousands of prisoners of war belonging to armies which the imperialists had organized exclusively in their own interests, having returned to Hungary, Germany, and Austria have effected that the *bacilli of Bolshevism have encompassed these countries completely*. If groups and parties who share a common cause with us are now in power there, this is due to this work, externally invisible, and, as depicted in

---

[2] *Izvestia*, December 12, 1917.

[3] *Pravda*, January 24, 1918.

146

the report [read at the Congress], unimportant and humble, performed by foreign groups. This work constitutes one of the most important aspects of the activities of the Russian Communist Party, as one of the cells of the World Communist Party.[4]

These two reserves—the extreme Left representatives of the socialist parties of Asia and the West, and the former prisoners of war—were used by Lenin to create the foundations of the world Communist movement at the First Congress in Moscow, March 2–6, 1919. Fifty-one delegates were present, representing the Russian Communist Party, the Communist Party of Germany, the American Socialist Labor Party, the Zimmerwald left wing of the French Socialists, the Communist Party of Austria, the Communist Party of Finland, the opposition Swedish Left Social Democratic Party, the Balkan Revolutionary Federation including Bulgaria and Rumania, the Communist Party of the Ukraine, the Communist Party of Latvia, the Communist Party of Lithuania, the Communist Party of Belorussia, the Communist Party of the German Colonies in Russia, and the United Group of the Eastern Peoples of Russia. The British, French, Swedish, Czech, Bulgarian, and Yugoslav groups, the Dutch Social Democratic Group, the American League for Socialist Propaganda, the Turkestanian, Turkish, Georgian, Azerbaidzhanian, and Persian sections of the Central Bureau of the Communist Organizations of the Eastern Peoples, the Chinese Socialist Labor Party, the Korean Labor Union, and the Zimmerwald Commission were represented at the Congress, but with advisory votes only.

The First Congress adopted a resolution setting up the Comintern and its executive organs—an Executive Committee and a Bureau—and discussed and approved reports by the Russian delegation, represented by Lenin, Trotsky, Zinoviev, Bukharin, and Osinsky, on program and tactics. The congress closed after adoption of a "Manifesto of the Communist International to the Proletarians of the Entire World." The Manifesto ended: "Under the banner of the Soviet, of the revolutionary struggle for the power and dictatorship of the proletariat, under the banner of the Third International—Proletarians of all Lands Unite!"[5]

The Executive Committee of the Comintern included Lenin, Zinoviev, Bukharin, and Trotsky as representatives of the Russian Communist Party. Bukharin was a permanent member of the Comintern Presidium and appeared at all congresses, where he read the directives. Stalin joined the Comintern Presidium in 1925, after Lenin's death, but once a member he began in his Stalinist manner to purge it of everything really idealistic or honest.

It would be naive and incorrect to believe that the membership of the Comintern was from the very beginning composed entirely of hirelings and agents of Moscow. There was of course no lack of these, as there never is in such circumstances. However, there were also old veterans of the international labor movement eager to regard the Russian Revolution as the beginning of the

---

[4] V. I. Lenin, *Sochineniya* (Works), 3rd ed., Moscow, 1926–37, Vol. XXIV, p. 128.

[5] *Pervy Kongress Kommunisticheskogo Internatsionala. Protocoly* (Minutes of the First Congress of the Communist International), Petrograd, 1921, pp. 189–90.

socialist era upon earth to the realization of which they had devoted themselves. There were also a few young enthusiasts who had quite seriously believed in the "liberation mission" of the Russian October Revolution. Deep disappointment awaited both. Many had their eyes opened by Lenin's "21 Conditions," which in practice reduced the foreign Communist parties and the Third International to the role of sections of the Central Committee of the Russian Communist Party. But if the foreign parties still enjoyed formal autonomy in Lenin's time, in Stalin's time even this type of autonomy became fictitious. At the same time that Stalin was carrying out his purges in the Soviet Communist Party he was also mercilessly purging the Comintern of all who failed to obey blindly and unconditionally the dictatorship of Stalin's cabinet within the Comintern. After the downfall of Trotsky and Zinoviev, effected with Bukharin's help, the only elements remaining in the Comintern were those which could be called agents of Moscow.

After these changes, Stalin found no difficulty in discrediting Bukharin in the Comintern. However, he approached the solution of this problem methodically and carefully, in 1928. Bukharin was head of the Comintern, though his official position was only that of political secretary, Stalin, out of jealousy, having abolished the post of Comintern chairman after the dismissal of Zinoviev. As political secretary, Bukharin was assigned to report on the international situation at the Sixth Congress of the Comintern in 1928. He drew up the main points of his report in full agreement with directives from the Politburo, including Stalin, and sent them to the various delegations in the Executive Committee of the Comintern. Then, without the knowledge of Bukharin or the approval of the Politburo Stalin circulated a number of "corrections" of Bukharin's points, in effect repudiating Bukharin. This action, which was completely unexpected and unprecedented in the experience of the Politburo and the Comintern, angered Bukharin but achieved its aim in the Comintern, whose foreign members made the sensational discovery that it was Stalin, not Bukharin, who was the theorist of Bolshevism.

Stalin described the event to the April Plenum as follows:

> The delegation of the All-Union Communist Party of Bolsheviks was forced to introduce about twenty corrections in the theses. This fact made Bukharin's position somewhat awkward. ... And so the delegation produced what were in effect new theses on the international situation which *the foreign delegations began to compare with the old theses signed by Bukharin.* ... I would like to note *four basic* corrections made in Bukharin's theses by the delegation of the All-Union Communist Party of Bolsheviks.
>
> The first question was that of the stabilization of capitalism. Bukharin seemed to think that ... capitalism was being reconstructed and was in general maintaining itself on a solid basis.
>
> The second question was that of the struggle with Social Democracy. It was said in Bukharin's theses that the struggle with Social Democracy was one of the basic tasks of the various sections of the Comintern. This, of course, is true. But it is not enough. The main emphasis must be put on the struggle with the so-called "left" wing of Social Democracy. ...

The third question was that of compromise in the sections of the Comintern. Bukharin's theses spoke of the necessity of combatting Right deviation, but contained not a word about combatting *compromise* with the Right. . . .

The fourth question was that of discipline. There was no mention in Bukharin's theses of the necessity of retaining iron discipline within the Communist parties. . . .[6]

After making these accusations, Stalin ended his speech with an emotional outburst: "We love Bukharin, but truth, but the Party, but the Comintern we love even more. Therefore the delegation of the Communist Party of the Soviet Union was forced to introduce these corrections in Bukharin's theses."[7]

I have no wish to justify Bukharin in his argument with Stalin. I merely wish to illustrate Stalin's original methods of carrying out polemics with his opponents. He consciously exaggerated his opponent's views in order to declare them heretical. He deliberately tore them to pieces in order to make them lose all sense. But if he failed to do either, he adopted a simpler method: Look, he would say, why have you said nothing about this, or this, or this? Bukharin's answer, made in his own style, seemed to me both suitable and clear, as he read aloud to the Sixth Congress of the Third International his ill-fated theses, keeping in mind Stalin's twenty corrections: "I have not covered all the questions, but Kuzma Prutkov has well said: 'Spit in the eye of anyone who says that you can encompass the unencompassable.' "

Stalin did not rest content with repudiating Bukharin this once within the Comintern itself. He had to destroy Bukharin's fame as the theorist of the Soviet Communist Party and the Comintern, as well as within the "fraternal parties." Three of Stalin's most trusted lieutenants undertook to fulfill this task—Thorez in France, Thaelmann in Germany and Gottwald in Czechoslovakia. Thaelmann went so far as to publicly criticize Bukharin's report at the Sixth Comintern Congress at a time when in the USSR not a word had been said against Bukharin, either publicly or in plenary sessions of the Central Committee. Since Bukharin was still considered the most orthodox of the orthodox, he was completely nonplussed by so daring an act on the part of Thaelmann. He demanded that Neumann, Thaelmann's representative in the Comintern Presidium, be immediately expelled from Moscow and Thaelmann himself called to order. Stalin sharply rejected Bukharin's demand, and accused Bukharin himself of aiding and abetting the right-wing elements in the German Communist Party.

The secret of Thaelmann's daring came to light during the April Plenum, when it became known that Stalin himself had written Thaelmann's speech against Bukharin. The background was as follows: Following the Sixth Congress of the Third International, a revolt had, with Bukharin's approval, been carried through in the Central Committee of the German Communist Party. Wittorf, Secretary of the Hamburg Party organization and a friend of Thaelmann, accused Thaelmann of embezzling Party funds. Thaelmann was then removed from his

---

[6] Stalin, *Sochineniya*, Vol. XII, 1949, pp. 20–23.
[7] *Ibid.*

post as Party chairman, by resolution of a majority in the Central Committee of the German Communist Party. Stalin, as may well be imagined, was incensed at this blow to his main supporter in the West. He complained at the April Plenum that the rebels, led by Ewert and Eisler, had "removed Thaelmann from the leadership, accused him of corruption, and published a resolution to that effect without the *knowledge and sanction of the Comintern*, . . . and instead of *giving a turn to the wheel* to right the course, Bukharin proposed in his famous letter to *sanction* the revolt of the compromisers, to hand over the German Communist Party to the compromisers, and to smear Comrade Thaelmann's good name in the press by again making a statement about his guilt."[8]

Stalin himself now "gave a turn to the wheel." By issuing a peremptory order on behalf of the Secretariat of the Central Committee of the Soviet Communist Party he forced the Presidium of the Comintern Central Committee to pass a resolution disavowing the revolt in the German Communist Party, restoring Thaelmann to his posts, and recalling the "compromisers" to Moscow from Berlin to be "placed at the disposal of the Comintern." The grateful Thaelmann, as chairman of the largest and most influential section of the Comintern abroad, reciprocated. What Stalin did not as yet dare to accomplish within the Politburo, the "foreigner" Thaelmann accomplished within the Comintern. In April 1929, Bukharin was removed from the post of political secretary of the Comintern, and at the Tenth Plenum of the Comintern Executive Committe in July 1929 Thaelmann and his friends proposed that "the ideologist of the Right deviation" be expelled from the Presidium of the Comintern.

Why did such persons as Thaelmann act as they did? Did they grasp the nature of the accusation against Bukharin? Did Stalin show them Bukharin's statement of January 30 or the "program of the three" of February 9? Of course not. Silone has described a similar case in connection with the discussion in the Presidium of the Comintern of a memorandum by Trotsky on the Chinese revolution, which resulted in his being expelled from the Comintern on the strength of the document. Apart from the Russian members, none of the foreign members of the Comintern Presidium had as much as seen the document itself. When the Italian representatives, Silone and Togliatti, asked to see Trotsky's memorandum before passing judgment on it, Thaelmann, who was present, replied quite coolly: "We have not seen the document ourselves." Silone, thinking that he had not understood Thaelmann correctly, asked him to repeat what he had said. Thaelmann repeated it word for word. Silone, supported by Togliatti, declared that although Trotsky's document quite possibly deserved condemnation, he was unable to condemn it without reading it first. Stalin now intervened in the argument. Giving as his reason the fact that the Italian comrades were unacquainted with the internal situation in the USSR, he proposed that discussion of the question be deferred until the following day and that in the meantime the Italians be informed of the situation. The part of informer was entrusted to Kolarov, the

---

[8] *Ibid.*, pp. 23–24.

leader of the Bulgarian Communists, who played his part in classic manner.[9] He invited Silone and Togliatti to his hotel, where he explained to them over a cup of tea the nature of the "internal situation" in the USSR.

"First," he said, "I have not read Trotsky's document myself; second, even if Trotsky had secretly sent me the document I would have refused to read it; third, the document frankly presents no interest for me; fourth, we are not seeking historical truth but merely establishing the fact of the existence of a struggle between two groups . . . for power in the Politburo. In this struggle, strength (the majority) is on Stalin's side and for this reason we are supporting Stalin rather than Trotsky."

---

[9] Later both Kolarov and Togliatti (Ercoli) lectured on international relations at the Institute of Red Professors, in excellent Russian.

Chapter XXI

The Capitulation of the Right Opposition
and the Celebration of Stalin's Fiftieth Birthday

It was seven months after the April Plenum and four months after Bukharin's expulsion from the Comintern before Stalin called the next plenary session of the Central Committee. The new plenum, which met in November 1929, discussed two main questions—the collectivization of agriculture, and the status of Bukharin's group.

On the first question a resolution was adopted calling for intensifying the pace of collectivization and stepping up "the offensive against the kulaks." There was as yet no mention of "total collectivization" or of "liquidation of the kulaks as a class." On the second question, a resolution, not published until 1933, read as follows:

After hearing the declaration made by Comrades Bukharin, Rykov, and Tomsky on November 12, 1929, the plenum of the Central Committee of the All-Union Communist Party of Bolsheviks establishes the following facts:

1. By accusing the April Plenum of the Central Committee and the Central Control Commission of allegedly placing them in a "status of inequality," the authors of the declaration are trying to wrest from the Party the "right" to set themselves up as a rival and equal body to the Politburo and freely to treat with the Party, i.e., they are trying to obtain legalization of the factional group of Right deviationists whose leaders they are.

2. Comrades Bukharin, Rykov, and Tomsky, now compelled—after the shameful failure of all their prophesies—to recognize the Party's indubitable successes, make hypocritical statements in their declaration about "the abolition of disagreements," yet at the same time refuse to recognize the mistakenness of their views as set forth in their program of January 30 and February 9 and condemned by the April Plenum of the Central Committee and the Central Control Commission as being incompatible with the Party general line.

3. By acting like demagogues, accusing the Party of failure to fulfill the plan for wages and salaries and for agriculture, and alleging that the extraordinary measures have "pushed" the medium-rich peasants toward the kulaks, the leaders of the Right deviationists (Comrades Bukharin, Rykov, Tomsky) are mounting a new attack on the Party and its Central Committee.

4. The resolution of Comrades Bukharin, Rykov, and Tomsky differs radically from the resolution of the Tenth Plenary Session of the Executive Committee of the Communist International, which condemned Comrade Bukharin's views as opportunistic and removed him from the membership of the Presidium of the Executive Committee of the Communist International.

Taking these facts into consideration, the Central Committee plenum is forced to regard the new document of Comrades Bukharin, Rykov, and Tomsky dated November 12 as a factious maneuver by political bankrupts. ...

The plenum of the Central Committee therefore rejects this declaration of Comrades Bukharin, Rykov, and Tomsky as a document hostile to the Party and resolves, *on the basis of the resolution of the Tenth Plenum of the Executive Committee of the Comintern on the subject of Comrade Bukharin, that* :

1. Comrade Bukharin, as leader and guide of the Right deviationists, is to be removed from the membership of the Politburo:

2. Comrades Rykov and Tomsky, as well as Ugarov, are to be warned that in case of the slightest attempt on their part to continue the struggle against the general line and decisions of the Executive Committee and the Central Committee of the All-Union Communist Party of Bolsheviks the Party will not hesitate to apply to them suitable organizational measures.[1]

The resolution was written by Stalin himself, but it was announced by Molotov in the name of the commission appointed to deal with Bukharin.[2]

Apart from what was contained in this resolution, there is no trace either in Party writings or in the publications by the Opposition of the joint declaration of November 12 by Bukharin, Rykov, and Tomsky. However, a cursory analysis of the resolution makes it possible to establish two very important facts—first, that the Rightists had continued to maintain the point of view expressed in their declaration of January 30 and their "program" of February 9, 1929, and second, that the Rightists had demanded "equality of both sides," that is, of the Stalinists and the Bukharinites. This demand was indubitably a reflection of the "plan" of Viktor and Sorokin set forth at the Podolsk conference.

As to the statement that the Right elements, in calling for the "abolition" of certain disagreements, intended to engage in a tactical maneuver, Stalin was probably correct. The Right remembered the treatment which it, together with Stalin, had meted out to the Left. For it was the Right—Bukharin, Rykov, and Tomsky—which, on Stalin's initiative, had prevented the leaders of the joint opposition—Trotsky and Zinoviev—from appealing to the Fifteenth Party Congress, by expelling them from the Party only a month before the opening of the Congress. The others, headed by Kamenev, had been expelled from the Party at the Congress itself, for the simple reason that their leaders were by then already considered to be "enemies of the Party." This procedure, which had then been completely successful, was what Stalin, Molotov, and Kaganovich now wished to apply again, this time to the Right. The Right, however, had no desire to give them an excuse for doing so. Therefore, while not repudiating the point of view expressed in their program, they were engaging in tactical maneuvers into which they had been forced by the serious disagreements on tactics between the "activists" and "pacifists" in their own ranks.

However, their maneuvers were useless. Bukharin was removed from the Politburo. Rykov and Tomsky were warned in writing and the others orally. The

---

[1] *VKP(b) v rezolyutsiyakh*, Vol. II, pp. 611–12.

[2] Stalin, *Sochineniya*, Vol. XII, 1949, p. 389.

fact that Stalin, Molotov, and Kaganovich did not dare to remove Ugarov and Tomsky from the Politburo immediately, as they had a perfect opportunity to do, indicated their uncertainty as to final victory. Even more disgraceful than the unjustified removals was the fact, unprecedented in the history of Bolshevism, that Stalin and his group concealed, not only from the country at large but even from their own Party, the program of the Right Opposition. From the point of view of their own interests, the Stalinists were, of course, correct. If they had followed the example of the action taken in and after Lenin's time in regard to such groups as the "Left Opposition" and the "New Opposition," they would have allowed the program of the Right Opposition to be published and the whole country would have seen that it was opposed to (1) predatory industrialization at the cost of the working class; (2) collectivization amounting to serfdom, and involving the "armed and feudal exploitation of the peasants;" and (3) international adventures at the cost of the vital interests of the peoples of the USSR.

Trotsky's program, irrespective of its author's intentions, looked like the reverse of Bukharin's, and the Stalinists had willingly allowed it to appear in the press and even to be freely discussed at Party meetings. Trotsky had lived in the revolutions of yesterday and in his heart had been anti-NEP, at a time when Russia, having adopted the NEP, was about to take a further step and become capitalist. Trotsky, who had barred the way, had broken not with Stalin but with the country. Therefore, just as Lenin had killed the inner counterrevolution by introducing the NEP, so Stalin in the name of the same NEP had been able to bury Trotsky after publishing his program and thus acquainting the whole country with it. The Stalinists could not deal in the same way with the program of the persons who had written on their standards the magic slogan of the spirit of the NEP: "Get rich!" Accordingly they did not dare to publish Bukharin's program. On the other hand, the entire press of the country screamed: "The Bukharinites want to restore in Russia the old tsarist regime of capitalists and landowners!" At the same time, the Politburo members Bukharin, Rykov, and Tomsky, who read the press together with the rest of the country, kept the absolute "silence" which is said to mark assent. "If they keep silent, it means they really are 'restorationists,'" argued the man in the street, who had no way of knowing that the lips of the Right had been sealed.

The program of the Bukharinites took advantage of the fact that they correctly gauged the spirit of the NEP, but their tactics were inferior to those of the Trotskyites, if tactics mean not only the art of passive maneuvering but also that of sudden diversion and decisive action at turning points in history. Trotsky and the Trotskyites were decisive and courageous men, willing to sacrifice themselves and not afraid to appeal to the crowd, as in the demonstrations of November 7, 1927, but their appeal was not in harmony with the epoch and therefore they lost out. The Bukharinites did not lose contact with their epoch, but no less than Stalin they were afraid of the "people" to whom they would have to appeal. Stalin was right in calling them "opportunists," but their "opportunism" benefitted Stalin himself.

After Bukharin's removal from the Politburo and the warning issued to the others, the question of the tactics to adopt toward the Stalinists again became acute. The only alternatives permitted by the Stalinists were complete capitulation or positive action. Stalin agreed to call a Party congress only on condition of complete capitulation. He went even farther in his demands. At previous meetings of the Central Committee it had been possible to state one's views on current policy either orally or in writing, even if they differed from the views of the Stalinists, but now this too was considered incompatible with the Party's requirements. Moreover, any Party member, from a member of the Central Committee down to the rank and file Communist, who did not publicly condemn the Bukharinites as Right Opportunists, was automatically placed on a list of "appeasers," a new category of "enemies of the Party." Stalin, Molotov, and Kaganovich deprived Party members of the advantage enjoyed by the leaders of the Right Opposition—the right to be silent. The entire mass of Party members—a million and a half strong—loudly condemned the program of the Right Opposition, which they had never seen, precisely as the members of the presidium of the Executive Committee of the Comintern had, according to Silone, done in the case of Trotsky. Everywhere they were forced to "reveal and expose . . . opportunists in practice," to use the words of the Party directive published in *Pravda* and *Izvestia* on the eve of the Sixteenth Party Congress. And secret and open Party directives demanded that "secret opportunists" who expressed agreement with the Party and even formally carried out its aims, but in their hearts remained "opportunists" and had "a stone in their bosoms," be mercilessly revealed and exposed. Such was the general atmosphere in the Party at the end of 1929.

It was no easy matter in an atmosphere of this kind to choose tactics that would guarantee success, particularly if they had to be tactics that required action. It was all the more difficult because the Stalinists by their shrewd maneuvers on the one hand and their moral and political repression on the other were able to bring about the first open split in the leadership of the Right Opposition. The Central Committee members Mikhailov, Kotov, Uglanov, and Kulikov submitted at the plenum a statement that they had broken with the Rightists. The political capitalist Stalin very skilfully took advantage of this capital. On November 1, 1929, *Pravda* published declarations by the four prominent Central Committee members indicating their complete capitulation to Stalin and their decisive condemnation of the program they had earlier shared with Bukharin.

Rykov, Tomsky, and Ugarov told the plenum that they retained their point of view but would submit to a majority decision. Only Bukharin threw out a challenge to Stalin. He declared that he did not recognize the decision of the Central Committee plenum and would not rest until he had acquainted the whole Party with his views. But even Rykov agreed with Stalin in condemning such action. Rykov, and to a certain extent Tomsky, believed that the best tactics to be adopted were those of "expectant inactivity." I am convinced that it was Rykov and Tomsky, and not Stalin, who persuaded Bukharin to state to the Politburo on November 25, 1929, that he would submit to the decision of the Stalinist majority within the Central Committee, although he had said in writing that he remained entirely faithful to his old point of view. Naturally, Stalin, unlike his action in the case of the statements by Kotov, Uglanov, and the others, did not publish Bukharin's statement, for capital of this kind brought in nothing but unfavorable interest, but it provided a sufficient basis for publishing in the press the news of Stalin's victory.

The collapse of the top level of the Opposition had an immediate effect on the rank and file. Such persons as Reznikov and the Commissar no longer saw their friends. Zinaida Nikolayevna became an open "appeaser." She ceased inviting persons to her apartment and anyone who did go there left with a feeling as if he had just left a cemetery after burying a dear friend: full of sorrow for the loss of the deceased and disillusioned by life in general.

To cap it all, the Stalinists began at the end of 1929 to publish mass editions of the anti-Bukharin literature which they had been secretly preparing from the middle of 1928 on. The manuscripts of these books had been held back until Bukharin had been defeated in the organization. Now that Bukharin was politically unmasked and organizationally defeated, even though he had not yet been discredited as a theorist in the eyes of the Party, new "works of red professors"— former pupils of Bukharin, as a matter of fact—were employed to complete the destruction of the "theorist and Party favorite." Among such works were a symposium entitled *Against the Threat from the Right and Appeasement* (Moscow and Leningrad, 1929); V. Sorin, *On Bukharin's Disagreement with Lenin: A Short Outline for Young Party Members* (Moscow and Leningrad, 1930); "Lenin Falsified," a review in *Lenin Symposium* (Vol. XI, 1929) of a book entitled *Economics of the Transitional Period* and so on and so forth.

It is true that the Stalinists gained nothing by publishing "Lenin Falsified," for Lenin's remarks on Bukharin's book written in 1920, i.e., a year before the NEP, made it clear to the Party how highly he had prized Bukharin as a theorist. Among many favorable remarks by Lenin on the margins of Bukharin's book, such as "Correct," "Good," "Excellent," there were also a few critical remarks. Where Bukharin had written, "financial capital did away with the anarchy of production within large capitalist countries," Lenin had underlined the words "did away with" and written in the margin "did *not* do away with." Bukharin had adopted this opinion of the organization of modern finance capitalism even before the Revolution, and had defended it against Lenin in 1919 at the Eighth Party Congress, in his report on the Party program. He refused to renounce it in Stalin's time. Now Stalin was placing theoretical views on a level with criminal acts and making the dead Lenin fight the living Bukharin. But in this case Lenin did Stalin a disservice. It seems strange that in making use of Lenin and misrepresenting him, Stalin did not exclude Lenin's general conclusion about Bukharin's book. The issue of the *Lenin Symposium* referred to above contains over Lenin's signature the statement: "I congratulate the Communist Academy on the brilliant work of one of its members." This oversight was probably due to what Stalin himself called "that damn disease—carelessness and rotten objectivism," and of which he himself was finally cured only after the period of the Yezhov terror, when he set to work to prepare faked editions, not only of Lenin's old works, but even of his own, such as the 4th edition of Lenin's works and the 1st edition of his own, not to mention the disgraceful *Short Course in the History of the All-Union Communist Party of Bolsheviks*.

Stalin reached his fiftieth birthday on December 21, 1929, just as he was concluding his victory over Bukharin and the Right Opposition. There was no tradition calling for the celebration of birthdays and other anniversaries of Party leaders. The celebration of Lenin's fiftieth birthday in 1920 had been an isolated exception. But now Molotov, Kaganovich, and Voroshilov decided to make use of the occasion to satisfy Stalin's ambition and to "legalize" the new "Party Leader." Up until this time all members of the Politburo had been called Party leaders. They were always listed in alphabetical order and if any member was mentioned he was referred to simply as one of the heads or leaders of the Party. Now, for the first time, the alphabetical order was dropped and Stalin was publicly declared to be "Lenin's first pupil" and the only "Party Leader." *Pravda* was filled with articles, greetings, letters, and telegrams speaking of the "Leader." (Adjectives such as "wise," "great," and "brilliant" came later as appetite developed.) *Pravda*'s initiative was taken up by other newspapers, by periodicals, the radio, the cinema, and the entire propaganda machinery of the Party. The entire press adopted a standard pattern, in which each article began with a reference to the "Leader" and ended with a bow of allegiance in his direction. Persons such as Yudin and Mekhlis, Vyshinsky and Varga showed great ingenuity in competing with each other for first place in eulogizing Stalin. All these "academicians" were later surpassed by a Kazakh minstrel, Djambul, who provided a brief but picturesque description of Stalin in *Pravda* : "Stalin is deeper than the ocean, higher than the Himalayas, brighter than the sun, he is the teacher of the universe!" Stalin responded to this flood of sugary obsequiousness laconically: "I am ready to give to the Party cause in the future, as in the past, all my strength and my talents and, if necessary, all my blood, drop by drop." (Stalin's enemies used to ask: "Why all this modesty about shedding it drop by drop, can't he give all his blood at once?")

Chapter XXII

Giddiness from Success

At the peak of this wave of adulation, Stalin, on December 27, 1929, condemned to death, on his own initiative and without any decision by the Central
Committee, many millions of peasants—the so-called kulaks—when he made his
famous statement to a conference of "Marxist agriculturists." "We are at a new
turning point in our policy and are beginning the liquidation of the kulaks as a
class on the basis of total collectivization." According to official statistics, there
were in the Soviet Union at the time five million kulaks and no less than thirteen
million others on the way to becoming kulaks—the "well-to-do" and the "sub-
kulaks."[1]

Stalin's speech marked the beginning of a real war aimed at the extermination
of the peasantry. It was not until I saw with my own eyes both in Central Russia
and in the Caucasus how this campaign of collectivization and liquidation was
being carried out that I grasped the meaning of our Dedodub's remark: "A real
war is taking place in the villages, worse than the Civil War and the German
War." I shall not attempt to depict here either the horrors of this war or its
consequences for the country; other witnesses have told this well and often. As
to the peculiar form taken by the war in districts inhabited by backward peoples,
I shall speak elsewhere. At this point I wish merely to record the reaction of the
Right Opposition to this new turn.

I have called attention to the fact that Stalin's speech took place unexpectedly
and without a decision by the Central Committee. A resolution on agriculture
adopted by the November plenary session of the Central Committee, a month
before, had made no mention of any new turn in the policy of the Party or of the
liquidation of the kulaks as a class. It had declared that "as a result of the kolkhoz
movement certain oblasts are faced with the problem of total collectivization,"
but as to the kulaks it had merely said that "the offensive against the kulaks must
be resolutely continued and their attempts at infiltration into kolkhozes must be
impeded and suppressed in every way."[2]

Invective of this kind against the kulaks had been frequent in the Soviet press
from the Eighth Party Congress in 1919 on. But the confiscation of the land and
other property of five million peasants, including all from babes-in-arms to old
men, and their banishment to the Siberian tundra without clothes or food or a roof
over their heads, was so incredible that at first we thought that Stalin had been

---

[1] Stalin, "On Questions of Agrarian Policy in the USSR," in *Voprosy leninizma*, pp. 306–26.

[2] *VKP(b) v rezolyutsiyakh*, Vol. II, pp. 594–603.

exaggerating or had simply blurted out an off-hand remark. But when it became apparent that Stalin meant what he said, there was an outburst of discontent not only in the ranks of the opposition but at the Party summit itself. Rykov and Tomsky lodged a protest with the Central Committee against what they described as Stalin's arbitrary action and his direct violation of the decision on agricultural policy adopted by the last plenary session. Uglanov, Kotov, and others who had just repented now hastened to associate themselves with the protest. Perplexed telegrams and letters began to pour in from local Party secretaries and members of the Central Committee and Central Control Commission. For a time the situation was unclear and touched with a mood of crisis. The Rightists, having caught Stalin red-handed, now had an opportunity to call him to account for having usurped the power, not only of the Politburo, but also of the Central Committee. Stalin rushed back and forth between Molotov and Kaganovich. The rank and file insistently pressed for an explanation, and the members of the Central Committee considered themselves to have been deceived. But the Rightists restricted themselves to solemn protests. Bukharin was silent. After handing over Rykov and Tomsky to Stalin to do with them as he liked, Bukharin seemed to be taking a passive revenge. "There you are, you fools, there is Stalin for you," he seemed to be saying; "admire him and plunge with him into the abyss!" But the greater the difficulties, the greater became Stalin's power. On January 5, 1930, the Politburo approved Stalin's speech of the week before, and adopted a resolution on "the tempo of collectivization" providing deadlines for collectivization throughout the USSR.[3] The Rightists abstained from action. Questions from the rank and file ceased and the uncertainty on the part of the Central Committee members vanished. Collectivization, blood-stained and violent, proceeded apace. Stalin's victory over the Central Committee was complete.

The extent of Stalin's victory over the Party and the people was later indicated by the success of his program of collectivization and liquidation of the kulaks. But at the time the outlook was grim. Isolated peasant outbreaks within the country, in connection with "extraordinary measures" taken to ensure grain collection in the autumn of 1929, were threatening to develop into mass peasant uprisings throughout the country. It was a repetition of the peasant uprising of 1905, but without the support of the city workers and with the intellectuals silent and the outside world indifferent. Peasants armed with pitchforks hurled themselves at Soviet tanks, which received their first battle honors in the war against the people. Women threw themselves on the bayonets of the Chekists, children wept on the bodies of their dead parents, while tanks, cannon, machine-guns, and bayonets collectivized some and liquidated others mercilessly and systematically. Battle communiqués from the front reported to the Central Committee that a clear majority of peasants preferred physical liquidation to enforced collectivization.

The "wise leader" persisted, but fresh communiqués arrived from the battle fronts, where here and there the Red Army was refusing to shoot down the

---

[3] *Ibid.*, p. 208.

kulaks. The "wise leader" issued orders to press on, attack, break and defeat the kulaks. But in vain. The peasants died but did not surrender. It is true that the resistance was unorganized and spontaneous, disconnected and at times insane. But at any moment a new Pugachev, a new peasant leader, might appear, to hold in his hands the fate of the Soviet regime. The countryside consisted of peasants and so did the army. The Revolution had been a peasants' and soldiers' revolution, even though it had been usurped by the city, but a peasant revolution can take a cruel revenge upon the city. Such thoughts, at last, occurred even to the realists and cowards in the Politburo. Now, following the resolution of the Politburo, Stalin made a new statement on March 2, 1930, when *Pravda* published his article cynically entitled, "Giddiness from Success." The Bolsheviks, he said, had become giddy from the great success in collectivization. And this giddiness had made local organizations collectivize the peasants by force. This, said Stalin, was a violation of the Leninist principle of voluntary action in the kolkhoz movement. On March 15, 1930, a new Central Committee decree was published confirming the views expressed in Stalin's article and announcing that the kolkhoz movement must be based on the principle of voluntary acceptance. These two documents are of exceptional importance, both as witnesses to developments in the countryside and as admissions of the fact that Central Committee policy regarding the kolkhoz movement was bankrupt.

"The kolkhozes must not be propagated by force," said Stalin in his article. "But what do we actually do sometimes? Can it be said that the principles of voluntariness and of making allowances for local peculiarities are not neglected in a number of districts? No, this cannot be said. . . ." In veiled phrases and references to "huge successes," Stalin attempted to transfer his own guilt to the local organizations. But it was known at the time and later on officially stated, that Stalin's article on "Giddiness from Success" had not been written of his own free will and on his own initiative, but had been dictated by the deathly frightened Central Committee, where his own collaborators had told him quite bluntly: "You got yourself into this mess, now you can get yourself out of it!"

In a second article on April 30, 1930, entitled "A Reply to the Comrade Kolkhozniks," Stalin adopted the innocent position of a simple executant of the will of the Central Committee. "Some people," he said, "think that the article 'Giddiness from Success' was written on Stalin's personal initiative. This, of course, is nonsense. The Central Committee does not exist in order to allow personal initiative by anyone in such cases. The Central Committee undertook to reconnoitre the situation. And when the depth and extent of the errors committed became clear, the Central Committee did not hesitate to strike against these errors with the full strength of its authority by publishing the famous decree of March 15, 1930."[4]

After pointing out his modest role in the all-powerful Central Committee, while carefully avoiding mention of the call for collectivization which he had issued on December 27, 1929, Stalin again referred in complimentary terms to the

---

[4] Stalin, *Voprosy leninizma*, pp. 311–12.

Central Committee, without which, he said, it would have been difficult "to stop people as they rushed madly in headlong flight toward the abyss and to turn them onto the right path." Reading between the lines, it is clear that Stalin was saying, he would have been rushing headlong toward the abyss at the head of the Central Committee if the Central Committee had not temporarily taken over the leadership from him. He himself confirmed the truth of this view by adding that "the danger arising from the issuance of decrees by individual Party representatives is very real. . . . I have in mind not only local workers, but also individual oblast workers and members of the Central Committee. The danger here consists in the fact that mistakes are leading us directly to discrediting of the kolkhoz movement, to *dissension with the medium peasantry*, to disorganization of the poor peasantry, to *confusion* in our ranks, [and are driving us] onto the path of undermining the proletarian dictatorship."[5]

Although this was precisely what the Right—Bukharin and the others—was charging him with doing, Stalin would not have been Stalin if he had not imputed his crime to the Right, even though it was obviously his and he had indirectly confessed to it in his reference to the mistakes of "individual members of the Central Committee." "The Left perpetrators of excesses are the allies of the Right deviationists," declared Stalin.[6]

As to the March 15, 1930, decree, this declared:

> Information received in the Central Committee of the Party on the progress of the kolkhoz movement shows . . . that the Party line is being distorted in *various* districts of the USSR. . . . In a number of districts, free will is being replaced by *compulsion* to enter the kolkhozes, under threat of de-kulakization, under threat of deprivation of the right to vote, etc. As a result, some of the medium peasants and even poor peasants are sometimes included among those de-kulakized. In some districts, the proportion of persons de-kulakized reaches 15%, while from 15% to 20% are deprived of voting rights. Examples can be cited of exceptionally rough, infamous, and criminal treatment of the population . . . (pillage, division of property, the arrest of the medium and even the poor peasants) . . . in some districts collectivization increased within a few days from 10% to 90% . . . churches have been closed by administrative order without the consent of the overwhelming majority of the village . . ., markets and bazaars have been abolished. . . .[7]

The proportions of the failure of Stalin's policy appear in the following data compiled from Soviet sources:

Dates of Collectivization	Percentage of Peasant Households Collectivized	Dates of Collectivization	Percentage of Peasant Households Collectivized
1928 (June)	1.7	1930 (April)	37.0
1929 (July)	3.9	1930 (May)	28.0
1929 (October)	4.1	1930 (June)	24.0
1930 (January)	21.0	1930 (September) . . .	21.0
1930 (March)	58.1		

SOURCE: V. Mertsalov, *Tragediya russkogo krestyanstva* (The Tragedy of the Russian Peasantry), Frankfurt am Main, 1950, p. 39.

---

[5] *Ibid.*

[6] *Ibid.*, p. 315.

[7] *VKP(b) v rezolyutsiyakh*, Vol. II, pp. 549–50.

While the Central Committee had its "wise leader" to thank for this "giddiness from success," the leader himself came out of the debacle unscathed. The aim of Stalin's article and the Central Committee's decree—abandonment of the policy of forcible collectivization and headlong mass liquidation of the kulaks, in order to save the situation—was reached. Stalin's policy had failed ignominiously, the main body of peasants left the kolkhozes, calm was restored in the villages. But the policy of the Right had failed no less ignominiously. The opportunity, unique in the entire history of Stalinism, of overthrowing the Stalinist régime by force was quite unforgivably allowed to slip. At a time when literally all predictions of the Right had come true, at a time when almost all Russia had reacted to the Stalinist policy by a series of peasant uprisings, at a time when Stalin himself had lost his head and did not know which way to turn, at a time when the Red Army, that is, the same peasants in Red Army uniforms, refused to shoot down their brothers, at a time when panic had seized the Party organizations and the Central Committee itself had fallen prey to confusion and uncertainty, the only correct policy would have been to break demonstratively with the Stalinist Central Committee, to appeal to the people, and to have recourse to arms. It is true that later on, in March 1938, Bukharin did state during his trial that he had been deceiving the Central Committee by his professions of loyalty, in order to prepare and head peasant uprisings against Stalin's régime. But this, unfortunately, was a monstrous lie, put into Bukharin's mouth by the Cheka itself. On the other hand it *was* true that among the rank and file of the Opposition, and among the Moscow groups, there were "activists" who wished their leaders to adopt energetic measures to overthrow Stalin by taking advantage of the peasant uprisings and the bankruptcy of Stalin's policy. I have already told of the failure of their leaders to respond.

Meanwhile, Stalin's policy of the stick having failed, he now held out a carrot to lure the peasants into the very kolkhozes against which they had risen so resolutely and so successfully. In the above-mentioned article entitled "A Reply to the Comrade Kolkhozniks" (who, by the way, had never asked Stalin any questions—these were simply invented by Stalin as his favorite way of presenting a case), Stalin described the carrot. The Soviet government, he said, had recently decided to lift for a period of two years all livestock taxes on all draft animals, such as horses and oxen, held in common on kolkhozes, and all cows, pigs, sheep and fowl, both in the collective possession of the kolkhozes and in the private ownership of kolkhoz peasants. The Soviet government had also decided to defer until the end of the year the payment of debts owed by kolkhoz peasants and to cancel all fines and legal penalties incurred up to April 1 by peasants who had joined the kolkhozes. And, finally, the government had decided to provide credits to kolkhoz farmers in the current year up to 500 million rubles. To make his meaning perfectly clear, he added that such benefits would not be extended to peasants who had left the kolkhozes, while those who had already left could become eligible only by returning to the kolkhozes.[8] Stalin deliberately refrained

---

[8] Stalin, *Problemy leninizma*, p. 318.

from saying that the Central Committee decree conferring these benefits upon peasants in or returning to kolkhozes was accompanied by another decree, still unpublished but strictly enforced, providing for the imposition of tax and other material penalties on poor and medium peasants who refused to enter kolkhozes voluntarily. The purpose of these "peaceful" penalties was to make obdurate peasants clearly understand and admit that it was completely impossible to live outside a kolkhoz. "The peasants," Stalin pointed out quite correctly, "are committing a mistake in leaving the kolkhozes." In the end the peasants themselves understood that there were only two paths open to them, one leading to the kolkhoz with its promises of a happy life and the other leading to Siberia, where the merciless NKVD had harsh nature as its faithful ally. There was no third path.

The outrageous failure of the policy of collectivization, which the Bukharinites had clearly foreseen and of which they had vainly given warning, gave rise to great confusion in the ranks of the Party. It was generally believed that the articles and the decrees of the Central Committee were mere lightning rods erected to relieve the electrically charged atmosphere within the Party and in the country as a whole. Meanwhile, the time was fast approaching when a plenary session of the Central Committee would have to be summoned, the last such session having taken place in November 1929.[9] But with even the fanatics in his following understanding that the failure of the Party policy on collectivization must be laid at the door of Stalin and his closest collaborators, it was clear that he and his friends must answer to the Central Committee for the failure, and under such circumstances it would have been political suicide to summon the Party's supreme organ.

Stalin was the last among the Central Committee members to be capable of such a desperate step. Instead he chose the well-tried method of using the Party apparatus to deal with those among his collaborators who were urging him in this direction. The Central Committee apparatus, that is, Stalin's cabinet and the Secretariat, began again to reshuffle Party cards throughout the country, throwing out in the process not only ordinary trumps but even the great Party aces, including all potentially dangerous members of local and central committees and control commissions. Those in charge of oblasts were discharged from Party work by the dozens in the Ukraine, in Belorussia, on the Volga, and in Siberia. The Party leaders were changed in the Turkestanian republics, the Transcaucasian republics and the republics and oblasts of the North Caucasus. Even the leaders of Moscow Oblast, including Bauman, who had until then been one of Stalin's most trusted lieutenants and who had recently been appointed straight from Stalin's cabinet, first as director of the rural section and later as secretary of the Moscow Oblast Committee, were removed. All were accused of the same crime—Left deviationism in applying the general Party line in regard to collectivization.

In the process, Stalin not only liquidated his potential critics, both in the provinces and in the Central Committee, by attaching to them the new Kremlin label

---

[9] "Statutes of the All-Union Communist Party of Bolsheviks," *Pravda*, Moscow, June 26, 1926.

marking them as Left deviationists, but he rehabilitated himself in the eyes of the peasants and the rank and file Party members by imputing his own crime to the conscientious executors of his policy. Those who were dismissed were rarely replaced by local people. The new officials sent out from Moscow were mainly persons who had worked in the Party itself in the apparatuses of the Central Committee and the Central Control Commission, where they had filled posts as heads or deputy heads of sections in the Central Committee, instructors in sections, "experts" in Stalin's cabinet, or lecturers in such higher Party schools under the Central Committee as the Sverdlov and Stalin Communist Universities, schools of Marxism, and the Institute of Red Professors.

At the same time, the Special Section liquidated all traces of Stalin's crime. All Central Committee directives on collectivization from the end of January to the beginning of March 1930 were hurriedly returned to the Central Committee through the messenger service of the NKVD from the special sections of oblast and district committees and the central committees of the national Communist Parties. It is possible that they were destroyed. In any case not a single one of these directives ever saw the light of day, even in Party publications issued after the dethroning of Stalin. Central Committee directives signed by Stalin personally in January and February had superseded, in effect, the Central Committee resolution of early January 1930, on "the tempo of collectivization." Whereas this resolution had provided for gradual collectivization, according to plan and over a period of almost five years, depending in each case on the area concerned, in the heat of the moment and incited by inflated plans and counterplans, or, to use Stalin's words, "giddy from success," Stalin himself had demanded "a more rapid rate of collectivization." Several directives issued at the time were among those recalled. Many of the local leaders now had to sacrifice their Party careers, either because they had refused to apply the directives in practice or because they could not go as fast as Stalin's views on the tempo of collectivization demanded, and they were dismissed as Rightists in practice. It might be thought that now, when life had cured Stalin himself of his excessive fever for collectivization, he would amnesty at least those who had been "Rightists in practice," and would thus partly repair his own mistake. But here, as throughout his life, while unobtrusively correcting his own mistakes, if possible at the expense of those who had been the most faithful executors of his mistaken orders, he destroyed those who had opposed his will and had turned out to be correct, and destroyed them all the more ruthlessly because they had proved to be correct.

So in the course of the 1930's the Right Bukharinites and the Left Deviationists would be replaced by the new post-October generation of Bolsheviks, such as Malenkov, Shcherbakov, Khrushchev, Mikhailov, Suslov, Ponomarenko, Patolichev, and Kozlov in the Central Committee apparatus; Bulganin, Pervukhin, Malyshev, Tevosian, Saburov, and Yefremov as directors of enterprises; Beria, Bagirov, Kruglov, Abakumov, Merkulov, and Serov in the Cheka; Mekhlis, Yudin, Mitin, and Pankratova as Academy members and Red Professors; Gromyko, Malik, Zarubin, Zorin, and Pavlov in Stalin's diplomatic service.

The list could be extended indefinitely. The Army was not involved as its officers, after the liquidation of the Trotskyites, were on the whole unconcerned with politics until the period of the Yezhov terror.

The new generation, free from past "errors" and deviations, lacking in self-will and ambition, efficient and devoted, ready to act and not to reason and, most important, having grown up under the eyes of Stalin himself and passed their lives as a part of a "collective," was capable of everything except independent thought.

Chapter XXIII

My Article in *Pravda* on the Nationality Problem
and my Expulsion from the Institute of Red Professors

Careful study of Party documents, and especially comparison with actual practice in the areas of the USSR inhabited by non-Russians made it abundantly clear that the so-called "national policy" of the Stalin leadership was an empty declaration characterized only by its elasticity and, to use Stalin's words, by its "indirect methods."

I therefore decided to write an article on the subject at the time of the discussions held prior to the Sixteenth Party Congress. I did not reject the national policy of the Lenin period, as outlined in the Tenth and Twelfth Party Congresses but called for putting in practice what in many cases had remained only on paper.

The Tenth and Twelfth Party Congresses in 1921 and 1922 had pronounced the slogans: "We must help the national borderlands to catch up with Central Russia in the fields of culture and economics," and "Let us abolish inequalities among the peoples of Russia." As to these goals I wrote that the rate of our economic and cultural development was such that the clear and precise directives of the Tenth and Twelfth Party Congresses could not be carried out either in the current Five-Year Plan or in the next two or three. But as my main theme, *I denied that collectivization was necessary for the national areas of the USSR.*

I had not yet finished my article when *Pravda* published the "Politburo Theses," that is, the outlines prepared by the Politburo of the papers to be read at the Sixteenth Party Congress by Yakovlev, People's Commissar for Agriculture, Kuibyshev, President of the Supreme Council of National Economy, and Shvernik, Chairman of the Central Trade Union Council. I decided to revise my article and devote it to "loyal" criticism of the Central Committee theses. I realized that I was risking expulsion from the Party and therefore from the Institute of Red Professors, it having been decided at the plenary session of the Central Committee in November that propaganda for the views of Right opportunism was incompatible with membership in the Soviet Communist Party. To write against collectivization, even as applied to the national areas of the USSR, would certainly be considered crass opportunism. But in my mood at the time, I was inclined to ignore the risk and consider my action as a heroic deed.

I did not tell Sorokin that I was preparing the article on the nationality problem, but when it was finished I placed it on his desk. Although Sorokin was keeping close watch over my progress, the article came as a complete surprise to him. I remember his first reaction as clearly as if it were today. Sorokin read the article carefully, occasionally going back to read over again certain pages. I could not tell by the expression on his face whether to expect to be greeted by sarcastic laughter or congratulations when he had finished. He finally came to the end and pronounced his verdict: "The mountain has come to Mahomet! Congratulations!" and shook me warmly by the hand. My national pride as well as my pride as an author were gratified. I mailed the article to *Pravda* on my way back through Tverskaya Street.

A week went by during which my article failed to appear. To Sorokin's questions I answered evasively, "not yet," or "I am revising it and will send it in later." Another week began. Early each morning I dashed off to the newspaper stand, bought a paper, scanned the table of contents with mounting impatience, turned over the pages, and then crumpled the paper in disgust—nothing again! Obviously, I thought, my creation had found its way where it belonged: at best in the editorial wastebasket of the vigilant Mekhlis, and at worst in Yaroslavsky's office. The worst could be tragicomic: I had simply denounced myself!

I had given up dashing out every morning to get a newspaper, and considered it beneath my dignity to inquire at the *Pravda* office. But on June 22 I was filled with both joy and despair when I read an announcement: "In today's *Pravda*— A. Avtorkhanov, 'The Party Directives Regarding the Nationality Problem Must be Carried Out.'" The article was being published as the first and main contribution to the discussions page. It covered nearly three columns of *Pravda*, and was unchanged except for the omission of a few sharp passages, especially those involving personal criticism of the Politburo members Andreyev and Kaganovich, who had been assigned by the Central Committee to carry out the first "experiment" in "mass collectivization." I had collected a great deal of material on the way in which the experiment had been imposed on the peasantry of the North Caucasus by Andreyev, the secretary of the krai district Party committee, and Kaganovich, who had been deputed to assist him. *Pravda* had allowed me to criticize the "Politburo Theses," but not their application by Andreyev and Kaganovich. As a result the article ended abruptly and ineffectively rather than as a bombshell. But I was satisfied.

The article evoked a sharp reaction at top Party level; first, in a number of articles attacking me in *Pravda*, and later, through the Institute of Red Professors. One such article was that written by the new Party theorist on the national problem, Kosta Tabolov, a member of the permanent Nationality Commission of the Central Committee and later secretary of the oblast committee in Alma-Ata where he was liquidated by Yezhov and Malenkov. His article appeared in *Pravda* on June 26. It constituted a violent attack "from the Party position" on the well-known Party figure Dimanshtein for a leading article in the magazine *Revolution and the Nationalities* and on me for my article in *Pravda*.

As to my article, Tabolov declared: "Comrade Dimanshtein may have overestimated our successes, tried to minimize the nationality problem and declared it solved in the main, but Comrade Avtorkhanov has gone just as far in the opposite direction by minimizing our successes in nationalities policy."

Citing my view that there was no immediate prospect of ensuring the execution in the near future of the directives of the Tenth and Twelfth Party Congresses, he added: "Therefore Comrade Avtorkhanov demands a forced rate of development for outlying nationalities, even if this is not economically expedient." These views he attacked as follows: "The first mistake in Comrade Avtorkhanov's formula is the assumption that all minorities are as backward as the most backward tribe of the Chechen people." Some of the directives in question, he claimed, had already been applied in full. "Secondly, Comrade Avtorkhanov separates nationality policy from general Party policy. Third, Comrade Avtorkhanov obviously slurs over and thus minimizes the enormous achievements of the nationality policy of the proletariat. Fourth, by not appreciating our successes and by spreading pessimism, Comrade Avtorkhanov provides material for local nationalist leaders in their attacks on the Party."

Tabolov then proceeded to define Party national policy for the kolkhozes, the gist of which was that the Party was opposed to making any concessions to nationality, to exaggerating the distinctive features of the republics and national oblasts, and to minimizing the successes accomplished. The Party was against local nationalism, which he declared was equivalent to various forms of "opportunism" in the borderlands. The nationality problem, in its new stage, must have room for such Party slogans as "liquidation of the kulaks as a class on the basis of total collectivization." He attacked my thesis that priority should be given to land distribution rather than to the creation of kolkhozes or voluntary land-working associations. Tackling the problem of the organization of land exploitation would not, he declared, accelerate socialist reform in the countryside but would perpetuate individual farming.

In conclusion Tabolov referred to my first thesis, regarding which he cited my statement that "it is necessary now, during the reconstruction period, to aim at a practical, rather than a forcible abolition of *actual inequalities among nationalities*." On this he commented: "Very characteristically the article contains a demand for 'practical measures' in the solution of these problems." And asked the rhetorical question: "Have we been approaching the problem of abolishing actual inequality impractically?" (It must have come as a surprise to Tabolov and his friends when the Sixteenth Party Congress soon after, in a resolution on a speech by Stalin, declared: "The Party must adopt more *practical* measures in applying Lenin's nationality policy, in abolishing the causes of national inequality, and in developing the national cultures of the peoples of the Soviet Union.")[1]

The main purpose of my article was more clearly understood by Lev Gotfrid, who also wrote an article on the nationality problem, which appeared in the June 30 issue of *Pravda*, after the Sixteenth Party Congress had already opened. Gotfrid, although not a member of the Central Committee, was a member of Stalin's cabinet, where he was considered an expert on the nationality problem. His article was entitled, "On Comrade Avtorkhanov's Correct and Right Opportunist Proposals."

---

[1] *VKP(b) v rezolyutsiyakh*, Vol. II, p. 624.

The article accordingly was divided into two parts. In the first, my criticism of the practice and the level of national-cultural development in the Soviet borderlands was recognized as correct, and was even supported by additional facts and figures furnished by the Central Committee (a direct answer to Tabolov's optimism). But my demand that collectivization be dropped in the national republics and oblasts was not only rejected but was described as the most pernicious Right opportunism (a crime for which persons were being expelled from the Party and dismissed from their positions, or, if students, from their educational institutions).

Gotfrid began by asserting that I had both correctly and opportunely drawn the attention of the Party to an urgent problem, that of the manner in which the directives of the Tenth and Twelfth Party Congresses on the nationality question had been applied in practice. He agreed that practical measures must be adopted, without forcing the issue, to iron out existing inequalities between the various nationality groups during the reconstruction period. However, he objected to my viewing special treatment of the national groups as a necessary sacrifice. The Party, he declared, had never regarded the problem of industrialization of the borderlands from this point of view. It was not a sacrifice but the only possible and correct policy. He recalled in this connection Lenin's well-known statement: "Scratch a Communist and you will find a Russian chauvinist." The article then went on to point out that the resistance of officialdom and bureaucratic elements in the state apparatus and economic organs to admitting the native population to the apparatus was enormous, and agreed that I was right in exposing how little had been done in this respect. When an Uzbek, a Turkman, or a Tadzhik was lucky enough to be taken on by a factory, he was in most cases doomed to remain for ever an unskilled workman. "We can safely say that on many sovkhozes in Central Asia, external conditions smack strongly of colonialism."

Gotfrid then went on to deal with the heart of the matter. "We find ourselves," he said, "in complete agreement with Comrade Avtorkhanov on the problem of industrialization of the national areas of the USSR, but we must emphatically disagree with his obviously 'liquidatory' and Right opportunist theories and proposals regarding the methods of collectivizing the borderlands, including Central Asia." As to my belief that preparatory work for mass kolkhoz and cooperative land exploitation movements must begin at the beginning with land distribution, he asserted that I was confusing agrarian reform in Uzbekistan with land distribution. . . . "What would happen if the line proposed by Comrade Avtorkhanov were followed? *It would mean dropping the slogan of total collectivization in the national districts in earnest and for long, . . . for distribution would entail the establishment of individual peasant holdings, and would mean the perpetuation of the status quo.*" He also insisted that I was wrong in claiming that mass and even anti-Soviet demonstrations had taken place on a larger scale in the national districts than in Russia proper. "It is a well-known fact," he declared, "that Kazakhstan and Central Asia are not one and the same, and it was under the leadership of the Central Committee of the Party that correction of the political mistakes undoubtedly made in the course of collectivization in Central Asia made possible fulfilling of sowing plans. This is why we cannot but consider Comrade Avtorkhanov's proposal as *an attempt to drag the Party backward, away from the general Party line and onto the path for which Right opportunist elements do nothing but whine and whimper.*"

In regard to my personal "political illness," Gotfrid offered the following diagnosis: "Comrade Avtorkhanov has definitely caught the disease of Right opportunist shortsightedness and panic. He is blind to what already exists in the national borderlands, but, as Lenin said, 'it is impossible not to acknowledge that which exists, for it will force its existence upon you.' Why do we so violently disagree with Comrade Avtorkhanov? Simply because, to quote Lenin again," and here he cited from Lenin's speech against Bukharin at the Eighth Party Congress: "In difficult times the problem becomes a million times more important and to fall ill just then is to compromise the revolution." He closed by saying, "the traitor ears of a master of Rightist affairs stick out from Avtorkhanov's arguments about the methods of collectivizing the national borderlands."

After attacks of this kind in *Pravda* it was usually the turn of the Chekists to speak, and there the "traitor" was invariably talked to in a different language and with more formidable arguments. In the meantime, quotations from Lenin were being bandied about and I was linked indirectly with Comrade Bukharin. The hint was too obvious for my peace of mind. A psychological attack was also launched from within the Institute. As soon as I arrived at the Institute that morning a crowd reminiscent of Yudin began to pester me. "Comrade Master of Rightist Affairs!" "How much are you paid by Comrade Bukharin?" "Comrade Red Professor, show us your traitor ears!" One man even thrust his face in mine, stuck his thumbs in his ears, spread out his fingers, and began to bray like a donkey. The crowd burst out laughing. I answered with a swinging blow in his face. Blood poured from his nose. He did not hit back, and the crowd immediately parted to let me pass.

Later I met Sorokin. I was terribly excited. He had been already informed of the incident and had read the article about me. Besides, he realized that his influence was at least partly responsible for my having become twice the hero of the day. He invited me to accompany him. An hour later we were sitting in the same restaurant in the Arbat where he had first begun to enlighten me. The fruits of this enlightenment were now obvious: the "traitor ears," the public bullying, my hitting my fellow-student. Sorokin ordered beer. I asked for vodka. "What's the matter with you, you don't generally drink vodka?" asked Sorokin in mock surprise.

"To complete the picture," I replied, and added, "the sages are right when they say, without vodka there is no understanding."

A decanter appeared on the table. I filled two glasses and emptied my glass at a gulp. The alcohol slowly crept to my head. I had another glass, and another. My brain began to work, to work rapidly, too rapidly . . . My sense of humiliation became even more acute, my thirst for revenge still greater. I mentally transposed the whole crowd of Institute asses to Russia as a whole, to the Turkestan deserts, and the Caucasian Mountains, where it, or a similar organized gang, represented the "dictatorship of the proletariat." If Gotfrid was right in saying that such burning hatred for them all was treason, I had become a traitor long before the appearance of Gotfrid's article.

"Well, many thanks for fighting for this kind of a Soviet régime, Comrade Sorokin," I said stiffly to Sorokin, as if he had been following my mental processes and was personally responsible for the present régime.

"Every nation," replied Sorokin, "gets the government it deserves, said a wise German. The cruelty of the Prussian Junkers was balanced by their chivalry, but the cruelty of our Kremlin Bashibazouks is eclipsed by their baseness. I must disappoint you—I did not fight to put power in the hands of these rascals. But if they are temporarily in power today, Hegel is profoundly right—we deserve it. If a Party a million strong contains not even a score of Taras Bulbas who can say, 'we begat you, and we shall kill you,' then we are all rascals. But the ideals of our revolution are as little to blame for the actions of Stalin as Christ was for the cruelties of the mediaeval inquisition. What can we conclude? As there are no Taras Bulbas, and as the captains are the first to abandon ship, there is nothing for it but to hide in deep catacombs, as did the early Christians in Rome. Party and country alike, we have been occupied by the police bayonets of internal foreigners. The occupation will last as long as it will take us to expiate our own baseness through suffering."

Sorokin's "new philosophy" left no doubt in my mind that the unconditional surrender of the Bukharinites at the Party congress then in session was already a fait accompli. Sorokin was not prepared to capitulate, nor were dozens of others around him, but they were individuals without reputations in the Party and country. The "revolution from above," the coup d'état which was Sorokin's dream, needed big names rather than striking slogans.

The "captains" of such an army—the leaders of Bukharin's group—absolutely refused to lend their names for the purpose. Rykov, the de jure head of the Soviet government, had no wish to become its head de facto. Bukharin, who still wielded immense authority in the Party, was frightened by his own authority. Stalin's régime, which had been in a critical stage from the fall of 1929 to the late fall of 1930, was saved, not by the wisdom of the Stalinists but by the doctrinaire attitude of the Bukharinites. The word "cowardice" springs to my lips, but I do not wish to be unfair. Even Stalin became a great coward only after his victory. Before then, he had risked his life with as much courage as his opponents of the day. They were certainly not cowards! They were slaves of the doctrine, which they shared with Stalin, of "social revolution," "dictatorship of the proletariat," and "socialism." The difference was that after reaching power, Stalin simply abandoned these high-sounding phrases while the Bukharinites continued to grasp at a mirage.

We sat for a long time discussing the ruin of our illusions: the miserable collapse of the last stand of the opposition in the Party. Regarding my personal political and psychological misfortunes, Sorokin comforted me by saying that because of developments in the Party congress the attacks against me would not stop until I had made public recantation of my alleged errors.

"However," he added, "be guided by your own conscience."

On the following day, July 1, I was called to a meeting of the cell bureau of the Institute of Red Professors. The agenda contained two items: (1) Comrade Avtorkhanov's Right opportunist article in *Pravda*, and (2) Comrade Avtorkhanov's rowdy behavior in the Institute. Nearly all members of the bureau were present, including Sorokin. The first item was quickly disposed of. The chairman asked me two questions: (1) Did I admit that my article in *Pravda* was an example of Right opportunism and (2) If so, was I prepared to admit that the article was a mistake? The chairman hinted that the decision on the second item depended on my answers to the first.

Quietly, but firmly, I answered: "Since I regard the first question as an act of provocation I refuse to answer the second."

The chairman then switched over to the attack. "You maintain that kolkhozes are not suited to the national republics and oblasts. You write that in those areas the Party should not carry out the policy of total collectivization and liquidation of the kulaks as a class; you say that the Party's policy in those areas should be to distribute the land, that is, to perpetuate individual landholding. And yet you want to convince us that this is not a Right opportunist theory? You want the Party to have two policies, a Leninist policy for Russians and a Bukharinite policy for the nationalities?"

"This," I replied, "is your own personal interpretation, based on the fantasies of Tabolov, Gotfrid and others, and so is not valid. I can recognize only one authority in this case, and that is the Party Congress. And the Fifteenth Party Congress has just announced a policy providing for land distribution."

"And Stalin is not an authority as far as you are concerned?" asked one of the members of the bureau with biting sarcasm.

"More so for me than for you," I answered, in an attempt to provoke him.

"Then read what Stalin said at the Sixteenth Congress about land exploitation. Four days after the appearance of your article Comrade Stalin declared, 'the Party has restudied the method of land distribution in favor of collectivization.' Do you agree with this?"

This was a direct, pointed, and most unpleasant question. Stalin had certainly been following our discussions and had in fact said what the member of the bureau had quoted. My position was critical. All eyes were fixed on me. The least indiscretion or false step on my part could be fatal. The deliverance for which I had been hoping from the beginning now came. Sorokin got up to speak.

"I feel that we are discussing Comrade Avtorkhanov's case in a one-sided and prejudiced manner. For purposes of analysis his article should be divided into two parts, as was done by Gotfrid. The first part is a very serious and correct presentation of the problem of the need for the Party to pay more attention to the nationality problem and the whole question of the nationalities. For this Comrade Avtorkhanov should be thanked and not blamed. The Central Committee has commented very favorably on this part of the article, and Comrade

172

Gotfrid has told me as much. Both the Central Committee and we consider that the second part contains a mistaken premise—the recommendation for promoting land distribution instead of collectivization for the national republics. On direct instructions from the Central Committee, Comrade Gotfrid has already corrected Comrade Avtorkhanov's error. To brand him as a Right opportunist after all this means consciously to push a young member of the Party into the abyss. I propose that we stop the discussion of this point and, as the second point is linked to the first, to remove both from the agenda."

Sorokin's speech provoked a stormy debate. Forgetting me for a time, they began to attack him. The fatal word "conciliator" was spoken and they began fulminating against Sorokin as a conciliator.

The decision adopted was one quite unexpected by either Sorokin or myself. It was (1) to expel Comrade Avtorkhanov from the Party as a "degenerate" and "Right opportunist" and to bring before the Central Committee the question of expelling him from the Institute; and (2) to reprimand Comrade Sorokin for his conciliatory attitude to Right opportunism.

The second item on the agenda—my "rowdy behavior"—was dropped automatically. The next day, July 2, Sorokin and I—he as a "conciliator"—went to the Central Committee. During an interval in the Congress we managed to speak to Stetsky, who listened carefully to our account of the bureau meeting and its decisions, but refused to go into details. He simply said: "Your argument has already been answered by the resolution of the Congress on Stalin's address," and referred us to the relevant passages in the resolution. These were definite and unambiguous:

> Right opportunists, who have openly expressed themselves against collectivization, have tried to exploit anti-Soviet tendencies and the difficulties of the kolkhoz movement in order to launch a new attack on the Central Committee and its policy. It has lately been observed that there have been a number of attacks by bankrupt Right opportunists trying to discredit all the work of collectivization [and] preaching the theory of voluntary action in the kolkhoz movement and the suppression at this stage of Party slogans such as total collectivization and liquidation of the kulaks as a class. . . . The Sixteenth Congress enjoins the Party Central Committee . . . to carry out without fail the liquidation of the kulaks as a class on the basis of total collectivization throughout the Soviet Union. The Congress declares the views of the Right opposition to be incompatible with membership in the All-Union Communist Party of Bolsheviks.[2]

Stetsky, after quoting these passages, addressed himself to me: "To carry out this decision of the Congress is obligatory for all of us. To carry out land distribution is out of the question. It was precisely your article that Stalin had in mind when he put an end to the discussion by saying, 'the Party has revised [its program by abandoning] land distribution in favor of collectivization,' and the Congress added, 'throughout the USSR.' There is only one course of action open to you—you must go to the *Pravda* office and immediately acknowledge your *gross* Right opportunist error."

---

[2] *Ibid.*, pp. 620, 624.

Stetsky asked me if this was quite clear and I answered that it was. Without asking me if I was willing to admit my error (it must have appeared to him quite natural that I would), Stetsky called his secretary on the telephone and in our presence dictated the following telegram:

"To the Secretary of the Cell Bureau of the Institute of Red Professors: Stop repression of Comrade Avtorkhanov. Destroy minutes regarding Comrades Avtorkhanov and Sorokin. Confirm execution of order. By order of the Central Committee, Stetsky."

On July 4, 1930, *Pravda* published the following letter from me:

COMRADE EDITOR:

In my article "The Party Directives Regarding the Nationality Problem Must be Carried Out" (*Pravda*, Discussion Page No. 17) I stated that collectivization among the nationalities in the borderlands must begin with land distribution. I thereby permitted a gross Right opportunist error and now repudiate this theory. Comrade Yakovlev is perfectly right when he says that "in certain non-grain-sowing areas and in the national areas of the Eastern USSR, the organization and spread of associations for joint land working will be carried out as a stage of transition to the artels, and side by side with them, particularly as the Party has revised the method of land distribution in favor of the collective farm system" [from Stalin's address at the Sixteenth Party Congress].

I have no doubts or hesitations about the correctness of the general Party line in the fields of industrialization, collectivization of agriculture, and decisive struggle on two fronts—first and foremost, against the danger of Right deviation and second, in the field of national policy.

With Communist greetings, A. AVTORKHANOV.

From the very beginning of Stalin's dictatorship, "six commandments for the safety of Soviet citizens" were current in the USSR. They were:

1. Do not think!
2. If you think, don't talk!
3. If you talk, don't write!
4. If you write, don't publish!
5. If you publish, don't sign!
6. If you have signed, repudiate it!

By writing the letter to *Pravda* I was repudiating my "gross Right opportunist error" and thus attempting to obey the sixth commandment and to mend my shaken position in the Institute. The letter was only partially effective. My greatest fear was realized. Two or three weeks later I was summoned by the manager of the Press Bureau of the Central Committee, Sergei Ingulov. I was received by one of his assistants, who conveyed to me very dryly the crux of the matter: "The Central Committee has decided to transfer you from the Institute of Red Professors and place you at the disposal of the national sector of the press bureau. Your duties in that organization will be explained to you by Comrade Rakhimbayev." (Rakhimbayev was in charge of this sector.)

"Will I have the chance to come back to the Institute, or is this all for the time being?" I asked.

"You will have every opportunity to obey Party discipline, and that is all," answered Ingulov's deputy, in a voice which clearly conveyed his wish not to prolong the conversation. I was wise enough not to insist.

"Man is the plaything of fate," it used to be said.

"Communists are the playthings of the Central Committee," it is said now.

Anyone who refuses to play this game finds himself in Siberia. I preferred to play the game.

Chapter XXIV

The Central Committee Press Bureau and Stalin's Letter
Outlining the Campaign Against Freedom of Thought

I did not return to the Institute of Red Professors until 1934. Meanwhile, my work in the national sector of the Central Committee Press Bureau gave me an opportunity to observe at close quarters both the propaganda activities of the Party and the Party manner of dealing with the national problem.

Before the Bolsheviks came into power, Lenin regarded the central press organ of the Party as even more important than the Central Committee itself. After the Party split at the Second Party Congress in 1903 into Bolshevik and Menshevik wings, Lenin did not become a member of the Central Committee, but preferred to join the editorial board of the Party's central press organ, the newspaper *Iskra*, to which Plekhanov and Martov were also assigned. However, when the Menshevik leader Martov, with Plekhanov's support, refused to join the new editorial board and demanded retention of the former six-man board made up of Plekhanov, Lenin, Martov, Zasulich, Potresov, and Axelrod, which the Bolsheviks had wished to replace, Lenin resigned and at his own suggestion became a member of the Central Committee.

At the Third Party Congress, in London in 1905, where the Bolsheviks met alone, Lenin was elected both to the Central Committee and to the central press organ, but at the Fourth Party Congress, in Stockholm in 1906, where the two wings temporarily reunited, he failed to obtain re-election to the Central Committee. At the Fifth Party Congress, in London in 1907, he was elected as an alternate. During this entire period, however, he was invariably elected to membership on the editorial board, which he considered to be of critical importance and to which he was always eager to belong. It was Lenin who provided, in *What Shall We Do?*, the famous Bolshevik definition of the role of the press: "A newspaper is not only a collective propagandist, it is also a collective organizer."

At the time when I was assigned to it, the Press Bureau was under the department of the Central Committee apparatus which dealt with culture and propaganda. About the time I returned to the Institute of Red Professors, in 1934, the Department of Culture and Propaganda was merged with the Department of Agitation and Mass Campaigns to form a Department of Propaganda and Agitation, as a part of a general reorganization along "production" lines, intended to tighten the totalitarian control of the Central Committee apparatus over all forms of life. Until 1929 the head of the Department of Propaganda and Agitation was Krinitsky. In that year he was replaced by Stetsky, who was later liquidated in the great purge of 1937. Ingulov, who was in charge of the Press Bureau at the time I was assigned to it, was later replaced by his assistant, B. Tal, at which time the Press Bureau was changed into a full department of the Central Committee, with increased authority and an expanded field of operations.

The Press Bureau and its successor the Press Department had three functions: (1) to issue guiding directives to the entire Party and Soviet press; (2) to control the press; and (3) to act as a research laboratory for working out new types, methods, and modes of operation for press propaganda. It worked through sectors for Party press, Soviet press, ministerial and departmental press, military press, youth press, nationality press, trade union press, the press of "fraternal Communist Parties," foreign press, and a sector for publication. TASS (Telegraphic Agency of the Soviet Union) had the status of an independent sector.

Each sector had at its disposal in addition to its permanent staff reporters a large number of expert consultants drawn from various central institutions and organizations such as institutes, the Communist Academy, the Institute of Red Professors, the editorial boards of the central press organs, the State Publishing House, the War Department, the Nationality Council of the Central Executive Committee of the USSR, the Central Committee of the Komsomol, the Central Trade Union Council, the Press Department of the Commissariat (later the Ministry) of Foreign Affairs, the Comintern, and so on.

Before the Central Committee worked out a "line of action" in connection with any particular problem, or started a new propaganda campaign, the relevant sector held one or more meetings of its staff specialists to discuss the problems and aims of the new campaign. (To the present day all propaganda is dealt with as part of a permanent series of campaigns.) The question asked at such meetings was not "What should be done?" (this was a matter for the Central Committee), but how to do it, that is, how to obtain the most effective psychological and practical results. Outside consultants as well as regular staff members participating in these discussions were allowed broad scope for initiative.

The Party organizations of the non-Russian nationalities had the same rights of initiative, in conformity with the cultural and other conditions of the national group concerned. Indeed, the local national organizations sometimes went far beyond Moscow in their "creative initiative" in propaganda campaigns. For instance the Department of Agitation and Propaganda of the Central Asian Bureau of the Party Central Committee suggested that Central Asian republics which lagged behind others in their propaganda zeal should be awarded plaster crocodiles. But the Central Committee intervened and the idea was never put into practice. A telegram was sent to Central Asia ordering the crocodiles to be removed from the Central Asian Bureau of the Central Committee. But where the rather stolid Turkestanians had failed, the more dashing Caucasians were able to succeed. At oil fields in Grozny which lagged behind the others, workers were called into meeting and were solemnly handed buffalos, with an honorary certificate reading: "You are loafers and I am your king!" Below-average kolkhozes were given a donkey bearing the placard: "You are donkeys and so am I. We are brothers."

Betal Kalmykov, a person at the time famous throughout the USSR, a former friend of Stalin and secretary of the Kabardino-Balkar Oblast Party committee and a member of the Central Control Commission of the Party Central Committee, did something even more original: he summoned a Congress of Loafers of the republic, with an agenda reading, "we are sitting on the necks of the workers." The oblast press made great propaganda of Kalmykov's congress while he himself triumphantly wired to the Central Committee recommending that a similar congress be held in Moscow for loafers throughout the USSR.

After several such local stunts, the right to initiate them was reserved to the Department of Agitation and Propaganda and the Press Department of the Central Committee.

Within the Press Department, the foreign sector had three functions, (1) censorship, (2) information, and (3) research.

Censorship boiled down to a strict foreign trade monopoly in ideas, whether expressed in newspapers, journals, or books. Not a single work—political, literary, scientific, or technical—could be exported from the USSR without the knowledge of the sector. In the same way, no newspapers, journals, books, etc. could be imported into the USSR without the knowledge of the sector. This, however, was not its main task, even though it was strictly performed. The chief aim of the "idea monopoly" was to prevent a harmful "smuggling of ideas" from the outside into Soviet publications—books, journals, and newspapers—as required by "Stalin's letter," of which more will be said later. The foreign press sector saw to it that Glavlit (the main censorship department) received up-to-date instructions regarding translations from other languages, as well as on the use of foreign sources by the Soviet press. Equally strict instructions were worked out for TASS on the extent to which the Soviet press could use information provided by foreign agents and its own foreign correspondents. These instructions were revised in accordance with changes in the foreign policy of the USSR concerning any particular state, party, or even person.

The functions of the foreign press sector, as the provider of information or rather misinformation, consisted in acting as a masked part of Soviet camouflaged propaganda diversionism, such as probing the enemy in order to find a sympathizer, or reconnaissance within the camp to subvert the enemy by misinforming world public opinion in regard to the Soviet Union. This work was usually done through foreign "progressive journals" in Moscow, through the neutral foreign press, and frequently through less discerning foreign politicians or famous literary figures. It was from this angle that the press sector viewed the publication of the works of foreign writers. It was enough for a formerly "reactionary" writer to make a couple of public statements favorable to the Kremlin for Moscow to enter him immediately on its list of "progressive" writers. In the meantime, the State Publishing House would be ordered by the Press Department of the Central Committee to translate the writer's works into Russian at once, while the writer himself would be advertised as a friend of the Russian people. A certain number of foreign writers were caught in this way. It would serve no purpose to cite their names here. Suffice it to mention the fact that André Gide was one of those who was not caught.

The research functions of the press sector had nothing to do with literary research. They dealt purely with reconnaissance for purposes of military, economic, and political espionage. Large and well-staffed research groups to analyze and classify the world press were attached to the Marx-Engels-Lenin Institute and to the Institute of World Politics and World Economy. These groups had access to the newspapers and journals of all countries and in all languages. They studied both the central and the provincial newspapers and journals of almost all the countries of the world. Once a month they supplied the press sector carefully analyzed data culled from the foreign press and divided into the three types of material—military, economic, and political—mentioned above. The press sector gave these analytical statements a "secret" classification and distributed them as bulletins among the relevant departments.

The nationality press sector had for the nationality press the same aims as the Press Department for the press as a whole, except for the Ukraine and Belorussia which were served by special publication sectors of the department. The nationality sector served only the non-Slav peoples—those of the Crimea, the Caucasus, Tataria, Central Asia, and Kazakhstan—for internal propaganda, and those of only the Eastern Asiatic countries—China, India, Afghanistan, Iran, Turkey, the Arab States, etc.—for foreign propaganda. The sector was headed by Rakhimbayev, a member of the nationality commission of the Central Committe and one of the future chairmen of the Central Executive Committee of the USSR. Among the outstanding specialists on the national questions who played important parts in the work of the sector were Broido, Dimanshtein, Ryskulov, Gabidullin, Pavlovich, Klimovich, Arsharuni, Tulepov, Tabolov, and Svanidze, the brother of Stalin's first wife. In addition, representatives of other Communist parties from the Comintern, diplomats from the Commissariat for Foreign Affairs, and specialists from the two Eastern Universities in Moscow—the Stalin Communist University for the Workers of the East and the Sun Yat-sen Communist University—were constantly used as outside consultants for the sector's propaganda in the East. The students of the Sun Yat-sen University were Chinese, Koreans, Malayans, Indians, Filippinos, Negroes and so on.

The sector's tasks in connection with foreign propaganda were particularly difficult. The general Communist propaganda line, with methods that hardly varied in the West, had little relevance to the needs of the Asian countries, which required special attention to such factors as feudal and pre-feudal conditions in countries subsisting side by side with highly developed industrial areas, as in the cases of China and India, the exceptional power and influence of local religions whose spirit was opposed to Communist infiltration, the existence of powerful nationalist movements which, in their ideas and social structure, denied the dogmas of Communism, etc. In such countries, Communist propaganda had to deal not with a proletariat which wished to socialize the wealth of capitalists, but with

179

peasants who were aiming at themselves becoming rural capitalists. However, all these countries had one thing in common—their status as dependent or semi-dependent colonies.

But it so happened that in these countries it was the nationalist-minded intelligentsia together with the clergy which preached the doctrine of independence. This intelligentsia was a main and a dangerous rival of "national Communism." The Central Committee took these facts into consideration and based its propaganda in the East on strict differentiation between countries and places, in accordance with theoretical principles openly expounded by Stalin as early as 1925 in a speech to the students of the Stalin Communist University for Workers of the East.[1]

In Moscow itself, only official Comintern documents and Marxist classics were translated and published for the benefit of Asian countries. I believe that documents and works prepared by foreign Communist parties in the East were not printed in Moscow for export purposes. It was Litvinov's job to see to it that this rule was adhered to. The People's Commissariat for Foreign Affairs invariably and vigorously protested to the Central Committee whenever the representatives of foreign Communist parties attempted to establish their own printing establishments in Moscow, even if their publications bore a false imprint indicating that they were published in Berlin or Calcutta. The commissariat protested no less vigorously against furnishing foreign agents of the Central Committee and the Comintern with the forged documents of export-import organizations under the Commissariat of Foreign Trade. As it was, however, common practice to furnish agents with forged documents of such organizations, the Comintern and the Commissariat for Foreign Affairs were in a state of perpetual cold war with each other.

Later on, after a number of such forgeries were discovered abroad, the question was, on Litvinov's urgent insistence, brought up before the Central Committee, where he argued that if the Comintern, like the Bolsheviks before their victory, did not wish to risk its personnel in revolutionary work, it was also true that the Commissariat for Foreign Affairs could not endanger the prestige of the Soviet government on an international scale. He succeeded in obtaining formal recognition of his statement that the Soviet government and the Comintern were not identical. But there was yet another channel, the secrets and possibilities of which were unknown even to Litvinov. This was the NKVD, which was able to help Comintern agents on one essential condition, that they be at the same time agents of the NKVD.

In all national republics and oblasts in the Soviet East, the press was in two languages—Russian and the local language. It was a simple enough matter to direct and control the portion of the press which appeared in Russian. But this portion was read by only the insignificant part of the population which consisted of the local intelligentsia. As a rule, over 90% of the native population did not understand Russian, and over 60% were illiterate in their own language, except in

---

[1] Stalin, *Sochineniya*, Vol. VII, 1950, pp. 146–51.

Georgia, Armenia, and to some extent Azerbaidzhan. Printed propaganda in the Soviet East began, therefore, with a campaign for the abolition of illiteracy. Primers were first issued, followed by translations of the Marxist classics—Marx, Engels, Lenin, and Stalin. What a vast amount of public money was spent on a cause which had absolutely no effect whatever! The languages of many backward nations had no political or philosophical terminology for the simple reason that before the Revolution they had had no alphabet. The Marxist classics were translated for them. Naturally enough this indigestible hodgepodge was quite useless, but the Central Committee persisted nevertheless.

At the same time, vast sums were earmarked for agitation and propaganda in the national areas. In addition to the Marxist classics, the entire mass of current political literature put out in Moscow, such as speeches, resolutions, etc., was immediately translated into the local languages. Special staffs of translators were trained. In order to avoid terminological chaos, special dictionaries approved by local Party committees were issued. The translations were strictly controlled. To begin with, the translator, who had to be approved by the local Party committee, was personally responsible for the quality and, which was most important, the political consistency of his translation. After that a literary editor, especially selected for the project, was made responsible for the accuracy of the translation. The third step was for the director of the publishing organization to send the translation to the political reviewer—a Party member appointed by the Party oblast or republic committee. The reviewer was required to furnish a detailed review, dealing with the political reliability of the translation. The translation was then returned to the publisher to be revised again in accordance with the reviewer's notes and instructions. After all this, the Party committee appointed a responsible editor, who was a Communist of some standing. The responsible editor read the manuscript in its final version and stamped it with his official approval, after making any corrections he thought fit. The manuscript was then sent to the censorship office, which checked the manuscript from the point of view of its own requirements. If the manuscript survived this checking, the head of the censorship office stamped it, "Passed for Publication," and gave it a censorship number. The manuscript was now at last sent to the printers. The type would be set, the proofs corrected, and the book printed, but it would not see the light of day until a so-called token copy had been officially stamped by the relevant sector of the NKVD, "Approved for Distribution." And so the book would come out and reach its readers. But alas, only then would its political errors be revealed. Who, in this case would be held responsible? All who had had anything to do with it, except the NKVD.

A similar procedure for the publication both of writings in the original Russian as well as in translation was worked out after Stalin wrote the famous letter referred to above.

So complex a procedure gives the impression of being completely fantastic, but it had one indubitable advantage for a Soviet régime: it provided maximum insurance for the state against an expensive mistake, even though it increased production costs. In many cases a Turkmenian or other publishing house would issue a large edition of a "great work of a Marxist classic," in which two or three expressions would be found which could be interpreted in two ways. Such a work would be immediately withdrawn from circulation, together with the people responsible for it. The people would be thrown into the prisons of the NKVD, and the books into the fire. As a result, people became very careful and, as always in such cases, would find a way out of the situation. If an expression had a double meaning in the native language, the original Russian word would be inserted in the text without being translated. The result was a Russian language in local dialect. Such Russianization was certainly not imposed by Moscow; it was simply the result of local preventive measures adopted for purposes of self-defense.

It is true that the new-alphabet committee of the Central Executive Committee of the USSR attempted to combat misuse of Russian terminology in the languages of the national minorities. The committee provided many examples in its publications and reports to the Central Committee of the manner in which national publishing houses and newspapers would, in order to insure themselves, use Russian words in Latin script even though the terms concerned could be easily translated into the local tongue particularly if it were Turkic. The local Party committee could usually defend itself by saying something to the effect that "our writers are perfectly right in preferring the great Russian language—the language of Lenin and Stalin (!)—to the Arabism of mediaeval obscurantism." The Central Committee itself was powerless to oppose such an argument. At the end of 1930, when I was sent to the Caucasus, this problem had not yet been solved. But in the summer of 1937, after I had graduated from the Institute of Red Professors, and two months before my arrest, I witnessed the easy and radical solution adopted for the problem of the national alphabet as well as terminology.

What happened was this. Bauman, the head of the Scientific Department of the Central Committee, summoned a special meeting of representatives of Moslem republics and provinces for a conference on "The Introduction of the Russian Alphabet in the Republics of Central Asia, Kazakhstan, Tataria, Bashkiria, Azerbaidzhan, and the North Caucasus." Bauman read aloud a draft resolution of the Central Committee on the question. Appended to the draft were resolutions by local national Party committees with requests that their alphabets be transliterated from the Latin into the Russian script. The reasons given were the same: the Russian alphabet was the alphabet of Lenin and Stalin. The participants in the meeting were given an opportunity to express their opinions on the draft. But no one spoke up. There was a tense silence, which can best be described in the words of the Russian proverbs: "Don't mention a rope in the house of a hanged man," or "It is no use weeping for the hair if the head has been cut off." Lenin had once referred to the Latin alphabet as the "revolution in the East," but in Lubyanka Prison the leaders of the October Revolution were now having their heads cut off. What use was there in arguing about an alphabet?

Bauman insisted that there should be a discussion. We remained silent. Probably there were not three persons present who agreed with the draft, but at the same time there were no volunteers for the Lubyanka. The fatal words "bourgeois nationalism" were by then being freely used by *Pravda* as a brand of iniquity. The basic argument of the Central Committee's draft resolution— "the Russian alphabet is the alphabet of Lenin and Stalin"—was in the circumstances completely unassailable. Besides, objections were pointless, the whole matter having been decided in advance.

When no one reacted to his repeated demands for a discussion, Bauman made a list of those present and proposed that Ryskulov be the first to speak. Ryskulov, a fat, squat, powerfully built little man, with a Mongol face and wearing horn-rimmed glasses and an elegant European suit, resembled a Japanese professor rather than the first Kazakh revolutionary. Up to that time, he had been carving out a good career for himself, in spite of a very unsuitable propensity for thinking independently. In Lenin's time, he had been able to manage it: he was both the ruler of Turkestan and Stalin's deputy in the Commissariat of Nationalities. He had also been a deputy chairman of the Council of People's Commissars of the Russian Soviet Republic when Rykov was chairman. At one time, Stalin had forecast a great future for him, but this failed to materialize as a result of Ryskulov's unaccountable character. He was gradually pushed aside, but his opinion was still listened to with respect. This was his opportunity to give his opinion. He did not let the opportunity slip. "Comrade Bauman insists," he said, "that we give our opinion on the question of Turkestan's reaction to the introduction of the Russian alphabet. I must reply quite honestly—there is none. If, instead of the Russian alphabet, you were to introduce the Georgian alphabet [a thrust at Stalin's native alphabet] or Chinese hieroglyphics, the result would be the same."

Others contented themselves with repeating the standard phrase: "I approve the Central Committee draft." Bauman read aloud the following resolution: "The draft resolution of the Central Committee dealing with the introduction of the Russian alphabet in the national republics is unanimously approved by the conference of nationalities." A month later all of us who had taken part in the conference, including Bauman and Ryskulov, were sitting, if not in one cell, at least in adjoining cells, of Lubyanka Prison. But the proposal for a Russian alphabet had been accepted "unanimously" and this alphabet is still thriving in the Moslem republics of the USSR.

Before leaving the subject of the Press Bureau and its place in the totalitarian scheme developed by Stalin, I must say a few words about Stalin's letter to which I have already referred, and also about Stetsky and the other leading figures in the Press Bureau with whom I came in contact.

I shall begin with Stetsky, who, as I have said, headed the Department of Agitation and Propaganda from 1929 to 1937.

Stetsky was an economist by profession, a graduate of the School of Economics of the Institute of Red Professors. He was an enthusiastic pupil of Bukharin, but left him in 1928. Although he himself came from a bourgeois family, he was tolerant toward bourgeois scholars, in spite of the fact that the reverse was usually the case: a Communist from an alien social background tried to make up for his "alienism" by applying repression to members of his own class. Vyshinsky, Bulganin, and Malenkov are good examples.

As a "dialectician and propagandist," Stetsky is probably best characterized by the following two examples.

At the height of fresh persecutions in a Ukrainian city, the agitation and propaganda section of the oblast Party committee confiscated the synagogue of the local Jewish community and turned it into a club for the oblast branch of the League of Militant Atheists, after making the necessary alterations. A group of believing Jews complained to Kalinin, who was chairman of the Central Executive Committee of the USSR. Kalinin's chancellery forwarded the complaint to the local executive committee with a note that a synagogue could be closed only after obtaining the agreement of the congregation. The chief of the oblast agitation and propaganda section then had the issue put to a vote; that is, the Komsomol members who represented him visited the homes of Jewish families with an open ballot on whether or not the citizen in question wished to have a club for "educational purposes" opened in the district. The unsuspecting Jews all signed voluntarily. The resulting approval was returned to Kalinin, whereupon his chancellery gave permission for the synagogue to be turned into a club. It was only after this that the congregation grasped the fact that it had been deceived and sent a protest to the Party Central Committee, personally addressed to Kaganovich, probably because he was a Central Committee Secretary and a Jew. The local rabbi wrote, in the name of his congregation, that his parish was prepared to let the Soviet government have another and smaller synagogue situated in the same city, but asked the authorities to let them retain the large old synagogue, which the parish regarded not only as a place of religious worship but also as a rare architectural relic of the spiritual and religious culture of the Jews in Russia. Kaganovich, irritated by the fact that the petition had been addressed personally to him, endorsed the rabbi's petition, "both synagogues to be closed." The petition was duly sent to the Agitation and Propaganda Department of the Central Committee and finally reached Stetsky. Stetsky, no less irritated than Kaganovich, wrote a new endorsement, "to be filed." At the same time, he wired to the local agitation and propaganda department that the recently requisitioned synagogue was to be restored at the expense of the oblast committee and immediately returned to the congregation. The rabbi, who had no way of knowing what had happened, wrote a letter of thanks addressed to Kaganovich. Kaganovich, exasperated by Stetsky's high-handedness, appealed to Stalin to arbitrate between them. Stalin, according to reports, very quickly set Kagonovich straight. "Lazar," he said, "no single Catholic can outdo the Pope, but an unwise Pope can make all the Catholics rise up. We do not want an uprising."

In 1934, after I had returned to the Institute, I ran into another good example of Stetsky's way of working. We had an Ancient History seminar conducted by the well-known Professor Preobrazhensky, who was not a member of the Communist Party. The subject of the seminar was the classical democracy of Athens in the time of Pericles. The aim of the main lecturer as well as that of the other participants was not only to present the official concept, but also to demonstrate an approach to the subject based on independent research. Everything went well until one of the participants began to quote from Marx and Engels in an attempt to prove that the situation in Athens was not as described by Thucydides. The usually calm and imperturbable professor tried for a long time to restrain himself and make the speaker return to his subject. When he saw that his attempts were in vain, the old man suddenly brought down his fist on the table and jumped up as if he had been stung. "This is scandalous," he cried, "monstrous! You are talking the most utter nonsense. You must know that Marx and Engels are no authorities on questions of ancient history. You are a disgrace to science and to your teachers. Sit down! I am giving you a mark of 'unsatisfactory!'"

The speaker sat down in confusion. We, too, were in confusion. The professor turned to the next speaker and asked him to proceed, but the group's Party organizer stood up and proposed that in view of the fact that both the professor and the students were tired the seminar be adjourned until the next day. The professor rejected the proposal, but those of us who knew what it was all about supported the Party organizer. The seminar was adjourned, the professor departed, and the Party organizer opened an extraordinary Party meeting to discuss one point only, "the counterrevolutionary and anti-Marxist outburst of Professor Preobrazhensky." The secretary of the Party committee, Kudryavtsev, and the director, Dubina, were hurriedly summoned to the meeting. The Party organizer gave a brief explanation of the affair, and a number of persons rose to speak, all, of course, condemning the professor. On the following day the subject was referred to a meeting of all Party members of the Institute. It was decided to elect a delegation to report the incident to Stetsky and to demand Professor Preobrazhensky's removal from the Institute. The delegation went off to Stetsky in a fighting mood. Stetsky listened to the report with cold indifference, before handing down his decision. "Professor Preobrazhensky," he said, "is not a Marxist but a bourgeois scholar; the Central Committee knows this better than you do, but we never knew before that you were such simpletons. Learn facts from people like Preobrazhensky until you surpass them in their own bourgeois science. Then, when this happens, we shall kick out all these Preobrazhenskys and put you in their places. But not a day earlier. Now go back to the Institute and continue your seminar." (As it happened, not only was Preobrazhensky kicked out in 1937, and kicked right into prison, but Stetsky was kicked out and into prison with him.)

Ingulov, the chairman of the Central Committee Press Bureau, was a person of quite different views. Rigidly orthodox, he used to boast that it gave him greater spiritual satisfaction to read Marx and Lenin than to listen to Tchaikovsky, read Tolstoy, or visit the Tretyakov Art Gallery. On the basis of this spiritual wealth, he wrote incredibly dull, ignorant, and therefore entirely pro-Stalinist books on *politgramota*, that is, elementary official Communist philosophy. In fact it was Ingulov who was the originator of that unified collection of well-worn phrases which afterward formed part of the "iron fund" of Stalinism, under the name of "Communist Upbringing" of the masses. Ingulov mercilessly prosecuted the slightest departure from this system in the Soviet press. Even his own works were subjected to pretentious "self-criticism" and "self-confession," whenever they failed to accord with the current trend in the famous "general line." Ingulov was one of those who could read aloud the leader's unexpressed thoughts. Such persons constituted Stalin's "reserve brains." The "basic brains" thought for everyone, but the "reserve brains" thought only for Stalin. They competed with each other in interpreting the dictator's will, while Stalin himself acted as umpire. He allowed only those of the competitors to make a career who proposed the most effective and the most dynamic recipes for the establishment of his personal dictatorship. In its first sensational article directed against Stalin, on March 28, 1956, *Pravda* attempted to explain the careers of such persons by saying that Stalin promoted to the leading posts only those who approved the cult of Stalin. This, of course, is quite wrong. Hundreds and even thousands of Stalinists who assisted in creating the cult of Stalin perished in Stalinist prisons. In order to make a career, it was not enough merely to praise Stalin, to be slavishly devoted to him, or to constitute his "reserve brains." The Stalinists who survived and made careers for themselves were those who were Stalinist not only in *thought* but also in *action*.

Ingulov's ideological career is an apt illustration. Ingulov both suggested and worked out the details of the organized campaign for the Stalinization of social sciences in the USSR which was launched in the beginning of the thirties. His initiative won him a career, but he was later liquidated because he was unable to put his proposals into effect. While still head of the Central Committee Press Bureau, Ingulov—over the heads of his immediate chief Stetsky and Stetsky's deputy Kerzhentsev—prepared for Stalin a detailed report on ideological "smugglers." This was the Stalinist idea, not yet formulated by Stalin himself, of a dictatorial regime in ideology. Stalin adopted Ingulov's plan and early in September 1931 the Organization Bureau of the Central Committee adopted two decisions on the matter. One called upon Stalin to publish in the press an article on anti-Leninist sorties on the literary front and to direct the Party's attention to the necessity for systematic exposure, both oral and written, of Trotskyite and other falsifications of history, to unmask them methodically, to declare war on liberalism in literature, and to stop all discussions "at the expense of the vital interests of Bolshevism." The other relieved Kerzhentsev from his post as deputy head of the Central Committee Department of Agitation and Propaganda and appointed Ingulov in his place.

The first of these decisions resulted in the publication in *Proletarian Revolution* of Stalin's famous letter entitled "Some Problems in the History of Bolshevism." In it Stalin did not spare even Yaroslavsky, a member of the Central Committee presidium and one of his most trusted assistants in defeating the Opposition. His criticism of Yaroslavsky was based on a passing remark in Yaroslavsky's *History of the All-Union Communist Party of Bolsheviks* to the effect that before Stalin's return from abroad in April 1917 the Bolsheviks leaders in Russia—Kamenev, Sverdlov, and "even Stalin"—had not adopted the correct Leninist policy of offering conditional support to the Provisional Government.

However, Stalin's letter went far beyond individual criticism. In the spiritual and ideological life of the USSR, it was as important as his speech at the conference of Marxist agriculturists in December 1929 had been in the life of the Russian peasantry. Although in form Stalin's letter was directed against historians, its basic principles were applied to the entire ideology of the country. With it there began the full and complete Stalinization of all social sciences in the USSR. All spheres of the cultural and spiritual activity of Soviet citizens—science, literature, painting, theater, music, cinema, and even the circus—were revised from the point of view of the requirements laid down in Stalin's letter. This spiritual dictatorship later assumed unbelievably ugly forms, even from the point of view of the interests of the régime itself. Not only suspicious books of all kinds, but even the stenographic reports of Party congresses and old articles, speeches, and pamphlets by Stalin himself, or by Kaganovich, Molotov, or other members of the Politburo, were withdrawn from Party libraries. In informing the local Party organs of this program, the Central Committee explained that these works by the Party leaders reflected what had been true in the past, but must now be re-edited and commented on by the authors themselves to purge them of anything that might seem to contradict the current policy and practice of the Party.

It was true that in speeches by Party leaders and in published minutes of the Central Committee, young Communists could easily find examples of the instability, lack of principle, and cynicism of Stalin and the Stalinists in their ideological struggle for power. In some such documents Stalin, Molotov, Kaganovich, Voroshilov, Mikoyan, Shvernik, and Andreyev were vigorously defending Bukharin, Rykov, and Tomsky against Zinoviev and Kamenev; in others they were categorically rejecting the "cult of the individual" and declaring that the highest principle of Leninism, as far as organization was concerned, was "collective leadership" by the entire Central Committee and not leadership by individual leaders. Stalin himself had loudly affirmed in his discussion with Trotsky and Zinoviev that it was absurd to think that after Lenin's death the Party could have only one leader. "We have no such leader and cannot have one. Collective leadership will be our leader." And in the speech at the Fourteenth Party Congress in which he had attacked Zinoviev and Kamenev, Stalin had stated several times (in itself a suspicious fact) that he was opposed to applying repression to Party leaders (which would include Zinoviev, Kamenev, Trotsky, Bukharin, and other members of the Politburo, who were at the time considered Party leaders). "We are against the policy of decapitation," he said. "This does not mean that the leaders will be allowed to do what they like in the Party. Oh no, there will be no kowtowing to the leaders. If any one of us goes too far he will be called to order—this is essential. It is impossible to lead the Party from outside the collective. It is stupid to dream of such a thing after the death of Ilyich, stupid to speak of it. . . . Collegiate leadership—that is what we need now."[2]

Since Stalin was steadfastly and consistently pursuing his aim of personal dictatorship while forbidding other Party leaders to so much as dream of such a

---

[2] *Ibid.*, pp. 390–91.

thing it is evident that his earlier writings had to be taken out of circulation. It was not until after World War II that Stalin and the members of the "collective leadership" which succeeded him decided to publish them in a large edition of Stalin's collected works. But by this time Stalin was a recognized dictator, and everyone saw that it would now be stupid to dream of "collective leadership" while the infallible "genius, teacher, and father" was still alive.

However, even so, the collected works of Stalin came out semialtered and semifalsified. The more "obsolete" of his works, such as articles and speeches in praise of Trotsky as the organizer of the October Revolution, and articles and speeches in defense of Zinoviev, Kamenev, Bukharin, and others, were not included.[3]

[3] P. Berlin, "Stalin under Self-Censorship," *Sotsialisticbesky vestnik*, New York and Paris, No. 11, 1951, pp. 211—212.

Chapter XXV

National and Other Opposition Movements in the Early Thirties

It was extraordinary that there should be powerful resistance after the Sixteenth Party Congress, at which Stalin, to all appearances, had won a complete victory and the leaders of all existing opposition groups had pleaded their repentance. It was also extraordinary that there should be resistance in the higher Party organs, elected at a Congress whose membership was restricted to the highest Party dignitaries, with impeccable records, while former oppositionists had been allowed to attend only if they had recognized Stalin as the Party leader. However, resistance there was. It came from three directions at once—from the Young Bolsheviks headed by Central Committee member Syrtsov, from the Old Bolsheviks headed by Central Committee member Smirnov, and from the National Bolsheviks headed by Central Committee member Skrypnik. All three were well known in the Party, and, which was particularly significant, had never been involved with any previous opposition groups.

Syrtsov's Group

A most unpleasant and unexpected event for Stalin was the "revolt of the Young Bolsheviks," made up of members of the Central Committee and the Central Control Commission, and headed by Syrtsov. The Young Bolsheviks represented the people upon whom Stalin relied for his "planned policy" of annihilating the Old Guard and creating a new Party. The head of the group, Syrtsov, was being groomed to succeed Rykov as chairman of the Council of People's Commissars of the USSR. He had been recalled to Moscow from his position as secretary of a Party district committee in Siberia and appointed chairman of the Council of People's Commissars of the Russian Soviet Republic in Rykov's place, although the latter still remained nominally chairman of the Council of People's Commissars of the USSR. By then it was clear to all that Rykov was a doomed man. Ever since Lenin's time, the chairman of the Council of People's Commissars of the Russian Soviet Republic had also been chairman of the Council of People's Commissars of the USSR; the fact that this tradition was now broken emphasized the inevitability of Rykov's doom and the certainty of his replacement by Syrtsov. The appointment of Syrtsov as alternate member of the Politburo, together with such future Politburo members as Mikoyan, Chubar, and Andreyev, made it absolutely clear that he had been chosen to head the Soviet government. His future depended entirely on himself—on the degree to which he would grasp the new policy and the importance of the role which he would have to play in its execution. Stalin for his part was doing all in his power to assist Syrtsov in this task. Although he was the youngest member of the Politburo both in age and in Party membership, and was not a full member but only an alternate member of the Politburo, he was given authority equal to that of some of the full members. The appointment of Syrtsov to Rykov's place within the Politburo itself, which was a question of the immediate future, would give him a place second only to that of Stalin within the one-party state. Stalin deliberately emphasized at every opportunity the role to be played by this new rising star and thus gained him the envy of his old companions in arms. And Stalin well remembered the great services which Syrtsov had rendered him in his attempt to carry out his plan for collectivization in Siberia and in the Urals.

Syrtsov's personal qualities for the role assigned to him were also beyond doubt: he possessed exceptional organizing ability, directness and decisiveness, an orthodox past, energy and will power, and an apparent complete lack of ambition to think independently in the sphere of policy. At a distance—when Syrtsov was still living in far-off Siberia—these qualities had appeared most impressive in connection with the natural selection of the new man. However, they concealed a potential danger. If Stalin were unable to utilize them in his own interests they could be turned against him. Stalin believed that by guaranteeing a spectacular political career, for which the competition was so fierce, he would remove the danger inherent in Syrtsov's personal qualities. However, in this he was mistaken. No sooner had Syrtsov come to live in the capital, no sooner had he gained access to the ante-chamber of Stalin's office, than his provincial innocence disappeared without a trace.

Syrtsov saw what Stalin was aiming at and what methods he was using to gain his ends. He saw, too, the members of Stalin's Secretariat, men unknown to the Party but able to decide the Party's fate in its name. To his great surprise he discovered, too, that the high-sounding title of "Politburo" was nothing but a legal cover for an all-powerful, illegal force—again that of Stalin's Secretariat. He saw more—he saw that the anonymous collective group known as the Party Central Committee was the collective pseudonym of Stalin's technical employees.

Under these circumstances, the newcomer's choice was strictly limited: he had either to serve in this apparatus with excellent chances of making a career for himself, or to oppose it with equally excellent chances of perishing in the attempt. Stalin's resounding victories over all opposition groups, right or wrong, spoke in favor of Stalin's apparatus. Not to choose Stalin needed considerable personal courage and a great store of the idealism typical of the old revolutionaries. And as it happened, Syrtsov had both.

Syrtsov decided that what the Old Bolsheviks—Bukharin and his followers—had failed to do, he and the Young Bolsheviks within the Central Committee and the Central Control Commission would be able to accomplish. Syrtsov's program was the same as that of the Bukharinites, but his methods and his means for carrying on the fight were different. Stalin, he saw, was no idealist, no seeker after truth. All debate with him on the ways and ideals of socialism was not only useless, but harmful. All attempts to appeal to the Party were equally harmful. The Party, Syrtsov understood, was composed entirely of careerists, and had no idealism. But even the section of the Party which had still remained true to the old principles and was capable of independent thought would never dare to undertake independent action while the Party was being run along the established lines. The whole policy of the Party, he decided, was dictated not by the interests of the country but by the interests of the apparatus. In order to correct the policy it was necessary to correct the organization, the apparatus, and the system of administration. In short, to deprive Stalin of the possibility of becoming a dictator it was essential to reorganize the Party's administration on entirely new principles. Should the raising of this question provoke Stalin's opposition, that would be the best evidence of his secret intentions, and would facilitate his removal from the Central Committee. And indeed, in what did Stalin's power within the Party apparatus consist? In the fact that he was both Secretary-General of the Secretariat—the executive organ of the Central Committee—and chairman of the Politburo—the legislative organ—while in a third and very important organ—the Orgburo—he was not only a member, but in practice the chief, although the nominal chairman was the Second Secretary of the Central Committee, a position filled at different times by Molotov, Kaganovich, Andreyev, Zhdanov, and Malenkov.

It was Syrtsov's intention to split up this unusual concentration of power in the hands of one man, unprecedented in the history of the Communist Party. The problem was how to achieve it. To this Syrtsov's answer was: by an organized demand presented by the secretaries of the oblast and district committees, who were the main links in the Party chain of command. It was on this theory that he formed the so-called Right-Left bloc of Syrtsov, Lominadze, and Shatskin. Vano Lominadze was a member of the Central Committee and Secretary of the Transcaucasus District Party Committee, made up of the central committees of the three national Communist parties, those of Azerbaidzhan, Armenia, and Georgia. Lazarus Shatskin was a member of the Central Control Commission and one of the leaders of the Communist Youth International. The bloc relied on the support of many secretaries and other local Communists. A considerable portion of the younger members of the Central Committee and the Central Control Commission, such as Chaplin, Milchakov, and Khitarov, showed open sympathy for the demands made by the bloc, even if they did not give it their direct support. The former oppositionists were represented in the bloc by Sten, a former member of the Central Control Commission.

Syrtsov's bloc, as Stalin referred to it, although it was merely a group of persons thinking along the same lines, intended to make known its organizational plan at the next joint plenary session of the Central Committee and the Central Control Commission, which was scheduled to take place not later than October 1930. But Syrtsov and his friends never had an opportunity to take part in the plenary session. The whole group was expelled from the Party and the plenum was not convened until December. This was the first occasion upon which members of the Central Committee and the Central Control Commission were expelled from the Party, not only without discussion but even without the consent of the Central Committee plenum. A number of local secretaries were removed, and those who abandoned Syrtsov at the last moment and went over to the other side received promotions, in accordance with the usual method of encouraging traitors and treachery. Syrtsov's former friend D. Sulimov, the secretary of the Urals Oblast committee, was appointed chairman of the Council of People's Commissars of the Russian Soviet Republic in Syrtsov's place.

Smirnov's and Other Groups

The expulsion of the Central Committee and Central Control Commission members who had belonged to Syrtsov's group showed that Stalin's enemies would henceforth discuss their programs not in plenary sessions of the Central Committee but in the dungeons of the OGPU. Nevertheless, Stalin did not feel master of the situation. The liquidation of one opposition group turned out to be the prologue to the appearance of another. The opposition to Stalin resembled the legendary hydra of ancient Greek mythology, which always sprouted new heads in the place of those which had been cut off. The members of Syrtsov's group had hardly had time to reach their places of exile—individuals were not usually shot at that time—before three new opposition groups turned up—those of Ryutin, Smirnov, and Skrypnik.

Although these groups had much in common in ideology and program, they had no organizational connection. Ryutin was a former Party secretary of the Krasnaya Presna District of Moscow and alternate member of the Central Committee after the Fifteenth Party Congress. His group, which was formed outside the Central Committee, was composed mainly of former members of the Right Opposition—Galkin, Astrov, Slepkov, and others. Smirnov had for many years been a member of the Central Committee and had at one time been Secretary of the Central Committee, and had been one of the active members of the St. Petersburg Union of Struggle for the Liberation of the Working Class founded by Lenin and Martov. His group was the most influential of the three. Smirnov's authority in the Party was enormous. He had belonged to Lenin's personal guard as one of the founders of Bolshevism. He was a member of the Central Committee Organization Bureau and was therefore familiar with the organizational policy of the apparatus as it was carried out behind the scenes. Smirnov's group brought together for the most part old Bolshevik workers who had never belonged to any opposition groups. It had cells in labor circles in Moscow, Leningrad, Ivanovo-Voznesensk, and Rostov-on-Don. Some of the more prominent participants in the Civil War, such as Eismont and Tolmachev, also belonged to the group. It was supported by important trade union officials. The group's program differed little from that of Bukharin's former group, but was more radical and specific. It demanded revision of the unbalanced "super-industrialization" which was developing some parts of the national economy at the expense of others, dissolution of kolkhozes and sovkhozes, reorganization of the OGPU and its subjection to legal control, removal of Stalin and his disciples from the Central Committee, and separation of trade unions from the state.

Smirnov's group understood of course that it was powerless to carry out its program by legal methods. It therefore decided to go underground and formed an independent group known as "Bolshevik Workers." Although its program was essentially a second edition of that of Bukharin's Right Opposition, there was one important difference—the difference in time—which made Smirnov's group more dangerous for Stalin's majority than Bukharin's group had been. The Bukharinites had proclaimed their program and formed their group at a time when the Central Committee, in alliance with the Bukharinites and carrying a right-of-center flag under the joint leadership of Bukharin and Stalin, had defeated the left-wing Trotskyites, and when Stalin's economic and organizational policies had not yet been tested in practice. Where the Bukharinites had attempted to anticipate the possible direction and consequences of Stalin's plan without having sufficient data to discredit it, Smirnov's group on the other hand was attacking Stalin's plan on the basis of its first practical results. These results had been very serious and very concrete. For agriculture they had included the failure of the plan for the compulsory collectivization of agriculture, the disastrous decline in grain cultivation, and the mass slaughtering of cattle and consequent famine throughout the country on an unprecedented scale, particularly in the Ukraine where, according to the most conservative data, up to five million people had died of starvation. For industry Stalin's plan had resulted in a striking imbalance in industrial development, as the emphasis on the development of heavy industry had led to a standstill in the progress of light industry and in the production of consumption goods. Finally, Stalin's plan had resulted in transformation of the OGPU into a force standing above both Party and state.

In reviving the old program of the Rightists, Smirnov's group was not acting on theory, but simply because it was taking stock of the practical results of Stalin's policy. For all Stalin's resourcefulness in dialectics, he would have been helpless in the face of such facts if they had been available to the Bukharinites. They were now available to Smirnov's group. But on the other hand Stalin, too, had a force at his disposal which he had not had in 1928—the "monolithic unity" within the Central Committee and the Central Control Commission, and the much improved local Party police apparatus.

Smirnov's group, however, had no intention of appealing to the Party and this fact constituted another, and indeed the main difference between it and Bukharin's opposition group. Smirnov's group decided for the first and last time in the history of Stalinism to subject the controversial problems, both economic and political, to the judgment of the workers and peasants in whose name Stalin was ruling. This could be done only by working underground without formal separation from the Party. His first efforts were devoted to the creation of illegal cells in the more important working-class centers and the drawing together of all oppositional elements within the Party.

The group regarded the overthrow of Stalin's leadership as an act aimed at restoration of the power of the Soviets which it claimed had been usurped by the Stalinists. It was to be a second edition of Lenin's plan for a "proletarian revolution," but this time directed against the dictatorship of the Party apparatus and the OGPU. Smirnov's main slogan was that of Lenin: "All power to the Soviets!" Smirnov's group sought to attract to this platform the former leaders of the Right Opposition. Bukharin categorically refused to have anything to do with Smirnov's group. Uglanov, Katov, Mikhailov, and others did the same. Rykov and Tomsky probably met Smirnov several times, but did nothing more. The Rightists had taken to heart the lessons of the years 1928–29.

Meanwhile Stalin lost no time. At the end of 1932, the Chekists uncovered Smirnov's group. In January 1933, a joint plenary session of the Central Committee and the Central Control Commission examined the whole case against the group as reported by Rudzutak. No incriminating documents against Smirnov were presented to the plenary session apart from evidence of OGPU secret agents to the effect that the group had drawn a contrast between the "power of the Soviets" and the Party apparatus. To protect their own interests, the leaders of the Right, to whom Smirnov had turned earlier in his activities, stated that Smirnov had never talked to them of anything other than ordinary current affairs. However, the resolution adopted by the plenary session was very severe. It was short, and typical of the manner in which such oppositions were dealt with. The resolution, prepared by Stalin and Rudzutak, declared that Smirnov's group had adopted the Rightist program and had found support among the workers, even those who turned bourgeois. No attempt was made to prove the existence of any organizational connection between the former Right leaders and Smirnov's group, but a last warning was nonetheless issued to Rykov, Tomsky, and Shmidt. Bukharin, who had definitely disavowed the Smirnov group in the course of the plenary session, was not mentioned. The text of the resolution was as follows:

The Anti-Party Group of Eismont, Tolmachev, A. P. Smirnov, and Others

I.

1. The joint plenary session of the Central Committee and the Central Control Commission makes it known that, while signifying their agreement with the Party line in theory, Eismont, Tolmachev, Smirnov, and others in fact carried on anti-Party activity and opposed the Party policy. They established a factional underground group, the members of which were drawn by Eismont and Tolmachev from among corrupt elements and bourgeois turncoats who have turned away from the working masses.

2. At the time when the Party is reaping the results of the great victories of the Five-Year Plan, the group in fact rejects the policy of industrialization and aims at the restoration of capitalism in general and of the kulaks in particular. In this it resembles the anti-Party group of Ryutin and Slepkov.

3. The joint plenary session of the Central Committee and the Central Control Commission therefore resolves:

(a) To approve the decision of the Central Control Commission Presidium to expel Eismont and Tolmachev from the Party as corrupt and treacherous anti-Soviet individuals, who have tried to organize opposition to the Party and the Party leadership;

(b) On the basis of the resolution of the Tenth Party Congress, to expel Smirnov from the Party Central Committee with a warning that if he fails to gain the confidence of the Party in his work, he will be expelled from the Party.

The joint plenary session of the Central Committee and the Central Control Commission declares that Central Committee members Comrades Tomsky and Rykov and Central Committee candidate member Comrade Shmidt have failed to combat anti-Party elements effectively and actively in defense of the general line of the Party and the practical policy of the Party Central Committee. Instead, they have stood aside from the struggle with anti-Party elements and even maintained relations with Smirnov and Eismont, thus in fact encouraging them in their anti-Party activities. Also, their entire behavior made it possible for various anti-Party elements to count on the support of the former leaders of the Right Opposition. The joint plenary session of the Central Committee and the Central Control Commission requires Comrades Rykov, Tomsky, and Shmidt radically to change their behavior insofar as combatting anti-Party elements is concerned and warns them that if they should continue with their present behavior they will be subject to severe measures of Party punishment.[1]

It is typical that Stalin did not make known in the resolution the fact that the Communists Eismont and Tolmachev had been arrested and were being kept in prison as "enemies of the Soviet régime" while their group was being discussed at the plenary session. However, the demand made by Stalin and Rudzutak that Smirnov be subjected to the same fate was rejected by the plenum and the resolution was equally silent on the subject of "All power to the Soviets!" In another connection, but at the same plenum, Stalin explained his conception of Soviets without Stalinists. "Too much stress," he said, "should not be laid on Soviets as a form of organization, even though this form is an immense revolutionary achievement: the main thing is the work performed by the Soviets, the character of their work; it is vital that the Soviets be headed by revolutionaries and not by counterrevolutionaries."[2]

"National Opposition" within the Party

In a letter written to Maxim Gorky from Vienna in 1912, Lenin said: "I quite agree with you about nationalism. We have a marvelous Georgian here, who has started writing a long article in *Prosveshchenie* (Enlightenment)."[3] The "marvelous Georgian" was of course Stalin and the article was "Marxism and the National Question."

After the October Revolution, Stalin received an appointment suited to his speciality and was made People's Commissar for Nationalities. Later his commissariat was given the definite task of fusing with Soviet Russia the Soviet

---

[1] *Pravda*, January 13, 1933.

[2] Stalin, *Voprosy leninizma*, pp. 403–05.

[3] Lenin, *Sochineniya*, Vol. XVI, 1930, p. 328.

republics which had known an independent existence—the Ukraine (1919), Belorussia (1919), Azerbaidzhan (1920), Armenia (1920), and Georgia (1921). The Central Asian republics—Kazakhstan, Tataro-Bashkiria, and the North Caucasus—had already been incorporated in the Russian Soviet Republic. All these republics had been sovietized but they had not yet been subjected to unified control by the central government at Moscow. Central control was exercised by the Party as represented by the Central Committee of the Russian Communist Party, which was in a sense a little Cominform with limited powers of control. The Central Committee's authority was ideological rather than organizational. Each Soviet republic enjoyed, so to speak, full "national and Communist sovereignty" in its national affairs. On paper the republics even had their own armed forces and conducted "independent" foreign policies. The Riga agreement with Poland in 1921, for instance, was signed by two Soviet republics, the Russian and the Ukrainian.

The first step toward setting up a Soviet federation had, it is true, been made as far back as December 1920, when the Russian, the Ukrainian, and the Belorussian Soviet Republics had concluded military and economic conventions with each other and later with the Caucasian republics. But this was still confederation with Russia, not federation. When the first step toward creating a federation was taken at the end of 1922, the National Communists made their appearance. The National Communists in Stalin's native land, the Caucasus, fought with particularly great bitterness against the loss of their country's independence. The Caucasian Communists rejected the draft of the first "Stalin Constitution" which sought to create an All-Union Federation in the form of a Union of Soviet Socialist Republics. On September 15, 1922, the Central Committee of the Communist Party of Georgia passed a resolution declaring that "the unification of *independent Republics* recommended by Comrade Stalin must be considered premature. The unification of economic effort and of policy as a whole must be considered essential, provided *all attributes of independence are preserved.*"[4]

This "separatist" resolution of the Georgian Communists, which R. Akhundov, Kadirli, and other leaders of Soviet Azerbaidzhan agreed to support and which threatened to ruin the whole scheme for the creation of the USSR, was rejected by Moscow. Stalin, Ordzhonikidze—then secretary of the Caucasus bureau of the Central Committee of the Russian Communist Party—Molotov, and Myasnikov, an Armenian, argued before the Central Committee that the Caucasian National Communists—later to be referred to as "national deviationists"—did not express the will of the Caucasian peoples. A month later the question was discussed at a plenary session of the Central Committee. On October 16, 1922, Stalin, as Secretary-General of the Central Committee, sent the following telegram to Georgia, with copies to the other national republics:

> The proposal of the Georgian Central Committee referring to the prematureness of unification and the preservation of independence has been unanimously rejected by the Central Committee plenum. In view of this unanimity, the representative of

[4] L. Beriya, *K voprosu ob istorii bolshevistskikh organizatsiyakh v Zakavkaze* (The History of Bolshevik Organizations in Transcaucasia), Moscow, 1948, p. 243.

the Central Committee of Georgia, Mdivani, was compelled to withdraw the demands of the Georgian Central Committee. The plenum has accepted, without amendment, the proposal made by members of the Commission—Stalin, Ordzhonikidze, Myasnikov, and Molotov—to preserve the Transcaucasian Federation and bring it, together with the Russian Socialist Federated Soviet Republic, the Ukraine, and Belorussia, into a Union of Socialist Soviet Republics—the USSR. . . . The Central Committee of the Russian Communist Party has no doubt at all that its directive will be applied enthusiastically. [5]

This "unanimous" resolution was accepted by the triumvirate of Stalin, Kamenev, and Zinoviev. Lenin was sick and did not take part in the activities of the Central Committee or the government. Trotsky was opposed to the triumvirate and was allied with Lenin. The resolution of the Central Committee was rejected by the Georgians. Stalin, under cover of the Central Committee's authority and taking advantage of Lenin's illness, began a purge in Georgia. This was the famous "Georgian Case" which occasioned Lenin's well-known "testament" demanding Stalin's dismissal from the post of Secretary-General of the Central Committee. Trotsky wrote of it as follows:

> Two of Lenin's secretaries, Fotieva and Glasser, served as liaison. This is what they report. Vladimir Ilyich [Lenin] was extremely worried by Stalin's preparations for the coming Party congress, particularly in connection with his factional intrigues in Georgia. "Vladimir Ilyich," were Fotieva's precise words, "is preparing a bomb to be thrown at Stalin at the Congress." The word "bomb" is Lenin's, not Fotieva's. "Vladimir Ilyich asks you to look into the Georgian case yourself and save him great worry." On March 5, [1923], Lenin dictated the following note to me: "Dear Comrade Trotsky, I beg you very much to take on the defense of the Georgian case in the Central Committee of the Party. At the moment, the case is being looked into by Stalin and Dzerzhinsky and I cannot be sure of their impartiality. Quite the contrary! . . ." I asked why the question had become so acute. It appeared that Stalin had once again betrayed Lenin's confidence: in order to obtain support for himself in Georgia, he, behind the backs of Lenin and the entire Central Committee, wiped out the best elements in the Party with the help of Ordzhonikidze, and not without Dzerzhinsky's assistance, while falsely claiming the authority of the Central Committee. Stalin took advantage of the fact that Lenin was too ill to see the other comrades and tried to feed him false information. . . . Fotieva again came to me with a message from Lenin addressed to the old revolutionary, Mdivani, and other opponents of Stalin's policy in Georgia. Lenin wrote to them: "Am following your case closely. Am shocked by Ordzhonikidze's roughness and the connivance of Stalin and Dzerzhinsky. Am getting notes and speech ready for you." [6]

But Stalin continued to thunder at the Georgian "national deviationists." Lenin was, of course, not a "separatist," but the leader of the "centralists." However, he wished to establish centralization ("federation") without repression against his own political adherents in the Caucasus. But Stalin's aim was not merely "centralist." He regarded Georgia as his own province. In the Georgian case, he was still too much of a Georgian and too much of a "provincial." Besides,

---

[5] *Ibid.*, p. 245.
[6] Trotsky, *Moya zhizn*, Vol. II, pp. 220–21.

the main threat to his successful career came from his native Georgia, where Lenin's personal friends, such Old Bolsheviks as Mdivani, Makharadze, Orakhelashvili, Okudzhava, etc., were then residing. Stalin, therefore, tried to do away with his enemies once and for all. Lenin asked his wife, Nadezhda Krupskaya, to telephone Stalin to demand that he desist from his Georgian campaign. Stalin called her "an intriguing woman" and used other insulting names. Trotsky writes as follows:

> Kamenev gave me some additional information. He had just visited Nadezhda Konstantinovna Krupskaya, who had asked him to come and see her. She was greatly worried and said to him: "Vladimir has just dictated a letter to Stalin telling him that he was breaking off all relations with him." The immediate cause of this was semi-personal. Stalin had attempted to isolate Lenin from sources of information and had been exceptionally rude to Krupskaya. "But you know what Ilyich is like," added Krupskaya, "he would never have gone so far as to break all personal relations if he had not considered it necessary to destroy Stalin politically."[7]

It was under these circumstances, and in direct connection with the Georgian Case, that Lenin's Testament of 1922 came into being, together with his additional note of January 4, 1923, demanding Stalin's dismissal from the post of Secretary-General on account of his "roughness and disloyalty." Documents published in 1956 provide official confirmation of these statements.[8]

Lenin's death saved Stalin but at the same time spelled the death sentence of the Georgian National Communists. The death sentence, however, was not carried out until twelve years later, in 1936. "In the years 1927 to 1935," Beria later reported, "national deviationism, having fused with counterrevolutionary Trotskyism, grew into an agency for Fascism [and] turned into an unprincipled and cynical gang of spies, wreckers, diversionists, informers, and murderers, a wild gang of mortal enemies of the working class. In 1936, a Trotskyite Center for spying, wrecking, and terrorist activities was discovered, which included B. Mdivani, M. Okudzhava, M. Toroshelidze, O. Gikhladze, N. Kiknadze, and others."[9]

The struggle of the National Communists for the sovereign rights of their republics continued even after Lenin's death. The question of adopting the Constitution was discussed at the Second Congress of Soviets of the USSR, which met March 26 to February 2, 1924. The congress again witnessed a difference of opinion as to the nature of the Constitution of the USSR. Stalin, Zinoviev, and Kamenev proposed federation, while the delegates from the Ukraine, Belorussia, and Georgia made proposals based on the idea of confederation. "The fraternal Soviet republics" claimed the right to conduct an independent foreign policy. (Stalin, of course, granted them the "right" twenty years later, but at a time when

---

[7] *Ibid.*, p. 223. See also *Rech Khrushcheva na zaktrytom zasedaniye XX sezda KPSS, 24–25 Fevralya 1956 g.* (Khrushchev's Speech at the Closed Session of the Twentieth Congress of the CPSU, February 24–25, 1956), Munich, pp. 6, 7. (Hereafter cited as *Rech Khrushcheva*).

[8] *Kommunist*, No. 5, 1956.

[9] L. Beriya, *op. cit.*, p. 256.

they had no right to make use of the right.) The Moscow plan, involving federation, was finally adopted although with important additions and improvements, proposed on the spot. It formed the basis of the Constitution of 1924.

Compared with the Stalin Constitution of 1936, it was super-democratic as far as the national question was concerned. According to it, the Union republics kept all the "attributes of independence" in all matters of internal self-government. The competence of the federal government of the Union in Moscow covered only four aspects of state life—foreign policy, armed forces (defense), transport, and communications (post and telegraph).

From 1924 on, the National Communists looked to the Constitution of 1924 as a basis for their fight for "autonomy" and against centralization. In this respect their efforts were perfectly legal. But after Stalin's victory over the Party, their struggle became "illegal" and "counterrevolutionary." Of the rights of the "fraternal republics" nothing remained but sweet memories. Centralization of the power of the government continued apace. The heads of the national republics and the national Communist parties were hired and fired, not even by Stalin, but by his personal chancellery.

It was under these circumstances—gripped by hopelessness and despair—that the last National Opposition was formed within the Soviet Communist Party. This was the opposition led by Skrypnik, a member of the Party Central Committee and of the Politburo of the Ukrainian Communist Party.

Stalin had little liking for, and even less confidence in, the Ukraine—the largest republic in the Soviet Union next to the Russian Republic. The Ukrainians were not a mere "national minority," without a history or civilization of their own, but were a great and compact people who could boast of outstanding intellectual and political cadres. But in the hour of historic decision, the hour of the Russian Revolution, a considerable part of the Ukrainian intellectuals had joined the camp of the "separatists." The victory of the Bolsheviks in Russia had hastened the movement for Ukrainian autonomy in January 1918 openly supported not only by Austro-German diplomacy but by Austro-German armed force. At the Peace Conference in Brest-Litovsk, at which a separate peace was concluded, the foreign minister of the Ukraine sat opposite the Soviet foreign minister, not as a "younger brother" but as the representative of an independent power.

Lenin, who needed a breathing space, even at the cost of what he called "the most obscene, the most shameful peace," recognized this independence de facto. But the collapse of the German Empire soon after buried in its ruins the independence of the Ukraine. Lenin, supported of course by the bayonets of the Red Army and a series of efficiently organized internal explosions, declared the Brest-Litovsk Peace Treaty null and void, and the Ukraine a Soviet Republic. The explosions, naturally, had internal supporters. Ideologically they were far from being in complete agreement—they were split into *Borotbists*, *Ukapists*, Anarcho-Communists and simple Communists—but they all shared the same political platform; that of a Soviet regime. And nothing more was needed at the time.

The Ukrainians were promised an "independent" but Soviet Ukraine. When the Soviet Ukraine became a fact and a greater degree of Communist centralization in the Ukraine a necessity, Molotov was appointed First Secretary of the Central Committee of the Ukrainian Communist Party, in 1920, and henceforth the Ukrainian Bolshevik throne was as a rule occupied by "centralists." At the same time, however, the resistance of local National Communism also grew.

Mikola Skrypnik was an outstanding representative and leader of Ukrainian National Communism. He had been a member of the Russian Social Democratic Labor Party from 1900 on. After the Party split into two, he became a Bolshevik, a "professional revolutionary" of the Leninist school, and repeatedly suffered for his actions. He played an important part in the Bolshevik coup d'état and the Civil War in the Ukraine, and became one of the leaders of the Party and the government—the Politburo and the Council of People's Commissars—of the Ukraine. He represented the Communist Party of the Ukraine in the Executive Committee of the Comintern and was a member of the Party Central Committee of the Soviet Union. From 1930 on, he headed the National Opposition in the Ukraine against the Kremlin.

"Skrypnik's fall from grace," as Stalin called it at the Seventeenth Party Congress in 1934, resulted from the fact that it coincided with the growth in the Ukraine of yet another power, this one a movement outside the Party—the revolutionary underground movement of Ukrainian nationalists. The underground nationalist groups included the Union for the Liberation of the Ukraine (SVU) created in 1930, the Ukrainian National Center created in 1931, and the Ukrainian Military Organization (UVO), in 1933. These organizations had only one main aim—national independence for a free Ukraine, while the task which Skrypnik and his group set for themselves was more modest; all they asked for was "internal independence" for a Communist Ukraine.

The national aims of all these groups differed little from each other, but their political aims were diametrically opposed. Stalin, however, was able to make friends into relatives and enemies into friends. The members of the Ukrainian nationalist organizations were arrested, thrown into Lubyanka Prison, and questioned on their alliances with Skrypnik's group. The persons arrested "testified" that they had contacted Skrypnik's group in order to separate the Ukraine from the USSR, and that they had done it on the demand of the Ukrainian centers abroad and of the Polish, Austrian, German, and French intelligence services. They asserted that they had supplied Skrypnik with money, while Skrypnik had supplied them in turn with information about the military power and economic situation of the USSR. Allegedly under orders from Ukrainian organizations abroad, the arrested nationalists, together with Skrypnik's group, were charged with having carried out wrecking activities in the sphere of education under the guise of "Ukrainization" (Skrypnik was Ukrainian People's Commissar for Education). Skrypnik learned of all this only after he was placed under house arrest. His arrest, however, did not last long: he committed suicide in

1933.[10] It is said that in his last letter, written before his death to the members of the Party Central Committee of the Soviet Union, he declared: "I have only one argument left with which to refute the monstrous lies of the Stalinist police; it consists in condemning the Stalinist system by depriving myself of life." The argument had no effect on Stalin. Mass arrests of members of "Skrypnik's group," many of whom Skrypnik had never seen, now took place in the Ukraine.

The same process of purges and arrests of National Communists and of nationalist members of the intelligentsia took place in the course of 1932 and 1933 in the other national republics. Although from the point of view of organization the influence of Skrypnik's group never extended beyond the Ukraine, the movement had adherents in all the republics—followers of Sultan-Galiyev in Tataro-Bashkiria, followers of Sadvokasov in Turkestan, former National Deviationists in the Caucasus, and so on.

The "centripetal revolution" from above, which meant the abolition of all local autonomy, brought with it its own internal reaction: the development of centrifugal forces in the border republics. The centralization of government power made allowances neither for national characteristics and ways of life nor for well-established traditions of national self-government.

Later on, at the Seventeenth Party Congress, Stalin attempted to gloss over the real situation by deceptive phrases about "survivals of capitalism," and thereby admitted to the fact that Skrypnik's "Ukrainian nationalism" had not been a fortuitous or even a unique development. "It should be noted," declared Stalin, "that traces of capitalism in the minds of men are more tenacious of life in the sphere of nationalism than in any other. They are able to survive because they can camouflage themselves conveniently in national traits. Many persons think that Skrypnik's fall is a unique case, an exception to the rule. This is not so. The fall from grace of Skrypnik and his group in the Ukraine is not an exception. The same type of distorted mentality can be seen in the case of other Comrades in other national republics."[11]

The campaign against the sinners was accordingly not incidental, but was both organized and general in all the republics. As a result the resistance within national Communist parties and organizations continued to grow against the new Stalinist nationality policy, a policy still "national in form" but in fact based only on police measures.

The general situation in the country, the Party, and its national organizations after the destruction of the Right Opposition was far from idyllic. The Party purge of 1929–30 had failed to achieve its aim. It had made the Party neither homogeneous nor monolithic nor even disciplined. Stalin and his assistants found more obstacles on the way to personal dictatorship than they had imagined. The old Party was dying, but it was not dying a natural death. Its last agony was to be accompanied by torment and strife and excesses were to be perpetuated which would place the régime itself in jeopardy.

---

[10] *Problemy istorii*, Moscow, No. 3, 1956. He was rehabilitated in 1956.
[11] Stalin, *Voprosy leninizma*, p. 474.

Chapter XXVI

The Party Purge of 1933 and the Seventeenth Party Congress

Hardly had Stalin's apparatus had time to deal with one opposition, when another took its place. And each new opposition, being both in composition and in ideology a Communist opposition, always reflected to a certain extent the hopes of the popular masses. This constituted the greatest danger of the oppositions for the Stalinists.

After the last legal forums for the expression of the popular will—the soviets and the trade unions—had been turned into paper organizations, the people pinned their hopes on a collapse of the régime as a result of internal struggle within the Party itself. The people's sympathies in this struggle were on the side of the opposition. In case of a conflict outside the framework of the Party, an appeal to the people from the opposing groups would certainly have led to Stalin's defeat. Stalin never lost sight of this danger. In short, Lenin's question "Who whom?"—i.e., in this instance whether Stalin would defeat the Party or the Party would defeat Stalin—had not yet found an answer. And yet without an answer to this question within the Party Stalin could not possibly hope to establish his personal dictatorship over the state. In other words, he had to turn the Party into as fictitious an organization as the soviets and the trade unions, but sufficiently imposing for him to be able to act in its name. And the Party, too, had to be made sufficiently obedient for him to be able to rely on it.

The events which had followed the Sixteenth Party Congress convinced Stalin that the Party was far from measuring up to his ideal. He needed a new Party purge, this time more radical and more universal. The decision for such a purge was made in a Politburo resolution of October 10, 1932.[1] It should be noted that the decision was taken not by a Party congress, nor by a plenary session of the Central Committee or of the Central Control Commission, nor even by a Party conference. It was decided upon by the Politburo, i.e., by Stalin. On January 12, 1933, a joint plenum of the Central Committee and the Central Control Commission ratified the Politburo decision retroactively. An even more characteristic and significant aspect of the whole affair was Stalin's choice of persons to be purged. There was no longer any talk of limiting it to "socially alien elements" as in the past. Neither was the scope of the purge narrowed by reference to categories, such as that of "former oppositionists." This time Stalin found a more elastic definition for those to be included in the purge:

---

[1] *Pravda*, December 2, 1932.

they were referred to simply as "unreliables." The purge had at last to make the Party more obedient. In the language of the Stalinists, "obedience" was spoken of as "proletarian iron discipline."

The attributes which Stalin now demanded of the new Party were incorporated in the resolution of the Central Committee and the Central Control Commission, and read as follows:

PARTY PURGE:

1. The plenum of the Central Committee and the Central Control Commission sitting in joint session, approves the decision of the Politburo of the Central Committee to carry through a Party purge in the course of 1933 and to halt the admission of new members until such time as the purge has ended.

2. The plenum of the Central Committee and the Central Control Commission sitting in joint session, entrusts the Politburo of the Central Committee with organization of the purge in such a way as to ensure *iron proletarian discipline* within the Party and the purging of the Party ranks of *all unreliable and unstable elements and other hangers-on.*[2]

The effect of the resolution was to assign to Stalin, in the name of the Central Committee and the Central Control Commission, the conduct of the Party purge.

A resolution of the Politburo of the Central Committee and the Presidium of the Central Control Commission dated April 28, 1933, defined the categories of Communists to be purged. There was of course for the record mention of "hostile and alien class elements" which were alleged to have infiltrated into the Party by stealth and to have remained there in order to decompose it. This category referred to former landowners, members of the middle class, kulaks, White Guardists, and Mensheviks, although all of these had long since ceased to exist, not only in the Party, but in the country as a whole. The few individuals of alien class extraction who still remained in the Party were a part of Stalin's personal guard, such persons as Molotov, Zhdanov, Vyshinsky, Bulganin, and Malenkov. A category of "alien class elements" was added in order to give the purge a "proletarian" character. The real target, however, was the newly "discovered" categories listed for expulsion from the Party. These categories were enumerated as follows:

2. *Double-Dealers* deceiving the Party, concealing from it their real purpose and trying to undermine the Party's policy under cover of a false oath of "allegiance" to the Party;

3. *Open and Secret Violaters* of Party and state iron discipline, who do not carry out Party and government decisions, but discredit and cast *doubt* upon the decisions and plans drawn up by the Party by calling them "unrealistic" and "unrealizable";

4. *Turncoats*, who have allied themselves with bourgeois elements, who do not want actually to combat the class enemy and who do not combat kulak elements, grafters, idlers, and robbers of communal property.[3]

---

[2] *VKP(b) v rezolyutsiyakh*, Vol. II, pp. 782–83.

[3] *BSE*, 1st ed., Vol. LXI, p. 655; Ye. Yaroslavsky, *Za bolshevistskuyu proverku i chistku partii* (For a Bolshevik Check and Purge of the Party), Moscow-Leningrad, 1933; M. Kaganovich, *O chistke partii* (The Party Purge), a collection of documents, Moscow, 1933.

Any Communist from a member of the rank and file to a member of the Central Committee and the Central Control Commission could be included in any one of these categories or in all three at once if any doubts were raised concerning his loyalty to Stalinism. In this respect, the resolution did not in practice make an exception for members of the Central Committee or the Central Control Commission. As elected delegates to Party congresses they were not subject to purge, but the resolution expressly stated that "members of the Central Committee and the Central Control Commission can also become liable to checking and purging provided a reasoned statement is first presented by a group of Party members."[4] Since the Politburo was elected by a plenary session of the Central Committee, and the Central Committee was elected by a Party Congress, the Politburo was according to Party statutes an executive and subordinate organ of the Central Committee as a whole. But in spite of this fact, it was given the right henceforth to expel members of the Central Committee independently of a Party congress or a plenary session of the Central Committee and merely as a result of a "statement" by a group of Communists, something which could of course be easily arranged.

Such was the situation when the Seventeenth Party Congress set up a most important landmark in the process of legitimizing the positions which Stalin had occupied de facto.

The Seventeenth Party Congress, which met in January and February 1934, has been called the "Congress of the Victors." In a certain sense this was true. The first Five-Year Plan had been fulfilled, the resistance of the peasants to collectivization had definitely been broken, new opposition groups within the Party had been rather easily destroyed, and the continued purge was having favorable results upon the creation of a "homogeneous" and obedient Party. The congress was the first in which Stalin's political triumph was complete. Stalin was right when, in his political report to the Congress, he said: "If, at the Fifteenth Party Congress, it was still necessary to attempt to prove the correctness of the Party line and fight certain anti-Leninist groups, while at the Sixteenth Congress we had to deal final blows to the last adherents of these groups, at this Congress there is nothing to prove and really nobody to deal blows to."[5]

What conclusion did Stalin draw from the fact of his victory over his enemies within the Party? What possibilities did he see for further development? Had he finally rid himself of his everlasting fear—sometimes well-founded, but often merely imagined—that a new opposition might destroy him?

The conclusions which Stalin drew were quite incomprehensible to his former enemies and equally unexpected to his followers. Stalin was not likely to have false illusions as to the stability of his victory. He had a higher opinion of his former and his potential enemies than his enemies had of themselves. He never, as he himself said at the Congress, took a childish delight in personal

---

[4] *BSE*, 1st ed., Vol. LXI, p. 655.
[5] Stalin, *Voprosy leninizma*, p. 465–67, 475–76.

success, and he was a total stranger to a feeling of magnanimity in victory. Although he had won a brilliant victory, he felt the need of insuring himself. How? By keeping the country, the Party, and the apparatus in a state of permanent tension, a state of never ending siege. By what means? By further developing the theory of the class struggle and by continuing the purge. What for? In order to concentrate state and Party power in a single organ, the apparatus of the Central Committee, and in a single post, that of Secretary-General of the Party. Such a concentration called for reconstruction of the mode and character of the work of the entire state and Party apparatus. And here it was policy on organization rather than policy in general that was of decisive significance. Previously, Stalin had been accustomed to saying: "Cadres decide everything." He now amended this motto to say in effect: "Cadres fully familiar with the technique of their work decide everything." The time was past when careers could be made simply by cheering Stalin. The need now was for practical Stalinists, who could act and carry out the will of their supreme leader. These considerations were reflected in Stalin's report to the congress and in the resolutions of the congress itself.

Stalin declared that although the Party was admittedly more united than ever before, this did not mean an end of difficulties in the Party, that it would never again suffer from divisions, and that the Party could therefore rest on its laurels. "A classless society cannot just occur: it must be fought for ... by strengthening the dictatorship of the proletariat, by developing the class struggle, by the destruction of classes." The Leftists, he asserted, had openly accepted the counterrevolutionary program of the Rightists in order to create a unified bloc and carry on with them a common struggle against the Party. The Party had undertaken the task of systematically unmasking the ideology of all currents of thought hostile to Leninism.[6]

As to organization and personnel policy, Stalin insisted that once the correct line was laid down, success depended on the organization of work, including activities aimed at carrying out the Party line in practice and assuring the right personnel by dismissing inefficient workers and selecting good ones, since the role of the Party organizations and their leaders had assumed decisive importance. It was necessary to do away with indifference, to abolish the principle of collegiate responsibility, and reorganize the Central Control Commission and the Workers' and Peasants' Inspectorate. All violaters of rules, "dispensers of eyewash," and chatterboxes must be replaced with men of action. All local government, agricultural, and industrial organizations must be purged. And lastly, the Party must be purged of all turncoats and unreliable elements.[7]

To sum up, the main factor in any organizational work, Stalin emphasized, was the selection of personnel and the control of their work.

The kind of functionaries who needed to be driven out of the governing apparatus, said Stalin, could be grouped into two main types: "One type of

---

[6] *Ibid.*, pp. 478–80.
[7] *Ibid.*

workers consists of men who can boast of certain services in the past, men who have become important personages and who consider that Party and Soviet laws are written for fools and not for them. . . . They must be dismissed from leading posts without hesitation irrespective of their services in the past. . . ." Here he was aiming at the Old Bolsheviks. The second type consisted of "babblers, honest babblers I would say, honest men devoted to the Soviet regime, but incapable of administrating anything, incapable of organizing." He illustrated what he meant by babblers by describing a conversation with "a highly respected Comrade but an incorrigible babbler." The conversation had gone as follows:

Stalin: "How is your grain sowing getting on?"
Reply: "Grain sowing, Comrade Stalin? We have mobilized ourselves." (Laughter)
Stalin: "Well then?"
Reply: "We are examining the problem." (Laughter)
Stalin: "And what else?"
Reply: "We have reached a turning point, Comrade Stalin, a turning point." (Laughter)
Stalin: "Yes, but. . . ?"
Reply: "We have improvements in view. . . ." (Laughter)
Stalin: "All right, but how are you getting on with your grain sowing?"
Reply: "Our grain sowing has been a failure up till now, Comrade Stalin." (General laughter in hall).[8]

Traditionally, any special decree enumerating the tasks of the Party was based on a report presented by the Party Central Committee. Now for the first time in the Party's history, a Party congress made the Secretary's report a directive for the whole Party. One of Stalin's most faithful henchmen, Sergei Kirov, recommended that the previous procedure be abandoned and Stalin's report adopted as a Party decree. The congress accordingly merely resolved "to approve Comrade Stalin's report and recommend to all Party organizations that they be guided in their work by the statements and tasks set forth in Comrade Stalin's report."[9]

Thenceforth, every word uttered or to be uttered by Stalin became law for the Politburo, the Central Committee, the Party, and the country as a whole. A situation which existed de facto was now recognized de jure. The state and Party apparatuses now had to be reorganized to correspond to the new situation. Two very important decisions were therefore adopted on the report presented by Kaganovich, the First Secretary of the Moscow Committee and Second Secretary of the Central Committee, one on organizational problems, entitled "The Party and Soviet Construction," and the other on new Party statutes.

The first decision read: "The Seventeenth Congress of the All-Union Communist Party of Bolsheviks considers that in spite of the successes achieved in refashioning the levers of the proletarian dictatorship, the work of practical

[8] *Ibid.*, p. 480.
[9] *KPSS v resolyutsiyakh*, Vol. II, p. 744.

organization still lags behind the requirements expressed by political directives and fails to satisfy the greatly increased requirements of the present time." The decision then went on to quote from Stalin: "It is unlikely that any of you would maintain that it is enough to provide a good political line and rest content with that. This is merely to do things by halves. After providing a correct political line, it is essential to select functionaries in such a way that the men appointed to the various posts will know how to apply directives and be able to accept them as if they were their own. . . ."[10]

The congress condemned the extreme weakness in individual direction, an absence of personal responsibility and impersonal administration under the guise of "collegiate leadership" and resolved:

1. To abolish all secretariats in oblast committees, district committees and central committees of national areas, leaving not more than two secretaries;

2. To abolish boards *(kollegia)*, except soviets, in all fields of Soviet and economic work;

3. To abolish boards in all people's commissariats, leaving at the head of each people's commissariat the people's commissar and not more than two vice-commissars;

4. To establish that chairmen of oblast and district executive committees and of republic and city councils of people's commissars shall have no more than two vice-chairmen;

5. To abolish the Central Control Commission of the All-Union Communist Party of Bolsheviks and create in its place a Commission of Party Control attached to the Central Committee and headed by one of the secretaries of the Central Committee of the Party.[11]

The abolition of the Central Control Commission was of great importance to Stalin. The commission had been originally created according to a plan proposed by Lenin at the Tenth Party Congress, in 1921. The intention was to make it an independent Party court able to prevent Party splits and the misuse by individual Party leaders of their Party positions for personal gain. The Central Control Commission was elected at congresses and was not subordinated to the Central Committee but itself maintained a check on the Central Committee and its members. Its local organs had similar rights in relation to local Party committees. After Stalin had become Secretary-General of the Party and his misuse of his position had become obvious, Lenin, even before writing his "Testament," had ordered Stalin and the entire staff of the Central Committee to be placed under strict supervision by the Central Control Commission. Lenin considered the situation to be so serious that he made a specific proposal to the forthcoming Twelfth Party Congress, in 1923, which he published in two *Pravda* articles. He declared that "the People's Commissar of Workers' and Peasants' Inspectorate, together with the Presidium of the Central Control Commission, should see to it that employees of the commission are continuously on duty at the Politburo to check all documents coming to it for consideration." Such a system would, he thought, not only be politically advantageous by keeping the

---

[10] *Ibid.*, p. 767.
[11] *Ibid.*, pp. 770–72.

members of the Central Committee and the Central Control Commission better informed, and better prepared for the meetings of the Politburo, but it would also tend to lessen the influence of purely personal and fortuitous circumstances in the Central Committee and thus decrease the danger of Party schisms.[12]

Although a resolution to this effect was adopted by the Twelfth Party Congress and embodied in the Party statutes, the Central Control Commission immediately became reduced to the status of another tool to be used by Stalin in fighting opposition groups. Stalin saw to it that it was headed by his personal friends and henchmen—Kuibyshev, Ordzhonikidze, and Andreyev in turn. Even so the Central Control Commission, as the highest official Party court, continued to be a potentially dangerous rival and resulted in a division of authority within the Party. Hence when the tools of the proletarian dictatorship were being refashioned, this particular tool became superfluous and Stalin abolished it. He made the recreated Commission of Party Control elected by the congress an executive organ of the Central Committee. He abolished the Workers' and Peasants' Inspectorate and replaced it by a Commission of Soviet Control attached to the Council of People's Commissars. These changes made the Party lawgiver at the same time the Party judge, both functions being concentrated in one person.

The Party constitution, known as the "statute," was revised along the same lines. The last constitution, dating from 1926, was obviously obsolete; it still retained large traces of "inner-Party democracy" and of the old theory of "collective leadership" which had been proclaimed by Stalin himself after Lenin's death. Now it, too, had to be brought into conformity with the conditions of "the period of reconstruction," to use the expression current at the time.

In the new constitution the sentence "within the Party discussion of all controversial subjects is entirely free until a decision is adopted" was omitted, and a provision that "all Party organizations have complete independence in deciding questions of local importance," was weakened by addition of the words "insofar as these decisions are consistent with the decisions of the Party."[13] Party congresses, previously required to be held each year, were now required only once every three years. The critically important right to effect a Party purge, previously reserved to the congress, was now delegated to the Central Committee, in practice meaning the Secretariat and Politburo, or, more exactly, Stalin himself. The provision for this permanent purge read as follows:

> 9. Periodical resolutions of the Central Committee of the All-Union Communist Party of Bolsheviks will provide for purges in order to cleanse the Party of: hostile elements and elements alien in their class allegiance; double-dealers who deceive the Party and conceal from it their real opinions . . .; open and secret violators of iron discipline . . .; turncoats who have merged with bourgeois elements . . .; time-servers and self-seekers . . .; the morally degenerate . . .; passive Party members who fail to perform their duties . . .[14]

---

[12] V. I. Lenin, "How to Reorganize the Workers' and Peasants' Inspectorate," and "Better Less but Better," *Sochineniya* (Works), 3rd ed., Vol. XXVII, Moscow, 1937, pp. 402–18.

[13] *VKP(b) v resolyutsiyakh*, Vol. II, pp. 221–22; *KPSS v resolyutsiyakh*, Vol. II, p. 779.

[14] *KPSS v resolyutsiyakh*, Vol. II, p. 777.

A drastic new clause provided that "Party members who refuse to give truthful answers to questions asked by the Commission of Party Control are liable to immediate expulsion from the Party."[15] It is clear that these provisions could be applied to any Communist from the highest-placed bureaucrat down to rank and file member, if it should become necessary to liquidate him.

In November 1934 the official control over local Party organizations was further centralized. Hitherto the Party Central Committee had appointed only secretaries of oblast committees and central committees of national areas. District secretaries were appointed by the oblast committees. A decree of the November 1934 plenary session of the Party Central Committee provided that oblast committees, and district committees and central committees of national areas, must submit all appointments of district Party secretaries to the Party Central Committee for ratification.[16] In practice this gave final control of such appointments to the Organization and Instruction section of the Party Central Committee.

Such was the situation in the Party when, in December 1934, Communist Leonid Nikolayev assassinated Communist Sergei Kirov in a corridor of the Smolny Institute Building in Leningrad, thus opening the way for the Great Purge.

[15] *Ibid.*, p. 787.
[16] *Ibid.*, p. 807.

Chapter XXVII

The Assassination of Kirov
and the Great Purge under Yagoda, Yezhov, and Beria

The literature on Stalin abounds with theories on the reasons for his Great Purge of 1934–39. "The revolution," says one theory, "devours its own children: a great experiment requires great sacrifices." "Stalin was a crazy and sadistic despot," runs another theory. Khrushchev provided the following theory in his secret speech at the Twentieth Party Congress: "Stalin," said Khrushchev, "regarded it all from the angle of working class interests, the toilers' interests, the interests of socialist and Communist victory. We cannot say that his actions were those of a crazy despot. He considered that such actions were made necessary by the interests of the Party, the working masses, and the defense of revolutionary conquests. Therein lies the tragedy."[1]

In my opinion the most convincing explanation of the Great Purge is to be found in an interview by Stalin with the actor, People's Artist N. K. Cherkasov, and the famous film director S. M. Eisenstein, as recorded in an interview described in N. K. Cherkasov's *An Actor's Notes*.

First a few words on the genuineness of the interview. While criticizing Stalin for his "un-Marxist" views on the main subject of the interview, Prof. S. M. Dubrovsky, an old and highly respected Soviet historian, writes: "N. K. Cherkasov's book, *An Actor's Notes*, was ready for publication while J. V. Stalin was still alive. No protest was made either by the latter or by others present at the interview. It was evidently considered that the interview had been correctly reported."[2]

The portion of the interview of particular interest in the present connection was as follows:

> In speaking of the state activity of Ivan the Terrible, Comrade Stalin remarked that Ivan IV had been *a great and wise ruler who had protected the country from the infiltration of foreign influence* and had tried to bring about the unification of Russia. In particular, talking about [Ivan] the Terrible's progressive activity, Comrade Stalin emphasized that Ivan IV had been the first to introduce a foreign trade monopoly in Russia, adding that Lenin had been the only one to have done this after him. J. V. Stalin also remarked on the *progressive role played by the Oprichnina* [the political police employed to suppress opposition] and said that the head of the Oprichnina, Malyuta Skuratov, was a great Russian general. . . .

---

[1] *Rech Khrushcheva*, p. 54.
[2] *Voprosy istorii*, Moscow, 1956, No. 8, p. 128.

In mentioning Ivan the Terrible's mistakes, J. V. Stalin remarked that they partly consisted in *a failure to liquidate the five remaining great feudal families, failure to fight the feudal lords to the end; had he done so Russia would have had no Time of Troubles* [the peasant wars in the beginning of the seventeenth century]. At that point Stalin added humorously "There God stood in Ivan's way": [Ivan] the Terrible would liquidate one feudal family, one boyar clan, and would then repent for a whole year and pray for forgiveness of his "sins" when he should have been acting with increasing decisiveness.[3]

Accordingly, Stalin regarded the mistakes of the "progressive tsar" and his political police as due to insufficient cruelty, itself a result of insufficient resolution. But for Ivan the Terrible's mildness, he believed, Russia would have escaped the peasant revolution that followed his death!

The Great Purge marked the final stage in the physical annihilation of past and potential Party boyars and feudal lords. Stalin did not repeat what he regarded as the mistakes of Ivan the Terrible.

The Great Purge itself passed through three stages, each characterized by the character of Stalin's assistant at the time in the NKVD (People's Commissariat for Internal Affairs): the Yagoda Purge of 1934–36, the Yezhov Purge of 1936–38, and the Beria Purge of 1938–39.

In the process of organizing the Great Purge, People's Commissar for Internal Affairs Genrikh Yagoda played a role no less important than that of his more notorious successor Nikolai Yezhov, and in a certain sense even more so. Yezhov merely continued, harshly and ruthlessly, the course of action worked out and set in motion by Yagoda on Stalin's order, with infinite finesse, in absolute secrecy, and no less perfidiously. During the trial of the Right-Wing Trotskyite Bloc in March 1938, Yagoda admitted to having planned and carried out the murder of Kirov, a member of the Politburo and Secretary of the Central Committee and the Leningrad Oblast committee, and to having poisoned the cabinet members Valerian Kuibyshev and Vyacheslav Menzhinsky (Yagoda's former chief), as well as the author Maxim Gorky and Gorky's son Maxim Peshkov. At the time just as little credence was given to Yagoda's admissions as to all the other evidence produced at the Moscow trials, a lack of credence due to causes well known to everyone. First, no one believed that old revolutionaries, such as Trotsky, Zinoviev, Kamenev, Bukharin, Rykov, and the others, could, toward the end of their lives, have turned into common murderers, hired spies, and professional poisoners. Second, all indictments were based on personal confessions of the accused, too fantastic to be believed. Third, no objective proof or evidence was supplied at the trial, unless what the prosecutor, Vyshinsky, called at the trial "objective logic" be considered as proof.

Khrushchev's report at the Twentieth Party Congress, however, makes it impossible to escape the conclusion that Yagoda was speaking the absolute truth regarding the assassination of Kirov and the poisoning of the others, but was lying about who had arranged the murders. In fact, of those who had arranged

---

[3] N. K. Cherkasov, *Zapiski aktera* (An Actor's Notes), Moscow, 1953, pp. 380–82.

the murder, only one, Yagoda himself, was sitting in the dock; the others—Stalin Molotov, Kaganovich, and Voroshilov—were in the Politburo of the Central Committee of the Party.

Trotsky had pointed this out, in his book, *Stalin*. And before Stalin was officially exposed, a former NKVD general, Alexander Orlow, had provided in *The Secret History of Stalin's Crimes* evidence that Kirov had been murdered at Stalin's instigation. Khrushchev's report at the Twentieth Party Congress provides indirect support for these views, in the following passage:

> It must be stated that the circumstances surrounding Kirov's murder are still in many ways unclear and mysterious and call for very careful investigation. There are reasons for suspecting that Kirov's assassin, Nikolayev, was aided by one of the men responsible for Kirov's personal security. Six weeks before Kirov's murder, Nikolayev was arrested for suspicious behavior, but was later freed and not even searched. Unusually suspicious, too, is the fact that the Chekist who had acted as one of Kirov's personal bodyguards was killed, while on his way to interrogation, in an automobile accident which claimed no other victim among the occupants of the car. After Kirov's murder the leading functionaries of the Leningrad NKVD were given very mild sentences, but in 1937 they were shot. Presumably they were shot in order to cover up the traces of the real organizers of Kirov's murder.[4]

Why did Stalin choose Kirov, Kuibyshev, Menzhinsky and Gorky as the first victims of his Great Purge? If we recall the nation-wide status and importance of each of these persons, if we take into account their personal qualities and their relationships to Stalin's future victims, it becomes obvious that Stalin's crime was neither fortuitous nor arbitrary. Kirov's tragedy, for instance, resulted from his immense popularity in the Party, his exceptional personal courage, and his independence verging on obstinacy. There were well-known cases in which Kirov had simply ignored the instructions of the Central Committee and the Council of People's Commissars if he believed they ran counter to the interests of his work in Leningrad, in connection with such matters as consumer goods for the workers, punitive measures by the NKVD against the intelligentsia, etc. He had earned great popularity among the masses, while at the same time maintaining the old revolutionary tradition of taking part in workers' and peasants' meetings, although this tradition had long since been abandoned by Stalin and the other members of the Politburo. The last time Stalin had been "among the people" was, according to Khrushchev, in 1928.

Kirov had other personal advantages as well, which in those days played an important role in a Communist career. Unlike Stalin—a semi-intellectual, student in an ecclesiastical seminary, and son of a petty-bourgeois Georgian cobbler—the *Russian* Kirov was the descendant of a long line of proletarians and was himself a proletarian who had joined the Bolshevik Party in 1904 at the age of eighteen. Stalin, on the other hand, at the age of nineteen, had joined the "Mesame-dasi" Georgian nationalist party, which had later become the Georgian Menshevik Party, and had maintained relations with this Menshevik group until 1917. During

---

[4] *Rech Khrushcheva*, p. 18.

World War I and the March Revolution Stalin had belonged to the Right wing of the Bolshevik Party, and, as the Bolsheviks themselves have admitted, had joined Kamenev in attacking Lenin's "April Theses." Kirov, on the other hand, had never wavered from the Leninist line since 1904.

As a theorist Stalin was a mere amateur, as a journalist he was a mediocrity, and as a speaker he was a bore, while Kirov was the most gifted speaker and journalist in the Bolshevik ranks next to Trotsky and Lunacharsky. In spite of his exceptionally high position as the second most important figure in Moscow and the first in Leningrad, Kirov, unlike his colleagues in the Politburo, had not turned into a bureaucrat poised at the summit of the Party oligarchy and outside the reach of common humanity. In fact, he was killed in one of the passages of the teeming Smolny Institute Building, and could easily have been killed at any workers' meeting. In the eyes of idealistic Communists, Kirov possessed yet another quality: he conceived of the "dictatorship of the proletariat" in its literal sense, in spite of the Stalinist training to which he had been subjected for ten years.

Stalin always considered the good qualities of his colleagues as his own defects. The megalomania of which Khrushchev spoke had as one of its sources a sense of his own deficiencies, which were particularly obvious in his relations with Trotsky, Zinoviev, and Bukharin. In the obituary which he wrote on his own victim, Stalin could not avoid mentioning the qualities of Kirov as a man and as a Communist which he himself lacked. "Comrade Kirov," declared the Central Committee, "represents the model Bolshevik, who recognized neither fear nor difficulties. . . . His straightforwardness, his amazing qualities as an inspired tribune of the revolution, were combined with the kindness and gentleness in his personal relations with friends and comrades, with the radiant warmth and modesty, inherent in a real follower of Lenin."[5]

Kirov's tragedy stands out in even sharper relief against the political and historical significance of the city in which he reigned as independent dictator. Leningrad was the first capital of the Revolution and the second capital of the country. Proletarian Petrograd, as Leningrad had been called at the time, had been the cradle of the Revolution, while Moscow, the city of merchants, was merely the illegitimate heir to Leningrad. Bureaucratic Moscow had emerged from merchant Moscow, but Petrograd had remained what it had always been, a proletarian center. In Moscow the proletariat had turned into a bourgeoisie but in Petrograd the bourgeoisie had turned into a proletariat. Petrograd had staged three revolutions, one after another, Moscow had staged none. There was danger that Petrograd might stage a fourth if Moscow should attempt to change the sham dictatorship of the proletariat into a real dictatorship by Stalin. Certainly Kirov had been a most convinced follower and friend of Stalin in his struggle against the Trotskyites and Zinovievites, but he had been an equally convinced opponent of their physical obliteration. He had opposed the Bukharinites without great enthusiasm, but he had never severed relations with Rykov, Tomsky, and Bukharin himself, whom he idolized as a theorist. It was not mere

---

[5] *Pravda*, December 2, 1934.

chance that the investigating committee (Stalin) made Yagoda say at the trial of Bukharin and Rykov: "The case could be summed up thus: Rykov's talks with me made me personally sympathetic to the right-wing program. Besides, Rykov told me that not only Bukharin, Uglanov, and he himself but the entire Moscow Party organization, the Leningrad organization, and the trade unions were all on the side of the Rightists and I therefore obtained the impression that the right-wing group might be victorious in its struggle against the Central Committee."[6] The Leningrad organization, then, which was headed by Kirov as the Moscow organization was headed by Uglanov, had supported the Rightists. And it is true that not one of Kirov's assistants, not one of his personal friends, not one of the members of the bureau and secretariat of the Leningrad Oblast Party committee survived the Great Purge. Even their wives were killed off. If all traces of the real organizers of Kirov's murder were to be destroyed, it had to be done thoroughly. For this purpose Stalin invented the theory that there had been a "Leningrad Center" composed of Kirov's former assistants Chudov, Second Secretary of the oblast committee and member of the Central Committee, Ugarov, Smorodin, Pozern, Chudov's wife Shaposhnikova, and others, all of whom were members of the bureau of the oblast committee.

The Seventeenth Party Congress in February 1934 had been an unprecedented personal triumph for Kirov. He had paid high tribute to Stalin's report as "an epoch making document" and it was he who, contrary to all Party tradition, had called upon the Congress not to adopt the Central Committee resolution but simply to accept Stalin's instructions contained in his report to the Central Committee. All this had been highly satisfactory and had fitted into the framework of Stalin's strategy. But what was less satisfactory was that the star of the congress was not Stalin, officially designated the "wise leader and faithful disciple of Lenin," but Kirov, the "inspired tribune" of the Revolution—a Revolution which had long since lost its impetus. A tempestuous and unbroken ovation, not officially inspired but genuinely spontaneous, had been accorded to Kirov. The congress had appeared to warn Stalin: "Take care," it had seemed to say, "do not be too rash, Kirov stands close to the throne of the Secretary-General." Stalin, ever suspicious, was made even more despondent by the results of the elections to the chief organs of the Central Committee. Kirov had been unanimously elected to all three—the Politburo, the Organization Bureau and the Secretariat, a privilege in the past accorded to Stalin alone. (It was in order to belittle this achievement that Stalin had brought Kaganovich into these organizations.) Kirov, the sincere friend of Stalin, the convinced fanatic of Leninism, the "hereditary proletarian," but a self-willed politician and dangerous idealist, had been openly recognized as the heir apparent to the Party leader. For such a friend Stalin could have nothing but hatred. He did not fit into the Molotov-Kaganovich-Voroshilov constellation. In spite of Kirov's panegyrics Stalin felt that Kirov was still a man of the old revolution and it was Stalin's services to the old revolution that Kirov had extolled in speaking of "Stalin—faithful disciple

---

[6] A. Ya. Vyshinsky, *Sudebnye rechi* (Court Speeches), Moscow, 1948, p. 533.

of Lenin." Such praise bore a subtle flavor of condescension. "After Lenin there is no other man who can so truly and so ably lead the Party along Lenin's path. All the Party must know this," Kirov had declaimed, but he had never said, like Molotov and Kaganovich, that "Stalin is the Lenin of today."

It was difficult to recruit into a conspiracy aiming at the very heart of Lenin's policy, a fanatic who adhered so closely to that policy. But how could he be disposed of? Could he be arrested and held in the Lubyanka Prison as an "enemy of the people?" Such a charge would not be believed either by the Party or the NKVD. Could he be declared another "deviationist" by a plenary session of the Central Committee? In that case Stalin might find himself branded as a deviationist. Kirov was not an ex-Menshevik like Trotsky, not a deserter from the October Revolution like Zinoviev and Kamenev, not a Left Communist and later Right Opportunist like Bukharin, not an "ex-nationalist" and later follower of Kamenev, like Stalin. Kirov, as Stalin himself said in his obituary speech, was an "exemplary Bolshevik." And Stalin himself had shown confidence in Kirov in 1926 when he had advanced him to the post of leader of the Leningrad Party organization, although Lenin had made him a mere secretary of the Central Committee in Azerbaidzhan in 1921. Stalin had confirmed his devotion to Kirov by autographing a copy of *Problems of Leninism*: "To my brother and friend, Sergei Mironovich Kirov, from the author, J. Stalin, 1924."

Kirov could not be removed politically, but could easily be removed physically, thus attaining two objects at once—the death of a rival and an excuse for the Great Purge. I presented this version of Kirov's murder in my book *Stalin au pouvoir* published in 1951 but I had my doubts about it at the time. However, since Khrushchev's report, historians can write: "Secretary of the Party Central Committee Kirov was murdered by Party member Nikolayev, under the direction of Chief of the Central NKVD Yagoda and chiefs of the Leningrad NKVD Medved and Zaporozhets, and on orders of Secretary-General of the Party Central Committee Stalin."

Why did Yagoda agree to his part? What if the plot had failed? What if he were exposed by Kirov's followers or by Kirov himself? To this Vyshinsky, the prosecutor, made the classic reply: "Yagoda was not an ordinary murderer, he was a murderer with a guarantee that he would not be found out."[7] The chief guarantor was the chief organizer of the crime—Stalin himself. But his guarantee was purely temporary. Following the assassination of Kirov, Yagoda was given the more difficult and responsible task of preparing several trials in Moscow and Leningrad to dispose first of those implicated in Kirov's murder and second, of Stalin's political enemies who had had nothing to do with the murder.

The first task was easy—Nikolayev and his personal friends Katalynov, Rumyantsev, Sositsky, and others who might have known something about who were the real organizers of the murder were arrested and executed early in January 1935, suspiciously soon after the assassination. The official announcement merely stated that the members of the "Nikolayev group" had been brought

[7] *Ibid.*, p. 523.

to trial and shot. It is still not known if there was a trial, what Nikolayev testified, what the defendants said, or whether they were shot within a month or, like Kirov's bodyguard, within a day. Medved and Zaporozhets were punished for having failed to ensure Kirov's safety by being transferred to other Chekist work in the Far East, Medved under official sentence of five years. The first trial of Zinoviev and Kamenev began in Moscow in mid-January 1935. They were accused of having instructed Nikolayev and his group to murder Kirov, and as indirect proof it was submitted that all members of the Nikolayev group were former followers of Zinoviev (although Nikolayev himself had always been a Stalinist). As physical torture was probably not applied in the course of interrogation, all the accused categorically refused to plead guilty. Kamenev said in the course of the trial: "I must say that I am not a coward, but I never wanted to fight." When the court announced that he was accused of being the leader of a terrorist group, the so-called "Moscow Center," Kamenev observed ironically: "I must be blind. I have reached the age of fifty but have never seen this 'center' of which it appears I have been a member."[8]

Zinoviev's testimony was roughly the same, except that he pointed out one important detail: there were several of the 16 members of the alleged Moscow Center whom he had never seen until he faced them in the courtroom.[9] (Throughout the Moscow trials the NKVD had completely unknown agents provocateurs sitting alongside well-known statesmen and Party dignitaries.) But Zinoviev and Kamenev did admit to moral responsibility to the extent that they shared the opinions of the alleged Leningrad Center Communists, i.e., Nikolayev's group. This was not exactly what Stalin needed but he had to be satisfied with it for the time being. Kamenev and Zinoviev were therefore convicted of moral responsibility for Kirov's murder and sentenced to prison.

The Zinovievites were wrong if they thought that they had so easily shaken Stalin off. Zinoviev and Kamenev were not sent to Siberia, but placed in solitary confinement in the Lubyanka Prison. Stalin now granted Yagoda unlimited power to get the necessary confessions. He threatened Yagoda as he later threatened Ignatyev during the famous Doctors Case: "If you do not get a confession from the doctors, we will make you a head shorter!" What methods were used to obtain the desired result? Khrushchev has told us. "The methods were simple: Beat them, beat them and beat them again!" Yagoda and his assistants beat the prisoners until they signed affidavits in which they confessed that they had not only killed Kirov but had intended to kill Stalin, Kaganovich, Voroshilov, Zhdanov, and even Kosior, Postyshev, Ordzhonikidze, and Yagoda as well. For some reason Molotov was not included in the list.

In August 1936 the first public political trial of those old friends of Lenin and organizers of Bolshevism was held in Moscow. The accused included Zinoviev, the former president of the Comintern, and Kamenev, Lenin's deputy in the Council of People's Commissars, both Old Bolsheviks and leaders of the October

---

[8] *Ibid.*, pp. 392, 394.
[9] *Ibid.*, p. 396.

Revolution and the Civil War, Yevdokimov, Smirnov, Bakayev, Mrakhkovsky, Ter-Vaganyan, and ten NKVD agents who had been put in to provide supporting testimony to the existence of a Trotskyite-Zinovievite Terrorist Center. There was really no need for the NKVD agents, because the accused now confessed to everything, made no excuses, and offered no such resistance as during the first trial in January 1935. Vyshinsky could say cynically: "It can be said that the trial of January 15 and 16, 1935, was for Zinoviev and Kamenev a kind of rehearsal which they probably did not expect, but which, like fate, they did not avoid."[10]

Although confessing to the murder of Kirov and to preparations for the murder of Stalin and his associates, Zinoviev and Kamenev categorically denied a second accusation, which had no bearing on the case but which Vyshinsky pressed, namely that if the plot had succeeded, they would also have killed those who had committed the murder. We certainly decided to kill Stalin, they said, but not Stalin's murderers. Vyshinsky was highly indignant. He declared:

> When I spoke about the methods which were used by these people, I showed, or tried to show, how deep was their moral and political degradation. . . . I am referring to their plan for obliterating all traces of their abominable crimes. . . . Their intention was to appoint Bakayev to the post of chairman of the OGPU. Zinoviev and Kamenev did not exclude [the fact] that the OGPU had at its disposal threads concerning the state conspiracy, and therefore they considered it a most important goal to appoint Bakayev chairman of the OGPU. He was to have seized these threads and destroyed them, as well as those who had physically carried out their own orders. Kamenev and Zinoviev do not deny the first part of this indictment, but they deny the second. It was too horrible, and Zinoviev said it was something out of Jules Verne. . . . It was fantastic, he said, like tales from the Arabian Nights. . . . But surely history can afford many examples of conspirators being murdered by the organizers of a conspiracy. . . .[11]

Zinoviev and Kamenev, together with their friends and the NKVD agents provocateurs were shot on August 25, 1936. But Yagoda's time had also come. Exactly one month later, on September 25, 1936, Stalin and Zhdanov cabled to Molotov and Kaganovich from Sochi on the Black Sea:

> We consider it absolutely necessary and urgent that Comrade Yezhov be appointed to the post of People's Commissar of Internal Affairs. Yagoda has clearly shown himself incapable of exposing the Trotskyite-Zinovievite bloc. The OGPU is lagging four years behind schedule for this task. This has been noted by all the Party workers and by the majority of the representatives of the NKVD.[12]

On this Khrushchev commented:

> Strictly speaking it must be emphasized that Stalin was not in contact with the Party workers and therefore could not know what they thought. Stalin's statement that the OGPU was four years behind in applying measures of mass repression and that it was necessary to catch up with the work pushed the NKVD workers onto the path of mass arrests and executions.[13]

---

[10] *Ibid.*, p. 383.
[11] *Ibid.*, pp. 403–04.
[12] *Rech Khrushcheva*, p. 18.
[13] *Ibid.*

The question arises, in what respect had Yagoda failed to deal adequately with the Trotskyite-Zinovievite bloc after having so brilliantly tried and executed Zinoviev and Kamenev? The answer is that Yagoda had managed the task well. The entire world was amazed at the fantastically detailed and seemingly voluntary confessions of the defendants, who had admitted to all the serious crimes of which they had been accused by the NKVD (Yagoda), the Public Prosecutor (Vyshinsky) and the Military Collegium of the Supreme Court of the USSR (Ulrich). The case had been concluded without a single hitch, the last words of the accused had been words of repentance for uncommitted crimes. Yagoda, who had expected another decoration and another similar assignment was instead dismissed from his post as NKVD chief and unceremoniously thrown into the dungeons of his own NKVD! Stalin could have been accused of ingratitude if this had not been the first really justified arrest during the entire period of Soviet rule. Yagoda's path was strewn with the corpses of hundreds of thousands of ordinary Soviet citizens. He was responsible for the corpses of only a few Soviet dignitaries, among them Kirov, Kuibyshev, Menzhinsky, Maxim Gorky and the score of members of the Zinoviev and Nikolayev groups. Stalin shot Yagoda for the murder of these Soviet dignitaries because he found it essential to liquidate the eyewitnesses and executors of his own crimes.

The day following receipt of the telegram from Stalin and Zhdanov, Yagoda was dismissed from the NKVD and appointed People's Commissar of Communications of the USSR, in place of Rykov, who had held the post after being dismissed as chairman of the Council of People's Commissars. Yagoda was replaced by Yezhov. Nikolay Ivanovich Yezhov was 40 years old, and was, in Soviet terminology, a classic product of the Stalin school. Until 1927, when he was engaged in Party work in Kazakhstan, Stalin took him into his secretariat on recommendation of his old friend Poskrebyshev. In 1930 he was appointed head of the Personnel Department of the Central Committee and at the Seventeenth Party Congress in 1934 was elected member of the Central Committee. By 1935 he was already a secretary of the Central Committee and chairman of the Commission of Party Control in place of Kaganovich, whose deputy he had been. But Yezhov was not merely one of the secretaries of the Central Committee: he was special secretary responsible for supervising the personnel of the NKVD, the courts, and the Public Prosecutor's office. This newly created special secretaryship has continued to exist to the present time.

As I have written elsewhere,[14] five months after Kirov's assassination, on May 13, 1935, the Party Central Committee adopted four decrees of immense importance for the lives of millions of persons. One provided for creation of a Defense Commission of the Politburo to direct preparation of the country for possible war against powers hostile to the USSR. This decree had in mind Germany and Japan in the first place and France and England as a second eventuality. Stalin, Molotov, Voroshilov, Kaganovich, and Ordzhonikidze were made members of the commission. The second decree created a Special Security

---

[14] Alexander Uralov [A. Avtorkhanov], *The Reign of Stalin*, London, 1953.

Commission of the Politburo to deal with the liquidation of "enemies of the people." The commission included Stalin, Zhdanov, Vyshinsky, Yezhov, Shkiryatov, Malenkov, and later Molotov and Kaganovich. The third decree called for two checks of the entire Party, one a public check of the documents of all Party members, by Party committees, and the other a secret check of the political reliability of each Party member, by the NKVD. The fourth decree provided that letters be sent to all Party members and alternates calling upon them to increase their "Bolshevik vigilance" and "mercilessly to unmask and liquidate all enemies of the people."

The only provision of these decrees to be published was that concerning the public check of Party documents. Stalin's political apparatus was now deeply involved in a great conspiracy against its own Party, people, and state.

While the Defense Commission acted on the principle formulated by Voroshilov: "We will defeat the enemy on his own territory," the Special Security Commission adopted Stalin's slogan: "Exterminate the enemy in the rear and you will defeat him at the front." Kirov's murder had been committed on this theory. But as the ubiquitous Soviet intelligence service was convinced that war with Germany and Japan was inevitable sooner or later, Stalin recalled the threats of the Trotskyites to resort to "Clemenceau's thesis" that when the enemy is at the gates of the capital a coup d'état should be carried out to save the country. He therefore ordered the Special Security Commission to work out a detailed operational plan for achieving "the moral and political unity of the Soviet people." After two years' intelligence work the commission was able to present a monstrous plan which the Soviet people christened the Yezhovshchina, or Yezhov purge.

As it was put into effect, the plan was substantially as follows:

1. The entire adult male and the educated portion of the female population of the USSR was classified into three groups—intelligentsia, workers, and peasants—and secretly checked for political reliability by the NKVD and its network of agents.

2. The percentage of each group to be liquidated was then determined.

3. A detailed "table of specifications" was drawn up as a basis for the liquidation of individuals.

4. A timetable was worked out providing for exact time limits for liquidating the groups by sub-districts, districts, oblasts, and national republics.

The plan divided those selected for liquidation into the following categories:

1. The remnants of the former enemy classes—gentry, landowners, bourgeoisie, tsarist civil servants, and officers, and their children.

2. Former members of political parties hostile to Bolshevism, members of former anti-Soviet groups and organizations and of the White Army Movement, and their children.

3. Clergy of various faiths.

4. Former kulaks and sub-kulaks.

5. Former participants in any anti-Soviet uprising from 1918 on, including such persons amnestied by the Soviet government.

6. Former participants in any anti-Party opposition movement within the Party, irrespective of present attitude and membership in the Soviet Communist Party.

7. Former members of any national-democratic party in a national republic of the USSR.

There might have been some "legal" justification for the liquidation of all these categories, since in every case a past record was involved, either of birth, or education, or conviction. But a new category was added of an entirely different kind. Members of this category were to be liquidated on the basis of specifications which could only have been discovered by the alchemists of the Politburo: this category consisted of "persons with anti-Soviet sentiments," or potential enemies of the Soviet régime. Persons of proletarian origin, Stakhanovite collective farmers, dyed-in-the-wool Bolsheviks, the reddest of red professors, famous heroes of the Civil War, legendary partisan leaders, army political commissars, army generals and marshals of the Soviet Union, hotel barbers, embassy porters, Foreign Office diplomats and Intourist prostitutes—all could fall under the heading of "persons with anti-Soviet sentiments." Later, in prisons in Moscow and the provinces, they could be promoted to the rank and profession of spies, terrorists, wreckers, rebels, none having anything to do with the past but all truly Soviet ranks and professions.

In 1935 and 1936, NKVD psychologists, guided by the Special Security Commission, used the "table of specifications" to draw up lists of former and future enemies of the Stalinist regime. As it was a question not of thousands or even of hundreds of thousands but of millions of people, there was no way of dealing with them through normal legal channels. It was therefore decided to set up a special tribunal under the Central NKVD and extraordinary three-man tribunals in republics, oblasts, and districts to try in absentia persons held under arrest.

Simultaneously a vast campaign was launched in the press calling for "unmasking and exterminating enemies of the people." Two thirds of all the material published in *Pravda* and in the local Party press was devoted to this task. Under the guise of "Bolshevik criticism and self-criticism" every member of the Party and every "non-Party Bolshevik" was required to submit evidence purporting to unmask enemies of the people.

"We need all criticism, even if it contains only five to ten percent of the truth," said Stalin, and this dictum was endlessly repeated orally and in the press, in order to sustain the morale of the vast army of informers. To unmask "enemies of the people," all institutions and factories, mines and pits, railways and waterways, kolkhozes and sovkhozes, schools, centers of art, culture, and science, had to submit to "criticism and self-criticism." A collective farmer from Tambov or a People's Commissar in Moscow could be talked about or written about with equal success if the informer's information contained "five percent of the truth" about the anti-Stalinist sympathies of his victim. Party members vied with Party members, Party committees with Party committees, oblasts with oblasts, republics with republics in their efforts to unmask "enemies of the people." The sincerity and ideological loyalty of a Party organization to the Party of Lenin and Stalin was judged by the number unmasked.

Orders and medals were awarded only to Chekists who had successfully arrested a large number of enemies of the people. Only their names were mentioned frequently in NKVD lists of agents, and only they received promotions in government and Party rank. Denunciations assumed the character of a plague and could boast of Stakhanovite efficiency. Brothers were urged to denounce brothers, sons to denounce their fathers, and wives their husbands; it was one against all and all against one. People of all ranks and age groups suffered from this peculiarly Soviet disease of denunciation mania. Many were forced into it. At a Party conference of the Krasnaya Presna district of Moscow in 1937, one of the delegates boasted that he had personally unmasked over one hundred enemies of the people in four months. One single report sufficed for Mitin and Yudin–NKVD workers on the "philosophy front"–to have the entire Communist Academy thrown into prison in spite of the fact that it was attached to the Central Executive Committee of the USSR and in the past had been considered the "theory laboratory" of the Party Central Committee.

Although in Moscow the "table of specifications" continued to form the basis of action, in the provinces the denunciation mania degenerated into denunciation chaos. As the local Party and NKVD establishments could not cope with the work involved in examining the denunciations, to say nothing of bringing some system into them, the Central Committee was forced to dispatch to their aid groups of "specialists" from the Central Committee and the NKVD with instructions to restore order in the Party management as well as to keep an eye on the local Party managers. But local organizations had no intention of lagging behind the capital. Some had their own "tables of specifications," to which Zhdanov referred at the Eighteenth Party Congress in March 1939, in reporting on the "mass killings of Party members." One organization, according to Zhdanov, determined to cope with this chaos of denunciations by its own efforts, and hit upon the expedient of introducing an element of fairness by classifying the "enemies" of the people according to the number of denunciations against them. The task of discovering and registering "enemies of the people" was performed on the largest scale and with the greatest energy not by Party committees, but in the offices of the NKVD. Special representatives from the All-Union NKVD and the Special Security Commission, who alone knew the aims and purpose of the coming general campaign, were sent to local NKVDs. They carried warrants signed by Stalin and Yezhov granting them complete freedom of action, including the right to arrest local Party chiefs and Cheka commissars at all levels. District and oblast NKVD branches were obliged to submit to them and their staffs their lists of "enemies" grouped according to the tables of specification.

In order to carry out so extensive and exceptional an operation, Yezhov was vested with correspondingly extensive and exceptional powers. He was a Secretary of the Central Committee, Chairman of the Commission of Party Control—the Party court—member of the Politburo, member of the Organization Bureau of the Central Committee, and People's Commissar for Internal Affairs of the USSR. Only Stalin himself was above him, and this by virtue of his Party authority, since Stalin was not yet a member of the government.

The appointment of Yezhov, who only twelve months before had been completely unknown in the country at large and little known to the Party, was welcomed with relief by the people as a whole. When a short time after, the news spread that Yezhov had thrown into prison the old and hated inquisitor Yagoda, there was general rejoicing. To pessimists who cautioned, "provided things don't get worse," the optimists answered, "things could not get worse."

Yezhov was a cruel disappointment to the optimists, for under his regime the criminal possibilities of Stalinism turned out to be truly unlimited. Yezhov was entrusted with four tasks concerned with carrying out a part of the plan which the Politburo had approved:

1. To invent an "anti-Soviet Trotskyite cell" headed by Old Bolsheviks and Central Committee members Pyatakov, Radek, Sokolnikov, Serebryakov and others, and to bring them to trial.

2. To invent an "anti-Soviet military cell" headed by Civil War officers Marshal Tukhachevsky, Generals Yakir, Uborevich, Kork, Eideman and others, and to try them in secret.

3. To invent an "anti-Soviet Right Trotskyite bloc" headed by former members of the Politburo Bukharin and Rykov, former chief of the NKVD Yagoda, and former members of the Party Central Committee Krestinsky, Rozengolts, Ivanov, Chernov, Grinko, Zelensky, Ikramov, Khodzhayev, etc. (none of whom, according to a later statement by Khrushchev, had been expelled from the Central Committee) and to bring them to trial.

4. To carry out mass arrests by oblasts and republics in order to put the above plan into effect and to process those arrested through the three-man NKVD tribunals.

Yezhov began his work in what were technically speaking highly unfavorable circumstances. He was not a Chekist by profession, the entire NKVD organization had been shattered from top to bottom after Yagoda's arrest in the attempt to purge it of his followers, and the new NKVD employees coopted from the Party apparatus and from the schools had had little experience in police work. Nevertheless, during his two and a half years in power, 1936–38, Yezhov inaugurated and conducted a terror the like of which the NKVD, the Cheka, and the OGPU had never attained during the twenty years of their existence. Khrushchev himself declared that "it is enough to state that the number of arrests following charges of counterrevolutionary activity increased more than ten-fold between 1936 and 1937."[15] For some reason, Khrushchev failed to add that the number in 1938 increased in geometrical progression in comparison to 1937.

---

[15] *Rech Khrushcheva*, p. 20.

It is easy to estimate the number of members of the Party arrested, and this I have done elsewhere. But it is quite impossible to calculate the number of non-members arrested. I know that in July 1937 the Central Committee of the Party sent out to local Party committees, to organs of the NKVD, and to prosecuting organs top secret instructions signed by Stalin, Yezhov, and Vyshinsky explaining how "elimination of the remnants of enemy classes" should be carried out and on what scale. The instructions indicated the actual percentages of the population to be arrested in each republic and oblast. They were fairly modest for that time—three to four percent of the total. For the entire USSR this involved the liquidation of five million people.

I am convinced that this plan for human liquidation was considerably over-fulfilled. The arrested victims were dealt with very simply. Some were sent to concentration camps by decision of local NKVD tribunals consisting of the head of the local NKVD, the secretary of the oblast Party committee, and the oblast prosecutor: others were shot in groups after trial in absentia by the same tribunals. In the latter case relatives were orally informed that the person arrested had been deported for 10 years without the right to carry on correspondence.

Yezhov carried out efficiently his task of "liquidating the remnants of the enemy classes" throughout the countryside, where the problem was the fairly simple one of arresting people, trying them in absentia according to lists submitted by the NKVD tribunals, and shooting them in groups or deporting them en masse to concentration camps. In Moscow, on the other hand, the trials did not run so smoothly, although the accused, as in the case of the Pyatakov and Radek groups in January 1937, continued to plead guilty. Whether the military group pleaded guilty or not remains a secret, as all were tried in secret. But the most important Yezhov trial, that of Bukharin and Rykov, was only on the face of it successful; in fact it was an unmitigated failure. (This trial is described in the next chapter.) It was generally believed that this unsuccessful trial would teach Stalin, if not Yezhov, to avoid embarking upon further legal tragicomedies. The foreign press raised the cry that the legal rigmarole had been a complete fake and that the "sincere confessions of the accused" had been sheer inventions. Within the USSR itself, they deceived no one.

In view of this debacle and because Stalin had already killed off his former competitors for power, there was some reason to believe that the purge was nearing its end. Such expectations proved to be vain. Stalin now set Yezhov two new tasks: (1) To invent a "parallel Bukharinite center" composed of persons who were still sitting side by side with Stalin in the Politburo—Kosior, Chubar, Eikhe, Rudzutak, Petrovsky, all members and alternate members of the Politburo who in the plenary session of the Central Committee in September 1936 had voted against trying Bukharin—and to bring them to trial; and (2) To invent a "parallel military center" composed of a group headed by Marshals Yegorov, Bluecher, and others, and to bring them to trial.

These two tasks proved Yezhov's undoing. He failed in both. The reason for his failure is closely bound up with the technique used for investigation and with the personal characteristics of the new arrestees; in other words, with the effectiveness of the physical methods of interrogation and the reactions of the accused.

There are two theories which purport to explain the reasons for the confessions at the Moscow trials. One is that under the stress of great moral and physical torture and in order to save the lives of friends and families, the accused would admit to anything. The other holds that the Old Bolsheviks continued in these trials to serve the cause of the revolution (cf. Rubashev in Arthur Koestler's *Darkness at Noon*). I believe both these theories are correct in certain particular cases, but they have no general application and no "law" can be deduced from them. There could be seen at the Moscow trials persons who under torture provided the evidence desired by Stalin, but there were no Rubashevs among them nor were there enemies of the Soviet regime. There were Rubashevs—I knew several of them myself—but only among the middle layers of the élite. They were people of politically limited vision who said: "There can be no revolutions without victims and I will carry out the orders of the Party and confirm my evidence before the court, in the interests of socialism." The Chekists had no hesitation in having such simpletons appear at trials and in shooting them afterward. They treated in the same way those who succumbed to torture. However, those brought to public trial were numbered in the tens, while the hundreds of thousands whom Stalin did not allow to appear at public trials were never seen at all. We saw Old Bolsheviks and members of the Party Central Committee who had only recently been openly opposing Stalin and his associates. But we never saw those who had not belonged to any opposition group, although they too were imprisoned and shot. As to this, Khrushchev reported in 1956:

> Out of 139 full and alternate members of the Party Central Committee elected at the Seventeenth Congress, 98 individuals, or 70%, were arrested and shot (mostly in 1937–38). But of these only about ten were brought to trial, the others were shot either after secret trial, or with no trial at all, although they included the above-mentioned full and alternate members of Stalin's Politburo. Did they not confess at preliminary interrogations? Many of them did, but as soon as they appeared in court they unanimously declared that their confessions had been extracted from them under torture and beatings, and were lies from beginning to end.[16]

Khrushchev cited several such examples connected with the efforts of Stalin and Yezhov and, later, Stalin and Beria, to invent a "parallel Bukharinite center."[17] His examples are so vivid and typical that they warrant quotation at some length:

1. The Eikhe Case. Khrushchev described this case as follows:

> The case of the former candidate member of the Politburo, one of the most prominent Party and government workers, Comrade Eikhe, a Party member from 1905 . . . (arrested in April 1938), is an example of wicked provocation and the most odious distortion of the truth. Eikhe was forced to sign, under torture, a previously prepared protocol of a "confession" in which he and some other prominent Party

---

[16] *Ibid.*, p. 16.
[17] *Ibid.*, pp. 21–25, 32.

functionaries were accused of anti-Soviet activities. On October 1, 1939, Eikhe sent Stalin a statement in which he categorically denied his guilt and demanded a review of his case. Eikhe's second statement, which he sent to Stalin on October 27, 1939, has survived. Eikhe wrote:

"On October 25 of this year I was informed that the investigation regarding my case had been concluded. . . . Had I been guilty of even the hundredth part of the crimes of which I am accused, I would not have dared to send you this statement before my death. But I am not guilty of any of these crimes. I have never lied to you and am not lying to you now, standing as I am with one foot in the grave. My entire case is a typical example of slander and provocation . . . my guilt consists in my admission to counterrevolutionary activity. . . . But the reason is that I was not able to bear the tortures inflicted on me by Ushakov and Nikolayev, especially by the former. He knew that my broken ribs had not yet healed, and making use of this knowledge caused me terrible pain during the interrogation. . . . Whenever something in the legend made up by Ushakov and signed by me did not tally I was forced to sign new variants."

The same treatment was meted out to Rukhimovich . . . as well as to the head of a *reserve network* allegedly established by Bukharin in 1935.

How did this case end? Khrushchev continued:

Eikhe was tried on February 2, 1940. He said: "None of my evidence contains a word of truth. The signatures which I put to this evidence were wrung from me by torture. I was never guilty of any kind of conspiracy. I shall die believing in the correctness of the Party's policy, as I have believed all my life." On February 4, Eikhe was shot.

2. The Cases of Full and Candidate Politburo Members Kosior, Rudzutak, Chubar, and Postyshev and Orgburo Member Kosarev. Khrushchev said:

Rudzutak, candidate member of the Politburo, a Party member since 1905, a man who had been for ten years in a tsarist prison, retracted at the trial the evidence which had been forced out of him. The minutes of the Military Board of the Supreme Court contain the following statement by Rudzutak:

"The only request which he made to the Court was to ask them to inform the Party Central Committee that there still remained a cell in the NKVD which had not been liquidated. Its work consisted in cleverly fabricating cases and forcing innocent persons to confess to crimes which they had not committed; the accused were not given the opportunity to prove that they had not participated in the crimes described in confessions obtained under torture. The methods of judicial investigation were such that people were forced to lie and slander innocent persons. . . . He asked the Court's permission to let him inform the Central Committee about it in writing. He assured the Court that he had never had any hostile intentions toward our Party's policy, because he had always agreed with the Party line. . . .

It took twenty minutes to pronounce the verdict and Rudzutak was shot. . . . The cases against the prominent Party and government workers Kosior, Chubar, Postyshev, Kosarev, and others were fabricated in the same way. The NKVD adopted a criminal method of preparing lists of persons whose cases were tried by military tribunals. *In these cases the verdicts were prepared beforehand.* Yezhov generally sent these lists personally to Stalin, who confirmed the penalty proposed. In 1937–38, Stalin was sent 383 such lists with the names of thousands of Party, Soviet, Komsomol, military, and economic workers. He ratified these lists.

3. The Case of the Army Leaders. As to these persons, Khrushchev said:

> The liquidation by Stalin of a great many officers had most dire consequences, especially at the beginning of the war ... during those years repressions were directed against the holders of certain ranks, quite literally from company and battalion commanders up to officers of the highest rank.... We had excellent military personnel, certainly loyal to the Party and the country. Suffice it to mention that those who managed to survive the severe tortures inflicted on them in prisons showed themselves to be real patriots from the first days of the war and fought to the glory of their country. I have in mind such comrades as Rokossovsky, Gorbatov, Meretskov (a delegate to the present Congress), Podlas (a remarkable commander, killed at the front) and many, many others. However, many such officers perished in concentration camps and prisons.

In November 1938, Yezhov was dismissed from his post in the NKVD and was appointed People's Commissar for Water Transportation. He was seen for the last time at the opening of the Eighteenth Party Congress in March 1939. Immediately after, he disappeared without trace. Whether he was shot after trial, or simply because his name had been placed on a list, remains unknown. Khrushchev said nothing specific on this point. He even tried to justify Yezhov to a certain degree in his usual attempt to place all the blame on Stalin. "We are quite right," said Khrushchev, "in blaming Yezhov for his iniquitous methods in 1937. But an answer should be given to the question: could such problems as the fate of prominent Party members be decided by Yezhov alone? They could not, and it would be naive to believe that they could. It is quite clear that Stalin settled such problems himself and that Yezhov could not act without his orders and his approval."[18]

When Stalin dismissed Yezhov in November 1938, he did so on his own initiative, such decisions being made by Stalin personally without consulting the Politburo, which now, according to Khrushchev, existed in name only. What was the reason for the fall from grace of this trusty executioner? In the light of Khrushchev's analysis, we can come to only one conclusion. Yezhov had managed fairly well the trial of Pyatakov and Radek, had been less successful in the trial of Bukharin and Rykov, and had failed completely in his attempt to invent the "parallel Bukharinite center" and the "parallel military center." In spite of beatings and broken ribs received in interrogations, and in spite of Yezhov's distortions of the truth, after the Bukharin trial people not only stopped confessing in secret trials to imaginary crimes, but wrote letters from their NKVD cells directly to Stalin and to the powerless Politburo to lay bare the practices employed by Stalin and Yezhov. In short, Yezhov had failed in his task. He had to go, but the only place to which he could go was the grave, because he knew too much.

The manner in which Beria carried on his activity in 1939–40 confirms the truth of the conclusion arrived at above regarding the reason for Yezhov's disgrace. Beria dropped the practice of holding public trials and shot members of the Central Committee and high ranking army officers after individual secret

---

[18] *Ibid.*, p. 26.

trials, regardless of whether or not the accused had confessed. He shot them even after acquittal by the Cheka. Khrushchev cited in his report an enlightening document illustrative of the political tragedy which befell Bolshevik fanatics thrown into Bolshevik prisons and the infinite amorality of the Stalinists in the Bolshevik Politburo. This document was a letter from an Old Bolshevik, Kedrov, to his personal friend Andreyev, at that time Secretary of the Central Committee of Party Control of the Central Committee and member of the Politburo and later a member of the Central Committee and of the Presidium of the Supreme Soviet of the USSR. It read as follows:

> I appeal to you for help from a grim cell of the Lefort Prison. May this cry of despair reach your ear! Do not remain deaf to this appeal; take me under your protection; I beg your help to stop this nightmare of interrogations and prove to them that it has all been a mistake. I suffer through no fault of mine. Please believe me. Time will prove the truth. I am not an agent provocateur of the tsarist okhranka; I am not a spy; I am not, as I have been denounced, a member of an anti-Soviet organization. Neither am I guilty of other crimes against the Party and the government. I am an Old Bolshevik, with no stain on my character. I fought conscientiously for nearly forty years for the welfare and prosperity of the country.... Today the prosecutors threaten me, an old man of sixty-two, with even more cruel and degrading methods of physical torture.... They are trying to justify their actions by painting me as an inveterate and hardened enemy, and demand new and ever more cruel tortures. But let the Party know that I am innocent and that there is no power on earth that could have transformed a true son of the Party into its enemy. I have no way out. I cannot protect myself against new and heavier blows that are about to fall on me. But everything has its limits. My sufferings have reached theirs. My health is broken, my strength and energy are melting away, the end is near. To die in a Soviet prison, branded as a foul traitor to one's country—what can be more monstrous for an honest man? How terrible it all is! My heart overflows with infinite sorrow and bitterness. No, this cannot be, I exclaim, it is impossible! Neither the Party nor the Soviet government, nor the People's Commissar, L. Beria, can allow such a cruel and irreparable injustice.... I have a profound belief in the triumph of truth and justice. I believe. I believe.[19]

Khrushchev went on to explain: "The military board found that Old Bolshevik Comrade Kedrov was innocent.... Nevertheless, he was shot on Beria's orders." Other Old Bolsheviks were treated even more summarily: Golubev and Baturin, for example, were shot without trial and the verdicts were not announced until after they had been carried out.[20]

Through Beria Stalin was able to accomplish what he had failed to do during Yezhov's term of office. Continuing to make use of physical torture and paying scant regard to legal formalities, Stalin and Beria went on to execute remaining members of the Central Committee. When, at the beginning of 1939, the local Party organizations began to look askance at the continuation of NKVD torture after the dismissal of Yezhov, Stalin sent the following coded telegram on

[19] *Ibid.*, pp. 43—44.
[20] *Ibid.*, pp. 43—44.

January 20, 1939, to secretaries of oblast and district committees, to republic central committees, to people's commissars of internal affairs in the various republics, and to the heads of other NKVD organizations:

> The Central Committee of the All-Union Communist Party of Bolsheviks explains that the use of physical force by the NKVD as from 1937 on was authorized by the Central Committee. The Central Committee considers that methods of physical coercion must continue to be applied in exceptional cases to well-known and inveterate enemies of the people, and these methods must then be considered both permissible and correct.[21]

Khrushchev maintained not only that Beria was an agent of a foreign intelligence service, but that Stalin, after being warned and placed in possession of the relevant facts, had made no move against Beria, because "Stalin believed in Beria and this was enough for him." These facts, said Khrushchev, had been reported to the plenum of the Central Committee in 1937, when Beria was still only Secretary of the Central Committee in Georgia, by a man named Kamensky, who had in his possession the archives of the Azerbaidzhan independent republic of 1918–20, headed at the time by the anti-Communist Mussavat Party. Kamensky had been a member of the Bolshevik Party since 1913, and in 1920 after the overthrow of the Mussavat régime First Secretary of the Central Committee of the Communist Party of Azerbaidzhan and chairman of the city soviet of the Azerbaidzhan capital of Baku. In 1930 he had been secretary of the Moscow Oblast Party Committee, and in 1937 People's Commissar of Health of the USSR. There could be no question that this first ruler of Soviet Azerbaidzhan was a competent witness as far as Beria was concerned. Beria had been educated in Baku and had worked there, first under Turkish rule and later under Mussavat rule during the British occupation. His connections with the Mussavat leaders had been generally known; regarding his connections with the Turks and the English there were various rumors in circulation until Beria became deputy chief of the Soviet intelligence organization in Baku. (The chief was Bagirov, who was shot after Beria.) Beria's rise to power had put a stop to these rumors. As to Kamensky's testimony, Khrushchev declared: "As early as 1937, Kamensky, the former People's Commissar of Health, said at a plenary session of the Central Committee that Beria had worked for the Mussavat intelligence service. However, the plenary session of the Central Committee had hardly been concluded when Kamensky was arrested and shot."[22]

It should be noted here that of all the secretaries of Party central committees in the union republics, only three survived Yezhov's firing squads and continued to make a career for themselves. The three were Beria in Georgia, Bagirov in Azerbaidzhan, and Khrushchev in the Ukraine. Was the advancement of at least the first two entirely fortuitous? Isaac Don Levine may well be correct in stating in his absorbing and well-documented book, *Stalin's Great Secret*, that Stalin himself had been an agent of the tsarist security police. Now, as

---

[21] *Ibid.*, p. 27.
[22] *Ibid.*, p. 42.

Beria and Bagirov had been agents of the Mussavat government, could it be a case of agents covering up each other's crimes against the Party? Stalin's entire active life before the Revolution had been spent in Baku and Tiflis, in centers where during Lenin's lifetime and until his own death he installed only his own personal followers. According to Khrushchev, Stalin had not trusted Ordzhonikidze, but had placed complete confidence in Beria. "Ordzhonikidze," said Khrushchev, "was always opposed to Beria and told Stalin so. But instead of investigating the case and taking appropriate measures, Stalin sanctioned the liquidation of Ordzhonikidze's brother and reduced Ordzhonikidze himself to such a state that he shot himself."[23]

For some reason Khrushchev did not tell the entire story. Ordzhonikidze was the only one of the old members of the Politburo to deliver an ultimatum to Stalin demanding a suspension of the Yezhov inquisition. This was at a time when Beria was still the "tsar" of Georgia. In response to Ordzhonikidze's ultimatum Stalin sent him several Chekists with a spare revolver. Ordzhonikidze was given the alternative of shooting himself in his own flat or dying in the cellars of the NKVD. Ordzhonikidze said farewell to his wife and shot himself in the presence of the Chekists. The doctor, who was waiting in the anteroom, certified that Ordzhonikidze had died of heart failure. Three days later the funeral service was held in the Red Square. His friends and murderers—Stalin, Molotov, Kaganovich, Voroshilov, Khrushchev, Mikoyan, Yezhov—stood with bowed heads on Lenin's mausoleum. Beria, who had been hurriedly summoned from Georgia, shed crocodile tears for the premature death of "the great revolutionary, Stalin's friend and comrade-in-arms, Sergo Ordzhonikidze." I was present and stood near enough to the mausoleum to see the sorrow, the suffering, the unbearable pain depicted on the face of that great actor, Comrade Stalin.

Khrushchev also failed to tell the whole truth regarding the scope of Beria's reign of terror. It is true that with regard to the members of the Central Committee, important Party workers, and top-ranking army officers, Beria finished without mercy the work begun by Yezhov. But except for these "famous enemies" he applied torture only to former Cheka officers appointed in Yezhov's time. Moreover, prisoners arrested by Yezhov's men were now set free wholesale. Executions in the provinces were suspended and the cases of people condemned to be executed were hurriedly reviewed. Many prisoners were even sent back from concentration camps for review of their cases. By the beginning of 1939, arrests and tortures had virtually come to a stop. I do not believe that Beria was less cruel than Yezhov or that Stalin's conscience had suddenly awakened, but a halt had to be made somewhere.

After arresting Yezhov and appointing Beria in his place, Stalin managed, as usual, to make capital out of his own crimes; the responsibility for the reign of terror was attributed to Yezhov personally, while the "spring of liberalism" was attributed to Stalin's loyal disciple Beria.

---

[23] *Ibid.*, p. 44.

Nevertheless, both during and after the war, Beria's inquisitorial talents, under Stalin's leadership, surpassed even those of Yezhov. Entire national populations were now deported to Siberia and Kazakhstan. The Chechens, Ingush, Karachai, Balkars, Kalmyks, Crimean Tatars, and Volga Germans were uprooted and deported, and the same fate was meted out to a part of the population of the Baltic states. Khrushchev declared with pretended indignation:

> Monstrous acts [were committed] on Stalin's initiative. We have in mind the mass deportations from their native lands of whole nationalities, including their Communist and Komsomol members, with no exceptions made for anyone. These deportations were not dictated by any military considerations. Thus, as early as the end of 1943, an order was issued to deport all Karachai. . . . At the same time, at the end of December 1943, the same fate was meted out to the whole of the population of the Kalmyk Autonomous Republic. In March 1944, the whole of the Chechen and Ingush peoples were deported, and the Chechen-Ingush Autonomous Republic was liquidated. In April 1944, all Balkars were deported to distant places from the territory of the Kabardino-Balkar Autonomous Republic.

"The Ukrainians," he added ironically, "escaped this fate only because there were so many of them, and there would not have been enough room for them all elsewhere."[24]

---

[24] *Ibid.*, p. 37.

Chapter XXVIII

The Trial and Execution of Bukharin

It was in the course of the Yezhov period of the Great Purge that Bukharin was finally tried and executed. Our information regarding his trial comes chiefly from the foreign press. Soviet citizens were excluded from such trials and knew only what the Soviet press censorship allowed to appear. The foreign press was in a vastly better position. Although it, too, was subject to strict controls, nevertheless several correspondents of foreign press agencies and one person from each embassy were permitted to be present and to inform their presses of the proceedings. The accused, of course, confessed to everything and sometimes even added to their own guilt in excess of Vyshinsky's requirements.

While at the time the foreign press was alone in reporting that these trials were based on falsifications, lies, political terror, and torture and that this was the only possible explanation of the fantastic "self-accusations" by the defendants, the Stalinists themselves later admitted that this was true. The "secret" methods used by Soviet investigators in political cases were first admitted and revealed by the Soviet government itself in April 1953, when the government declared publicly that the case of the Kremlin doctors had been fabricated by the use of "illegal methods," i.e., of torture and beating, and that the "confessions" of non-existent crimes reported by the press on January 13, 1953, in Stalin's lifetime, had resulted from use of these types of "interrogation technique" by the NKVD, then headed by Deputy Minister Ryumin. The same type of charge was made later regarding the Leningrad Case in the course of the trial of former Minister of State Security Abakumov.

These revelations, however, were merely a beginning. After the dethroning of Stalin at the Twentieth Party Congress the Kremlin was forced to admit to the whole world that all of Stalin's political cases, both in the USSR and in the satellite states, had been manufactured by the same methods as those used in the Doctors Case.

Khrushchev in his famous speech hinted that he had opposed the trial of Bukharin in March 1938. If so, he would have had very solid grounds for his action, not, of course, because he was in principle opposed to having Bukharin tried, but because the trial turned out to be the most unsatisfactory of all those carried out by Stalin. Even the "miraculous" technique of the Chekists failed completely, if its aim was to present Bukharin as a spy, a murderer, and a traitor.

An eyewitness, Brigadier Fitzroy Maclean of the British Embassy in Moscow, who was present at all the sessions of the Military Board of the Supreme Court of the USSR which tried Bukharin, gives an interesting description of the trial and of the behavior of Bukharin himself. As the trial progressed, says Maclean, it became clearer that the underlying purpose of every piece of testimony was to blacken the leaders of the alleged bloc by representing them not as political offenders but as common criminals, murderers, poisoners, and spies. Bukharin particularly was picked out as arch-fiend in this grim pantomime. He, said the witnesses, had planned to murder Lenin, had decided to dismember the Soviet Union, had plotted with Tukhachevsky to open up the front to the Germans in the event of war and with Yagoda to murder Kirov and Maxim Gorky, Menzhinsky, and Kuibyshev, had instructed his followers to establish contact with the agents of Britain, Japan, Poland, and Germany, with the White Russians, with Trotsky, with the Second International, had organized agricultural and industrial sabotage in the Ukraine, in Siberia, in the Caucasus, in Central Asia, had planned first a peasant uprising and civil war, and then a palace revolution and a coup d'état. Each defendant, as he blackened himself, was careful at the same time to blacken Bukharin. The old picture of the revolutionary fighter, the Marxist theorist, the friend of Lenin, the member of the Politburo, the President of the Communist International, was methodically demolished and replaced by a new portrait, that of a demon, a traitor, a spy, for whom no one could feel sympathy.[1]

The method, says Maclean, was having the desired effect as long as Bukharin himself was not on the stand. But when Vyshinsky turned to Bukharin for confirmation matters went less smoothly. Even when he admitted to the crimes with which he was charged, he had an awkward way of qualifying his admissions in such a way as largely to invalidate them, of slipping in little asides which made complete nonsense of them. Moreover, he did not reply to the Public Prosecutor with the same deference as the other prisoners, but seemed to treat him as an equal and at times to be actually poking fun at him.

On the evening of March 5, Ulrich announced that it was Bukharin's turn to be cross-examined. As Bukharin rose to his feet there was a stir of interest in the crowd. The accused made full confession of his guilt, almost too full, for having declared himself the leader of the Right-Trotskyite bloc, he forthwith announced that he accepted entire responsibility for any and every misdeed which might have been committed by the bloc, whether he had known of it or not. This of course was satisfactory, but not, it seemed, exactly what was wanted. Vyshinsky attempted to elicit more details. But it was not easy to pin down the defendant to concrete facts, for he tended to launch into an account of the bloc's economic program or to relate how he had given consideration to a coup d'état against the present rulers of the Soviet Union.

Ulrich and Vyshinsky, says Maclean, began to look annoyed. This was not at all what was wanted. It was essential for Bukharin to be made to appear not a theorist, but a common criminal, but here he was, quite his old self, evolving a reasoned political and economic theory, and, which was worse, one that for some people might not be unattractive. It was unprecedented for a defendant

---

[1] Fitzroy Maclean, *Eastern Approaches*, London, 1949, pp. 94–97.

232

in a state trial to declare that he had opposed Stalin's policy because he had come to the conclusion that it was wrong. Yet this in effect was what Bukharin was doing.

Hastily Vyshinsky turned to the question of espionage. Bukharin had been in Austria before the Revolution, in 1912 and 1913. Had he not had contacts with the Austrian police? Had they not recruited him as a spy? The answer came back like a flash: "My only contact with the Austrian police was when they imprisoned me in a fortress as a revolutionary." And almost immediately he was back in the realm of political theory. When the court adjourned later that night, Vyshinsky had made little progress in the desired direction.

On the next day, March 6, the court recessed, permitting twenty-four hours in which to prepare Bukharin for the next phase of his cross-examination and to induce in him a more amenable frame of mind. But when the court reassembled on March 7, Bukharin, though showing signs of strain, was a resilient as ever. To some charges he replied as before that he personally had no knowledge of the events referred to, but was nevertheless prepared to accept responsibility for them on behalf of the bloc. To others, his answer was that he did not happen to have committed the crimes with which he was charged, but that it would have been a logical consequence of his conduct if he had done so, and that he was therefore quite ready to admit his guilt if it would give any pleasure to the Public Prosecutor. At times, displaying all his old dialectical skill, he amused himself by picking holes in the arguments advanced by the prosecution, making free use of such terms as "nonsense" and "absurd."

On several points he remained absolutely firm. He refused to admit that he had ever contemplated murdering Lenin, or that he had ever been the agent of a foreign power, or that he had ever agreed to dismember the Soviet Union or to open up the front to the Germans in time of war. Nor did he once consent to dance to the prosecution's pipe by incriminating his fellow prisoners. Vyshinsky tried arguing, he tried blustering, he used every trick known to a slippery second-rate lawyer. Still Bukharin stood firm. Vyshinsky reinterrogated several of the other defendants and elicited from them the most damning statements. Bukharin flatly contradicted some of these witnesses and dismissed others as agents provocateurs.

On March 12, Bukharin made his last statement. Against all previous practice, these last words by an important defendant were not published in the Soviet press, with the exception of brief extracts in which he admitted to being politically guilty of being a "counterrevolutionary bandit" and a "conspirator."

Maclean's report of Bukharin's statement makes it clear why Stalin did not allow it to be published although the closing speeches of Kamenev, Zinoviev, Radek, and others filled whole pages of *Pravda* and *Izvestia*.[2]

After admitting in principle the justice of the case made against him, he proceeded, this time without interruption, to tear it to bits, while Vyshinsky, powerless to intervene, sat uneasily in his place, looking embarrassed and yawning

[2] *Ibid.*, pp. 109–111.

ostentatiously. In the first place, said Bukharin, it was alleged that there was a bloc. It might, therefore, be assumed that the members of such a bloc would at least have known each other. But before coming into court he had never seen or heard of Sharangovich or Maximov, had never in his life spoken to Pletnev, Kazakov, or Bulanov (all codefendants of Bukharin and Rykov as leaders of the alleged bloc) had never had any counterrevolutionary talks with Rozengolts or Rakovsky. In fact, he asserted it was impossible to make any claim under law that the accused constituted a Right-Trotskyite bloc. "There had been," said Bukharin, "no such group."

Besides, Bukharin continued, there was an obvious lack of connection between the crimes with which the members of the alleged bloc were charged. Yagoda, for example, was known to have murdered Maxim Peshkov for personal reasons. This crime had had nothing to do with any bloc. Menzhinsky was known to have been dying. What could have been the purpose of murdering him? The weakness of the prosecution's arguments, he commented, was painfully apparent. Because Tomsky, also now dead, had once said to him in the course of a conversation that the Trotskyites were opposed to Maxim Gorky, he, Bukharin, was now being accused of having given orders for Gorky to be murdered. In fact Vyshinsky was assuming what he was trying to prove. Vyshinsky's assumption that because he had talked politics with Khodzhayev in Tashkent, he had instructed him to get in touch with British agents in Tadzhikistan was a typical instance. He categorically denied having had any connection with any foreign espionage organizations. Nor had he advocated opening the front to the enemy in case of war, or given instructions for sabotage. He denied having had anything to do with the murders of Kirov, Menzhinsky, Kuibyshev, Gorky, or Peshkov. Finally, he denied having ever contemplated the assassination of Lenin.

The main points of Maclean's eyewitness account of the trial are confirmed by the few facts about the trial which the Stalin censorship allowed to be published. For instance, the Soviet press quoted Bukharin's statement to the effect that he admitted being guilty of counterrevolution as charged. According to *Pravda*, he had stated during the cross-examination on March 5: "We all turned into rabid counterrevolutionaries, traitors, and restorers of capitalism. We embarked on treason, perfidy, and crimes. We became an insurgent group, became wreckers, and wanted to overthrow the Soviet proletarian regime."[3] But although Bukharin appeared to have confessed to all the sins imputed to him in the verdict, in fact when Vyshinsky tried to find out what these crimes were, it transpired that Bukharin was a "spy," a "traitor," a "murderer," and a "counterrevolutionary" who had never committed an act of espionage, of treason, of murder, or of counterrevolution. When Vyshinsky said: "Tell me, defendant Bukharin, what form did your anti-Soviet activity take?" Bukharin, according to *Pravda*, tried to evade answering the basic question, but replied that it had been "as a politician and as the former leader of the Right Opposition. If I were to formulate my program in practical terms, it would be, in regard to economics, as state capitalism,

---

[3] *Pravda*, March 7, 1938.

individual peasant owners, reduction in the number of kolkhozes, foreign concessions, modifications in the foreign trade monopoly, and as the result, capitalization of the country."[4]

But this was not counterrevolution or treason or murder, but was the most orthodox Leninist New Economic Policy. It certainly was not the answer required by Vyshinsky and Stalin. All peasant Russia mentally applauded Bukharin's "counterrevolution!" In fact, he was making use of the dock for purposes of anti-Stalin propaganda—a dangerous procedure. Bukharin had to be "unmasked" as spy and assassin with all possible speed. Vyshinsky hastened to put a concrete question: "What was your connection with the murder of Kirov? Was this murder committed with the knowledge and on the orders of the Right-Trotskyite bloc?" To this Bukharin replied: "I knew nothing about it." Kirov was the only top-ranking Party leader in the USSR who had been murdered. The crime had been ascribed to everyone—to the White Guard, to the Trotskyites, to Zinoviev's followers. And all had confessed to it. There were apparently so many in the USSR who had wanted to kill Kirov that the only surprising thing about the assassination was that it had been committed so late. Now it had been decided to have Kirov murdered by the Bukharinites. But Bukharin refused to murder Kirov once more. His refusal threatened to reveal the well-established technique of Kirov's "permanent" assassination. Vyshinsky hastened to produce as witness some alleged collaborators in order to convict Bukharin. But Bukharin simply ignored some and branded others as agents provocateurs. Vyshinsky then resorted to a trick which seemed to him to promise better results: he announced that he would question Bukharin's friend Rykov, whom Bukharin could not suspect of provocation, and who usually gave Vyshinsky the desired answers. But again he was unsuccessful. "Defendant Rykov," he asked, "what do you know about Kirov's murder?" Rykov replied: "I know nothing about any participation by Rightists or by a Right part of a bloc in Kirov's murder."[5]

Rykov having proved to be a broken reed, perhaps something could be done with an alleged "murder" which had never taken place, but which Bukharin had planned, according to evidence unanimously given by many of the accused.

Vyshinsky: "In 1918 were you not in favor of killing the leaders of our Party and government?"

Bukharin: "No, I was not."

Vyshinsky: "What about the murder of Comrades Lenin, Stalin, and Sverdlov?"

Bukharin: "Under no circumstances."[6]

Vyshinsky, of course, was beside himself. He had invited to the trial the old leaders of the Left Social Revolutionaries in order to convict Bukharin of conspiracy against Lenin (Stalin and Sverdlov were dragged in for no reason at all), but the only sensation created by their appearance was that the world discovered that they were still alive. And so the Lenin gambit also proved a failure.

---

[4] *Ibid.*

[5] *Ibid.*

[6] *Ibid.*

Finally Vyshinsky came to the main charge against Bukharin—that of espionage. Surely here Bukharin could have no defense, with Ivanov, Sharangovich, and Faizulla Khodzhayev at his side, and all describing in fantastic details the espionage assignments which he had entrusted to them. And Bukharin himself had admitted to having become a spy and traitor.[7] But again Bukharin refused to admit to concrete acts of espionage. Questioned as to periods of residence in Austria, the United States, and Japan, he replied stubbornly that he had in none of these countries gotten in touch with the police.

Vyshinsky: "Why then did you so easily join the bloc, which was engaged in espionage?"

Bukharin: "I know nothing of any espionage work."

Vyshinsky: "What did the bloc do?"

Bukharin: "Evidence regarding espionage has been given by two persons, Sharangovich and by Ivanov, that is, by two agents provocateurs. . . . My connection with the Austrian police consisted in being imprisoned in an Austrian fortress. I was imprisoned in Sweden, twice in Russia, and also in Germany."

Having despaired of making Bukharin confess to anything like treason to the Fatherland, even to old tsarist Russia, and seeing that Bukharin had publicly branded the two chief witnesses as NKVD agents provocateurs, Vyshinsky was forced to resort to a third witness, Faizulla Khodzhayev—former head of the Uzbekistan government and member of the Party Central Committee.

Vyshinsky: "Did you have conversations with Khodzhayev of a defeatist and treasonable nature?"

Bukharin: "I had only one conversation with Khodzhayev, in 1936."

Vyshinsky: "Did you tell Khodzhayev that there was already an agreement with Nazi Germany?"

Bukharin: "No, I did not."

Vyshinsky: (to Khodzhayev): "Did Bukharin speak with you?"

Khodzhayev: "He did. He said that we must so direct our activity that it would result in the defeat of the Soviet Union, and that there was an agreement with Nazi Germany . . ."

Vyshinsky: "Bukharin, did you visit Khodzhayev's country house?"

Bukharin: "I did."

Vyshinsky: "Did you have a conversation with him?"

Bukharin: "Not that kind of conversation, but another, also conspiratorial."

Vyshinsky: "I am not asking you about conversations in general, but about *that* conversation."

Bukharin: "In Hegel's *Logic*, the word *that* is considered the most difficult . . ." (the omissions are *Pravda*'s).[8]

---

[7] *Ibid.*

[8] *Ibid.*, March 8, 1938.

What led Bukharin to admit his guilt in general while rejecting concrete charges of espionage, treason, murder, and counterrevolution? The question has been discussed many times. Was it a split personality? Was it a desire to serve the Party's high ideals? Was it the wish to stay alive? To all these questions the answer is quite definitely "No!" Bukharin's tactics, I am entirely convinced, consisted in getting himself publicly tried with only one end in view—to make a last attack on the Stalinist regime. While orally admitting his guilt, Bukharin was in fact not only revealing the technique of the Stalin inquisition, but was enabled publicly to state his old program of "restoration." He was the only one in the Stalin trials to oppose publicly the political program of his enemy Stalin. If Bukharin had chosen the other tactic—that of denying all guilt—he would certainly have been shot without trial, as were many other members of the Central Committee and even of the Politburo. There is no doubt whatever that Bukharin had also been beaten and physically tortured, even more so than the others. Nevertheless, he had not been broken. After all, it was in the same trial that Krestinsky, in his first cross-examination, had denied his guilt, thus frightening not only the court but Vyshinsky himself. But it had taken only one night to bring Krestinsky to his senses, and the next day, to Vyshinsky's question whether he still insisted on his innocence, Krestinsky had hastily replied that he admitted everything and that on the previous day, finding himself in new surroundings in the court and in the presence of the public, he had been overwhelmed with shame for his crimes, a typically Stalinist explanation successfully placed in his mouth after several hours of "physical work" in Yezhov's office.

The attempt to do the same to Bukharin failed. He could have been tortured to death, but Stalin preferred to process him through the court, if only to get from him a half-confession. Bukharin accepted the compromise and gave the people a riddle which was no riddle at all. Both Bukharin and Rykov, as well as the NKVD agents provocateurs Sharangovich and Ivanov, were sentenced to death and executed on March 15, 1938.

Chapter XXIX

The Party after the Great Purge

The period of Stalin's rise to power was a period of ideological degeneration and of physical liquidation of the basic membership of the old Bolshevik Party. It was also, however, the period in which a new Party was created—the Party of Stalin, even though it continued to bear the old name right up to 1952, when the word "Bolshevik" was dropped.

It was entirely logical that there should be ideological degeneration as a result of the conflict between doctrine and the realities of life. It was also entirely logical that in the course of the insoluble contradictions between theoretical dogmas and the circumstances of life itself, numerous splinter and opposition groups should have arisen within the Party, each eager to suggest its own recipes, methods, and remedies for saving whatever could still be saved. But the tragedy inherent in all opposition and opposition groups within the Party lay in their failure or refusal to see a fact of world significance—the bankruptcy of the basic tenets of theoretical Communism whenever theory had to give way to practice. Stalin approached the matter at hand as a practical man. He had something to save and something to fight for—power. But in order for power to be strong, invulnerable, and monolithic, the Party of oppositionists, romantics, and doctrinaire theorists had to be transformed into a Party of realists, devoted to one leader, obedient and efficient. As long as the old revolutionary phraseology was preserved, the Party could be given any meaning and be used for any particular aim. The method of creating a Party of this kind was duly found: it consisted first in periodic purges of old Party members and second in a mass enrollment of new members selected to meet new requirements.

In Stalin's time there were six such purges:

1. The purge of city soviet and university cells in 1925.
2. The purge of rural cells in 1926.
3. The general purge of 1929–30.
4. The general purge of 1933.
5. The general purge of 1935–36 ("the check of Party documents").
6. The Yezhov and Beria Purges of 1936–39.

What were the results of these purges?

Before replying to the question, let us examine the dynamics of Party growth:

1905 (January 1)	Total Number of Members and Candidates	Workers	Peasants (Percentage of Total)	Employees
1905 (January 1)	8,400	61.7	4.7	33.6
1917 (January 1)	23,600	60.2	7.6	32.2
1917 (October 1)	70,000	—	—	—
1921 (March)	732,521	—	—	—
1922 (March)	401,000	44.4	26.7	28.9
1924	446,080	44.0	28.8	27.2
1925	741,117	57.9	25.3	16.8
1926	1,002,490	58.1	24.6	17.3
1927	1,131,254	56.1	26.3	17.6
1928	1,220,836	57.8	22.3	19.9
1929	1,439,082	62.1	21.0	16.9
1930	1,572,164	65.8	19.7	11.5
1931	2,066,400	66.6	22.3	11.1
1932	3,172,215	64.5	27.8	7.7
1934 (February)	2,809,786	—	—	—
1939 (March)	2,477,666*	—	—	—

* 888,814 are candidates.

SOURCES: *Malaya Sovetskaya Entsiklopediya* (Small Soviet Encyclopedia), 2nd ed., Moscow, 1934, article "VKP(b)"; *Kommunisticheskaya partiya Sovetskogo Soyuza v rezolyutsiyakh i resheniyakh sezdov, konferentsii i plenumov TsK, 1898—1953* (The Communist Party of the Soviet Union in Resolutions and Decisions of the Congresses, Conferences, and Plenums of the Central Committee, 1898—1953), 2 vols., Moscow, 1953; Reports by Malenkov at the Nineteenth Party Congress and in *Soveshchaniya nekotorykh kompartii v Varshave v kontse sentyabrya 1947g.* (A Conference of Several Communist Parties in Warsaw at the End of September 1947). The error in the breakdown of the figures for 1930 is in the source, the *Malaya Sovetskaya Entsiklopediya.*

As to the figures for social groups within the Party, the following must be borne in mind:

1. In referring to "workers" and "peasants," Party statistics included not only workers and peasants actually performing physical labor but also all who were "workers" or "peasants" by social origin. Hence the percentage given for "employees" reflected by no means the actual number of "employees" in the Party.

2. From 1934 on the Central Committee ceased to publish data on the social origins of Party members. There is accordingly no way of determining the social structure of the present membership.

3. Beginning with 1939, the statutes adopted at the Eighteenth Party Congress abolished the former class restrictions on intellectuals and the special privileges granted workers for admission to the Party. The "Party of the working class" thus gradually became a Party of employed intellectuals.

4. Until 1933 Party purges were accompanied by the enrollment of new members, which makes it difficult to calculate the number of Party members purged and reaccepted previous to the general purge of 1933. However, general data for all purges previous to that time can be found in an article in the *Large Soviet Encyclopedia* written by no less an authority on purges than Yaroslavsky. "As a result of this systematic purge and of the periodical purges," he reported, "almost a million members and candidates were either expelled from the Party or resigned voluntarily between 1917 and 1933."[1]

Yaroslavsky's blanket use of the long period "from 1917 to 1933" was intentional, and was aimed at concealing the scale of purges in Stalin's time. But before Stalin's rise to power, there had been only one purge, what might be called

[1] *BSE*, lst ed., Vol. LXI, col. 655.

a voluntary purge, which consisted in the general reregistration of Communist Party members in 1921. All those who failed to become reregistered were considered expelled from the Party or, to use Yaroslavsky's expression, to have "resigned voluntarily." It is true that the former Mensheviks were expelled on account of their past records and that in their case Lenin was inexorable: he proposed to leave in the Party no more than one percent of all former Mensheviks and even that one percent had to be checked and rechecked hundreds of times (one such "Menshevik" Bolshevik who remained in the Party was Vyshinsky). But, according to Yaroslavsky, the total number of those who had been expelled or had resigned in 1921 was 219,650. In other words, about 800,000 Communists were expelled from the Party in the course of the first Stalinist purges—those of 1925, 1926, and 1930.

The net results of the general purge of 1933 can be inferred from the same table, which shows that, in 1933 alone, 362,429 Communists were expelled from the Party, i.e., almost as many as the total Party membership of 401,000 in 1922, at the time when Stalin became Secretary-General.

To turn to Yezhov's purge, it is generally accepted that the beginning of this purge coincided with the date of Kirov's murder in 1934. Many assume that without Kirov's murder there would have been no Yezhov terror. This, of course, is not true. The new general purge had been decided upon before Kirov's murder and it was intended that he should play a leading part in it. The resolution providing for the new general purge was adopted by the joint plenary session of the Central Committee and the Central Control Commission on January 12, 1933. The resolution read as follows:

> 1. The joint plenary session of the Central Committee and the Central Control Commission approves the decision of the Politburo to carry out a Party purge in the course of 1933 and to suspend enrollment in the Party until the end of the purge.
> 2. The joint plenary session of the Central Committee and the Central Control Commission requests the Politburo and the Presidium of the Central Control Commission to organize the Party purge in such a way as to ensure the preservation of iron proletarian discipline within the Party and the cleansing of the Party of all unreliable and unstable elements and hangers-on.[2]

The purge did not end till March 1939. It did indeed pass through a number of stages, rising and falling in intensity and even slacking off for a time. But in the course of these stages it was merely the outward forms and methods of the purge that underwent changes; the purge itself never ceased. Kirov's murder, regardless of whether he was killed by Stalinists or anti-Stalinists, provided a highly convenient pretext not only for enlarging the scale of the purge, but for making it terroristic. Whereas Party purges had formerly been carried out in open meetings by commissions of the Central Control Commission, after Kirov's murder the Party was purged by the Party apparatus itself, working behind the closed doors of the offices of the Party secretaries of the provincial committees and the Central

---

[2] *VKP (b) v resolyutsiyakh*, Vol. II, 1933, pp. 782–83.

Committee, as appears from a decree of May 13, 1935, "On the Exchange of Party Documents." Finally, even this was considered insufficient. Yezhov, who was now Secretary of the Party Central Committee and Chairman of the Commission of Party Control, was also appointed People's Commissar of Internal Affairs of the USSR with the title of "General Commissar of State Security of the USSR." The Party purge was turned over to the officials of the NKVD, marking the beginning of Yezhov's reign of terror.

What were the net results of this phase of the purges? It would be vain to seek any direct data in official Party documents. Even Stalin—past master as he was at juggling both concepts and figures—sought to evade this question in his report to the Eighteenth Party Congress. He confessed that the 1933 purge continued after 1933, but assured his listeners that it had not continued until October 1936:

> It was decided to continue the purge of Party members and candidates which began as early as 1933 and it was continued until May 1935. It was further decided to cease enrollment of new members in the Party and it was duly stopped right up to September 1936. . . . Moreover, as a result of the dastardly murder of Comrade Kirov, which proved that the Party contained many suspicious characters, it was decided to carry out a check and an exchange of Party documents, both of which operations were only concluded by September 1936.[3]

As to the net results of the Party purge to September 1936 Stalin reported:

> The purge of 1933–36 was inevitable and in the main was beneficial. The present Eighteenth Congress represents about 1,600,000 Party members, i.e., 270,000 members less than the Seventeenth Party Congress.

According to Stalin, then, the great purge was concluded in September 1936 and resulted in the expulsion of only 270,000 Communists from the Party. Even for Stalin this was an unprecedented distortion of historical fact. One need hardly have lived through the events to know that this was the case. A cursory examination of the local and national press of the time establishes three facts: first, that the Yezhov stage of the great purge did not begin until 1936, with the Zinoviev-Kamenev trial; second, that the purge assumed really universal proportions in 1937, with the Pyatakov and Tukhachevsky trials and others; and third, that it reached its culminating point in 1938, with the trial of Bukharin and others.

It should be borne in mind that these trials were the trials of "privileged" personalities, while hundreds and thousands and millions of Soviet citizens were liquidated without trial by extraordinary tribunals of local NKVD branches and by the "special tribunal" of the NKVD in Moscow. The number of persons who did not belong to the Party but were liquidated in this way cannot of course be calculated. It is, however, quite easy to estimate the number of Communists liquidated, not by guessing, but by using official data published by the Party Central Committee.

Stalin deduced the number of persons eliminated by the purge of 1933-36 by comparing the 1,588,852 Party members represented at the Eighteenth Party

---

[3] Stalin, *Voprosy leninizma*, 2nd ed., 1947, p. 593.

Congress with the 1,874,488 represented at the Seventeenth Party Congress. But he deliberately excluded from his calculations the following significant facts:

1. In addition to the 1,874,488 full Party members represented at the Seventeenth Party Congress there were also represented 935,298 candidate members[4] who, after enrollment in the Party was resumed in the second half of 1934, automatically became full members.[5] Thus by May 1935, i.e., before enrollment was again halted, the Party should have had 2,809,786 members, not counting those admitted from among new candidates.[6]

2. The overwhelming majority of the Party members represented at the Eighteenth Party Congress joined the Party after enrollment was resumed in November 1936, i.e., they had not been included among the Communists represented at the Seventeenth Party Congress, a fact for which indirect confirmation will appear in connection with analysis of representation at the Nineteenth Party Congress.

In order to conceal the real scale of the Yezhov purge Stalin had accordingly set back the date for the end of the purge and had compared figures which, whether falsified or not, were not comparable. He had good reason for this tampering with facts, as a valid comparison would have shown that the 2,809,786 Party members as of May 1, 1935, minus the 1,588,852 as of March 1, 1939, meant that 1,220,934 had been purged and liquidated, those purged at the time being automatically liquidated. Even if many of the candidates of 1934 did not become full members, the general conclusion would not be materially affected, for such persons did not remain candidate members right up to 1939, and the candidate members represented at the Eighteenth Party Congress had been recruited in the late 1930's. Accordingly, the net result of Communists purged from the Party from 1917 to 1939, as shown by official data, was as follows:

1917—22	219,650
1925—33	800,000
1933—34	362,429
1934—39	1,220,934
Total	2,603,013

This complete destruction of the old Leninist party and the creation of a new Stalinist party was reflected in a rout of the old Party leadership. Stalin declared at the Eighteenth Party Congress that "the Party Central Committee has data indicating that during the period under review the Party was able to appoint over 500,000 young Bolsheviks to leading posts in the state and Party."[7] It is quite clear that he did not create new positions for these "young Bolsheviks," who merely took the places of Communists who had been removed as secretaries

---

[4] *Ibid.*, p. 594.

[5] *KPSS v resolyutsiyakh*, Part II, 1953, p. 742.

[6] Applicants were at this time required to spend between one and two years as "candidates" (alternates) before admission as full members. *Ibid.*, p. 778.

[7] Stalin, *Voprosy leninizma*, p. 597.

of district and oblast committees and executive committees, members of the governments and central committees of national republics, directors of enterprises, administrators in the Red Army, etc.

The Party Central Committee elected at the Seventeenth Party Congress in February 1934 was completely destroyed. Of the 71 full Central Committee members of 1934, by 1939 4 had died of natural causes, 51 had been shot or otherwise punished, and only 16 survived to participate in the Eighteenth Party Congress. Of the 68 candidate members of 1934, none had died of natural causes, 63 had been shot or had disappeared, and only 5 were present at the Eighteenth Party Congress in 1939. The full members of 1934 still present in 1939 were Andreyev, Badayev, Beria, Voroshilov, Zhdanov, Kaganovich, Kalinin, Krzhizhanovsky, Litvinov, Manuilsky, Mikoyan, Molotov, Nikolayeva, Stalin, Khrushchev, and Shvernik. The candidate members who were still in favor were Lozovsky, Bagirov, Budenny, Poskrebyshev, and Bulganin. Nearly all the full members and the majority of the candidate members of the Central Committee of 1934 who had been done away with by 1939 had been members of the Party before the Revolution.

By 1939 the lengthy process leading not only to the creation of a new Party but also to a radical revision of its former organizational principles of "democratic centralism," "inner-Party democracy," "election of secretaries," etc., had come to an end. Henceforth the Party was based on the "leader principle," precisely in the same way as Hitler's National Socialist Party was based on the "Führer principle." Formerly, the hierarchical pryamid of the Party, beginning from the top, had been both in theory and in practice as follows: Party Congress, Central Committee Plenum, Central Committee Politburo, Central Committee Organization Bureau, Central Committee Secretariat, Secretary-General of the Central Committee. After the Eighteenth Party Congress, the pyramid remained, but had been turned upside down. The Secretary-General had assumed legislative functions, the Central Committee organs executive functions, and the Party Congress had become a consultative assembly.

This entire Party reconstruction took place in accordance with Stalin's demand at the Seventeenth Party Congress that "organizational leadership be raised to the level of political leadership."[8] The qualifications required for personnel selected to fill leading positions in the Party and state were set to fit this demand. Stalin defined them at the plenary session of the Central Committee in February and March 1937 as follows: "What does correctly selecting workers and correctly assigning them to work mean? It means selecting workers first for political qualifications, i.e., for political reliability, and second, for practical qualifications, i.e., depending on whether they are suited to the given work."[9]

And in fact the entire personnel of the Party and state apparatus as it existed on the eve of World War II had been selected on the basis of these qualifications.

---

[8] Stalin's report at the Seventeenth Party Congress.

[9] In his speech entitled, "Liquidation of the Trotskyites and other Double-Dealers."

It is the main reason why they proved faithful to its leader to the very end, even in the days of immense danger for the existence of the Soviet state and of equally immense mistakes and errors committed by Stalin himself.

The chief political feature of the new personnel was that they were not only disciplined like so many soldiers, but also possessed the quality most valuable under the existing régime, that of being immune to independent thought. Their chief feature as far as work was concerned was a gift for organization combined with obedience and ability to get things done. Provided the political trustworthiness of two candidates was the same, preference was given to men of action and knowledge. Past services as well as social origin had long ceased to be of interest. This principle considerably raised the level of the leading Party organs, particularly in the most important arm of the Party apparatus—the district and oblast Party committees.

According to official data, the educational background of secretaries of district committees and chairmen of district executive committees in 1946 and 1954 was as follows (in percentages):

	— University — Graduates		— Graduates of — Secondary Schools		— Graduates of — Primary Schools	
	1946	1954	1946	1954	1946	1954
First Secretaries of District Committees	12.2	24.3	40.3	70.4	47.5	5.3
Secretaries of District Committees	9.9	14.7	40.3	79.1	49.1	6.2
Chairmen of District Executive Committees ...	7.5	14.6	31.2	69.6	61.3	15.8

SOURCE: *Partiinaya zhizn*, No. 9, 1954, p. 10.

As the table shows, the percentage of district committee secretaries who had completed the secondary school and had in many cases gone on to acquire a partial or complete university education increased in the years from 1946 to 1954 from about 50% to 95%, while the percentage with no more than a primary education fell from about 50% to about 6%. Most of the secretaries and chairmen with university education were specialists working in some field of economic life, such as engineers, agricultural experts, etc. There are few figures concerning secretaries of oblast committees or of central committees of the union republics, or concerning government personnel at the same levels. However, the little information available indicates that as in the case of Party organizations, there are at present no oblast Party committees without at least several specialists—engineers, economists, or agricultural experts—on their staffs.

According to the report of the mandate commission, of the 1,192 full members represented at the Nineteenth Party Congress, i.e., the leading Party personnel, 709 were university graduates, 84 had partial university educations, 223 had completed secondary schools, and 176 had partial secondary school education. Of the total 282 were engineers, 68 agricultural and livestock experts, 98 professors, 18 economists, 11 doctors, and 7 lawyers. It is interesting that almost 60% of the top Party personnel were professionals of some type.

Accordingly the Soviet Communist Party, which had formerly boasted of being a workers' Party, had under Stalin and his heirs become a party of engineers, professors, and bureaucrats, a party of professional employees.

This transformation had been brought about by polytechnizing Party cadres, and politicizing economic cadres. This did not, of course, mean that there were no workers and peasants in the Party, or that it did not grow by increasing the number of such persons in the Party. On the contrary, the Party grew by enrolling workers and peasants but, as has been pointed out, the Central Committee was careful to conceal, from the mid-1930's on, the proportion of the various social groups, as a result of which it is difficult to say upon which social groups it drew in the process of growth.

In any case the Party growth, particularly during the war, when stimulated for propaganda purposes, was very rapid. From 3,600,000 full and candidate members in 1941 it grew to 6,300,000 in 1947 and nearly 7,000,000 (6,888,145 to be exact) in 1952.[10]

At the Warsaw Cominform Conference in September 1947, Malenkov noted that about half the Party consisted of Communists who had joined it during or after the war, but that "the overwhelming majority joined it in the period when the Fatherland was in mortal danger." The artificial growth during the war had led, as Malenkov remarked, to a dilution of the Party membership. In the same speech Malenkov stated: "A certain discrepancy developed between the quantitative growth of the Party ranks and the level of political enlightenment of the members and candidate members. . . . The Party, therefore, has now decided not to encourage the further growth of its ranks."[11]

The rapid growth was accordingly halted after the war. Malenkov, speaking for the Central Committee, at the Nineteenth Party Congress, said that "the Party is strong, not in quantity but in quality."[12] In other words, the Party was returning to the old policy of strengthening the Party by increasing the number of members with practical experience or education. In this the Central Committee has probably been successful. Even assuming that the Party is growing by taking in workers and peasants rather than bureaucrats, it must not be forgotten that the chief real reason for joining the Party in the USSR is the desire to make a career. Workers and peasants join the Party in order to cease being workers and peasants. All else being equal, the Party ticket is a "passport to life," a ticket of admission to the top layers of Soviet society. The Party was and is a reservoir from which the Central Committee draws the Party, agricultural and industrial, government, cultural, and military bureaucracy.

This bureaucracy is in effect the Party itself. It is the "Party within the Party." Its membership must be severely limited. It is limited, and its size can be estimated quite precisely. Entry is also restricted. Party tickets are not enough; diplomas are required as well, as they have always been, and still are, required by every bureaucracy in the world. Nowadays it is not possible for "any cook," as Lenin

---

[10] The figures and the following quotations are from G. M. Malenkov, "The Activity of the Party Central Committee," *Informatsionnoye soveshchaniye nekotorykh kompartii* (Information Conference of Several Communist Parties), Moscow, 1948, p. 144. See also his report to the Nineteenth Party Congress, in *Pravda*, October 6, 1952.

[11] Malenkov, *op. cit.*, pp. 144—45.

[12] *Pravda*, October 9, 1952.

hoped might one day be the case, to govern the state. Cooks, of course, can still vote in meetings of the Supreme Soviet, but can no longer head even local governing bodies. Nor are the sons of the cooks better off than the cooks themselves. The doors and windows of universities stand wide open for the sons and daughters of bureaucrats, but the sons of the cooks must go to trade schools, and, if they are clever enough to finish their secondary education, they can go straight to work—in factories or mines or on kolkhozes. In fact it is difficult to conceive of the son of a Central Committee member, a cabinet minister, a Party secretary, or the director of an enterprise sitting in a trade school, standing behind a lathe in a factory, or walking behind a plough on a kolkhoz. It is not enough to be a member of the Party to enjoy rights and privileges—one must belong to the bureaucratic caste. Such rights and privileges are not, of course, hereditary, but they are handed down: the children of Party workers go to universities of their own choice, the children of industrial managers to higher technical schools, and the children of generals to military academies. Legally all Party members have equal rights, but in practice their rights depend upon the rung occupied on the social ladder.

The very concept of the Party as a "leading and directing force" is pure fiction. In actual fact the leading force within the Party is the "secretarial corps," and within the government it is the "committee corps" working under the direction of the secretarial corps. Paragraph 50 of the Statutes of the Soviet Communist Party reads: "Secretaries of city and district committees are *ratified* by oblast and district committee and the central committee of the Communist Party of the union republic." The same principle applies to secretaries of oblast committees, and even to secretaries of the Party central committees of union republics. Paragraph 42 of the same statutes reads: "Oblast [and] district committees and the Party central committees of union republics elect their executive organs, the membership of which must not exceed 11 persons, including 3 secretaries [5 after the Twentieth Party Congress], whose appointment is *ratified* by the Party Central Committee."[13]

Accordingly the careers of Party secretaries, from those in the primary organizations up to secretaries of Party central committees of union republics, are dependent not on the mass membership of the Party but on the Party apparatus of the next higher committee. All these secretaries together are in fact the "guiding and directing" force of the Party and the state which determines the fate of rank and file Communists and leading state civil servants outside the Party. The higher up the Party ladder the more restricted is the membership and the greater the power wielded by it. Numerically, the "secretarial corps" represents a fairly impressive force, whose total can be estimated from the number of territorial organizations reported by the Mandate Commission of the Nineteenth Party Congress. According to this report, there were in 1952 in the USSR 15 central committees of union republics, 8 district (krai) committees, 167 oblast committees, 36 okrug committees, 544 city committees, 4,886 raion committees.[14] According to official data of the Twentieth Party Congress, there were in 1956, 350,000

---

[13] *Ustav KPSS* (Statutes of the Communist Party of the Soviet Union), Moscow, 1952, Paragraph 11.
[14] *Pravda*, October 9, 1952.

primary Party organizations, each with its Party committee or secretary.[15] Finally, by decision of the September 1953 plenary session of the Central Committee, the rural district committees were to have one secretary for each "machine-and-tractor station zone": there were at the beginning of 1954 9,000 such zones.[16] Counting 8 secretaries for the Party Central Committee, 5 for each of the 770 union republic, district, oblast, okrug, and city committees, 3 for each of the 4,886 raion committees, 1 for each of the 9,000 special machine-and-tractor zones, and 1 committee, bureau, or secretary for each of the 350,000 primary organizations, there were at the beginning of 1954 377,516 persons in the secretarial corps of the Party.

The nucleus of this secretarial corps is of course made up of the relatively few 27,566 secretaries at levels above the primary organizations. The members of this group appoint and discharge each other without reference to the nominal electoral rights of the mass membership. Elections are held, but the Party statutes legalize the appointment procedure by providing that elections of secretaries be ratified by members of the Party apparatus at higher levels.

The statutes protect the rights and privileges not only of the secreterial corps but also of all members of committees from the raion committee up. It is impossible to give the exact total of committee members, since the statutes do not provide rules for the sizes of the various committees. Even the size of the Central Committee varies, as is evident from the reports of the Party congresses. Committees vary in size depending upon the number of members of the Party organization, the economic importance of the area, provision for "autonomy" for the Party organization in the case of central committees of union republics, oblast committees of autonomous republics, and committees of national okrugs, or territorial and administrative status. However, data for the elections of 1955 and 1956 indicate that as a fairly constant minimum each raion committee has 40 members, each city and okrug committee 60 members, each oblast committee 80 members, each central committee of a union republic 100 members, and the Party Central Committee 133 members and 122 candidate members.

Based on these figures, and using the number of committees already indicated it appears that the minimum total membership of all committees from the raion committee up is 245,995. There are however at all levels except the raion, persons holding membership on more than one committee. Deducting half of the 50,555 persons at these levels leaves a total "committee corps" of 221,118.

It is this committee corps of 221,118 which constitutes the top Party elite. In fact, it is the Party itself, and has its own Party name of "Party *aktiv*." What social and professional groups are represented in this Party aktiv? There are official breakdowns, but one thing is fairly certain—there are no workers or peasants. As the official journal of the Party Central Committee reported in connection with local Party organs on the eve of the Twentieth Party Congress, "few or no

[15] *BSE*, 2nd ed., Vol. XXVI, p. 565.

[16] *Ustav KPSS* (Statutes of the Communist Party of the Soviet Union), Moscow, 1952, Paragraph 11.

ordinary workers were elected to leading posts in Party organs."[17] For a Party which calls itself a Party of the working class and the vanguard of the "dictatorship of the proletariat," such a situation is clearly abnormal.

The Party statutes provide special rights and privileges for the committee corps which make its members independent of the rank and file Communists and primary Party organizations in general. The following paragraph is devoted to this subject:

> 11. A primary Party organization cannot decide on the expulsion from the Party, or transfer to [status of] candidate, of a Communist if he is a member of the Central Committee of the Communist Party of a union republic, a krai committee, an oblast committee, [or] a raion committee of the Party.
>
> The question of expulsion from a Party committee of a member of the central committee of a union republic, a krai committee, an oblast committee, an okrug committee, a city committee [or] a raion committee of the Party and also expulsion from the Party or transfer to [status of] candidate is decided at a plenary session, provided the plenary session, by a two thirds vote, finds this necessary.[18]

Over this body of officials, Stalin, at the peak of his power, ruled as absolute dictator.

---

[17] *Partiinaya zhizn*, 1955, No. 10.

[18] *Ustav KPSS* (Statutes of the Communist Party of the Soviet Union), Moscow, 1952, Paragraph 11.

Chapter XXX

Preparations for a Postwar Purge, and the Death of Stalin

After Stalin's exposure by the Stalinists, the reasons for his long delay in calling a Party congress are clear. In the first place, before calling such a congress, he wished to "legitimize" his personal dictatorship in the Party and the state by having a cult of Stalin officially recognized both in the Party program and in the Party statutes. An important preliminary to this step was the decision of the Nineteenth Party Congress to base the new Party program on Stalin's *Economic Problems*. His second means of preparing for a new Party congress was to effect a new great purge in Party and state of potential "enemies of the people," also, as in the case of the Yezhov Purge, on the basis of the old theory of the class struggle. The Doctors Case is an indication of this part of his general goal.

Stalin almost succeeded in his first aim, but ruined his cause in his attempt to reach the second.

After being recognized as a "classic of Marxism," on an equal with Marx, Engels, and Lenin, Stalin considered it particularly important to have the entire nation recognize that he was a genius as a military leader. He attempted to base this belief on the history of World War II. He himself made the first suggestion to the Soviet propaganda machine along this line immediately after the end of the war, in a well-known letter to Colonel Razin in 1946. In this letter, with no false modesty, he declared to his surprised "disciples and companions-in-arms" that Lenin was not competent in military science and had frequently told the members of the Central Committee that he was too old to learn, but that they, the young members of the Central Committee, must study it. Stalin, of course, had only one "young member" in mind—himself. The conclusion he intended to be drawn was clear: Stalin was not an amateur in the art and science of war, but a professional. Indeed, he was the founder of a new military strategy and tactics. He was a new Napoleon. The proof was the triumph of his strategic "genius" during World War II. The central thesis of the postwar "cult of Stalin" was accordingly that the war had been won not by the people, not by the army, not even by the Party, but only by Stalin's "genius for strategy."

Possibly Stalin himself did not have so definite an opinion of the part he had played in the war and of his military genius. Before the war he had been used to saying, against his own convictions, that the time was past when leaders alone made history; nowadays, he had declared, history was made by the masses, the people. This thesis was in complete agreement with the spirit of historical material- ism, of which Stalin regarded himself as the only true representative. At an evening reception for the participants in the Victory Parade in May 1945, Stalin with perfect truth ascribed the victory to "the great Russian people—wise, patient, and heroic." But of course even then he was not sincere. He said on other occasions that the victory was due less to the Russian people than to his own system of government. "It is one of the lessons of this war," he declared at one time, "that the Soviet régime proved that it had the best method of mobilizing the entire strength of the nation for repulsing the enemy in time of war." And again: "The socialist régime given birth by the October Revolution has given our people and our army great and unconquerable power."[1]

But to his propaganda machine Stalin gave a different task: that of ascribing the victory to him personally. Typical of many descriptions of Stalin's role as the sole savior of Russia was the statement by the Politburo member Kaganovich, who wrote on the occasion of Stalin's 70th birthday that "as in the days of the Civil War and the foreign military intervention Comrade Stalin, together with Lenin, saved the young Soviet Republic, defended it by organizing the victories of the Red Army, so during the Second World War Stalin saved our Fatherland, the heroes, the freedom, and the independence of the peoples of the USSR from the Fascist invaders." Or, as an official biography declared, "Stalin brought the Soviet people to victory."[2]

Not only was Stalin credited with the overall strategy of victory, but he was praised for his skill in detailed tactics. "At every stage of the war, Stalin's genius was able to find correct solutions, which took fully into account all the given circumstances in any situation. Stalin's military genius showed itself both in defense and in attack.... Comrade Stalin worked out and applied new tactics for simultaneous break-throughs of the enemy's front in several sectors, intended to make it impossible for the enemy to gather his forces for a strong blow, tactics for sectors, one break-through after another, intended to force the enemy to lose time and effort in reorganizing his troops, tactics of break-through of the enemy flanks, turning them, encircling and destroying large enemy groupings.... The battles in which Comrade Stalin led Soviet troops embody outstanding examples of military operational science."[3]

During the last years of Stalin's life, those about him, who were later to claim that he himself had created the "cult of the individual," vied with one another in raising the cult of Stalin to what Khrushchev called "a new and higher level."

Khrushchev: Millions of people nurture feelings of deepest love and devotion for Stalin who, together with Lenin, created the Bolshevik Party and our socialist state, who enriched the theory of Marxism-Leninism and raised it to a new and higher level. This is why all the peoples inhabiting our land so warmly and with such filial love refer to the great Stalin as their father, great leader, and teacher of genius .... Comrade Stalin like a loving gardener tends and cares for all the men and women.

---

[1] J. V. Stalin, *O velikoi otechestvennoi voine SSSR* (The Great Patriotic War of the USSR), Moscow, 1946 and 1950.

[2] *Pravda*, December 21, 1949.

[3] *I. V. Stalin, Kratkaya biografiya* (J. V. Stalin, A Short Biography), Moscow, 1947, pp. 231—32.

Kaganovich: Glory to Comrade Stalin, the great general and the leader of nations!

Malenkov: Together with Lenin, Stalin guided and directed the Socialist Revolution. Together with the great Lenin, Comrade Stalin created the first socialist state in the world.

Molotov: ... so infinite is the confidence that the workers of our country have for Stalin's wise leadership, so strong is their feeling for Stalin's genius, so great is the love of the Soviet people and the workers of all the world for Comrade Stalin.

Voroshilov: Stalin is the greatest man on our planet, a wise leader and teacher and a general of genius .... Glory to the wise and great leader of progressive and toiling humanity!

Mikoyan: Comrade Stalin is the great continuator of Lenin's work.

Comrade Stalin is the Lenin of today.

Comrade Stalin is the genius of socialism.

Comrade Stalin is the great architect of Communism.

Bulganin : Comrade Stalin is what toiling humanity holds nearest and dearest.

Stalin is a symbol for all that is progressive and advanced.

Stalin is the great continuator of Lenin's immortal work.

Stalin is the creator of the Soviet armed forces and the great General of modern times.

Stalin is the creator of progressive military science.

Stalin is the standard, the pride, and the hope of the whole of progressive humanity.[4]

Where Marx was regarded as an economist, Engels as a sociologist, and Lenin as a practical politician, Stalin allowed it to be said of him that he was a "pillar of all science," both technical and otherwise. "Mention must also be made of Comrade Stalin as a scholar and scientist, who was also an initiator of new ideas in certain specialist branches of science," said Poskrebyshev, Stalin's personal secretary.[5]

At the same time Stalin, also according to Proskrebyshev, was a great humanitarian, living only to help mankind. "... it is impossible to enumerate even approximately all the facts proving Comrade Stalin's love and devotion to others .... Comrade Stalin's love for children is well known to all."

Even this was not enough. Stalin was not merely the universal superman. He was a magic superman, a fabulous magician. Georgy Guliya, a member of the editorial board of the influential *Literary Gazette*, wrote in *Pravda:* "... if in meeting difficulties in your work and struggles you ever begin to doubt your strength, think of him, of Stalin, and faith in yourself will immediately return.

---

[4] *Pravda*, December 21, 1949.
[5] *Ibid.*

If you feel fatigued at a time when you should not feel fatigued, think of him, of Stalin, and all fatigue will disappear. If you plan something great, something essential to the people, think of him, of Stalin, and your work will thrive."[6]

(Only three years after Stalin's death, the collective leadership divulged in Khrushchev's speech at the Twentieth Party Congress the emptiness of Stalin's military "genius" and "generalship." To begin with, according to Khrushchev, Stalin's belief in Hitler was so strong that he would not admit the thought that Hitler could declare war on him. In spite of serious warnings, he had failed to adopt necessary measures for defense of the country. Stalin had simply lost his head and all self-control. Khrushchev said: "It would be wrong to forget that after the first reversals and defeats at the front, Stalin thought that the end had come. In one of his speeches delivered at the time, he said: 'All that Lenin created, we have lost forever.' For a long time after, Stalin was not in practical control of military operations and ceased to do anything at all. He did not return to active leadership until after a visit by several members of the Politburo, who told him that certain specific measures had to be adopted immediately in order to improve the situation at the front." And so on. Although Khrushchev, speaking in the name of the collective leadership, thus expressed his disgust that in films, on the stage, in pictures, in literature, and in "scholarly" historical works, people had irresponsibly created "the cult of Stalin's military genius," it should be noted that Khrushchev and his fellows had played their part in creating the cult which was one of the means by which Stalin hoped to maintain his personal dictatorship.)

Stalin's other means of laying the way for a new Party congress was, as has been noted, a fresh purge. Preparations for such a purge were made by the tested method used in the 1930's—ideological warfare. The ideological war was launched by the issue of two decrees by the Party Central Committee, the first, "On the Periodicals *Zvezda* and *Leningrad*," on August 14, 1946, and the second, "On Theater Repertories and Measures for their Improvement," on August 26, 1946. Stalin assigned Zhdanov, his closest assistant in the Party at the time, to organize the purge. The campaign involved the unmasking of "bootlickers," "cosmopolitans," and "regenerates" in literature, the arts, philosophy, and history. Its driving power was an attack upon "Westerners." Its chief slogan was the resurrection of a neo-Bolshevik Slavophilism based on the "exceptional character" and the "primacy" of "Russianness" in all the sciences. But in fact the campaign was launched for ideological reasons and not to emphasize the Russian spirit. It was inaugurated not so much to combat imagined "cosmopolitans" as to create a psychological atmosphere in the country conducive to a large-scale purge among top-ranking members of the Party, the sciences, and the state.

Before the purge had time to emerge from the ideological stage, Zhdanov died in 1948. His death seriously upset Stalin's plans, but did not halt them. It merely marked the end of the first stage. It was probably Stalin's intention to let Suslov take over Zhdanov's role in the second stage that now followed, in 1949–52. Typical of this stage was Suslov's *Pravda* article in December 1952 attacking

---

[6] *Pravda*, February 17, 1950.

Voznesensky and Fedoseyev and, indirectly, Shepilov. In this second stage the scope of the ideological purge was widened, to include in linguistics an attack on Academician Marr, in physiology one on the pupils of Academician Pavlov, in political economy one on friends of Voznesensky, and in agronomy one on the enemies of Lysenko. During this stage Stalin carried the purge to what had always been its real targets—the Party, the army, and the administrative staffs.

Dismissals, transfers, and even arrests of leading Party and army officials now began. The Leningrad Party heads, including the Politburo member Voznesensky as well as Kuznetsov, Rodionov, and others, were arrested. Popov and other heads of the Moscow Party organization were replaced. Well-known military leaders of World War II were dismissed. Marshal Zhukov, at that time already in disgrace, headed the list. Others were Admiral Yumashev, Commander-in-Chief of the Navy (replaced by Vice-Admiral Kuznetsov); Air Marshal Novikov, Commander-in-Chief of the Air Force; Air Marshal Vershinin (replaced by Zhigarev); Marshal Bogdanov, commander of tank troops (replaced by Lieutenant General Radziyevsky); Marshal Voronov, commander of artillery (replaced by Marshal Nedelin); and General Shikin, head of the chief political directorate (replaced by Zheltov). Beginning early in 1949, all members of the Politburo were dismissed from independent ministerial posts: Molotov (replaced by Vyshinsky), Bulganin (replaced by Vasilevsky), and Kaganovich, Mikoyan, and Kosygin, all replaced by minor officials. Beria had already been dismissed from direct administration of the NKVD in 1945; Voroshilov had had no independent post since 1940 when he had been replaced by Timoshenko. Khrushchev and Malenkov were members of the Central Committee Secretariat, Andreyev had already been eliminated from the Secretariat in 1947 and was officially chairman of the Central Committee Commission of Party Control, but all except Khrushchev were included in the honorary "institute of deputies" of Stalin in the Council of Ministers of the USSR; that is, they were ministers without portfolio.

In the light of the facts revealed after Stalin's death and in view of Beria's execution there can be no doubt whatever that the beginning of the second stage of the preparations for the purge was accompanied both by tension and by a struggle at the summit of the Central Committee. The tension was due to the fact that Stalin's disciples had at last guessed their teacher's intention: to exterminate the Politburo members and the top-ranking officers of the army. In this struggle Stalin no longer relied on the Party apparatus, in which he had lost his faith. He did not even trust the Central Committee as a whole: from February 1947 to mid-1952, i.e. for five years, no plenary session was convened although according to the statutes one should have been convened at least every four months. The same, of course, was true of the Party congresses. Stalin relied only on his Secretariat in the Party and on the NKVD in the country as a whole.

The purge in the top ranks of the Party began with the Leningrad Case already mentioned. To carry it out Stalin made Abakumov Minister of State Security in place of Merkulov, who had not come up to expectations. Not much is known about his earlier life, but during the war, in his role as head of the famous

"Smersh" ("Death to Spies") organization, in which he had acted as "mass inquisitor," he had astonished even Stalin. Abakumov now had to play the part of another Yezhov.

The first task entrusted to Abakumov he carried out brilliantly, as can be seen from the report on his activities published by the "collective leadership" during his trial in December 1954. (The report makes no allusion to Stalin but refers entirely to Beria as the one responsible for his crimes, although later on, in his secret speech, Khrushchev named Stalin as the main instigator of Abakumov's acts.) After Beria had appointed him Minister of State Security, said the report, Abakumov had collaborated directly with a group of criminal conspirators, and carried out Beria's instructions aimed at injuring the Communist Party and the Soviet state. He had made use of intrigue and political provocation. He had forged documents on individual workers in the Party and state apparatuses and on members of the Soviet intelligentsia, and had then arrested them. By applying criminal methods of investigation, forbidden by Soviet law, he had extorted fictitious confessions. He had used this method to forge documents in the Leningrad Case, as a result of which a number of Party and local government workers had been arrested, charged with grave crimes against the state.[7]

The point, of course, was not the methods used by Abakumov. They had been used before him, and will continue to be used as long as the Cheka system exists. The point was that Abakumov, following the recipe of the 1930's and the logic of Stalin's will, was to have prepared a new case—the Moscow Case—in which any member of the Politburo might be implicated.

The Leningrad Case was to have been a rehearsal for the Moscow drama. The rehearsal was successful, but the drama did not come off. At the end of 1950 or the beginning of 1951 the Politburo won its first important victory over Stalin: Abakumov, the head of the Ministry of State Security and the one who had helped Stalin to frame the Leningrad Case and to have Politburo member Voznesensky and his friends shot, was dismissed from his post. Malenkov's disciple Ignatyev, who had previously been employed in Party work in Bashkiria and Central Asia, was appointed in his place.

There was also a second and even more important victory: it was decided that the Nineteenth Party Congress, which Stalin had wished to avoid convening at all costs before the start of the new purge, was to meet at last in the summer of 1952. The announcement was made more sensational by the news released at the same time that, contrary to usual practice, the report of the Central Committee would be read not by Stalin, the Secretary-General, but by Malenkov. Did Stalin on his own initiative surrender to Malenkov, his closest disciple and heir, his right to read "the epoch-making report" together with its directives? It is doubtful, especially in view of what is known of events at the first plenary session of the new Central Committee after the Nineteenth Party Congress. In this plenary session, Stalin, in addition to enlarging the Presidium and Secretariat of the Central Committee and appointing new members to both bodies, created for the

---

[7] *Pravda*, December 24, 1954.

first time and contrary to the statutes a small inner bureau, made up of members of the Presidium. Its existence was first made known in a Central Committee decree of March 6, 1953, and its composition is still a secret. Which of the Old Guard were members? In any case, not all and not even the majority. The "Bureau of the Central Committee Presidium" (a "Politburo within the Politburo") was really intended as an offset to the Old Guard. At the same plenary session of the Central Committee, according to Khrushchev, Stalin quite openly attacked Molotov, Mikoyan, and perhaps other members of the Politburo. Nevertheless the historical significance of the plenary session consisted in an event which to those outside the Kremlin appeared totally inconceivable: Stalin had been removed from his post as Secretary-General and the post itself had been abolished.

There is nothing about this event in the version of Khrushchev's speech which has become available. But the biographical sketch of Stalin's life published in the 1955 edition of the *Encyclopedic Dictionary* states that "After the Eleventh Party Congress, on April 3, 1922, the Plenum of the Central Committee, on V. I. Lenin's motion, elected Stalin as Secretary-General of the Central Committee of the Party; Stalin served in this post until October 1952, and from then until the end of his life he was Secretary of the Central Committee."[8]

It is true that Stalin's name continued to head the lists of Presidium and Secretariat members, out of alphabetical order, but the minutes no longer, as in previous years, stated that he had been elected Secretary-General. Did Stalin resign this post of his own free will? Such an act would be completely at variance with the psychology of a dictator. What happened was quite different. The apparatus of power which Stalin had established had outgrown him. His control over this apparatus was slipping from his grasp in proportion as the apparatus itself began, if not to control, at least to sabotage the extravagant acts of its former manipulator. Besides, Stalin had disregarded the law of interdependence which underlay his system. The members of the Politburo were indebted to Stalin for their careers, but Stalin himself had become a dictator because these very members had so willed it and had given him their support. At the moment when Stalin definitely decided to get rid of these supporters, the end was inevitable. His disciples and companions-in-arms could say: "We begat you and we shall kill you."

The struggle between Stalin and the Stalinists now entered its third, last, and most dramatic stage. Stalin arrested the Kremlin court physicians of the Politburo.

The Doctors Case had only incidentally to do with those who were arrested. As in the Leningrad Case it concerned the Party oligarchy belonging to the Presidium and the Army High Command. Its apparently anti-Semitic aspect served simultaneously as a safety-valve (for the benefit of the less enlightened part of the population, the Party and the army) and as a piece of camouflage (for the benefit of the oligarchy and the Army High Command). Nevertheless, Stalin's companions could not have been unaware, if only from the experience of the 1930's, of what the dictator was aiming at. Those arrested were not ordinary

---

[8] *Entsiklopedichesky slovar* (Encyclopedic Dictionary), Vol. III, Moscow, 1955, p. 310.

doctors but—according to Khrushchev—personal physicians of long standing to Politburo members and marshals of the Soviet Union, and, moreover, they had been arrested without the knowledge of the Politburo. Furthermore, members of the Politburo were denied the right of personal contact with their former doctors, and, again according to Khruschhev, had to rest content with reading their written confessions—and only those confessions which Stalin deemed it expedient to show them. But the experience of the thirties showed, first, that Central Committee members and army marshals were never arrested until after their personal assistants had been arrested, and second, that the depositions of those arrested were shown to the Politburo members only after they themselves had been apprehended. Such had been the case in connection with Kosior, Rudzutak, Eikhe, Chubar, and Postyshev. In sanctioning the arrest of their collaborators in order to divert suspicion from themselves, these members and alternate members of the Politburo had never suspected that in so doing they were sanctioning their own future arrests. But the old procedure was now too well known. Stalin committed a fatal mistake when he decided to repeat this routine of the thirties, for he was now no longer surrounded by the politically naive amateurs of those days but by sophisticated masters of the art of purges, whom he himself had trained.

In spite of Khrushchev's assertions in his famous speech, these masters had not been mere spectators of the acts of Stalin, Yagoda, and Beria during the thirties but had been active participants and organizers of the Great Purge. They had so thoroughly learned the Stalinist technique that they could quite successfully compete with him. Perhaps another of Stalin's mistakes was that, without giving thought to the future, he had earlier divulged the secret of his phenomenal skill to his ungrateful disciples, who now showed so much virtuosity in employing them. It is true that Stalin took the precaution to surround himself with persons uninitiated in his methods, intending under cover of them to repeat the exploits of Yezhov. The increase in the membership of the Central Committee Presidium after the Nineteenth Party Congress was a pointer in this direction. But it was precisely these measures that put his former disciples even more on guard. Khrushchev in fact declared in his speech that Stalin had packed the Presidium with "inexperienced persons" to make it easier to discharge the Old Guard and then settle accounts with it.

What little Stalin revealed to the outside world regarding the Doctors Case (according to Khrushchev he did not reveal any more to the Presidium of the Central Committee), should have been enough to indicate, even to the uninitiated, where the main blow would fall. The official Kremlin announcement of January 13, 1953, regarding the Doctors Case stated that the doctors had intended by means of medical malpractice to shorten the lifes of persons active in Soviet affairs. They had murdered Zhdanov and Shcherbakov, both members of the Politburo, and had intended to murder Marshals Vasilevsky and Govorov, General Shtemenko, Admiral Levchenko and others. Two spy organizations were allegedly involved—one American, working though the Jewish "Joint" philanthropic organization and involving Doctors Vovsi, M. Kogan, B. Klin, A. Feldman,

Ya. Etinger, A. Grünstein, and G. Mayorov, and one British, which "recruited" mainly Russians—Doctors Vinogradov and Yegorov. Since it would have been awkward for Stalin to have to include persons of purely Russian blood in the Zionist group, he had found it necessary to divide the doctors between different spy organizations. But why should the doctors wish to murder only Marshals Vasilevsky and Govorov? Why not Zhukov, Voroshilov, and Bulganin? Why had they, as alleged, killed Shcherbakov and Zhdanov, but had not thought of murdering Khrushchev, Molotov, Mikoyan, Kaganovich, and even Malenkov? Khrushchev's revelations give an answer to these questions, but Khrushchev and his friends knew the answer even before Stalin's death. "If Stalin were still alive, Molotov and Mikoyan would not have been able to speak at this Congress," said Khrushchev. This is certainly true, although it is not the whole truth.

Stalin was aiming not only at these two but also at the entire oligarchy and at the part of the High Command connected with Zhukov. The *Pravda* editorial of January 13, 1953, whose author was undoubtedly Stalin himself, stated that as a result of the establishment of socialism in the USSR and as a consequence of postwar progress "certain people draw the conclusion that wrecking and espionage no longer constitute a danger. . . . But only Right Opportunists can think and reason in this way. They hold the anti-Marxist viewpoint that class war is dying out. They do not, or cannot, understand that our progress is leading not to the dying out but to the sharpening of the struggle; that the more rapid our progress the more acute will become the struggle against enemies of the people."

Who were these nameless "Right Opportunists," who according to Stalin's logic might any day be declared enemies of the people? With what group of Rightists was Stalin in conflict? From what Khrushchev told the Twentieth Party Congress in 1956, that "Stalin's incorrect theory of the class struggle" dated as far back as the February-March plenum of the Central Committee in 1937, and from what the Stalinists themselves have written in their attacks on Stalin, it is clear that Stalin had in mind the adherents of Khrushchev and Molotov. The following excerpts from the editorial hint at the scale of the purge and the identity of its probable first victims. "Certain of our Soviet organs, and their heads," said the editorial, "have lost all sense of vigilance, and have become infected with indifference." "The organs of security," it complained, "failed to discover promptly the wrecking terrorist organization of the doctors." And: "History has already had examples of traitors to the Fatherland masquerading as doctors; witness the case of the doctors Levin and Pletnev, who, on the orders of enemies of the USSR murdered the great Russian writer Maxim Gorky and the distinguished Soviet statesmen Kuibyshev and Menzhinsky." The editorial concluded with a warning against the "foreign masters" of the doctors and against their instigators at home. "As to the inspirers of these hirelings and murderers, they can be sure that vengeance will not forget them, but will find a way to pronounce its weighty judgment."

Such language was in the true Yezhov tradition, dating from the time when Stalin had "found the way" to the inspirers of Levin and Pletnev, and had disposed of more than 70% of the members of the 1934–38 Central Committee after having first had the doctors shot. Khrushchev, Bulganin, Molotov, Kaganovich, and their fellows were thoroughly familiar with this language and knew what their fate would be if Stalin remained in power. "Stalin," said Khrushchev in his speech to the Twentieth Party Congress, "evidently meant to finish off all the old members of the Politburo. He often used to say that members of the Politburo must be replaced by new blood. His proposal after the Nineteenth Congress, that 25 persons be elected to the Presidium of the Central Committee, was directed at the removal of old members from the Politburo and the inclusion of less experienced persons who would praise Stalin in every possible way. Presumably the intention existed to liquidate at some future date the old members of the Politburo and thus conceal Stalin's shameful acts, the acts which we are now examining."

It is difficult to believe that these thoughts regarding Stalin's intentions did not occur to the "old members of the Politburo" until after Stalin's death. Stalin's plan for a new purge, as Khrushchev says, must have become clear to them at that first plenary session of the Central Committee in October 1952, after the Nineteenth Party Congress. But the details of the plan did not become apparent until after the arrest of the doctors. Then a *Pravda* note on an article of June 18, 1956, by Eugene Dennis revealed that Ukrainian doctors, i.e., Khrushchev's own doctors, had also been arrested. The date of their arrest is still not known. The official communiqué merely stated that they had been arrested "some time ago." Nevertheless, judging from the fact that by January 13, 1953, the doctors had had time to "confess" and the so-called "investigation" had been completed, it must be presumed that the doctors had been kept under arrest at the NKVD for at least three months, and must therefore have been arrested immediately after the Nineteenth Party Congress, after Stalin had created what he thought was a reliable rearguard by assuring himself of a majority of inexperienced members in the Central Committee Presidium, where the old members had been reduced to a minority of 8 out of 25.

Stalin succeeded in arresting the doctors, but not in trying them. The doctors were, in a sense, fortunate in their misfortune: Stalin was not in the least interested in having them die, but he did want the deaths of their "patrons" and "inspirers" in the old Politburo. The "inspirers," aware of this aim, fought for the lives of the doctors in order to escape death themselves. There will be proof some day that the conspiracy against Stalin, which has been called "the struggle against Stalin's cult of the individual" was hatched in the course of a period beginning January 13, 1953. As soon as it dawned on the old members of the Politburo that Stalin was determined to bring the Doctors Case to a logical conclusion, they had no recourse left but to fight for their lives. It was a choice between Stalin and them. Ideological convictions, disagreements on Party program, a political opposition by an imagined Lenin nucleus—none of these things existed. It was simply a desperate fight for survival.

The *Pravda* article of January 13 announcing the discovery of the doctors plot ended with the statement: "The investigation will be concluded in the immediate future." To judge from the proceedings in the thirties, this meant that the indictment would be published, and the date of the trial announced, within a week, or, at most, a fortnight. However, a week passed, then a fortnight, and finally seven weeks before an announcement was published, and then it dealt not with the doctors' trial, but with Stalin's fatal illness.

What had happened? Khrushchev's speech throws some light on the question:

> Soon after the arrest of the doctors, we members of the Politburo received the minutes of evidence in which the doctors confessed their guilt. The case was presented in such a way that no one could verify the facts on which the accusation was based. It was impossible to verify them by contacting those who had confessed to their guilt. We felt however, that the whole case of the arrested doctors had a doubtful validity. We knew some of the people personally, for they had attended us at one time or another in their professional capacity. When we came to review the case after Stalin's death, we arrived at the conclusion that it was a fabrication from beginning to end. This shameful case was fabricated entirely by Stalin. However, he did not have time to carry it through to the end he had planned.[9]

Stalin did not have time because Stalin's disciples could imagine only too well the kind of end which their master had planned. It is, of course, impossible to expect people who could wait three years after his death before revealing Stalin's crimes to give a frank account of his last days. Nevertheless it seems clear, especially in the light of Khrushchev's speech, that by the time of Stalin's death—regardless of how he died—a conspiracy against him already existed within the Central Committee. The famous Central Committee resolution of June 30, 1956, regarding the "cult of the individual" reveals it plainly, although its basic character is obscured by appeals to the name of Lenin. The relevant passage of the resolution reads: "The Twentieth Party Congress and the entire Central Committee policy after Stalin's death show clearly that a nucleus of Leninist leaders existed within the Central Committee."[10]

The fact that the conspirators have declared themselves to be a "Leninist nucleus of leaders" does not alter the essence of the matter. As Stalin was not a member of this nucleus, it must have been directed against him, and against the few in the Central Committee who remained loyal to him.

So Stalin died in the arms (or at the hands) of this "nucleus." In the very first government communiqué regarding Stalin's illness, issued on March 4, 1953, it was found necessary to inform the country of three facts: (1) Stalin's cerebral hemorrhage occurred during the night of March 2, "while he was in his own apartment in Moscow." (Why was it so important to report that it happened in Moscow and in his apartment?); (2) "The medical treatment of Comrade Stalin is being carried out under the constant supervision of the Central Committee and the Soviet government" (the Leninist nucleus?); and (3) "Stalin's grave illness will prevent him from taking part in government activities for a more or less lengthy period of time" (this by way of preparing the population for Stalin's absence).

---

[9] *Rech Khrushcheva*, p. 41.
[10] *Pravda*, July 2, 1956.

Bulletins about Stalin's sickness became progressively graver: the people were obviously being prepared for his inevitable death. The bulletins were signed by members of a commission composed of famous medical authorities, headed by Tretyakov, the Minister of Health, and Kuperin, the head of the Sanitary and Medical Administration of the Kremlin. After Stalin died on March 5, "the Central Committee and the Soviet government" resorted to a measure which had not been adopted even after the death of Lenin—they created a new medical commission, composed of completely new people, to confirm the correctness of the diagnosis by the first commission and the quality of the treatment given under the direct supervision of the Central Committee and the Soviet government, and the inevitability of Stalin's death.

This second commission, composed of nine professors, also headed by Tretyakov and Kuperin, signed a report which if true precluded any possibility that Stalin had been deliberately given medical mistreatment. "The result of the post-mortem examination," said the report, "fully confirms the diagnosis of the professors of medicine who attended J. V. Stalin. The post-mortem examination has established the incurable nature of J. V. Stalin's illness from the moment when cerebral hemorrhage set in. Therefore the energetic measures taken could not have favorable results and prevent a fatal outcome."

If it be admitted that Stalin died while under solicitous care by his old disciples and comrades-in-arms, how can the following facts be explained?

1. On March 6, 1953, the day following Stalin's death, the Presidium of the Central Committee, composed of 25 full members and 11 alternate members and created by Stalin after the Nineteenth Party Congress, was dissolved and the old Politburo, composed of its eight old members plus Saburov and Pervukhin, was restored.

2. On the day of Stalin's death all the members of the "inner cabinet," headed by Poskrebyshev, "died" or at any rate diappeared.

3. The following also "died" (or disappeared) on the day of Stalin's death: (a) the Commandant of the Kremlin, Lieutenant-General Spiridonov (replaced by General Vedenin); (b) the Commandant of Moscow, General Sinilov (replaced by General Kolesnikov); and (c) the commanding officer of the Moscow Military Area, Colonel-General Artemyev (replaced by General, later Marshal, Moskalenko).

4. Two former members of "the Secretariat of Comrade Stalin," Chesnokov and Andrianov—both members of the Central Committee—also disappeared.

5. Even Stalin's son, General Vasily Stalin, disappeared.

6. The USSR Minister of Health, Tretyakov (replaced by Kovrygina) disappeared directly after the drafting of the Stalin health bulletins.

7. The entire Sanitary and Health Administration of the Kremlin, headed by Professor Kuperin, was abolished and a new special department for attending the Kremlin leaders was created, under the Ministry of Health. Kuperin himself disappeared.

These facts have a direct and logical bearing on the main event—the death of Stalin. If the dictator's death had occurred under normal circumstances, as the medical bulletins attempted to prove, there would have been no need for dealing so radically and speedily not only with Stalin's Secretariat but also with his military police guard inside the Kremlin and with the staff of the Moscow Military Area headed by Generals Artemyev, Sinilov, and the younger Stalin, all loyal to Stalin. The open NKVD (MGB), was similarly dealt with, although the arrest of Deputy Minister of State Security Ryumin was only announced later, in connection with the rehabilitation of the "doctors group," on April 4, 1953. The heads of the Political Administration of the Soviet Naval Ministry who had been appointed personally by Stalin were removed immediately. Retribution did not touch either the old Politburo, including Beria, or the apparatus of the Party Central Committee, or the Moscow Party Committee, or the editorial board of *Pravda*. Judging from subsequent events it is more than likely that the main threads of the conspiracy both for organizational purposes and in political affiliation led mainly to the Central Committee Presidium, including all the old Politburo members with the possible exception that Voroshilov and Molotov remained neutral; the Party Central Committee, with Malenkov and Suslov; the Moscow Party Committee, with Khrushchev and Furtseva; and the *Pravda* editorial board, with Shepilov and Satyukov. The suspicious role of the then Minister of State Security, Ignatyev, became clear after Khrushchev's report. When Beria was appointed Minister of the amalgamated Ministries of State Security and of Internal Affairs (MGB and MVD), Ignatyev was not simply dismissed, but was made a Secretary of the Party Central Committee. After the doctors were freed and Ryumin was arrested, Ignatyev was removed on charges of "political blindness" regarding Ryumin. Nevertheless he was not liquidated, but was appointed First Secretary of the Bashkir Oblast Party Committee, in which he had worked before his appointment as Minister of State Security.

How is one to explain so lenient an attitude toward the person who was chiefly responsible for the management of the Doctors Case and the purge for which it was a preparation, the person, as Khrushchev pointed out, to whom Stalin had personally given instructions regarding the Doctors Case. "Former Minister of State Security Comrade Ignatyev," reported Khrushchev, "was present at this congress as a delegate. Stalin turned to him and said sharply: 'If you don't get the doctors to confess, we'll make you a head shorter.'"[11] Stalin, said Khrushchev, had then sent for the investigator and told him what methods he should use during the investigation. These methods were simple: "Beat them, beat them, and beat them again!"

Khrushchev's account clears up the picture. Ignatyev, by then certain that success in the case, directed as it was less against the doctors than against the older members of the Politburo, would inevitably spell for him the fate of Yagoda and Yezhov, betrayed the Stalin conspiracy to Stalin's disciples. The Stalinists then countered Stalin's conspiracy with a conspiracy of their own. Beria undoubtedly

[11] *Rech Khrushcheva*, p. 41.

took part in this counterplot. The announcement of the discovery of the doctors' plot pointed out that the Ministry of State Security had been directly responsible at a time when Beria had headed it. (The group of doctors—Vinogradov, Yegorov, and Kogan—alleged to belong to the British intelligence, were referred to in the announcement as "long-term agents of the English" and Beria had always been regarded inside the Party as a former spy of the English in the Caucasus).

Having quarrelled with the Politburo and the army generals, Stalin had made the fatal mistake of driving the members of his only sure support—the NKVD (Beria, Serov, Kruglov, Merkulov, Dekanozov, Kobulov, Goglidze, and others)—into the arms of the conspirators. However, the anti-Stalin conspirators, while admitting Beria and his group to their ranks, intended to deal with them in the manner of Stalin, that is, to use them as temporary allies against the main enemy, Stalin, and to destroy them in turn. Accordingly, within the major conspiracy directed against Stalin a minor one, directed against Beria and his group with the exception of Serov, gradually took shape.

There were more than enough reasons for this minor conspiracy. Khrushchev's report proves what had long been known—that Stalin's power had been based for more than 20 years on Beria's apparatus. Khrushchev and his co-conspirators may well have been right when, in liquidating Beria, they accused him of having organized a conspiracy or counterconspiracy against the Politburo, since he could not have helped knowing that in the final analysis, if Stalin had to pay for crimes committed by him jointly with Beria, he, Beria, would be next in line. The appointment of Beria as Minister of Internal Affairs and his elevation to an importance next only to that of Malenkov, represents a serious objection to this theory, for the real power was again concentrated in his hands, making him a particularly dangerous rival for the "collective leadership." What may have happened is that in the conspiracy against Stalin, Beria played a leading part, more important perhaps than that of Malenkov, Khrushchev, Bulganin, and the others, and this would have pushed him into the front ranks of the new rulers. But here the conspirators could surround him with persons whom they trusted, in order to forestall any possible action on his part against the Central Committee Presidium.

Beria also controlled the MVD armed forces, but against this there was a reliable counterweight in the form, first, of the Moscow Garrison commanded by General Moskalenko, a new figure representing the interests of the "collective leadership," and, second, of the Soviet Army headed by Generals Bulganin and Zhukov. Moreover the secret Kremlin NKVD (intelligence, guards, and troops) was, as in Stalin's day, probably outside Beria's sphere of action, being, as before, subordinate to the Secretariat of the Party Central Committee. Under such circumstances, Beria could not act except to sabotage the Central Committee. His sabotage amounted to this: having readily freed the doctors and arrested Ryumin, Beria declared that the measures to be taken against the NKVD had been completed. He had no intention of revealing the crimes committed by Stalin before the arrest of the doctors. The last stage of the Great Purge (1938–40) and the Leningrad Case (1949), i.e., the very acts which were not being condemned by the collective leadership, had been the joint work of Stalin and Beria. Beria well knew that if he were to help rake over these events, he would be destroying himself. After the Twentieth Party Congress it became obvious that this was precisely what the collective leadership had been trying to get done. The *Pravda* editorial of July 10, 1953, dealing with Beria's dismissal emphasized his efforts at sabotage. "Faced with the instructions of the Central Committee and the government that he enforce Soviet legality and abolish all possibility of such illegal and arbitrary action as took place on a number of occasions, Beria deliberately delayed execution of these instructions and in some cases attempted to distort them." It became clear that as long as Beria remained in the government, the Kremlin could not embark on its policy of exposing Stalin, and that short of agreeing to have his own crimes revealed Beria could not help opposing this policy if he remained in the Kremlin.

Stalin's death, whether due to the law of nature or to the law of politics, still remains, and will remain for a long time, one of the deepest mysteries of the Kremlin. Stalin's age and the circumstances surrounding his life do not preclude the assumption that he died a natural death, although his disciples complained of his extraordinary energy immediately before his death. However, on the other hand, no moral considerations or sense of duty to Stalin on account of his past services could have held back the Stalinists from taking action when it became a question of life or death for them. The "moral code" of Stalin's disciples had been worked out by Stalin himself, and for many years past they had had before them the example of his own behavior. While Stalin was using against the Bukharinites and Trotskyites the "unworthy" methods of which they complained, the disciples expressed nothing but admiration. However, as soon as he threatened to apply them against these disciples themselves, they may well have retaliated in true Stalinist fashion, for "the school shapes its pupils."

Chapter XXXI

Khrushchev's Revelations of the Stalin System

There is no need to doubt the authenticity of Khrushchev's secret speech at the closed meeting of the Twentieth Party Congress. All the main political statements made in the speech were later embodied in the decree of the Party Central Committee dated June 30, 1956, on "Elimination of the Cult of the Individual and its Consequences."[1] The *Pravda* reprint on June 27, 1956, of the article by Eugene Dennis speaks of the "special report" as an authentic document. And finally, the minutes of the Twentieth Party Congress refer not only to a report on the cult of the individual delivered by Khrushchev at the closing session of the congress but also to the passing of a resolution.[2]

It is quite impossible to analyze here the entire report. To some extent, everything that has been said up to this point has been a commentary on it. But certain questions call for further discussion.

Khrushchev's report was a new version of a "Short Course in the History of Stalinism." But historical scholarship was farthest from his mind. His aims were political, with an eye to the more immediate problems. For this purpose he was attempting (1) to represent the crimes of the Stalin regime as errors by Stalin and Stalin alone; (2) to divorce the Stalinist party from Stalin himself; and (3) to outline a new and "scientific" history of the Soviet Communist Party. In order to accomplish these purposes, Khrushchev was forced to begin where Stalin himself had begun—by falsifying history. His purposes, in fact, permitted no other approach. Nevertheless, his speech is a document of great historical value. This is not because it reveals anything basically new in the history of the establishment of Stalin's personal dictatorship and the commission of Stalin's crimes. Khrushchev's new evidence on these subjects merely provides details and illustrations of events which were being discussed at length in the outside world at a time when Khrushchev and his group were included among the loyal "companions-in-arms and disciples" of Stalin. The historical importance of the speech lies in the fact that through Khrushchev the collective leadership admitted that the Party and government of the USSR were personally conducted for 20 years by a thoroughly evil figure. This admission, although made with many reservations, is pregnant with implications so far-reaching that it is difficult to foresee a limit to their consequences.

---

[1] *Pravda*, July 2, 1956.

[2] *XX sezd kommunisticheskoi partii Sovetskogo Soyuza: Stenografichesky otchet* (The Twentieth Party Congress of the Soviet Communist Party: Stenographic Report), Moscow, 1956, Vol. II, p. 402.

The first question to be considered in connection with Khrushchev's report is that of the sources of Stalin's crimes. These according to Khrushchev were: (1) Stalin's cult of the individual, with its gross perversions of Party democracy and of the principles of revolutionary legality; and (2) Stalin's personal qualities, which were quite correctly described by Lenin, who at the same time pointed out that it was essential to dismiss Stalin from the post of Secretary-General.[3]

The effect of this description of the sources of Stalin's crimes is to create before our very eyes a new legend, that of "the cult of the individual," as an explanation for all the crimes of the present regime. Not the Cheka system, not the one-Party dictatorship, not even Stalin himself, but "Stalin's cult of the individual" and "the deficiencies of Stalin's character" (defined by Lenin as "rudeness, disloyalty, instability") were the sources of Stalin's crimes. The cult of the individual explains the crimes, and the crimes explain the cult of the individual.

Khrushchev turned round and round in this vicious circle throughout his entire speech, to the considerable embarrassment of his foreign companions-in-arms—Togliatti, Thorez, and the others. The Central Committee decree of June 30, 1956, represented a belated attempt to break out of the vicious circle, but the attempt turned out to be as unconvincing as it was hopeless. In this attempt to explain the historical process by objective facts through determinist "Marxist analysis," the Central Committee came to the same conclusions as Khrushchev, namely, that Stalin's cult of the individual was to blame for everything. From the orthodox Marxist point of view, or, as Plekhanov would have said, in the "monistic view of history," this is pernicious "idealism."

But what was the source of Stalin's cult of the individual? Khrushchev did not even raise this question, but merely remarked that the cult "has been cultivated among us for many years." The Central Committee decree stated that it had resulted from (1) capitalist encirclement; (2) the class struggle; and (3) deficiencies in Stalin's character. This statement is so obviously worthless that the decree hastens to add: "All this explains but does not justify the cult of the individual."[4] It certainly does not justify it, and, of course, does not explain it.

But what does justify it? The Central Committee did not even try to answer this question, but cited the reply already made in the free world. "Our enemies," said the decree, "declare that Stalin's cult of the individual was engendered not by specific historical conditions, which have by now receded into the past, but by the system itself, and by what is from their point of view its undemocratic nature, etc. . . ." This reply, said Khrushchev and his Central Committee, was a slander, and to prove it they turned to Lenin. When Stalin used terror and mass repression, said Khrushchev, this was contrary to the instructions of Lenin. On closer examination, however, the appeal to Lenin turned out to be unfortunate. "The scientific concept of dictatorship," Lenin had written,

---

[3] Lenin's "Testament" in *Kommunist*, No. 9, 1956, p. 15.
[4] *Pravda*, July 2, 1956.

"means nothing but absolute power untrammelled by any laws or regulations whatsoever and based entirely on force."[5] As to this, Khrushchev and his followers asserted that Lenin was speaking of class dictatorship, while Stalin had established a personal dictatorship by a "leader." But as to this distinction Lenin had also spoken unequivocally: "The very fact that the question, 'dictatorship of the Party or dictatorship of the masses,' is raised, testifies to an unbelievable confusion of ideas. . . . It is ridiculous absurdity and stupidity to talk about a contrast between dictatorship of the masses and dictatorship of the leaders."[6]

Khrushchev cited one of Lenin's propagandist pronouncements dating back to 1920, in which he had justified mass Red Terror on the grounds of intervention by the Entente and had promised to stop the terror and to abolish capital punishment by the end of the Civil War. Stalin, charged Khrushchev, had failed to carry out Lenin's direct and clear instructions. "Stalin forced the Party and the NKVD to use mass terror when there were no longer any exploiting classes in our country." But in this, too, Khrushchev's argument was not in accord with historical fact:

1. The Cheka-OGPU-NKVD-MGB-MVD-KGB regime was created by a personal decree by Lenin on December 20, 1917, a little more than a month after the October Revolution and before the beginning of the Civil War;

2. Capital punishment was never abolished during Lenin's lifetime (the collegium of the OGPU had the same "extraordinary powers" of extra-legal execution by shooting as the Cheka);

3. At the end of the Civil War the terror was extended, and was even directed against former "Soviet parties" (Mensheviks and Left Social Revolutionaries), which had fought against the White Army during the Civil War).[7]

But what was most important was that when Khrushchev cited Lenin's February 1920 propaganda speech to the Central Executive Committee meeting at which the Russian Social Democratic Labor Party (RSDRP) headed by Martov still formed the opposition, he forgot to cite another directive written by Lenin two years later. It was contained in a letter of May 17, 1922, from Lenin to the People's Commissar of Justice, Dmitry Kursky, and read as follows:

> Comrade Kursky, with reference to our conversation I am sending you the preliminary draft of a paragraph to be added to the criminal code. Its main idea is clear, I hope: openly to present the basically and politically true situation motivating the essential nature and justification of terror, and its necessity. The court must not stop this terror—to promise this would be self-deception and deception—but it must explain and legalize it clearly in principle, without falsehood and without whitewash.[8]

---

[5] Lenin, *Sochineniye* (Works), 3rd ed., Vol. XXV, Moscow, 1935, p. 441.

[6] *Ibid.*, p. 188.

[7] B. Nikolayevsky, "Contributions to the Pre-History of the Sotsialistichesky Vestnik," and P. Abramovich, "The Ideological Line of the Sotsialistichesky Vestnik," *Sotsialistichesky Vestnik*, New York and Paris, 1956, No. 2–3.

[8] Lenin, *Sochineniya* (Works), 3rd ed., Vol. XXVII, Moscow, 1936, p. 297.

The editors of Lenin's *Works* appended the following footnote to this letter: "The letter to D. I. Kursky on the subject of terror was written by Lenin when the first Criminal Code of the RSFSR was being discussed. Lenin himself proposed the preliminary draft. . . . This draft was adopted as the basis of Article 57 [58?] of the Criminal Code of the RSFSR."[9]

Terror, then, is the essence of the Soviet system and Soviet "legality." Stalin neither created the system of legalized terror nor abolished it, nor, of course, transgressed it. To use the Soviet phraseology, Stalin merely raised it to the "higher plane" of a universal inquisition. The only innovation which he introduced was to abolish its Leninist "dualism." Under him the country was no longer ruled by the Party and the NKVD jointly, but by the political police alone.

Accordingly Togliatti, the leader of the Italian Communists, came very close to the truth of the matter, both from the point of view of scientific sociology and from that of "historical materialism," when in his well-known interview with the editor of the Italian magazine *Nuovi argumenti* in June 1956 he asked a question far from acceptable to the collective leadership:

> In the past everything good was ascribed to the superhuman qualities of one person, now everything bad is explained by his no less extraordinary vices. But as long as everything is explained by the actions of one person and the cult of the individual, the main problem remains unsolved—how and why could the Soviet government allow, as in fact it did, such a violation of legality, such a departure from democratic standards, and even such a degeneration of public life.[10]

The Soviet Central Committee called Togliatti's statement "interesting and informative" but waved aside its main argument. "We cannot agree," said a Central Committee resolution, "with the possibility implied in the statement that Soviet society may in some ways have undergone degeneration." However, the question of the possibility of the rise of a cult of the individual under socialism and the degeneration of the Soviet system was being publicly asked by friends, not by enemies, and had to be publicly answered. But the members of the collective leadership did not bother their heads about the "sophistry" of the Communist philosopher from Rome. The reply of the Central Committee, although essentially naive as far as content was concerned, was vigorous:

> To imagine that individual personalities, be they as powerful as Stalin, can alter our social and political system is to be in complete contradiction with the facts, with Marxism and with the truth, [it is] to adopt an idealist point of view . . . All the world knows that the October Revolution and the victory of socialism have introduced a socialist method of production in our country and that for nearly 40 years the government has been in the hands of the working class and the peasants.[11]

This answer contains two implications: (1) that Stalin could not alter the socialist nature of the USSR (socialist methods of production); and (2) that

---

[9] *Ibid.*, p. 544, note 141.
[10] *The New York Times*, International Edition, June 5, 1956.
[11] *Pravda*, July 2, 1956.

power in the USSR had been for nearly 40 years in the hands of the working class and the peasants. The second point was meant for the more simple-minded, the first merely explained the essence of the matter. The quality peculiar to the Communist totalitarian system, making it different from other totalitarian systems such as Fascism and National Socialism, is that under Communism the seizure of the means of production (capital) and the abolition of the right of personal economic initiative ("a socialist method of production") reinforce the earlier abolition of civil rights and political freedom.

A political dictatorship which must take into consideration the people's economic independence of the state government is always vulnerable. This was especially true of such a country as Russia which was essentially a country of small property owners with an overwhelming peasant population. Lenin grasped this fact from the first days of the Revolution. In order to neutralize the opposition of this class—the most important in the country—Lenin adopted the Social-Revolutionary land program of "socialization" instead of the Bolshevik program of "nationalization." He also delayed "nationalization" of large industrial concerns and introduced an intermediate stage known as "state control of production." Small-scale, and, to a certain extent, medium-scale, industry was not to be nationalized. State capitalism by leases and concessions was also permitted in order to attract private capital at home and abroad. As a result, five methods of production, or, as Lenin put it, "five systems of economic management," were able to co-exist: (1) the "patriarchal form," (2) small-scale production for trading purposes, with the majority of the peasants permitted to deal in grain, (3) private capitalism, (4) state capitalism, and (5) "socialism." But Lenin also understood that in order for the Bolsheviks to remain in power it was necessary to have one universal system—a system of state socialism. From this point of view, War Communism was not only a purely military measure, but also a first experiment in economic management. But the experiment failed—the Kronstadt uprising was the last warning.[12] The warning was heeded by both Lenin and the other Bolsheviks, although such unanimity was rare at the time. Together they introduced the New Economic Policy in 1921.

All five methods of production then acquired legal status and were given the opportunity of competing peacefully with each other, on condition, of course, that the posts of direction and command be held by the "dictatorship of the proletariat." However, as a result of this peaceful competition, small-scale producers for the market (peasants) and private capitalism (craftsmen and small-scale and medium-scale industry) so thoroughly demonstrated the advantages of private initiative that after one year Lenin had to change his tactics. "The retreat has stopped, forces are now being re-grouped," said Lenin at the Eleventh Party Congress in 1922. Agriculture was especially successful. There was such

---

[12] "In February 1920, close observation of peasant life in the Urals led me to demand the adoption of a new economic policy. Lenin at that time was against it. The switch over to the NEP was accomplished only a year later. The decision was unanimous, it is true, but with the roar of the Kronstadt uprising in our ears and with the army in a very ugly mood." See Trotsky, *Moya zhizn*, Vol. II, 1930, p. 168.

an abundance of grain that the Twelfth Party Congress in 1923 passed a resolution declaring that "the regularization of Russian grain exports has now become an objective of first-rate importance."[13]

Accordingly, by the time Stalin had seized control of the Party apparatus the "grain problem" had been solved. The solution, however, had its disadvantages from the point of view of the regime. There was plenty of grain, but it belonged to the peasants and not to the state or the Party. As agriculture was the mainstay of the national economy, the Communist dictatorship found itself economically dependent on the peasants. As Stalin described the situation in April 1929: "The wealthier elements of the rural population have considerable grain surpluses in their hands and decide the conditions of the grain market, but they refuse to supply us voluntarily with the necessary amount of grain at prices fixed by the Soviet government."[14]

Stalin could see only one way out of this dilemma, and he took it uncompromisingly: it was the collectivization of peasant property and the nationalization of peasant labor. Henceforth the peasants were dependent upon the state. "War Communism" had acquired a new pseudonym—"kolkhoz production." Stalin admitted in a conversation with Churchill that some ten million peasants had perished during the introduction of the "socialist method of production." But although this unprecedented crime against humanity had enabled Stalin to establish his autocratic dictatorship, it had not solved the grain problem or the livestock problem, in spite of the claim repeatedly made in the Stalin era that both had been solved.

The political dictatorship of the Party, on the other hand, had been enabled to become even more absolute than before by its establishment of an economic dictatorship over the people. This, in fact, was the essence of Stalin's strategy. But the seizure of power from the Party in order to set up a personal dictatorship was not a question of strategy; it was simply the question of a technique for manipulating the Party apparatus. This is the next question to be considered in the light of Khrushchev's speech.

Bolsheviks like to use such terms as "dictatorship of the working class," "workers' and peasants' regime," and "Soviet democracy," but have great hesitation in mentioning "dictatorship of the Party," or "dictatorship of the leaders." This was not true of Lenin, however. "When," he said, "we are accused of having established a Party dictatorship we reply: We have, indeed—the dictatorship of one Party; we stand by it and cannot abandon it."[15] In complete agreement with Lenin, the Twelfth Party Congress, in 1923, incorporated this idea in a resolution which affirmed, "the dictatorship of the working class cannot be guaranteed otherwise than in the form of the dictatorship of its vanguard, that is, the Communist Party."[16]

---

[13] *KPSS v rezolyutsiyakh*, Vol. I, 1953, p. 628.
[14] Stalin, *Voprosy leninizma*, p. 258.
[15] Lenin, *Sochineniya* (Works), 3rd ed., Vol. XXIV, Moscow, 1936, p. 423.
[16] *KPSS v rezolyutsiyakh*, Vol. I, 1953, p. 683.

During the period when he was still trying to seize power, Stalin was most indignant whenever the question was phrased in this manner. He considered it a distortion of the spirit of Leninism and maintained that the formula "dictatorship of the Party" had been implied in the resolution of the Twelfth Party Congress.[17] "If we go in this direction," he said, "we would have to say that 'the dictatorship of the proletariat is the dictatorship of our leaders.' For this is the absurdity to which we are led by identifying the 'dictatorship' of the Party with the dictatorship of the proletariat."[18]

Party dictatorship, or more correctly, the dictatorship of the Central Committee, or what Khrushchev called the "collective leadership," has passed through five stages since the October Revolution: (1) the dictatorship of the Party headed by Lenin (1917–22); (2) the dictatorship of a triumvirate of Zinoviev, Kamenev, and Stalin during Lenin's illness and after his death (1922–25); (3) the dictatorship of the right-wing Stalinist bloc headed by Stalin, Bukharin, and Rykov (1925–29); (4) the dictatorship of the Stalinists—Molotov, Kaganovich, Kirov, Voroshilov, and Stalin himself, headed by Stalin (1929—34); and (5) the personal dictatorship of Stalin nominally assisted by the Politburo (1934–53).

Khrushchev began his story of the manner in which Stalin had established his personal power with the second stage (1922–25). Historically, this was perfectly correct. Lenin's testament, as reported by Khrushchev, indicates the tremendous power which Stalin already wielded during Lenin's lifetime, a power which could pit itself boldly against Lenin by ignoring him, insulting Krupskaya, making reprisals against the Georgian Leninists, and so on.

The Party Central Committee, where Lenin was nominally chairman of the Politburo, was in fact in the hands of the Organization Bureau, whose chairman was Stalin. The ailing Lenin felt that his power over the Party was slipping from his hands. The authority of the Secretary-General's apparatus under Stalin's elastic tactics was gradually becoming greater than the moral authority of the invalid Lenin. The shrewd Zinoviev and Kamenev regarded Stalin as a dependable tool in the fight against Trotsky, the main pretender to Lenin's throne, while Stalin regarded "Lenin's old companions-in-arms" as a weapon to be used against Trotsky. Of the three, Stalin was the most dynamic. Moreover, he was in charge of the Party apparatus. His aim was unlimited power, but the only two persons to understand this, Lenin and Trotsky, decided to combine against Stalin. This, be it recalled, was at a time when, according to Khrushchev, 99% of the delegates whom he was addressing at the Twentieth Party Congress had never even heard of Stalin. Trotsky tells the following story of the formation of this bloc:

> Lenin thought a little and then asked without further ado: "You propose then to start an open war not only against the state bureaucracy, but also against the Organization Bureau of the Central Committee?" I could not help laughing from sheer surprise: the Organization Bureau of the Central Committee was the very center of the Stalinist apparatus. "Well, it rather looks like it." "Then," continued Lenin, obviously pleased that the crux of the matter was being referred to by its

17 Stalin, *Sochineniya*, Vol. VI, 1950, p. 258.
18 Stalin, *Voprosy leninizma*, p. 133.

right name, "I propose forming a bloc against bureaucracy in general, and the Organization Bureau in particular." "It flatters me to form a bloc in such excellent company," I answered. We decided to meet again. Lenin proposed to think about the organizational side. He thought of forming a commission of the Central Committee . . . We were both to be members of it. The main function of this commission would be to act as a lever for the destruction of the Stalinist faction . . . and to create conditions in the Party which would enable me to become Lenin's deputy, as he thought of it, his successor as chairman of the Council of People's Commissars.[19]

This, says Trotsky, was the origin of Lenin's testament, which was intended to prepare the way for the dismissal of Stalin at the Twelfth Party Congress and thus strike a blow at "rudeness, disloyalty, and instability."[20]

Trotsky continues:

Our combined attack against the Central Committee, at the beginning of 1923, would have resulted in certain victory. Furthermore, I have no doubt that if on the eve of the Twelfth Party Congress I had acted in the spirit of a "Lenin-Trotsky bloc" against the Stalin bureaucracy, I would have won a victory without even having to drag in Lenin.[21]

But Stalin was also on the alert:

Stalin again betrayed Lenin's trust. In order to ensure the support of Georgia for himself, he struck out against the best elements of the Party there, falsely pretending to have the Central Committee behind him. In fact he did this behind the backs both of Lenin and of the Central Committee as a whole, assisted only by Ordzhonikidze and, to a certain extent, by Dzerzhinsky. Taking advantage of Lenin's illness, which prevented him from seeing his friends, Stalin allowed only false information to reach him. He tried to cut him off from all sources of information and in the process behaved with exceptional rudeness toward Nadezhda Konstantinovna [Krupskaya—Lenin's wife].[22]

Stalin also had luck on his side. On Trotsky's advice conveyed through Kamenev, Stalin wrote a letter of apology to Lenin's wife, in accordance with a demand by Lenin. In the meantime, Lenin, before he had time to read the letter, suffered another stroke and could no longer write or speak. Nor did Trotsky's courage last for any length of time. He wanted, he told Kamenev, "to preserve the status quo. I am against the liquidation of Stalin, the expulsion of Ordzhonikidze, and the dismissal of Dzerzhinsky. But I agree with Lenin in principle."[23]

Lenin never recovered from this last stroke. He died on January 21, 1924, just at the moment when his death was the only event which could guarantee Stalin's continued political life. Trotsky even suggests the possibility that Lenin's death had occurred not without help from Stalin. According to Trotsky, Lenin asked Stalin for poison to put an end to the terrible sufferings caused by his fatal illness. "Lenin knew whom to ask for poison," remarks Trotsky.[24]

---

[19] Trotsky, *Moya zhizn*, Part II, pp. 216–17.
[20] *Ibid.*, p. 218.
[21] *Ibid.*, p. 219.
[22] *Ibid.*, p. 223.
[23] *Ibid.*
[24] Trotsky, *Stalin* (German Edition), Koeln-Berlin, 1952, p. 478.

Trotsky is somewhat in error in stating that Stalin carefully concealed Lenin's testament from the Party by keeping it in his archives.[25] By an irony of fate, the testament proved to be of service not to its intended beneficiaries—Trotsky, Zinoviev, Kamenev, Bukharin, and Pyatakov—but to those whom it was intended to "liquidate." Stalin preserved it carefully in his files to be brought out whenever he intended to liquidate one of the persons named in it. This was all the easier because Lenin, in mentioning the good qualities of all the Party leaders except Stalin, also described their bad qualities. Stalin boldly omitted all mention of the favorable traits, and, in order to emphasize the unfavorable, cited Lenin's testament against Trotsky during the period of the Left Opposition of 1924, against Zinoviev and Kamenev at the time of the New Opposition of 1925–26, and against Bukharin during his attack on the Right Opposition in 1928–29. When Lenin's testament came to be published in the USSR, the part relating to Stalin was not published until after Stalin's death.

But the testament was not the only document which Stalin found useful. In taking over Lenin's heritage and liquidating the "Leninist guard," he held a magic key which, in sufficiently able hands, could lead him to success—namely the resolutions of the Tenth Party Congress, in 1921, abolishing the last remnants of so-called inner Party democracy and placing the apparatus above the Party. The resolutions were entitled, "On the Unity of the Party." One read as follows:

> The Congress directs all organizations to see strictly to the avoidance of all factional activities. Failure to carry out this resolution of the Congress will result in immediate and unconditional expulsion from the Party. In order to enforce strict discipline within the Party and in all spheres of Soviet activity, and also to achieve the greatest possible unity, while preventing the formation of factions, the Congress authorizes the Central Committee, in case discipline should be infringed upon or factions be formed or allowed to be formed, to adopt all possible measures of punishment available to the Party, including expulsion from it. Full members of the Central Committee will be demoted to the rank of candidate members, and, in extreme cases, will be expelled from the Party.[26]

Another resolution provided for the creation of control commissions, "in order to consolidate the unity and authority of the Party,"[27] in order, in other words, to combat any manifestations of freedom of thought within the Party.

Stalin was not yet Secretary-General when these resolutions were adopted. They were written in Lenin's own hand, but it was Stalin who made use of them when he became Secretary-General in 1922. He and his apparatus had in practice almost unlimited power to apply these resolutions to any Party member up to and including Trotsky, Zinoviev, and Bukharin, and to have them tried by the Party court, the Central Control Commission. As resolutions of a congress, they became "Party law"; as directives from Lenin, they were not open to discussion. In striving to liquidate opposition groups within the Party, in other words to

---

[25] *Ibid.*, p. 205.
[26] *KPSS v rezolyutsiyakh*, Vol. I, 1953, p. 529.
[27] *Ibid.*, p. 533.

liquidate the Party of Lenin and set up one of his own, Stalin invariably made use of these resolutions of the Tenth Party Congress both in spirit and in letter.

Khrushchev, in his secret speech, remained silent on this subject. On the other hand, he quite arbitrarily saddled Stalin with "original sin" which was not his—the sin of inventing the concept, "enemy of the people."

> Stalin created the concept, "enemy of the people." This term made it unnecessary to produce proofs of ideological errors committed by *individuals* or by a *group of individuals*. It made possible the most barbarous prosecution . . . of anyone who disagreed with Stalin on any subject . . . The concept, "enemy of the people," was sufficient to *exclude in practice any possibility of an opposition on ideological grounds, just as it made impossible the expression of any personal opinion on any subject whatever.*

Comparison of the italicized words with the passages cited from the Tenth Party Congress resolutions makes it obvious that the concept, "enemy of the people," although it dated back in fact to the French Revolution, was first applied in Russia as a result of the spirit of the Tenth Party Congress resolutions. These resolutions attempted to establish a direct connection between inner-Party groups in disagreement with the Party on the one hand and "counterrevolutionary" activities on the other. The relevant passage reads as follows:

> Propaganda must explain the experience of earlier revolutions when the counter-revolution gave its support to small bourgeois groups closest to the extreme revolutionary parties, in order to undermine and overthrow the revolutionary dictatorship, thus opening the way to complete the victory of the counterrevolution of capitalists and landowners.[28]

The followers of Trotsky, Zinoviev, and Bukharin, who had originally voted for these Leninist resolutions, as had, indeed, the followers of Stalin, later of course blamed Stalin for his unjustified repression of Party members who were in "ideological" disagreement with him, although repression, at that time, was limited to such relatively humane acts as expulsion or deportation. Stalin, even then, had quite a reasonable answer: "In the arsenal of our Party, repression was never regarded as excluded. Our actions are based on the well-known resolution of the Tenth Congress of our Party, drawn up and confirmed at that Congress by Comrade Lenin."[2]

Khrushchev's criticism that Stalin was unlike Lenin in not tolerating either freedom of "ideological opposition" or the expression of "personal opinions" on any question, rings false both historically and politically. Did Khrushchev's collective leadership tolerate "ideological opposition" and "personal opinions?" After all, it was after Stalin's death that attacks were made on "pseudo-economists" based on the charge that their works were unpublished schoolboy essays. It was *after* the dethroning of Stalin that Yaroshenko and his group were dubbed turncoats on the basis of unpublished speeches, the contents of which are unknown to the Party and the country at large to this day.

---

[28] *Ibid.*, pp. 528–29.
[29] Stalin, *Sochineniya*, Vol. X, 1953, p. 83.

However, according to Khrushchev, there were two Stalins—the Stalin who was Lenin's follower up to the Seventeenth Party Congress in 1934, and the Stalin who was a despot from then on to the end of his life. This statement, too, must be examined.

First, what was the reason behind the theory of the two Stalins?

The theory served to conceal the crimes of the Stalinists themselves. Khrushchev was as ruthless in his attitude to Stalin's personal failings as he was gentle in his treatment of the individuals around Stalin. The same reason prevented him from asking the main question: Who bears the original responsibility for creating both Stalin and his cult—particularly the former?

Trotsky wrote: "Stalin systematically surrounded himself either with people of the same type as himself, or with simpletons who wanted to live without troubling their heads with too much thought, or with people who felt themselves offended and let down. There was no lack of any of these types."[30]

This description applies to the first Stalin, the "good Stalin." Khrushchev gave in his secret speech the following description of the "second Stalin," the "bad Stalin."

> Before the Seventeenth Party Congress, Stalin still paid some attention to the opinions of the collective leadership. However, after the complete political liquidation of the Trotskyites, Zinovievites, and Bukharinites . . . he paid progressively less attention to the opinions expressed by members of the Central Committee of the Party or even by members of the Politburo. Stalin thought that he could now decide everything by himself and that all he needed was stage extras. His treatment of others left them with no choice but to obey and praise him.

These statements made by two of Stalin's colleagues in the Politburo differ in time but not in substance. Their similarity merely confirms the fact that the theory of the two Stalins was necessary for the rehabilitation of the Stalinists themselves.

The above passage from Khrushchev's speech also contains an answer to the questions why and how Stalin managed to transform the members of the Politburo into mere extras. First, Stalin selected only those who chose to live and not to think; second, with the aid of these very extras Stalin had liquidated all the Leninist élite of the Party and thus reached his objective—the establishment of a personal dictatorship.

Khrushchev regarded, or claimed to regard, the struggle against the oppositions carried on by Stalin with the backing of the Party apparatus and the NKVD as a struggle for "socialism." But socialism, in the sense of a well-ordered life for the people, was never Stalin's objective, but only a slogan used for the achievement of his personal dictatorship. Until this objective was reached, and while the main obstacles to it—the Trotskyites, Zinovievites, and Bukharinites—remained, Stalin pretended to pay attention to the opinions of the collective leadership. After reaching his objective of dictatorship, he was able to allocate a new

---

[30] Trotsky, *Moya zhizn*, Vol. II, p. 214.

function to the collective leadership—the right only "to obey and praise him." Khrushchev apparently approved entirely of Stalin's liquidation of the political opposition and disagreed with Stalin only regarding the physical liquidation of the oppositionists—Zinoviev, Kamenev, and the Trotskyites and Bukharinites. Khrushchev's words are:

> In the days preceding the October Revolution, two members of the Central Committee of the Bolshevik Party, Kamenev and Zinoviev, came out against Lenin's plan for an armed uprising . . .
>
> Lenin proposed expelling Kamenev and Zinoviev from the Party. Nevertheless, after the October Revolution, they were appointed to important posts. Lenin made them responsible for putting into practice some of the most important Party decisions . . . In his "testament" Lenin emphasized that "the case of Zinoviev and Kamenev was no accident." But he did not suggest that they be arrested or even less that they be shot . . . Trotsky was surrounded by people who could in no way be described as bourgeois . . . These people had taken an active part in the labor movement before the October Revolution as well as during it, and had also helped to consolidate the victory of this, the greatest of all revolutions. Many of them broke away from the Trotskyite position and rejoined the Leninists. Was it really necessary to liquidate these people? We are absolutely convinced that had Lenin been alive, such extreme measures would not have been taken.

Here Khrushchev was continuing to pursue the two parallel aims which run through his entire report, first to prove that there were two Stalins, the early Stalin and the later Stalin; and second, to separate Stalin from Lenin.

Psychologically, and, in a sense, historically, such an approach was to a certain degree justified in the eyes of the Party and even of the people. Attacks against Stalin by all opposition groups within the Party began and ended with one slogan: "Back to Lenin!" Public opinion, at the height of the Stalin reaction, also appealed to Lenin: "If only Lenin were alive. . . ." But the public thought of Lenin not in connection with the policy of War Communism and the Committees of Poor Peasants, but with the NEP. The Opposition, on the other hand, thought of him in connection with freedom of internal Party discussion. Khrushchev could not achieve either of these goals, and consequently he had to leave inviolate the Stalin who liquidated the NEP, carried out compulsory collectivization, and introduced intensive industrialization. But he could contrast with Lenin the Stalin responsible for the physical liquidation of his own followers in the Party. The famous Khrushchev amnesty for "physically liquidated" Stalinists was, it is true, extended to anti-Stalinists as well, but only very conditionally and in a very restricted sense: it was right to isolate them politically ("private opinions and discussions within the Party are quite unnecessary when the apparatus is there to think for everyone"), but it was wrong to shoot them. ("We are convinced that had Lenin been alive he would not have acted in this way.")

Of course it is difficult to judge how Lenin would have acted. Politically Stalin had merely carried Lenin's precepts through to their logical conclusion. Khrushchev and his friends had had good reason to teach the Party for thirty years to say: "Stalin is the Lenin of today." Psychologically and intellectually

Lenin was, of course, a person of a different type, heavily loaded with every kind of "bourgeois prejudice," such, for instance, as morals, honor, sense of duty, and loyalty, even if only on a purely Party level. Stalin was completely devoid of such "prejudices," and this lack constituted his great superiority, as a Bolshevik politician, even over Lenin. But even Lenin, whose teachings had their moral roots in Machiavellianism, possessed no immunity against infection by Stalinism, and might well have succumbed to it if he had been forced to act in the same circumstances and with the same end in view as Stalin. In this respect, Khrushchev's argument is not convincing. After all, Lenin did write: "History knows of all kinds of transformations: to rely on conviction, on loyalty, and on other excellent moral qualities is not to treat politics seriously."[31]

There was yet another and very fundamental difference between Lenin and Stalin. It may sound like a paradox, but it was nevertheless true that Lenin was a confirmed Communist, which Stalin never was. To Lenin, power was a means to the end of Communism; to Stalin, Communism itself was merely a means to the attainment of power. Hence, Lenin, before setting out to destroy his companions, would have considered the interests of his ultimate objective, the extent to which these "erring" Communists were still convinced Communists and the degree to which their destruction was useful or harmful to the cause of Communism. Stalin's objective on the other hand, that of power, demanded another approach. The question which he asked himself was the extent to which any particular Communist could promote or harm his chances of establishing his personal dictatorship. And it was precisely for this reason that ideologically convinced Communists were for Stalin the most dangerous group in the Party. They alone could form an opposition to Stalin if they thought that he was not striving to attain a social ideal but was aiming at purely personal and unlimited power for himself. Here we arrive at the portion of Stalin's career—the Yezhov terror—which evoked Khrushchev's greatest indignation.

Before examining Khrushchev's version of the history of the Yezhov reign of terror, the circumstances of the time and the personnel of the main organs of the Central Committee on the eve of the Great Purge should be briefly reviewed. The circumstances were as follows:

1. Most members of the former opposition groups had long since capitulated to the Stalinist apparatus and had ceased to play a part in Party life. Their former leaders were employed in Stalin's propaganda service and were, in common with the rest of the Party, singing hymns of praise to the "great genius"—Zinoviev in the magazine *Bolshevik*, Kamenev in the "Academia" press, Bukharin in the newspaper *Izvestia*, Radek in the newspaper *Pravda*, Tomsky in the State Publishing House, etc.

2. The Central Committee elected at the Seventeenth Party Congress in 1934 contained the most orthodox Communists in the history of the Party, with the exception of three regular members—Pyatakov, K. L. Nikolayev, and Krupskaya—who had once been Trotskyites but had been rendered powerless, and three

[31] Lenin, *Sochineniya*, Vol. XXVII, 1936, p. 243.

alternate members—Bukharin, Rykov, and Tomsky—who had belonged to the Right, but had also capitulated. The majority of the regular and alternate members of the Central Committee had been members of the Party before the Revolution.

3. The executive organs of the Central Committee elected at the Seventeenth Party Congress were as follows:

Politburo : Members—Stalin, Molotov, L. Kaganovich, Voroshilov, Kalinin, Ordzhonikidze, Kuibyshev, Kirov, Andreyev, Kosior, and from 1935, Mikoyan and Zhdanov. Alternates—Mikoyan, Chubar, Petrovsky, Postyshev, Rudzutak.

Organization Bureau (Orgburo) : Members—Stalin, Kaganovich, Kirov, Zhdanov, Yezhov, Shvernik, Kosarev, Stetsky, Gamarnik, and Kuibyshev. Alternates—Krinitsky and M. Kaganovich.

Secretariat : Stalin, L. Kaganovich, Kirov, and Zhdanov.

Neither in the Central Committee nor in its top organs did Stalin have any opponents with the exception of the former oppositionists mentioned above. The Central Committee and its organs contained only Communists who had by word and deed helped Stalin to smash the Party opposition after Lenin's death, to carry out collectivization, to fulfill the first Five-Year Plan, and to consolidate his position as the official and actual leader of the Party. They alone were found at the head of all local Party committees. "Leadership but not dictatorship" might have been the slogan of the Central Committee in 1934. The loyalty of the Central Committee to the ideals of Communism is quite beyond doubt. But the same cannot be said of its loyalty to Stalin. That the first of these statements is true was confirmed by Khrushchev; of the second loyalty he made no mention. He said:

> Stalin's high-handed treatment of the Party and its Central Committee became quite obvious after the Seventeenth Party Congress in 1934. After collecting a considerable number of facts illustrating Stalin's gross disregard of the opinions of Party members, the Central Committee appointed a Party commission under the control of the Presidium of the Central Committee to investigate the reasons for measures of mass repression taken against most members and alternate members of the Central Committee. The commission examined the material in the NKVD archives and other documents and established the existence of many cases of rigged-up charges against Communists, false accusations, and blatant miscarriages of justice resulting in the deaths of innocent people. It was revealed that many ["tens of thousands" says Khrushchev elsewhere] Party and Soviet workers, as well as persons prominent in economic life, who had been branded in 1937–38 as enemies had in fact never been either enemies or spies or wreckers, but had always been honest Communists. They had merely been libeled, and being unable to bear the barbarous tortures to which they were subjected, frequently accused themselves of the most terrible and improbable crimes. This they did at the orders of the investigators, who had themselves faked all the evidence. The commission submitted to the Presidium of the Central Committee very extensive and well-documented material . . . It has been established that out of a total of 139 full and alternate members elected at the Seventeenth Party Congress, 98, or 70%, were arrested and shot. ("Indignation in the hall.")

Khrushchev added that the delegates to the Seventeenth Party Congress as a whole suffered the same fate as the members of the Central Committee which it had elected. According to him, 80% of the Congress delegates had joined the Party before the Revolution or during the Civil War. Of the delegates, 60% were of working class origin. Nevertheless:

> Of 1,956 delegates to the Congress with deciding or advisory votes, 1,108 were arrested and accused of counterrevolutionary crimes. This fact alone shows how absurd, wild, and senseless were the charges of counterrevolutionary crimes leveled against the majority of the delegates to the Seventeenth Party Congress. ("Indignation in the hall.")

What reason did Khrushchev give for Stalin's rough treatment of his own Party? Khrushchev gave an answer which was anything but an answer to this important and, indeed, decisive question. He said: "The only reason why 70% of the regular and alternate members of the Central Committee were branded as enemies of the Party and the people was that fabricated evidence was used to libel honest Communists."

This was all.

This disingenuous answer at once suggests four questions: How was the evidence fabricated? Who had sanctioned the faking? Why, to use Khrushchev's words, was it possible to apply such "absurd" and "wild" measures against the Party in the name of the Party itself? Were there any members of the Central Committee who opposed these measures?

To the first two of these questions Khrushchev gave concrete and convincing replies:

> Under such circumstances there was no need for sanction by anyone; besides, what question could there be of anyone's sanctioning anything when Stalin decided everything himself? He was himself the chief prosecutor in all these cases. Stalin not only agreed to all these arrests, but ordered them as well, on his own initiative.

Were there any persons in the top ranks of the Party who doubted the correctness of Stalin's policy aiming at the physical liquidation of the Party? If there were, did they have enough courage to express their doubts aloud? If only to justify both himself and his colleagues in the Politburo, Khrushchev did not admit that there were any such persons. He frankly said:

> Wielding unlimited power, he could have men destroyed, both morally and physically, without reference to anyone. The result was that nobody could express his own wishes. If Stalin said that this or that man must be arrested, it had to be taken on trust that the man in question was an enemy of the people.

Khrushchev admitted indirectly that the Politburo had sanctioned such acts, while taking Stalin's decisions on trust. Elsewhere in his speech, Khrushchev indicated even more explicitly on whom Stalin leaned for support in initiating his program of mass terror, and the role played by the Politburo and some of its members.

Khrushchev's first such statement dealt with the preparations for the purge. On the evening of December 1, 1934, immediately after Kirov's murder, the

Presidium of the Central Executive Committee of the USSR published a decree which according to Khrushchev was signed by Yenukidze, but which obviously would have been legally invalid without the signature of the chairman of the Central Executive Committee of the USSR, Kalinin. The decree read as follows:

1. The investigating departments are directed to deal more rapidly with the cases of persons accused of the preparation and carrying out of acts of terrorism.

2. The organs of the judiciary are directed not to delay the execution of death sentences.

3. The organs of the Commissariat for Internal Affairs [NKVD] are directed to execute death sentences . . . directly after they are pronounced.

Khrushchev commented on this as follows:

This directive gave rise to numerous abuses of socialist legality. During the many fabricated trials, the accused were charged with having "prepared" terrorist acts. This alone made review of their cases impossible, even when they made statements to the court that their "confessions" had been obtained by force, and had conclusively proved the falsity of the accusations against them.

This first legislative act, which legalized all the other crimes, was ratified by the Politburo. It is true that according to Khrushchev it was ratified post factum, but it was ratified. "On the evening of December 1, 1934, on Stalin's initiative, but without a Politburo resolution, which followed, by the way, two days later, the Secretary of the Central Committee Presidium signed the following directive. . . ."

Khrushchev's second statement, referred to earlier in another connection, declared that Yezhov was appointed People's Commissar for Internal Affairs of the USSR in place of Yagoda on the mere authority of a telegram from Stalin and Zhdanov, who were absent from Moscow at the time.

Mass repressions had assumed immense proportions from the end of 1936, after a telegram from Stalin and Zhdanov dated Sochi, September 25, 1936, and addressed to Kaganovich, Molotov, and other members of the Politburo. Its contents were as follows: "We consider it absolutely essential and immediate that Comrade Yezhov be appointed to the position of People's Commissar of Internal Affairs. Yagoda has definitely shown himself to be incapable of uncovering the Trotskyite-Zinovievite bloc. The OGPU is four years behind in this matter" . . .

After quoting this telegram, Khrushchev commented:

Stalin's use of the phrase "the OGPU is four years behind" in carrying out mass repressions, and his expression of the need to "catch up" with the neglected work, pushed the NKVD workers along the path of mass arrests and executions.

If Khrushchev's love for historical truth had been as great as his personal hatred of Stalin, and if he had had no share in the responsibility for the crimes committed, he would have made a third statement to the effect that both the appointment of Yezhov and the Yezhov purge were sanctioned by the Politburo in the absence of Stalin, and in response to reports by Kaganovich, the Second Secretary of the Central Committee, and Molotov, the chairman of the Council of Ministers of the USSR. Whenever he committed a crime—on whatever scale, whether great or small—Stalin, with the inborn instinct of a professional criminal, always made sure of an alibi, and it was doubtless for this reason that he had proposed that this problem, so heavy with consequences for himself and for the country, be decided in his absence. If necessary, he could always say (and probably did at the time of Yezhov's liquidation): "Come now, Comrades, all I did was to send you a wire, made a suggestion so to speak; it was you who voted and took all the decisions. I was not there, and you could see things more clearly for yourselves." Moreover, it is probable that Stalin was absolutely convinced that the action which he proposed was of vital and mutual concern to all his "companions-in-arms and disciples."

Khrushchev deliberately remained silent as to this aspect of the Yezhov reign of terror. But he said enough to warrant the conclusion that Stalin acted not only with the knowledge, but also with the full approval, of the members of the Politburo—Molotov, Kaganovich, Voroshilov, Mikoyan, Zhdanov, Andreyev, and Kalinin; in other words, of all those who survived the Yezhov terror. Knowing this, Khrushchev preferred to disassociate himself from *that* Politburo, although indirectly. In describing to the congress delegates the terrible tortures inflicted by the NKVD on the Old Bolsheviks, and relating how, in letters to Stalin, those Old Bolsheviks had withdrawn the "confessions" which had been forced out of them, Khrushchev reminded his listeners as if in passing: "At the same time Stalin, as we have been informed by members of the Politburo of that time, did not show them the statements made by many of the accused political figures." It is true that Khrushchev had not been a member of the Politburo, but in order to include him, Malenkov, Bulganin, Beria, and others, the Stalin-Molotov-Kaganovich team had to dismiss and liquidate nine out of the sixteen persons comprising the Politburo, including Kirov, Ordzhonikidze, Kuibyshev, and Yezhov himself. Of these nine, only Petrovsky remained alive.

As to the statements made by members of the Politburo "of that time" that Stalin had concealed from them "letters" written by Old Bolsheviks, Stalin hardly needed to do this. For of the 21 members of the Council of People's Commissars presided over by Molotov, only three had retained their freedom—Kaganovich, Voroshilov, and Mikoyan. All the others, including Molotov's deputies Rudzutak, Mezhlauk, and Antipov, were in the NKVD prison. These individuals wrote presumably not only to the Secretary of the Party but also to their Prime Minister. Likewise persons in positions of economic responsibility wrote presumably to Kaganovich and Mikoyan, Party workers to Andreyev, Malenkov, and Khrushchev, and army commanders to Voroshilov and Budenny. From whom then did those companions-in-arms of Stalin hide the letters they received? On this subject Khrushchev claimed not to have been informed.

While describing Stalin as a terrorist and despot, Khrushchev never once cited an illustration of the manner in which Stalin and his Party systematically annihilated, on a preconceived plan, millions of non-Party peasants, workers, and intellectuals. This omission was only to be expected. If the annihilation of the upper ranks of the Party was the work of Stalin and the Politburo, the annihilation of the people was the work of the entire Stalinist Party. Stalin can be accused of having compiled personal lists of members of the higher establishment of the Party and the state destined for physical annihilation. ("In 1937–38, 383 such lists were sent to Stalin, with the names of thousands of Party, Soviet, military, Komsomol, and industrial and agricultural workers. He ratified these lists," said Khrushchev). But who ratified the lists of those millions who had passed through the hands of the Extraordinary Tribunals in the oblasts and republics? Each such tribunal was composed of three members of the bureau of the local Party committee–the First Secretary of the Party Committee, the Public Prosecutor, and the head of the local NKVD unit.

Khrushchev provided no statistical data regarding the monstrous crimes thus committed by the Stalinist Party, and was not prepared to appoint a state commission (analogous to the Party commission) to investigate them. Nor did Khrushchev make any mention of the total number of rank and file Party members executed, in spite of the great number affected. As I have shown earlier, 1,220,942 Communists were expelled from the Party and therefore arrested during the years 1934–39. Another source estimates that 1,116,500 Communists were expelled and arrested in the years 1935–38.[32]

Why then did Khrushchev not report these mass figures to the Congress, and why, even after the unmasking of Stalin, are statistics on the length of membership of its members kept secret? The answer is clear: because those responsible for repression against the Party members as a whole were the Stalinists themselves: Malenkov, Kaganovich, and Andreyev (secretaries of the Central Committee and members of the Politburo Commission for State Security) at the center, Khrushchev himself in the areas under his direct control, i.e., in Moscow and the Ukraine, and Suslov in Rostov-on-Don.

---

[32] Z. K. Brzezinski, *The Permanent Purge*, cited in *Ost-Probleme*, 1956, No. 23. p. 798.

Chapter XXXII

Stalin's Successors: The "Collective Leadership"

"Many articles and biographical descriptions in the *Large Soviet Encyclopedia* fail to give a true portrayal of the part played by this or that Party leader," declared the Soviet journal *Problems of History* in 1956.[1]

The "collective leadership" which succeeded Stalin attempted to blame him alone for all the errors committed during his period of dictatorship. But there is an apparent lack of logic in the fact that while accusing Stalin of doing away with Lenin's "collective leadership" and of establishing a personal dictatorship over Party and people, at the same time they accused his opponents, the Trotskyites and Bukharinites, of being the "fiercest enemies" of Leninism. Those who laid down their lives in an effort to forestall Stalin and his crimes are criminals, and Stalin's victory over them is "an unquestionable achievement."

Is this really lack of logic? On the contrary. The logic of this view is profound and rests on one all-important fact: the post-Stalin "collective leaders" were themselves the force but for which Stalin would not have become "Stalin," while they in turn would not have become the "collective leaders."

A cursory glance at the histories of these leaders will go far to make clear the logic of the behavior of those who, to the bitter end, were Stalin's trusted "companions-in-arms and disciples" and who lived to curse their teacher:*

Vyacheslav Molotov: (Born 1890, Party member from 1906). Although not a member of the Politburo, Molotov preceded Stalin as Secretary of the Central Committee. His membership in the Committee depended on prior removal of Trotsky, Zinoviev, and Kamenev, and in the struggle to liquidate them he surrendered body and soul to Stalin. "Molotov is not a living being—he is Stalin's robot," it was said of him in the Party. The "robot" earned his reward and in 1926 was appointed member of the Politburo. It would be a mistake to call Molotov a careerist by nature. There was, however, one amazing trait in his character which made of him a robot: this was his machine-like lack of feeling and his automation in execution. Both these traits were fully used by Stalin when he was preparing the ground for his campaign against the Bukharinites. There was no more need to "indoctrinate" or "convince" Molotov than there is to indoctrinate or convince a machine. He had only to be greased and put in the proper place, which is exactly what Stalin did.

---

[1] *Problemy istorii*, No. 5, 1956, p. 145.

* The author has not found it necessary to bring these biographies up to date, as his main purpose in presenting them is to picture the types of Soviet leaders brought to the top by the Stalinist system. For further biographical details on these and other Soviet figures see *Biographic Directory of the USSR*, New York, 1958.

During the struggle with the Right, Molotov showed greater ability than in the struggle with the Trotskyites and Zinovievites. Yet there was nothing personal in his contribution, nothing that expressed Molotov's own individuality: he merely carried out to perfection the will of his operator. It was at this time that Stalin discerned in him both the long-sought-for screen behind which he could conceal his dictatorship and the perfect and obedient tool for putting it into practice. In 1930 he appointed Molotov to the quite nominal position of Chairman of the Council of People's Commissars in place of Rykov. He used him in this capacity as long as he felt the need for some kind of a screen.

Before the outbreak of the war in 1941, Stalin relieved Molotov of his post, in spite of the part he had played in purging his own cabinet. Of the 21 members of the cabinet of ministers of the USSR serving under Molotov in 1937, only three accomplices of Molotov and Stalin—Kaganovich, Mikoyan, and Voroshilov— escaped death. (Litvinov had been removed from office and had died a natural death.) All the others, although they were neither Trotskyites nor Bukharinites, were found guilty of being in German pay as "spies of German Fascism." All of the ministers executed were arrested on warrants signed either by the Prime Minister, Molotov, or by the head of the Central Executive Committee of the Supreme Soviet of the USSR, Kalinin, or the Chief State Prosecutor, Vyshinsky. No member of the cabinet of ministers could be arrested without the signature of one of these persons together with that of the allpowerful Yezhov. Even Stalin's signature was invalid, as he had no administrative position, being at the time only Secretary of the Central Committee, and member of the Presidium of the Central Executive Committee of the Supreme Soviet of the USSR.

But this is only half the picture. In order to appreciate the extent and magnitude of Molotov's share in the purges of 1933–39, it is not enough to examine the facts which appear on the surface. Molotov's activities behind the scenes, or at least those in the plenary sessions of the Central Committee of the Party in 1935–36 and 1937 must also be taken into account.

During this entire period one matter, although differently formulated, invariably formed the subject of discussion at all the plenary sessions of the Central Committee. This was the Party purge. The December 1935 session discussed "The Results of the Check of Party Membership Cards," and was marked by the election of Mikoyan as full member and Zhdanov as alternate member of the Politburo. The June 1936 plenary session considered "The Exchange of Membership Cards." The February-March 1937 plenary session dealt with "The Expulsion from the Party of Bukharin and Rykov." The March 1938 plenary session worked on completion of the purge under the pretext of ridding the Party of Left Deviationists, and admitted Khrushchev as alternate member of the Politburo and Mekhlis as member of the Organization Bureau. The most important of these plenary meetings, that of September 1936, which failed to give Stalin a vote of confidence, was not even mentioned in the Party press.

At all these sessions the formal duties as chairman, such as opening the meeting, steering discussions, moving resolutions, and closing the meeting, were performed not by Stalin but by Molotov. If the minutes are ever published, the surprising fact will come to light that although Stalin was the real organizer of the purges, he rarely appeared as such. In his few utterances, to answer an occasional query or to make a speech, he played the part of "pacifier" and "peace-lover," or, up to the time of the arrests of Bukharin and Rykov in February 1937, spoke on any subject except that of the purges. On the other hand Molotov, Kaganovich, Andreyev, Shkiryatov, Shvernik, Mekhlis, and, of course, Yezhov, were all intensely active. Molotov set the tone on government matters, Kaganovich on ideological principles, and Yezhov on police proceedings.

Molotov, accordingly, particularly from the legal point of view, as the official head of the Soviet cabinet must share with Yezhov, who was only one of his ministers, responsibility for the Yezhov purge of 1936–38.

Mention has been made of the part played by Molotov in the destruction of the peasant class in the USSR through enforced collectivization and predatory industrialization. In this process his influence was only little less than that of Stalin. The "Plan for the Liquidation of the Kulaks as a Class" approved by the Polit-buro in January 1930 was based on a report submitted by the Rural Commission of the Politburo, of which Molotov was chairman. Furthermore, all the pre-war Five-Year Plans, with their continued lowering of the Soviet worker's already low standard of living, were approved by plenums and congresses of the Party on the basis of reports submitted by Molotov. He was likewise the "legal" father of the "Stalin Constitution" approved by the December 1935 plenary session of the Party Central Committee, and adopted by the Supreme Soviet in December 1936.

When the purge came to an end in 1939 and some of its promoters, including Malenkov, Khrushchev, Suslov, Bulganin, Vyshinsky, and others, were granted their rewards, Molotov was allowed to form a new cabinet. This time he included among the ministers not only his personal friends but even his wife, Paulina Zhemchuzhina. The family idyll, however, was short-lived. Before two years had elapsed Malenkov had removed Molotov's wife from the cabinet and Stalin had dropped Molotov as prime minister, although retaining him as Deputy Prime Minister and Minister for Foreign Affairs. In the field of foreign affairs, the only monument bequeathed by Molotov to posterity was the Molotov-Ribbentrop pact. It was Molotov who at 5 a.m. June 22, 1941, received from German Ambassador von Schulenburg the note informing the government of the German invasion of the USSR. His panic-stricken and bewildered answer at this tragic moment indicates the complete vacuity of this alleged "statesman:" "Tell me, Your Excellency, what have we done to merit such treatment?" Before the morning was over he pulled himself together and addressed the nation by radio—something which Stalin did not do until two weeks later. "Our cause is just," said Molotov, "we shall vanquish the foe and victory will be ours." This was the only message he could give to the citizens of the USSR to justify his pro-Hitler policy which had culminated in war.

During the war years, as deputy chairman of the State Committee of Defense, he was again useful to Stalin as a "front" for Russian patriotism. At all the Allied war conferences—Teheran, Yalta, and Potsdam—it was Molotov who presented the extreme demands of the Soviet government while the "concessions" were granted by Stalin. However, in matters of decisive importance to the Kremlin, Stalin could, on occasions, be as obdurate as Molotov, either on pretext of inability to convince the Politburo, or by arguing that he and Molotov feared being charged with defending the interests of Russia less ably than the Russian tsars.

In the "cold war" which followed, the kind of weapon required by Stalin was perhaps morally less scrupulous but intellectually more keen than Molotov. Early in 1949 Vyshinsky, Molotov's deputy, was appointed Minister of Foreign Affairs, while Molotov was relegated to the status of Minister without Portfolio. Before he died Stalin showed his gratitude to Molotov by having his wife arrested.

Notwithstanding all the injustices he and his family had suffered at Stalin's hands, Molotov remained a faithful disciple to the last. He never abjured the declaration of loyalty made in December 1930 when he took over the chairmanship of the Council of People's Commissars from the deposed Rykov. "In connection with my new appointment, I cannot but say a few words about myself and my work. In the course of the last few years, as Secretary of the Central Committee, I have been schooled and personally instructed in Bolshevik work by Lenin's most able disciple, Comrade Stalin. I am proud of this fact."[2]

Such, then, in brief, were the services rendered by Molotov to the late dictator. His removal from the post of Minister for Foreign Affairs in 1956 was a direct consequence of these services. To the "Young Leninists" of the new collective leadership he was persona non grata, not because of the crimes he had committed for Stalin, but mainly because he was a living symbol of the era of the deceased dictator.

His appointment as Minister for State Control, while a tribute to his individual qualities of bureaucratic insensitivity and administrative pedantry nevertheless placed him on the plane of the ordinary mortal. The logical consequences of a return to Stalinism, should this ever prove possible in the future, should be a new triumph for Molotov.

Lazar Kaganovich: (Born 1893, Party member from 1911). Within the Party Kaganovich has the reputation of being a gifted organizer. This particular ability has been unfailingly stressed in all his official biographies, and foreign authors have generally been content to repeat this Soviet appraisal of his character. His abilities as organizer are indisputable, but the real question is, where, what and how does he "organize?"

Take, for instance, Mikoyan. Like Kaganovich, he is a member of the Bolshevik Old Guard, a member of the Presidium of the Party Central Committee, and First Deputy Premier. He, too, is a gifted organizer. Yet there can be no comparison between the two. Not, of course, because of a difference in convictions, but mainly because of their totally different mentalities and the limited "creative" breadth of Mikoyan in the organizational technique of Bolshevism.

In this field Kaganovich is virtually as unique as was Stalin. Of all Stalin's successors he comes closest to being a copy of Stalin himself as a Stalinist Bolshevik, in fact so true a copy that at times it is difficult to distinguish between the

[2] V. Molotov, *V borbe za sotzializm* (In the Fight for Socialism), 2nd ed., Moscow, 1935, p. 76.

original and the copy. If the laws of biology were effective in politics, it would be possible to say that all members of the Politburo were brothers but Stalin and Kaganovich were twins. This kinship between Stalin and Kaganovich is psychological, not physical, although it must be admitted that Kaganovich did his best to look like Stalin. During Lenin's lifetime he wore western clothes and grew a short beard like Lenin's; in Stalin's day, he changed his European suit for a Stalinist jacket and grew a moustache like Stalin's. It is, however, quite wrong to think of Kaganovich as a mere robot or tool in the hands of Stalin.

The official biographers of Kaganovich, by juggling facts and events, have succeeded in embellishing the story of his life and in presenting him as one of the leaders of the October Revolution and the Civil War and even as one of the organizers of the Red Army. This is invention, as fictitious as parts of Stalin's biography; a fact which even his disciples unwillingly admit.

Kaganovich's career began in Nizhny Novgorod in 1919. In 1920, in Turkestan, he became a member of the Muslim Bureau for Central Asia of the Party Central Committee. Until 1922 his duties consisted in personally informing Stalin, the People's Commissar for Nationalities, on matters concerning Central Asia and Kazakhstan. His official position in Turkestan corresponded to that of Stalin in Moscow, where Stalin was People's Commissar for Nationalities and People's Commissar of Workers' and Peasants' Inspection. All the most important measures adopted to Sovietize and Bolshevize Central Asia were suggested to Stalin by Kaganovich over the heads of the local leaders, and the methods he employed were dictated to Kaganovich by Stalin and, consequently, were those of his immediate chief, namely conspiracy and terror.

Stalin soon recognized that here was a man after his own heart, and one well qualified to enter the group he was then building around himself—a master plotter and kindred spirit in applying his methods. When Stalin was promoted in 1922 to Secretary-General of the Central Committee, it was only natural for him to transfer Kaganovich to the apparatus of the Central Committee and to make him his principal assistant in the forces he was preparing to use against the Trotskyites. Here Kaganovich was head of the Organization and Instruction Department of the Central Committee, and later head of the Organization and Allocation Department. At the Twelfth Party Congress in 1923, Stalin had him accepted as candidate member of the Central Committee and at the Thirteenth Party Congress in 1924, after the death of Lenin, as regular member, in recognition of his share in the defeat of Trotsky. Two years of collaboration confirmed Stalin in the wisdom of his choice and in 1924, with the support of Zinoviev and Kamenev, he secured Kaganovich's appointment as one of the secretaries of the Party Central Committee.

The victory over Trotsky had ended the first stage of the struggle. The second, the struggle with the Zinovievites and "bourgeois nationalists," was about to begin. It was generally accepted that in this forthcoming clash the Ukraine would play a major part, second in importance only to that of Leningrad and Moscow. In May 1925, six months before the opening of the campaign against the Zinoviev-

Kamenev bloc and later the Trotsky-Zinoviev-Kamenev bloc, Stalin dispatched Kaganovich to the Ukraine, as Secretary-General of the Ukrainian Communist Party. There, by copying Stalin's tactics in Moscow and with equal talent, Kaganovich decimated the Zinovievites and Trotskyites of the Ukraine, as well as the Ukrainian Communist intelligentsia, headed by Shumsky.

By 1928 the Trotskyite-Zinovievite bloc and the "bourgeois nationalists" had been defeated, and Stalin was moving on to the next campaign on his list—the liquidation of Bukharin, Rykov, and Tomsky. The main base of the Rightists was Moscow, where their leaders enjoyed considerable authority and held prominent positions in the government, the press, the Comintern, and the trade unions. Stalin realized that the Bukharin-Rykov-Tomsky triumvirate would have to be opposed by a triumvirate of Secretaries of the Party Central Committee. Apart from Stalin and Molotov, the only man suitable to fill a seat was Kaganovich. In 1928, a few months before the actual beginning of the struggle with the Rightists, Kaganovich was recalled to Moscow from the Ukraine and was appointed Third Secretary of the Central Committee, under Stalin and Molotov. Later in the same year, when the campaign was well under way, Kaganovich was made "political commissar" of the Central Committee and a member of the Trade Union Council presidium, to be used against Tomsky. In 1930, after the annihilation of the Rightists and their eviction from the Politburo, Kaganovich was appointed member of that body and thus at last reached his coveted goal.

He was now settled in Moscow for good, with the exception of a short term of office in the Ukraine, where he was sent to relieve Khrushchev, who had been appointed prime minister of the Ukraine.

These milestones in Kaganovich's career fade into insignificance in comparison with his role after the early thirties, when he was given the opportunity to apply his organizing ability to the full. During this period he was singularly reminiscent of Stalin during Lenin's lifetime. Whenever someone was needed to "liquidate," "annihilate," or "destroy"—in short when an "organizer of repression" was called for—Kaganovich was immediately dispatched to the seat of trouble. On occasions when some new form of coercion, physical or moral, could suitably be suggested to his chief, it was suggested by Kaganovich. Whenever it was expedient to find some form of ideological justification for the vilest of crimes against the nation or the Party, it was invariably found by Kaganovich. An anecdote current in Moscow ran: "Stalin works twenty-four hours a day." "How can he do it?" "Quite simple. He works eight hours a day under his own name and sixteen by using Kaganovich and Molotov as pseudonyms."

During the winter of 1930, practically the entire Soviet Union was engulfed by a wave of peasant uprisings against forcible collectivizations. In a few areas these uprisings assumed the character of open and armed revolt, while in the main agricultural districts, the Ukraine, the North Caucasus, Voronezh Oblast, and Western Siberia, agitation against the kolkhozes acquired ugly and dangerous proportions.

From 1930 to 1934 Kaganovich, as one of the "Plenipotentiaries Extraordinary of the Central Committee and the Council of People's Commissars for Collectivization and Grain Deliveries," was constantly on the move, touring the affected areas. The practical importance of the post now held by Kaganovich was immense. Every such plenipotentiary was furnished with a mandate signed by Stalin and Molotov which baldly stated that in the local district, oblast, or republic, supreme authority was temporarily vested in the plenipotentiary, who was authorized to make all decisions at his own discretion and to impose in the name of the Central Committee and the Soviet government such measures as he might deem appropriate. Such decisions could not be appealed and could not be referred to Moscow.

Supported by special detachments of Cheka troops, and adopting as his motto, "the complete defeat of kulak sabotage," Kaganovich proceeded to a ruthless deportation of women, children, and old people from Voronezh, the Ukraine, and the North Caucasus to Siberia, and from Siberia to the wastes of the northern tundra. In Moscow Oblast, where he was made First Secretary of the oblast committee in April 1935, he applied similar tactics of mass deportation. However, the theory of "kulak sabotage" was soon contradicted by the realities of life. After liquidation of the kulaks the most important part of the rural population, i.e., the "middle" peasants, replied to enforced collectivization and grain delivery by joining the kolkhozes in order to avoid deportation to Siberia, but not in order to work for the Party.

The kolkhozes were primarily created, apart from other considerations, for the purpose of enabling the government to requisition grain more easily from an organized peasantry. The peasants, on the other hand, tended to regard the kolkhoz grain as their private property and to withhold it from the government. In January 1933 Stalin declared that "the main deficiency [in connection with reduced delivery in 1932] lay in the increased difficulty encountered in obtaining delivery of grain as compared with the previous year ... The enemy has correctly appreciated the altered circumstances and, by changing his dispositions and modifying his tactics, has passed from a frontal assault to undermining and sapping the kolkhozes ... In the villages the kulaks of today and their henchmen, the anti-Soviet elements, usually masquerade as docile, sweet tempered, virtually saintly men. There is no need to hunt for them outside the kolkhozes—they are there, right inside them. ..."[3]

How was the campaign against these peasants to be organized, and what were the most effective methods to be used? "In my opinion," said Stalin, "our aims can best be achieved by political sections of the machine-and-tractor stations and sovkhozes."[4] The next question was to decide who could best be entrusted with direction of the entire campaign. Stalin's choice fell upon Kaganovich.

The man who was First Secretary of the Moscow City Committee, First Secretary of the Moscow Oblast Committee, and Second Secretary of the Party

---

[3] Stalin, *Voprosy leninizma*, pp. 398, 406.

[4] *Ibid.*, p. 409.

Central Committee, was now named All-Union Chief of Political Sections and was placed in charge of the Agricultural Department of the Party Central Committee. A total of 5,389 political sections, including 3,368 for machine-and-tractor stations and 2,021 for sovkhozes, were created, with 17,000 workers allocated to the former and 8,000 to the latter. Each political section was headed by a plenipotentiary extraordinary for agriculture, assisted by a deputy who was an OGPU worker and by a staff of overt and secret assistants.

The campaign against the peasants thus directed by Kaganovich lasted until November 1934. Additional millions of peasants were deported to Turkestan from Central Russia, the Ukraine, and the Caucasus, from Turkestan to Siberia, and from Siberia to Kolyma. A resolution of the November 1934 plenary session of the Central Committee, based on a report presented by Kaganovich, praised the policy adopted and the methods employed. "The Party," said the resolution, "assisted by the political sections, has to a great extent exposed and expelled from the kolkhozes and sovkhozes the anti-Soviet, anti-collective farm sabotaging and wrecking elements, kulaks and their supporters . . . Millions of kolkhoz workers have begun to understand the vital importance of granting *top priority* to fulfillment of their obligations to the state."[5]

Although the names of Kaganovich and Stalin will be linked together in history for their campaign of repression against the peasants under Kaganovich, in the eyes of Stalin, Kaganovich's main contribution was in a totally different field, namely, in creating conditions which made it possible to liquidate the old Leninist Party on the one hand, and to create a new Stalinist Party on the other, a step essential to the establishment of Stalin's personal dictatorship.

In order to attain this double objective the new general purge of the Party was required, the preceding purges having been inconclusive. This was the purge decided upon by the Politbureau in November 1932 and ratified by a plenary session of the Central Committee in January 1933. A central commission for purging the Party was appointed but the question of chairmanship proved difficult, as Kaganovich was absent "purging" the peasants. However, as the number of suitable candidates was limited, Stalin had no choice but to place Kaganovich at the head of the commission. The methods which he employed were the same as those he had applied to the peasantry—terror and provocation.

The 1937 edition of the *Small Soviet Encyclopedia* reported on Kaganovich's activities as follows: "Kaganovich, Secretary of the Central Commission and head of the Agricultural Section of the Central Commission in 1929–34, personally directed . . . the campaign against the sabotage of the peasants' liabilities to the government organized by the kulaks. As chairman of the central commission appointed to purge the Party, 1933–34, he directed the purge of the Party ranks."[6] In the course of a single year, Kaganovich was responsible for removing 362,429

---

[5] *KPSS v rezolyutsiyakh*, Vol. II, pp. 804–05.

[6] *Malaya Sovetskaya Entsiklopediya* (Small Soviet Encyclopedia), 2nd ed., Vol. V, Moscow, 1937, p. 128.

members.[7] His services received due recognition and at the Seventeenth Party Congress were rewarded by his election as Chairman of the Central Committee Commission on Party Control.

The purge had now reached its final stage—that of physical liquidation of "enemies of the people" both inside and outside the Party. Despite his great organizing ability it seemed probable that Kaganovich could not tackle this task singlehanded and at his request Yezhov was placed at his disposal, as deputy chairman of the Commission on Party Control. In 1935, after two years of collaboration between Kaganovich and Yezhov, Stalin decided that the deputy was as efficient as his chief and made Yezhov chairman of the commission and a Secretary of the Central Committee. A year later, in September 1936, Yezhov added to his duties that of People's Commissar of the Interior. Kaganovich retained his post as Second Secretary of the Central Committee up to the Eighteenth Party Congress in 1939, meanwhile taking a leading part in Yezhov's purge of the Party.

In 1935 Kaganovich handed over his duties as First Secretary of the Moscow Party Committee to another of his assistants—Khrushchev. From that time on Kaganovich was constantly shifted from one bottleneck to another. In the course of a few years, he headed at one time or another practically every economic department of the government—transport, heavy industry, fuel, oil, and building materials. Wherever he went, there followed a marked improvement in output. What was the secret of his "organizing ability?" Why was he so extraordinarily successful in solving the most intricate problems of economic leadership, in view of the fact that he was a self-taught man who lacked even an elementary education? It is true that in his youth Kaganovich had gained some experience in methods of industrial production. His official biographers relate that from the age of fourteen he went through a tough school as shoemaker, cutter, packer, loader, and private in World War I in reserve regiments in Saratov and Gomel. But with no more experience than this Kaganovich never hesitated to assume direction in industry and succeeded in ironing out many industrial problems.

The secret of Kaganovich's success was his use of the method he had so successfully applied in collectivization of the peasants and forcible delivery of grain; in short, not economic leadership, but wielding the heavy truncheon of the policeman. This is confirmed in his Soviet biography. "Between March 1935 and the end of 1937 the People's Commissar of Transport broke down the wrecking theory that railway transport was working 'to capacity.' Within a few months, under the direction of Kaganovich, the daily loading capacity of the railways was raised from 56,000 to 75,000 freight cars."[8]

Wherever Kaganovich appeared he at once found "wreckers" and began liquidation of the bottlenecks by liquidating the people concerned. During his term of office in 1935–39 as the head of the People's Commissariat of Transport and Heavy Industry every single director of the main directorates, every single director of a trust, every railway manager, every chairman of a political department of a railway, and every director of a larger enterprise was arrested.

---

[7] A. Abramov, in *ibid.*, 2nd ed., Vol. II, pp. 523–24.

[8] *Politichesky slovar* (Political Dictionary), Moscow, 1940, p. 236.

In his dual capacity as People's Commissar and Secretary of the Party Central Committee, Kaganovich faced a newly appointed official with the same unvarying condition—"fulfillment of the plan, or expulsion from the Party." In the circumstances of the time expulsion spelled imprisonment as a "wrecker" or "saboteur." The victim was left with no choice but to apply in his department the same methods of repression and coercion as those used by Kaganovich in Moscow. When it was found that even this system failed to produce the required results recourse was made to the rediscovered remedy of "eye-wash." The essence of this cure consisted in reports of "victory" which were submitted by local Party or state officials in the field of economy to Stalin and Kaganovich, with fictitious figures purporting to show the "fulfillment and overfulfillment" of the particular plan. This ingenious method rapidly became accepted practice as an effective measure of self-defense among officials responsible for Party economic policies. The very term "eye-wash" as a means of self-defense entered the Soviet dictionary. There is no doubt that the practice results from Kaganovich's methods of administration.

Stalin's disciples are now apt to speak of Stalin's anti-Semitism. Numerically, the hardest hit section of the intelligentsia, especially in the Party, were the Jews. Kaganovich is the only surviving member of the Old Bolsheviks of Jewish extraction. In the treatment of the Jews he played a shameful part. When Mikhailov, secretary of the Kalinin Oblast Party committee and a close relative of Mikhail Kalinin, the Chairman of the Supreme Soviet of the USSR, was arrested, even this weak-willed man was moved to send an ultimatum to Stalin demanding the release of Mikhailov under threat of refusal to sign future decrees of the Supreme Soviet. Mikhailov was at once set free, as Kalinin's signature was of greater value to Stalin than Mikhailov's dead body. Kaganovich, however, behaved quite differently when his own brothers were being "purged": (1) the manager of the Univermag department store in Kiev, (2) the secretary of the district committee in Gorky, and (3) the People's Commissar of the Aviation Industry in Moscow. It was reported that when their wives and children besought him to intervene in their behalf, his only answer was: "I have but one brother, and his name is Stalin!"

Many served Stalin because of fear. Kaganovich served him from conviction. The *Large Soviet Encyclopedia* (1937 edition) rightly said: "Kaganovich developed as political figure and Party leader under the personal tutorship of Comrade Stalin; he is now one of his most loyal disciples and assistants."[9] It is noteworthy that although Stalin's other disciples and comrades were described as "loyal," Kaganovich alone was called "most loyal."

After the war Stalin once more availed himself of Kaganovich's talent for organization and applied it in new repressions and purges. In the liberated Ukraine, where Khrushchev was patently unable to cope with the task, he was removed by Stalin in 1947 and replaced by Kaganovich as Secretary of the Party Central

---

[9] *BSE*, 1st ed., Vol. XXX, col. 517.

Committee of the Republic. Kaganovich soon proved that he had lost none of his former skill: hundreds of thousands of Ukrainians were deported to Central Asia, Kazakhstan, and Siberia as "Fascists" or "enemies of the people."

After Stalin's death the collective leadership concluded that the fate of the government's economic policy hinged, in the long run, on "productivity of labor," i.e., on the degree of exploitation to which the working classes could be subjected. A State Committee on Labor and Wages was formed. Kaganovich devoted his organizing ability to the work of the committee, but failed miserably. It was no longer possible to organize by terrorist methods while at the same time condemning Stalin for having used them. The government even found itself compelled to rescind the law treating tardiness and absenteeism as criminal offenses. The law, first introduced in 1940, had long since been rendered inoperative by the workers themselves.

For the time being, at least, the methods of coercion on which Kaganovich had built his reputation were no longer in demand, and neither was Kaganovich. In June 1956 he was relieved of his post and appointed Minister of Construction Industry.

Klim Voroshilov: (Born 1881, Party member from 1903). The biography of Voroshilov in the 1929 edition of the *Large Soviet Encyclopedia* described him as "a man of outstanding courage, exceptional energy, quick at finding his bearings in any circumstances, firm in his decisions, and ready unflinchingly to put these decisions into practice."[10] This description was deleted from later biographies. Time has shown that of all the qualities enumerated the ability to "find his bearings" rapidly was the only one that Voroshilov really possessed.

Voroshilov and Stalin had met at the Fourth and Fifth Party Congresses but the close association between them began in Tsaritsin in 1918. Voroshilov quickly discerned in Stalin a powerful personality whom it would be to his advantage to back in order to promote his own career. History has amply proven the wisdom of his decision.

Like many other Old Bolsheviks who were factory workers and who had joined the Party, but who during the Revolution were little more than passive representatives of the masses, Voroshilov lacked the special qualities needed for making a career after victory. He had joined the Party as a rebel against social injustice and not from ideological conviction. His life had been a hard one. At the age of seven he had been employed in a pyrite mine; at ten he and his father had herded cattle for a landowner. After that he had followed a variety of trades until at last he found work as a machinist in Lugansk. At the age of twelve, when he entered a rural primary school, which he attended for two winters only, he could neither read nor write, and this short period of study comprised his entire education at the time of the October Revolution.

Politically, however, he had a wider outlook than his friends, for at the time of the Revolution he was among the leaders of the Bolshevik city council of

---

[10] *Ibid.*, Vol. XIII, col. 175.

Lugansk, although prior to 1918 his fame had spread no farther than his native town. In 1918, when, after the breakdown of the Brest-Litovsk negotiations for a separate peace the Germans renewed their advance into the Ukraine, Voroshilov sent a telegram to Lenin and Trotsky saying that he was marching against the German Army "at the head of 600 men" with the intention of destroying these "butchers of the proletarian revolution."

The authorities in Moscow accepted his suggestion for organizing a "partisan movement" quite separate from the regular Red Army. With no previous military training of any kind (he had never served as a soldier), Voroshilov first quickly increased the size of his force and then gained official recognition from the two opposing sides: from the generals of the White Army, because of his daring raids, and from the Red High Command, impressed by the very idea of organizing guerilla warfare. Soon his detachment was reformed as the Fifth Ukrainian Army and dispatched to Tsaritsin, where it was renamed the Tenth Army. It was at Tsaritsin that Voroshilov received his political baptism and became Stalin's "friend and companion-in-arms." It must be added that this friendship rested upon a somewhat negative foundation, based as it was on a common policy of intrigue against Trotsky, the Commander in Chief of the Red Army.

The famous Military Opposition to Trotsky, led by Voroshilov, Yegorov, Minkin and a few others at the Eighth Party Congress in 1919, dated back to the days of Tsaritsin. The "Tsaritsin group" of proletarian commanders, consisting of Voroshilov and his friends, criticized Trotsky's policy of employing "bourgeois" and "tsarist" professional soldiers in responsible Red Army posts and the Army Staff. Trotsky's line of reasoning was both logical and simple. First, "the proletariat lacks properly trained general staff officers," and second "by the hands and brains of one set of bourgeois we are beating other bourgeois." The moving spirit and behind-the-scenes organizer of the Military Opposition was Stalin himself, but he kept out of sight until he could learn what Lenin had to say on the subject.

As soon as it was apparent that Lenin strongly disapproved of the line taken by the partisan commanders and that he wholeheartedly supported Trotsky, Stalin came into the open and severely censored Voroshilov and his friends. Voroshilov again proved his quick grasp of essentials. He realized at once that Stalin was merely manoeuvring for position while waiting for better days to come and that he was doing so both in his own interest and in that of Voroshilov. The better days dawned after the end of the Civil War. In 1921, on Stalin's recommendation, the "partisan leader" Voroshilov was appointed commanding officer of the North Caucasus Military District. At the Tenth Party Congress, in 1921, again on Stalin's recommendation, Voroshilov was elected to membership in the Party Central Committee.

In 1924, when making preparations for the struggle with Trotsky, Stalin obtained for Voroshilov appointment as commander of the Moscow Military District in place of the Trotskyite Muralov. On January 8, 1925, Trotsky was relieved of his post as Chairman of the Revolutionary Military Council of the

USSR and People's Commissar for the Army and Navy. Stalin obviously wished, even in these early days, to push Voroshilov into the posts vacated by Trotsky, but Trotsky's deputy, Mikhail Frunze, had universally and irrevocably been recognized as his successor. Accepting the inevitable, and also wishing to draw Frunze into his own camp, Stalin supported his candidature at the January 1925 plenary session of the Party Central Committee. Frunze took Trotsky's place, while Voroshilov was compelled to wait. However, he did not have to wait long: Frunze died in the summer of the same year.

Voroshilov now became the chief of the armed forces of the USSR. He was duly grateful and henceforth had an active part in all the crimes committed by Stalin in the name of the Red Army. After the rout of both the Trotskyite Left Opposition and the New Opposition of Kamenev and Zinoviev, Voroshilov, together with Molotov, was granted membership in the Politburo in 1926, a position which he continued to hold thereafter.

Voroshilov was never of great importance as a political leader and became head of the Red Army, not because of his ability as military leader, but because of his status as a politician of the Stalinist school. That he was in this school at all was due, not to conviction, but to the shrewd suspicion that it would benefit his career.

Stalin was well aware of the foibles of his disciples and knew how to exploit them to further his own ends. An inordinate partiality for the fair sex, fondness for vodka, and a passion for decorations were Voroshilov's weak points. According to Trotsky, Stalin knew from the early years of his ascent to power how to gratify such weaknesses on the part of his followers. However, Stalin practiced this policy of "bread and circuses" with moderation in regard to himself and his friends, an appearance of asceticism being dictated by the eventual but as yet unknown outcome of his struggle for power. He wished to convince the people that the men in the Kremlin were near-saints, a group of idealists who, for the sake of the Communist morrow, were ready to sacrifice their personal lives of today. Of all his followers Voroshilov was least suited to fill this role. For this reason Stalin made him a private drinking companion. It is of interest that of all the members of the Politburo Voroshilov was the only one referred to in the official press as Stalin's "companion-in-arms and personal friend."

In the matter of bestowing decorations Stalin was far more generous. At the end of the Civil War Voroshilov could only boast of two "Orders of the Red Banner" as against five apiece for Bluecher, Fedko, and Fabricius. By World War II Stalin had raised the number of Voroshilov's orders to four, and when, during the Yezhov purge, the holders of five orders were all executed with Voroshilov's assistance (except Fabricius who is reported to have died earlier in an air crash) Voroshilov automatically became the "first cavalier" and "first marshal" of the USSR.

Stalin needed Voroshilov less as a political worker than as a tool for furthering his own policy. At the time, Voroshilov was the only member of the Politburo who could rightly claim that "among all of you former petty bourgeois, I am the only proletarian straight from the lathe." He was also the only "Red

Commander" of the Civil War in the Politburo. In the early twenties, in his attempt to emphasize his own part in the Civil War, Stalin popularized Tsaritsin and the role of Voroshilov and in 1925 had Tsaritsin renamed Stalingrad at the suggestion of Voroshilov and his friends. Stalin returned the compliment by changing the name of Lugansk to Voroshilovgrad.

This building of Voroshilov's reputation as the first "Red Officer" (there was a song of that title) and an Old Bolshevik and "locksmith from Lugansk" was aimed at aiding Stalin in reaching his goal of seizing personal power. In this respect the services which Voroshilov could render to Stalin may only be compared with the help he received from Molotov and Kaganovich. Stalin well knew what he was about when he claimed for Voroshilov the titles of "Hero of the Civil War" and "Proletarian General." He was deliberately establishing the trustworthiness of a witness who would publicly confess to his own worthlessness in order to enhance the fame of his benefactor. The story of Stalin's former life, before and during the Revolution and Civil War, was much too drab, colorless, and unsuitable for "Lenin's foremost helper and disciple," as he was now being described. A new biography had to be invented.

In the new biography of Stalin the history of the Party was ably dealt with by two civilians, Molotov and Kaganovich. An expert was needed to edit the military part. This avowed expert was Voroshilov. Aided by Stalin's personal archives he was given the task, unthinkable before 1929, of substituting Stalin for Trotsky as the real leader of the Red Army in the Civil War.

The deliberate distortion of history is no easy task at any time, and particularly so if the majority of the protagonists are still alive. Voroshilov's falsification of the history of the Civil War was a stupendous achievement. In a preliminary sketch, "Stalin and the Red Army," published December 21, 1929, Voroshilov wrote:

> Much has happened within the past five or six years, during which Comrade Stalin has stood at the very center of the developing struggle for the Party and for socialism. It is exclusively due to this fact that the full importance of Comrade Stalin's share in the planning of our victories in the Civil War has as yet not received the recognition it deserves and has to a certain extent been overshadowed by these events. Today, on the fiftieth anniversary of our friend, it is my wish at least partly to amend this omission.[11]

What was so important about Stalin's share in the victories of the Civil War? Voroshilov revealed it as a sensational piece of news:

> From 1918 to 1920 Stalin was in all probability the only man moved by the Central Committee from one battlefront to another and dispatched to the sectors where the Revolution faced the greatest dangers and was most seriously threatened. No one saw Stalin either on relatively quiet sectors of the front or in those areas where we were victorious. But Comrade Stalin was ever present where. . . the Red Armies were on the point of breaking, or where the counterrevolutionary forces seemed to threaten the very existence of the Soviet state.[12]

---

[11] K. Voroshilov, *Stalin i vooruzhennye sily SSSR* (Stalin and the Armed Forces of the USSR), Moscow, 1951, pp. 7—8.

[12] *Ibid.*

After thus boldly contradicting the facts and records of history, Voroshilov went on to prove that "the Supreme Command of the Red Army, headed by Trotsky and his staff, sabotaged the victory of the Army on all the fronts in the Civil War, while Stalin, battling on two fronts—against the leaders of the Red Army and against the White Armies—saved the Soviet regime."

Ten years later, in 1939, it appeared to Voroshilov that even he had undervalued Stalin in the article written in 1929. He had then referred to him as "one of the planners of the victories in the Civil War," albeit an "omnipresent" planner. Now, in harmony with Stalin's progress along the road to "the cult of the individual" it transpired that he was no longer merely one of the planners but had been solely responsible for the Red Army's victories and had also been its creator. "Many volumes will be written about Stalin, the creator of the Red Army, the organizer of its victories, the genius by whom it was inspired, the author of the strategy and tactics of the proletarian revolution."[13]

Very soon, however, this too struck Voroshilov, i.e., Stalin, as inadequate. As far as the Civil War was concerned, Stalin had long since taken the place of Trotsky; he had even substituted himself for Lenin as "the author of the strategy and tactics of the proletarian revolution." What Stalin required now was removal of Lenin from his seat as the "leader" of the Revolution and recognition by the Party Central Committee of himself as a "companion-in-arms" rather than a "disciple" of Lenin. These new "facts" were promptly confirmed by Voroshilov. "Only Stalin, Lenin's closest companion-in-arms, was the direct organizer and leader of the proletarian revolution and of its armed forces." (In the interests of historical truth it should be noted that in 1938 a mythical "Party Center" responsible for directing the October coup d'état and allegedly presided over by Stalin had been mentioned in the *Short Course in the History of the Communist Party of Bolsheviks*. In fact there had been only two centers at the time: the Politburo, under Lenin, and the Military Revolutionary Committee, under Trotsky.)

A decade later, in 1949, having exhausted his entire stock of nouns and adjectives in his glorification of Stalin, Voroshilov resorted to planetary terminology:

> The Soviet people, together with the entire human race, is today celebrating the seventieth anniversary of the greatest man on our planet, Joseph Vissarionovich Stalin. . . . The Great Patriotic War and its victory will be recorded in history as a triumphant and glorious testimony to the strategic genius and leadership of the great Stalin.[14]

Voroshilov's part was not, of course, limited to the composition of panegyrics to Stalin. For twenty-six years he was a leading member of Stalin's Politburo, throughout the period when, according to Stalin's disciples, Stalin committed his most atrocious crimes. History will prove that not one of them was perpetrated without the signed approval of Voroshilov, Molotov, Kaganovich, Mikoyan, or others.

---

[13] *Ibid.*, p. 66.
[14] *Ibid.*, *pp.* 89, 129.

Throughout the purge from 1936 to 1939, for which Stalin was later blamed by his successors, Voroshilov's behavior was particularly revolting. All of his comrades among the highranking officers of the Red Army, his former superiors in the Civil War, his peacetime subordinates, were betrayed by him to be butchered by Yezhov. He may not have been responsible for initiating the slaughter, yet the fact remains that he never once raised his voice to mitigate this wholesale butchery of loyal generals and army commanders. Even after such members and alternate members of the Politburo as Rudzutak, Ordzhonikidze, Kosior, Chubar, and Postyshev had demanded that Stalin abandon this senseless extermination of army and civilian personnel, Voroshilov, together with Molotov, Kaganovich, and Mikoyan, not only insisted on continuation of the purge, but even called for liquidation of the protesting members as "Bukharinite appeasers." According to data carefully checked and verified, Voroshilov's contribution to the purge of Red Army commanders resulted in the execution of 3 out of 5 marshals, 13 out of 15 army commanders, 57 out of 85 corps commanders, 110 out of 195 division commanders, and 220 out of 406 brigadier generals. These figures relate to the command staff alone. Khrushchev cited a total of 5,000 officers executed. An Army order of the time read: "No highranking or senior command-ing officer may be arrested without the approval of the People's Commissar for Defense." Voroshilov could not have acted otherwise. Stalin and he were bound to each other by a common tie of mutual responsibility for these crimes.

The main factor which enabled Voroshilov to maintain his position until Stalin's death was his personal loyalty to the dictator. If, as Khrushchev has stated, Stalin toward the end of his days refused to allow Voroshilov to continue in the Politburo because he was an English spy, this was not an indication of treachery on the part of Voroshilov, but reflected a firm determination by Stalin to rid himself of political deadwood. In Voroshilov's case this was easier for Stalin to accomplish because World War II soon shattered the legend of in-vincibility built around the "proletarian general" and "first marshal" of the USSR. As commander in chief of the Northwestern Group of Armies at the beginning of the war, Voroshilov proved himself utterly incapable and later on, in 1944, Stalin removed him from the State Committee of Defense. It was at this time that he was given the task for which he was best suited, that of chief of staff of the partisan movement.

His subsequent appointment to the innocuous chairmanship of the Supreme Soviet of the USSR, after the death of Stalin, followed in the natural course of events.

Anastas Mikoyan: (Born 1895, Party member from 1915). Mikoyan was born in Georgia as the son of a small Armenian merchant (long since officially transferred by his biographers to the class of "workers"). Intending to become a priest of the Armenian Gregorian Church, Mikoyan attended the Armenian theological seminary in Tiflis. His interest in politics dates back to his days in the seminary, where he became a member of a group of young Constitutional Democrats. Later his thinking was influenced by the Georgian Socialists (he spoke Georgian fluently) and in 1915 he transferred to a group of Social Democrats. His sympathies wavered between the Bolsheviks, Mensheviks, and the Armenian nationalist Dashnaks until the Bolsheviks were victorious in Central Russia.

There was, however, in Mikoyan's prerevolutionary life one black spot which provided Stalin with an excuse for blackmailing him throughout the rest of his life. This was in connection with the case of the "26 Baku commissars" (Shaumyan, Dzhaparidze, Fioletov, Azizbekov, and others) shot by the British in September 1918. The details were as follows:

At the time of the Revolution, Mikoyan was living in Baku, where he remained during the subsequent occupation of the city first by the Turks and then by the British. His latest biography describes him as a prominent and active Bolshevik and credits him with editing the newspapers *Social Democrat* and *Izvestia of the Baku Soviet* (predominantly Menshevik and Social Revolutionary). The fact remains, however, that although he was arrested together with the 26 commissars, he was not shot, whereas some of those executed were non-Party office workers of the Baku Soviet. Not only was his life spared, but he was soon released from prison and returned as a free man to British-occupied Baku from Krasnovodsk to which the arrested commissars had been removed. Why had the British and the anti-Bolshevik Transcaucasian government, which executed even the non-Party members of the Baku Soviet, released Mikoyan, a Bolshevik since 1915?

Mikoyan's official biographer gives the answer furnished by Mikoyan himself: "Mikoyan's name was not included in the list of arrested persons published by the Baku newspapers, nor on the rations list—a fact to which he owes his life, whereas several non-Party members, three officials of the Baku Soviet (Mishne and others), were shot."[15]

After the execution of the "26," Mikoyan spent some time in prison but again benefitted mysteriously from what appears to have been inexplicable magnanimity or even weakness on the part of the British, at any rate as described by Mikoyan's biographer:

> Mikoyan's great wish was to reach Baku. He was planning an escape from jail, but as it turned out this proved unnecessary, since the British forces of occupation were compelled to release him at the demand of the Baku workers and, together with a group of Baku deportees, return him to Baku under convoy from beyond the Caspian.[16]

After Mikoyan was returned to occupied Baku in March 1919 he was soon "at the head of the Bolshevik organization of Baku." Although twice more detained by the British in Baku itself, on each occasion he was quickly released. After a short time he settled in Social Democratic Georgia, where he was once more arrested but where, according to his biographer, he succeeded in "bribing" his way to freedom—proof that he was well supplied with funds. From Georgia

---

[15] *BSE*, 1st ed., Vol. XXXIX, col. 344.
[16] *Ibid.*

he journeyed to Moscow in order to obtain "instructions from Lenin and Stalin," and "returned to Baku on April 28, 1920, on the first armored train of the Red Army."[17]

If this career had been examined through Stalin's criminal lens, it would have been easy for Vyshinsky, in the course of the Moscow trials, to furnish him with a far more credible biography than any of those which he and Stalin had concocted for the other Old Bolsheviks. It is not too difficult to imagine that it would have read as follows: "Mikoyan came from a bourgeois family and was an agent of the Constitutional Democrat secret service. He was a German and Turkish spy, enlisted during the German occupation of Azerbaidzhan. During the British occupation of Baku he was employed by the British. He was then an agent provocateur of the British secret service and it was he who had betrayed the 26 Baku commissars to the British, his arrest being a blind staged by the British in order to provide suitable cover for their agent." This was the black spot in Mikoyan's life which gave Stalin a means of blackmailing him during his entire career.

It was quite in keeping with Stalin's character to surround himself with persons whose reputations were blemished or who were in some other way vulnerable. Men of this stamp blindly shared in Stalin's crimes for fear of being called to account for real or imaginary misdeeds, for instance such former Mensheviks as Menzhinsky, Yaroslavsky, Kuibyshev, and Vyshinsky. Mikoyan was such a person.

Although not a Stalinist by nature, Mikoyan was caught in Stalin's net from the very beginning of the Secretary-General's career. He served him not from conviction but from fear. The perpetual threat of being exposed as a spy and agent provocateur compelled him to subscribe to all of Stalin's crimes, which he probably would not have done under normal circumstances. It was this factor, too, which helped him to outdo his colleagues in the Politburo in their panegyrics of Stalin. The Byzantine flattery which he lavished on the dictator was so cunningly molded and expressed that it never betrayed the inner falsehood of its author. And yet, to the last, Stalin never completely trusted him. Of all the former and present members of the Politburo, Mikoyan was the only one to spend nine years (1926–35) as alternate member, and to be by-passed by his colleagues Andreyev, Kosior, Ordzhonikidze, and so on, who were at once admitted as full members.

At first, Stalin had certain plans mapped out for Mikoyan's future which he afterward transferred to Kaganovich. As soon as he was appointed Secretary-General of the Central Committee, Stalin procured for Mikoyan in 1922 the position of Secretary of the Southeastern Bureau of the Party Central Committee (later the North Caucasus district committee) in Rostov-on-Don; later, at the Eleventh Party Congress, and before Kaganovich, he was elected member of the Party Central Committee. In 1926 Stalin replaced Kamenev by Mikoyan

---

[17] *Ibid.*, pp. 345–46.

as USSR People's Commissar of Trade and immediately made him an alternate member of the then all-powerful Politburo.

At the age of 30 Mikoyan was the youngest minister in the USSR. A certain parallellism in their lives probably influenced Stalin in his choice of Mikoyan. Both were Caucasians, both spoke Georgian, both had studied in theological seminaries, and both were acquainted with each other's past failures and flaws. Mikoyan thus seemed a far more suitable tool for furthering Stalin's policy than Molotov, Kaganovich, or Voroshilov. But there came the day when Mikoyan's qualities were put to the test. The campaign against the Rightists was about to start the last decisive and culminating stage in Stalin's struggle for personal dictatorship and the last, and decisive, chance for gifted demagogues and plotters to win promotion from "activist" to member of the Central Committee, from member of the Central Committee to alternate member of the Politburo, and from alternate member to full member. In this struggle a few hitherto quite unknown individuals who, under Lenin, would not have been allowed to cross the threshold of the Central Committee succeeded in making brilliant careers for themselves and at once finding their way into the Politburo, while Mikoyan, after the final defeat of the Rightists, lingered on as an alternate member for another five years.

It is, of course, quite impossible to believe that Mikoyan had offered any opposition to the débâcle of the Rightists or to the measures taken preparatory to the Great Purge. (Such fairy tales can only be told in the Kremlin, post factum, today.) The real reason was that the Georgian Cheka officials, headed by Beria, had for years besieged Stalin with denunciations of Mikoyan, founded on reports unearthed from former archives. Stalin had carefully stored them and used them as a means of frightening Mikoyan, while keeping them in the background pending events.

The last stage, that of physical destruction of the opposition, both active and potential, was finally reached. Its details need not be repeated here. It was in Mikoyan's favor that his life offered no potential threat to Stalin. His star, which by then was shining rather dimly, began to rise the moment Stalin had shown his hand and openly set his course on the worst aspects of Bolshevism. In 1935, together with Zhdanov, he was admitted to full membership in the Politburo, while Yezhov was made Secretary of the Central Committee and Chairman of the Party Control Commission.

At the Twentieth Party Congress, in 1956, the wily Mikoyan attempted to produce political and historical alibis both for himself and for the other members of the inquisition. His statement that "we have had no collective leadership for about 20 years" implied that from 1933–34 on Stalin had ruled the country as sole dictator and was thus solely responsible for all the crimes committed, including the Great Purge. As a result of this really "historical" speech by Mikoyan many foreign observers, and particularly the American press, took the view that Mikoyan was the real initiator of Stalin's dethroning at the Twentieth Party Congress and that it was he who compelled the "wavering"

Khrushchev and the other members of the Central Committee Presidium to launch the campaign against "the cult of Stalin" and Stalin's crimes. Some even went so far as to assert that Mikoyan was Khrushchev's rival for leadership of the Party!

It requires no special insight into the Party affairs of the Kremlin, but merely a fairly accurate appreciation of Mikoyan's character, to be quite sure that his speech had been stenciled and given final editing by the majority of the Politburo, led by Khrushchev himself. Why was Mikoyan allotted this particular role? There are several possibilities, but one aspect is quite clear: the dethroning of Stalin would have to be announced by one of the older members of the Politburo and, preferably, by one of the least personally implicated in the crimes of Stalin and the NKVD. From this point of view, Molotov, Kaganovich, and Voroshilov were obviously unsuitable. There remained only Mikoyan, who had served out of fear, not devotion or conviction.

I shall not dwell on a description of Mikoyan's business ability, with which I am not well acquainted. Apparently his official reputation as a gifted "Red merchant" is based on fact, although the scale and scope of his commercial transactions was never particularly impressive. There is an anecdote in which a group of peasants and workers recommends to the Academy of Sciences of the USSR the abolition of the letter "M" in the Russian alphabet, as being of no further use. The reason given was the fact that there was no longer any margarine, any macaroni, any meat, or any manufactured goods. There was only Mikoyan and it was hardly worth while retaining the letter solely for his sake.

Georgy Malenkov: (Born 1902, Party member since 1920.) The present Communist Party of the Soviet Union was fathered by two men—Stalin and Malenkov. It is true that it was built up by Stalin, but only with Malenkov's aid. Malenkov entered upon technical work in the Party Central Committee in 1925, after studying for four years at the Moscow Higher Technical School. Until 1930 he worked under Poskrebyshev, first in the Special Section and later, which was more important, in Comrade Stalin's Secretariat.

Not all the members of the Central Committee were acquainted with what went on in the Politburo; Malenkov was its recording secretary. Only a few members of the Politburo knew what took place in Comrade Stalin's Secretariat; Malenkov was in charge of the personnel section. He had been "discovered" by Kaganovich and it was with his help that he received the official Party status which was a prerequisite for becoming a member of the Central Committee and the Politburo. His first official appearance was in 1930 when Kaganovich was appointed First Secretary of the Moscow Party Committee and made Malenkov his personnel chief. Under the personal direction of Kaganovich, Malenkov was able to demonstrate in practice the full possibilities of the Stalinist technique of using personnel.

The Moscow Party organization—the largest and most important local Party organization—had for long been led and influenced by such Rightists as Uglanov, Kotov, Ukhanov, and Ryutin. Only the top echelons of the organization had suffered after the defeat of the Bukharinites and of Uglanov's Moscow leadership, while the lower and middle echelons had remained unaffected. Malenkov now took them in hand. But his authority spread beyond the personnel of Moscow City and Moscow Oblast to the Party organizations of the People's Commissariats in Moscow. During his four years of work in the Moscow Committee Malenkov drastically purged the Party organization, on all these levels, of former right-wing "compromisers" and of all who had failed correctly to gauge the temper of the times.

Malenkov's work was duly given recognition as an excellent example of "Stalinist organizational leadership." The Seventeenth Party Congress was convened—the last congress under the old "collective leadership." In his report to the congress Stalin devoted the entire closing portion to "problems of organizational leadership." In this connection he sounded his new note on the role and importance of "organizational policy." "Good resolutions and declarations in favor of the general Party line," he said, "are only a beginning; they express a will to conquer but not victory. Once the right Party line is given, success must depend on organization: organization of the struggle to apply the general Party line in practice and on the right choice of men." Among other aims, the new "organizational policy" must include a tightened check on performance, "the unmasking and dismissal of incorrigible bureaucrats in administrative apparatuses," the dismissal of persons infringing Party decisions, the purging of Soviet economic organizations, and the purging of "unreliable and degenerate elements from the Party."[18]

Who within the Party could tackle these decisive problems involved in the new "organizational policy" on which depended the success or failure of the political line? Who could most consistently and efficiently prepare the Party personnel administration for the great purge of both Party and country thus foreshadowed by Stalin? Stalin could find no such person in the Central Committee elected by the Twelfth Party Congress. He entrusted the application of the new "organizational policy" to Malenkov, whom he placed in charge of the section responsible for personnel of the leading organs of the Party Central Committee.

Henceforth the fate of the members of the Central Committee no longer depended on a member of the Central Committee. The sides of the inner "triangle" of the forthcoming purge were now joined together, with Kaganovich as Secretary of the Central Committee and Chairman of the Party Control Commission, Yezhov as member of the Organization Bureau and vice-chairman of the Party Control Commission, and Malenkov in charge of the Organization and Political Section of the Central Committee. Stalin had merely to lay down the "correct political line." The "triangle" decided the fate of that line. The organization apparatus of the Central Committee was involved to the hilt in a deep conspiracy against its own Party.

---

[18] Stalin, *Voprosy leninizma*, pp. 476–79.

The so-called "check of Party membership cards" in 1935, conducted under the personal guidance of Yezhov and Malenkov, was in reality a preliminary, although thoroughly prepared, investigation into the character of each individual Communist. Previously, the Central Committee had held only the registration cards of Party members. From now on a personal file was kept on each Communist. These files contained, in addition to questionnaires filled in by the person himself, other questionnaires completed by special sections of the Party apparatus and by secret political sections of the NKVD, in which "specialists" of the special sections and "psychologists" of the NKVD assessed at their own discretion the value of the Communist in the past and his potential worth in future, including a prophecy whether he would be an obedient tool of the apparatus or a potential "enemy of the people."

By the spring of 1935 Yezhov was firmly established as Chairman of the Party Control Commission and Secretary of the Central Committee. In September 1935 a meeting was convened of Malenkov's section and its subordinate organs attended by the heads of the Organization and Political Sections, to make a preliminary evaluation of the results of the Party check. Malenkov conducted the meeting and Yezhov was the chief speaker. He pointed out the defects in the work done and outlined the new problems facing the Party apparatus in probing deeper into the internal life of the Party. Malenkov, according to reports of the meeting, concurred completely with every statement made by Yezhov: "Comrade Yezhov is quite right. . . . Comrade Yezhov has fully explained all the problems. . . ."[19]

The gigantic task, still on an exploratory basis, performed by the Party apparatus in preparation for the purge was not completed within the year assigned and was continued in 1936. By then Yezhov had begun to assume an air of importance and even presumed occasionally to "teach" Malenkov. In May 1936, having temporarily forgotten the existence of Stalin, Malenkov, as editor-in-chief of *Party Construction*, referred to Yezhov in terms which had hitherto been exclusively reserved for Stalin. "Comrade Yezhov," said Malenkov's press organ, "teaches us how we should reshape our Party work and raise the level of our organizational work to a higher level [and] we must carry out these instructions."[20]

Malenkov was not attempting to create a "Cult of Yezhov" (this was being successfully done by *Pravda*): he was making an admission of defeat as a badly beaten competitor. Stalin had chosen to favor Yezhov, and Malenkov and Kaganovich had to be content with being Yezhov's assistants.

Soon after the appointment of Yezhov as Commissar of Internal Affairs, in September 1936, Malenkov changed his tone from one of bitter admission to one of exaggerated flattery, in accordance with the desire of Stalin. At the height of the purge, in December 1937, his magazine declared:

---

[19] *Partiinoye stroieltstvo*, February 1935, cited in M. Ebon, *Malenkov*, London, 1953, p. 35.
[20] *Ibid.*

Directed by the Stalinist People's Commissar, Comrade Yezhov, the Soviet intelligence service is mercilessly liquidating the Fascist bandits. The trusted guardian of socialism—the NKVD—under the leadership of the Stalinist People's Commissar, Comrade Yezhov, will continue to destroy and eradicate the enemies of the people.... The NKVD, the punitive arm of the Soviet people, will complete their destruction! We send our ardent greetings to the Stalinist People's Commissar of Internal Affairs, Nicholai Ivanovich Yezhov.[21]

Malenkov, was, of course, telling the truth. The "organizational policy" worked out by the "triangle" prior to Yezhov's appointment had been handed over to the NKVD "for implementation." Nevertheless, he was only an executor, not an organizer; the real promoters responsible for the purge were Stalin, Kaganovich, Molotov, Yezhov, Vyshinsky, Andreyev, and Malenkov in the Politburo.

Vyshinsky and Malenkov were the only two of the seven named above who were neither members nor alternate members of the Central Committee, but they were jointly responsible with their colleagues for the activities of Yezhov. Malenkov's role in the ultimate downfall of Yezhov has never been ascertained; whatever it was, it could only have been that of a competitor, not a foe. Notwithstanding the present-day protests of Stalin's disciples against charges of collaboration either with Stalin or with Yezhov, the fact remains that Yezhov, at the time, was genuinely interpreting the collective policy of the men in the Politburo who had managed to survive the purge or had gained admittance to the Politburo as a result of it, such as Khrushchev, Zhdanov, Beria, and Malenkov, not one of whom would have had the slightest chance of getting into the Politburo without prior liquidation of the old Party and its members.

Neither the high opinion he had formed of Malenkov nor the important role which he had planned for him in the future were sufficiently compelling reasons to give even Stalin the necessary courage to recommend Malenkov to the Seventeenth Party Congress as a possible alternate member of the Central Committee, although Khrushchev and Beria were elected as members and Bulganin as an alternate. The old Leninist Party had to be liquidated before Malenkov could gain de jure recognition of his de facto status as architect of the Party. It was only after this that Malenkov was elected member of the Central Committee, member of the Organization Bureau and personnel secretary of the Central Committee.

The services rendered to Stalin by Malenkov during the Great Purge are only comparable to those of Yezhov and Vyshinsky. I have described elsewhere the results of the purge from 1933 to 1939 as it affected the Party. The arresting of millions of Party Communists was primarily the work of Malenkov.

At the same time when he was destroying the old Leninist Party, Malenkov was building up the new Stalinist Party. During the six months from April to October, 1939, 800,000 new Communists were admitted to the Party to replace those who had been liquidated, although under normal conditions of voluntary

---

[21] *Ibid.*, p. 36.

entry the Party never added more than 100,000 members in a full year. Malenkov proved that his "organizational policy" was able to perform miracles in this field. After the Yezhov reign of terror the conscription of members presented no difficulties. There were few who had the temerity to decline the "honor" of joining the Party whenever the suggestion to do so was made by the secretary of the local Party committee. Yezhov had departed, but Beria and Malenkov were very much present.

The average Soviet citizen, intimidated and terrorized, much preferred a membership card to denunciation to the NKVD by a Party secretary. Naturally there were some who joined the Party voluntarily, but they were job hunters, not idealists. However, both categories—the conscripts and the volunteers—were now convinced that the Central Committee no longer existed for them, but that they existed for the Central Committee. As a result of this belief there grew up a new concept of the Party, still generally held, that the Party meant the Secretariat of the Central Committee. This, too, was a brilliant victory for Malenkov's "organizational policy." It was far easier to direct and control the cells of a Party based on these principles than to deal with the kolkhozes. There was no need for reports, congresses, or elections.

For thirteen years Malenkov held his post as Secretary of the Central Committee of a Party organized along these lines. During the thirteen years only one Party congress was convened—a reflection of Malenkov's success in molding for Stalin a monolithic Party devoid of any pretentions of its own. The massive achievements of Malenkov were genuinely appreciated by Stalin, who rewarded his work of destroying the old Party by making him Secretary of the Central Committee, and his help in creating a new one by making him an alternate member of the Politburo.

On the outbreak of war the Committee of State Defense created on June 30, 1941, assumed all powers vested in the Politburo and the cabinet. Originally the Committee consisted of five members—Stalin as chairman, Molotov as deputy chairman, Voroshilov, Beria, and Malenkov—and passed over such old members of the Politburo as Kaganovich, Mikoyan, Kalinin, Andreyev, Zhdanov, and Khrushchev. When, after the end of the war, Malenkov became a full member of the Politburo in 1946 this was considered a matter of course.

Malenkov, the son of a tsarist civil servant, the "volunteer" who had spent a year (1919–20) as clerk in the political section of a Red Army regiment in Turkestan when the Civil War had virtually come to an end, the student who had failed to complete his course in a technical school, the undistinguished recording secretary of the Central Committee apparatus, now became the second most influential figure in the great "proletarian" state, so powerful that he alone of those who later survived to become members of the "collective leadership" had the temerity openly to contradict Stalin.

By the time of Stalin's death the Party and the entire Party apparatus were in fact in Malenkov's hands. Unlike the others, he had established an association with Lenin while Stalin was still alive, when, in the presence of the Party Central

Committee and the Council of Ministers of the USSR on the occasion of his fiftieth anniversary, he was spoken of as "the disciple of Lenin and companion-in-arms of Stalin."[22] Although he had never seen Lenin and had been the disciple of Stalin to the marrow of his bones, he was unwilling to be called his disciple in public. People had been dispatched by the dictator to the next world for such insolence. But nothing happened to Malenkov. On the contrary, at the Nineteenth Party Congress in October 1952 it was Malenkov who read the political report for the Party Central Committee, something which should have been done by Stalin himself.

After this it was clear to all that he either enjoyed the complete confidence of Stalin, who had earmarked him as his successor, or had developed into a power which even Stalin had to take into account. In the light of events after Stalin's death the last seems most probable.

There are grounds for believing that at the first plenary session of the Central Committee after the Nineteenth Party Congress, while Stalin was still alive, Malenkov assumed the position of First Secretary of the Central Committee when Stalin relinquished his position as Secretary-General. As it is highly improbable that Stalin voluntarily abandoned his Party position to Malenkov, it must be accepted that Stalin was seeking revenge. The case of the Kremlin doctors was the beginning. It was Malenkov's rivals, the former secretaries of the Central Committee and members of the Politburo Zhdanov and Shcherbakov, that the doctors were accused of murdering.

Versed as he was in Stalin's methods, Malenkov could not but know at whom he was really aiming. Stalin succeeded in arresting the doctors, but failed to bring them to trial. He died and they were released. After Stalin's death Malenkov became Prime Minister and First Secretary of the Central Committee.

However, the Old Guard of the Politburo was not inclined to approve the emergence of another Stalin, and even Malenkov must have fully realized that this was a goal beyond his powers. When he relinquished his post as First Secretary of the Central Committee to Khrushchev without a struggle, this was the beginning of his downfall. Cut off from the Party apparatus and member of a Central Committee Presidium from which all his supporters had been expelled, he was forced to recognize "the Leninist principle of collective leadership," in a speech of March 15, 1953.

In February 1955 he was removed from his post as Prime Minister. On this occasion, too, he gave in without a fight, in the deep conviction that the time of a "second edition" of his rule was yet to come

His self-discipline, his exceptional patience, his reticence, his dry realism in practical matters, his wealth of experience in political intrigue, and his elastic Communist conscience combined to make Malenkov a dangerous rival of other members of the collective leadership.

---

[22] *Pravda*, April 8, 1952.

Nikolai Bulganin: (Born 1896, Party member since 1917.) Bulganin's career to the middle thirties was not particularly outstanding, although he had taken part in the Civil War, had joined the Party in 1917 during the Revolution, and for some years had worked in various departments of the Cheka in Nizhny Novgorod (Gorky) and Turkestan. He had no easy road to success, notwithstanding the exceptionally important part he played in forging Stalin's conspiratorial technique at the time when Uglanov's leadership in Moscow was being broken and the Right Opposition destroyed. He was always battling against a handicap, which in those days counted for much: his origin in a "socially alien stratum," to use the contemporary expression. His father was an important industrialist, a member of the bourgeoisie, and his place of birth, Nizhny Novgorod, was a typical Russian commercial center.

From the very beginning of the Bolshevik uprising, Bulganin participated vigorously in the Cheka activities in order to stress his personal animosity to his own class. For many of the opportunists in the Bolshevik Party, this was the road to social rehabilitation. The Cheka was composed of persons of two kinds. It was headed by such Bolshevik fanatics as Dzerzhinsky, Menzhinsky, Yagoda, and Yezhov, while its agents, informers, and spies were "renegades" and former "bourgeois." It is probable that Bulganin belonged to this second group. During the period of Lenin, Trotsky, and Bukharin, when the universal cult of the "dictatorship of the proletariat" was in style, the members of this second group had no possibility of moving up to the top posts in the regime, being handicapped by the stigma of their social origin. Bulganin was one of those prepared to accept any assignment, provided the regime would grant him recognition.

In 1918–19 these efforts brought him into contact with the Old Bolshevik Lazar Kaganovich, who was then a member of the Party provincial committee in Bulganin's native city of Nizhny Novgorod. In 1920, when Kaganovich was appointed as a Party leader in Turkestan and made a member of the Military Revolutionary Council for the Turkestan Front he took Bulganin with him and placed him in the Special Section and the Political Administration of the Red Army in Turkestan.

In 1922 Bulganin accompanied Kaganovich to Moscow. Kaganovich probably intended to make use of the "Chekist and political worker" Bulganin in the Central Committee apparatus, but in this he was unsuccessful, solely on account of Bulganin's unfortunate "bourgeois" origin.

Shortly after, Kaganovich was transferred to the Ukraine as Secretary of the Party Central Committee there. On his return to Moscow as Third Secretary of the Central Committee he found that Bulganin, although holding only a minor position as manager of an electrical power station, now enjoyed an excellent reputation and had acquired such powerful patrons as Kuibyshev and Molotov. Bulganin was aiming at the same targets as Kaganovich—at Bukharin, to make a vacancy in the Politburo for Kaganovich; at Rykov, to clear the way for Molotov to become head of the government; and at Uglanov, in order to replace him himself. However, while Molotov and Kaganovich succeeded in securing the positions at which they were aiming, Bulganin had to be content with replacing Ukhanov as chairman of the Moscow Soviet and then only after Molotov was firmly established in Rykov's former post. Molotov soon made of Bulganin a still closer associate and had him made Chairman of the Council of People's Commissars of the Russian Soviet Republic. In this capacity he came to the attention of the severe appraiser of the talents of the "second generation," Stalin himself, and, as a result, became Deputy Chairman of the Council of People's Commissars of the USSR, which assured membership in the Politburo. The war gave him both the earned position and the quite undeserved rank of Marshal of the Soviet Union.

Rise to power always created the necessity for new biographies. In some cases the "bourgeois" past became "proletarian." In others, biographical descriptions unsuitable because of past failures and "unorthodox" stages were altered and enriched with the requisite attributes of "orthodox Communism." Lives hitherto described in the most general terms, shorn of "heroic episodes," were now embellished with striking and individual characteristics. A new and rigidly orthodox biography was now composed for Bulganin, which related that, starting from the February Revolution in 1917 he had consistently and everywhere played a leading part. Not a word remained about his "bourgeois" origin. The *Small Soviet Encyclopedia* of 1934 described him as the son of a factory official[23] whereas the *Large Soviet Encyclopedia* of 1951 gave him rebirth in the family of a worker.[24]

Bulganin was first made an alternate member of the Central Committee at the Seventeenth Party Congress, as a reward for his share in the defeat of the Bukharin opposition. At the Eighteenth Party Congress, in 1939, after Stalin had become personal dictator he became a full member of the Central Committee.

At the beginning of the war, when he was Deputy Chairman of the Council of Ministers of the USSR, Bulganin was given the rank of lieutenant-general and made a member of the Military Council, in which capacity he visited various sectors of the front as a special plenipotentiary of the Party Central Committee and the State Committee of Defense, such a member of the Military Council being allocated to each commander. Of all Stalin's political generals in the war Bulganin alone was given proof of Stalin's highest appreciation: in 1944 Stalin removed his personal friend Voroshilov, a member of the Politburo and "First Marshal of the USSR," from the State Committee of Defense and replaced him with Bulganin, although Bulganin was at the time not even an alternate member of the Politburo. At the same time he made Bulganin his first deputy in the Ministry of Defense.

After the war, while still continuing as Stalin's deputy in the Ministry of Defense, Bulganin carried out effectively and consistently three tasks set him by Stalin—playing down the importance of the Soviet Army's real leaders in the war, falsifying the history of the war in order to inflate Stalin's own reputation as the invincible leader responsible for all the Army's victories and the author of a

---

[23] *Malaya Sovetskaya Entsiklopediya* (Small Soviet Encyclopedia), 2nd. ed., Vol. II, Moscow, 1939, p. 140.

[24] *BSE*, 2nd. ed., 1951, Vol. VI, p. 260.

mythical military science of his own, and purging the top personnel of the Soviet Army, whom Stalin regarded as potential enemies. Stalin duly showed his appreciation of these services by making Bulganin Minister of Defense and Vice-Chairman of the Council of Ministers, in March 1947. These facts bear out the description of Bulganin published during Stalin's lifetime in the *Large Soviet Encyclopedia* : "Bulganin is one of those Party politicians and statesmen who were reared by Comrade Stalin, developed under his personal leadership, and later tempered by him in the hard struggle between the Party of Lenin-Stalin and the enemies of the people."[25]

In 1948, Bulganin was made a full member of the Politburo. Like the other cabinet ministers who were members of the Politburo, he was freed from ministerial duties and included in the group of Stalin's deputies attached to the Council of Ministers of the USSR. After Stalin's death he was again made Minister of Defense until he superseded Malenkov as prime minister in February 1955. When Khrushchev, speaking in the name of the Central Committee, recommended Bulganin for this position, he called him "a faithful pupil of Lenin and companion-in-arms of Stalin."

Bulganin thus had long and varied experience as a member of the bureaucracy of Stalin's time, having been in turn Chekist, practicing industrialist as a factory manager, communal worker as chairman of the Moscow Soviet, administrator in the state apparatus as Chairman of the Council of People's Commissars of the Russian Soviet Republic, financier as director of the State Bank of the USSR, soldier as Marshal and Minister of Defense, and three times deputy prime minister. In each position which he filled by order of Stalin he remained true to himself and to his master—a highly disciplined bureaucratic executive. Meticulous to the point of pedantry in carrying out the will of the dictator, he had no ambition to "teach" him, and it was probably this quality that Stalin valued most highly. Except for the period of struggle with the right-wing elements, which opened up for him the road to the higher levels of the state bureaucracy, his various promotions rested precisely on his ability as a Chekist and bureaucrat rather than on ability as a politician and organizer. After Stalin had long ceased to pay any attention to the social origin or the past successes and failures of his Communists, Bulganin was still perpetually "oppressed" by his origin.

Bulganin to the last appears to have suffered from this sense of being an outsider, particularly as after the death of Stalin the "proletarians," headed by Khrushchev, again set the tone, as in the days of Lenin. Khrushchev has stressed his own "proletarian origin" in season and out, as in his interview with the Komsomol members and that with the American Ambassador in Belgrade.

There are strong grounds for believing that Bulganin continued to hold his position as prime minister, not for reasons of statesmanship or personal ambition but as a result of a compromise between the various groupings in the Central Committee. With the exception of Pervukhin and Saburov he was the junior member of the Politburo and in his past activities the least bound to the Party. In

---

[25] *Ibid.*

distinction to his colleagues, he had never served in the Party apparatus. He had begun his career under Kaganovich, continued it under Khrushchev, and reached the post of deputy prime minister under Molotov. To which of these was he most indebted? Most likely to all three equally, as he had attempted to please each in turn to the extent that this did not clash with the oft-changing facets of Stalin's personal policy. If his appointment as prime minister after the retirement of Malenkov was the result of a compromise in the collective leadership between the factions of Molotov and Khrushchev, this was probably due to his personal qualities.

There was, however, a contradiction in Bulganin's position thereafter. He had been put forward by a faction, that of Molotov, to which he was indebted for his past career, but with which he had, in all likelihood, little sympathy later on. Molotov was a past chapter in the history of Stalinism, while Khrushchev represented the chapter now being read. Bulganin was too much the realist to snatch at yesterday. And yet Khrushchev did not allow him to travel abroad alone, accompanied only by his Minister for Foreign Affairs: "A member of the Presidium of the Supreme Soviet of the USSR" preferred to be personally present. This could be interpreted as distrust of Bulganin, and was, of course, open disparagement of Stalin—but matters were safer so.

Nikita Khrushchev: (Born 1894, Party member since 1918). "The ideology of the big bourgeoisie can be perfectly expressed by someone who is not even a small shopkeeper," said Marx. Probably Khrushchev's father Sergei was a person of the type suggested. In any case, in speaking of his father in the course of an interview with foreign journalists, Khrushchev said: "My father was an ordinary worker—a miner, but all his life he dreamed of becoming a capitalist. It is a good thing he didn't succeed." But what may be a "good thing" for the leader of "the dictatorship of the proletariat" was not so good for a proletarian who was ideologically a "big bourgeois."

Khrushchev grew up in the family of such a father and was a hired cow-herd. If Marx's premise that "life determines consciousness" is correct, the younger Khrushchev should have thought like his father. Was not this the one large flaw in his biography which it was impossible to erase or doctor, even at a time when brazen distortion of facts by Stalin's historical school was the order of the day? Of all the prewar members of the Politburo, Khrushchev was the only one who joined the Party after the Bolshevik Revolution. He joined at the age of 24, later than any of the other members of the post-Stalin collective leadership and even, perhaps, than any of the other members of the Central Committee. At the time of the February Revolution in 1917 he was 23, but had not as yet joined the Party. Nor did he join it eight months later in the days of the Bolshevik October Revolution. It was a year later, in 1918, that Khrushchev, then a machinist 24 years old, took out his membership card, a step which, incidentally, was of no great use to him until 1930. Also in 1918 Khrushchev was conscripted into the Red Army. Toward the end of the War, he became a batallion commissar in the Caucasus. Apparently this fact was considered a sufficient basis for the statement in 1938, after he had become an alternate member of the Politburo, that "the political education of the Red Army was in the hands of men like Lenin, Stalin, Molotov, Khrushchev."[26]

It is very doubtful if anyone in the Central Committee had ever heard of Khrushchev before 1929, with the possible exception of Kaganovich, who had been Secretary-General of the Central Committee in the Ukraine while Khrushchev was working at a low level in the Party apparatus as secretary of the Marino District Committee in the Donbas. It is surprising that Khrushchev did not advance in the Ukraine under Kaganovich, who ruled there virtually without any supervision.

A year after Kaganovich left the Ukraine, Khrushchev decided to make his own way by starting at the school level and in 1929 entered the Stalin Industrial Academy in Moscow, admission to which depended upon no qualifications other than literacy and the possession of a Party membership card. (Some time later the practically illiterate but famous Stakhanov studied there.) Khrushchev's secondary education had been limited to attendance at a *rabfak* or workers' college. For a Party or government career, even of average prominence, such qualifications were quite inadequate; some sort of school certificate was required, and this was the reason for his enrollment in the Industrial Academy.

In addition to general education, including intermediate mathematics, physics, chemistry, and Russian, the curriculum included two supplementary courses—a general one in Marxism-Leninism conducted by Suslov and Pospelov, and a special course in the organization of industry. Later on the entrance requirements were raised and candidates were required to be graduates of a secondary school, thus permitting the Academy to graduate students farther advanced in technical knowledge. Similar academies were founded in the provinces in addition to the one in Moscow attended by Khrushchev. However, after being reorganized these academies continued to produce graduates who were "technical organizers" and not "policy experts." After graduation, the students went into industry in mines, factories, or plants, as shop stewards, supervisors, etc., and the ablest as "Red managers." Consequently, the best that Khrushchev could hope for was a career as the "Red manager" of a plant in the South.

But fate willed otherwise. Some eighteen months later Khrushchev was "leader of the Moscow Bolsheviks" and in another five or six years member of the Politburo. His was the giddy, puzzling, and unprecedented career of a person quite unknown in the Party and one which, at first sight, appears inexplicable, if viewed from the angle of Khrushchev's personal qualities.

In the Ukraine Khrushchev would have failed to make even a moderately successful career. It is open to doubt that he had even a personal acquaintance with Kaganovich at the time, and he had only a year at the Academy. He was, it is true, elected secretary of the Party cell there, but only because he was a "proletarian from the lathe" and senior to his fellows both in years and in length of

---

[26] *Istoriya VKP (b). Kratky kurs* (Short Course in the History of the Communist Party of Bolsheviks), Moscow, 1950, p. 235.

Party membership. As a speaker he was not outstanding, except as he displayed temperament and activity at meetings of all kinds. Always prepared to talk on any subject, he appeared to many to be a mere windbag. In fact he was the founder of the new school of Bolshevik oratory which has replaced the style of the brilliant Trotsky and the academic Bukharin. Trotsky's speeches bore an individual stamp as unmistakable as that of Bukharin's writings. The speeches of the Old Bolshevik leaders Lenin, Lunacharsky, and Kamenev all had this personal quality while the speeches of Molotov, Kaganovich, Khrushchev, Malenkov, and Bulganin differ only in regard to the name of the actual speaker. Any of Bulganin's speeches could easily be attributed to Khrushchev, Khrushchev's to Malenkov, or vice versa. The new style was impersonal, "collective," uniformly limited in vocabularly, with set, standard sentences, utterly devoid of rhetorical mannerisms, catch phrases, literary references, or even personal pronouns. But of course these new orators never spoke in their own names, or evinced their own individual opinions. Every statement was made in the name of the Party and especially in the name of Stalin. He alone maintained an individual style of oratory, shorn of lyricism and generally impersonal.

The new style of the Khrushchev school has been universally adopted by the public press. The leading articles of any Soviet newspaper, from *Pravda* and *Izvestia* to the smallest provincial sheet, could as far as language and style are concerned have been written by one and the same person. The impersonal style does, however, possess an outstanding asset: notwithstanding its verbosity, it is concentrated on a single target and belabors a single point. In spite of an apparent tendency to "generalities," it is exhaustive, meaty, and specific. The public press says all that should be said today on a given subject and nothing more. In Leningrad and Moscow, in Vladivostok, Tashkent, and Tbilisi, hundreds of leading articles, astonishingly similar in style and content, daily express identical views, down to the finest shades of opinion, on any particular subject at home or abroad. In people widely different in character and individuality, such uniformity of thought could be achieved by Stalinism only through the medium of Khrushchev's school.

However Khrushchev, the founder of the school, attained success only after he had climbed to power, and the art of oratory had little to do with his achievements. What, then, is the explanation of his swift and puzzling career? In Moscow in the thirties this question was asked by many of Khrushchev's outstripped rivals and by all who were secretly jealous of his success, but no satisfactory answer was ever found. His rivals attempted to solve the mystery by saying that he was a featureless person of no individuality and that his tongue had brought him not only to Kiev, but as far as Moscow. The theory of the envious that he was merely lucky, was less picturesque and hardly more convincing. The reasons given for Khrushchev's luck were mainly centered round Stalin's wife, Nadezhda Alliluyeva, who was also studying at the Academy. It was Stalin's habit to visit the Academy unofficially from time to time, and on occasion, on graduation days and holidays, to receive groups of students. He did this not only because his wife was at the Academy, but because it was one of his duties: the Academy bore his name and he had agreed to be its personal patron. Besides, the Academy was a first trial establishment of its kind and had been founded by special decision of the Central Committee, on Stalin's initiative. It enjoyed exceptional privileges, such as having the students "personally registered" in the Central Committee, being supported from special funds, receiving medical service from the Kremlin clinic, and being issued individual holiday travel orders and medical recuperation grants by the health commission of the Central Committee. The members were allowed separate apartments or rooms and were paid monthly salaries, the so-called "Party maximum." (Party members at the time, irrespective of rank, were subject to "maximum" salary limits which varied according to geographic zones.) But, more important than all these blessings, the Academy was under the direct control of the only "super-capitalist" in the State—the Supreme Council of National Economy, which granted its future "Red managers" supplementary financial assistance. The heads of the council, in favoring the Academy, knew quite well that they were at the same time helping Stalin's family.

Fortunate indeed was the school in which the chief's wife was studying. The heads (and Khrushchev as secretary of the Party cell was also a "head") and even the rank and file of the students were persons to be reckoned with; so thought the job hunters and flunkeys at the summit. One never knew! This particular unknown student might be sitting on the same school bench as the wife of the chief.

What, then, can be said of Khrushchev, who was, in fact, the Party chief of the wife of the supreme chief? Khrushchev was publicly admitted to the chief's house, was invited to family parties at the Kremlin, and brought with him to this bureaucratized, stuffy, and official environment, long cut off from the people, a whiff of proletarian fresh air, expressed by his whole manner—his uncouthness, his originality, his closeness to the people, and his strikingly practical turn of mind. Yet he was no drawing-room fop or court jester—there was a surfeit of both in the Kremlin. He was the classical personification of the second generation of Bolshevism, stubbornly striving for power, something that hitherto had never been witnessed there. This generation had taken no part in the October Revolution, some, like Malenkov, because of their youth and others, like Khrushchev, through a lack of political flair. But it had fought in Stalin's Party battles against the generation of October, with the same dash and abandon as that generation had fought on the October barricades or on the battlefronts of the civil war against the Whites. It was moved by conviction against Trotsky and by calculation against Bukharin.

As a result of Stalin's victory the October generation had been withdrawn from circulation at the top. In and around the Kremlin there were vacant seats, into which the second generation, that of the Khrushchevs, was avidly scrambling, literally elbowing each other out of the way, tripping up the forward ranks, treading on the corns of the sensitive, and vying with each other in uttering loud cheers to the glory of Stalin, never for a moment losing sight of the main objective —not Stalin himself, but his heritage. Khrushchev was the first representative of the lower ranks of this second generation. His luck lay in the fact that Stalin had occasion to watch him directly, to study his personal characteristics, and to discern in him "exceptional gifts as a Party organizer."

Officially Khrushchev was not responsible for the decision of Stalin's apparatus and of the Stalinist Politburo to proceed with the Great Purge and to wipe out physically the "enemies of the people." On the other hand he cannot be accused of being too soft in helping to put the purge into effect. The old Moscow Party organization was almost completely destroyed at the time when Khrushchev was its secretary. For this operation alone Stalin rewarded him by making him alternate member of the Politburo in January 1938, three years earlier then Malenkov. In the same month Khrushchev was sent to the Ukraine as First Secretary of the Central Committee there, with orders to complete the purge. This he did by destroying both the Communist and the national-minded Ukrainian intelligentsias. By way of reward Stalin moved him up a year later, in 1939, from alternate to full membership in the Politburo, seven years before Malenkov and nearly ten years before Bulganin. Such rapid advancement—to member of the Central Committee at the Seventeenth Party Congress and member of the Polit-buro at the Eighteenth—was without parallel among the members of Stalin's entourage. Mikoyan, who became Khrushchev's friend for reasons of personal gain, was made member of the Politburo so that he could vote in favor of the purge, but Khrushchev gained his seat for carrying it out. In fact, this is the sole distinction between the two in their joint responsibility for Stalin's purge in the thirties.

At the Twentieth Party Congress both Khrushchev and Mikoyan denied responsibility. (Khrushchev is alleged to have said that he even protested against the execution of the "deviationists.") Speaking through Mikoyan he completely rehabilitated Kosior, his predecessor in the Ukraine, and through Ulbricht another predecessor, Postyshev.

According to Khrushchev, the purge which he had so mercilessly conducted in Moscow and the Ukraine was entirely attributable to the arbitrary will of Stalin himself. One is, however, inclined to agree with Khrushchev's biographer, who wrote in the *Small Soviet Encyclopedia*: "Khrushchev is Stalin's former disciple and companion-in-arms . . . He carried on a merciless struggle against the Trotsky-Bukharinite band of enemies of the people."[27] Of course after Stalin's death the encyclopedias lost no time in changing their descriptions of Khrushchev from that of "disciple of Stalin" to "disciple of Lenin," without, however, denying his connection with Stalin. His new biographer (or, perhaps, autobio-grapher) says, "Khrushchev was Lenin's faithful disciple and one of Stalin's closest companions-in-arms."[28] There is little doubt that in the next editions following the dethroning of Stalin at the Twentieth Party Congress, Khrushchev and he will have parted company.

Khrushchev's career before and after the war was uneven. Although a member of the Politburo and present on the main sector of the front, in the Ukraine, he was not brought into the State Committee of Defense either at the opening stages of the war or later on, while such non-members as Malenkov, Beria, Bulganin,

---

[27] *Malaya Sovetskaya Entsiklopediya* (Small Soviet Encyclopedia), Vol. XI, Moscow, 1931, pp. 493—94.
[28] *Entsiklopedichesky slovar* (Encyclopedic Dictionary), Vol. III, Moscow, 1955, p. 567.

and Voznesensky and such members as Molotov, Voroshilov, Kaganovich, and Mikoyan were on the committee. He also gained no promotion in rank. In 1942 he was made lieutenant-general and remained so until the end of the war, whereas the other political lieutenant-generals–Zhdanov, Mekhlis, and Shcherbakov–were promoted to colonel-general and Bulganin to marshal.

After the end of the war Stalin surprised Khrushchev by removing him from his responsible post as Secretary-General of the Ukrainian Central Committee and giving him the subordinate position of Prime Minister of the Ukrainian Soviet Republic, which he held from March to December, 1947, under Kaganovich as Secretary-General of the Party there. Khrushchev had returned to the starting point of his career, which he had begun under Kaganovich. He was now fated either to bring it to a close or to start afresh under the same man. Again luck was with him. Stalin relented, Khrushchev was reinstated in his former position, and Kaganovich was retransferred to Moscow. In 1949 Khrushchev, too, was brought there, as Secretary of the Moscow Party Committee and of the Party Central Committee of the Soviet Union.

He held these positions until Stalin's death. The events surrounding the death of the dictator and the liquidation of Beria brought Khrushchev to the forefront of the political stage. That he played a leading role in these events is beyond doubt. If Stalin died as the result of a conspiracy it can be said with certainty that Khrushchev was its ringleader. He must certainly have been the leading figure in the destruction of Stalin's "inner cabinet," headed by Poskrebyshev, and of the MVD apparatus under Beria, if only because at the time he was in practice and from September 1953 officially First Secretary of the Central Committee, with full control of the entire Central Committee apparatus, and consequently of the reorganized security service in the Kremlin. Furthermore, Khrushchev was the truly lucky man who discovered Stalin's secret archives and has since had them in his possession, including the reports of Stalin's spies on members of the Politburo, the reports of the members of the Politburo on each other, Stalin's notes on these members, plans for future purges and "physical liquidations," and so on. He has plenty to divulge and he can "expose" many persons on the basis of this material. In fact, he holds in the palm of his hand the fate of every member of the Presidium of the Central Committee, no matter how independent they may pretend to be. It is equally probable that these personal archives of Stalin's were of no small value to Khrushchev in unmasking Stalin himself.

Khrushchev, with his apparent simplicity, is extremely complicated psychologically. Stalin's death offered him the opportunity to reveal the manifold contradictions of his character. His latent potentialities, formerly kept in check by the iron jaws of Stalinism and the dictator's tyrannous will, only after the departure of Stalin could make themselves felt. Khrushchev is the only person, even among the members of the collective leadership, who has attained unrestricted inner freedom both of mind and action and who has struck a heavy blow at the golden rule of Stalin's diplomacy: "Do not say what you think and do not think what you say!" In the realm of the Kremlin's international politics he substituted a cutting, ungarnished cynical style for Vyshinsky's pharisaical formulas or Molotov's prefabricated mouthings to the effect that "of course we are enemies, but let us trade—in politics, in economics, or even in conscience." As a result, post-Stalin diplomacy at once emerged from a blind alley: Korea, Indochina, Yugoslavia, Austria, Geneva, India, Burma, Afghanistan, Egypt, the German Federal Republic, were but the first stages of Khrushchev's promising "trade."

Khrushchev does not, of course, trade in principles; what he offers up in exchange for advantages is Molotov's dullwittedness and Stalin's recklessness; his trade, in other words, is financed by the negative capital of Stalin's diplomacy. He is trading time for space. He is fully alive both to his own power and possibilities and to the potentialities of his customers; he is trading on the universal fear of war on the part of other nations, demanding in exchange concessions from foreign governments. It is precisely in this field that he has found Stalin's negative capital so useful.

There are many who are sceptical regarding Khrushchev's diplomatic skill. He is obviously no Talleyrand, he is not even a Litvinov—he is yesterday's cowherd who is today at the head of one of the most powerful countries in the world. The etiquette of diplomatic protocol is as foreign to his nature as the smooth conjurings of a Vyshinsky. He offers this cynical century a cynical formula: "You dislike Communism, we dislike capitalism, but why resort to war? We shall bury you without fighting. In the meantime let us trade." Offensive to the ear and derogatory to classical diplomacy? Certainly. But why should there be surprise or indignation at Khrushchev's undiplomatic conduct of affairs? The person who reveals his sincere though terrifying secret deserves recognition, not censure. A general of the Red Army who prematurely divulged his strategic plans would be hanged by Khrushchev, but Khrushchev himself deserves recognition for repeating after Stalin's death the same unvarying truth: "Our aim was, is, and ever shall be World Communism." The world is openly clamouring, as it always does, for an illusion: "Stalin's era has come to an end and the aims of the Kremlin may change." Khrushchev could, of course, have made profitable use of this illusion. Stalin during his best years would certainly have done so, and did, in the classical manner, but Khrushchev has reacted in his own way and has freed the world of this dangerous illusion.

Khrushchev's downfall was widely prophesied. He was accused of being too "active," too self-assured, too authoritarian, too eager, perhaps, to become another Stalin. However, he has maintained himself in power for many years; if he had been another man he would probably not have lasted three days.

Khrushchev's self-confidence and inner freedom are based on imponderables no less than on his personal qualities. Quite independently of what may happen to him in the future he has perpetuated his name in history as the man who in the space of three hours shattered the authority of one who for three decades had been regarded as a Communist demi-god. There is not the slightest doubt that this was done not only at Khrushchev's initiative, but in his characteristic manner of dealing with an enemy—insolent, authoritarian, provocative, self-assured, revolutionary, and cynical. It appeared at the time, and still appears, that the unmasking of Stalin involved enormous danger for Communism, a risk not justified by any reasons of state. The danger was not that there might be Stalinist sympathizers within the Party or within any of the Soviet Union republics, all of them in any case anti-Stalinist, but that after damning Stalin, Khrushchev might find himself compelled to follow in his footsteps.

The danger was fully appreciated by Molotov and his group and it was for this reason that they so long resisted the debunking of Stalin. But Khrushchev was not to be deterred—the advantages were too obvious: "I am not Stalin. I am working for co-existence with the outer world, but primarily with the peoples of our country. I am not Stalin—by killing Stalin the dictator, I am saving the dictatorship. I am not a Stalinist, but a disciple of Lenin. By treating Stalin as I have done, I am fulfilling the testament of Lenin. And, in particular, I realize the ardent hatred of the people for Stalin's regime and by debunking Stalin I am saving the régime." Such were probably his thoughts.

Khrushchev could not but know that the obvious question: "And what were you disciples and companions-in-arms of Stalin doing?" would follow immediately. That this question would be asked by the outside world worried him not at all. To his own people and Party he answered with inimitable frankness and conviction: "We, like you, feared him!"

If he could succeed in removing the Molotov group from the Presidium of the Central Committee he would gain full and unrestricted freedom of action. Strong-willed, temperamental, free from the shackles of ideology, Khrushchev is inclined to experiment in politics in order to outwit history. Khrushchev's first experiment of world-wide significance dealt with "the cult of Stalin." His aim was the de-Stalinization of the outward form of the regime, not its essence, the debunking of an individual, not the abolition of an established practice, the destruction of a symbol, not the revision of a doctrine. In short, what he wanted was to follow in the footsteps of Stalin the teacher, while condemning Stalin the man. Here lay the main contradiction inherent in the unmasking of Stalin.

This contradiction cannot be removed by Khrushchev within the framework of the existing system. Khrushchev's great service, however, consists in the fact that by debunking Stalin he has placed before the regime the fateful dilemma of either proceeding with de-Stalinization and thus temporarily deferring its own downfall, or of returning to Stalinist orthodoxy at the cost of an even greater inherent contradiction.

Chapter XXXIII

Back to Stalin?

In rejecting the cult of the individual and exposing the crimes of Stalin, the collective leadership did not succeed in doing away with three fundamental self-contradictions. On the practical level there was a self-contradiction in the fact that Stalin's terrorist methods of rule were declared illegal and anti-Party, yet without them it is impossible to maintain a dictatorship: Stalin's terrorist methods, and these methods alone have made possible the continued existence of Communism, both in the USSR and in the satellite states. The second self-contradiction, on the level of theory, lay in the fact that while the collective leadership condemned as anti-Leninist and anti-Party the theories bequeathed by Stalin, in particular those on the class struggle during the period of socialism and on "enemies of the people," in fact Stalin's views were indispensable as a means of reconciling Communist practice with theoretical dogma. Finally, on the moral level, while the charge was made that Stalin's treachery, suspiciousness, and duplicity were personal characteristics of the dictator, in fact these characteristics constitute the "moral code" upon which the entire philosophy of the present system is based.

In deciding to divorce Stalin's system from Stalin himself, his successors committed a grave error. They attempted to separate Stalin's personality from his system by ascribing, as Togliatti said, all the achievements of the system to themselves, while saddling Stalin with responsibility for its monstrous crimes. Togliatti was undoubtedly correct in declaring such an approach un-Marxist. Marx said in the preface to *Das Kapital:* "From my point of view, least of all can an individual be considered responsible for conditions whose product in a social sense he remains, however much he may rise above them subjectively."[1]

The consequences of this error on the part of the Kremlin leaders soon became apparent: (1) in the ideological crisis within the world Communist movement; (2) in the political crisis within the satellite countries; and (3) in the psychological crisis within the USSR itself. The cause of all these crises was the same: the repudiation and exposure of Stalin—the creator of the system and its model operator.

However, the exposure and debunking of Stalin was not the only cause of the ideological crisis within the world Communist movement. Khrushchev in his published speech forecast the forthcoming revision of a large number of dogmatic and tactical concepts of Communism, in keeping with the new circumstances of

---

[1] See preface to Marx's 1st edition.

international life. This, however, was a revision of Lenin, and not of Stalin. A comparison of Khrushchev's statements with the basic tenets of Leninism makes this clear. At the Twentieth Party Congress Khrushchev said:

1. In free countries it is possible for Communists to achieve power through the parliamentary system.

2. The parliament itself through its Communist majority will be transformed from "an organ of bourgeois democracy into a weapon of the true will of the people."

3. The assertion that we recognize violence and civil war as *the only way* to reform society has no basis in truth.

4. War is not absolutely inevitable.[2]

The tactical aims of these new "discoveries" in the body of the Leninist doctrine were clear: (1) to form a "united front" with the Socialists and thus be in a better position to seize control of the international workers' movement from within; (2) to reassure the satellites; (3) to provide a theoretical justification for "co-existence" in order to infiltrate the free world through the back door, politically, economically, and ideologically.

However, these "discoveries" in the field of the "further development of Marxism-Leninism" turned out to be of little value to the Kremlin and only served to aggravate the crisis in world Communism brought about by the exposure of Stalin, since the Kremlin's new tactical maneuvers could not possibly be reconciled with Lenin's old rules of strategy, which were as follows:

1. Lenin on the *tactics of Bolshevism:*

These tactics were proved right by their enormous success, for Bolshevism has become *world* Bolshevism.... Bolshevism made the whole world familiar with the idea of the dictatorship of the proletariat, was the first to translate the words from Latin into Russian, then into all the languages of the world.... For the masses of the proletariat of all countries, it becomes clearer every day... that *Bolshevism can serve as a model of tactics for everyone.*[3] (Lenin's italics).

2. Lenin on *the different forms of Socialism:*

In Russia the dictatorship of the proletariat must necessarily be distinguished by certain features peculiar to itself.... But the basic forces—and the basic economic framework—are the same in Russia as in any other capitalist country, so that these features can only apply to matters of secondary importance.[4]

3. Lenin on *parliamentarism:*

Communism rejects parliamentarism as a future form of society.... It rejects the possibility of a long-drawn-out conquest of parliaments: it aims at the *destruction* of parliamentarism. There can therefore be no question of making use of bourgeois government institutions for any purpose but that of their destruction. In this sense, and this sense only, can the question be considered at all.... Communist Parties join

---

[2] See Khrushchev, *Full Report of the Central Committee of the Communist Party of the Soviet Union to the Party Congress*, Moscow, 1956, pp. 40–44.

[3] Lenin, *Sochineniya*, Vol. XXIII, 1936, pp. 385–386.

[4] Lenin, *Sochineniya*, Vol. XXIV, 1936, p. 508.

these institutions not in order to perform constructive work but in order to help the masses blow up the bourgeois government machine and parliament itself by action from within.[5]

4. Lenin on *co-existence*:

We live not only within a state, but within a system of states. The existence of the Soviet Republic side by side with imperialist states for any length of time is *unthinkable*. In the end, either one or the other will prevail. And before the end comes, a series of the most terrible clashes between the Soviet Republic and the bourgeois states is inevitable.[6]

5. Lenin on *forms of government*:

The republic of workers', soldiers', and peasants' deputies united in soviets constitutes the highest form of democratic institution, and the only form.[7]

In Stalin's hands, Lenin's internationalism had changed into completely undisguised rule by Soviet chauvinism over the satellites. Tito's National Communism was a direct reaction against this chauvinism. The Communist crisis assumed virtually catastrophic proportions when the Kremlin recognized the National Communism of Tito as an acceptable form of international Communism on a national scale. As a system of government, Tito's Communism was in no way different from Lenin's system, but Tito introduced a completely new element—the element of *national dynamism*. Tito triumphed over Stalin not as a Communist, but as a nationalist. Even to a Communist the concept of nationalism had proved stronger than Communist doctrine.

This new concept was a serious warning to the leaders of the Communist empire headed by the USSR. Stalin rightly recognized it as a precedent fatal to world Communism. While refraining for the time being from armed intervention in order to destroy Titoism, he hastened to brand Tito's regime as Fascist in order to abolish the precedent. Meanwhile the liquidation of potential Titoists in the other lands infected by "people's democracy" began. Death, however, prevented Stalin from completing this work, while his less astute successors recognized National Communism as a legal form of Communism in two declarations—that of Belgrade in 1955, and of Moscow in 1956. Tito's precedent then begat imitators and successors, and a trend set in toward an independent system of socialism in almost all the European satellites, in China, and even in the Communist Parties of the free world. It was accompanied by a movement for decentralization of Communist absolutism, aiming at the creation of three Meccas of Communism— Moscow, Belgrade, and Peking. Hitherto the strength of Soviet Communism had lain in the fact that the Soviet approach to the Communist Revolution had been recognized as the only correct one, the Soviet formula of "the dictatorship of the proletariat" as of universal application, "the tactics of Bolshevism as a model for all," and Moscow as the only supreme center. The exposure of Stalin and the political reorientation at the Twentieth Party Congress in connection with the

---

[5] Lenin, "Resolution of the Second Comintern Congress, 1920," *Sochineniya*, Vol. XXV, 1935, pp. 581, 582.

[6] Lenin, *Sochineniya*, Vol. XXIV, 1936, pp. 122.

[7] Lenin, *Sochineniya*, Vol. XXII, 1929, p. 131.

"forms, ways, and methods" of Communism dealt a crushing blow to this whole conception. The logical result was the emergence of as many roads to socialism as there are Communist parties in the world.

While the theory of "different roads to Communism" served the Kremlin as the most elastic tactics for preserving its own domination, some of the Communist parties abroad interpreted it as the formula of self-determination which they had been seeking. Even the orthodox Stalinist Communist Party in Italy began to speak of an "Italian road to Socialism." China went even farther after the exposure of Stalin, to develop not only an independent road, but an independent doctrine regarding the methods to be employed. Meanwhile Gomulka's successful venture in Poland, and the tragic fate of Nagy, were part of the same process. When matters had come to a head, Stalin's successors suddenly awakened and did what even Stalin had not done: Bulganin's Communist government declared war on the Communist government of Nagy. Poland was saved, for the time being, entirely by the skill of Gomulka, the unusual degree of unanimity on the part of the Polish people, and possible differences of opinion in the Kremlin. The conclusion to be drawn from these events proved to be of great significance in historical perspective: they proved that wars are possible between Communist states, in the form of imperialistic wars waged by great powers (the USSR) and national wars of liberation waged by small powers (Hungary and, potentially, Poland and Yugoslavia).

Events in Poland and Hungary, having greatly increased opposition movements within the USSR itself, led to a temporary strengthening of the Stalinist wing within the Party leadership. The neo-Leninists, alarmed by these events no less than the orthodox Stalinists, betrayed by a careless remark by Tito to the effect that there were both Stalinists and non-Stalinists in the collective leadership,[8] and, above all, keen to safeguard their present position, decided to compromise. They agreed, therefore, to revision of the pronouncements of the Twentieth Party Congress on questions of foreign policy, to a rehabilitation of Stalin, to a deterioration in relations with Tito, to an ostentatious courting of the satellites for a deliberate front against Tito, and to renewed tension in international relations. One of the most important alleged discoveries made by Khrushchev, to the effect that foreign Communists could achieve power by peaceful parliamentary means, had already been revised before the Polish and Hungarian events. An editor of *Kommunist*, Sobolev, even declared in September 1956: "What does 'peaceful' mean? The word 'peaceful' has been interpreted by some persons as a repudiation of all struggle and of all violence, implying a purely evolutionary development without the revolutionary destruction of the old way of life. . . . This is a complete misconception."[9]

After Poland and Hungary, three other important "discoveries" by Khrushchev were also revised, although quietly and without reference to the Twentieth Party Congress. These were: (1) On the class struggle during the period of socialism; (2) On different roads to socialism; (3) On the nature of peaceful co-existence.

---

[8] Marshal Tito's speech in Pula, November 11, 1956.

[9] *Kommunist*, No. 14, 1956, p. 28.

Stalin's basic error in the field of theory, according to the Party Central Committee's decree of June 30, 1956, on the cult of the individual, was his theory of the class struggle during the period of socialism. The decree declared:

> Great harm was done to the cause of socialist construction and to the development of democracy within the Party and the state by Stalin's erroneous formula which implied that the class struggle would increase with the advance of the Soviet Union toward socialism. . . . In practice this erroneous formula served to explain away both mass repressions and the most outrageous violation of socialist legality.[10]

In February 1956 *Party Life*, a press organ of the Party Central Committee, contradicted this view. "The events in Hungary have shown once again that the construction of socialism cannot proceed without a class struggle and without the merciless suppression of the exploiting classes after their overthrow. . . . Thus are the basic tenets of Marxism-Leninism confirmed time and again."[11]

Shortly after, in June 1956, the periodical *Kommunist* declared: "Once again life has shown that socialism is born of actual reality, of the keenest class struggle."[12] The Bolsheviks, of course, being experienced "dialecticians" say what they do not believe and do not believe what they say. But even so it took the Hungarian revolution to make the Kremlin openly rehabilitate not only Stalin's "erroneous formula," but also Lenin's theory of the "dictatorship of the proletariat."

As to the question of the various roads to socialism, the Kremlin reinstated Lenin and his teaching of the one road to socialism, without any philosophizing. *Pravda*, in an article attacking Marshal Tito, said with no equivocation: "Creative diversity regarding the *one road* of socialist development is determined in various countries by actual, objective circumstances."[13]

As regards co-existence, Shepilov gave this principle a new interpretation which fitted perfectly into the framework of classical Leninism. "Peaceful co-existence is a struggle—a political struggle, an economic struggle, an ideological struggle."[14] Such an interpretation implies something more than a cold war. Political struggle includes class struggle carried to its ultimate conclusion—uprising and civil war, economic struggle means setting a clear course for economic expansion abroad, while the aim of ideological struggle is the internal disintegration of free peoples and the triumph of Communist ideology throughout the world.

Here is a return to classical Leninism! But does this mean that there is no such thing as "Stalinism" as a specific phenomenon and as a new chapter in Communism? Of course not. There is admittedly no such thing as Stalinism as a sociological or a philosophical stage in Communism, but there is as a practical interpretation of the theory of Communism. In this sense, Stalinism is the most comprehensive and most consistent application of Lenin's theoretical principles

---

[10] *Pravda*, July 2, 1956.

[11] *Partiinaya zhizn*, No. 20, 1956, pp. 43, 44.

[12] *Kommunist* No. 16, 1956, p. 5.

[13] *Pravda*, November 23, 1956.

[14] *Pravda*, February 2, 1957.

of the "dictatorship of the proletariat" in the spheres of administration, political economy, and ideology. Stalinism is an ideological system and a practical means of preserving, strengthening, and expanding absolute power. To seize power is a relatively easy task, but to maintain and preserve it is a much more difficult achievement, said Lenin. The first and easier task was accomplished by Lenin; the second and more difficult by Stalin. It is for this reason that Stalin's contributions to Communism originated not in speculative generalizations in the realm of abstract theory but in the practical needs of a dictatorship.

Of this nature were his apparently theoretical but in fact practical "innovations," of which the following are only a few:

1. The theory of the construction of socialism in one country.

2. The theory of full collectivization and the liquidation of the kulaks, serving to complete the usurpation of the political and economic freedom of the peasants.

3. The theory of priority for the development of heavy industry, serving to develop the armaments industry for strategic warfare.

4. The theory of intensification of the class struggle under socialism, serving to justify mass terror.

5. The theory of the preservation and consolidation of the state under socialism and under Communism, serving to justify expansion of the absolute power vested in the state, the growth and consolidation of the police, a centralized bureaucracy, an army, concentration camps, etc.

6. The theory of revolutionary vigilance and capitalist encirclement, serving to justify Cheka espionage at home and abroad, and the permanent purge.

7. The theory of "socialist" and "bourgeois" nations, serving to cultivate hatred toward free nations.

The list could be continued indefinitely, but these examples of Stalin's theories are sufficient to show that the distinctive features of Stalinism are doubly useful: his entire theoretical system was intended for application in the present Soviet empire as well as in the future Communist utopia. His theories were concerned not with finding roads to Communism as a basis for a harmonious community of peoples but with ways, methods, and forms for perpetuation of the status quo—the dictatorial regime.

The collective leaders, by maintaining that Stalin is no longer to be regarded as a founder of Marxism but was and is an "outstanding Marxist-Leninist," are themselves accepting Stalin's criminal practices as part of their current code of morality, thereby admitting that Stalin's crimes were perpetrated within the framework, and as a consequence, of Marxism-Leninism. Although this view is not devoid of a certain logic of its own, its political purpose is obscure. Accordingly it is difficult to understand why it was accepted by so many persons with ulterior aims. The reasons behind the Kremlin's acceptance were obvious—since attacks on Stalin become attacks on the regime, the Kremlin rushed to the opposite extreme in order to forestall such attacks, and attempted to rehabilitate Stalin.

But this was naive reasoning: Khrushchev's speech will go down in history as a severe judgment on the entire epoch, while his remark about Stalin at the Chinese Embassy will go down as proof of the political artlessness of Stalin's successors.

But was Stalin really rehabilitated by this remark of Khrushchev's, at least in the eyes of the Communists, and did the Kremlin thereby achieve its objective? Far from it. Communism does not recognize inconsistent and fallible prophets, guilty of errors and defects. Khrushchev's rehabilitation of Stalin having been vitiated by references to his errors, Stalin as a symbol of authority and leadership remains irretrievably lost to Communism.

Does the rehabilitation of Stalin mean a return to Stalinism in the USSR? This question is not as easily answered as might appear at first sight. We must not take the shadow for the substance. If we speak of a return, we must be clear as to what constitutes a departure from Stalin. We have already seen that in matters of dogma the statement issued by the Twentieth Party Congress represented not a departure from Stalin but a departure on specific points from Lenin. A return to the old doctrine on the subject of revolutionary strategy and tactics was in fact a return not to Stalin but to Lenin.

Of what did the departure from Stalin consist? It consisted of the following:

1. The cult of Stalin's personality was condemned and the cult of Lenin's personality was reestablished. (The principle of the cult of the individual was not condemned).

2. The principle of collective dictatorship by the Party and the state was proclaimed in place of dictatorship by an individual. (The principle of dictatorship remained).

3. Stalin's practice of terrorism directed against the Party oligarchy was condemned. (The principle of terrorism directed against the people was not condemned).

4. Stalin's transfer of power from the Party apparatus to the police was condemned. (The principle of the police system was not condemned).

5. The exaggerated centralization of the bureaucratic government apparatus was condemned.

6. Stalin's nationality policy of destroying small ethnographic groups was condemned.

7. An attack was launched on certain specific theories inherited from Stalin.

8. Stalin's ruthless interference in the internal affairs of the Communist parties in the "people's democracies" was condemned (e.g., Yugoslavia).

There now arose the problem of correcting or liquidating the consequences of the cult of the individual. The solution of this problem was envisaged in terms of a controlled form of de-Stalinization. Of all the departures listed, only the last two indicate a partial revision of the policy adopted at the Twentieth Party Congress. The rest indicate that de-Stalinization is to be continued in practice.

Forced by circumstances to rehabilitate Stalin, the collective leadership has not deviated, and is not deviating, from its set course—"liquidation of the consequences of the cult of the individual."

Events following the exposure of Stalin constituted a dire warning that calculated de-Stalinization was in fact passing beyond the control of the Kremlin. The optimistic assumption that the exposure of Stalin would clear up the atmosphere at home and abroad proved erroneous. From now on the Kremlin found itself in a vicious circle: a return to Stalin was psychologically impossible, while a continuation along the course of de-Stalinization threatened the very foundations to the system itself.

Has the Kremlin been able to break out of this circle? Does the policy of the collective leadership represent a return to Stalin? Which is progress—de-Stalinization or re-Stalinization?

Full and convincing answers to these questions can be made only after first defining the term "de-Stalinization," both as it is understood by the leaders of the Soviet Communist Party and as it is understood in the West.

In the West, the term "de-Stalinization" has been given a meaning which it never had in the Kremlin. Whereas in the West de-Stalinization has been taken to mean a gradual departure from the existing system in the USSR, the leaders of the Soviet Communist Party have interpreted de-Stalinization (they do not, of course, use this term, but speak of "liquidation of the consequences of the Stalinist cult of the individual") to mean:

1. The debunking of Stalin's fame and name as a classic of Marxism, in order to gain freedom of action both in dogma and in practice.

2. A revision of Stalin's methods of government, in order to place the Party over the police.

3. The creation of certain psychological and political conditions preliminary to carrying out economic and administrative "reforms from above," reforms which were forced upon the leaders and were in any case quite inevitable.

If the Kremlin leaders had plans for serious changes within the framework of the present system, they had, first of all, to expose Stalin's inadequacy as a classic of Marxism. This was the one indispensable condition necessary to justify the introduction of the new measures. The political, economic, and ideological impasse to which Stalin had brought the country on the eve of his death, and from which he had planned to extricate himself by means of a new, large-scale purge and an adventurous foreign policy, was described by the Kremlin as "the consequences of the cult of the individual," and the Kremlin proceeded to concentrate its attention on their removal.

How was this problem in fact approached by the Twentieth Party Congress? Following Khrushchev's official speech, the congress passed the following short resolution:

> The Twentieth Party Congress of the Communist Party of the Soviet Union has heard the speech of Comrade N. S. Khrushchev on the cult of the individual and its consequences. It approves the proposal contained in the Central Committee's report

and empowers the Central Committee of the Communist Party of the Soviet Union consistently to adopt all necessary measures for the complete suppression of the cult of the individual, so alien to Marxism-Leninism; *for the liquidation of its consequences in all spheres of Party, state and ideological activity*, and for the strict observance of the rules of Party life and the principles of collective Party leadership evolved by the great Lenin.[15]

In the light of this interpretation it cannot be said that re-Stalinization is being effected. There are, of course, factors which appear to suggest that it is, such as the armed intervention in Hungary, the recent deterioration of relations with the West and with Tito, the revival of religious persecution in the USSR, and the rehabilitation of Stalin. However, analysis of the general and specific reasons for these events shows that they are not manifestations of re-Stalinization. The tragedy of unfortunate Hungary must not be viewed exclusively in terms of Stalin—her fate was decided by the Allies in the agreements made during the war and in the peace treaty signed in Paris after the war. The Kremlin can and should be condemned for putting its own interpretation on these documents, but there is no possible denying of the fact that the Soviet army's intervention in Hungary took place in what according to these documents was the Soviet sphere of influence. Moreover, the Soviet intervention in Hungary was not a specifically Stalinist action; it was a most ruthless manifestation of pure imperialism, or what the Germans call *Machtpolitik*. But even if this type of action is regarded as being entirely Stalinist, it was not put into operation in Poland. There a manifestly anti-Stalinist compromise was reached, for the Polish uprising was not directed against Soviet military strategy or against Communism in general, as was the case in Hungary.

The relative and temporary cessation of the "thaw" in the USSR itself was already in its initial stages when these events took place. Indeed, it began at the time when the Kremlin realized that the campaign against the cult of the individual was spreading beyond the limits foreseen by the Party apparatus. The Kremlin was worried not so much by criticism of Stalin as by criticism of the régime; hence the necessity for putting the brakes on the anti-Stalinist campaign. This did not mean that the Kremlin had given up de-Stalinization in practice, within the specific limits intended.

The widespread belief that de-Stalinization began only after the Twentieth Party Congress is mistaken. It began immediately after Stalin's death, and was reflected in the following acts:

1. The amnesty for prisoners serving sentences of five years or less (Decree of the Presidium of the Supreme Soviet of the USSR, March 27, 1953).

2. Release of the Kremlin doctors (April, 1953).

3. The execution of Beria and his group (July, 1953).

4. The abolition of the military tribunals of the MVD (Decree of the Presidium of the Supreme Soviet of the USSR, September 11, 1953).

---

[15] *XX sezd kommunisticheskoi partii Sovetskogo Soyuza : Stenografichesky otchet* (The Twentieth Party Congress of the Soviet Communist Party: Stenographic Report), Moscow, 1956, Vol. II, p. 402.

5. The abolition of the Special Council of the MVD of the USSR (September, 1953).

6. Repeal of the decree of the Central Executive Committee of the USSR, December 1, 1934 (dealing with the organization and execution of terrorist acts) and repeal of the decrees of December 1, 1934, and September 14, 1937, amending criminal law to forbid appeals to a higher court in cases of sabotage, terrorism, or diversionary activity (Decree of the Presidium of the Supreme Soviet of the USSR, September 1953).

7. The amnesty for Soviet citizens who had collaborated with the Germans during the war (Decree of the Presidium of the Supreme Soviet of the USSR, September 17, 1955).

8. The abolition of a single State Security Administration, and establishment of central and local Committees of State Securty.

9. The publication of regulations governing the supervision of prosecutors in the USSR (Decree of the Presidium of the Supreme Soviet of the USSR, March 24, 1955).

10. The creation of committees of the Presidium of the Party Central Committee to investigate Stalin's crimes committed in the course of the Great Purge (1954. See Khrushchev's secret speech).

11. Re-examination of the cases of all political prisoners.[16]

These official actions had one aim—that of placing the Party over the police, with an obvious trend toward liberalization of the régime. They did not, of course, alter the character of the Soviet penal system, but they reduced, or were intended to reduce, to a minimum the arbitrary tyranny exercised under Stalin. In this sense they constituted de-Stalinization in practice before the dethroning of Stalin at the Twentieth Party Congress.

The first intention of the Party Central Committee was evidently to carry out de-Stalinization or to "liquidate the consequences of the cult of the individual" without implicating Stalin, and, indeed, by quoting him as an authority. *Pravda*, for instance, first mentioned the harmfulness of the cult of the individual on June 10, 1953, but in doing so referred to a "fundamentally important" directive by Stalin himself. On the other hand, Lenin's principle of collective leadership was discussed immediately after Stalin's death, in Malenkov's speech on March 14, 1953. But consistent de-Stalinization obviously could not long be carried out in the name of Stalin himself. Continued acceptance of Stalin as an infallible authority and classic of Marxism-Leninism could only result in interpreting collective leadership as an anti-Marxist practice. For the sake of de-Stalinization, apart from all other reasons, it was imperative to exclude Stalin from the "great quadrumvirate" of Marx, Engels, Lenin, and Stalin, while presenting de-Stalinization as the restoration of Lenin's principles of rule.

A long battle was waged around this fateful decision. It now appears that the question of the cult of Stalin was discussed as early as the July 1953 plenary

---

[16] *Partiinaya zhizn*, No. 4, 1957, pp. 67–70.

session of the Central Committee in connection with Beria's execution.[17] However, no final decision was arrived at, for in January 1956, on the eve of the Twentieth Party Congress, Kirichenko, a member of the Central Committee Presidium, was still speaking in his report to the Ukrainian Congress of January 21, 1956, of the "great teaching of Marx-Engels-Lenin and Stalin."[18] The final decision to expose and debunk Stalin was only reached immediately before the beginning of the Twentieth Party Congress. From that point on, de-Stalinization went hand in hand with attempts to place all the sins of the Soviet regime at the door of Stalin.

At the same time, until a partial halt was called to the campaign against the cult of the individual, the following steps were taken:

1. A decision of the Congress to continue the campaign against the consequences of the cult of the individual in all spheres of Party, government, and ideological life.

2. A decree of the Presidium of the Supreme Soviet of the USSR making it no longer a legally punishable offense for workers and employees to leave enterprises and institutions of their own accord and to absent themselves therefrom for no valid reason.[19]

3. Abolition of the Ministry of Justice of the USSR and transfer of its functions to the union republics.[20]

4. A series of resolutions of the Council of Ministers and the Party Central Committee adopted May–November 1956, extending the rights of the union republics for purposes of decentralization and budgetary control.

5. Decree of the Council of Ministers of the USSR, June 6, 1956, abolishing tuition fees in secondary and higher schools.

6. A series of legislative acts of the Council of Ministers and the Party Central Committee, and of the Presidium of the Supreme Soviet, dealing with social policy, March–November, 1956, covering reduction of the working day, state pensions, wage increases for low-paid workers, monthly credits to collective farmers, extension of leave during and after pregnancy, etc.[21]

These acts and decrees, particularly those concerned with social policy, were among other things also intended to remove the burden of the Stalin inheritance insofar as it affected the basic day-to-day interests of the population. Stalin always maintained a policy of permitting only a "fixed maximum living standard," as if in accordance with Engels's comment to the effect that primitive man discovered "philosophy" when he could eat his fill and make provision for the morrow.

The next question is the nature and extent of the influence exerted upon the development of internal Soviet policy by the events in Poland and Hungary, and whether they tended toward de-Stalinization or re-Stalinization.

---

[17] *Voprosy istorii KPSS*, Moscow, 1957, No. 1, pp. 215, 217.

[18] *Pravda*, January 23, 1956.

[19] *Vedomosti Verkhovnogo Soveta SSSR* (Reports of the Supreme Soviet of the USSR), Moscow, No. 15, 1956, p. 322.

[20] Decree of the Supreme Soviet of May 30, 1956, *Partiinaya zhizn*, No. 24, 1956, p. 43.

[21] *Partiinaya zhizn*, No. 34, 1956, pp. 39–45.

In the sphere of ideology, as has been seen, these events drove the Party leaders back not to Stalin but to Lenin, a fact which partly served to justify the rehabilitation of Stalin's name. This return to Leninism in ideology, together with the rehabilitation of Stalin's name, checked de-Stalinization in the USSR but did not stop it in practice. What might be called "de-Stalinization in practice" continued after the events in Eastern Europe, as is indicated by the following actions:

1. Issuance in the autumn of 1956 of two highly important government decrees dealing with the MVD (Ministry of the Interior), and the concentration camps. These decrees were not published in full but were summarized in the press. One decree provided that "within each oblast the MVD and the police directorates have been reorganized to form a single directorate for the interior attached to the executive committee." The other dealt with the concentration camps:

> The continued existence of corrective labor camps is recognized as no longer serving a useful purpose. It has therefore been decided to reorganize them into corrective labor colonies. . . . To tighten the control over the activities of the corrective labor institutions, observer committees, composed of representatives of the trade unions and the Komsomol organizations, have been attached to the executive committees of the local Soviets.[22]

2. Resolutions of the December 1956 plenary session of the Party Central Committee on decentralization of industrial administration.

3. Ratification by the Supreme Soviet of the USSR in February 1957 of a number of laws regarding administrative and legislative decentralization, including: (a) Placing within the competence of the union republics all legislation dealing with the organization of union republic courts and providing that civil and criminal law as well as codes of civil and criminal procedure would be administered by the union republics themselves; (b) Transferring to the competence of the union republics all matters concerning local, regional, and territorial administration; and (c) Limiting the control exercised by the Supreme Court of the USSR in favor of the supreme courts of the union republics.

4. Repatriation of the deported Caucasian peoples and restoration of their national autonomies.

5. The decree of the February 1957 plenary session of the Party Central Committee on further decentralization of industry.

6. A Central Committee resolution of April 19, 1957, adopted on advice of the Council of Ministers, on suspension of compulsory annual loans.

7. Ratification by the May 1957 session of the Supreme Soviet of a law for "further improvement of administration in building and industry,"[23] providing for continued decentralization.

8. Announcement of the "Khrushchev Plan" for catching up with the United States in the output of meat and dairy produce, and for exempting kolkhozes from the former obligation to make deliveries in kind.

---

[22] *Ibid.*, No. 4, 1957, p. 67.
[23] *Pravda*, May 24, 1957.

9. Publication, in place of Stalin's works, of new works on Marxism-Leninism and on the history of the Party, including: (a) *A Popular History of the CPSU*, a symposium edited by Chief of the Foreign Department of the Central Committee Ponamarev; (b) *Foundations of Marxism-Leninism*, a textbook symposium edited by Chief of the Department of Agitation and Propaganda of the Central Committee Konstantinov; (c) *Foundations of Marxism-Leninism*, a source book edited by member of the Presidium of the Supreme Soviet of the USSR Kuusinen; (d) *Political Economy*, a third revised edition of a source book prepared by Shepilov, Ostrovityanov, Yudin, and others.[24]

These examples of steps taken toward de-Stalinization in practice are corroborated by the Party leaders. Khrushchev, in an interview with Turner Catledge, managing editor of *The New York Times*, on May 10, 1957, said as reported in that paper:

> Stalin had big deficiencies and drawbacks, about which we had occasion to speak and will continue to speak. And we are not sorry to have done so. However, he was a devoted revolutionary and a devoted follower of Marx and Lenin. He made many mistakes, but he also made many great contributions to our Party, to our working people and to our country.[25]

It is typical that in the official Soviet text of the interview, the words "Stalin had big deficiencies and drawbacks about which we had occasion to speak and will continue to speak. And we are not sorry to have done so" were omitted.[26] Another difference in the texts of the interview is equally typical of Soviet censorship. According to Turner Catledge, Khrushchev, when asked what place Stalin would occupy in the history of the USSR, replied, "very great," while according to *Pravda* he merely said: "Stalin will occupy the place that is his due."

What, then, are the conclusions to be drawn as to the general tendency of the future development of the Soviet regime? Since the inner stability achieved by the collective leadership is relative and conditional, any answer to these questions must also be relative and conditional. Moreover, the development of Soviet domestic policy is dependent upon the Soviet international position. Any deterioration in the international status of the Soviet Union will automatically result in a strengthening of the Stalinist group and in increased use of Stalinist methods by the collective leadership, while a general relaxation of international tension may result in the total loss by the group of all influence not only in foreign policy but in domestic policy as well.

With these reservations in mind, we may draw the following conclusions regarding the future of Stalinism in the USSR:

1. De-Stalinization in the USSR is continuing, under strict supervision from above, and within certain definite limits. Lapses back into Stalinism or tendencies towards re-Stalinization after the events in Eastern Europe were reflected in domestic policy, chiefly in the sphere of dogma, without affecting practical

---

[24] *V pomoshch politicheskomu samoobrazovaniyu*, Moscow, No. 5, 1957, pp. 3—12.

[25] *The New York Times* (International Edition), May 11, 1957, p. 3.

[26] *Pravda*, May 13, 1957.

330

measures of administration. Closer examination of this relative re-Staliniz
makes it evident that what is involved is not a return to Stalin, but a return
ideology of Leninism, subjected to considerable revision at the Twentieth Party
Congress.

2. The strength and essence of Stalinism lay not in the realm of theory, but
in the practical system of government. This form of government rested on two
principles—a primary principle of preventive terror, and a secondary principle
of purposive propaganda. These two principles have now been reversed: purposive propaganda has the priority, while terror is no longer preventive.

3. The system of government at present taking shape in the USSR cannot be
called purely Stalinist. Before our eyes, a reformation is taking place. Definitely,
sometimes radically, the form if not the substance of the method of government
is changing. Of course the system has not ceased to be a police system, but the
police is no longer omnipotent. The system of compulsory labor is beginning to
give way to a system of compulsory "voluntariness." The centralized bureaucracy is being decentralized. The standard of living is showing a tendency to
outstrip Stalin's "fixed maximum." Propaganda seeks to entice people rather than
to order them about.

4. The Kremlin is entering upon an era of experimentation and reform from
above in order to modernize the regime, lead it out of Stalin's blind alley, and
thus forestall a possible eruption from below. On the analogy of a socially similar
phenomenon—if such analogies are at all permissible—the regime now emerging
in the USSR may be tentatively called a regime of "enlightened Stalinism," on
the analogy of the "enlightened absolutism" of the second half of the eighteenth
century. But enlightened absolutism was a transitional stage; in Western Europe
it paved the way for the complete abolition of absolutism, while in Russia, on
the contrary, the enlightened absolutism of Catherine II was replaced by the
military-bureaucratic government of Paul I, of Arakcheyev under Alexander I,
and of Nicholas I.

"Enlightened Stalinism" is also a transitional stage—pending either a return to
classical Stalinism, or its complete abolition. Not only does this dilemma constitute a serious danger but it is also extremely difficult to resolve. The present—and
entirely new—situation in the USSR is such that a return to classical Stalinism
would need a new dictator, but of a higher order than Stalin—a difficult thing
to imagine, even in theory. Yet a development tending toward the total abolition
of Stalinism must proceed from a certain minimum of freedom of thought.

Henceforth the USSR must grapple with the problem of resolving this fateful
dilemma. Theoretical considerations and historical experience alike suggest that
the outcome will not depend on the will of the collective leadership alone.

Chapter XXXIV

Revolution in the Kremlin

The June 1957 plenary session of the Party Central Committee expelled Molotov, Kaganovich, Malenkov, and Shepilov from the Presidium and from the Central Committee itself.

If Khrushchev's revelations concerning Stalin at the Twentieth Party Congress were referred to in the press as "Stalin's second funeral," this revolution in the Kremlin could be called his third funeral. From what has been said it is clear that without Molotov, Kaganovich, and Malenkov, Stalin would never have reached the summit of power which he reached in the years before the war. In unmasking the dead Stalin, Khrushchev was unmasking the live creators of Stalin. It was therefore quite natural that the First Secretary should meet with opposition from them, sometimes concealed and sometimes open, whenever he went too far.

It may be objected that Khrushchev, Bulganin, Voroshilov, Mikoyan, Shvernik, Kuusinen, Suslov, and the others had also helped to create Stalin and Stalin's crimes. The statement as it stands seems obvious, but historically it is not valid and politically it is meaningless. Of course the post-Stalin Presidium did not contain a single person who was not implicated directly or morally in Stalin's crimes. But the degree, the character, and the scale of this participation was different in each case. At the time when Stalin, with the support of Molotov and Kaganovich, was creating the Soviet Communist Party, Khrushchev was still a student and Suslov a teacher, while 80% of the post-Stalin members of the Central Committee were not yet members of the Party.

This first period of Stalin's climb to power ended at the time of the Sixteenth Party Congress in 1930 with the total political liquidation of Lenin's Old Guard and official recognition of Stalin as the Party's sole leader. Molotov became head of the government, and Kaganovich Second Secretary of the Central Committee next to Stalin. Before Stalin could become dictator a second stage had to be passed, in 1930–34, during which the triumvirate prepared the liquidation of the Party itself as a political force able to direct its own apparatus. There is no point in repeating here the details given earlier in this book, but it should be noted in passing that in the most critical phase of Stalin's preparations for establishing a personal dictatorship Molotov continued to act as his right hand and Kaganovich as his left. However, it was often true just at that time that Stalin's left hand worked far more efficiently than his right. Molotov's rigid, naturally bureaucratic

mind was devoid of creative imagination. As a fence, a tool, and a scrupulou
executor of a higher will he was of course irreplaceable and Stalin never put
anyone else in his place.

Only during the third phase, that of 1934–39, at the Seventeenth Party Congress in 1934, called by Stalinist historians the Congress of the Victors, did Khrushchev and Bulganin first join the ranks of the "victors," the former as full member
of the Central Committee and the latter as alternate member. According to
Khrushchev's secret speech, 60% of the delegates to the congress and 70% of
the full and alternate members of the Central Committee were arrested and shot on
orders of the triumvirate, which by that time had become a quadrumvirate consisting of Stalin, Molotov, Kaganovich, and Malenkov. The victims had all been
part of the "victors." The few survivors included Khrushchev and Bulganin.
The physical annihilation of the Party, army, and administrative personnel (entirely Stalinist by then) was directed by a Politburo commission which included
the quadrumvirate among its members, but did not include either Khrushchev
and Bulganin or Voroshilov and Mikoyan. It was for this reason that such persons as Khrushchev and Bulganin, and, of course, Suslov and Belyayev have
alibis and can prove, if necessary, that the famous "Yezhov lists" for the purging
and extra-judicial execution of Party members, politicians, and service officers
were signed not by Stalin alone, as Khrushchev reported at the Twentieth Party
Congress, but also by Molotov, Kaganovich, and Malenkov as members of the
Politburo commission.

But neither, of course, was Khrushchev simply idling away his time in the
areas committed to his care, and on this account he did not repudiate the whole of
Stalin but had to invent the theory of the existence of "two Stalins," the "anti-
Leninist Stalin" being the Stalin whose crimes had been committed in company
with Molotov, Malenkov, Kaganovich, and Beria, and the "Leninist Stalin"
being the Stalin whose crimes had been committed in the company of Khrushchev, Bulganin, Voroshilov, Shvernik, and Mikoyan. Therefore, in his general
appraisal of Stalin after the liquidation of the Molotov group, Khrushchev said:

> Our respect for Stalin was sincere, as we stood weeping at his coffin. Sincere,
> too, is our present appreciation of the part he had played—insofar as it was useful. . . .
> Each of us had faith in Stalin, and our faith was based on our conviction that the
> task Stalin and we were performing together was being done in the interests of the
> revolution. . . . We all have no hesitation in blaming Stalin for the gross errors and
> mistakes which have caused serious harm to the Party and to the people. We have
> lost many honest and devoted men, Party functionaries, civil servants, innocent of
> calumny.[1]

And again:

> To be able rightly to understand the essence of the Party's criticism of the cult
> of the individual, it must be fully grasped that we see *two* sides to Comrade Stalin's
> activities: the useful side which has our support and which we highly prize, and the
> evil side which we criticize, condemn, and reject.[2]

[1] *Kommunist*, No. 12, 1957, p. 20.
[2] *Ibid.*, p. 19.

This "useful side" of the "Leninist Stalin" included, according to Khrushchev, the struggle of Stalin and the Stalinists against "bourgeois nationalists and the followers of Trotsky, Zinoviev, and Bukharin." But here, too, Khrushchev provided a new and a significant description of the events:

> It was a political struggle. The Party was right in showing them up as opponents of Leninism, opponents of socialist construction in our land. They have been condemned, and rightly condemned, on political grounds.[3]

But were they, in fact, condemned "on political grounds" alone, as "opponents of Leninism?" Were they not also condemned as "enemies of the people," as "wreckers," "traitors," "spies," and "murderers?" Was this condemnation, when they were found guilty after trial by a criminal court of law, really legitimate? Khrushchev's new description, which expressed the view that the Trotskyites and Bukharinites were merely "opponents of Leninism," that is, only ideological opponents, represents a veiled rehabilitation by omitting the accusation that they were criminal "bandits" and "spies." They could therefore be publicly rehabilitated in the press only after the liquidation of Molotov, Kaganovich, and Malenkov.

But who, then, was responsible for the terror in the Party and in the country as a whole after Khrushchev himself became a member of the Politburo? For it was after that that Kosior, Chubar, Eikhe, and Rudzutak were shot in 1939–40 and that Voznesensky, Kuznetsov, Rodionov, and Popkov met the same fate in 1948. Yet for this question too, Khrushchev had a ready answer: "Beria, that mortal enemy of the Party and the people, incited Stalin and took advantage of his defects. Comrade Malenkov is also much to blame. He fell completely under the influence of Beria and became his shadow and his tool."[4] It would be vain to ask Khrushchev why Beria or Malenkov, who became members of the Politburo long after Khrushchev, should be held more responsible than he for the crimes of Stalin and his Politburo. Khrushchev's general answer to the question of responsibility was more convincing than his answer to the question of whose responsibility was greatest. "We were afraid of him," said Khrushchev. And Bulganin: "You would go to see Stalin on a friendly visit, but you would never know where you would end up on the way back: at home or in prison." And Politburo member Voroshilov telephoning obsequiously to Stalin's Secretariat: "Would you be kind enough to ask Comrade Stalin if I may be present at the meeting of the Politburo?"

It was, after all, Khrushchev himself who was describing the past to the members of the Twentieth Party Congress.

Before considering in detail Khrushchev's charges against Molotov, Kaganovich, Malenkov, and Shepilov as stated in the resolution of the June 1957 plenary session of the Central Committee, the following should be noted:

1. Absolutely nothing is known of the counter-charges and counter-arguments leveled at Khrushchev by the Molotov group.

---

[3] *Ibid.*, p. 19.
[4] *Ibid.*, p. 20.

2. Several of the charges leveled by Khrushchev at the Molotov group throw less light on Khrushchev's views than on his desire to give expression to the mood of the Party rank and file and of the population as a whole and to take advantage for propaganda purposes of the popular discontent with Stalin's methods of government.

3. Khrushchev did not immediately recover from the bitter personal attack which his opponents launched against him openly at the plenary session and which was probably not unjustified from the point of view of the interests of the regime; he was therefore obliged to be circumspect in his experiments for some time after the meeting.

4. The presence in the Central Committee Presidium of Voroshilov—an old friend of Stalin's and one of the founders of the "cult of Stalin"—as well as of the three old Stalinists Shvernik, Kuusinen, and Mikoyan, all served for a time to restrain Khrushchev from a more thorough destruction of the "cult of Stalin."

As to the technical aspects of the resolution, the following may be said:

1. In spite of its length, the resolution was general and somewhat abstract, while the charges, serious as they were, were based on no argument at all.

2. The resolution clearly bore the imprint of improvisation and haste. It had no logical consistency or even stylistic unity. Argument flitted from one point to another. The same charges were frequently repeated in different places.

3. Contrary to former practice in "unmasking anti-Party groups" the resolution mentioned only points with which members of the group were not in agreement and said nothing about the constructive measures which they had proposed.

4. The resolution called attention to the fact that all Central Committee members "with one abstention in the person of Comrade Molotov" voted for the expulsion from the Central Committee of Molotov, Kaganovich, Malenkov, and Shepilov. In other words, Kaganovich, Malenkov, and Shepilov had voted for their own expulsion from the Central Committee. (In Stalin's time all the accused always ended by confessing to their guilt, but they never voted for their own political death sentences, as they are doing under Khrushchev).

5. Now that Khrushchev is at the head of the Party, it appears that not only the full members of the Central Committee but even the alternate members as well, although according to the Party statutes, they possess consultative powers only,[5] vote for the expulsion of members of the Central Committee and of the Presidium of the Central Committee. Even members of the Central Control Commission, who, according to the same statutes,[6] do not even have the right to be consulted at plenary sessions of the Central Committee, also voted for expulsion. Even Stalin never disregarded these provisions of the statutes which had existed ever since the founding of the Party.

[5] *Ustav KPSS* (Statutes of the Communist Party of the Soviet Union), Moscow, 1952, Paragraph 33.
[6] *Ibid.*, Paragraph 39.

As to the substance of Khrushchev's charges, the main points boil down to the following:

Domestic Policy. 1. The members of the group "for three to four years," that is, from the day of Stalin's death, "offered direct and indirect resistance to the policy approved by the Twentieth Party Congress," particularly to "the correction of errors and mistakes resulting from the cult of the individual."

2. "They were against expansion of the rights of the union republics."

3. "The anti-Party group resisted the measures adopted by the Party to combat the spirit of bureaucracy. . . . The group stubbornly resisted and attempted to sabotage such an important measure as the reorganization of industrial control and the creation of economic councils for economic regions. . . ."

4. "They refused to admit the need for giving the collective farmers greater incentives for expanding agricultural production. . . . They argued against the abolition of the old bureaucratic planning system in collective farming and the introduction of a new planning system. . . . the members of the anti-Party group opposed the abolition of compulsory deliveries of agricultural products from the private plots of collective farmers. . . ."

5. "They opposed the Party's appeal to overtake the per capita production of milk, butter, and meat in the United States within the next few years. By acting in this way, members of the anti-Party group showed a scornful indifference to the vital daily needs of the population. . . ."

6. "Comrade Molotov showed a conservative and unenterprising attitude in resisting the plowing of 35 million hectares of new agricultural land. . . ."

7. "Comrades Malenkov, Kaganovich, and Molotov offered stubborn resistance to the measures adopted by the Central Committee and our entire Party for liquidation of the consequences of the cult of the individual. . . ."

Foreign Policy. 1. "In the sphere of foreign policy, the group, and in particular Comrade Molotov, showed a lack of enterprise and tried in every way to prevent the adoption of necessary new measures for the easing of international tension. . . ."

2. "Comrade Molotov frequently spoke against the measures put into effect by the Presidium of the Central Committee for the improvement of relations with Yugoslavia."

3. "Comrade Molotov delayed the conclusion of the political agreement with Austria. . . . and did not want relations with Japan placed on a more normal basis. . . ."

4. "He expressed himself against the Party's considered policy for the prevention of war in the present circumstances and against its policy which admitted the possibility of *different roads to socialism* in various countries and the necessity for strengthening contacts of the Soviet Communist Party with progressive parties in foreign countries."

336

5. "Comrade Molotov frequently spoke against the Soviet government's ṇ and necessary steps undertaken for the defense of peace and the security c nations. ... He denied the usefulness of personal contacts between the leading statesmen of the USSR on the one hand and the statesmen of foreign countries on the other—an essential measure in the interests of mutual understanding and the improvement of international relations."

6. "In a number of these questions, Comrade Molotov's opinion was supported by Comrade Kaganovich and on many occasions by Comrade Malenkov."

The resolution held that the political position taken by the Molotov group had its origin in the fact that "Comrades Malenkov, Kaganovich, and Molotov were and are hidebound by old concepts and methods; they ignore changed circumstances and conditions, show a conservative attitude, cling grimly to... obsolete forms and methods of work, and reject all natural innovations and all consequences of the development of Soviet society. ... Both in domestic and foreign policy their behavior is sectarian and dogmatic...."[7] The resolution noted that Molotov, Kaganovich, and Malenkov had not only tried to defend their policy within the Presidium of the Central Committee but "took to intrigue and arrived at a secret agreement directed against the Central Committee."[8] They were joined by Shepilov, who had for a short time been Minister of Foreign Affairs and was also Secretary of the Central Committee for matters of ideology.

The resolution had nothing to say about the contents of the "secret agreement" or how broad was the circle of its participants apart from the persons already mentioned, or what support they were counting on in the country. But the authors of the resolution solemnly bestowed praise on themselves: "The plenary session of the Central Committee notes with immense satisfaction the monolithic unity and solidarity of all full and alternate members of the Central Committee and of the members of the Central Control Commission, who have unanimously condemned the anti-Party group. There was not a single person among the members of the plenary session of the Central Committee who supported this group."[9]

The resolution made no mention of speeches made at the session by members of the Molotov group, leaving the inference that they did not speak at all. But in that case, it is difficult to understand why the session went on for seven whole days. The resolution did hint at a speech made by one of the group at the end of the session in a passage reading: "Faced by the unanimous condemnation by the Central Committee plenary session of the group's anti-Party activity, when the members of the Central Committee unanimously demanded the group's ejection from the Central Committee and its expulsion from the Party, they admitted the existence of an agreement and the harmfulness of their anti-Party activity, and promised to submit to the decisions of the Party."[10] Moreover, he

---

[7] All quotations are from the "Resolution of the Central Committee of the Communist Party of the Soviet Union on the Anti-Party Group of G.M. Malenkov, L. M. Kaganovich and V. M. Molotov," *Voprosy istorii KPSS*, Moscow, No. 1, 1957, pp. 4–7.

[8] *Ibid.*, p. 7.

[9] *Ibid.*

[10] *Ibid.*, p. 78.

considered it important to emphasize that the resolution was "adopted unanimously"—the word "unanimously" was repeated seven times in the last three paragraphs of the resolution.

Khrushchev may be believed when he says that Molotov and his followers admitted "the harmfulness of their anti-Party activity and promised to submit to the decisions of the Party," but how can this be reconciled with the action of Molotov, the head of the group, who "abstained from voting," thus disturbing the idyllic unanimity of this highly monolithic meeting? Something is wrong with the picture. Stalin was a far more skillful stage manager in matters of this kind. Khrushchev might say that he had condemned Stalin's methods and did not compel people to "practice self-abasement." But "self-abasement" by "dogmatics and schismatics" would have presented a more convincing argument than the frequent "unanimity" of Khrushchev with himself.

It must be admitted that "Stalin's methods" of dealing with opponents appear almost "democratic" compared to Khrushchev's modernized Stalinism. The Trotskyites were granted an opportunity to publish in *Pravda* their counterarguments against Stalin. Zinoviev made to the Fourteenth Party Congress a counterreport against Stalin. Bukharin, Rykov, Tomsky openly expounded their views in "manifestos" and in speeches at plenary sessions of the Central Committee, and enjoyed for a long time the right to belong to the Central Committee and to the Party while disagreeing with Stalin. Meanwhile, the Party discussed their programs for months and sometimes years until a Congress, and not merely a Central Committee plenary session, took a decision "on the incompatability between making propaganda for their views on the one hand and holding Party membership on the other." But Khrushchev within his narrow circle of Party functionaries, and without asking the opinion of the so-called Party, took only a few days to decide the fate of persons who had created both Khrushchev and the "wise and great Party."

The three main points of the indictment of the Molotov group were that the group had opposed:

1. The easing of international tension.
2. The exposure of Stalin and his methods of government.
3. The raising of the standard of living of the people.

If the group had really opposed these things, while Khrushchev condemned their opposition, this would mean that Khrushchev: (1) supported the return of normal international relations; (2) emphasized the policy of exposing Stalin and rejected Stalin's methods of government; and (3) was revising Stalin's economic policy of giving priority to the development of heavy industry as the basic foundation of Soviet economy, and was in favor of restoring a normal division of investment among heavy, light, and food industries. Was he in fact doing these things? Did anything change in the foreign and domestic policy of the Kremlin after the expulsion of the Molotov group? In foreign policy the course set by Molotov remained unchanged. Indeed, there were definite facts to indicate that the course was tending to bring Soviet foreign policy back to the point of departure—the "pure methods" of the "Stalin era." The facts showed unequivocally that the new Kremlin leadership was implementing Molotov's policy more consistently than Molotov himself. Even more startling was the fact that the Kremlin's foreign policy was still symbolized by the grim Gromyko, who combined the three qualities of the three founders of Moscow's present policy—Molotov's obstinacy, Vyshinsky's hypocrisy, and Stalin's absolute amorality.

What about "Stalin's methods," or, as the resolution put it, the "obsolete methods and forms"? As we have seen, the "obsolete methods" were applied first of all to the Molotov group itself. Then came the turn of the potentially more dangerous part of the population—the intelligentsia, and particularly the cultural intelligentsia. In "unmasking" Molotov and his group, as well as "Shepilov who had joined it," the periodical *Kommunist* reported that at congresses of Soviet artists and writers, as well as at a conference in Moscow to celebrate the 86th anniversary of Lenin's birth, Shepilov had advocated a cultural policy which ran counter to the decisions of the Twentieth Party Congress and the policy of the Central Committee. Of what had Shepilov's separate policy consisted? The answer as given by *Kommunist* was as follows:

> As the man responsible for the ideological sphere, Shepilov betrayed the trust of the Central Committee. He departed from the policy indicated by the Twentieth Party Congress of the CPSU in questions of literature and art. . . . He assumed a. . . liberal position. . . . In his bid for personal popularity he tried flirting with demagogues. . . . The general tenor of his speeches is invariably liberal.[11]

Kommunist's leading article was particularly incensed at the fact that in order to justify his "liberal policy" Shepilov had referred to Lenin by "quoting [him] out of context." One such quotation which Shepilov had allegedly cited out of context was: "It is certainly essential to ensure a great deal of freedom for personal initiative, individual leanings, thought and imagination, form and content."[12] Of this *Kommunist* complained: "And not a word more! Shepilov did not quote a single other thought of Lenin's regarding art and literature."[13] Apparently Shepilov should have quoted not this passage, but another concerning "the Party spirit in literature." In other words, he should have quoted the full text of Stalin's and Zhdanov's directives on literature and art issued in 1946–48 when Zhdanov first began to purge "cosmopolitans" and "bootlickers." As to these directives, *Kommunist* went on:

> In his speech at the Writers' Congress, Shepilov mentioned these directives. But how? Only in passing. He mentioned some of the problems discussed in these documents but did no more than name them as part of a list. He did not even mention Lenin's principle demanding a Party spirit in everything, the principle which underlies all these documents.[14]

---

[11] *Kommunist*, No. 10, 1957, p. 16.
[12] *Ibid.*, p. 17.
[13] *Ibid.*
[14] *Ibid.*, pp. 16, 17.

But clearly this accusation merely charged Shepilov with having opposed Zhdanov's and Stalin's methods of literary criticism, and these had been condemned not only by the Twentieth Party Congress but also by *Kommunist* itself in articles published following the congress. Also to be noted in defense of Shepilov is that his speech, like every responsible speech made by a Central Committee Secretary or a member of the Presidium, was first censored by the Secretariat and the Presidium of the Central Committee! Why then had the Central Committee (Khrushchev) not removed the anti-Leninist and "liberal" heresies contained in Shepilov's reports to the congress? In any case, how could Shepilov belong to Molotov's group if he was a "liberal"?

As to the charge that the members of the Molotov group supported Stalin's cult of the individual, this too appears to have little basis. The Stalin debunked at the Twentieth Party Congress and whom Lenin proposed to remove from the Central Committee has still not been removed from Lenin's mausoleum. Innumerable cities and villages, factories, kolkhozes, and schools still bear the name of Stalin. Even the "Stalin prizes," which had been renamed "Lenin prizes" while the Molotov group was in power, again received their old name immediately after liquidation of the worshippers of the cult of Stalin. In a speech published in *Kommunist* and reprinted in *Pravda*, Khrushchev declared with his usual candor: "I consider that anyone who has received a Stalin prize must be proud to wear the emblem. If I had a Stalin prize, I would be wearing the emblem."[15] And in another speech, delivered November 7, 1957, Khrushchev declared: "The Party has fought and will continue to fight all those who defame Stalin, who, under the pretext of criticizing the cult of the individual, distort the whole historical period of activity of our Party when Stalin was at the head of the Central Committee."[16]

Of all the domestic problems confronting the régime, agriculture still remains the most intractable. In this respect Khrushchev has made such far-reaching promises, incorporated in actual obligations assumed by all the union republics, that their fulfillment has become for him not only a question of peronal prestige but also in the eyes of the Party a general test of the correctness of his policy as against that of the group which has been isolated from the main body of the Party but not entirely liquidated.

Khrushchev returned to this problem after the Central Committee's June 1957 plenary session. He promised to put a final end to Stalin's agricultural policy by allowing freedom of action for peasant initiative within the kolkhozes. His criticism of the old policy was so devastating that it is worth while examining it again:

> Why has our agriculture been so backward for so long a time? The reason is that no one in Moscow wished to deal effectively with the situation in the countryside. Stalin, of course, never went anywhere, did not ask the opinion of agriculturists, did not listen to what people on the spot had to say. . . . The principle of increased rewards for greater production was grossly violated. . . . Let me give you a few examples. Soon after the end of the war, I visited the village where I was born and

[15] *Kommunist*, No. 12, 1957, p. 21.
[16] *Pravda*, November 7, 1957.

went to see my cousin. She had an orchard. I said to her: "You have wonderful apples." She replied: "I am going to cut the trees down in fall." "Why?" I asked. "I have to pay heavy taxes on them," she said, "it is not at all profitable to have an orchard."

I reported this conversation to J. V. Stalin and told him that the collective farmers were doing away with their gardens. Afterward he told me that I was a populist *(narodnik)*, that I had a populist approach to things and that I was losing my proletarian class feeling.

Here is another example. . . . We used to send thousands of townspeople to harvest potatoes on kolkhozes, while the collective farmers themselves took no part at all in harvesting potatoes. Why did the collective farmers not want to take part in this work? Because we paid very low prices for potato deliveries. The cost of transporting potatoes to the delivery center was higher than the entire price received by the collective farmer for the potatoes.[17]

The June 1957 events also cast light on the balance of power and the top strata of the Kremlin hierarchy after the war and after Stalin's death. After the war Zhdanov appeared to be the one who, of all the members of the Politburo, had the greatest chance to be Stalin's heir, but as soon as Malenkov joined the Politburo in 1946 it became less clear who would be the heir, particularly as Zhdanov dealt only with propaganda, whereas Malenkov continued to deal with Party personnel. The silent struggle which was waged between the two pretenders continued with varying success. Stalin needed them both, and he needed them as rivals. For they competed not with Stalin but with each other on behalf of Stalin, each trying to prove that he was more reliable than the other in understanding and carrying out the dictator's will. But at the precise moment when it seemed as if Stalin had made his final choice, and that this choice had fallen to Zhdanov, the unforeseen happened: Zhdanov died. Stalin, it is true, came to believe that his death had been foreseen and prepared for, and this belief found an outlet in the Doctors Case, but immediately after Zhdanov's death, Stalin himself either organized, or at least gave his blessing to, the liquidation of Zhdanov's followers, in the Leningrad Case. Why? Khrushchev answered this question at the Twentieth Party Congress as follows:

> The rise of Voznesensky and Kuznetsov worried Beria. As we have just shown, it was Beria who suggested to Stalin that he and his assistants fabricate the necessary documents. . . . Stalin personally followed the "Leningrad Case." . . . When Stalin received these documents from Beria and Abakumov, he did not examine this libellous material, but simply ordered further investigation of the Voznesensky-Kuznetsov case to be stopped. This sealed their fate.[18]

After the June 1957 plenary session of the Central Committee, Khrushchev gave a different answer in a speech in Leningrad. He said: "Malenkov, who was one of the chief organizers of the so-called Leningrad Case, was simply afraid to visit you here."[19] And in a conversation with Aneurin Bevan he offered a third

---

[17] *Kommunist*, No. 42, 1957.
[18] *Rech Khrushcheva*, p. 38.
[19] *Pravda*, July 7, 1957.

solution of the mystery of Voznesensky's death. According to Bevan, at the end of the war the members of the Presidium had initiated a study of the Soviet economy as a basis for future planning. The results of the study convinced them that it was necessary to allow more private initiative and decentralization in many sectors of the national economy. They prepared a detailed project along these lines, which Voznesensky, in charge of Soviet planning, presented to Stalin. Voznesensky, on his return from an interview with Stalin, reported that Stalin had attacked him as "a traitor to socialism." On the following day, several Presidium members went to Stalin to say that the plan had not been Voznesensky's but had represented the collective views of the Presidium, and to ask Stalin to apologize to Voznesensky for having treated him unfairly. Stalin had replied: "I cannot do this, he was executed this morning."[20]

In summing up the crimes committed by Stalin, Khrushchev said at the Twentieth Party Congress that it was Beria himself who had encouraged Stalin to commit these crimes and that at the time it had been impossible to unmask Beria as he had known how to take advantage of Stalin's weaknesses.[21]

It is interesting to note that Khrushchev, after the June 1957 plenary session of the Central Committee, made the same accusation of Malenkov: "While holding a high position in the Party and the state, Comrade Malenkov not only failed to restrain J. V. Stalin but very cleverly made use of Stalin's weaknesses and habits during the last year of his life. Frequently he encouraged him to commit acts which deserve to be severely condemned."[22]

Which of these two accusations was correct? Probably both. But the reasons given by Khrushchev for the great powers enjoyed in Stalin's lifetime by these two members of the Politburo rather than by others were obviously false. Malenkov had created and controlled the entire Party apparatus while Beria had perfected and controlled the police administration. They had held their positions under Stalin not because they were cunning manipulators and shrewd intriguers able to make use of a weak master but because Stalin had based his own position on the smooth interplay of these two organizations and their chiefs. If "tens of thousands of Party and government officials," in addition to millions of non-Party citizens, had been done away with in the process, this too had been done in the interests of the system and not in the interests of Beria and Malenkov alone.

Khrushchev's statement that "Malenkov not only failed to restrain Stalin but even encouraged him to commit his crimes" leads to another important conclusion, namely, that within the system as a whole Malenkov had become the leading power, whom everyone had to respect, including Stalin. The first to note this was B. I. Nikolayevsky. A number of facts previously overlooked assumed new significance in the light of Khrushchev's statement. These facts are as follows:

1. After Zhdanov's death and the liquidation of his followers, in 1949, Malenkov become the Second Secretary of the Central Committee, after Stalin.

[20] *New York Herald Tribune*, Dezember 16, 1957.
[21] *Rech Khrushcheva*, p. 44.
[22] *Kommunist*, No. 12, 1957, p. 20.

2. A short time after, in 1950, he became Stalin's deputy prime minister.

3. The Political Report to the Party Central Committee at the Nineteenth Party Congress was made not by Stalin but by Malenkov.

4. At the first plenary session of the Central Committee after the Nineteenth Party Congress, the small Politburo was replaced by an expanded Central Committee Presidium consisting of 25 members, of whom 15 were direct followers of Malenkov. (Khrushchev had earlier attributed the creation of this Presidium to Stalin's evil influence, but he could not attribute the same act to Malenkov, as all of Malenkov's followers had gone over to Khrushchev.)

5. In the course of this plenary session, Stalin was relieved of his post as Secretary-General of the Central Committee and left as merely one of the secretaries, while Malenkov became in practice First Secretary of the Central Committee.

There can be no doubt that Malenkov became the principal member of the Politburo after Stalin, but it is impossible to maintain with any certainty that Malenkov had been earmarked as heir by Stalin himself. Even Khrushchev did not say so directly, although he attempted to create the impression that such was the case. It may be said that Malenkov, after Stalin's death, became head of the Party and of the state not because of a "testament" by Stalin (assuming that Stalin had time to draw up such a testament), but quite automatically as the First Secretary of the Central Committee. It is also true that the Central Committee Presidium created by the Nineteenth Party Congress was dissolved and a new and smaller Presidium created, with approximately the same membership as that of the old Politburo, with the balance of power within the Presidium and the place of each member of the Presidium within the whole pyramid of power remaining almost the same as before Stalin's death, as is shown by comparison of the following two published lists, bearing in mind that such lists were at the time drawn up in order of importance in the pyramid of power. One list is that of members of the Poliburo published in *Pravda*, December 21, 1949, and the other is the list of members of the new Central Committee Presidium, published in *Pravda*, March, 7, 1953:

POLITBURO December 21, 1949	CENTRAL COMMITTEE PRESIDIUM March 7, 1953
Malenkov	Malenkov
Molotov	Beria
Beria	Molotov
Voroshilov	Voroshilov
Mikoyan	Khrushchev
Kaganovich	Kaganovich
Bulganin	Bulganin
Andreyev	Mikoyan
Khrushchev	Pervukin
Kosygin	Saburov

As the lists show, after Stalin's death changes within the old Politburo were very insignificant. Malenkov had retained his place, Beria and Molotov had exchanged theirs. Khrushchev, who in Stalin's time had occupied the next to the last place (admittedly a dangerous place from the point of view of purges) had moved up to occupy fifth place, ousting Mikoyan who was now eighth. Andreyev and Kosygin had been excluded at the first plenary session of the Central Committee elected by the Nineteenth Party Congress. Voroshilov, Kaganovich, and Bulganin had retained their former places.

It may be asked why Malenkov and Beria had retained their places within the pyramid of power after Stalin's death. Whose weaknesses were they now able to exploit? Obviously they were now able to exploit the weaknesses of all other Politburo members who, though they might be well known as individuals, had no apparatus of power at their disposal. The status of such persons was so uncertain that they did not dare to raise a question of vital importance to them, that of collective leadership. In this connection, it is significant that the new leadership never took the trouble to have an odd number of members in the Presidium, as Stalin's Politburo invariably had, in case a question arising in the Presidium had to be decided by majority vote. At this stage there was no necessity for such refinements. Power as a whole was concentrated in the hands of the Party apparatus, under Malenkov, and the police, under Beria. Besides, Beria was Malenkov's first deputy in the cabinet.

But this stage lasted for only a week. On March 14, 1953, Malenkov asked to be relieved of his post as First Secretary of the Party Central Committee and for the first time spoke of a "collective leadership." This was the beginning of the end, both for Malenkov and for Beria. Khrushchev became Acting First Secretary and prepared the way for Beria's liquidation in order to liquidate Malenkov as well. Khrushchev and the others were probably able to convince Malenkov that Beria was aiming to occupy his place and wished to put the MVD above Party and government. Malenkov, who had been foolish enough to relinquish his own Party apparatus, was now equally foolish in sacrificing the police apparatus. He agreed to liquidate Beria and his group, and it was he who reported Beria's liquidation to a Central Committee plenary session in July 1953. About a month later, a Central Committee plenary session in September approved the appointment of Khrushchev as First Secretary of the Central Committee.

The "palace etiquette" was gradually revised and members of the Central Committee Presidium were officially listed in alphabetical order. At almost the same time, Malenkov announced at the August 1953 session of the Supreme Soviet his own "Plan for the Speedy Development of Light and Food Industries." Throughout the country the new plan raised high hopes and even aroused considerable enthusiasm. By 1954 the first results of Malenkov's plan had become evident. Goods, in some cases from state reserves, began to appear in the shops. Some consumption goods were even bought abroad for foreign exchange, something which Stalin had never permitted. Malenkov, who until then had been considered a soulless favorite of Stalin, became a popular figure. Although "Malenkov's Plan" was in fact the plan prepared by the entire Central Committee Presidium and adopted immediately after Stalin's death and Beria's execution, the people credited Malenkov for it, and the members of the Presidium began to have doubts. In January 1955, they commissioned Shepilov, the chief editor of *Pravda*, to criticize the plan as "anti-Leninist" and "anti-Stalinist," Khrushchev at that time still needing the authority of Stalin's name. Shepilov's article bore an awesome title reminiscent of Stalin's style: "The General Line of the Party and Vulgarisers of Marxism."[23] The main theme of Shepilov's article was that Lenin and Stalin had always emphasized that priority for the development of heavy industry was the basic foundation of Soviet economic policy. The article did not, of course, mention Malenkov by name, but criticized severely what it called "the policy of rapid development of light industry."

Why did the article appear on January 24 and not on any other day? Because January 25, 1955, was the day set for the opening of the plenary session of the Central Committee which was to decide the fate of Malenkov's Plan and of Malenkov himself as Prime Minister. It was obviously addressed to the members of the Central Committee as a warning regarding their behavior during discussion of the Malenkov question. The session opened on January 25 with a report by Khrushchev on livestock raising. It continued until January 31.[24]

In the introduction to his report, Khrushchev repeated almost word for word the basic assumptions of Shepilov's article, describing the policy of promoting light industry as a policy of capitulation similar to that preached by Bukharin and Rykov.[25] It now became clear that Shepilov's article had not been an exercise in literary composition but represented the political program of the First Secretary of the Central Committee.

Much of the force behind Khrushchev's plan derived from the fact that it not only represented his own views but also reflected fully the program of Molotov and Kaganovich who, together with Stalin, had founded the "general line." Passed over in favor of Malenkov and Beria during the allocation of positions after Stalin's death, they now saw in the attacks on Malenkov the eagerly awaited opportunity of seizing the reins of power. The result was the creation of a temporary bloc, consisting of Molotov's and Khrushchev's groups, directed against Malenkov. Malenkov's fate as Prime Minister was now sealed. He was relieved of his post, although his removal was not announced until a week later, at a session of the Supreme Soviet. In a statement read to the Supreme Soviet, Malenkov emphasized the fact that he considered preferential development for heavy industry as basic to Soviet economic policy and added that he had been responsible for the collapse of agriculture during his tenure of office as Secretary of the Central Committee. He excused the deficiencies of his leadership and his wish to surrender his post as being due to a lack of experience in state affairs. This from a man who for an uninterrupted period of almost twenty years (1934–53) had been in charge of all government and Party personnel for the USSR and for fourteen years (1939–53) a secretary of the Party Central Committee.

---

[23] *Pravda*, January, 24, 1955.

[24] *Pravda*, February 2, 1955.

[25] *Pravda*, February 3, 1955.

Although Molotov and Kaganovich had helped Khrushchev to remove Malenkov they failed to achieve their own aims. Khrushchev offered the post of prime minister to his old Moscow friend Bulganin, probably not without Malenkov's assistance, in order to keep it out of Molotov's hands. In recommending Bulganin to the Supreme Soviet in the name of the Party Central Committee, Khrushchev did not stint words of praise: "Comrade Bulganin, a worthy disciple of the great Lenin and one of the closest collaborators of J. V. Stalin, is a prominent statesman and Party member."[26]

Molotov had become the deputy of his own former deputy, Bulganin, but for him there was worse to come. He apparently had failed to foresee that in helping to remove first Beria and then Malenkov he was digging his own grave. As a pretender to the post of Party leader after Stalin, Molotov was an exceptionally dangerous figure. For almost thirty years his name had been mentioned in the Party side by side with that of Stalin. For nine years (1921–30) he had been a secretary of the Central Committee, for eleven years (1930–41) Prime Minister, throughout the war Deputy Chairman of the Committee of State Defense of the USSR, and the only survivor in the Central Committee from Lenin's Old Guard. Moreover, although an Old Bolshevik, he had never been in any opposition or deviationist group. And he was the Party's main theorist after Stalin. In normal circumstances, he would have been the recognized and lawful successor to Stalin.

To remove such a person was no easy task, even for Stalin, although Stalin, as Khrushchev told the Twentieth Party Congress, had made the attempt. But what Stalin had failed to do, perhaps from lack of time, Khrushchev was able to achieve. He opened his first attack on Molotov at the plenary session of the Party Central Committee in July 1955. The discussions centered around the foreign policy of the USSR, for which Molotov was responsible. The press did not report on the discussions. But a resolution adopted at the close of the June 1957 plenary session of the Central Committee stated that "Comrade Molotov's mistaken policy regarding Yugoslavia was unanimously condemned by the plenary session of the Party Central Committee in July 1955."[27]

Khrushchev was also able at the July 1955 plenary session to expand the Presidium of the Central Committee by making Kirichenko and Suslov members. At the same time Aristov, Belyayev, and Shepilov were made members of the Central Committee Secretariat. Shepilov having not only betrayed his old patron Malenkov but also his new one, Molotov, by approving Khrushchev's Yugoslav policy, Khrushchev showed his gratitude by appointing him Secretary of the Central Committee.

A second attack on Molotov took place in the pages of *Pravda*, of which Shepilov was editor-in-chief. The excuse was an innocent remark by Molotov to the Supreme Soviet in February 1955 to the effect that the USSR had built no more than the "foundations of socialism." In speaking of "foundations" in the broad sense, he had committed no error even from the point of view of orthodoxy.

---

[26] *Izvestia*, February 9, 1955.
[27] *Voprosy istorii KPSS*, Moscow, No. 1, 1957, p. 6.

In ordinary circumstances, nobody would have paid the slightest attention. But circumstances, as far as Molotov was concerned, were obviously ceasing to be ordinary. Molotov was asked to confess publicly to his error. Molotov, as a well disciplined bureaucrat, succumbed to pressure and hastened to disavow himself publicly as a Party theorist. In a letter to the editorial board of *Kommunist*, he said: "I consider my statement regarding the creation of a socialist society in the USSR given at the February 8, 1955 session of the Supreme Soviet of the USSR theoretically erroneous and politically harmful, for it can lead to the conclusion that no more than the foundations of a socialist society have been built in the USSR."[28]

It was thus proved to the satisfaction of Party fanatics that Molotov was no longer a Party theorist. In the Soviet Communist Party this was an important victory for Khrushchev. He cemented it by having Molotov's error condemned again in a resolution of the Twentieth Party Congress. However, these attacks were no more than pin-pricks in comparison with what lay in store for Molotov, as well as for Kaganovich and Malenkov, at the Twentieth Party Congress. First, Khrushchev took full charge of the entire apparatus of the Party by creating a new Central Committee Secretariat, of the police, through Serov, the new chief of the Committee of State Defense and Dudorov, of the MVD, and of the army, through a complete new leadership consisting of Zhukov, Sokolovsky, Moskalenko, Biryuzov, Malinovsky, and Bagramyan. He also made sure of the support of Mikoyan, Bulganin, Suslov, and Kirichenko in the Central Committee Presidium. Having done all this, he made his famous speech against Stalin.

The speech was ultimately aimed not only against Stalin but also against the future anti-Party group of Molotov, Kaganovich, and Malenkov. Khrushchev's special report on the cult of the individual had not been written by the collective leadership. It was an ably drafted and convincingly argued indictment drawn up by the Khrushchev wing within the Presidium. That it bore the obvious imprint of Khrushchev's own personality is evident from the somewhat romantic digression, the examples from Khrushchev's own experience, and the not always orthodox phrasing. The report named Molotov and Kaganovich in connection with the Yezhov purge, by citing the telegram sent by Stalin and Zhdanov from Sochi, and Malenkov in connection with the erroneous directives issued during the war by Stalin, Malenkov, and Vasilevsky from General Headquarters. The anti-Molotov edge of Khrushchev's report was not allowed to protrude too sharply. Nevertheless, the prestige and future careers of Molotov, Kaganovich, and Malenkov had been dealt a crippling blow. Whereas the names of the rank and file members of the Politburo had been connected with certain of Stalin's crimes on certain occasions, the names of these three had been connected with all his crimes on all occasions.

The main theme of Khrushchev's report—"liquidation of the consequences of the cult of the individual"—spelled in the last analysis liquidation of the Molotov group. In consequence Molotov, Kaganovich, and Malenkov again found a

---

[28] *Kommunist*, No. 14, 1955, p. 127, 128.

common link and established a common bloc against Khrushchev. The bloc's program, as defined by Rumyantsev, the managing editor of *Kommunist*, consisted of one point: "Back from the Twentieth Party Congress!"[29]

Khrushchev was quite correct in reporting later on that the bloc had been created because "all the members of this group were particularly deeply implicated in the worst errors and mistakes taking place in the past."[30] Shvernik, a new member of the Central Committee Presidium, explained that "in trying to correct violations of revolutionary legality permitted by Malenkov, Kaganovich, and Molotov during the period of mass repressions, the Commission of Party Control in 1957 examined many personal files of former Party members cleared by special tribunals; most of these former members were allowed to rejoin the Party."[31] Marshal Zhukov was even more specific. In a speech in Leningrad in July 1957, following a speech by Khrushchev, he said:

> The anti-Party group of Malenkov, Kaganovich, and Molotov stubbornly resisted the measures adopted by the Party for the liquidation of the consequences of the cult of the individual, particularly those that led to the exposure and trial of the men mainly responsible for the violation of legality. It is now obvious why they were opposed to the exposure of the iniquities that had been committed. They were afraid of the responsibility which they bore for exceeding their prerogatives, and for their illegal actions.[32]

What compelled the Molotov group to abandon its cautious "tactics of self-preservation" in favor of an offensive was the conviction that Khrushchev, alluding to crimes jointly committed by Stalin, Yezhov, and Beria together with Molotov, Kaganovich, and Malenkov, was not in the least interested in the dead Stalin's honor, but was aiming at the group itself in an attempt to prepare the ground for their eventual liquidation. It was only at the Twentieth Party Congress and after that they realized what a fatal mistake they had committed by removing Beria and making Khrushchev First Secretary of the Central Committee. The history of the Party was being repeated. To prevent the seizure of power by Trotsky after Lenin's death, Zinoviev and Kamenev had made Stalin Secretary-General of the Central Committee. To prevent the seizure of power by Kamenev and Zinoviev in this manner, Bukharin, Rykov and Tomsky had preferred to retain Stalin as Secretary-General in the belief that he was a person of no distinction and lacking in ambition. To prevent a coup d'état by Beria, the Molotov group had appointed Khrushchev acting First Secretary of the Central Committee. To prevent Malenkov, with his strong personality, from seizing power for himself, the group had then appointed the undistinguished Khrushchev regular First Secretary of the Central Committee.

Khrushchev was still regarded as a political figure helpless in the face of intrigue, with no ambition to become a leader—an individual with whom it would be easy to deal after Malenkov was removed. But Khrushchev thought otherwise

[29] *Kommunist*, No. 11, 1957, p. 13.
[30] *Pravda*, July 7, 1957.
[31] *Pravda*, July 7, 1957.
[32] *Pravda*, July 16, 1957.

and acted like Stalin. It was important for him to prepare for a new Party congress by selecting the future delegates and organizing the necessary disposition of forces in the local Party apparatuses, local conferences, and local congresses before he could reveal his plans. The thoroughness with which he set about this task is shown by official information regarding the delegates to the Twentieth Party Congress. Approximately 37% of these delegates were persons appointed to responsible posts after Stalin's death and the others were persons who unconditionally recognized Khrushchev as their new patron. Backed by such an assembly, Khrushchev could allow himself the luxury not only of exposing Stalin, but even of "creatively developing Marxism-Leninism." When the discussion turned to the last point on the agenda—the election of members of the Central Committee—the congress let it to be understood that it recognized as its sole leader not the victorious "collective leadership" but Khrushchev and Khrushchev alone. The minutes of the congress show that the reading of the names of all other members of the new Presidium in the elections was greeted with simple "applause," but Khrushchev's name alone was greeted with "stormy applause."[33]

The resolution passed at the close of the June 1957 plenary session of the Central Committee shows that the period after the Twentieth Party Congress was a time of continuous conflicts, quarrels, and intrigues by the Molotov-Kaganovich-Malenkov bloc against Khrushchev. The resolution gives no details, but speaks of a "secret plot" organized by the group to overthrow the Party leadership, that is, Khrushchev. Shvernik, in the Leningrad speech cited above, declared that "the anti-Party group used factional methods to obtain supporters, organized secret meetings behind the back of the Central Committee Presidium, and appointed its own men at strategic points in preparation for a seizure of power both in the Party and in the country at large."[34]

Meanwhile Khrushchev was not wasting his time. In July 1956, the day of Marshal Tito's arrival on a visit to Moscow, the Central Committee Presidium and the Presidium of the Supreme Soviet relieved Molotov of his post as Minister of Foreign Affairs. This was done without a plenary session of the Central Committee, and simply as a routine act. Shepilov, Secretary of the Party Central Committee and Chairman of the Party Foreign Affairs Commission gave his assistance and was rewarded by appointment as Foreign Minister in place of Molotov. In October 1956 there came, first, the unexpected stormy events in Poland, and then, in October and November, the general revolt by the heroic Hungarians. In all likelihood the Molotov group now felt justified in saying to Khrushchev: "Here are the fruits of your unmasking of Stalin."

The events in Poland and Hungary provoked discontent not only in the other Eastern European satellites but in the USSR itself. The Molotov group felt the mortal threat of this discontent to the entire Soviet empire. This threat of

---

[33] *XX sezd kommunisticheskoi partii Sovetskogo Soyuza : Stenograficbesky otchet* (The Twentieth Party Congress of the Soviet Communist Party: Stenographic Report), Moscow, 1956, Vol. II, p. 403.

[34] *Pravda*, July 7, 1957.

destruction temporarily reunited the opponents: the times were too grave and the danger too great to allow for wrangling between the followers of Khrushchev and of Molotov. Again history seemed to be repeating itself, although on a different scale and in a different place: when Kornilov was advancing upon Petrograd and the fate of Kerensky's government was hanging by a thread, the Bolsheviks, including Molotov, wanted Lenin to take advantage of the attack to finish off Kerensky. Lenin answered: "Kerensky is ours, he will not escape us. But now we must all attack Kornilov."

It is probable that the followers of Molotov were thinking in these terms when, after capitulating in Poland, they joined hands with Khrushchev's followers to launch their cruel and merciless attack on unfortunate Hungary. They would, they thought, be able to deal with Khrushchev afterward.

And in fact Khrushchev's fate was hanging by a thread, not because of pressure from the opposition, but because the Party and the police apparatus created by Khrushchev were undergoing a serious crisis. Khrushchev himself was the only member of the apparatus not to lose his head. With the energy of a youth, a Stalinist talent for intrigue, and the hard cunning of a peasant, he translated into the language of politics the old military truism of Clausewitz: "The best defense is the attack." He launched his attack by turning the attention of the Party and the people to domestic problems. The program which he proposed affected the everyday life of the people, injured the opposition, and increased his own popularity. It called for:

1. Liquidating the centralized government bureaucracy (representing concessions to the union republics by increasing their authority and degree of sovereignty).

2. Freeing collective farmers from the obligation to deliver produce raised on their private plots (representing a concession to the peasants).

3. Overtaking the United States in the next two to three years in per capita production of meat, milk, and butter (representing a concession to industrial workers, employees, and intellectuals).

On none of these points, of course, could Molotov or Kaganovich come to an agreement with Khrushchev. They recognized that decentralization meant authorization for a new purge, this time affecting the vast army of bureaucrats which Molotov and his followers had taken years to create and from which they were recruiting their supporters. Their attitude to the peasants continued to be that of Stalin, namely, that any concession in the direction of peasant private property was a blow against the principle of collective farming, a precedent which might eventually result in destruction of the entire kolkhoz system. The slogan calling for the USSR to overtake the United States in output of meat and dairy products they regarded as a demagogic bid for popularity, not based on any real possibilities of achievement. But they did not want to enter into an open discussion with Khrushchev on these explosive themes, preferring discussion in the closed rooms of the Central Committee Presidium, where they still enjoyed support. But Khrushchev, with his usual recklessness, broke through the framework of formal discipline and dragged all the problems which were being discussed in the secret chambers of the Kremlin out into the light of day, to be discussed in public. He "took counsel with the people," as the Soviet press phrased it. He raised the main points of his new program at meetings attended by collective farmers, workers, employees, and Party workers, and asked the people for their opinion. Khrushchev of course knew beforehand what their opinion was, but it was important for him to make the people the official arbiter of the unofficial debate carried on in the Presidium. "There you have it," he could say afterward, "the people think as I do, but you, Comrades Molotov and Kaganovich, think otherwise. You have cut yourselves off from the people." That Khrushchev was now supporting the plan which had proved Malenkov's undoing made no difference. Khrushchev had received his training from Stalin himself, and Stalin had often given his opponents the compliment of stealing their programs.

In the end, the Molotov group could do little to combat Khrushchev's economic concessions. But they fought stubbornly—this time together with Malenkov—to ward off the most fatal blow: the proposal to abolish the bureaucratic apparatus in Moscow. In this fight they had the whole "bureaucratic population" of Moscow on their side. The plan called for the abolition of some forty economic ministries, leaving untouched only the "classic ministries." Khrushchev attempted to have his plan ratified at the December 1956 plenary session of the Central Committee (see Bulganin's report) but was defeated: the opposition of the leaders of the bureaucracy who were members of the Presidium—Molotov, Kaganovich, Malenkov, Pervukhin, and Saburov—was still too great. Bulganin and Voroshilov were probably equally opposed to aggravating the situation. The events in Poland and Hungary, and Khrushchev's moral responsibility for them, were still fresh in the public mind.

The plenary session decided on a compromise solution providing for partial decentralization, with the Moscow ministries retained. However, the rights of local ministries were extended. The State Planning Commission was divided into two parts—the *Gosplan* (State Planning Commission) dealing with long-term plans and the *Gosekonomkomissiya* (State Economic Commission) for short-term planning. The latter, however, was allowed to exercise administrative and operational functions far wider than those exercised by any other government body except the Council of Ministers of the USSR itself. Pervukhin was appointed head of the *Gosekonomkomissiya*, as a kind of economic dictator for the USSR. The "partial" decentralization turned out to be nothing short of centralization with absolute powers. That was not what Khrushchev had wanted, and he had no intention of leaving matters in this state. He removed his spineless friend Bulganin, and attempted to put through his plan himself. He toured the country and dispatched to the republics and local areas members of the Central Committee Secretariat and of the Bureau of the Party Central Committee of the Russian Soviet Republic to indoctrinate members of the Central Committee as to how they should vote.

He ordered the press to continue writing about "Lenin's democratic centralism," and, about a month after the December plenary session, summoned another plenary session in February 1957. Here, speaking for himself, he described the method of achieving decentralization. This time he was able to rely on the indoctrinated majority of the Central Committee rank and file: the decisions of the December session were to all intents and purposes annulled, Pervukhin's *Gosekonomkomissiya* was abolished, and the Central Committee Presidium was instructed to draft a new decentralization plan for ratification by the Supreme Soviet of the USSR.

After his victory at the June 1956 plenary session, Khrushchev still had at least five members of the Presidium—Molotov, Kaganovich, Malenkov, Saburov, and Pervukhin—definitely ranged against him. On the very probable assumption that one of the remaining six would adopt a compromise attitude, the Presidium would be unable to implement the decision of the February plenary session to submit the draft of the new law to the Supreme Soviet for ratification. Again Khrushchev took independent action. On March 30, 1957, he had the so-called "Khrushchev Theses" published in the entire central press without the consent of the Molotov faction. The unusual title immediately drew wide attention. Why "Khrushchev's Theses" and not the theses of the Central Committee and the Council of Ministers, as such proposals were traditionally called? (After liquidation of the Molotov group, it turned out that they were really "Khrushchev's Theses" and not those of the entire Central Committee Presidium and Council of Ministers.) Khrushchev again "took counsel with the people" to ask the population at large to voice its opinion and to suggest corrections and amendments to his theses.

The "theses" provided for the abolition of all central economic ministries and the transfer of many of their functions to the local republics and oblasts by creating economic regions with independent economic councils. The people "advised" Khrushchev to transform his "theses" into law. The opposition of the Molotov group against the "theses" continued. In order to avoid the appearance of a split, they took no part in the "discussion of the theses by the people" but continued to fight against them from within the Central Committee. Here they enjoyed a minor success: of the forty ministries earmarked for abolition only twenty-seven were in fact dissolved.[35] Khrushchev now set a six weeks' deadline for the dissolution of the ministries, requiring the employees of the twenty-seven ministries scheduled for closing to leave the capital by July 1, 1957. He even gave them a parting message. "Can there be any doubt," said the introduction to the theses, "that these comrades will rightly understand the measures adopted by the Party and the government and will resume their efficient administrative activities at the production level?"[36]

Khrushchev's second victory was also of great importance. Under the guise of increasing the authority and "sovereign rights" of the union republics, he

---

[35] *Izvestia*, May 11, 1957.

[36] *Pravda*, March 30, 1957.

brought into the Council of Ministers of the USSR the entire fifteen prime ministers of the union republics, all of them persons selected and appointed by the Secretariat of the Party Central Committee. Henceforth, the First Deputy Prime Ministers—Molotov, Kaganovich, Saburov, and Pervukhin—and Deputy Prime Minister Malenkov were members of a cabinet dominated by a pro-Khrushchev majority.

If the resolution of the June 1957 plenary session of the Central Committee is to be believed, the Molotov group continued to fight decentralization even after "Khrushchev's Theses" became law upon ratification by the Supreme Soviet.[37] The resolution read:

> They were opposed to the extension of the rights of the union republics. . . . The anti-Party group not only failed to understand, it even fought against the measures adopted by the Party to deal with "red tape" and to cut down the grossly inflated state administration. . . . The group stubbornly opposed and tried to sabotage such an extremely important measure as the reorganization of the administration of industry. . . . The group went so far as to continue the fight against the reorganization of industrial administration even after the above-mentioned measures were approved by popular discussion and their adoption as law by the Supreme Soviet of the USSR.[38]

In the middle of June, the struggle within the cabinet reached its most dramatic point. A more or less complete story of the drama played out in the Kremlin between June 18 and 29, 1957, appeared in the organ of the Central Committee of the Italian Communist Party, the newspaper *Unità*, on July 8, 1957.

Before describing the struggle as reported in *Unità* it must be cautioned that the article appeared in the central organ of the Italian Communist Party and was therefore semi-official. It reported events as told to the *Unità* Moscow correspondent by members of the Soviet Central Committee and thus came from the side which was victorious in the dispute. It naturally described the struggle and its outcome in the light most favorable to the victors. The Central Committee's source, in turn, according to the *Unità* correspondent, was a sealed letter from the Central Committee of the Soviet Communist Party addressed to local Party organizations, containing a report on the discussions in the Presidium of the Central Committee and describing the manner in which the Molotov group was censured by the Central Committee plenary session. The letter was said to have as enclosures the minutes of the meetings of the Central Committee Presidium and of the plenary session. The *Unità* story then was as follows:

Molotov's group had worked out a plan for removing Khrushchev as First Secretary of the Central Committee. Taking advantage of the absence from Moscow of the three members of the Central Committee Presidium, the group demanded that a meeting of the Presidium be held to discuss the texts of the speeches to be made by the Presidium members at the 250th anniversary of the

[37] *Izvestia*, May 11, 1957.
[38] *Voprosy istorii KPSS*, Moscow, No. 1, 1957, p. 415.

founding of Leningrad. However, when the Presidium met on June 18, the Molotov group immediately demanded that the membership of the Central Committee Secretariat and of the Cabinet of Ministers be changed on the plea that Khrushchev's policy was both Trotskyite and opportunist. The group presented a list of the proposed new members and demanded an immediate vote. Khrushchev's name was not included in the list.

Several members of the Central Committee Presidium, the *Unità* story continued, opposed this demand, stating that decisions of such importance must be made by the full Presidium membership. They succeeded in delaying the vote till the arrival of the absent members. After their arrival, Khrushchev's followers declared that only a plenary session of the Central Committee was entitled to rule on a decision involving changes in the membership of the Central Committee Secretariat and of the Presidium itself. However, Molotov, Kaganovich, and Malenkov insisted that a decision be made regarding changes in the leadership before summoning a plenary session of the Central Committee and that the decision be published immediately in the press, together with a political statement, the text of which had been prepared by Shepilov. The discussion on this subject continued in the Presidium for several days. Members of the Central Committee who had been informed of these events now began to arrive in Moscow, where they demanded the immediate convocation of a plenary session.

The plenary session opened on June 22. Suslov, who was both a Secretary of the Central Committee and member of the Presidium, reported on the events that had taken place in the Presidium. When Suslov finished, Molotov, Malenkov, Kaganovich, and Shepilov pressed their demand for a change in the leadership. However, their demand failed to gain the support of a majority of the members. As soon as they realized that they had become isolated, they attempted to retreat, but the members of the Central Committee accused the Molotov group of attempting to seize power by illegal means and insisted upon removal of the entire group from the central Party organs.

The report in *Unità* is supplemented by a story from the Associated Press correspondent in Warsaw, who received his information from leaders of the Polish United Workers' (Communist) Party. According to this correspondent, the first clash between Khrushchev and Molotov occurred on June 22 at the opening meeting of the Central Committee plenary session. In an attempt to destroy the Molotov group, Khrushchev proposed that the first point on the agenda be made "The Situation within the Soviet Communist Party." Molotov on the other hand proposed that the discussion begin with "The International Situation of the USSR in Connection with the Attempted Imperialist *Putsches* in Poznanie and Hungary." He also wished to discuss at the beginning of the session "Relations with Communist Parties in Poland, Italy, Japan, and the United States," in other words, the Communist parties whose leaders had not subscribed to the official Soviet view regarding the imperialist origin of the revolts in Poznanie and Hungary. Molotov was immediately opposed by Kirilenko, the

Secretary of the Sverdlovsk Oblast Party committee, who said: "The men responsible for the world-wide storm of indignation which arose after the Hungarian events are right here, within our own Party." And he added: "The conservative outlook of Molotov's group caused the revolt in Hungary and was responsible for the fall in the international prestige of the Soviet Union after the suppression of the Hungarian revolt."

According to the Polish leaders who provided the story, the first session lasted for thirty-five hours without a break. Khrushchev addressed it in a three-hour speech, in which he declared that the anti-Party group of Molotov, Malenkov, Kaganovich, and Shepilov had its center in Moscow and was using emissaries to spread its influence throughout the Party apparatus. Molotov, he said, had used the Ministry of Foreign Affairs and the Soviet diplomatic corps abroad to promote his own personal policy. Among other things he had sabotaged the reconciliation between the USSR and Yugoslavia which had become possible in 1954 but had been delayed for an entire year by Molotov's intrigues.

The stories provided by *Unità* and the Warsaw correspondent are confirmed in general not only by the text of the resolution of the June plenary session but also by various details which can be culled from the speeches made by members of the Presidium of the Party Central Committee in Leningrad on July 6, 1957.

Molotov and Kaganovich were hoisted on their own petard. Khrushchev had used against them the same methods as those which Stalin, it will be recalled, had used to overthrow the leaders of the Moscow Committee, headed by Uglanov, in October 1928. Khrushchev's behavior, involving as it did the entire Central Committee, simply points to the superiority of a gifted but ungrateful pupil over his former teachers.

We must now examine the higher Party and state organs to determine the changes made in them at the June plenary session. What was the political and professional make-up of the congress which cleared the road to power for Khrushchev? According to the report of Aristov, Secretary of the Central Committee and Chairman of the Mandate Commission of the Twentieth Party Congress, 1,355 delegates with full voting powers were present, representing the following groups:

Party Workers	506
Government Workers	177
Trade Union Workers	12
Komsomol Workers	8
Workers in Industrial and Agricultural Administration	438
Military Workers	116
Propaganda Workers	98
Total	1,355

SOURCE: The last four figures are taken from A. Avtorkhanov, "The Political Results of the Twentieth Party Congress and the Future of the Collective Leadership," *Vestnik*, Munich, No. 2, 1956, p. 9. The other figures are compilations from primary sources.

The length of Party membership of the delegates was as follows:

Date of Admission	Percentage
1917 (October or Before)	1.6
1917—20	4.5
1921—30	24.9
1931—40	34.0
1941—45	21.6
1946 (and later)	13.4

SOURCE: A. Avtorkhanov, "The Political Results of the Twentieth Party Congress and the Future of Collective Leadership," *Vestnik*, Munich, No. 2, 1956, p. 10. The 1.6% of pre-October 1917 members numbered only 22 persons, and the 4.5% from 1917—20 only 60 persons.

Accordingly, of the delegates to the Twentieth Party Congress, 69% were persons who had joined the Party after Stalin had established his personal dictatorship, that is, after the liquidation of the *thinking* Party. Over 500 delegates had become Party members afters Stalin's death. To a congress so composed, Khrushchev could present any program he wished and expose anyone he thought fit without fear of retribution, provided he could dominate the actual apparatus of power. It was this congress which elected the Central Committee which judged and removed from the Party scene the persons who had been responsible for creating it. And who were the judges? They were the following:

Admission Date to Party	Number
1917 (October or Before)	6
1917—20	14
1921—24	7
1925—30	44
1931—37	13
1938—42	28
Dead or Missing	7
Date of Admission Unknown	14
Total	133

SOURCE: *XX sezd kommunisticheskoi partii Sovetskogo Soyuza : Stenograficbesky otchet* (The Twentieth Congress of the Soviet Communist Party: Stenographic Report), Moscow, 1956, Vol. II.

The table indicates that out of the 133 persons who sat in judgment over Molotov (a Party member from 1906), Kaganovich (a Party member from 1911), and Malenkov (a Party member from 1920), 124, including Khrushchev, had joined the Party after the Bolshevik seizure of power, and of these, 110 had joined it at the time when Molotov, Kaganovich, and later Malenkov were Secretaries of the Party Central Committee. On the other hand, of the 255 full and alternate members, 100, or about 40%, had been elected for the first time by this congress, that is, Khrushchev's congress. Of the total of 236 full and alternate members of the Central Committee present at the Nineteenth Party Congress (the Stalin-Malenkov Congress) 90, or about 38%, had been purged, providing an excellent object lesson for all who had survived from the Nineteenth Party Congress and a good reason why the voting was unanimous for Khrushchev in the June plenary session.[39]

In summing up the results of the June plenary session *Kommunist* wrote:

> It can be said without exaggeration that the plenary session proved the salvation of the principle of unity. .... The dissenters have failed to understand that the bad old days of the cult of the individual are gone for ever, never to return. It was quite wrong for the Central Committee to play a subsidiary role while organizations elected by it were considered superior to it and could presume to decide questions which belonged to the exclusive competence of a plenary session of the Central Committee.[40]

It was, of course, Khrushchev's salvation that was meant by the "unity" allegedly saved by the Central Committee.

But had the Central Committee really become a supreme body able to dictate its collective will to the Presidium and the Secretariat? According to *Kommunist*, it had. "The defeat of the anti-Party group," said *Kommunist*, "has confirmed once more the immense strength of the collective Party leadership and the full significance of the fact that the Party is led not by individuals or groups, but by an authoritative and collective body elected by a congress."[41] However, closer examination reveals that this categorical statement merely confirmed what it attempted to deny. The Bolshevik leadership has always drawn strength from the fact that the so-called legislative body (a Party congress or a plenary session of the Party Central Committee) served as a signpost and a useful cover helping to justify the current practices of the executive organs. The Party through its congresses and Central Committee plenary sessions "voted" in favor of whatever was presented to it by the executive, irrespective of who was at its head—Lenin or Stalin or Malenkov or Khrushchev or anyone else. This was the heart of Lenin's famous "democratic centralism." One of Lenin's former colleagues, S. Dmitrievsky, tells how Lenin taught Stalin at a Russian Social Democratic Party conference in Tammerfors in 1905 what "democratic centralism" was and why it must be the basic principle of Bolshevik leadership. Stalin could not quite follow Lenin's argument and "maintained a sullen silence." He was repelled by any kind of democratic principle. "What is it all for?" he asked; "a fighting Party must have a permanent staff of leaders, independent of election hazards. Commanders are not elected in an army during a war." Lenin smiled wryly. "There is nothing to be done about it," he replied. "New circumstances call for new forms. .... After all nothing has changed in fact. The rulers are those who rule and not those who vote, and it depends on the skill of those who rule to see to it that they are always elected. ...." At the

---

[39] Bertram D. Wolfe in his brilliant analysis of Khrushchev's report, in his book *Khrushchev and Stalin's Ghost*, p. 28, quotes another figure: According to him, 113 persons, or 44% of the members of the old Central Committee, were purged. He probably included persons expelled from the Central Committee but remaining in the Commission of Party Control. It is worth noting that 12 of the 37 members of the Commission were removed and 38 new members added, making a total of 63.

[40] *Kommunist*, No. 10, 1957, p. 8.

[41] *Ibid.*, p. 9.

time, Stalin was not satisfied. It was only many years later, says Dmitrievsky, that he understood that "democratic centralism" was an excellent thing if you knew how to manipulate it.[42]

Despite the assertion of *Kommunist* that the June plenary session had proved that the Party was not led by individuals or groups, in fact the control of the session by an individual, Khrushchev, and a group, the Central Committee Secretariat, proved the opposite. And in the main Central Committee organs, the Secretariat and the Presidium, elected at the session, this type of "democratic centralism" was carried to further extremes. Khrushchev, in a step which even Stalin had never ventured to take, placed the members of the Party executive organ, the Secretariat, in the top position in the Party legislative organ, the Presidium. Of the ten members of the Secretariat elected at the June plenary session, Suslov, Aristov, Belyayev, Brezhnev, Kuusinen, Furtseva, Kirichenko (former Secretary of the Ukrainian Party Central Committee), Mukhitdinov, and Ignatov (former Secretary of the Gorky Oblast Committee) were all members of the Presidium. Other Presidium members close to Khrushchev were Shvernik, Chairman of the Commission of Party Control; Kozlov, a former secretary of the Leningrad Oblast Committee and now Prime Minister of the Russian Soviet Republic; Bulganin, Prime Minister of the USSR; and Mikoyan, a Deputy Prime Minister of the USSR.

Not only did the members of the Secretariat hold the top positions in the Presidium, but, including the Chairman of the Commission of Party Control, an agency of the Secretariat, they made up a majority of eleven out of the fourteen members. By reorganizing the Presidium, Khrushchev had created a kind of "small plenum of the Central Committee" entirely controlled by the Secretariat. This innovation, under which the legislature was not so much fused with, as absorbed by, the apparatus, provided a guarantee against an accidental and unforeseen revolt within the Presidium such as had occured in the old Presidium where the apparatus controlled only three votes—those of Khrushchev, Suslov, and Kirichenko—out of eleven, and when there was always the risk that appeals would be made from the Presidium to the Central Committee plenum. Repeated appeals to the plenum of the Central Committee as an impartial tribunal could be not only inconvenient in practice but also politically dangerous, for they might lead the plenum to arrogate to itself rights which it has according to the statutes, but which it could not be allowed to exercise in practice if Khrushchev wished to avoid the fate of Molotov and his companions and to keep firmly in his hands the reins of power in Party and state.

In selecting personnel, Khrushchev acted in precisely the same way as Stalin. It was Khrushchev who said:

> The proposal [by Stalin] after the Nineteenth Party Congress that 25 persons be elected to the Central Committee Presidium was due to his desire to remove all the old members from the Politburo and to introduce into it men who had less experience but who never tired of singing Stalin's praises.

---

[42] S. Dmitrievsky, *Stalin*, Berlin, 1931.

After Stalin's death, the Presidium thus selected by Stalin had been disbanded, but now Khrushchev was recalling eight of Stalin's "inexperienced" Presidium members: Aristov, Kirichenko, Kuusinen, Brezhnev, Ignatov, Kosygin, and Suslov (the last in 1955).

As to the most important strata of the Soviet social structure, the new Presidium lacked representatives of the social groups which, in Stalin's time, had always been represented—the political police, the industrial managers, and the trade unions. The alternate members of the Central Committee Presidium were also almost exclusively Party workers. There were no representatives of the police, the trade unions, or the Komsomol. On the other hand, five of the eight alternate members were directly under the Central Committee Secretariat. Thus the principle that the executive branch must always dominate the legislative was retained, the proportion being the same as among the four members of the Presidium. Serov, the head of the Secretariat, and Dudorov, the head of the MVD, were not members of the Presidium, but their absence was no sign of a decrease in the power of the police. Party workers, for the sake of their own Secretariat, wished to avoid a return to the status under Stalinism, when a junior police officer wielded more power than the secretary of an oblast Party committee, and the head of the NKVD was more powerful than all the Politburo members together with the exception of Stalin himself. Stalin ruled the country through the police and made the Party apparatus serve the police; Khrushchev wished to rule the country through the Party apparatus and to make the police serve the apparatus. Although this change in detail changed nothing in principle, in case of a new crisis it would be the police and not the Party workers who would have to pay with their heads.

The June 1957 plenary session of the Central Committee saw the end of the era in Party history known as that of collective leadership of the Central Committee. By liquidating Molotov's group at the June 1956 session, Marshal Zhukov at the October 1957 session, and Bulganin at the September 1958 session, Khrushchev acquired as much power as Stalin had enjoyed toward the end of the 1930's. The Central Committee Presidium itself recognized that Khrushchev held this power. The Uzbek Mukhitdinov, a member of the Presidium, declared: "Khrushchev, the director of the government, the Party, and the people, is a true pupil and continuer of the great work of Lenin."[43] Formerly, only Stalin had been spoken of in such terms. However, while Khrushchev shared this power in the cabinet with Bulganin and Mikoyan, and in the Party with the Secretariat, it was the latter with its eleven members which really constituted the government of the USSR. The other organs—the Council of Ministers, the Supreme Soviet, even the Central Committee—were merely a facade. The revolt of the Presidium against Khrushchev had been easily put down because the real power was concentrated in the hands of the Secretariat. Mention should be made here of another organ exercising personal control on behalf of the First Secretary over his subordinates. This was the so-called Technical Secretariat.

---

[43] *Pravda*, September 30, 1958.

With a large staff of specialists in every field of governmental activity and under orders from the First Secretary himself, it acts behind the scenes but is extremely important. Stalin controlled the Party, and the police, and the state through this Secretariat, which for over 30 years was headed by Poskrebyshev, who had the title of "Assistant to the Secretariat." Under Khrushchev he was replaced by A. S. Shevchenko, with the title of "Assistant to the Secretaries." Little is known about his functions and powers, but the arrest of the Beria group, the rapid convocation of a plenary session of the Central Committee to dethrone the Molotov group, and the secret plan to remove Zhukov all indicate that Shevchenko wielded no less power than his predecessor.

After the June session of the Central Committee, a great country-wide propaganda campaign against "dissenters" was unleashed through Party and non-Party conferences and meetings. Molotov, Kaganovich, and Malenkov were referred to not only as "conspirators" against the Central Committee leadership but also as persons devoid of ability as statesmen. Baibakov, the chairman of the Gosplan of the Russian Soviet Republic, declared: "Though claiming to be the Party's theorist, Molotov long ago lost all connection with Leninist teaching. He was unable to grasp the essentials of various problems. . . . Kaganovich showed himself to be incapable of performing the tasks with which he was entrusted. He was so far behind the times and so poor at understanding our new technical policy that he became the subject of anecdotes."[44] Minister of Agriculture Matskevich asserted:

> Malenkov acted as a brake on all attempts to solve basic problems of agricultural development. . . . At the same time, in order to raise himself and gain personal popularity, Malenkov ascribed to his own initiative measures for reducing the agricultural tax which in fact were adopted by the Central Committee. . . . Due to his conservative attitude and tendency to mark time, Molotov not only failed to understand the necessity for bringing virgin lands under cultivation, but stubbornly opposed the adoption of this very important measure. . . . Though he had no idea of agriculture, Kaganovich opposed the Party's policy in questions of agriculture.[45]

Much the same charges were made by Khrushchev's propagandists in "speaking to the people." Their main emphasis was laid on the opposition by Malenkov, Kaganovich, and Molotov to a rise in the standard of living. The following description by a Soviet author of a conversation between two collective farmers overheard on the banks of the Don is typical:

> "There is one thing I cannot understand," said the man in the coat slowly. "What is it they are aiming at, what do they want? How can they possibly know what we farmers want? Did Malenkov, or say Kaganovich, ever travel around the kolkhozes or chat simply and naturally with the people? Of course they didn't; they just sat in their studies like marmots in their burrows."
>
> "They ought to have been put on harvesters and given pitchforks. Then they would know what it costs the people to get their daily bread," said the second man

---

[44] *Pravda*, July 5, 1957.
[45] *Pravda*, July 14, 1957 and July 12, 1957.

sullenly. "Harvesters have nothing to do with it," interrupted the first. . . . . "They only know our life because they have read about it on scraps of paper or seen it in the movies."

"You cannot throw dust in the people's eyes, bluff your way into their confidence." "Yes, that's right. We are a country of literate people now."[46]

In the course of the censuring of the Molotov anti-Party group, Khrushchev again referred to the December 1958 plenum of the Central Committee. He now revealed for the first time that Bulganin had been a member of the group but had spoken to the plenum to confess his errors and denounce his former comrades. Finally, at the Twenty-First Party Congress, in January-February 1959, Khrushchev's supporters stated that there were still two more Presidium members, Pervukhin and Saburov, who had belonged to the group. It can accordingly be assumed that of the 11 members of the Presidium, six—Bulganin, Molotov, Malenkov, Kaganovich, Pervukhin, and Saburov—had voted for the removal of Khrushchev. These six members had constituted a majority in the Central Committee Presidium and had full legal authority to depose Khrushchev. It is highly probably that Voroshilov voted with the group and that Mikoyan, as usual, played both sides or waited to see who would win. Khrushchev, however, adroitly declared this majority a minority and even more anti-Party.

At the Twenty-First Party Congress, under the able direction of Khrushchev, all the delegates referred to these old Bolshevik-Stalinists as "thrice-despised," "conspiratorial," "traitorous," "abominable," and "wretched." In a manner reminiscent of Stalin's reign, the Congress demanded that the members of the Molotov group openly confess their errors and repent.

The most pressing demand was presented by I. Spiridonov, a young pupil of Khrushchev's and First Secretary of the Leningrad Oblast Committee, who said:

> Whereas up to this time an answer was demanded by the Central Committee from those participating in this group, it now follows that they must answer to the highest organ of the Party, the entire Congress. This especially refers to those members still remaining in the Party Central Committee. You already know about Bulganin's speech at the December plenum of the Central Committee. Remember how he spoke of his own compatriots who participated in the anti-Party group; of Molotov that he had lost contact with life; of Kaganovich as a phrase-maker, which in good Russian means a wind-bag; of Malenkov as an intriguer ready to perform any wretched task. We can believe Bulganin when he says that these characteristics had developed long ago. After all, Bulganin had worked with these persons not one or two years, but 20-odd years: How did Bulganin get into such a congenial family?[47]

Pervukhin, however, was the only one to speak up at the Congress and to make his repentance. Evidently Molotov, Kaganovich, Malenkov, and Saburov did not find it necessary to confess their sins. In fact, Voroshilov, who up to now had said nothing against the Molotov group, also failed to make a statement. Mikoyan's speech was ambiguous; although he spoke of the anti-Party group in

---

[46] *Literaturnaya gazeta*, July 25, 1957.
[47] *Pravda*, January 30, 1959.

general, he did not mention any names. And when Mikoyan was junketing through the United States, he spoke of Molotov and Kaganovich only to point out their services in the past.

The logic governing the history of the Party indicates that the Molotov group will necessarily finish its career either in the Kremlin or the Lubyanka.

At the Congress, the discussion no longer centered on the theme of the collective leadership but on the Party Central Committee under the leadership of Khrushchev. All the delegates to the Congress emphasized the wisdom and the personal services of Khrushchev. In fact, D. Ustinov, Deputy Chairman of the Council of Ministers of the USSR, even declared: "For the success in launching the Sputnik and the cosmic rocket, we are indebted to the Presidium of the Central Committee and personally to Nikita Sergeyevich Khrushchev."[48]

How did the official propagandists explain the reasons for the opposition of Molotov and his group to Khrushchev's leadership? "The main grounds for their anti-Party activity," said Deputy Prime Minister Kosygin, "were ambition and a sense of personal ill-treatment. They considered that they did not hold sufficient power in their hands."[49]

This explanation of the conflict as a naked struggle for power between two groups within a single Communist oligarchy is only partially true. That all political struggle is a struggle for power is a truism. However, to the extent that power is not an aim in itself, but a means toward the achievement of a certain policy, Kosygin's statement explains nothing. Molotov's group did not, and of course could not, have any other program than that of Khrushchev. The competing groups had argued not about programs but about tactics, not about the ideological "general line," but about the methods of applying it, not about reforms, but about the rate and scale of their application, not even about Stalin, but about Stalinism.

The Molotov group saw farther and deeper than Khrushchev into the consequences of Khrushchev's campaign against the Stalinist inheritance. They understood only too well that the present regime in the USSR could continue only as a Stalinist regime or perish altogether. It could and must be corrected and modernized, but its basic methods could not be subjected to revision. If Khrushchev's ideal of government as an unlimited dictatorship by the Party oligarchy should, like Molotov's, remain unchanged, the Stalinist system of government, irrespective of the personal characteristics of the late Master, would remain as a perfect and universal example. Any criticism of the Stalinist system and particularly of the Stalinist methods would lead to suicide. In short, men compelled by the very nature of the regime to rule as Stalin did, could not, the Molotov group believed, condemn Stalin's methods.

The inner motive of the "anti-Party activities" on the part of Molotov's group seems to have been not a lust for power (they had enough power), but a well-founded fear that the regime would collapse. In Khrushchev they saw

[48] *Pravda*, February 2, 1956.
[49] *Pravda*, July 4, 1957.

the most likely gravedigger of the regime, and their entire struggle was accordingly concentrated on him. For seven days in the course of the June 1957 plenary session they tried in vain to prove the unprovable: that the First Secretary was made for the Central Committee and not the Central Committee for the First Secretary. In this struggle the members of the Molotov group placed their trust in their moral capital—their past authority and services. But their hopes were in vain. The Party, which the day before had dragged its demigod down from his pedestal, now showed itself completely immune to feelings of remorse when it became necessary to put an end to the demigod's chief apostles.

Stalin, Molotov, Kaganovich, and Malenkov had taught the Party to serve not the ideals of the life of society but the workers in the Party apparatus. And the lesson had been well learned. Nothing could make it swerve from this path—neither ideological arguments, nor the former services of former leaders, nor their dire warnings of danger to come. These former leaders, moreover, overlooked the enormous psychological shock which the new leader gave to the conscience of the Party and the country by dragging Stalin from his pedestal. Even after he had done so, they continued to cling stubbornly to the Party's past, failing to see that in the meantime the First Secretary had boldly begun to write a new chapter in the history of the Communist Party.

Khrushchev's political experience suggests that this new chapter may turn out to be the last in the over-long history of the régime. So thought Molotov and Kaganovich; and it is also my view.

Khrushchev himself has different views on the subject and different aims in view. Being by nature "a permanent revolutionary," he wishes to be remembered in the history of Russia as the great Communist reformer. Stalin had promised that the great-grandsons of the present generation would not go hungry. Khrushchev wants the Russian people to eat their fill while he himself is still alive. But if he is successful, his very success will put an end to his historic mission: well-fed people will become interested in politics. No one has as yet expressed this "Marxist" truth better than Khrushchev when he said to a group of Soviet authors:

> I know people who are supposed to be theorists, and yet all their theoretical "wisdom" in fact boils down to juggling, in and out of season, quotations from the classics of Marxism-Leninism. All such pseudo-scholars, although they may claim to be theorists, cannot understand the important Marxist truth that men must first eat, drink, dress, and have a place to live before they can become interested in politics, art, and science.[50]

Khrushchev has my sincere wishes for success in the practical application of this truth. He has them because I am a firm believer in the wisdom of the saying that revolutions are made not by those who go hungry every day, but by the well-fed who have had to go hungry for one day.

---

[50] *Kommunist*, No. 12, 1957, p. 17.

Bibliography

Beriya, L., *K voprosu ob istorii bolshevistskikh organizatsiyakh v Zakavkaze* (The History of Bolshevik Organizations in Transcaucasia), Moscow, 1948,

Biographic Directory of the USSR, New York, 1958.

Bolshaya Sovetskaya Entsiklopediya (The Large Soviet Encyclopedia), Moscow, 1st ed., 65 vols., 1926—47; 2nd ed., 51 vols., 1949—58.

Cherkasov, N. K., *Zapiski aktera* (An Actor's Notes), Moscow, 1933.

Die Welt, Hamburg.

Dmitrievsky, S., *Stalin*, Berlin, 1931.

Ebon, M., *Malenkov*, London, 1953.

Entsiklopedichesky slovar (Encyclopedic Dictionary), 3 vols., Moscow, 1953—55.

Informationnoye soveshchaniye predstavitelei nekotorykh kompartii v Polshe v kontse sentyabrya 1947 goda (Information Conference of Representatives of Several Communist Parties in Poland at the End of 1947), Moscow, 1948.

Istoriya VKP(b). Kratky kurs (Short Course in the History of the Communist Party of Bolsheviks), Moscow, 1945.

I. V. Stalin : Kratkaya biografiya (J. V. Stalin: A Short Biography), Moscow, 1951.

Izvestia, Moscow.

Kaganovich, L., *Ot XVI k XVII sezdu partii* (From the Sixteenth to the Seventeenth Party Congresses), Moscow, 1934.

Kaganovich, M., *O chistke partii* (The Party Purge), Moscow, 1934.

Kirov, S., *Izbranniye stati i rechi* (Selected Articles and Speeches), Moscow, 1939.

Kommunist, Moscow.

Kommunistecheskaya partiya Sovetskoga Soyuza v rezolyutsiyakh i resheniyakh sezdov, konferentsii i plenumov TsK, 1898—1954 (The Communist Party of the Soviet Union in Resolutions and Decisions of Congresses, Conferences, and Plenums of the Central Committee, 1898—1954), 3 vols., 7th ed., Moscow, 1954.

Khrushchev, N. K., *Otchetny doklad Tsentralnogo Komiteta Kommunisticheskoi partii Sovetskogo Soyuza XX sezdu partii ; 14 fevralya 1956 goda* (Report of the Central Committee of the Communist Party of the Soviet Union to the Twentieth Party Congress, February 14, 1956), Moscow, 1956, pp. 40—44.

Lenin, V. I., *Sochineniya* (Works), 3rd ed., Moscow, 1926—37.

Literaturnaya gazeta, Moscow.

Maclean, Fitzroy, *Eastern Approaches*, London, 1949.

Malaya Sovetskaya Entsiklopediya (The Small Soviet Encyclopedia), 2nd ed., 10 vols., Moscow, 1933—41.

Malenkov, G. M., *Informationnoye soveshchaniye neketorykh kompartii* (Information Conference of Several Communist Parties), Moscow, 1948.

Marx, Karl, *Das Kapital*, Preface to First Edition.

Mertsalov, V., *Tragediya russkogo krestyanstva* (The Tragedy of the Russian Peasantry), Frankfurt am Main, 1950.

Molotov, V., *V borbe za sotsializm* (In the Fight for Socialism), 2nd ed., Moscow, 1935.

New York Herald Tribune, New York.

The New York Times, International Edition, Amsterdam.

O chistke partii (The Party Purge), a collection of documents, Moscow, 1933.

Ogonek, Moscow.

Ost-Probleme, Bonn.

Partiinoye stroitelstvo, Moscow.

Partiinaya zhizn, Moscow.

Pervy Kongress Kommunisticheskogo Internationala. Protocoly (Minutes of the First Congress of the Communist International), Petrograd, 1921.

Pokrovsky, M. N., *Russkaya istoriya v samom szhatom ocherke* (A Brief Sketch of Russian History), Moscow, 1933.

Pravda, Moscow.

Problemy istorii, Moscow.

Problemy istorii KPSS, Moscow.

Rech Khrushcheva na zaktrytom zasedaniye XX sezda KPSS, 24—25 fevralya 1956 g. (Khrushchev's Speech at the Closed Session of the Twentieth Congress of the CPSU, February 24—25, 1956), Munich, 1956.

Sotsialistichesky Vestnik, New York and Paris.

Stalin, J. V., *O velikoi otechestvennoi voine SSSR* (The Great Patriotic War of the USSR), Moscow, 1946 and 1950.

——, *Sochineniya* (Works), 13 vols., Moscow, 1946—54.

——, *Voprosy leninizma* (Problems of Leninism), 11th ed., Leningrad, 1940—47.

Trotsky, L., *Moya Zhizn* (My Life), 2 vols., Riga, 1940.

——, *Nasha revolyutsiya* (Our Revolution), St. Petersburg, 1906.

——, *Novy kurs* (The New Course), Moscow, 1923.

——, *Stalin*, Koeln-Berlin, 1952.

——, *Stalinskaya shkola falshifikatsii* (Stalin's School of Falsification), Berlin, 1932.

Uralov, Alexander [A. Avtorkhanov], *The Reign of Stalin*, London, 1953.

Ustav KPSS (Statutes of the Soviet Communist Party), Moscow, 1952.

Vedomosti Verkhovnogo Soveta SSSR (Bulletin of the Supreme Soviet of the USSR), Moscow.

Vestnik Instituta, Munich.

Virta, N., *Stalingradskaya Bitva* (The Battle of Stalingrad), Moscow, 1948.

VKP(b) v rezolyutsiyakh i resheniyakh sezdov, konferentsii i plenumov TsK (The All-Union Communist Party of Bolsheviks in Resolutions and Decisions of the Congresses, Conferences, and Plenums of the Central Committee), 2 vols., 2nd ed., Moscow, 1933.

Voprosy istorii, Moscow.

Voroshilov, K., *Stalin i vooruzhennye sily SSSR* (Stalin and the Armed Forces of the USSR), Moscow, 1951.

V pomoshch politicheskomu samoobrazovaniyu, Moscow.

Vyshinsky, A. Ya., *Sudebnye rechi* (Court Speeches), Moscow, 1948.

Wolfe, Bertram D., *Khrushchev and Stalin's Ghost*, New York, 1956.

Yaroslavaky, Ye., *Za bolshevistskuyu proverku i chistku partii* (For a Bolshevik Check and Purge of the Party), Moscow-Leningrad, 1933.

Znamya, Moscow.

XX sezd Vsesoyuznoi kommunisticheskoi partii Sovetskogo Soyuza : Stenografichesky otchet (Twentieth Congress of the Soviet Communist Party, Stenographic Report), 2 vols., Moscow, 1956.

Index

Chinese Socialist Labor Party, 147
Chou-Teh, 45
Chubar, V. Ya., 31, 101, 189, 223, 225, 256, 277, 297, 334
Chudov, M. S., 214
Civil War, 9, 20, 26, 27, 36, 55, 64, 99, 158, 192, 199, 217, 220, 222, 250, 266, 278, 286, 293-97, 305, 307, 313
Class Struggle, 76, 205, 323
"Class Struggle and the Theory of Equilibrium, The," 46
Clausewitz, Karl von, 350
Co-existence, 320
Collective agreement by trade unions, 31
Collective farmers, 328, 350, 351, 360. *See also* Kolkhozes.
Collective leadership, 134, 188, 208, 252, 254, 262, 263, 270, 273, 275, 282, 292, 302, 305, 306, 310, 318, 321, 323, 325, 330, 344, 347, 349
Collectivization, 8, 15, 84-86, 117, 152, 154, 158, 159, 162-64, 166-69, 172-74, 187, 193, 204, 288. *See also* Kolkhozes.
"Collegiate principle," 125
Colonialism, 169
Cominform press organ, 22
Comintern, 6, 21-23, 45, 72, 81, 92, 118-20, 145-50, 152, 153, 155, 177, 179, 180, 200, 206, 232; Congresses, First (1919), 147; Second (1919), 145; Sixth (1928), 148, 149; Presidium, 23, 24, 113, 137
"Comintern and Right-Wing Deviation, The," pamphlet, 46
Commission of Party Control, 105, 218, 222, 241, 253, 348, 357, 358. *See also* Central Control Commission.
Committee for a New Alphabet, 95
Committees of Poor Peasants, 275
Communes, 7
Communists, 13, 36, 64, 82, 91, 100, 127, 128, 136, 169, 179, 187, 240-42, 276, 281, 309, 316-18
Communist Academy, 4, 5, 16, 19, 22, 28, 55-58, 60, 68, 72, 74, 76, 80, 83, 91, 94, 133, 135, 137, 156, 177, 221
"Communist education," 21
Communist Manifesto, 17
Communist Party, 2, 3, 5, 8, 13, 15, 17, 20-22, 27, 28, 30, 33, 40, 43, 44, 48, 49, 52, 54, 62, 64, 68, 70, 71, 74, 78, 80, 81, 83, 88, 91,

98, 103, 105, 116, 121, 123, 127, 134, 142, 143, 148, 163, 166, 191, 201, 205, 206, 215, 220, 244, 253, 326, 363; activists, 54, 64, 76, 82, 83, 87, 108, 116, 122, 245; apparatus, 51, 55, 74, 76, 91, 93, 101, 102, 106, 108, 109, 114, 137, 194, 205, 206, 222, 240, 243, 244, 253, 254, 269, 270, 274, 303, 305, 310, 311, 324, 326, 342, 347, 349, 355, 358, 359; of Austria, 147; of Bulgaria, 151; bureaucratization, 117; Party card, 43, 67, 69; collegium of the Central Control Commission, 114; discipline, 64; elite, 133; growth, 238-39; history, 20; leaders, 44, 187, 189; line ,53, 55, 75, 140, 152, 170, 174, 302; "Party maximum," 313; members, 75, 76, 81, 96, 109, 190, 220, 221, 223, 240, 356; organizations, 86, 87; publications, 164; rank and file members, 74, 126, 140, 155, 164, 204; referendum, 142; statutes, 38, 95, 102, 106, 113-15, 122, 142-44, 208, 246-49, 355; theory, 75, 115, 133, 347; workers, 359. *See also* Central Committee, Central Control Commission, Commission of Party Control.
Communist Party Congresses, Second in 1903, 176; Third in 1905, 176; Fourth in 1906, 176, 292; Fifth in 1907, 176, 292; Sixth in 1912, 24, 52, 130, 132; Seventh in 1919, 146; Eighth in 1919, 99, 156, 158, 170, 293; Tenth in 1921, 166, 168, 169, 207, 272, 273, 293; Eleventh in 1922, 255, 268, 299; Twelfth in 1923, 51, 52, 166, 168, 169, 207, 208, 269-71, 286; Thirteenth in 1924, 50, 286; Fourteenth in 1925, 84, 86, 94, 113, 187, 338; Fifteenth in 1927, 11, 15, 84, 86, 88, 90, 94, 114, 153, 172, 192, 204; Sixteenth in 1930, 93, 125, 129, 131, 133, 138-41, 155, 166, 168, 171, 173, 174, 189, 202, 302, 332; Seventeenth in 1934, 104, 199, 200, 202-09 *passim*, 214, 226, 241-43, 274, 276-78, 302, 304, 308, 314, 333; Eighteenth in 1939, 221, 226, 239, 241-43, 290, 308, 314; Nineteenth in 1952, 242, 244-46, 249, 254, 256, 258, 260, 306, 343, 344, 356, 358, 360; Twentieth in

1945, 210, 231, 246, 247, 252, 257-59, 263, 264, 300, 314, 339, 347-49, 355, 356. (*See also* Khrushchev, secret report at the Twentieth Party Congress).
Communist Youth International, 191
"Communist upbringing," 185
Compulsory food distribution, 15
Congress of Loafers, 178
Congress of Soviets of the USSR, Second in 1924, 198
"Congress of the Victors." *See* Communist Party Congresses, Seventeenth.
Constantinople, 39
Constituent Assembly, 23
Constitution of 1924, 199
Constitution of 1936, 196, 199
Constitutional Democrats, 297, 299
"Construction of socialism in one country," 323
Council of Ministers of the USSR, 253, 308, 351, 352, 359. *See also* Council of People's Commissars of the USSR.
Council of National Economy, 31
Council of People's Commissars of RSFSR, 18, 183, 189
Council of People's Commissars of USSR, 4, 11, 18, 29, 30, 92, 93, 98, 118, 189, 212, 216, 308. *See also* Council of Ministers of USSR.
Counterrevolution, 28-30, 38, 41, 139, 154, 185, 195, 199, 235, 295
Cracow, 23
"Creative Marxists," 18
Crimea, 179
Crimean Tatars, 230
Criminal Code of the RSFSR, 12, 13, 267
Crypto-Trotskyites, 38-41
Cult of the individual, 187, 250, 265, 296, 322, 324, 325, 327, 340, 347. *See also* Stalin.
Czechs, 146, 147, 149

D

Dagestan, 70
Darkness at Noon (Koestler), cited, 226
Das Kapital (Marx), cited 17, 318
Dashnaks, 298
Deborin, A. M., 21, 44
Decentralization, 350-52; of industry, 329
"Declaration of the 46," 50
Dedodub, 2, 10, 45, 72, 80, 158

Defense Commission of Politburo, 218, 219
Defense, Ministry of, 308
Dekanozov, V. G., 262
"Democratic centralism," 243, 352, 357, 358
Denikin, Gen. A. I., 37, 82
Dennis, Eugene, 258, 264
Department of Agitation and Mass Campaigns of the Central Committee, 176
Department of Agitation and Propaganda of the Central Committee, 22, 55, 67, 76, 126, 127, 176, 178, 183, 184, 186
Department of Culture and Propaganda of the Central Committee, 176
De-Stalinization, 317, 318-31 *passim*
Dictatorship of the proletariat, 8, 96, 129, 130, 161, 171, 205, 213, 248, 320, 322, 323
Different roads to Communism, 321, 336
Dimanshtein, S. M., 103, 167, 179
Djambul, D., 157
Djugashvili, J. V., 5. 49. *See* Stalin, J.V.
Dmitrievsky, S., cited, 358
Doctors Case, 216, 231, 249, 255, 256, 258, 259, 261, 306, 326, 341
Dogadov, A. I., 33, 96, 101
Domestic policy, 27, 120, 122, 336, 338
Don River, 360
Donbas, 29, 311
Dubina, T., 185
Dubrovsky, S. M., cited, 210
Dudorov, N. P., 347, 359
Duma, 43, 128
Dutch Social Democratic Group, 147
Dzerzhinsky, F. E., 50, 51, 53, 197, 271, 307
Dzhaparidze, U.M., 298

E

"Economic materialism," 19
Economic Problems (Voprosy ekonomiki), (Stalin), 249
Economics, 19-22, 31, 166; Party policy on, 87
Economics of the Transitional Period (Ekonomika perekhodnogo perioda), (Bukharin), 77, 156
Education Committee of People's Commissariat of Education, 16
Egypt, 316
Eideman, R. P., 21, 222

Eikhe, R. I., 223-25, 256, 334
Eikhenwald, Yu., 22, 33
Eisenstein, S. M., 210
Eisler, Gerhart, 118, 150
Eismont, V.V., 33, 192, 195
Ember-Dro, Zh., 120
Encyclopedic Dictionary, cited, 255
"Enemies of the people," 21
Engels, Friedrich, 17, 129, 181, 249, 251, 327, 328. *See also* Marx *and* Engels.
England, 23, 218
Enlightenment (Prosveshchenie), (magazine), 23, 195
Entente, 82
Ercoli-Togliatti. *See* Togliatti.
Erdeli, General, 37
Espionage, 236
Etinger, Dr. Ya., 257
Eastern Europe, 21, 329
Ewert, A., 118, 150
Extraordinary Tribunals, 281

F

Fabricius, Ya. F., 111, 294
Factionalism, 113
"Factory proletarian," 16, 52
Famine, 193
Fascism, 268
February Revolution, 23, 25, 48, 146, 308, 310. *See also* Revolution.
"Federation of Foreign Groups" of Communists, 146
Fedko, I. F., 294
Fedoseyev, P. N., 22, 79, 253
Fedotov, D. M., 29
Feldman, Dr. A., 256
Fifth Ukrainian Army, 293
Figner, Vera, 26
Filippinos, 179
Finland, Communist Party of, 147
Fioletov, I., 298
Five-year plans, 31, 85, 86, 125, 129, 166, 284; First, 39, 84, 204, 277
Foreign Affairs, People's Commissariat and Ministry for, 26, 101, 177, 179, 180
Foreign policy, 120, 122, 178, 198, 336-39, 346, 356
Foreign Section of Central Committee, 104
Foreign Trade, Commissariat of, 180
Fotieva, L. A., 197
Foundations of Marxism-Leninism (Osnovy marksizma-leninizma) (Kuusinen, ed.), 330

Foundations of Marxism-Leninism (Osnovy marksizma-leninizma) (Konstantinov, ed.), 330
"Foundations of Leninism" (Stalin), 5
France, 23, 147, 149, 200, 218
French Revolution, 273
Freedom of thought, pp. 176-88 *passim*
Frumkin, I., 34, 120; letter, 34, 35
Frunze, M. V., 99, 100, 294
Furtseva, Ye. A., 261, 358

G

Gabidullin, M., 179
Galkin, L. F., 192
Gamarnik, Ya. B., 277
"General, The," 26, 27, 46, 66, 98-100, 108, 110-13, 122, 126, 139, 141-43
"General Commissar of State Security of the USSR," 241
"General line," 33, 54, 62, 92, 186
Geneva, 316
Genghis Khan, 123
Georgia, 40, 48, 95, 111, 147, 181, 191, 196-98, 229, 230, 270, 297, 298
Georgian Case, 197
Georgian Menshevik Party, 212
Georgian Socialists, 297
Germany, 23, 124, 146, 149, 200, 218, 219, 232, 233, 236, 283; army, 293; colonies, 147; Communist Party, 147-50; Empire, 199; Federal Republic, 316; independents, 145; philosophers, 23; war, 158
"Giddiness from Success" (Stalin), 160, 162, 164
Gide, André, 179
Gikhladze, O., 198
Gladkov, F. V., 79
Glasser, M. I., 197
Glavlit Publishing House, 178
Goglidze, S. A., 262
Goldberg, 33
Gomulka, Wladyslav, 321
Gorbatov, A. V., 228
Gorky, city, 4
Gorky, Maxim, 132, 195, 211, 212, 218, 232, 234, 257, 291
Gorky Oblast Committee, 358
Gosekonomkomissiya (State Economic Commission), 351, 352
Gosplan (State Planning Commission), 84, 351, 360
Gotfrid, Lev, 168-73
Gottwald, Klement, 149
Govorov, Marshal L. A., 256, 257

Grain, 1-18, 34, 193, 206, 269; confiscation, 34, 117; collection, 12-14, 39, 128, 288; prices, 128
"Grain Front, The" (Stalin's lecture), 5
Gratsiansky, N. P., 21
Great Purge of 1934-39, 209-28 passim, 231, 238-43 passim, 256, 262, 276, 300, 304, 314. See also Purges.
Grekov, B. D., 21
Grinko, G. F., 222
Groman, V. G., 21
Gromyko, A. A., 164, 339
Grozny oil field, 177
Grunstein, Dr. A., 257
Guliya, Georgy, 251

H

Hamburg, 149
Hanover, 23
Hegel, Georg W. F., 45, 171, 236
History of the All-Russian Communist Party of Bolsheviks (Istoriya VKP (b)), (Yaroslavsky et al), 43
History of the All-Union Communist Party of Bolsheviks (Istoriya VKP (b)), (Yaroslavsky), 44
Historical materialism, 19, 20, 267
Historiography, 19
Hitler, Adolph, 5, 243, 252
Höglund, C., 23
"Honorary Chekists," 30
Hungary, 146, 321, 322, 326, 328, 349-51, 354, 355

I

Ideology, 22, 75, 96, 205, 329. See also Theory.
Ignatyev, S. D., 254
Ignatov, N. G., 358, 359
Ikramov, Akmal, 95, 222
Ilyichev, L. F., 22
India, 179, 316
Indochina, 316
Industrial commission of Politburo, 84
Industrial Party, Case of, 30
Industrialization, 39, 84, 86, 117, 128, 154, 169, 174, 192
Industry, 34, 84, 85, 128, 193, 311, 338, 345
Ingulov, Sergei, 174, 176, 185, 186
Ingush, 230
Inner-Party Center, 142, 143
"Inner-Party democracy," 40, 62, 106, 114, 117, 208, 243

Institute of Red Professors, 1-10 passim, 16, 19-24 passim, 25-35 passim, 36-42 passim, 44, 46, 54-56, 67, 68, 71-73, 74-80 passim, 81, 83, 84, 86, 94, 110, 115, 124, 126-28, 133, 137, 164, 166, 167, 170, 172-77, 182, 183, 185
Institute of World Politics and World Economy, 179
Intelligentsia, 180, 201, 212, 239
"Internal emigration," 20
Second International, 232
International Organization for Aid to Revolutionary Fighters (MOPR), 81
Iran, 179
Iskra, 176
Italy, 321, 354; Communists, 267, 353
Ivan (IV) the Terrible, 210, 211
Ivanov, W. I., 222, 236, 237
Ivanovo-Voznesensk, 83, 192
Izvestia, 9, 22, 155, 233, 276, 312
Izvestia of the Baku Soviet, 298

J

Japan and Japanese, 21, 23, 218, 219, 232, 236, 354
Jews, 71, 184, 291
Joffe, A. A., 8, 53
"Joint" Jewish organization, 256

K

Kabakov, G. I., 15, 83
Kabardino-Balkar Autonomous Republic, 230
Kabardino-Balkar Oblast, 178
Kadirli, 196
Kaganovich, L. M., 15-17, 21, 41, 42, 47, 56-59, 62-65, 67, 69, 71, 72, 76, 77, 81, 85, 92, 96-98, 101, 103, 108-10, 118, 133-38, 153-55, 157, 159, 167, 184, 187, 191, 206, 212, 214-16, 218, 219, 230, 243, 250, 251, 253, 257, 258, 270, 277, 279-81, 283-86, 295-98, 300, 301, 303-05, 307, 310-12, 315, 332-37, 343-48, 351-56, 360-63; biography, 285-92
Kaganovich, M. M., 277
Kalinin, M. I., 1, 2, 10, 11, 21, 28, 58, 83, 86, 101, 119, 120, 184, 243, 277, 279, 280, 283, 291, 305
Kalinin Oblast, 291
Kalmyk Autonomous Republic, 230
Kalmykov, Betal, 178
Kalmyks, 230

Kamegulov, 132
Kamenev, L. B., 32, 37, 53, 71, 89, 90, 94, 102, 115, 128, 153, 186-88, 197, 198, 211, 213, 215-18, 233, 270-72, 275, 276, 282, 286, 294, 299, 312
Kamensky, G. N., 228
Karachai, 230
Karavayev, A. L., 62
Karev, N. A., 10, 22, 41, 44, 94
Karib, G., 70
Katalinov, I. N., 215
Katov, P. I., 33, 61, 62, 116, 124, 138, 142, 155, 156, 159, 194, 301
Kautsky, Karl, 24
Kazakhstan, 12, 169, 179, 182, 183, 196, 218, 230, 292
Kazakov, M. I., 234
Kedrov, M. S., 227
Kerensky, A. F., 43, 350
Kerzhentsev, P. M., 186
Khamovniky district committees, 61
Kharkov, 83, 95
Khitarov, R., 191
Khodorovsky, I. I., 16
Khodzhayev, Faizulla, 95, 222, 234, 236
Khrushchev, Nikita I., 17, 164, 210, 216, 217, 222, 225-30, 243, 250, 254, 256, 258, 261, 284, 290, 301, 304, 305, 309-18, 332-63 passim; cited, 210, 212, 217, 222, 226-32, 261, 263, 279-82, 321, 332, 335, 336, 343, 363; secret report at Twentieth Party Congress, 211-13, 226, 231, 252, 255, 257, 259, 261, 262, 264-72 passim, 318-31 passim
"Khrushchev's Theses," 352, 353
Khrushchev, Sergei, 310
Kiev, 25, 74, 291, 312
Kiknadze, N. D., 198
Kin, B., 43, 135
Kirichenko, A. I., 328, 346, 347, 356, 358, 359
Kirilenko, A. P., 354
Kirov, S. M., 47, 85, 101, 206, 209, 211-16, 218, 232, 234, 241, 270, 277, 280; murder of, 212, 217, 219, 235, 240, 278
Klimovich, L. I., 179
Klin, Dr. B., 256
Knorin, W. G., 135
Kobulov, B. Z., 262
Koestler, Arthur, 224
Kogan, Dr. M., 256, 262
Kolarov, V., 150
Kolchak, Admiral A. V., 21
Kolesnikov, Gen. P. K., 260

M

Machiavelli, Niccolo, 48, 106, 276
Machine-and-tractor stations, 289
Machtpolitik, 326
Maclean, Fitzroy, cited, 231-34
Madagascar, 28
Madyar, 22, 94
Makharadze, Philip, 11, 198
Malayans, 179
Malenkov, G. M., 11, 15-18, 48, 103, 105, 164, 167, 184, 191, 203, 219, 245, 251, 254, 257, 261, 262, 280, 281, 284, 301-06, 309, 310, 312, 314, 327, 332-337, 341-48, 351-57, 359, 360, 363; biography, 301-06
"Malenkov Plan," 54, 91, 344, 345
Malik, Ya. A., 164
Malinovsky, Marshal R. Ya., 347
Malyshev, A. P., 164
"Manifesto of the Communist International to the Proletarians of the Entire World," 147
Manuilsky, D. Z., 21, 92, 118, 243
March Revolution, 213
March on Rome, 5
Maretsky, D., 22, 33, 47
Marr, N. Ya., 21, 253
Martov, L., 176, 192, 266
Marx, Karl, 17, 181, 249, 251, 310, 327, 328, 330. *See also* Marx *and* Engels.
"Marx and the Contemporary World," (Bukharin), 24
Marx and Engels, 4, 17, 23, 24, 47, 76, 116, 136, 185. *See also* Marx *and* Engels.
Marx-Engels-Lenin Institute, 22, 179
Marxism, 1, 17, 18, 23, 24, 49, 56, 57, 61, 64, 124, 129, 132, 267, 325, 345
Marxism-Leninism, 72, 77, 135, 311, 319, 322, 323, 326, 327, 349, 363
Marxism and the National Question (Marksizm i natsionalny vopros), (Stalin), 23, 195
Marxist agriculturists, conference in 1929, 187
Marxist theory, 20, 74, 78; classics of, 180-82; of crises, 79; history, 19; science, 56; schools of, 164. *See also* Marxism.
Mass proletariat, 48, 52
Materialism and Empirio-Criticism (Materializm i empiriokrititsizm), (Lenin), 44, 56
Maximov, V. A., 232
Mayorov, Dr. G., 257

Mdivani, Budu, 95, 197, 198
Medved, F. D., 215, 216
Mekhlis, L. Z., 10, 22, 24, 76-78, 80, 92, 103, 134-37, 157, 164, 167, 283, 284, 315
Melnichansky G. N., 33, 96
Mensheviks, 38, 75, 111, 176, 203, 240, 266, 298
Menzhinsky, V. R., 28-30, 62, 211, 212, 218, 232, 234, 257, 299, 307
Meretskov, K. A., 226
Merkulov, M. A., 164, 253, 262
"Mesame-dasi" Georgian nationalist party, 212
Meshchaninov, I. I., 21
Messianism, 48
Metternich, 105
Mexico, 52
Mezhlauk, I. I., 280
MGB (Ministry of State Security), 261. *See also* Cheka, GPU, MVD, NKVD, OGPU.
Mif, P., 21, 94
Mikhailov, V. M., 22, 101, 116, 124, 155, 164, 194
Mikhailovsky (N. Garin), 142
Mikoyan, Anastas I., 71, 85, 101, 187, 189, 230, 243, 251, 253, 255, 257, 277, 280, 283, 285, 296-308, 314, 315, 332, 333, 335, 343, 344, 347, 358, 359, 361, 362; biography, 297-301
Milchakov, A. I., 191
Military Collegium of the Supreme Court of the USSR, 218, 225, 231
Military Council, 308
Military Opposition, 99, 100, 293
Military Revolutionary Committee, 296
Military Section of Central Committee, 104
Milyutin, V. P., 53
Minkin, A. Ye., 99, 293
Mints, I. I., 43, 44, 135
Minsk, 74
Mirzoyan, L. I., 111
Mishne, 298
Mishulin, E., 21
Mitin, M. B., 10, 22, 24, 41, 42, 44, 46, 78, 79, 134-36, 164
Molotov, Vyacheslav, M., 9, 28, 31, 46, 47, 61, 63-65, 67, 72, 77, 84-86, 92, 96, 97, 101, 109, 118-20, 128, 134, 153-55, 157, 159, 187, 191, 196, 200, 203, 212, 214, 215, 218, 219, 230, 243, 251, 253, 255, 257, 258, 261, 270, 277, 279, 280, 282-88, 294-97, 300, 301, 304, 307,

310-12, 315, 316, 332-37, 339, 343, 345-54, 358-63; biography, 282-85; group, 317, 333-35, 337-40, 345, 347, 348, 351-56, 361, 363
Molotov-Ribbentrop pact, 284
MOPR. *See* International Organization for Aid to Revolutionary Fighters.
Moscow, 1, 11, 12, 15, 18, 22, 23, 26-29, 40, 45, 56, 58, 70, 73, 74, 88, 89, 91, 95-98, 105-07, 116, 118, 124, 126, 137, 140, 141, 143, 144, 146-48, 150, 164, 177, 178, 180-82, 189, 192, 195, 196, 198, 206, 213, 215, 216, 220, 223, 241, 259, 279, 281, 286, 287, 291, 299, 307, 312, 320, 339, 346, 349, 351, 354, 355; activists 64, 110; "Center" 218; Control Commission 63, 82; district committees 33, 34; Electric Power Plant 62; garrison 262; Higher Technical School 16, 301; military district 91; Oblast 163, 231, 288, 302; Party 33, 214, 253, 314; Party Committee 60-66 *passim*, 74, 261, 315; "proletarian cells" 51; Soviet (city council) 75, 308, 309; trials 211, 226, 254, 299; university 19, 22
Moskalenko, Marshal K. S., 260, 262, 347
Moskvin, V. A., 101
Moslem republics of the USSR, 182, 183
Mrakhovsky, S., 91, 217
Mukhitdinov, N. A., 358, 359
Muralov, N., 53, 91, 293
Musabekov, G. K., 95
Muslim Bureau for Central Asia, of Central Committee, 286
Mussavat Party, 228, 229
Mussolini, Benito, 5, 78
MVD (Ministry of Interior), 261, 315, 326, 327, 329, 347, 359. *See also* Cheka, CPU, MGB, NKVD, OGPU.
Myasnikov, A. F., 196
My Life (Moya zhizn), (Trotsky), cited, 27n, 39, 99, 197-98, 268n, 271, 274

N

Nagy, Ferenc, 321
Napoleon, 249
Natanson, M. A., 146
National areas, 181, 207, 209
See also National republics.

Viktor, 141-44, 153
Vinogradov, Dr. V. N., 257, 262
Vladivostok, 312
Volga River, 163
Volga Germans, 230
Volunteer Army, 20
Voronezh, city, 288; Oblast, 287
Voronov, Marshal N. N., 253
Voroshilov, Marshal K. Ye., 28, 62, 85, 99-101, 119, 120, 134, 157, 187, 212, 214, 216, 218, 219, 230, 243, 251, 257, 261, 270, 277, 280, 283, 292-97, 300, 301, 305, 308, 315, 332-35, 343, 344, 351; biography, 292-97
Vovsi, Dr. M. S., 256
Voznesensky, N., 253, 254, 315, 334, 341, 342
Vyshinsky, A. Ya., 21, 157, 184, 203, 211, 215, 217-19, 223, 231-36, 240, 253, 283-85, 299, 304, 316, 339

W

War Communism, 8, 34, 48, 117, 268, 269, 275
Warsaw, 354, 355; Cominform Conference, 245
Ways of Communication, People's Commissariat of, 141
Western Europe, 45
Western Siberia, 287
Western trade-unionists, 96
What Shall We Do?, 49, 54, 176
White Army, 3, 37, 38, 70, 82, 134, 203, 219, 232, 235, 266, 293, 296
Wieser, F., 23
Wittorf, 149
Workers, 15, 91, 94, 193, 194, 212, 239, 245, 248, 328, 351. *See also* Trade Unions.

Workers' and Peasants' Inspectorate, 205, 207, 208
Works (Stalin), cited, 49
World Communist movement, 318, 319
World War I, 145, 213
World War II, 145, 188, 243, 249, 250, 253, 294, 297
Writers' Union, 22

Y

Yagoda, G. S., 33, 210-12, 214-16, 218, 222, 232, 256, 261, 279, 307. *See also* Purges.
Yakir, Gen. I. E., 222
Yakovlev, I. D., 84, 166, 174
Yalta, 284
Yanson, N. M., 105, 114
Yaroshenko, A. G., 273
Yaroslavsky, Ye. M., 9, 21, 43, 44, 58, 59, 83, 86, 105, 114, 115, 125, 136, 167, 186, 239, 240, 299
Yefremov, L. N., 164
Yegorov, Marshal A. I., 99, 223, 293
Yegorov, Dr. B. G., 257, 262
Yenukidze, A. S., 83, 115, 142, 279
Yevdokimov, Ye. G., 28-30, 217
Yezhov, N. I., 29, 48, 103, 105, 167, 210, 211, 219, 221-28, 230, 231, 237, 254, 256, 257, 261, 277, 279, 280, 283, 284, 290, 297, 300, 302-04, 307, 348. *See also* Purges.
Young Bolsheviks, 189, 190, 242
Youth International (Internatsional molodezhi), magazine, 129, 130
Yudin, P. F., 9, 22, 24, 41, 43-46, 56, 60, 61, 72, 78-80, 126, 127, 134-38, 157, 164, 170, 221, 330

Yugoslavia, 147, 316, 321, 324, 346, 355
Yumashev, Admiral A. B., 253

Z

Zapolsky, 35
Zaporozhets, I. V., 215, 216
Zarubin, G. N., 164
Zasulich, Vera, 26, 176
Zelensky, I. A., 222
Zemlyachka, R. S., 114
Zhdanov, A. A., 15, 191, 203, 216, 219, 221, 243, 252, 256, 257, 277, 279, 280, 283, 300, 304-06, 315, 339-42, 347
Zheltov, Col. Gen. A. S., 253
Zhemchuzhina, Paulina (Molotov's wife), 284
Zhigarev, Marshal P. F., 253
Zhukov, Marshal G. K., 253, 257, 262, 347, 348, 360
Zimmerwald Commission, 145, 147
Zinaida Nikolayevna. *See* Koroleva, Z. N.
Zinoviev, G. Ye., 1, 22, 23, 37, 53, 71, 88-90, 92, 94, 96, 102, 133, 146-48, 153, 187, 188, 197, 198, 211, 213, 215-18, 233, 235, 270, 272, 273, 275, 276, 282, 286, 294, 334, 338, 348
Zinovievites, 88, 90, 92, 101, 213, 218, 274, 282, 286
Zinoviev-Kamenev bloc, 286; trial, 241
Zionists, 257
Zorin, V. A., 164
Zubatov, 31
Zvezda, cited, 252